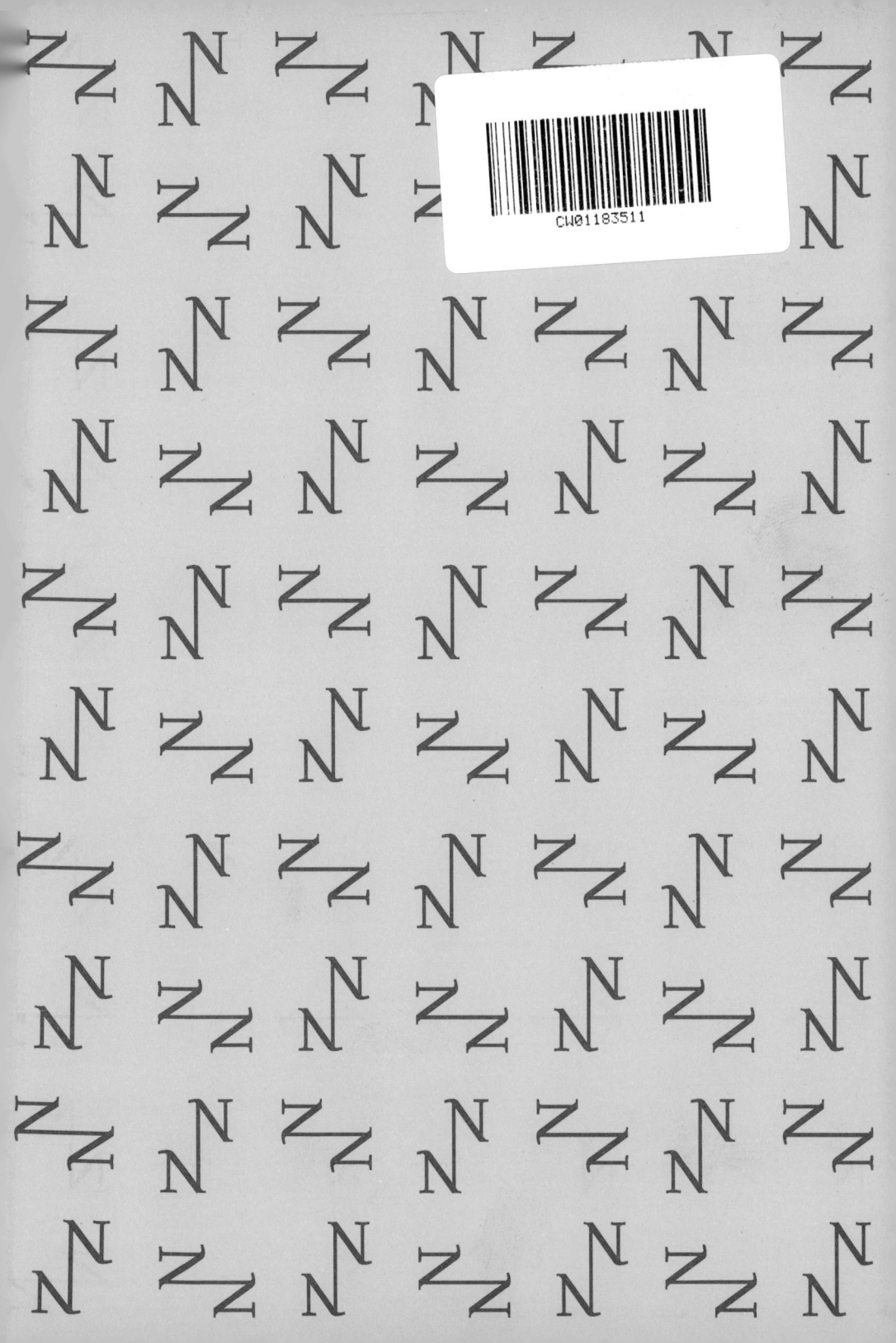

THE NEW NATURALIST LIBRARY

A SURVEY OF BRITISH NATURAL HISTORY

FALCONS

EDITORS
SARAH A. CORBET, ScD
DAVID STREETER, MBE, FIBiol
JIM FLEGG, OBE, FIHort
Prof. JONATHAN SILVERTOWN
Prof. BRIAN SHORT

*

The aim of this series is to interest the general reader in the wildlife of Britain by recapturing the enquiring spirit of the old naturalists. The editors believe that the natural pride of the British public in the native flora and fauna, to which must be added concern for their conservation, is best fostered by maintaining a high standard of accuracy combined with clarity of exposition in presenting the results of modern scientific research.

THE NEW NATURALIST LIBRARY

FALCONS

RICHARD SALE

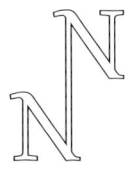

WILLIAM COLLINS

This edition published in 2016 by William Collins,
an imprint of HarperCollins Publishers

HarperCollins Publishers
1 London Bridge Street
London SE1 9GF

WilliamCollinsBooks.com

First published 2016

© Richard Sale, 2016

Photo credits
Except where stated photographs are copyright ©:
Peregrine and Hobby, Richard Sale;
Kestrel and Merlin, Graham Anderson, Keith Burgoyne and Richard Sale.

All rights reserved. No part of this publication may be reproduced, stored in a retrieval system or transmitted in any form or by any means, electronic, mechanical, photocopying, recording or otherwise, without the prior written permission of the copyright owner.

A CIP catalogue record for this book is available from the British Library.

Set in FF Nexus

Edited and designed by
D & N Publishing
Baydon, Wiltshire

Printed in Hong Kong by Printing Express

Hardback
ISBN 978-0-00-751141-9

Paperback
ISBN 978-0-00-751142-6

All reasonable efforts have been made by the author to trace the copyright owners of the material quoted in this book and of any images reproduced in this book. In the event that the author or publishers are notified of any mistakes or omissions by copyright owners after publication of this book, the author and the publisher will endeavour to rectify the position accordingly for any subsequent printing.

Contents

Editors' Preface   vii
Author's Foreword and Acknowledgements   ix

1　The Falcons   1

2　The Four Falcons: a Comparative Study   13

3　Hunter and Hunted   57

4　The Peregrine   97

5　The Kestrel   197

6　The Hobby   305

7　The Merlin   387

8　Populations: Past, Present and Future   481

Endnotes   521
References and Further Reading   535
Index   567

Editors' Preface

ALTHOUGH THERE ARE ONLY four species of falcon resident in Britain and Ireland, and even if most naturalists are favoured with only occasional encounters with them, the falcons command, even demand, our attention. In the chapters of this New Naturalist on *Falcons* Richard Sale explains just why.

Readily recognised as birds of prey by their hooked beaks, piercing eyes and formidable talons, falcons are to many perhaps most familiar as constituents of popular falconry centres and displays. However, True Falcons in these cases play a lesser role than other international and more numerous raptors such as hawks, buzzards and even occasional eagles and vultures.

Although they are clearly taxonomically related, we are fortunate that our four falcon species differ so much in distribution and particularly in behaviour. These similarities and differences are woven by Richard Sale into a fascinating and eminently readable text.

Not many years ago, the Kestrel was the commonplace falcon, regularly seen hovering characteristically over roadside, even motorway, verges and rough grassland, but sadly it is now in decline. In contrast, the Peregrine, once a bird of cliff-girt coasts and remote uplands, can now be found by alert observers in many of our larger towns and cities, exploiting the ledges of grand buildings for nesting sites and the humble Feral Pigeons as a source of food. Scanning the list of Peregrine prey species remains from three city nests, the author reports that unsurprisingly the Feral Pigeon was the most numerous, amounting to about 70% by weight, but has some surprises in store with the inclusion, amongst some thirty other quarry species, of Snipe, Woodcock, Golden Plover and even a Little Grebe.

Before discussing each species individually, the author describes 'our' falcons concisely in the context of their related species and subspecies around the globe. Even here there are striking differences among our four resident falcons – from the Peregrine, one of the five most cosmopolitan of the world's birds and with numerous subspecies whose precise relationship is much debated, to the Merlin, which remains an enigmatic moorland and marshland bird, with a pronounced northerly distribution and with little or nothing in the way of near relatives.

The opportunity is still there for many of us to watch a hovering Kestrel (being mindful of road traffic!) and marvel at how static the head – and therefore the hunting eyes, with amazing acuity of vision – is held despite flapping wings and tail twisting to counter the wind. Likewise, over favoured wetland areas on a summer evening, enthusiasts can enjoy the spectacle of a Hobby catching dragonflies in mid-air before, still in flight, consuming them held in one foot – like a child with an ice-cream cone. But the ultimate 'red-letter day' for any birdwatcher, and an extremely rare event for most, is to see a Peregrine at full speed in a diving stoop plummeting towards its unsuspecting prey.

Richard Sale explains in his foreword that his training in physics, with a mathematical slant, provided skills that enhance his discussion of falcon hunting techniques. Linked to a passion for the icy polar regions, this led to ecological studies above the Arctic Circle, where his inbred ornithology re-emerged. There, his observations of hunting Gyrfalcons (only very occasional visitors to Britain and Ireland) led, ultimately, to this book.

This volume is a fascinating and detailed account of a family of spectacular birds and their ways of life. It is a welcome and most worthy addition to the New Naturalist Library.

Author's Foreword and Acknowledgements

In recent years the Kestrel has been added to the Amber list of British birds, a listing which identifies those species with an 'unfavourable conservation status', because their populations are either small or are in decline. The Kestrel joins the Merlin and the Peregrine on the list; though the populations of these two falcons are thought to be increasing slowly (or, at least, to be stable), in both cases numbers are relatively low, making the species vulnerable. Such vulnerability was well illustrated some fifty years ago, when the increased usage of organochlorine pesticides led to sudden population declines in both Merlin and Peregrine which, if the problem had not been addressed in time, could have been irreversible. It is ironic that of the four British breeding falcons the only one whose population is definitely increasing is the Hobby – a bird which, just a few generations ago, was so rare and elusive that a birdwatcher might spend a lifetime of casual observation without seeing one.

This book deals with the four species mentioned above, the four British breeding falcons. Other falcons may occasionally be seen in Britain – six further species appear on the latest (8th) edition of the British Ornithologists' Union (BOU) British List – but the American Kestrel, Amur Falcon, Eleonora's Falcon and Lesser Kestrel are accidentals, with fewer than ten records each, and although the Gyrfalcon and Red-footed Falcon are more often seen, the former occurs only as a migrant, the latter as an increasingly frequent visitor. As non-breeding, occasional visitors, these six species are not considered here.

My interest in birds is life-long, stemming directly from the enthusiasm of my father. An amateur birdwatcher who tailored family holidays and days out around areas rich in birdlife, and timed them with the breeding season, he had hoped that I might follow a career in natural history. But being good at sums led me down a path to a PhD in physics. Birds remained a passion, but one which had to share its time with another, for snow and ice. Ultimately these twin passions took me to the Arctic, and to a shift in career to polar ecology and wildlife. One day, time spent watching hunting Gyrfalcons on Bylot Island in Arctic Canada led to an interest in exactly how the birds were tracking their prey. And that day led, eventually, to this book.

The book starts with a general introduction to the world's falcons, followed by a chapter comparing the four British breeding species. There is then a chapter focusing on the hunting techniques of each species, much of the information for which has been accumulated through my own studies on falconry birds. The remainder of the book is then divided into four chapters, one for each breeding species, exploring its form, habitat, breeding biology and status. And finally, in Chapter 8, the recent population history of the four species is considered, with an assessment of the present population and some thoughts on the future.

ACKNOWLEDGEMENTS

This book would not have been possible without the help of many people. In particular I thank Graham Anderson and Keith Burgoyne, both of whom helped with the photographic work that illustrates much of the book, and whose companionship and never-ending good humour in occasionally very trying conditions in the field was absolutely invaluable.

I would also like to thank Steve Barton, Denis Corley, Nick Corley, Steve Davies, Chris Dobbs, Mervyn Greening, Nathan Guttridge, Alan Heavisides, Malcolm Henderson, Rob Husbands, Dave Pearce, Mike Price, Graham Rebecca, Nathan Sale, James Sellen and George Smith, all of whom were immensely helpful in the field and shared their expertise. In addition, I would like to register my thanks to Klaus-Dietrich Fiuczynski, one of the world's leading authorities on the Hobby, with whom I shared many happy hours watching and discussing the birds, who sadly died during the production of this book. I also thank colleagues too numerous to mention in Belarus, Canada, Estonia, Germany, Iceland, Mongolia, the Netherlands, Russia – from west to far east – and the USA for both valuable discussions and assistance in the field.

I thank falconers Steve Barton, Nick Havemann-Mart, Gerard Sulter and Alan van Vynck for allowing me to fix inertial measurement units (IMUs) to their birds, and I thank Polly Barton, Lyn Havemann-Mart, Gemma Sulter and Sue van Vynck for their hospitality. Thanks also to Christian Habich, Andy Hollidge, Nigel King and Steve Rose for their hospitality and patience during the experimental work on their birds. Experiments in the field can be frustrating for many reasons, and they all showed continuous enthusiasm and remarkable tolerance. Thanks too to Lloyd and Rose Buck for allowing their Kestrel to be used for high-speed filming, a time-consuming operation during which they showed great forbearance. On the latter work, a big thank-you is also due to Adam Cook, Mark Johnson, Nick Pitt and Nathan Sale, who all displayed the same doggedness. I also thank Waldo Cervantes, Natan Moran, Calum Roke and Nathan Sale for their considerable assistance and equally remarkable patience with the experimental work.

I would also like to thank the library services of Oxford University for their help, in particular Sophie Wilcox of the Alexander Library for her unfailing assistance.

Finally I thank my wife Susan for her tireless assistance. The book involved my absence from home for many extended periods, all of which she tolerated without complaint, intervening times of coping with a tired and often frustrated husband, and all-too-frequent occasions when she was pressed into service carrying far-too-heavy rucsacs to remote areas in order to assist in the placing of hides. She bore it all with unfailing good grace and humour.

CHAPTER 1

The Falcons

THE ORIGINS OF FALCONRY ARE still debated, but it is certainly a sport which is several thousand years old and is likely to have originated in central Asia. That origin supports a minority opinion that the word *falcon* is of Germanic ancestry, tribes of what are now the countries of Germany and eastern Europe learning their skills from further east. Majority opinion, however, claims that this theory is false, and that the Germanic tribes learned the sport from the Romans (though historic evidence does appear to suggest the reverse), who had acquired it from the east. The word *falcon* derives from the Latin *falx* (genitive *falcis*), a curved blade or sickle, probably from the shape of the bird's talons or beak, perhaps even the shape of the wing. In old French *faucon* was the word for a diurnal raptor (*raptor* itself derives from the Latin *rapere*, to snatch or carry off), and as French was the language of the English nobility after William's 1066 conquest, *faucon* became the old English form until around the fifteenth century, when scholarly Englanders inserted an L to conform to the assumed Latin origins.

Other terms for falcons which also derive from the sport of falconry, and which are in (relatively) common use, include *tiercel* (occasionally *tercel*) for a male falcon. This probably derives from the Latin *tertius*, meaning one-third, through the old French *terçuel* (occasionally *tiercelet*), because the male birds are, in general, one-third smaller than the females. Another term is eyas (occasionally eyass) for a nest-bound chick, which is assumed to derive from the Latin *nidus*, nest, through the old French *niais*, with *un niais* being modified over time to 'an eyas'. Chicks are also occasionally referred to as *pulli*, though this is often used to refer to any chicks, rather than specifically those of a falcon or raptor. Here the derivation is more certain, the Latin *pullus* meaning a young animal, though as it was also the Latin for chicken (the base of the French *poulet*, which became Middle English *polet* and hence *pullet* for a hen) there is room for negotiation, particularly as *pullulare* was the Latin verb 'to sprout', which could also be used to imply young growth.

The debates over the origins of the word *falcon* and of falconry are mirrored by those concerning the classification of the falcons themselves. The Family Falconidae of the Order Falconiformes (the diurnal raptors) is divided into two subfamilies, the Polyborinae, which are largely confined to neotropical South America and include the caracaras and the forest falcons, and the Falconinae, which are more widespread and include the falconets and pygmy falcons, as well as the 'true' falcons (of the genus *Falco*). As the behaviour of the caracaras resembles that of vultures and, to a lesser extent, buzzards, while the forest-falcons are hawk-like, this has led to the suggestion that there is a close evolutionary link between the Falconidae and the Accipitridae. That is still a matter of debate, as is the suggestion of a South American origin for the Falconidae, though the latter is supported by the number of genera and endemics found there. Although fossil forms indicate that the two families have origins in the Eocene (some 35 million years ago) there are structural differences between the 'falcons' and the 'hawks', as well as differences in the moult sequence, though the often-quoted primary difference, that 'falcons' do not build nests whereas 'hawks' do, ignores the fact that caracaras do construct untidy piles of sticks.

Griffiths (1994a, 1994b, 1997, 1999) used a combination of morphological differences (specifically of the syrinx of various bird families) and genetics (specifically sequences based on mitochondrial cytochrome *b*) and suggested that all Falconiformes have evolved from a single ancestral family. Though the ancestral line of the falcons is still debated, particularly in the field of genetics, it is undoubtedly true that the True Falcons are more closely related to the falconets – the Spot-winged Falconet (*Spiziapteryx circumcinctus*), the two *Polihierax* pygmy falcons and the *Microhierax* falconet species – than they are to the *Dapritius*, *Milvago*, *Phalcoboenus* and *Polyborus* caracaras, the Laughing Falcon (*Herpetotheres cachinnans*) and the *Micrastur* forest-falcons.

More recent molecular phylogenetic analyses imply a link between parrots and falcons at the ancestral level (Hackett *et al.* 2008). Others have noted a similar link, and have suggested that an ancestral form of parrots and falcons originated on the supercontinent of Gondwanaland during the Cretaceous (Wright *et al.* 2008). The work of Pyle (2013) supports the close relationship between parrots and falcons, noting that they share a moult sequence which is not seen in any other order of birds. (One parrot, the Kakapo (*Strigops habroptila*) does not share the sequence, but Pyle considers it probable that this species split from the other parrots prior to the divergence between the Psittaciformes and the Falconidae.) Very recently, the link between parrots and falcons has been confirmed by work of the Avian Phylogenomics Consortium, a group of some 200 or so scientists from 20 countries. Late in 2014 the Consortium produced around two-dozen papers across the entire spectrum of ornithological scientific journals suggesting an ancient link between falcons, parrots, the seriemas of South America and all passerines (Passeriformes). The Consortium suggest these four groups form the Australaves clade, one of two clades which comprise core landbirds, the other being the Afroaves which include, among others, the remaining diurnal birds of prey and the owls. For more information on the Consortium's work see, for instance, Jarvis *et al.* (2014).

However, while this relationship has merit, genetics is an evolving subject and there are discrepancies between the results of genetic methods and data based on both palaeoenvironmental and palaeontological (particularly morphological) evidence, which is perhaps not surprising, as there is no reason to suppose that the rates of evolution of morphology and molecules are equal. It is therefore worth noting the cautions expressed by some experts. Galtier *et al.* (2009) when considering the application of mtDNA analysis to the evolutionary reconstruction of species note that mtDNA is 'far from neutrally evolving and certainly not clock-like', while Ballard & Whitlock (2004) note 'it is not safe to assume a priori that mtDNA evolves as a strictly neutral marker because both direct and indirect selection influence mitochondrial'. Nonetheless, in the 53rd supplement to the American Ornithologists' Union check-list (Chesser *et al.* 2012) the linear sequence of orders has been changed, with Falconiformes and Psittaciformes being placed immediately before Passeriformes, a change 'reflecting the close relationship among these orders'.

Whatever their origins, the True Falcons have proved extremely successful and have colonised all of Earth's ecozones except Antarctica. The failure to colonise that continent is probably due to its isolation, though whether a falcon could survive Antarctica's climate is another matter – the Gyrfalcon (the world's largest True Falcon) is an Arctic dweller, but the southern winter is far harsher than that of the northern polar region.

It is now thought that the True Falcons evolved in the Miocene, probably in Africa, which is consistent with the earliest known fossils in Europe, which date from the late Miocene/early Pliocene (about 2 million years ago; Milkovský 2002).

The grouping of species within the genus *Falco* is as contentious as the genus, with all suggested groupings having as many critics as adherents. Below, I list four groups which are agreed in principle by most falcon scientists. These four groups accord with the current best estimate for the evolution of the falcons as a whole, which sees the hierofalcons branch off the ancestral line first, followed by the kestrels, the hobbies and then the peregrines. There are still complications with this four-group structure, however – not least, the number of species which do not readily fit into any of the groups. This classification is presented here with the proviso that it is as much a way of listing the members of the genus *Falco* as of examining the way in which the members of genus are truly related.

THE HIEROFALCONS

- Gyrfalcon (*Falco rusticolus*), which has a circumpolar Arctic distribution
- Saker Falcon (*Falco cherrug*), of central Asia
- Laggar Falcon (*Falco jugger*), of India
- Lanner Falcon (*Falco biarmicus*), of southern Europe and north Africa

The name hierofalcon was coined by Otto Kleinschmidt (1870–1954), a German pastor and ornithologist who developed the theory of 'form circles' (self-contained stable units of 'hidden nature'). Kleinschmidt probably meant *hiero* to derive from the Greek for 'hawk' because of the usual hawk-like hunting strategy of the larger falcons as opposed to the stooping technique favoured by peregrines. However, in view of the pastor's creationist views, it has been suggested he might have favoured the Greek for 'sacred'. For more information on Kleinschmidt and his ideas see Potapov & Sale (2005).

An alternative name for the group is 'desert falcons', because of their preferred habitat. (The Gyrfalcon is a true Arctic species, so the definition of desert has to be expanded to include the polar desert of the tundra.) Of the four hierofalcons, the Gyr is a not infrequent visitor to Britain and Ireland, and it is also well known as a popular falconry bird, either pure-bred or as a hybrid. Lanners and Sakers may also be seen at falconry demonstrations.

Despite most specialists now considering the hierofalcons to include just four species, unscrambling their evolution has not been easy (see Potapov & Sale 2005 and references therein) and is still debated. The Prairie Falcon has also been included on occasions, although that species would appear much more closely associated with the peregrines (Wink & Sauer-Gürth 2000, Nittinger et al. 2005). In another complication, Wink *et al.* (2004) consider that the Brown Falcon of Australia (see below) is associated with the hiero group.

Nittinger *et al.* (2005) also consider that Africa was the probable origin of the hierofalcons, while in a subsequent paper suggesting that the Lanner is the closest species to the African ancestor of the group, subsequent phases of

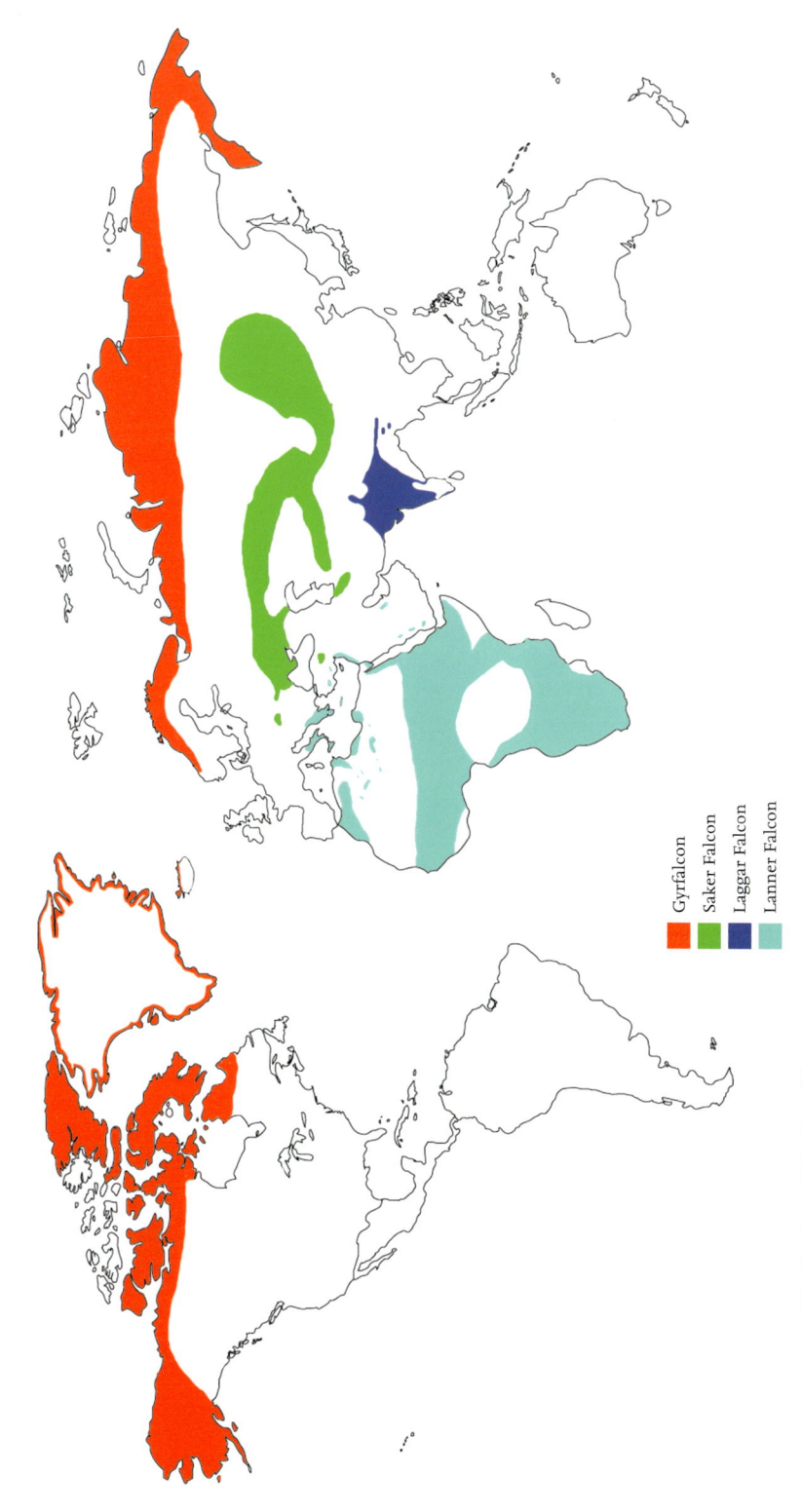

FIG 1. Distributions of the hierofalcons.

emigration splitting off into Eurasia and south Asia to form the Gyr, Saker and Lagger falcons (Nittinger *et al.* 2007). Potapov & Sale (2005) suggest that the Gyr and Saker falcons were initially a single species, separation by the growth of the taiga forming the two species we see today.

THE PEREGRINES

- Peregrine Falcon (*Falco peregrinus*), of all continents apart from Antarctica
- Barbary Falcon (*Falco pelegrinoides*), of North Africa, the Middle East and west central Asia
- Prairie Falcon (*Falco mexicanus*), of North America

Given the range of the Peregrine, the number of subspecies which have been identified across that range (20 are identified in the superb recent book on the species by White *et al.* 2013a), the debate about the authenticity of those subspecies (White *et al.* 2013a sensibly decline to get involved with the various pros and cons of the subspecies in favour of dealing with the current 'agreed' status), and the sheer majesty of the bird, it is not surprising that copious material has appeared in the scientific press regarding the Peregrine's evolution

FIG 2. Adult Peregrine.

and family tree. White *et al.* (2013a) present a brief, but cogent, assessment of the position and reference the relevant papers.

For the purposes of this book it is sufficient to note that some authorities consider the Barbary Falcon to be a subspecies of the Peregrine, not a full species, and that the debate over the position of the Prairie Falcon (Peregrine–Prairie hybrids are known to occur naturally) is ongoing. Recently, further genetic analysis has suggested that an ancestral falcon may have evolved into both the Prairie Falcon and another line, which itself then branched to produce a line which was ancestral to the hiero and peregrine falcons, and a line which was ancestral to the kestrels, hobbies and, presumably, other falcons which do not comfortably fit the four-group pattern (White *et al.* 2013b).

THE KESTRELS

- Eurasian or Common Kestrel (*Falco tinnunculus*), of Eurasia and Africa
- Lesser Kestrel (*Falco naumanni*), of southern Europe and central Asia
- American Kestrel (*Falco sparverius*), of North and South America
- Greater or White-eyed Kestrel (*Falco rupicoloides*), of southern and eastern Africa
- Fox Kestrel (*Falco alopex*), which ranges across central Africa
- Seychelles Kestrel (*Falco araea*), which is endemic to the Seychelles
- Mauritius Kestrel (*Falco punctatus*), which is endemic to Mauritius
- Madagascar Kestrel (*Falco newtoni*), of Madagascar, Mayotte and Comoros, together with an Aldabran subspecies
- Moluccan or Spotted Kestrel (*Falco moluccensis*), of Indonesia
- Australian or Nankeen Kestrel (*Falco cenchroides*), of Australia and New Guinea
- Grey Kestrel (*Falco ardosiaceus*), of central Africa
- Dickinson's Kestrel (*Falco dickinsoni*), of central Africa
- Madagascan Banded Kestrel (*Falco zoniventris*), endemic to Madagascar

Some experts also include the following species within the kestrel group:

- Eastern Red-footed or Amur Falcon (*Falco amurensis*), of China
- Western Red-footed Falcon (*Falco vespertinus*), of eastern Europe and west central Asia (though the species is now spreading westward)
- Red-necked or Red-headed Falcon (*Falco chicquera*), of India

The kestrels are a complex group, with both rufous and grey forms. Though many kestrels are to be found in Africa, which Groombridge *et al.* (2002) considered

FIG 3. Female Kestrel.

the evolutionary home of the group, the Eurasian Kestrel is the most widespread form, a falcon which breeds on Atlantic coasts in Europe and above the Arctic Circle in Fennoscandia, but is also found in Japan and South Africa. Groombridge *et al.* (2002) used genetic analysis to study not only kestrel evolution, but the interdependence of various African/near-African subspecies. The work supported the idea of an African origin for kestrels, with an ancient move to the Nearctic and a more recent move from Africa towards Madagascar and on to Mauritius and the Seychelles, though the timing of the movement to Australia is ambiguous.

However, while the idea that kestrels evolved in Africa fits with the distribution of species, it is not the only interpretation, complicating factors being the position of the Red-footed falcons, which may be related to the American Kestrel, and the fact that the Lesser Kestrel is so distinct from the other Palearctic kestrels that it seems basal to all.

THE HOBBIES

Occasionally referred to as a subgenus, *Hypotriorchis*, this group consists of four tree-nesting species:

- Eurasian Hobby (*Falco subbuteo*), of central Eurasia
- African Hobby (*Falco cuvierii*), of central Africa

- Oriental Hobby (*Falco severus*), ranging from northeast India to Indochina
- Australian Hobby (*Falco longipennis*), of Australia

Some experts consider that the following two cliff-nesting species are also hobbies:

- Sooty Falcon (*Falco concolor*), of the Middle East
- Eleonora's Falcon (*Falco eleonorae*), of the Mediterranean coasts of Europe and Africa

The behavioural and morphological similarities between these two species and the Eurasian Hobby are supported by molecular data (Wink *et al.* 1998) and certainly imply a close relationship. Wink and co-workers suggest that an ancestral *Falco* branch gave rise to the Merlin and a branch which then split, with the Sooty Falcon taking one path, while a second path branched again to form the Eurasian Hobby and Eleonora's Falcon.

The Bat Falcon (*Falco rufigularis*) of Central and South America is also very hobby-like both in plumage (having red leg feathers and vent, a characteristic shared by the 'true' hobbies and by Eleonora's Falcon, though not by the Sooty Falcon), hunting technique, and diet, with males specialising in hunting insects.

FIG 4. Juvenile female Hobby.

However, it nests in tree holes rather than the stick nests favoured by the hobbies. The Aplomado Falcon (*Falco femoralis*) of South and Central America and the southern USA has also been considered to be allied to the hobbies by some. Olsen *et al.* (1989) linked the Aplomado to the hobbies on the basis of feather protein similarities (but suggested other falcon linkages which are not favoured by more recent genetic studies). The Aplomado has red leg feathers and vent, and there are also behavioural similarities: Fiuczynski & Sömmer (2000) noted the similarities between the prey and urban breeding habits of the Aplomado (in Rio de Janeiro) and Eurasian Hobby (in Berlin).

The four-group classification presented above leaves several species adrift, these forming distinct continental or country groups:

- Orange-breasted Falcon (*Falco deiroleucus*), of Central and South America
- Aplomado Falcon (*Falco femoralis*), of southern USA, Central and South America
- Bat Falcon (*Falco rufigularis*), of Central and South America, if the Bat and Aplomado falcons are not grouped with the hobbies
- Taita Falcon (*Falco fasciinucha*), a rare species of east and southern Africa, which has occasionally been placed with the hobbies, but more recently has been suggested as being part of the peregrine group as a consequence of mitochondrial DNA sequencing (White *et al.* 2013b, Bell *et al.* 2014)
- Black Falcon (*Falco subniger*), endemic to Australia
- Brown Falcon (*Falco berigora*), endemic to Australia (occasionally placed with the hobbies by some experts)
- Grey Falcon (*Falco hypoleucus*), of Australia and New Guinea (?)
- New Zealand Falcon (*Falco novaeseelandiae*), which is endemic to New Zealand – one of only two diurnal birds of prey in New Zealand (the other being the Australasian or Swamp Harrier, *Circus approximans*) – with characteristics which suggest it fills the role of both falcon and sparrowhawk

The above groupings leave a single falcon species, the Merlin (*Falco columbarius*), of northern Eurasia and North America. Merlins share characteristics with the hobbies and the peregrines, but are distinct from both. The position of the Merlin is complicated further by the fact that while most falcons are birds of temperate climates (warm and damp maritime, warm and dry continental) the Merlin is a cold-climate species.

While the Peregrine Falcon is found as far or further north than the Merlin, the only other cold-climate specialist falcon is the Gyrfalcon. The Peregrine's northward range extension appears to be less a specialism than a natural

FIG 5. Female Merlin.

by-product of the species' astonishing success as a predator, breeding on all continents except Antarctica. This is a feature it shares with only five other terrestrial birds – Barn Owl (*Tyto alba*), Cattle Egret (*Bubulcus ibis*), Glossy Ibis (*Plegadis falcinellus*), Great Egret (*Ardea alba*) and Osprey (*Pandion haliaetus*) (Note 1.1). (It should be noted though that Peregrines are largely absent from South America and equatorial Africa.) Having adapted to the cold Arctic climate, the subspecies *F. p. tundrius* (the Tundra Peregrine Falcon) has exceeded the specialist Merlin in terms of northerly breeding records, perhaps in some areas even competing with the Gyrfalcon as the northernmost breeding falcon.

Genetic analysis has shed some light on the evolution of the Merlin, Wink & Sauer-Gürth (2000) constructing a family history which sees an ancestral falcon branch dividing to create two arms, one of which resulted in the kestrels, the other branching again, one arm forming the hiero and peregrine falcons, the other being ancestral to the hobby group and the Merlin. The analysis of Wink & Sauer-Gürth also supported the opinion of Wink *et al.* (1998), who suggested that the Nearctic and Palearctic forms of the Merlin were now separate species rather than subspecies. Wink *et al.* (1998) used an assumed 2% sequence divergence per million years molecular clock to calculate that separation of the two forms occurred about a million years ago. DNA therefore supports the idea of speciation, which some experts had already seen in the morphology, size and distribution of the two forms, although the size and morphological differences do not seem as clear-cut as some would suggest.

In Britain and Ireland, therefore, the bird lover is blessed with a single representative of each of three of the groups of True Falcons, and is compensated in the lack of a breeding hierofalcon by the breeding of the Merlin, one of the more enigmatic falcons, at least in taxonomic terms.

Having begun this general look at the falcon family with references to falconry, it seems appropriate to end it by returning to the topic and quoting from the *Book of St Albans*, a source for one of the most famous recent books in English which makes a falcon a central character. Printed in 1486, the *Book of St Albans* was the last of only eight from the St Albans Press, which had been established in 1479 in the Benedictine Monastery of St Albans. The book was a compilation of information of interest to gentlemen of the day, covering the topics of falconry, hunting and heraldry. The falconry section is the supposed work of Dame Juliana Barnes or Berners, 'dame' in this context meaning prioress. Though no reference to the existence of a prioress of that name at Sopwell Priory, which lies close to St Albans, exists, Sopwell's records are not complete so it is possible that Juliana existed: perhaps she was the daughter of nobility, for a position as head of the priory would often have been taken by such a person. Dame Juliana does not offer much in the way of viable information for would-be falconers, and her list is not always easy to unscramble, as some of the spellings do not allow an unambiguous definition of the bird in question, while some are clearly wrong – vultures, for example, are not the chosen falconry bird of emperors, three Peregrines of differing types are mentioned, and most dukes would not be at all content to be given a bustard as a sporting bird (though it is now generally considered that 'bustard' is a misspelling of 'bastard' and refers to a hybrid falcon). Her list must also surely not be seen as indicating which noble had to have which bird. It was, rather, a list of avian raptor hierarchy set against the hierarchy of English nobility, a list which would likely have been crucial in the class-steeped society of the time. And so we read that a King must have a Gyrfalcon, for a Prince it must be a Peregrine, a Lady must have a Merlin, for a Young Man it must be a Hobby, while a Kestrel is for a Knave. Hence the title Barry Hines' *A Kestrel for a Knave* (1968), subsequently adapted for the screen as *Kes*, directed by Ken Loach and released in 1969.

CHAPTER 2

The Four Falcons: a Comparative Study

ASSUME THAT YOU HAVE BEEN hatched a falcon, one which evolution has decided should have a body weight larger than the other falcon species in the country you inhabit. Physics as well as biology will now decide that you will hunt larger prey, as you have the strength to stop and hold such prey, and it has the biomass to satisfy your hunger. Physics also decrees that you will make the most of your body weight by utilising gravity to turn potential energy into kinetic energy as you stoop from height to collect your prey. Your habitat will be open country where you can use your speed and strength, as long as it has enough prey to satisfy your needs. The coast will do, as auks, gulls and doves abound; moorland and mountain is fine, as there will be grouse; farmland can work, because there are partridge and pheasants. You can try urban living, as towns and cities have large pigeon populations living, in part, on the detritus of their human residents. But you also have to think about breeding. Because your prey is resident and you are almost as adept at catching adults as fledglings, you can nest early in the year. Nest sites have to be large, to accommodate a growing brood, but there are few birds which build such nests and you are not accomplished at tree-living. The coast is again fine, as the cliffs offer spacious ledges, and perhaps even an old Raven (*Corvus corax*) nest. Mountains and some moors also offer cliff sites, as do cities, where the resident humans have constructed usable cliffs. But farmland looks less agreeable now unless the humans have excavated quarries. At your nest, just as at the one you were hatched in, there will probably be four eggs. Your preferred prey is resident in Britain, so you can be too, though you may need to move in winter if the prey does. The British climate can be harsh occasionally in winter, but your large mass will aid in keeping you warm. You are a Peregrine.

Now assume that you are a much smaller falcon. You have the same body shape as other falcons, but a longer tail, which physics says is ideal for allowing you to hang in the wind (as long as it is not blowing too hard, or not blowing at all). That means you can watch the ground for prey, descending quickly when you spot it. So your prey will be ground-based – rodents, shrews and lizards, and insects – beetles and the like – if you happen across them. Of course you can still fly fast and with enough agility to catch birds, particularly youngsters. There are rodents more or less everywhere – farmland, moorland, at the coast, in the cities, though not always in abundance on very high land. So you can live anywhere which isn't a high, windswept mountain where both you and the rodents find life hard. Humans are good at providing food for rodents, so you can live in towns, and they are also good at providing environments for rodents, so you can dine on roadside verges, railway embankments and industrial sites. When it comes to breeding, spring is the best time, as it is for your prey, and there are more opportunities. You can utilise the wide range of possibilities your equally wide range of habitats offers – stick nests in trees, tree holes, ledges on cliffs, on the ground, on buildings and in nest boxes. At the nest there may be as many as seven eggs, perhaps a result of your ancestors altering their egg-laying habits because of the cyclic populations of rodents. As your preferred prey is abundant at all times, you can reside in Britain, but being smaller than your Peregrine cousin you prefer warmer weather and may choose to move, though if you stay there is always the possibility of a draught-free barn to take the edge off the worst of the weather. You are a Kestrel.

Now assume you are slightly smaller than your Kestrel cousins, but do not have the longer tail. Your falcon shape means you are fast, but you also have low wing loading. Physics says that this makes you highly manoeuvrable, which means you are agile enough to catch insects in flight. There is not much meat on an insect, but they have the advantage of being available in vast numbers. You will hunt where the insects are, on farmland where they abound around stock, on marshland and above some water bodies. But raising youngsters on a diet of insects would be very hard work, so you will change to larger aerial prey – birds and bats – when breeding. The sensible choice is to choose a species which no one else chases, to reduce competition, but that means Swifts (*Apus apus*) and hirundines, which are too fast for most predators to catch. Despite your speed and agility the adults are difficult to catch, though you do take them by surprise sometimes, so a better strategy is to take the youngsters, as their flying skills are poorer – so best breed later in the year when they are available. Your farmland habitat always has a good number of corvids, so you can readily find a stick nest and have less need than other falcons to search for alternatives. In your nest you probably only had two siblings, which might have been because your parents were nervous about whether there would be enough young hirundines to raise a bigger brood. You are, as many of your True Falcon cousins, a lover of warm weather, so you will leave Britain when autumn comes, heading south to tropical Africa, perhaps even crossing the equator. On your journey south, and also on the long journey north again next spring, you can try to travel with the hirundines and so supplement the continuous swarms of insects in the countries you cross with the occasional old or exhausted bird. You are a Hobby.

And now assume you are the smallest of the quartet of British falcons. Oddly for a falcon you prefer a harsher climate, preferring upland areas which are generally cooler and usually windswept. So you are found on the moors and lower hills of Britain. As with your Hobby cousin, you are fast because of your falcon shape, but your wing loading is higher. So you are fast, but less agile. You feed on birds, but many of the moorland birds you hunt are fast too, so you will mostly hunt by surprise. Your prey may also be faster at ascending than you, so if you fail to catch them by surprise you may have to chase them upwards in ringing flights, hoping they tire before you do. You breed at the same time as your prey so that you can take fledglings as well as adults. Your habitat offers limited places to nest. If there is woodland close by then you might be lucky and find a stick nest built by a corvid or a Buzzard (*Buteo buteo*). You might even be able to use a basket mounted in a tree. But often there will be no trees. You can then use cliff ledges, or the odd isolated boulder, but in many cases the only option will be the ground, setting your nest in dense heather so as to avoid detection by foxes and mustelids. The safest places for your nest will be on managed moorland where the number of terrestrial predators is controlled, but that control might extend to endangering your own life as well. At the nest you hatched you probably had three siblings, and when you breed you or your mate will also probably lay four eggs. In winter, despite your liking for a harsher environment, the lack of prey will force you to lower ground. Some of your cousins may actually fly south, even reaching the continent. But most will move only to estuaries, where waders will offer an alternative to moorland prey. You are a Merlin.

It has already been noted in Chapter 1 that the United Kingdom is fortunate in having one species from three of the four major groupings of True Falcons, together with the Merlin. But how do those four falcons compare? Here we explore their similarities and differences, though one of the major differences, the flight characteristics of the hunting falcon, is dealt with in the next chapter. Further details on much of what appears below are also given, species by species, in Chapters 4 to 7.

SIMILARITIES

Predatory adaptations

Falcons are diurnal raptors, adapted for predation. The eyes are enlarged, to such an extent that they cannot be manoeuvred in the way human eyes can, the falcon needing to move its head in order to change its field of view. The falcon's eye also has two foveas (from the Latin for a pit) or positions of maximal visual acuity, rather than the one in the human eye. One fovea is positioned to give forward binocular vision, the other positioned at an angle of about 40 degrees to the axis of the bird, which is probably associated with the tracking of prey. The function of the fovea in hunting in considered in detail in Chapter 3.

The upper mandible (maxilla) of the beak is decurved, and hooked at the tip for tearing at the flesh of prey. The tomia (cutting edges) of the maxilla have a distinct notch creating the tomial tooth, which is used to sever the spine of the prey by biting the base of the neck. In killing in this manner falcons differ from hawks which tend to kill by squeezing their prey with their talons, death occurring by asphyxiation or by penetrating the skin with damage to vital organs and causing death by multiple body trauma, or by a combination of the two. The

FIG 6. Kestrel chick, showing both the egg tooth and the tomial tooth.

FIG 7. Peregrine chick. Note how the tomial tooth of the upper mandible fits neatly into the notch on the lower mandible.

muscles which control the falcon beak are large, resulting in a powerful bite and allowing falcons to deal with prey larger than themselves. Use of the bill to kill is inherited rather than learned, appearing to be an automatic reaction when faced with live prey. That said, adult falcons overcome this auto-function during the fledgling stage of their offspring's development, as they occasionally deliver live prey for the young to deal with as part of the learning process.

Falcons also have hooked claws (talons) on their toes which are used to seize prey in an unremitting grip which may actually be fatal (causing death, as in hawks), even if the main purpose is to ensure capture. The toes also have a ratchet-like tendon which means that once prey is gripped no muscular effort is required to maintain the grip, a useful attribute when prey must be carried away to a nest or secure place for consumption.

Table 1 indicates the length of the middle toe as a percentage of the tarsus for the British falcons. The table suggests that the bird specialists have longer toes than the ground-feeding Kestrel, emphasising the usefulness of long toes for grabbing prey in mid-air. However, it is interesting that the Merlin, which preys on birds to an even greater extent than the Hobby, has a relatively shorter foot. One explanation could be the Hobby's enthusiasm for feeding on the wing,

FIG 8. The foot of a Peregrine chick, showing the hooked talons. These inflict damage not only on prey, but on those attempting to ring young birds.

which places a greater emphasis on being able to hold prey firmly. Cade (1982) also suggests that the tarsi of avian specialists might be shorter to better absorb the shock of hitting the prey, while those of rodent feeders have longer tarsi because the attack may be into long vegetation.

The talons may also be used to deliver a blow to prey during a stoop. If the blow causes the talons to rake across the prey, this may cause severe damage, perhaps even death. Prey stunned by the blow, or injured by the talons, usually

TABLE 1 Middle toe length as a percentage of tarsus length. Data from Cade (1982).

	Male	*Female*
Peregrine	100.6	100.4
Kestrel	66.9	68.2
Hobby	94.9	94.5
Merlin	80.0	81.7

falls to the ground, and after a sharp turn the falcon will reach it and deliver a final fatal bite. The blow delivered by the feet of a stooping falcon has long been the subject of debate – is the foot closed or open? How does the bird avoid injury? The best available evidence is that the toes are extended so that the blow is associated with a potential raking by the talons. Extended toes also allow the prey to be grabbed if contact allows. But why falcons do not injure their toes or legs more frequently is not entirely clear.

Reversed sexual dimorphism (RSD)

Reversed sexual dimorphism (RSD) means that males of a species are smaller than females, a reverse of the 'normal' situation. But while all raptors exhibit RSD it is worth noting that despite what is occasionally seen in popular writing, RSD is not exclusive to raptors. In several other bird families – for example, Stercorariidae (the skuas/jaegers), Scolopacidae (the sandpipers) and Sulidae (the boobies/gannets) – males are also smaller than females with no suggestion of predatory behaviour. It is also noteworthy that Laniidae (the shrikes), which predate birds, rodents and lizards, do not exhibit RSD.

The effect of body mass on flight characteristics is a good starting point for considering why falcons (and other raptors) exhibit RSD, and the work of Andersson & Norberg (1981) – which will be mentioned again in Chapter 3 – was carried out in an attempt to shed light on the phenomenon.

Andersson & Norberg (1981) suggested that RSD in raptors had evolved as a consequence of three factors. First, role partitioning favoured one sex being larger to guard the nest while the other hunted for the pair and their offspring. This did not of itself favour larger females, but once it was accepted a second

FIG 9. Reversed sexual dimorphism is clear in this photo of a Peregrine pair – male left and female right.

factor, that it made more sense for the female to be the nest guard, did suggest RSD. The reasoning was that the female risked injury to her eggs while attacking prey, and that her role in egg laying predisposed her to be close to the nest. Once her role as a guard was established, a larger female was a more formidable opponent. The third suggestion of Andersson & Norberg was that as smaller body mass favoured better hunting (as their work on flight characteristics had shown) males of species which hunted birds would tend to be smaller. In support of this, Andersson & Norberg pointed out that RSD was more pronounced in species which attacked birds. This is true of the British falcons, where the size differential of Peregrines, Hobbies and Merlins is greater than that of the rodent-feeding Kestrel.

RSD has been the subject of a considerable number of papers over the years, both before and after the work of Andersson & Norberg (1981), but no consensus has emerged, either on the reasons for it or on whether it emerged in ancestral falcons because males became smaller or because females became larger (though data to support either would be difficult to obtain). In excess of 20 theories of RSD have been put forward, with varying levels of success in terms of both explaining the phenomenon and achieving a degree of measured scientific acceptance. The 'most successful' theories fall into three main groups. The first is ecologically based, from the idea that the sexes operate in specific niches, in this case prey size, to avoid competing with each other on a shared territory. Evidence in support of this theory is contradictory, and in recent years has been the source of a debate between researchers in India and Australia. Pande & Dahanukar (2012) noted that their work on Barn Owls in India indicated that the mean mass of prey brought to the nest by males was significantly lower than that of prey brought by females. However, males brought a greater number of prey items. Olsen (2013), replying from Australia, pointed out that a study across all raptors showed that while males did indeed carry lower-mass prey than females in many species, in others the mean mass was the same for both sexes, while in some species males carried heavier prey than the larger females.

In Britain a number of studies have examined Peregrine Falcons, which show a high degree of RSD. In Cornwall, Treleaven (1977) could find no difference in the mean size of prey delivered to the nest by the two parent birds, while Parker (1979) in Pembrokeshire and Martin (1980) in the Lake District noted that the prey delivered by males was significantly smaller than the prey of females. In a recent Spanish study Zuberogoitia *et al.* (2013) found no difference in the size of prey delivered to the nest by male and female Peregrines. In other studies it has been noted that in single-chick broods the male does much of the provisioning of the youngster, while in broods of three or four the female brings more of the prey:

as she is larger, she is able to carry larger prey, which is helpful when feeding a larger brood. This adds a further argument to the ecological theory, positing that females are larger so that they can carry larger prey to the nest: in some studies it has been noted that male Peregrines consistently bring small prey items to the nest even if they are killing larger prey, for instance grouse, which they feed on themselves. The ecological theory therefore has much to recommend it – but it does not explain why females are larger than males rather than vice versa.

The second RSD theory is behavioural, suggesting that females are larger so that they can dominate males, and so maintain the pair bond and ensure food deliveries; because larger females can out-compete conspecifics in competition for males; or because males compete for females and smaller males can make superior (more agile) display flights.

The third hypothesis is physiological, the idea being that smaller males, being more agile, are better hunters and so better providers for their mates and broods, or that larger females can produce larger eggs and/or clutches and so enhance breeding success. An adjunct to this idea was the *starvation* hypothesis, which posited that larger females were better able to withstand food shortages during the breeding season. A physiological basis for RSD is certainly supported by the observation by Newton (1979) that in female falcons body condition is critical for reproduction and that females are at their heaviest during the laying phase of the breeding cycle and remain heavy (though weight is lost) during incubation and the early nestling phase. Although it is in the reproductive interests of the male to feed his mate and so increase her weight, the increased size of the female would also allow her to dominate her mate, 'bullying' him into hunting. In a study of Tengmalm's Owl (*Aegolius funereus*) Korpimäki (1986a) found no evidence to support the idea that larger females are superior nest guardians, but some support for the starvation hypothesis, and also for the idea that smaller, more agile males are preferentially chosen by females.

More recently, further evidence for a physiological aspect to RSD has come from the work of a Norwegian group. This began with a report by Slagsvold & Sonerud (2007) which noted that the ingestion rate of prey was variable, and that this might influence dimorphism. Ingestion rates were higher for smaller prey, and for mammalian rather than avian prey. Mammalian prey was also ingested faster by raptors which were primarily mammal feeders. Slagsvold & Sonerud argue that the differing roles of breeding raptors, the male hunting, the female at the nest feeding the young, offers a potential solution to the ingestion-rate problem. In later studies the Norwegians noted that video evidence from a number of nests of Eurasian Kestrels suggested that the assumption that females delivered larger prey to the nest was flawed (Sonerud *et al.* 2013, 2014a, 2014b). It seemed that females intercepted larger prey items, which they then consumed as well as feeding them to the chicks, while the male delivered smaller, more easily handled prey items directly to the chicks once they could handle these. The change from the male passing food to the female and directly provisioning the chicks occurred first for insect prey, then lizards, mammals and birds, and occurred earlier for small mammals than for larger mammals. The female's ability to intercept prey deliveries depended on her size (allowing her to bully the male), while the male's ability to return quickly to hunting also depended on his size, lending support to the contention that ingestion rates may have been influential in the development of RSD.

While it is a personal opinion, of the numerous papers to date, one of the more interesting ones resulted from the work of Krüger (2005), who collected data on 237 species of Accipitridae (hawks), 61 species of Falconidae (falcons) and 212 Strigiformes (owls) and used comparative studies of 26 variables – physiological (body mass, wing length etc.), behavioural (breeding system, displays etc.) and ecological (habitat, range size etc.) – to investigate potential correlations with RSD. Krüger found slightly different correlations between the three raptor forms, but in all three the dominant correlation appeared to be in support of the third of the hypotheses mentioned above: that small males evolved so as to efficiently hunt small agile prey. Krüger's findings suggest that the trend for smaller males occurred before falcons began to attack larger prey, which would explain why males are relatively smaller in larger falcon species.

However, while the work of Krüger (2005) seems to narrow the choices in terms of RSD theories, it is likely that debate on the topic will continue.

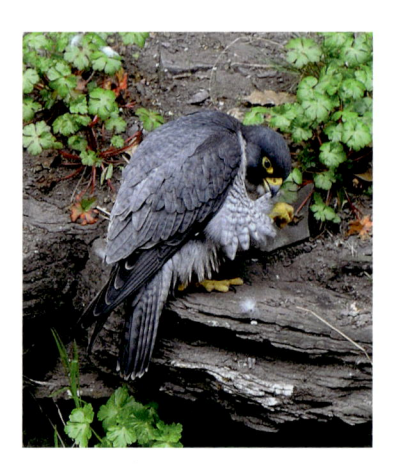

FIG 10. Male Peregrine preening.

Feather care

To maintain feathers in good condition all birds preen often, and the falcons are no exception, nestlings beginning to preen as early as 6–8 days, when they are still prone, or experimenting with standing. Nestlings will also preen each other.

Adults also bathe regularly. Walton (in White *et al.* 2002) observed Peregrines in the Yosemite National Park, California, USA, 'bathing' by flying through the mist generated by a waterfall. Both dust bathing (e.g. Ostermüller, cited in Schmidl 1988) and sunbathing have also been

FIG 11. Juvenile Kestrel preening.

observed, with both behaviours observed in Arctic-breeding Peregrines (personal observations). One very interesting example of bathing was reported by Ford (2007), who observed a female Peregrine hitting the sea off Portland, Dorset, after binding to a pigeon. The falcon spent 20 minutes making her way to shore, using her wings to perform a 'butterfly stroke'. The following day the same bird was seen standing in rain with outstretched wings which she shook periodically in what appeared to be an attempt to remove salt from her plumage. Fledgling Peregrines have also been seen to bathe in rain and make bathing movements in rain or dew-stained grass.

Shrubb (1993a) observed an adult Kestrel which deliberately sat at the top of a tree so as to take a shower in pouring rain; he also discovered a Kestrel drowned in a farm water trough, though this could, of course, have been the result of a failed attempt to drink. However, bathing seems to be rare behaviour for Kestrels, not mentioned by the group at the University of Groningen (which carried out a remarkable series of studies on captive and wild Kestrels, as detailed in Chapter 5). No observations of dust bathing have been identified.

Hobbies have been observed sand and dust bathing (e.g. Ganzeboom 2014b), though Fiuczynski & Sömmer (2011) caution against assuming Hobbies seen on the ground on sunny days are sunbathing, as ground hunting has also been observed (personal observations include a Hobby on the ground which appeared to be hunting rather than consuming prey). Schnurre, in Fiuczynski & Sömmer (2011), observed a Hobby in Berlin evidently bathing by deliberately flying around in fine drizzle, as did Andersen (1975) in Crete, while Grünhagen (1983) recorded seeing two young Hobbies, fledged about four weeks before, also deliberately flying among oaks (*Quercus* spp.) in the rain. The young falcons then perched on branches which were barely able to hold their weight. The birds leaned forward as the branches sagged and fell through the wet foliage below with their wings open. Grünhagen considered the activity, which continued for nearly 30 minutes, to have been 'bathing in foliage'.

Wright (2005) records fledgling Merlins bathing in a stream – behaviour which was perhaps associated with ridding themselves of parasites, as Wright notes that young chicks often carry louse flies (Hippoboscidae). From other reports, bathing would seem to be rare behaviour, though Merlins have been seen to take deliberate showers in rain, extending wings and tail. However, in a study in south Wales, Haffield (2012) records that the breeding Merlins he observed bathed almost every day. Rebecca (1987) observed dust bathing, noting a female Merlin in Scotland which flew down to a patch of sand and gravel beside a busy road. The bird fluffed her feathers, pushed her underside into the 'dust', then walked slowly forward and flapped her wings, presumably ensuring the 'dust' was widely scattered. The bird dusted for a period of four minutes and was then disturbed by a car, but returned for a further two minutes of dusting before moving to a perch to preen. Similar behaviour has been seen in North American Merlins, with one bird noted dusting seven times in an hour (Sodhi *et al.* 2005). The bird was parasite-infested, which may explain this particular intense session of dusting. Haak & Buchanan (2012) report a Black Merlin (*F. c. suckleyi*) bathing. This bird was also drinking, behaviour which has been observed in captive Merlins, but is rarely seen in the wild, though Morozov *et al.* (2013) note that in the warmer climate of the steppes Merlins often seek out water to drink. In addition to water and dust bathing, Merlins have also been observed sunbathing, both in summer (Rolle 1999, Dickson 2003) and in winter (Dickson 1998b).

However, despite the fastidious care birds take in ensuring their feathers stay in good condition, feathers are damaged, raptor feathers probably sustaining a higher level of damage than those of non-raptors because they may add collisions, struggles and so on to the normal wear and tear experienced as a result of landing and take-off. In addition, feathers are subject to the attention of a myriad of parasitic feather mites which degrade both the vanes and quills (as well as infesting the skin and subcutaneous tissues, blood etc.) In a review of the parasitic mites of falcons and owls Philips (2000) found a total of 21 families infesting falcons (and 17 infesting owls), including at least six species which infested the feathers of Peregrines; ten species on the feathers and nasal cavities, or found subcutaneously, in Kestrels; four species on the feathers or on or beneath the skin of Hobbies; and four species on the feathers or on the skin of Merlins.

To maintain good feather condition, all the feathers of adult birds are replaced once annually, the requirement to maintain flight ability at all times in order to be able to hunt meaning that replacement is over an extended period. For further details of the annual moult see the chapters on the four species.

Gastroliths

Falcons consume grit or small stones, officially known as gastroliths, but frequently termed rangle by falconers. While this is common behaviour in herbivorous birds, where the gastroliths grind the forage, the reason for it in falcons is less well understood, though the fact that it is necessary for the health of the birds has probably been known since the beginnings of falconry: Symon Latham, whose books on falconry, published in the early seventeenth century, are still considered to be among the best ever produced, wrote 'washed meat and stones maketh a hawk to fly'. Present opinion is that gastroliths aid in cleaning the stomach of mucus or the grease from prey, or in shedding of the gizzard lining. They may also, of course, assist in grinding the food. Though well known in falconry circles, the use of gastroliths by wild falcons is assumed, but rarely observed, though Albuquerque (1982) did note it in a female Peregrine overwintering in Brazil.

Pellets

Though falcons usually prepare their food, plucking birds and removing the fur of mammals, some feathers and fur will be consumed and will be added to remaining indigestible parts – teeth and bone, claws and bill, the chitinous parts of insects – which cannot easily pass through the digestive tract. This detritus is formed into a pellet within the bird's gizzard, pellets being regurgitated at regular intervals, and the regurgitation has the added advantage of purging the upper section of the digestive tract. (Pellets are known as casts by falconers, the action of regurgitating being called 'casting'.) Pellets are normally regurgitated at dawn, and as the bird is then at its roost, or at the nest in the breeding season,

26 · FALCONS

FIG 12. Pellet of a nestling Kestrel. Down feathers have been ingested while preening, then regurgitated in the pellet.

FIG 13. Pellet of an adult Kestrel.

this aids recovery of many pellets for analysis. Carefully separation and analysis of the contents of the pellet reveals the prey consumed.

Food caching

All falcons cache food, and the behaviour is not restricted to wild birds, as falconry birds will also cache despite their meals being delivered regularly (assuming, of course, that the bird is aware that this will be the case). Since

FIG 14. Merlin cache. The cached Meadow Pipit (*Anthus pratensis*) has been moved very slightly forward from underneath the branches so as to be visible.

FIG 15. The cached Meadow Pipit of Fig. 14 was removed for photographing, then replaced. Care was taken to avoid tainting the prey with human scent.

cached food will, if discovered, be eaten by the discoverer, falcons are furtive when caching, moving the food if, presumably, they believe they have been watched or if they believe the hiding place offers inadequate protection against discovery. Once the food has been cached, the falcon will observe the site from a short distance or after taking off, presumably to fix it in its memory. Caching is used when prey is abundant, particularly if the falcon catches several prey items, such as chicks from a nest or several juveniles in a flock, or if it catches prey which is more abundant at certain times of day (e.g. bats as they emerge at dusk, or certain seabirds which fly far out to sea to feed). It is also used in winter, allowing the bird to benefit before or after enduring the long hours of darkness; it may also be useful if winter weather prevents hunting. Caching may also be used occasionally as a form of food pass, a male caching prey in full view of a female, then departing.

Voice

Though comfortably distinguished by pitch and, to a lesser extent, speed of delivery, the basic call of all four falcons is a repetitive '*ke-ke-ke*'. This call is most frequently heard by the human observer in the form used by breeding pairs if the nest site is approached, when it is harsh and staccato, but a gentler version is also used between the birds of a pair. A gentler call, variously described but essentially a nasal chupping, is also used, particularly between the female and her brood, but also between the breeding pair at food passes.

Breeding

Falcons are essentially monogamous, and pairs may be maintained from year to year, though evidence for this is weaker in Merlins than in the other three species. In both Hobbies and Peregrines there is evidence that pairs may be lifelong. Evidence for extra-pair copulations exists for all species except Hobbies, but in all cases it is very limited in extent.

Territory and displays

All four falcons have hunting ranges which extend beyond the territories surrounding their nest sites. The size of the territory depends partly on the characteristics of the local environment and partly on the individual breeding pair. The falcons will fiercely defend that territory against interlopers, while within the hunting range a degree of tolerance is shown, though antagonism may arise if circumstances bring two birds into close contact.

Initial displays by a male falcon involves high circling above the territory, together with fast swoops, a combination which indicates to a female both site ownership and flight abilities, each of which are important if breeding is to be successful. Other displays tend to follow a pattern which involves either flying with wings held in a V-shape, somewhat in the manner of pigeons, or the delightfully named *Zitterflug*, in which the wings are shivered. There are differences – Hobbies corkscrewing to show off their agility, Merlins and Peregrines rocking to flash their underwings – but all are variations on similar themes.

Courtship feeding

The feeding of the female of a falcon pair by the male bird, which is described in the individual species chapters, is usually referred to as courtship feeding. While many experts consider this the correct term, it is worth noting that Nelson (1970) feels the term is not appropriate to describe the food exchange. Although in its very earliest form it is likely that the giving and accepting of food cements the pair bond, Nelson considers the continued instances of food passing are as much related to the two birds ensuring that the female acquires the reserves necessary for egg laying and, consequently, reproductive success, and that it is therefore in the interests of both that the male continues to pass food to his mate after the 'courtship' phase.

Incubation and chick development

Incubation times are similar for the four falcons at 30 ± 3 days. Usually hatching is synchronous. In all cases chicks are semi-altricial and nidicolous, with closed eyes and weights appropriate to the adult bird (Merlins 16 g, Hobbies about 17 g, Kestrels about 18 g and Peregrines about 36 g). Newly hatched chicks need more or less constant brooding for about ten days, as they are unable to thermoregulate until that age. Chick growth follows a standard S-shaped curve, with fledging times varying from about 30 days for the smaller species to 35 days for Peregrines.

Fidelity

In addition to evidence of mate fidelity, all the falcons show territorial fidelity. In some cases this fidelity is reflected in nest site, with some sites becoming traditional. In the case of both Merlins and Peregrines traditional use may last for decades, outliving many pairs. For Merlins, Rowan (1921–1922 part I) records a site that was occupied every year from 1898 to 1916 despite the fact that in each year both birds of a pair were trapped and killed and no egg was hatched. Kestrels using the same nest box year on year are also known, though over more limited periods, as the use of boxes is a relatively new phenomenon. Stick nests have limited lifetimes, so in the case of the Hobby a traditional site means the same general area of countryside rather than a specific nest site.

Age of first breeding

There is evidence for Hobbies, Merlins and Peregrines, and weaker evidence for Kestrels, that birds are less likely to breed in their first year, with males significantly less likely to do so than females. This raises the questions of why, and why there is a difference between males and females. One hypothesis, the *differential mortality* hypothesis, suggests that reproduction is exhausting and may affect the life span of both sexes. A male has to provision the female and the brood, which means hard work and hunting skills: the former might take its toll on the bird, the latter needs experience, which might mean a year spent acquiring skills before mating. Females must acquire the bodily reserves for egg laying and, later in the breeding cycle, must assist in provisioning a growing brood: both will take their toll on the bird, though neither will prevent a female from mating in her first year, as lack of hunting skills will be alleviated by a good partner during the latter stages of brood raising. After surviving their first winter both sexes will likely be in a poorer condition than older birds. For males this potential reduction in body condition will be exacerbated, if they attempt to breed in their first year, by the need not only to feed themselves, but to feed their mates during courtship and egg laying, and then to provision the brood. For first-year females the time to regain body condition will be shorter, as they will be fed by their male partner.

In a study of urban-breeding Merlins (*F. c. richardsonii*) in Saskatoon, Canada, Espie *et al.* (2000) attempted to explore differential breeding by considering the brood size of birds of differing ages, the hatch dates of the chicks, and the total number of fledglings produced by birds over their lifetime (the lifetime reproductive success, LRS). Espie and colleagues also studied the number of young produced by individual birds which survived and returned to the study area. The results indicated that brood size was positively correlated with the age of parent birds, though the increase was more pronounced for males than for females. However, what was interesting was that the increase was apparent only for birds younger than the mean age of the population: for birds older than the mean age the brood size declined. In other words, birds which survived to breed again had larger broods until they reached the mean age, but then had smaller broods, increasing the likelihood of surviving to breed again. The results also indicated that the hatch date of chicks was earlier for older parents, both males and females; and that LRS was positively correlated with age for both sexes.

Considering their results, Espie *et al.* (2000) concluded that there was support for the differential mortality hypothesis for both sexes, though support was much more pronounced for females. Overall, as would definitely be expected, the longer a Merlin lives the more chicks it will successfully raise (Fig. 16), i.e. the higher the LRS. The researchers found that a female will produce a mean of 9.2 ± 6.2 fledglings in her lifetime, a male will produce 7.4 ± 5.9. The reduction in male LRS is a result of losing a year to gain experience: in other words, male Merlins are trading loss of first-year breeding for long-term reproductive success. The LRS for the female Merlins in Canada was higher than that calculated in a study of Merlins in northern Sweden, where Wiklund (1995) measured 6.4 ± 4.6, with a range of 2–24. While the high standard deviations in both cases mean that there is considerable overlap in the two LRS distributions, the higher value for the urban-dwelling Merlins probably relates to the reduced nest predation of that population.

An alternative theory for delayed breeding posits that older males arrive earlier than first-year males at breeding sites and so are able to establish territories which are richer in food resources, and it is certainly the case that adult–adult pairs tend to breed earlier than pairs in which one bird is a first-year, and that earlier breeding usually results in higher numbers of fledglings. By contrast, later breeders, which often means pairs which either are both first-years or include one first-year, have lower reproductive success. Warkentin *et al.* (1992), studying urban Merlins in Saskatoon, noted that adult–adult pairs fledged,

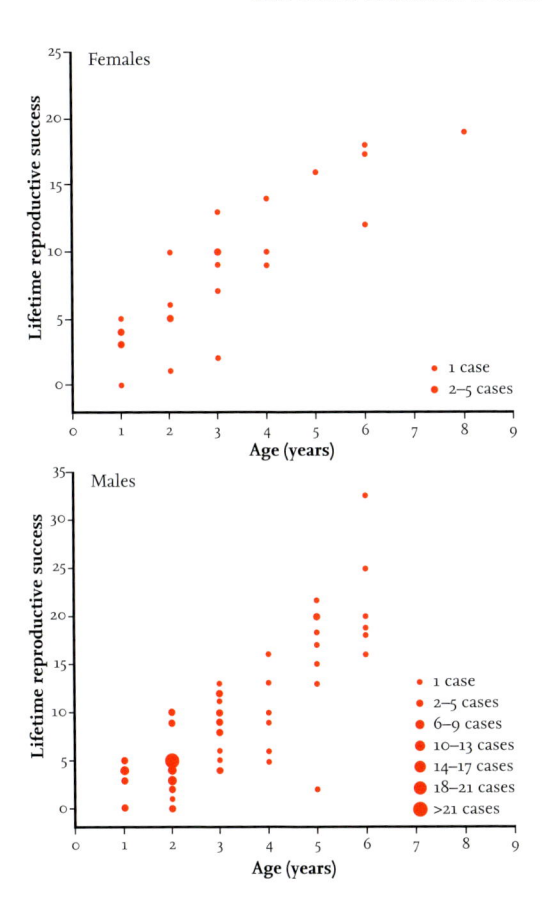

FIG 16. Scatter diagram of age attained and reproductive success of male and female Merlins. Redrawn from Espie *et al.* 2000.

on average, 4.2 ± 1.2 young, while pairs with at least one first-year bird bred later and produced 2.6 ± 1.6 fledglings. This theory suggests that first-year birds, and particularly first-year males, need to gather experience before they can mate, the males needing not only to acquire better territories, but the hunting skills required to provision a mate and brood. Further support for this theory comes from the numerous observations of third birds at nest sites. Often these are males, which appear to be helping with provisioning the brood, and sometimes the female, and which may even accompany the male parent on hunting trips as if to gain experience.

However, some observations of third birds suggest that the situation may be more complex. James & Oliphant (1986) report particularly interesting behaviour in urban-dwelling Merlins in Saskatoon, where there were several observations of a third bird aiding nest defence and food provision. In one case a first-year male was taking food from an adult male which he consumed, and also taking food which he passed on to the female at the nest. The younger bird accompanied the adult male on hunting trips but was never seen hunting himself. The younger male also defended the nest, attacking both American Crows (*Corvus brachyrhynchos*) and Black-billed Magpies (*Pica hudsonia*), when the adult male was absent. Similar behaviour has also been seen in Britain (Rebecca *et al.* 1988). Newton (1979) also records instances of male birds being replaced during the breeding season when the first male was shot.

In observations of other three-bird groups, the female was seen to copulate with the third bird. James & Oliphant (1986) observed this in urban-dwelling Merlins. As first-year males are capable of breeding, if copulation occurs (James & Oliphant saw this much less often than nest defence and food provisioning) the younger male may actually benefit much more directly: in such situations, while it is clear that the female Merlin may benefit from enhanced nest protection and more secure food provision, it is unclear what benefit the adult male gains.

Third birds are also seen in species other than falcons, the fact that in some cases their behaviour is apparently more complex than the 'helpers' in some falcon observations leading them to be called 'floaters'. In work on Purple Martins (*Progne subis*), Stutchbury (1991) noted that male floaters did not intrude on all occupied territories equally, but preferentially choose 3–5 territories. While attempts to usurp these territories usually failed in conflicts with the male holding the territory, the floaters fought a war of attrition which was sometimes rewarded with long-term success. Another idea is that late dispersal of juveniles might explain their presence in the nest area in the following year, though this theory would only explain floaters in non-migratory species: Kimball *et al.* (2003) also note that in most cases floaters are not family members, so late dispersal cannot be the sole reason for their existence.

More recently, Campioni *et al.* (2010), in a study of Eagle Owls (*Bubo bubo*) in Spain, noted that the behaviour of territory holders and floaters differed, the former sitting on prominent posts to emphasise their territory ownership, the latter being more secretive. This suggested that female floaters might actually be using the ability to move through occupied territories without being subject to an aggressive response as a way of comparing them for future occupation. This is consistent with the finding of Bruinzeel & van de Pol (2004), who, in a study in the Netherlands, removed one breeding bird of a pair of Oystercatchers (*Haematopus ostralegus*) and observed how the resulting vacancy was filled. In 80% of cases it was filled by an 'intruding floater', i.e. a non-paired bird which had been seen to spend time within the territory of a breeding pair. Bruinzeel

& van de Pol found that intruding male floaters were more successful at filling vacancies than females. While the breeding behaviours of Oystercatchers and falcons differ, the Dutch study suggests that it is possible that both male and female floaters in falcon species are gathering not only breeding experience prior to their own first breeding, but also territorial information which might be of value later. For males this might allow a decision to be made on which territories to compete for, while for females it might indicate which males/territories would be favourable to partner.

Further studies are required before differential breeding is fully understood: for an excellent review of the position for a raptor (the Sparrowhawk, *Accipiter nisus*) see Newton & Rothery (2001).

Survival

In general falcons are not long-lived birds, the life expectancy being 3–5 years for Merlins, 4–5 years for Kestrels and 6–7 years for Peregrines. In a study of German Hobbies it was found that the life expectancy of males was lower (at 3.3–5.4 years) than that of females (4.8–6.9 years), which might also be reflected in the other three falcons once further studies of the sexes have been made. These lifetimes are for those birds which survive their first winter, as the attrition rate of young falcons is remarkably high, with 50–60% of newly hatched birds failing to survive to the following spring. Longer-lived birds are known, with a British Kestrel having made it to 15 years, a German Hobby living almost as long, an Irish Merlin reaching 13 years and a British Peregrine dying at 17 years of age. Peregrines in the USA are known to have lived longer, one female having been trapped alive 19 years after being ringed as a nestling. Falconry Peregrines have lived 20–25 years, but of course they do not have to survive the rigours of climate and erratic feeding (though soft living has its dangers, of course). While Hobby chicks do not have to survive a British winter, they do face the hazards of a long migration which involves crossing both the Sahara Desert and the equatorial rainforest. Interestingly, the mortality of first-year falcons wintering in Britain and that of Hobbies making the long return journey to Africa is the same. (It should be noted that some other falcons also migrate, with British Kestrels occasionally reaching north Africa and British Peregrines having been recovered in southwestern Europe, but in the main British populations of Kestrels, Merlins and Peregrines are essentially resident, while all Hobbies migrate.)

Of the falcons recovered post-mortem, most have died as a consequence of collisions – with buildings, windows, cars etc. – or as a result of human activities. While it is, of course, the case that birds which die close to human habitation are more likely to be found, it is nevertheless the case that the greatest threat to falcons – as eggs, nestlings, juveniles or adults – is humans.

Friends and foes
There is evidence to suggest that in parts of their range Curlews (*Numenius arquata*) nest close to Kestrels, Wood Pigeons (*Columba palumbus*) close to Hobbies, Fieldfares (*Turdus pilaris*) close to Merlins, and several species, including Wrens (*Troglodytes troglodytes*), Twites (*Carduelis flavirostris*) and Ring Ouzels (*Turdus torquatus*), close to Peregrines, in each case gaining a greater advantage in terms of protection from predators than they lose in predation by the falcon, though the relationship between Merlins and Fieldfares is more complex. There are also observations of tolerant behaviour between the falcon species during breeding – particularly it would seem between Kestrel and Peregrine, and in some cases this could even be termed friendly, although in others that might be a significant over-statement.

Antagonistic behaviour between adult falcons is more prevalent, with all four British species having been seen to interact aggressively on occasions – perhaps not surprisingly, as Peregrines are known to predate Merlins and will likely also sometimes take Kestrels and Hobbies. The smaller falcons are also preyed upon by Goshawks (*Accipiter gentilis*), Sparrowhawks and Tawny Owls (*Strix aluco*), and Merlins are known to have been preyed upon by Short-eared Owls (*Asio flammeus*). In northern Britain Golden Eagles (*Aquila chrysaetos*) have taken both Kestrels and Merlins. Buzzards have also taken Merlins, and there are known territorial disputes between Buzzards and Kestrels which may occasionally have resulted in the death of the falcon. The falcons will all attack corvids, all of the larger species being predators of falcon eggs and chicks.

DIFFERENCES

The differences in the four falcons are primarily seen in habitat, diet and hunting techniques. All three are interlinked, and also influence the breeding biology of the birds. Here we consider habitat first, as diet leads naturally into consideration of hunting techniques.

Habitat
The habitats of the four species differ significantly, ranging from farmland to mountains and the coast. The Hobby is a bird of open woodland, both deciduous and coniferous, though dense woodland is avoided. In Britain when Hobbies are

not breeding they are invariably found near bodies of water or over marshland when insects, particularly large insects, become the principal prey. During the breeding season Hobbies require avian prey, and they specialise in Swifts and hirundines, which in Britain are usually associated with human habitation. The falcon's habitat is therefore lowland farmland, where there are also isolated trees or small copses which provide the stick nests essential for breeding. In continental parts of their range Hobbies are not confined to the lowlands, breeding as high as 3,000 m in places, though in all situations there have to be trees so that they can utilise the stick nests of corvids. More recently in Germany Hobbies have been invading the suburbs, with breeding pairs being seen in cemeteries, parks and large gardens in Berlin. Since Hobbies in Britain show a marked reluctance to breed close to houses or farms (though they are much less reluctant to breed close to busy roads) it will be interesting to see whether a continuing increase in the breeding population leads to an expansion of range or a move to suburban living within the current range (or, of course, to both).

Kestrels are predominantly a lowland bird, though the fact that rodents (the primary prey) are found in any habitat which will sustain them means that moorland and even the lower slopes of mountain areas are occupied, provided that suitable nest sites can be found. While in other parts of their vast range Kestrels are found to heights of 3,000 m, in Britain the limit is around 500 m. Kestrels are also found on riverbanks, woodland edges, at coastal sites and, most obviously for the general public, on the verges of railways and motorways. They have even been seen hovering above the central reservations of motorways, apparently oblivious to the streams of fast-moving cars. Because rodents move in wherever humans set up home or work, Kestrels are also found in cities and industrial sites. Indeed, their enthusiasm for such sites has led to their being called *Turmfalke* – Tower Falcon – in Germany. In a study in Wales 37% of Kestrel habitats covered were farmland, 29% hill grazing, 26.5% coastal areas, 6% urban or industrial sites and 1.5% forest (Shrubb 2003). The fractions mirror, to a first approximation, the geographical-economic make up of much of Wales and so reflect the fact that rodents are found almost everywhere, though the flexibility of the Kestrel diet has enabled the species to adapt to a broad spectrum of habitats. The low fraction of forested land is not surprising, as the Kestrel's preferred hunting technique is far more difficult (and therefore less efficient) in forests. However, a study in Finland suggested that 71% of the avian prey of Kestrels consists of forest species (Korpimäki 1985b), suggesting that other Kestrel hunting techniques work well in forests.

The Merlin is a falcon of remote, undeveloped land, usually at higher elevations than those at which Hobbies and Kestrels are seen. The principal habitat is dry heather moorland, though Merlins are also found on wet or mixed moorland. Across much of their British range Merlins occur on moorland managed for grouse, but hill grazing land is occupied, as is farmland which abuts moorland. Merlins are also found nesting at the edges of forestry plantations, if suitable nests sites are available, though they infrequently hunt in forests. One study in the Kielder Forest, close to the border of England and Scotland, noted that while the local Sparrowhawk population followed periodic eruptions of forest species, that of the Merlin did not: despite breeding at the forest margins, the falcons were hunting their open country prey (Petty *et al.* 1995). Since the 1970s North American Merlins have become urban dwellers, utilising corvid stick nests in trees of cemeteries, parks and gardens and feeding on town birds, chiefly House Sparrows (*Passer domesticus*). As the sparrows are resident, and are joined in winter by immigrants seeking the warmth of the city and the food on offer – chiefly Bohemian Waxwings (*Bombycilla garrulus*), drawn by the autumnal fruits on trees planted by the thoughtful city inhabitants – the Merlins have also been able to overwinter, hunting the resident and immigrant species. This trend has yet to be seen in Britain, and as our Merlins winter mainly on estuaries with their large wader populations, it is possible it may not be seen. However, if wader populations continue to decline perhaps Merlins will join Kestrels and Peregrines as part of the winter town landscape.

As primarily a predator of avian prey, the Peregrine needs open country over which to hunt, but also requires cliffs on which to breed, a fact which explains the absence of the falcon from East Anglia. Coastal areas with a ready supply of steep cliffs are therefore favoured, a habitat which takes in part of southern England, the Southwest Peninsula, almost all of Wales, much of northern England and Scotland, some areas of Ireland and many British islands. Inland sites include mountain areas with rock outcrops (including most of Britain's national parks and the Scottish Highlands), quarries and river gorges. Since to a Peregrine's eye cities are filled with steep cliffs and hold large populations of pigeons, a favoured prey, it is perhaps no surprise that Peregrines have become urban dwellers, a co-habitation with humans which has a much longer history than that for (non-British) Hobbies and Merlins, though perhaps not for Kestrels. The more recent enthusiasm for mounting nesting boxes or platforms on buildings, particularly churches, has aided the urban population to increase, the use of video links to nest activity adding to the falcon's iconic status.

Diet and hunting techniques

The diets of the four falcons cover the range of available prey. One is primarily a mammal hunter, one preys mainly on insects, and two are specialist avian hunters.

Kestrels are primarily hunters of rodents, principally *Microtus* voles. They also take mice (including the diminutive Harvest Mouse, *Micromys minutus*), shrews, Moles (*Talpa europaea*, driven to the surface by waterlogged burrows), bats (taken crepuscularly), reptiles (particularly lizards), amphibians and earthworms, and have also been seen eating fish and crabs. Insects are taken, these making up a large fraction of the diet of fledgling falcons as they learn to hunt. Kestrels will also pirate foods from other birds, including other Kestrels, Sparrowhawks, Barn Owls and Short-eared Owls, and have even been seen attempting to pirate food from Weasels (*Mustela nivalis*). Rodents form the bulk of the prey in all habitats apart from heavily built-up urban areas. There, with fewer 'wild' areas for the hunting of rodents avian prey predominates, the chief victim being the House Sparrow. Surprisingly, in a study in Manchester where it was found that sparrows constituted 90% of the avian prey, the next largest fraction (4%) was pigeons, a species which would seem, intuitively, too large for a Kestrel. But Kestrels have also been known to kill Lapwings (*Vanellus vanellus*). For Kestrels in non-urban habitats the percentage of avian prey in the diet peaked during the time when the young of prey species were fledging, reflecting the relative ease of capture of young, inexperienced birds. The Kestrel's preferred hunting technique is hovering, now more usually called flight-hunting, but avian prey is taken in surprise attacks, usually from a perch. Insects may be taken on the wing or from the ground, occasionally after a flight-hunting attack has failed.

Hobbies are primarily insect feeders, an 18-year study in France finding 700 invertebrates in the falcon's diet (Dronneau & Wassmer 2008). Although Hobbies are most often seen during the heat of the day, they also hunt at dawn and dusk. At such times Hobbies often take bats, and they have also been observed hunting the mammals by the light of a full moon. During the breeding season Hobbies take avian prey, although there are observations of the falcons provisioning a brood entirely on insects, a task which required extraordinary delivery rates. The major prey is then Swifts and hirundines, but larks, pipits, small waders, wagtails, finches and other small passerines are taken as well. Hobbies will also take rodents, and have been observed to prey on reptiles and amphibians. Insect prey is usually consumed on the wing, and both bats and birds may also be consumed in flight on occasions, though in general these are taken to a perch to be eaten.

The Hobby's preferred hunting technique against insect prey is fast, agile flight, plucking the insect from the air. When hunting birds, the falcon uses the same technique, but must ally this with surprise even when chasing juvenile hirundines. Such surprise attacks are usually made from perches, but the falcon will also use a short stoop to gather speed and then swing up to capture the prey from below. Ringing flights to capture, as employed by Merlins (see Chapter 7), have also been recorded, as has hovering, chiefly for mammal prey, and hunting on the ground for insects. Hobbies are also kleptoparasites, with attacks on Kestrel, Red-footed Falcon, Montagu's Harrier (*Circus pygargus*) and Common Tern (*Sterna hirundo*) recorded, but are themselves the victim of piratical attacks by Peregrines.

My own observations and those of others suggest that success rates in hunting insect prey are extremely high, with few misses, and there is one observation of 11 attacks against Sand Martins (*Riparia riparia*) all being successful (Mead & Pepler 1975), but it is very unlikely that such high rates are either normal or can be sustained. It is probable that the overall success rate against avian prey is comparable with that of Merlins and Peregrines.

Merlins are chiefly avian predators, taking small species (mainly weighing no more than 40 g). The main prey are open country species – Meadow Pipit (*Anthus pratensis*), Skylark (*Alauda arvensis*), Wheatear (*Oenanthe oenanthe*) and Starling (*Sturnus vulgaris*) – but others are taken opportunistically, the list including some surprising entries, such as Goldcrest (*Regulus regulus*), which weighs only 5 g, and Green Woodpecker (*Picus viridis*), which is comparable in weight to a female Merlin, Mistle Thrush (*Turdus viscivorus*), Cuckoo (*Cuculus canorus*) and pigeons. The diet includes insects such as butterflies, moths, beetles and dragonflies, lizards and frogs, and across its vast circumpolar range the falcons take such exotic prey as scorpions and snakes. Merlins will also take rodents: indeed, studies in Scandinavia suggested that when the lemming population peaked, Merlins were capable of living on a diet composed almost entirely of rodents (Rudebeck 1951). In other parts of the Merlin's range, including Britain, mammals are usually a small fraction of the diet, and in Iceland, where there are no indigenous terrestrial mammals, Merlins survive entirely on an avian diet. In winter, those Merlins which stay in Britain (the majority) often move to estuaries where they feed on waders, as well as finches and other local residents.

As a falconry bird the Merlin was famous for its ringing flights against larks, but while this technique is regularly observed in the wild, it is not the preferred option, that being a fast, surprise attack on prey observed from a perch chosen to offer an expansive view of the local country. In studies in Scotland it was noted that most Merlin attacks on birds were from perches (about 80%) rather than from the air, and aimed mostly at prey which was perched or on the ground (again about 80%) rather than airborne (Cresswell 1996). Merlins will also fly fast and low, often following the rise and fall of the land, or below tree tops so as to flush prey. If avian prey is spotted on the ground the Merlin may also swoop at it – termed 'bouncing' by one observer – in an effort to make it take off. Since rodents must be taken on the ground it is likely that birds may also be seized there. Merlins may hover, though this is rarely seen, and will also stoop on prey, though this is also an infrequently used technique. There are observations of piracy on Merlins by corvids and by Peregrines in the USA, but none by Merlins themselves, though this may be because the falcon is relatively poorly studied in comparison to the other British falcons. Studies of the success rate of Merlins hunting waders in winter suggest that the falcon is successful on about one in ten occasions (Dickson 1988). However, it is possible that this figure includes a number of first-year birds, and adults in the breeding season may achieve better rates.

Peregrines are renowned for their diet of pigeons in cities and grouse on moorland, but it is no surprise that a species with such a vast range across six continents has a much more flexible diet. In central Europe one study concluded that over 200 prey species formed the Peregrine diet. Peregrines are powerful birds, males taking prey with weights up about 190 g, females up to 250 g, though much heavier prey has been observed. However, throughout Britain pigeons and grouse do represent the bulk of the diet (in terms of biomass), with pigeons forming the greatest fraction by number. In cities, of course, grouse are absent, pigeons forming some 50% of the diet, while at coastal sites grouse are replaced by gulls, auks and Fulmars (*Fulmarus glacialis*). Mammals are also taken, as are bats, and occasionally even fish.

Peregrines are famous for their stoop attacks (high-speed dives – see Chapter 3), and many attacks do indeed use this technique, though most start from a perch, the falcon climbing to acquire the height to stoop, rather than from aerial searches. However, stooping does not necessarily take the often-assumed form of a near-vertical plunge, many stoops being at a much shallower angle so that the Peregrine appears to be chasing down the prey. Peregrines will also fly fast and low across the country in order to flush prey. While Peregrines are chiefly diurnal raptors, they also hunt bats at dawn and dusk, and urban falcons are now taking advantage of city lights to hunt birds at night, many migrating species that make nocturnal flights being attracted towards the lights. In the USA Peregrines are known to pirate prey from other raptors, and also to be subject to piracy by larger raptors such as Gyrfalcons and Bald Eagles (*Haliaeetus leucocephalus*). In Europe piratical attacks on corvids are known, and doubtless if the opportunity arose Peregrines would pirate the three smaller falcons.

It is often reported that Peregrines have a 100% success rate when hunting, and one well-attested falconry bird had success rates in successive years varying between 73% and 100%. Such figures are remarkable, but the hunts were likely artificial in that the falconer and/or his dog were raising the prey for the waiting falcon. However, in studies of wild birds very high rates (35–70%) have been recorded, though these are at odds with studies in Scotland of

FIG 17. Brunel's Clifton Suspension Bridge, Bristol. Peregrines breed in the Avon Gorge, which is spanned by the bridge. City lighting helps the falcons to hunt nocturnally, taking night-flying migratory species. (Nathan Sale)

winter attempts to catch waders where figures of no more than 10% have been seen. However, two factors must be borne in mind. Firstly winter studies may include data of inexperienced first-year birds, whose success rate is liable to be much lower that of adults, and secondly there is good evidence to suggest that Peregrines may make dummy attacks, perhaps as a prelude to real attacks – gauging the strength of the opposition, as it were – or simply as practice or for the 'pleasure' of doing so.

Live prey

Any observer who has spent time with breeding Peregrine Falcons will know that the adult birds will occasionally drop not only dead but live prey, apparently as a teaching aid for their young. Instances also occur of adult Peregrines 'herding' a pigeon into a quarry which holds the nest site and then circling to ensure the pigeon does not escape while the young Peregrines practise their hunting. In a study of the use of live prey Spofford & Amadon (1993) investigated known instances not only of its use, but of other instances where live prey has been seen in nests, and also curious adoptive behaviour by falcons and other raptors. Spofford & Amadon (and references therein) noted instances where prey had blundered into raptor nests and also where prey had been brought in alive, but had escaped before being killed and fed to the chicks. In most instances provision of live prey is avoided because, Spofford & Amadon suggest, with elevated nests any struggle between nestlings and prey might result in the nestlings falling to their deaths. There is also no evidence that raptor chicks 'play' with prey in the manner, for instance, that domestic cats do, so there is no specific advantage in the practice. Spofford & Amadon also reported instances where raptors had adopted chicks which they had brought to their nests and not killed, mentioning several instances in which Bald Eagles had adopted Red-tailed Hawks (*Buteo jamaicensis*). In another instance a pair of American Kestrels, whose brood had apparently been preyed upon, ousted adult Starlings from a nest box and reared the young Starlings on a diet of mice.

Spofford & Amadon conclude that only Peregrines are known to definitely use the dropping of live prey as a teaching method. However, the behaviour has also been seen in New Zealand Falcons and is suspected (anecdotally) in other falcons.

Breeding

Nest sites

As falcons do not build nests, the availability of suitable nest sites may limit the breeding population, particularly if suitable habitat is in short supply. This was probably true in the past for both Merlins and Peregrines, the former because of limited habitat, the latter because of limited nest sites. Within available habitat Merlins were restricted across much of northern England by the lack of stick nests, or, more correctly, by the lack of trees in which corvids and Buzzards could build nests. Merlins therefore nested on boulders or cliff ledges, or, more frequently, on the ground: in a study of nesting across Britain 78% of nests were on the ground, with 20% in trees, the small residual number on boulders or crags (Rebecca 2011). Ground nesting is also known in Scandinavia, but is virtually absent in North America. Ground nesting has its dangers, as both eggs and chicks may be preyed upon by terrestrial mammals: on managed grouse moors the numbers of Red Fox (*Vulpes vulpes*) and mustelids are controlled, reducing the likelihood of predation of ground-nesting Merlins. Across the Merlin's range buildings and tree holes have also been utilised, but such sites are rare. While the data for nesting across Britain suggest that Merlins prefer ground nesting even if there are alternatives, there is some evidence that stick-nest usage has increased in some conifer plantations. The falcons have also begun to use artificial nests

FIG 18. Merlins are now nesting in artificial sites, though usually not as indecorous as this old bucket in Belarus. (Vladimir Ivanovski)

placed in trees, which may aid the population in areas where stick nests are in short supply. Some of these artificial sites can be of remarkably strange form.

Peregrines generally nest on steep cliffs, choosing essentially flat ledges large enough to accommodate the brood. On the ledge the female will scrape a shallow dish for her eggs, though stick nests on ledges are used if these are available. Stick nest of Ravens are most frequently used, but those of Buzzards, crows and Golden Eagles are also utilised. Stick nests have the advantage that they make some sloping ledges usable for the falcons, which can make sites with the benefit of overhanging rock cover available. Some sites are traditional, with Peregrines having used them for decades, the advantages being clear to generations of falcons. There is also good evidence to suggest that 'better-quality' falcon pairs command the most advantageous sites, these in general being higher on the cliff, more inaccessible and providing better shelter for nestlings. More recently, with Peregrines becoming urban dwellers, building ledges and boxes placed in inaccessible positions, particularly on churches, have been used.

In other parts of their range Peregrines use stick nests in trees, and this has also occurred in Britain, as has ground nesting (I have seen a nest on a peat hag

THE FOUR FALCONS: A COMPARATIVE STUDY · 43

FIG 19. Single Peregrine chick on a peat hag in northern England.

FIG 20. Tree-nesting Peregrines in Germany. (Torsten Pröhl)

FIG 21. Peregrines nesting in a wicker basket, Germany. (Torsten Pröhl)

on sloping ground), which is common in Arctic areas where neither trees nor cliffs are found.

Kestrels are the most eclectic falcon in terms of nest sites, a fact which, with their dietary flexibility, doubtless aided their spread across the country. Kestrels will use natural sites – tree holes, rock clefts, cliff ledges, flat areas on sloping ground, and even ground sites, though the latter are rare – and they will also utilise stick nests, mainly of corvids, as well as boxes, both open and closed forms, baskets, occasionally of surprising form, and also ledges on buildings.

By contrast to Kestrels, Hobbies are much more particular about their sites, nesting almost exclusively in stick nests (chiefly of corvids, though nests of Goshawks, Sparrowhawks, Grey Herons (*Ardea cinerea*) and Wood Pigeons have been used across the falcon's range). Hobbies have also utilised squirrel dreys. However, in some parts of the Hobby's range cliff ledges have been used, and there is one observation of a ground nest. More recently they have taken to using baskets, a study in Germany suggesting that the falcons have preferentially used baskets even when stick nests were available. It will be interesting to see if the increase in Britain's Hobby population results in basket use here.

Laying dates
While the laying of the first egg will vary with the timing of spring, in general female Kestrels lay in late April or early May, Merlins at much the same time,

though spring arrival times on high moorland may extend the period until late May/early June, and Peregrines a little earlier, usually in the last week of March or the first week of April. By sharp contrast Hobbies do not lay their first eggs until mid-June, perhaps later in the month if spring is delayed. The timing of the three smaller falcons seems defined by the arrival of young of their preferred prey, with young rodents being available in May for Kestrels, young pipits and larks available in June for Merlins, and young hirundines arriving in late June and July at the same time as dragonflies and damselflies are emerging and Hobby parents start to feed their hatchlings.

Peregrines appear to have a different breeding regime, but there are several issues which have to be borne in mind. Peregrines primarily hunt pigeons throughout the year. Feral Pigeons, which form a fraction of the diet in most Peregrine habitats, and the bulk of the diet in cities, breed at any time that food is available, so young birds, which are likely to be the easier prey (though the preferred Peregrine hunting technique is effective against both young and adult birds), are available at most times of the year. At coastal sites Rock Doves (*Columba livia*) share the same breeding habits as their feral cousins (Rock Doves are the forebears of domestic and Feral Pigeons) and so usually offer the falcons easier targets. Grouse tend to breed later than Peregrines, but their incubation time is shorter (around 20 days in comparison to 30 days) and the chicks are precocial and nidifugous. Development is therefore more rapid, young grouse flying within 14 days of hatching and being essentially adult within 28 days. They therefore represent a significant target for a Peregrine while its chicks are still nest-bound.

While the Hobby's late breeding period coincides with the flying of juvenile hirundines and dragonflies, the juveniles which are being raised on this aerial bounty have to gain the flying and hunting experience necessary to carry out an exceptionally long and difficult migration to central/southern Africa. It is therefore worth considering the timings of adult breeding in more detail. The first Hobbies start to arrive in Britain in mid- to late April, but the mean arrival date is the end of the first week in May (Goodenough *et al.* 2015). Pair formation cannot therefore be complete much before early/mid-May. The birds have arrived after a long and probably exhausting flight, and while migration has been timed to coincide with that of hirundines, which may provide food on the wing, the Hobbies need to feed in order to be ready for the rigours of breeding. At this time of year Hobbies are seen in numbers feeding on insects above water bodies and marshland in southern England, the time spent feeding, notwithstanding the limited nutrition available from a single insect, suggesting that the falcons are recovering from the migration flight. It is not surprising therefore that egg laying does not begin until mid-June. For the juveniles the race to be in condition for the long flight south, and experienced enough to undertake it successfully, is a hard one: the youngsters may accompany juvenile hirundines south, these offering an easier target than the adults, but it is still a journey fraught with dangers. The marvel is that the mortality of juvenile Hobbies is similar to that of the juveniles of the other three falcons rather than significantly worse. (As an aside, Eleonora's Falcon, which is considered by many to be related to the Hobby, breeds even later than the Hobby so as to be able to take advantage of juvenile birds as they migrate south.)

Clutch sizes

While Merlins and Peregrines lay a 'standard' number of eggs in a clutch, both Kestrels, with larger clutches, and Hobbies, with smaller, differ.

Merlins normally lay 3–5 eggs, though clutches as low as one and as high as seven have been recorded. Seven eggs are extremely rare and have only been observed in Scandinavia during seasons of peak lemming populations. Peregrines lay clutches of 2–5 eggs (with a mean of about 3.5), single eggs being seen in about 1 in 50 nests. There is a record from North America of a clutch of seven, with a repeat clutch of six when the first clutch was lost. Females tend to lay the same size clutch in successive years.

FIG 22. Seven-egg Kestrel clutch in a nest box in southern Scotland.

Kestrels usually lay clutches of 4–6 eggs, with seven eggs being seen in about 1 in 100 nests. Clutches of one or two are very rare. A clutch of ten has been claimed, nine of the eggs hatching and eight chicks fledging. Throughout much of the Kestrel's range, though to a much lesser extent in Britain, the populations of the rodents which form the bulk of its diet are cyclical. Population peaks often produce increased clutch sizes in their avian predators, arguably the most extreme case being that of the Snowy Owl (*Bubo scandiacus*), where clutches from 2 to 14 eggs have been observed (Potapov & Sale 2012). It is possible that the Kestrel has evolved to take similar advantage of rodent availability and consequently shows a greater degree of variation in clutch size than is common in the other falcons.

Hobbies invariably lay three eggs, with two or four more rarely seen (a combined total of about 15%) and single eggs very rare. In a ten-year study of over 100 nests in Derbyshire the average clutch was 2.96 (Messenger & Roome

FIG 23. Rare single chick in a Hobby nest in England. The 11-day old chick has recently been fed and has a full crop.

2007). An intuitive thought is that the rigours of a long migration might result in exhausted parent birds laying smaller clutches so as to raise fewer chicks. However, a recent study has suggested it is not the migrants that lay unusually small clutches but the non-migratory species that have evolved larger ones, because the rigours of the northern winter reduce reproductive life (see Chapter 6, Note 6.8). It is interesting to speculate whether this low clutch size reflects the possibility that the male may need to provision the nestlings on a diet of insects if avian prey is in short supply (or too difficult to catch). Equally interesting is the suggestion that after Goshawks moved into the suburbs of Berlin and took a toll of adult Hobbies, the average clutch size of the falcons increased to four.

Movements
The four British breeding falcons differ radically in their annual movements. Peregrines are resident and usually move only relatively short distances between breeding and wintering quarters. One female hatched on a church in the English Midlands bred in a quarry a few kilometres from the natal site, but returned to the town each winter. Of over 500 ringed and recovered birds, the mean distance travelled was only 45 km, with few travelling more than 200 km. The longest journeys were made by Scottish falcons moving to England or Wales. However, there have been instances of British Peregrines crossing to continental Europe, with birds recovered in France and Portugal.

Both Kestrels and Merlins are partially migratory, those breeding in the most remote areas moving to areas where winters are less harsh. Most migratory Kestrels move south, or to lower country, but some make longer journeys, reaching Spain and north Africa. Merlins which migrate tend to move short distances (on average about 100 km) from high moors to estuaries where they hunt wintering waders. However, some ringed and recovered birds have travelled much further, to continental Europe.

By contrast, Hobbies travel huge distances, migrating to central Africa with some potentially reaching southern Africa. A Hobby fitted with a satellite tracker in Scotland flew to Ghana, while tracked birds from Sweden and Germany travelled around 8,000 km in each direction during their migration flights.

Populations
The Hobby differs from the other three falcons in several ways: it is insectivorous or preys upon insectivorous birds, it is a relative newcomer to Britain, and it avoids the managed grouse moors of northern Britain. It has consequently been less vulnerable to the major threats which have limited the populations of the other species.

Persecution

The Inclosure Act of 1773 permitted landowners to enclose land which had formerly either been a shared resource – an open field system with parcels of land occupied by peasant farmers, sometimes working for their feudal lord as well as themselves – or common land used for grazing. Although in principle enclosure had to be agreed between all relevant parties before parliament could be petitioned and royal assent granted, unscrupulous landowners frequently avoided informing or seeking the opinion of those affected. Although the Act was later amended to demand that the petition be mounted on the local church door for a period to allow locals to see what was proposed and object, by then much of Britain's commons had been enclosed. One effect of the enclosures was to allow formerly common land to become available for shooting. With shooting, even if it was not initially on a commercial basis, came gamekeeping, the job of the keeper being to maintain a sufficient level of game for the enjoyment of the shooters. Inevitably gamekeepers saw any species that hunted game as enemies, and the large-scale shooting, trapping and poisoning of raptors, and of terrestrial predators, followed. On some shooting estates hundreds of raptors were killed annually. Ratcliffe (1993) quotes the inventory from the Glen Carry estate in the county of Inverness which noted the killing of 1,799 raptors, including 98 Peregrines, during the four years between 1837 and 1840. Ratcliffe also notes that on the Isle of Arran the bounty for Peregrines was 2s.6d. (two shillings and sixpence, 12½ p in today's decimal currency) for an individual bird and 10s.6d. (52½ p) for a nest. In each case the amounts represented considerable sums to the locals, and it is no surprise that much effort went into the killings.

Neither was the slaughter confined to those raptors which took game birds, even smaller birds such as Hobby, Kestrel and Merlin being seen as potential threats, if not to adult game birds, then to their chicks. And, of course, a gin trap placed on a post suitable as a perch catches whatever species is unlucky enough to use it. For the Kestrel, a rodent feeder, which could not take adult game birds and rarely took chicks, indiscriminate killing seems particularly dreadful. But in its case the problem was that the rearing of Pheasants (*Phasianus colchicus*) for estate shooting involved the use of surrogate hen chickens which were cooped while the young Pheasants they were helping raise ran free in wire enclosures. Such chicks were extremely vulnerable to Kestrels, as a consequence of which the species was seen as just as much a threat as the larger raptors.

The most comprehensive account of the persecution of raptors, and other species deemed a risk to game birds, has been provided by McMillan (2011), who analysed data on record cards kept by the gamekeepers of the nine beats which covered the 56,650 ha (140,000 acre) Atholl estate close to Pitlochry. McMillan's analysis covered two periods, 1867/68 to 1910/11, when the records were collated from the returns of the nine beats, and from 1915/16 onwards, when, following the 1914–1918 war, individual records for the nine beats were available. In the first period, covering 44 years, the records show that 659,975 Red Grouse (*Lagopus lagopus scoticus*) were killed (an annual mean of 14,999), together with 19,972 (mean 454) Black Grouse (*Lyrurus tetrix*), 4,886 (mean 110) Capercaillie (*T. urogallus*), 2,827 (mean 64) Ptarmigan (*Lagopus mutus*), and 78,067 (mean 1,774) Pheasant. During the same period the estate's gamekeepers killed 13,272 'crows' (an annual mean of 302), 11,428 (mean 260) 'hawks', 3,731 (mean 85) 'owls', 1,434 (mean 33) Ravens, and 777 (mean 18) Magpies (*Pica pica*). The 'crows' were probably Hooded Crow (*Corvus cornix*) rather than Carrion Crow (*C. corone*). The 'hawks' are likely to include all the raptors which could have been seen on the estate – Buzzard, Golden Eagle, Hen Harrier (*Circus cyaneus*), Kestrel, Merlin, Peregrine and Sparrowhawk – which were recorded throughout the period – and, potentially, Goshawk, Osprey, Red Kite (*Milvus milvus*) and White-tailed Eagle (*Haliaeetus albicilla*), which became extinct during the period. The 'owls' were likely to be Barn Owl, Long-eared Owl (*Asio otus*), Short-eared Owl and Tawny Owl. The killing of avian 'vermin' would, of course, have been accompanied by the killing of terrestrial predators.

Not until 1880 was an Act of Parliament passed to protect birds from indiscriminate slaughter, but of the 86 species listed (some of which were duplicated because of the use of local names) none were raptors. Not until 1896 were raptors protected (though even then the Red Kite was excluded from the schedule), at least during the closed (breeding) season, and only then in certain areas. The effect was to allow continued persecution at other times, and the closed season was largely ignored in any case. The data presented by McMillan suggest a more or less uniform annual toll for all 'vermin' types apart from Ravens, where the numbers killed fell sharply after 1896/97, and for Magpies, where the numbers fell after 1903/04 and were zero after 1909/10; while Raven numbers have recovered somewhat, Magpies were driven virtually to extinction and are still essentially absent from the area. It would appear, therefore, that even the first attempts at legislation against the wholesale slaughter of raptors (and owls) were ignored.

Only with the passing of the Protection of Birds Act 1954 did the shooting of any raptor seen on a game bird estate become significantly less than routine, though the data which McMillan presents suggest that as far as the Atholl estate was concerned the new, stronger legislation made little difference to the nine gamekeepers, individual beat records suggesting that on some the killing continued more or less unabated until 1988/89, when someone noticed that the records were noting the slaughter of protected species and the forms were altered to avoid that unfortunate occurrence. McMillan notes that the records for the individual beats show that some gamekeepers were not killing raptors, and were teaching their successors to behave in the same way, while others were continuing the slaughter. The fact that the gamekeepers acted entirely as they saw fit suggests that neither the landowner nor the estate manager was responsible for encouraging the law to be flouted, but the fact that there were individual differences strongly suggests there was no guidance that they should obey it either. Apparently even after the police became involved and there were meetings between the Royal Society for the Protection of Birds (RSPB) and the estate, the situation continued as before. Most telling in McMillan's data is the indication that during the years 1980/81 to 1987/88 (when recording ceased), only in one year was the return from a single estate beat (one of nine, it must be remembered) for the number of 'hawks' killed lower than the number reported illegally killed for Scotland as a whole. Overall, over the eight-year period, the return from that single beat (controlled by a single gamekeeper) suggested twice as many hawks and owls killed as were recorded by the RSPB for the whole of Scotland. In a study by Amar *et al.* (2012), data from 1,081 nests across northern England between 1980 and 2006 were analysed against areas of grouse shooting. Though clutch and brood sizes were the same for grouse managed areas and non-grouse areas, suggesting that neither cohort was food-resource limited, the productivity of the falcons on actively managed grouse moors was 50% lower. Analysis of wildlife crime data indicated that persecution of the Peregrine was more frequent on the actively managed moors (Note 2.1).

While the story set down above is dispiriting, it must be remembered that on the Atholl estate there were enlightened gamekeepers, and that elsewhere there were others, both gamekeepers and landowners, who recognised that the effect of raptors was limited and that their presence enhanced, rather than diminished, the countryside. These individuals were supported by the evidence of studies on Red Grouse ecology (Jenkins *et al.* 1963, 1964) which showed that while the turnover of adult territorial grouse was 60–70% and mortality of first-year birds was comparable, losses to predation were small, representing about 6.5% of eggs (compared with 14.5% to other causes) and 20% of adults (of which about half were due to foxes, the remainder to avian predators, among which Golden Eagles and Hen Harriers were the most significant).

However, despite the statistics, there remain landowners and gamekeepers who see the situation completely differently and continue to illegally kill protected avian predators. Thompson (2013) discusses more recent events in Scotland, and though his report concludes with cautious optimism, during the production of this book the RSPB reported a rise in the illegal persecution of raptors, with 238 reports of killings in 2013 (RSPB 2014). Of these, 74 were poisonings, though this was actually a drop from the 153 reported in 2009, 128 in 2010 and 101 in 2011; there were 70 reported poisonings in 2012. The remaining 164 reports were of shooting or destruction. The report notes that these figures represent only a fraction of the actual number of events. In its report the RSPB recommended a change in the law in England and Wales to include the offence of vicarious liability so that landowners would be liable for the actions of their staff, as was introduced in Scotland in 2011. The change in the law seemed to have been reflected in data collected in 2012 (RSPB 2013) when only seven cases of poisoning, four shootings and four spring-trap incidents were confirmed. Of the poisonings only three involved raptors (a Golden Eagle and two Buzzards), the other victims being two cats, a Raven and one case where the poisoned bait (two Rabbits, *Oryctolagus cuniculus*) was discovered before the intended casualty had taken it. The three raptor victims compared with the more than 500 that had occurred in the years since 1989: there were also a further 400 non-raptor and mammalian poisoning deaths. The shooting victims were two Golden Eagles, a Hen Harrier and a Short-eared Owl. In addition, a Golden Eagle, two Buzzards and a Peregrine were caught in illegal spring traps, with two Goshawks, a Buzzard and a Tawny Owl also caught in illegal Larsen or crow traps. A Goshawk nest was also shot out. This total of 13 incidents compared to more than 340 in the years from 1989. While the report notes that inevitably the true extent of illegal killing exceeds the confirmed incidents, the drop in victim numbers was encouraging. In December 2014 the first conviction of a landowner for vicarious liability occurred, and in January 2015 a gamekeeper became the first to be imprisoned for raptor persecution. However, 2014 also saw a horrific incident in the Black Isle, with 16 Red Kites and six Buzzards being found dead: at least 12 of the raptors had definitely been poisoned (RSPB 2015), so there is no room for complacency.

In England and Wales the major areas of concern are the Peak District, the Yorkshire Dales and Northumberland, pointing to a continuing problem with grouse moors, their owners and agents, though there were also incidents in other areas of England, in Wales and in Northern Ireland (RSPB 2015). The situation was also not aided by news (mid-2013) that the government had secretly agreed to allow the destruction of Buzzard nests on a Pheasant shoot in order to preserve the few birds which the raptors were taking for the enjoyment of shooters. That the government attempted to keep the deal secret (it was discovered by an individual who became suspicious and demanded details under the Freedom of Information Act) can only have been seen as a green light by less scrupulous gamekeepers elsewhere.

It is ironic therefore that the gamekeeper can be friend as well as foe to raptors. Baines & Richardson (2013) studied the population of Hen Harriers on a moor managed for grouse shooting in southern Scotland and noted that the effect of a reduction in the shooting of the harriers led to a tenfold increase in the number of breeding pairs over a five-year period, but the cessation of management of the moor (and, therefore, the absence of keepers) led to an increase in the population of crows and Red Foxes and a reversal of the harrier population increase.

Before leaving the subject of game management, it is worth noting that in addition to the concerns over the activities of some gamekeepers, many environmentalists have expressed concern that the annual rearing and release of around 50 million game into the wild – with a biomass comparable to that of all wild bird species – is having an impact on the ecology of the countryside (see, for instance, Neumann *et al.* 2015, who noted the change in local invertebrate communities following the release of Pheasants for shooting). There has also been important recent work on the effect of the burning of moorland heather on the local ecology, the burning being carried out because it is necessary for the moor to carry the grouse population density required for economic shooting (a density significantly above the natural carrying capacity). The Leeds University EMBER project found that the burning adversely affected moorland (peat) hydrology and chemistry, as well as the ecology of local rivers, the latter due to alterations in water chemistry which reduced invertebrate populations (Brown *et al.* 2014). In a related study at Leeds, heather burning was shown to alter water colour, which had economic implications for companies providing water to local populations (Holden *et al.* 2012). The illegal destruction of Hen Harriers has recently been specifically highlighted because of the near-extinction of the species in England: in 2015 almost half the male harriers of the dozen pairs which attempted to breed in England 'disappeared'. Interestingly, the often-used argument by the shooting community that antipathy to driven grouse moors is based on class warfare and the ignorance of 'townies' was not supported by the results of an e-petition organised by Dr Mark Avery, formerly the Conservation Director of the RSPB, which suggested that Conservative voters were more opposed than Labour voters, and rural voters of both parties more opposed than urban dwellers (http://markavery.info/2015/08/18/it-really-is, retrieved 19 August 2015): urban lefties, it would seem, are not the primary objectors to driven grouse moors.

Pigeon fanciers/racers also continue to believe that raptors, and particularly Peregrines, are responsible for all failures to return to lofts, and all losses during races, even if the evidence does not support the contention. In his assessment of predation on domestic pigeons Ratcliffe (1993) considered that the likely predation rate of homing (i.e. racing) pigeons was probably $\leq 3\%$ per annum, but suggested that this figure was open to debate. Given the total number of pigeons likely to be taken by the British population of Peregrines, based on at most one pigeon per day throughout the year, in comparison to the number of registered pigeons in the country, the figure does seem to be of the correct order, but it is lower than that proposed by some studies (which suggest a figure as high as 14%). This implies that losses from Peregrine predation are small in comparison to losses from other causes, 85% being due to collisions, bad weather, illegal shooting and so on.

In an edition of *British Homing World*, the official publication of the Royal Pigeon Racing Association (RPRA) on 25 April 2014 there was a list of known Peregrine nesting sites in Britain, with the comment that many readers had found such lists useful, and that 'fanciers must be vigilant for new locations'. The latter may have been the reason a Facebook page followed with a list of further sites. The magazine did not suggest exactly how readers had found such lists useful, and would doubtless argue that its usefulness was in allowing fanciers to avoid such places when flying their birds rather than there being any more sinister motives. 2014 was a bad year for the destruction of Peregrine sites and the theft of nestlings. In July 2015 the Raptor Alliance, which lobbies on behalf of pigeon fanciers for a relaxation of laws protecting raptors which hunt pigeons, and of which the RPRA is a constituent member, produced a letter that it suggested all its members should send to their own Member of Parliament, the essence of which was to amend the Wildlife and Countryside Act 1981 to allow 'relocation' of individual raptors (the Peregrine and Sparrowhawk were mentioned as specific examples) which threatened homing and racing pigeons, particularly as the populations of these raptors were increasing. One concern for those opposed to any change is that the suggestion of population increases is not borne out by recent studies. A more major concern is that any raptor, not just the quoted examples, could be defined as a threat, and that as pigeons cover large swathes of the country during races the effect of 'local' nuisance raptors could lead to more wholesale relocation. A further problem, of course, is that relocation of a species with the nesting habits of the Peregrine would inevitably require long-term 'removal', as birds would return to their territories or their territories would be taken over by incomers.

Contamination

The effects of organochlorine contamination on Kestrels, Merlins and Peregrines is considered in the chapters on those species – and particularly in Chapter 8, where the work of Derek Ratcliffe in identifying the root cause of the decline in Peregrine numbers and the effect of organochlorine pesticides on the shell thickness of the falcons is described in detail. Later work has concentrated on other contaminants, particularly mercury: this is also covered in the species chapters. More recently concerns have been raised over the effect of a new generation of insecticides, the neonicotinoids. These now account for about 25% of insecticide sales across the world, although the effect they appeared to be having on bee populations eventually persuaded the European Union to impose a moratorium on three compounds – clothianidin, thiamethoxam and imidacloprid – which are used as seed coatings in flowering crops that attract bees (European Commission 2013).

There were protests over the ban, the main argument against it being that it was based on poor science, because the studies which had been carried out to suggest a causal link between the insecticides and bee population declines were trials in which bees had been artificially fed neonicotinoids and so were unrepresentative. In order to investigate whether the criticism was valid (and therefore the ban was an overreaction), a trial in southern Sweden investigated the effect on wild bees of the use of the insecticides in 'real world' agriculture (Rundlöf et al. 2015). The Swedish team grew Oilseed Rape (*Brassica napus*) from seed coated with a proprietary insecticide containing a combination of the systemic neonicotinoid clothianidin and the non-systemic pyrethroid β-cyfluthrin, together with a fungicide, at eight sites, each of which was paired with another site at which seed treated only with the fungicide was sown. The site pairs were separated by a minimum of 4 km, and for each site the local density and activity of the Buff-tailed Bumblebee (*Bombus terrestris*), the solitary Red Mason Bee (*Osmia bicornis*) and the European Honeybee (*Apis mellifera*) were determined prior to the trial. It was found that in the sites at which neonicotinoid-coated seeds were grown the densities of both the bumblebees and the solitary bees were reduced, as was nesting of the solitary bees and colony growth and reproduction of the bumblebees. Cellular investigation of the bees showed significant uptake of the neonicotinoid, but no (non-systemic) pyrethroid β-cyfluthrin was detected. By contrast there was no significant impact on the honeybees, in line with other studies which suggest that this species is better at self-detoxifying after exposure than the wild bees. However, Rundlöf et al. caution that the absence of short-term effects does not imply that there will not be a long-term effect. This caution is particularly relevant, as another study has noted that both the Buff-tailed Bumblebee and the European Honeybee prefer sucrose solutions contaminated with the neonicotinoids imidacloprid and thiamethoxam to sucrose solutions without (Kessler et al. 2015).

More recently Hallmann et al. (2014) noted that in a study in Holland there was a clear negative correlation between the populations of 15 insectivorous bird species and the surface-water concentrations of imidacloprid, the most widely used neonicotinoid, populations declining by an average of 3.5% per year in areas where the concentration of imidacloprid was higher than 20 nanograms per litre, even after correcting for land-use changes. These declines have been observed only since the introduction of neonicitinoids to the environment in the last decade. This raises very real fears that in the future populations of avian predators will begin to show declines. Most affected of the studied species was the Barn Swallow (*Hirundo rustica*), a significant prey species of the Hobby. Neonicotinoids are water-soluble and persistent in the soil. It is estimated that 95% of the pesticides applied to crops is taken up by the plant, the rest reaching the soil. And while the study of Hallmann and co-workers noted the effect of 20 nanograms per litre of imidacloprid, in places concentrations up to 50 times higher were noted.

Other studies have also shown that neonicitinoids are lethal to non-target insects at very low doses (e.g. Charpentier *et al.* 2014), leading to fears that over time accumulation of the chemicals in species further along the food chain may be significant. Because of time delays, as with the organochlorines, such significance may not become apparent until the effects are profound and long-lasting, as has been the recently revealed problem of diclofenac (a non-steroidal anti-inflammatory) in Asian vulture species which had fed on the carcasses of cattle treated with the drug. As the vultures do not have the enzyme required to break down the drug, it acts as an antiuricosuric and the birds die of renal failure or the inability to secrete uric acid. Concerns over neonicitinoids are heightened by the fact that despite the Asian problem, the safety of European vultures has now been threatened by the approved use of diclofenac in cattle in both Italy and Spain.

Concerns over the effects of neonicotinoids on insects and birds had been alleviated somewhat by the EU ban, which explains the outrage of environmentalists and others at the decision of the British government to offer a derogation of the EU directive to farmers allowing two of the banned compounds to be used for 120 days on 5% (about 30,000 ha) of Oilseed Rape as protection against Cabbage Stem Flea Beetle (*Psylliodes chrysocephala*) in response to a National Farmers' Union (NFU) claim that the crop was being devastated. Opponents of the derogation, which included academics and politicians as well as environmentalists, were also outraged that the government had chosen not to publicly announce a decision taken in May 2015 until Parliament had gone into summer recession, so that no questions could be raised in the House, and even more so when the yield figures for 2015 were shown to be above recent average yields.

While all the falcons, but primarily the three smaller species, take insects, it may be that the chiefly insectivorous Hobby will be most affected if there are long-term effects of neonicotinoid use. It would be tragic if the recent population increase in this beautiful falcon were to be reversed.

CHAPTER 3

Hunter and Hunted

Chapters 4 to 7 will discuss in detail the strategies employed by each of the four falcons to find and catch prey. It is obvious that in order to do this falcons must be able to see prey and then have sufficient flight abilities to reach it before the prey can move to a position of safety. Here we consider aspects of both vision and flight, considering first the Peregrine, whose abilities to spot distant prey and to stoop speedily on to it are legendary, and then the Kestrel, whose skill in locating small prey while hovering utilises vision and flight in a very different way. Merlin and Hobby will also be considered, but we start by looking at aspects of the flight of all birds, with particular reference to the four British falcons, and then consider the escape tactics which may be employed by avian prey species. The data on falcon flights presented here are part of an ongoing research programme, the results of which will be published in due course.

AVIAN FLIGHT

Falcons share the design details of all birds – the fusion and elimination of some bones, the hollowing of others to reduce weight (but with the use of strut-reinforcing to increase strength), and a respiratory system which maximises oxygen uptake – so as to allow flight. The True Falcon wing is the classic design for rapid flight, the leading edge outboard of the wrist being swept back and tapering to a point: the falcon wing shape defines it as a hunter, rather than a soaring raptor which searches for prey on the wing. However, it is not the case that the falcon wing is modified solely for rapid flight. The outer primaries (the last two,

P9 and P10, in the Peregrine, the last three in the Kestrel) are notched on the inner vane so that a degree of wing-slotting (as seen in the classic soaring birds) exists, enough to allow all the falcons to soar, though this flight mode is only used for limited periods by the larger falcons – see comments on wing loading below.

Avian flight is complex, the mathematics used to explore it no less so, and the mathematical problems are compounded by the fact that flight is more than mere wing shape and beat frequency: flying is very energetic and so involves biology as well as physics. For interested readers, the books of Pennycuick (2008) and Videler (2005) represent good starting points. Here we briefly discuss the basic features of falcon flight. In a classic paper on the flight of avian predators, Andersson & Norberg (1981) defined six flight characteristics which are important in the capture of prey. These are: linear acceleration in flapping flight; maximum speed in horizontal flapping flight; terminal dive speed; maximum rate of climb; angular acceleration; and turning ability. The last two define the manoeuvrability of the bird. What Andersson & Norberg found was that of the six, only terminal dive speed was improved by body mass, all the others varying with the inverse of mass – in other words, smaller birds fare better (Note 3.1). Higher body mass allows a diving (stooping) falcon to accelerate faster under gravity, the bird closing its wings to reduce its frontal profile and so minimise drag. However, body mass reduces rate of climb as the bird gains height initially to achieve a position where stooping is beneficial. While stooping is, consequently, most usually associated with the larger falcons, the smaller falcons also use it as a hunting technique.

Of particular interest in the work of Andersson & Norberg was the finding that in the two characteristics which affect the manoeuvrability of an avian predator (angular acceleration and turning ability), wing loading was important. While falcons, primarily hunting birds, have high wing loading, which underpins fast flight, high wing loading also decreases manoeuvrability. Falcons which feed on insects therefore have lower wing loadings and can make tighter turns, as the radius of the turn is proportional to the wing loading.

Lower the wing loading further and lift is increased, allowing Hobbies to soar when they are searching for prey, and Kestrels to hover, a useful ability when searching for the mammals that are the primary food resource of the birds. Kestrels have proportionately longer tails than the other falcons, which also aids hovering; shorter tails are seen on faster fliers. As noted above, Kestrels may also use stooping when attacking avian prey, as their low wing loading precludes fast pursuit.

Wing loading also affects take-off speed, as a lower number means the bird can take off with minimal effort (in comparison, say, to swans and other water birds, which have to run across the water in order to generate the speed necessary to produce the lift required to become airborne). A quick take-off aids initial acceleration, though low body mass is then required for improved acceleration in flapping flight. For a surprise hunter such as the Merlin, becoming airborne quickly and without frantic wing beating which might alert the prey, and accelerating quickly, is of enormous value (Note 3.1). The wing loadings of the four British falcons are given in Table 2.

FIG 24. A female Merlin takes off from a moorland boulder.

TABLE 2 Wing loadings of British falcons (g/cm^2). Data from Cade (1982).

	Male	*Female*
Peregrine	0.52	0.66
Merlin	0.30	0.33
Hobby	0.21	0.25
Kestrel[1]	0.19	0.22

1. Kestrels are heavier in winter and their wing loading then increases, to 0.26 for males and 0.29 for females.

FIG 25. An adult Peregrine making a tight turn as it comes in to land near its eyrie.

FLIGHT SPEED

Birds have a range of potential flight speeds, dependent on circumstances. A stooping Peregrine uses gravity to accelerate and so may reach a speed in a stoop which is different from the maximum speed it could sustain in flapping flight (an aerobic speed limit) or which it could reach in a short sprint (an anaerobic speed limit). The latter speeds apply to all birds and may actually be employed during displays or while hunting or avoiding capture by a predator. There are also foraging flight speeds, and migration flight speeds, the former defined by the minimum energy input per unit time (and usually called minimum power velocity, V_{mp}), while the latter (usually called maximum range speed, V_{mr}) is defined by the minimum energy input per unit distance, as migration is not usually time-constrained while the former often is: see Hedenström & Alerstam (1995) for a good, if somewhat mathematical, consideration of the various forms. The physics and mathematics of bird flight are highly complex, and this is not the correct forum for an in-depth consideration, with interested readers being pointed towards Hedenström & Alerstam, or the books of Pennycuick (2008) and Videler (2005) for more general studies of birds in flight.

All of these various speeds are of interest, but the easiest one to measure is V_{mr}, as observations of migrating birds are possible at well-known migration sites. Bruderer & Boldt (2001) used radar to measure migration speeds at several sites in Germany, Israel and Switzerland, providing data on 139 Western Palearctic species. Observations of three of the four British falcons were made (the Merlin not being present) – as well as Barbary Falcon, Eleonora's Falcon, Lanner Falcon, Lesser Kestrel, Red-footed Falcon and Sooty Falcon. From the measured air speed, Bruderer & Boldt were able to calculate the equivalent sea-level speed and a range of ground speeds allowing for wind speed. Most of the falcons were migrating, but both the Lanner and Barbary falcons were resident where observed and so speeds for them are likely to be closer to V_{mp} than V_{mr}. The status of the Sooty Falcon (i.e. resident or migrant) was unknown. Speeds for the falcons are set down in Table 3.

In a second study, filming and radar observations were used, with wing-beat frequency of the birds being studied by both techniques (Bruderer *et al.* 2010). In most cases birds alternate periods of power flying, in which the wings beat, with periods of gliding. Wing-beat frequencies were computed from the power flying periods. In the study, data from 200 species, chiefly from the Palearctic, were accumulated. The same group of falcons was observed as in the earlier study, though in this case migrating Merlins were also included. Data on wing-beat frequencies are also shown in Table 3.

TABLE 3 Speed and wing-beat frequency of falcons during migratory flapping flight periods. From Bruderer & Boldt (2001) and Bruderer et al. (2010).

Species	Air-speed (km/h)	Equivalent mean sea-level speed ± SD (m/s)	Ground speed range allowing for wind (m/s)	Mean wing-beat frequency (Hz)	Mean equivalent sea-level wing-beat frequency (Hz)
Hobby	25.2–57.6	40.7 ± 7.9	21.6–64.8	5.2 5.8[3]	5.0 5.6[3]
Kestrel	21.6–68.4	44.3 ± 9.0	14.4–72.0	5.1 5.8[3]	4.9 5.5[3]
Merlin[1]	—	—	—	6.1	5.9
Peregrine	25.2–64.8	43.6 ± 12.6	25.2–75.6	5.1	4.9
Barbary[2]	50.4	51.8 ± 0.4	50.4–61.2	4.7 5.6[3]	4.7 5.6[3]
Eleonora's	43.2–50.4	46.1 ± 8.3	43.2	5.1	5.1
Lesser Kestrel	28.8–68.4	41.0 ± 10.1	28.8–64.8	5.1	4.9
Lanner	36.0–54.0	40.0 ± 9.7	39.6–61.2	4.4	4.2
Red-footed	43.2–50.4	46.1 ± 3.6	43.2–61.2	5.2	5.1
Sooty	50.4–64.8	54.7 ± 6.8	43.2–72.0	4.5	4.4

1. Merlins were not observed in the study of Bruderer & Boldt (2001). Only two Merlins were observed in the study of Bruderer et al. (2010).
2. Only two observations in Bruderer & Boldt (2001).
3. These frequencies were obtained from filming. The remaining frequencies were obtained using the variation in intensity of the radar echoes which are created by wing-beats. The wing-beat variations could be distinguished from phases of the flight which involved no wing-beats.

FIG 26. Adult Hobbies in flight. (Left: Dave Soons)

TABLE 4 Mean flight speeds of migrating Merlins and Peregrines measured on straight paths to the nearest 0.5 km/h. From Cochrane & Applegate (1986).

Species	Duration (minutes)[1]	Ground speed (km/h)	Air speed (km/h)
Merlin, immature male	20	48.5	48.5
Merlin, immature male	28.5	30	30.5
Merlin, adult female	30.5	74	44
Merlin, immature female	40.5	30	44
Mean		45.6	39.3
Peregrine, adult female	55[2]	50	49
Peregrine, immature female	83	49.5	36.5
Peregrine, immature female	9	53	53.5
Peregrine, immature male	9	36.5	36.5
Peregrine, immature male	17	70	50.5
Peregrine, immature male	129.5[2]	35	36
Mean		48.8	43.7

1. Time over which speed was calculated.
2. The falcon was flying in a strong cross-wind.

Cochrane & Applegate (1986) measured the migration speeds of Peregrines and Merlins in the USA using a combination of radiotelemetry and visual observation. The researchers noted that both species soared during migration and rarely flew in straight lines when hunting, but collected data from periods of flapping flight: these are set down in Table 4. The data for migratory Peregrines in Table 4 show reasonable agreement with those in Table 3.

AVIAN PREY ESCAPE STRATEGIES

Flocking by prey species, as a defence strategy against predation, is discussed in Chapter 7. Here we consider the potential strategies employed by individual birds when they are attacked. There are four main possibilities. The prey bird can dive in an attempt to reach cover before being overtaken; it can attempt to outfly the predator in a horizontal chase, a tactic often employed if there is no time to reach ground cover but tree/shrub cover is available at flying height, or if distance can be gained which can be converted into time for a controlled ground landing, or which persuades the predator to abandon the chase; it can out-manoeuvre the predator by making one or more tight turns in order to gain the time needed to reach cover or to persuade the predator to look elsewhere; or it can fly upwards in an attempt to outfly the predator vertically, again hoping to persuade the predator to abandon the pursuit.

Diving for cover is a tactic which requires sufficient time to be available for a controlled landing on the ground, and so is dependent on where the prey bird is situated when it comes under attack. In general, therefore, it does not require specific flight abilities by the prey: rather it requires sensible foraging and vigilance. The remaining three escape strategies are dependent on flight capability. Hedenström & Rosén (2001) explored these options with particular reference to hunting Eleonora's Falcons, but the modelling they present has relevance for all avian-prey–avian-predator interactions. The climbing ability of a bird depends upon morphological data (mass, mass of flight muscle, wing-beat frequency and wing span) as well as air density, but these parameters combine in a complex way which does not lend itself to an easy explanation. Hedenström & Rosén therefore provide data from measurements of climbing speed of some potential prey species. They note that the decision of a Skylark to outclimb a pursuing Merlin – the classic ringing flight (see Chapter 7 for further details) – is a good strategy, as about 25% of the mass of a Skylark is flight muscle, which gives them good climbing ability. But, surprisingly, the data of Hedenström & Rosén suggest that Dunlin (*Calidris alpina*) also have good climbing ability, which raises the question of why the waders, which are winter prey of both Merlin and Peregrine, rarely attempt to outclimb a pursuing falcon (though such behaviour has been seen – see, for instance, Lima 1993). Presumably the rarity of outclimbing attempts is a consequence of the flocking behaviour of Dunlin taking precedence over the potential response of an individual bird, whereas the solitary Skylark naturally adopts the best defence strategy. It is also the case that waders will dive into the sea to escape attack (see, for instance, Boyce 1985), this perhaps offering a more immediate escape strategy.

Fast horizontal flight and tight turning require specific morphological features, the former necessitating large flight muscles and a drag-reducing shape, the latter low wing loading. Low wing loading is a characteristic of hirundines, and it is no surprise that the Hobby, which predates them, has a similarly low loading value. The Merlin, with its higher wing loading, seeks prey which is less agile. The response of a grouse to an attack by a Peregrine is to attempt outflying by fast horizontal flight, the aim being to reach safety before being captured. In a study by Pennycuick *et al.* (1994) on the contest between the Peregrine and the Sage Grouse (*Centrocercus urophasianus*), a North American grouse species, calculations of maximum flight speed indicated that the grouse was faster than the falcon in level flight, but that the morphology of the grouse was not suited for aerobic flight and that the power input for acceleration and fast flight would fairly rapidly result in oxygen debt. The grouse would therefore need to reach safety quickly and to have created a sufficient time gap to allow a safe landing if a short run to cover was needed. Similar reasoning would apply to the smaller British grouse species: the Red Grouse has been timed at speeds to 100 km/h, but again has a limited range at such speeds. As grouse have very high wing loadings – being heavy, in part because of large flight muscles, and having short wings which are excellent for acceleration and fast flight – they cannot make fast turns and, when pursued, make fast flights in straight lines, using their knowledge of their territory to head for the nearest position of good cover.

Diving as a strategy – diving through the air, that is, rather than diving into a water body – is not often used as predators, being invariably heavier, have the advantage in diving speed. Some passerines are, however, known to employ the tactic, often using a tight vertical turn as a modification of the horizontal flight and turn to gain time and position.

THE HUNTING TECHNIQUES OF BRITISH FALCONS

Peregrine
Flight
When considering Kestrels below, vision is considered before flight, but when the species of interest is the Peregrine it is natural to consider flight first, as the falcon's oft-quoted position as the fastest creature on Earth and the (occasionally exaggerated) claims for its top speed make the Peregrine's stoop an obvious candidate for observation and research. Both Cade (1982) and Ratcliffe (1993) quote claimed speeds for Peregrines from early observers, but not until the 1980s are claims from 'modern' equipment available for assessment. Alerstam (1987), while using tracking radar to monitor bird migration in southern Sweden, observed two stoops (and an aborted stoop) by a Peregrine apparently against Skylarks. The average stoop speeds for the falcon were 25 m/s (90 km/h) over stoop periods of about 50 seconds for the two full stoops, with a maximum speed of 39 m/s (140 km/h) during one ten-second time interval. The Peregrine's stoop angle was 30 degrees for the first attack, 64 degrees for the second (in each case relative to the horizontal). Alerstam also measured stoops by a Goshawk, which averaged 25 m/s (90 km/h)

on two stoops with a top speed of about 30 m/s (108 km/h). Later Tucker *et al.* (1998) measured a speed of 58 m/s (209 km/h) for a falconry (i.e. captive) Gyrfalcon, at which time the speed was the highest ever recorded for a bird. Peter & Kestenholz (1998) measured 51 m/s (184 km/h) for a wild Peregrine (and 44 m/s – 158 km/h – for a Barbary falcon).

More recently various much higher speeds have been claimed for Peregrines, usually as a result of stoops associated with chasing a skydiver. However, such claims are rarely published in peer-reviewed journals. In an article describing the series of dives and the various body shapes a Peregrine assumed in following a skydiver (Franklin 1999) there seems little doubt that a speed of about 290 km/h was reached, with the possibility of speeds in excess of 320 km/h having been attained. During the stoop, as speed increased, Franklin states that the falcon went through four identifiable shape phases. The first was the 'classic falcon diamond', the wings folded back so that the wing tips and tail tip meet, but with the shoulders still discernible, the head forming the fourth point of the elongated diamond. In the second phase, the 'tight vertical tuck', the space between shoulders and body is reduced. In the 'mummy wrap' phase the interspace between shoulders and body at the base of the neck is zero, the shoulders being forced towards the crop to produce the 'mummy' shape. In the final shape the body appears elongated, the width reduced. Franklin refers to this phase as 'warpdrive vacuum pack'. In this final phase Franklin believes a large (i.e. heavy) Peregrine could reach 250 miles per hour (400 km/h), perhaps even 300 miles per hour (480 km/h).

Such speeds seem improbable, but in his consideration of the capabilities of an 'ideal' falcon (a falcon with morphological and aerodynamic properties which mirror those of real birds, but idealised to avoid the constraints which would inevitably apply to a real bird as a consequence of changes in drag during stooping) Tucker (1998) considered that a large ideal falcon could have a top speed of 174 m/s (626 km/h), which would almost certainly make falcons the world's fastest creatures (Note 3.2).

Here, some general thoughts on stooping falcons and the limitations on stoop speed in the wild are presented, with minimal mathematics. On Earth, an object falling through any medium is subject to gravity, which accelerates it, converting potential energy into kinetic energy. The falling is also subject to drag as a consequence of the resistance to movement of the medium. This resistance clearly depends on the density of the medium – for instance, things fall faster through air than through water. Drag is itself a complex aerodynamic force which comprises several differing forces dependent on the profile of the object, the density of the medium, and the interference of the air patterns flowing over the

FIG 27. A diving Perlin (a Peregrine–Merlin cross falconry bird).

FIG 28. A falconry Peregrine executing a high-speed turn.

FIG 29. A stoop by a falconry Peregrine.

object. In addition, for a bird which evolution has formed to maximise lift, there is an induced drag as a consequence of the inherent lift generated by that shape in any non-vertical dive. A further complication in birds is the distinction that is often made between parasitic drag, due to the bird's body, and profile drag, which is contributed by the wings after exclusion of induced drag.

As the speed of the falling object increases, so does the drag, but gravity remains constant so that ultimately gravity and drag are in equilibrium: the object has reached terminal velocity.

Terminal velocity (*V*) can be calculated from the equation:

$$V = \frac{\sqrt{2mg}}{\rho A C_d}$$

where *m* is the mass of the object, *g* is the acceleration due to gravity (= 9.81 m/s²), ρ is the density of the medium through which the object is falling, *A* is the profile (cross-sectional area) of the object as seen by the medium, C_d is the drag coefficient of the object.

This equation can be used to calculate the fastest speed of a falcon diving vertically – provided a value for *A* and C_d can be derived. In practice deriving either is no easy task.

But there is a problem with the equation above. Falcons rarely dive vertically, and the inclusion of a glide angle complicates the equation significantly, requiring solution in the form of quartic (fourth-order quadratic) equation. The solution of such an equation allows the terminal velocity of a diving 'ideal' falcon to be calculated at various dive angles, and underpins the work presented by Tucker (1998).

Ideal falcons differ from real ones in not having to concern themselves with time and distance. While terminal velocity is a handy concept, the nature of it – the balance of drag and gravity – means it is approached asymptotically and, as such, is never reached. Figure 30 shows the variation of speed with time for an ideal falcon stooping at various glide angles, while Fig. 31 shows the altitude loss against time for the same angles. In each case the time is that required to reach 95% of terminal velocity. The two figures are from the work of Tucker (1998), which, interestingly, showed that the total distance travelled by the falcon (the combination of horizontal distance and altitude loss) was almost independent of glide angle (within 6% of the mean in all cases) and was about 1,200 m. As Tucker also notes, if the drag coefficient is assumed to be smaller (the parasitic drag coefficient was assumed to be 0.18 to produce Figs 30 & 31) the terminal speed of the falcon will be higher, but the distance travelled will be greater: if a coefficient of 0.07 is assumed, the value which yields a speed of 174 m/s, then the total distance travelled must be almost 3,000 m.

Figures 30 and 31 illustrate one of the problems with assessing the flight speed capabilities of Peregrines – there is, in all probability, a great difference between how fast a falcon can dive and how fast it does dive. While they may indeed be able to travel at or above 300 km/h, in the wild they are very unlikely to do so because to attain such speeds they need to be so far from their prey they may have difficulty in spotting it (despite their excellent eyesight – see below) and may, in any case, be travelling so fast that striking the prey would incur

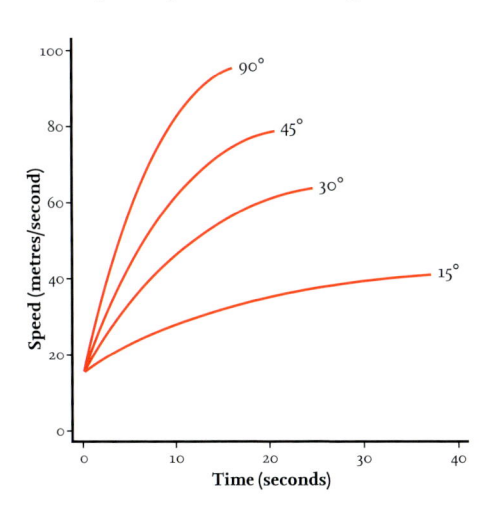

FIG 30. Variation of speed with time for an ideal falcon with a weight of 1 kg at different dive angles. The falcon is assumed to start the dive at 15 m/s, and times are to reach 95% of terminal velocity. Redrawn from Tucker 1998.

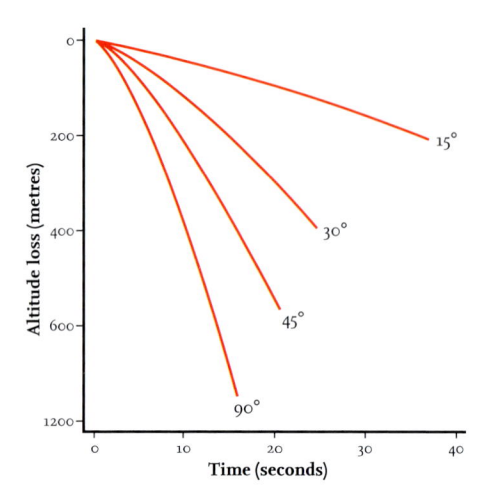

FIG 31. Variation of altitude loss with time for an ideal falcon with a weight of 1 kg at different dive angles. The falcon is assumed to start the dive at 15 m/s and times are to reach 95% of terminal velocity. Redrawn from Tucker 1998.

significant physical damage. Speed has to be regulated in such a way as to reach the prey before it has time to make its escape, but at a velocity which allows the falcon to be uninjured and able to fly again tomorrow. This regulation of speed by the falcon was illustrated with a falconry bird (a Gyrfalcon weighing 1.02 kg) in a study reported in Tucker *et al.* (1998). As noted above, the falcon attained a speed of 58 m/s (209 km/h). Such speeds were recorded in steep dives: as an example, Tucker and colleagues noted one dive at an angle of 62 degrees (from the horizontal): the falcon dived from a height of 500 m and travelled 250 m horizontally to reach the falconer.

In calculations of an ideal falcon following a similar dive path, the researchers suggest an acceleration phase followed by a flight at constant speed and a deceleration phase. To maintain a constant speed while continuing to dive, the falcon increases its drag coefficient, then increases it again more radically to decelerate. In each case the falcon has a number of options – it can change the angle of attack of the wing to vary induced drag, or lower its feet to increase parasitic drag. While, clearly, the bird was diving towards a lure rather than prey, it is probable that wild birds will follow the same general pattern, though observations of wild falcons accelerating into a dive by energetic wing flapping suggest that they may attain higher dive speeds, perhaps to 250 km/h. During the rapid deceleration phase the falcon experiences a negative *g*-force, though the exact size of this depends entirely on timescale. Tucker (1999), on the basis of accelerometers attached to falconry birds, suggests that in very rapid decelerations the bird may experience 5–10 *g*, which is extraordinarily high –

high enough to tear the wings off most aircraft and to endanger even those built specifically for aerobatics, and to induce unconsciousness in pilots. However, the latter requires a sustained high negative g-force for several seconds on a seated pilot, with blood unable to reach the brain, while the falcon is horizontal and the deceleration is for fractions of a second (Note 3.3). That the falcon's wings remain intact is much more impressive, as aircraft wing damage is sustained very quickly. But, of course, suggesting that falcons can experience such high decelerations does not, again, mean that wild birds routinely do so. Experienced wild birds are almost certainly capable of moderating both speed and deceleration in ways which minimise stress on their bodies while allowing success rates at reaching prey that are high enough to avoid starvation.

Vision

As well as being capable of speeds which raise the Peregrine to the level of myth and legend, falcons are also renowned for having excellent eyesight, with suggestions that it is better than that of humans by factors of up to ten. Here again the reality is somewhat more measured. Consideration of falcon vision must start with the physiology of the falcon eye, which differs from that of humans in having two foveas. The human fovea lies in the centre of the macular region of the retina and is the position of visual acuity, about half the fibres of the optic nerve carrying information from it. Falcons have two foveas, one positioned as in humans, the other being offset (Fig. 32).

In a study of a male American Kestrel, Hirsch (1982) considered that the visual acuity of the falcon and a human were comparable, despite the eye of the former being only half the size of a human eye, the difference being explained by superior optics and closer-packed photoreceptors. Vision was further enhanced by the second, deep, fovea which afforded the bird a further magnification, suggesting that the falcon's vision was at least 1.33 times more acute than that of the human eye. Reymond (1985), working with the Wedge-tailed Eagle (*Aquila audax*), suggested the eagle's vision was probably twice that of a human, but

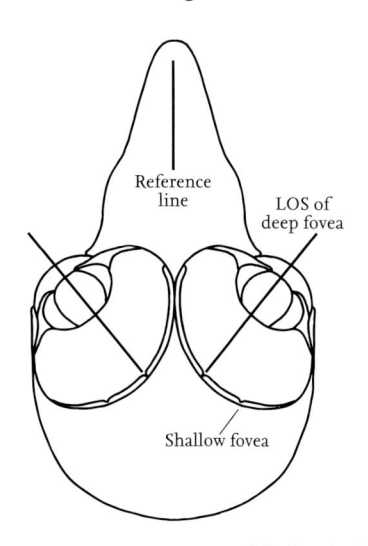

FIG 32. Representation of the head of a falcon with eye positions in the skull, fovea positions within the eye and line of sight (LOS) marked.

FIG 33. Male Kestrel. The size of the eye relative to head size is remarkable.

did note that the eagle's vision was more sensitive to light levels than that of a human, performance deteriorating more rapidly as luminance declined: this finding confirmed an earlier study of Fox *et al.* (1976) which had shown a similar decline in falcon vision with declining luminance. Building on Reymond's work, Martin (1986) was able to suggest that for the eyes of large falcons the visual acuity might be twice that of a human. Jones *et al.* (2007) came to the same conclusion. If a factor-of-two vision improvement does not sound enough, it has to be remembered that human vision is itself remarkably acute, so that falcon vision is extraordinarily good (Note 3.4).

As noted above, the falcon's deep fovea provides maximum visual acuity. This explains why when an observer stands in front of a falcon the bird will move its head from side to side (behaviour which is well known to anyone who has spent time with a falcon), using the deep fovea for closer examination. This is necessary because falcon eyes have minimal movement within their sockets – about 2–5 degrees only (see, for instance, Jones et al. 2007) – so the bird must move its head to allow the deep fovea to scan the object of interest.

While observing Gyrfalcons in the wild in Arctic Canada about 10 years ago in locations where they were chiefly hunting Ptarmigan and Arctic Ground Squirrel (*Urocitellus parryii*), but also waders and gulls, I was surprised to see that when stooping after prey the falcons were not travelling in straight lines. Discovering that the falcon eye was twin-fovea, and that the more visually acute fovea was set at an angle of about 40 degrees to the main linear axis of the bird (i.e. the axis running through the bill, the centre of the head, back and tail), and knowing that falcon eyes do not move in their sockets, I calculated the path a falcon would travel if it maintained the deep fovea on the prey. The flight path is shown in Fig. 34. At any instant the angle (Ψ) subtended by the tangent to the falcon's flight path and the line of sight to the prey is constant (assuming the prey remains stationary), and in polar coordinates the equation of the flight path is

$$r = ae^{b\theta}$$

with r and θ as defined in Fig. 34, e the base of natural logarithms, a and b are constants which define the tightness of curvature of the resulting curved path. b is dependent on Ψ, the relationship between them being

$$b = \frac{1}{\tan \Psi}$$

If $\Psi = 90°$, then $b = 0$ and the curve is a circle of radius a. As Ψ reduces towards zero, b increases and the curvature becomes less tight: ultimately, $\Psi = 0°$, b approaches, and the spiral becomes a straight line.

In mathematics the curve is well known and is called a logarithmic spiral: Fig. 35 shows a typical spiral. It is well known in nature as well – fossil ammonites and *Nautilus* species illustrate the spiral, which in their case is formed by the production of new *camerae* (chambers) into which the animal

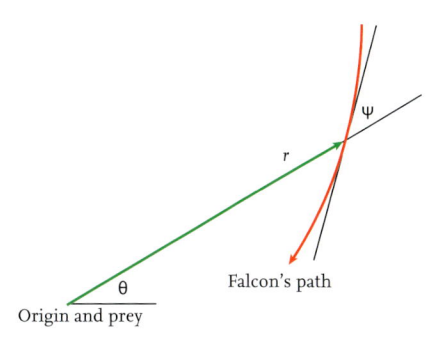

FIG 34. Flight path of a falcon relative to its prey. Assuming the prey remains stationary, the distance, r, to the prey and the angle, θ, between the line of sight of the falcon and the ground plane changes as the falcon moves, but the angle Ψ remains constant. Ψ is the angle between the tangent to the falcon's path and the line of sight at any instance.

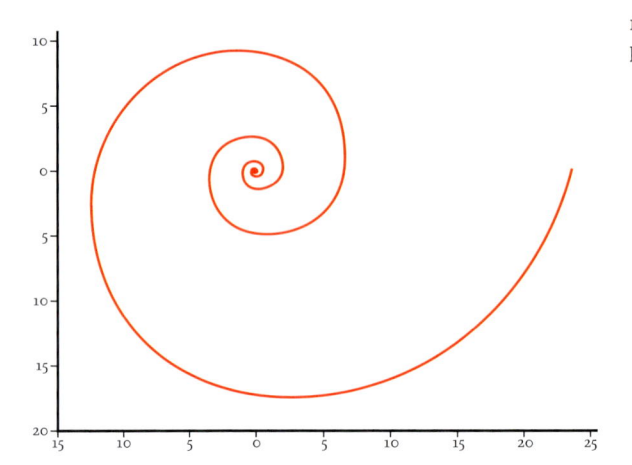

FIG 35. Typical logarithmic spiral.

moves as it grows (Figs 36a & b). Romanesco, also known as Romanesque cauliflower or Romanesque broccoli, a vegetable which has become popular in recent times though it has been grown for many years, also grows in a logarithmic spiral (Fig. 36c). Insects will also fly in logarithmic spirals, though in this case the reason is not the eye, but the fact that they fly in straight lines by keeping a light source at a constant angle to the direction of travel. When the light source is the sun or moon, it is effectively at infinity and so, as noted above, the 'curved' flight path is a straight line. But when the light source is a light bulb or a candle flame the insect spirals into it along a curve of form as in Fig. 35.

Once the form of flight path of the hunting Gyrfalcons on Bylot Island had been defined, the obvious question was, why were the falcons choosing to deviate from the idea that the shortest distance between two points is a straight line? While working on the underlying mathematics, my attention was drawn

FIG 36. Examples of logarithmic spirals in nature. (a) An ammonite, a common fossil found in the UK. (b) Section through the shell of a nautilus. (c) A Romanesque.

to a paper by Tucker (2000a), who had already identified the logarithmic spiral as the likely flight path and investigated the effect of following curved paths. In deference to the primary author, the nomenclature of Fig. 34 follows that of Tucker, and what follows also refers to that paper.

If the falcon were to follow a straight-line path to its prey, then to maintain observation with the deep fovea the bird would need to move its head sideways by 40 degrees, a turn which would inevitably increase drag. While this seemingly makes the reason why the falcon chooses the spiral path clear, this obvious reasoning works only if the decrease in speed (caused by increased drag) along the straight path is such that the falcon will always reach the prey quicker along the spiral path. Importantly, Tucker considered this issue in his work. He noted that there was a value of the ratio of drag coefficients in the two cases (falcon flies with head bent off axis (C_{db}) or falcon flies with head straight (C_{ds})) at which the increased speed on the spiral path and the increased drag on the straight path compensated and the falcon reached the prey at the same time whichever path was chosen. One extremely useful property of logarithmic spirals is that the ratio of the curved and straight path lengths is essentially constant at all times. If the ratio of drag coefficients was lower than this 'break-even' value then the straight path is still the best route. If not, the spiral path wins. Tucker calculated that the break-even value of C_{db}/C_{ds} was 1.8. In a separate paper Tucker (2000b) noted that the ratio was in the range 2–6 as speed increased, and so was always above the break-even value.

So, having calculated theoretically for an ideal falcon that a spiral path was better than a straight path with the head bent to one side, the next objective was to see if real falcons were following spiral paths. This was tested by observing a pair of Peregrines hunting from an eyrie in central Colorado, using the naked eye, binoculars, tripod-mounted telescopes and an optical tracing device fitted to a telescope (Tucker *et al.* 2000). Over three weeks of observation Tucker and co-workers were certain that curved flight paths were being observed, though the researchers had some reservations. Principal of these was the difficulty of being precise about the path being followed by a fast-travelling falcon viewed at a distance, though the tracking device employed eliminated most of this concern. The Peregrines were also noted as invariably curving to the right, and observations were almost exclusively in the morning when such a path would bring the falcon out of the sun as it approached its prey. Since Peregrines are known to dive out of the sun, this might therefore explain the observations. However, the preponderance of right-curving paths did suggest that the falcons favoured their right eye. Tucker *et al.* also considered the possibility that a curved path might mislead prey into believing they were not under attack. However, the number of curved paths observed seemed to justify the idea that use of the deep fovea for prey monitoring was the explanation for the behaviour.

More recently, the use of video cameras on falconry birds – attached either to the falcon's back or mounted on a modified hood – have suggested that hunting falcons may occasionally use saccadic (i.e. very fast) head movements so as to scan prey with the deep fovea, with minimal impact on drag and that use of such movements may negate the need for a spiral flight path (Kane & Zamani 2014; a subsequent paper, Kane *et al.* 2015, extended the study of hood cameras to the Goshawk). However, the falcons involved in the study were hunting birds in flight and, it would seem, from relatively short distances, which would favour the use of the binocular vision afforded by the shallow fovea: even if the deep fovea and a spiral flight path are used in pursuit of ground, or close-to-ground, prey, when acute vision is required to observe small prey from a significant distance and to isolate it from a confusing background, it is assumed that for the final metres before interception a falcon would change from deep-fovea to shallow-fovea vision, as binocular vision would be required for attack. However, Kane & Zamani do also suggest that for longer falcon–prey distances their data are still consistent with use of the shallow fovea, though it is not clear what definition of longer distance is referred to. In the wild, falcons will sometimes fly at heights above 300–400 m. Spotting small prey from such heights, and perhaps at significant horizontal distances as well, would certainly seem to require use of the deep fovea for tracking, at least in the early stages of a stoop.

Observations of curved falcon flight paths encouraged me to consider the construction of an inertial measurement unit (IMU) which would fly on a falconry bird and pinpoint the exact hunting track. With the assistance of others (as noted, with thanks, in the Acknowledgements) a small IMU was constructed which included a Global Positioning System (GPS) unit. Size and mass were, of course, a critical element of the design. The mass of a carried device has a direct effect on the bird, as it represents an immediate increase in weight without the advantage of an increase in fitness which might otherwise compensate in the longer term. In studies by the team at the University of Groningen who trained Kestrels to fly specific routes along corridors, i.e. in still air, male and female falcons were loaded with 31 g or 61 g of lead (Videler *et al.* 1988a, 1988b). Unloaded, the falcons flew at speeds close to the V_{mr} (maximum range speed) predicted by theoretical models, but as the payload increased speeds declined, approaching the V_{mp} (minimum power speed) predicted by the same models. As the payload mass increased, the decline in speed was accompanied by an increase in wing-beat frequency and an increase in tail inclination. However, the payloads carried by the falcons were large. The male weighed 160 g, the female 190 g, so 31 g represented 19% and 16% of body weight respectively for male and female, while 61 g represented 38% and 32%. In the wild lower alterations in body mass are likely on a short-term, perhaps daily, basis.

Hambly et al. (2004), looking at the variation in flight energy costs and flight speeds in the Cockatiel (*Nymphicus hollandicus* – an endemic Australian species also known as the Quarrion), noted that daily weight changes of 5–10% were normal. In a study that used the elimination of injected ^{13}C (a stable isotope of carbon) rather than the double-labelled water technique (see Chapter 5, Note 5.3), Hambly and colleagues noted declines in flight speed with payloads of 5%, 10% and 15%, but then a reversion to control flight speed (i.e. 0% payload) at 20%. The decreases in speed for lower payloads were initially small (of order 1% at 5% payload, 3% at 10% payload), but rose to 7% at 15% payload, a statistically significant difference). The reversion to normal flight speed at the higher payload was accompanied by a significant increase in wing-beat frequency: the Cockatiels were changing their behaviour rather than simply reducing their speed. The energy cost of flying increased with payload, but was not significantly higher than unloaded flight for any payload. While this is surprising, Hambly et al. noted that Cockatiels regularly increase their body mass by 20% prior to migration, suggesting that the observed behavioural change at the higher payload was an inherent strategy.

While falcons differ from Cockatiels in many ways, the results of the study by Hambly et al. suggest that, provided the mass of a unit added to a falcon was minimised, the effect on flight characteristics would be limited. This was further confirmed by a study by Pennycuick et al. (2012) using Rose-coloured Starlings (*Pastor roseus*), though a separate issue was noted in that work, namely the interference with the air flowing over the back of the bird. In the work of Pennycuick et al. the payload (a dummy transmitter) projected 6 mm above the back of the bird. This increased the drag coefficient of the bird (as measured in a wind tunnel) by 50%, but the addition of an angled aerial increased the drag coefficient by almost 200%. Pennycuick and co-workers then simulated the effect of the mass and drag coefficient increases by considering the actual flight of a Barnacle Goose (*Branta leucopsis*) which had been fitted with a satellite transmitter to study its migration. The simulation suggested that the effect of increased mass due to the transmitter would have been small, but the effect of drag coefficient increase would have reduced range and decreased energy reserves on arrival (Note 3.5).

In preparing an IMU to fly on falcons it was therefore clear that both mass and profile were important. While mass would need to be no more than 10% of body weight, a UK ethics committee considering university proposals for fitting transmitters and other devices on birds suggests a limit of 5%, and so this was set as a target. In addition, a minimal profile was sought. Proprietary units were soon discarded in favour of one constructed on a purpose-designed printed circuit board (pcb). An integral-aerial GPS unit was chosen, as this would eliminate the need for an external aerial. Data from the GPS were stored in solid-state memory on the bird to eliminate the need for, and weight of, a radio transmitter. The first units collected GPS data at 10 Hz, but it was soon apparent that at this speed the GPS unit was occasionally unstable, adding spurious data to its output. The second units therefore slowed the speed to 1 Hz, but added a tri-axial gyroscope, accelerometer and magnetometer which operated at higher speeds and which could be used to interpret the flight path between GPS readings, as well as allowing roll, pitch and yaw to be calculated. This unit weighed about 9 g and had a square profile 12 mm × 6 mm. It clipped to a standard harness which many falconry birds wear, a 'backpack' which sits between the wings and so offers a stable platform for the IMU. The IMUs are powered by small LiPo batteries. The first units were used on Peregrine and Peregrine hybrid falcons, though later units could also be flown by all the British falcons.

One other factor must be considered before assuming that data obtained by fitting the IMUs to falconry birds reflected the behaviour of wild birds. While clearly it is difficult to be definitive, particularly for an individual falcon, the work of Feenders & Bateson (2013) on groups of age-matched Starlings, one group hand-reared, the other not, suggests that basic cognitive performance was identical in the two groups, though some emotional responses differed (for example, the hand-reared birds were less neophobic). It is therefore considered reasonable to assume that falconry birds and wild falcons do not differ significantly in their flight behaviour.

FIG 37. An inertial measurement unit (IMU) attached to a Peregrine, and the bird about to take off.

Figures 38 and 39 are the profile and plan of the final dive in a successful Peregrine attack on a Red Grouse in Scotland. The Peregrine had been released in order to fly to a kite on a very windy day. The wind speed at ground level was steady at about 7 m/s, occasionally gusting stronger, but had increased by the time the kite was at altitude, being about 10 m/s at 2 m above the ground when the kite broke free of its line and disappeared. The falconer was about to bring the Peregrine down to the lure when a grouse broke cover a short distance behind, presumably alarmed by the noise and activity which accompanied the kite failure. The grouse rose and was immediately attacked by the falcon. The 'elbow' in Fig. 38 is curious and is more likely to represent uncertainty in height position, which may occur if a small number of satellites are viewed by the IMU (to overcome this problem a barometer was added to later IMUs). Superimposed on Fig. 39 is a logarithmic spiral with $\Psi = 40$ degrees.

During the early part of the stoop the falcon was at a height of about 100 m above the ground, but it dropped and remained steady at a height of about 50 m, before the final dive took it more or less to ground level, the grouse being taken (and held) at about 8 m above the ground. What is not clear is whether the falcon locked onto the grouse at Point A in Fig. 38 then carried on for a few metres (to Point B in Fig. 38), or whether Point A represents the falcon's change in speed to allow it to catch, rather than strike, the prey. The latter would seem more likely, in which case Point B represents the point at which the falcon

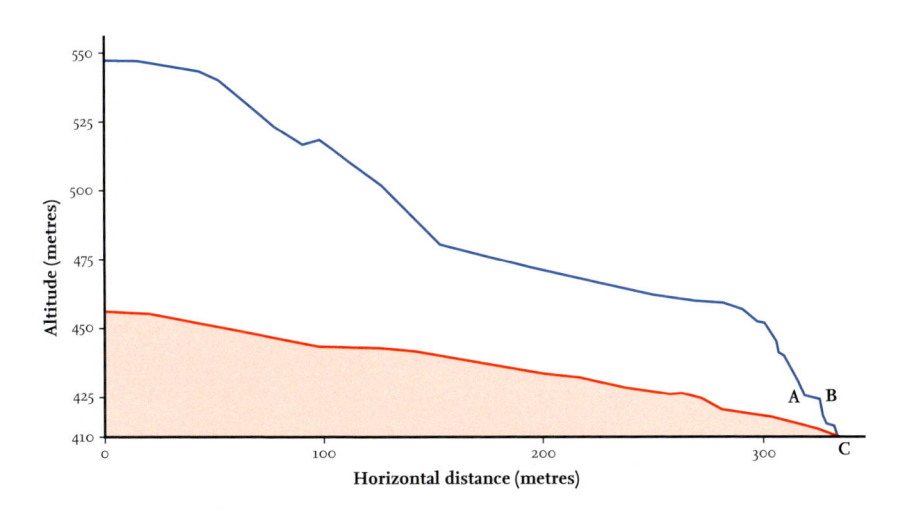

FIG 38. Profile of the final stoop of a successful Peregrine attack on a Red Grouse.

locked onto to the prey. Either way, the falcon and prey then dropped more or less vertically to the ground (Point C in Fig. 38).

The falcon covered the first 280 m of horizontal distance, dropping about 130 m, at an average speed of 12.4 m/s, then dropped much more steeply onto the grouse at a speed of 16.7 m/s. These speeds are not high, but wind must be taken into account. The wind was rising up the slope down which the falcon flew, and so represented a persistent headwind (as was also true for the grouse). Frictional effects mean that wind speed varies with height above the ground. The variation is complicated by the roughness of the ground and the stability of the air column, but for heights below about 100 m is best described by a power law relationship:

$$\frac{V_h}{V_r} = \left(\frac{h}{r}\right)^c$$

FIG 39. Plan of the final stoop of the successful attack shown in Fig. 38. The red line is the track of the Peregrine; the dotted curve is a section of a logarithmic spiral.

where V_h is the wind speed at height h, V_r is reference (measured) windspeed at height r, and c is a constant dependent on local conditions. In general, for a uniform surface and stable atmosphere, $c = 0.143$.

Assuming $r = 2$ m, the height at which the measuring anemometer was set, the air speed of the falcon would have been 17.5 m/s higher than the calculated ground speed, i.e. 29.9 m/s (107.6 km/h) during the early part of the stoop. The final stoop was closer to the ground, but the Peregrine would still have been battling a wind of 15.5–17.5 m/s, and would have increased its drag as its profile to the wind would have increased as it turned more vertical. It seems reasonable therefore to assume that the same wind-speed correction applies, and that the falcon was travelling at a speed of about 120 km/h during the final phase of the attack.

Figure 39 suggests that at point A the Peregrine's flight path altered to a straight line, presumably as stereo vision took over for the final attack. During the main part of the stoop the path followed is very close to the theoretical curve for $\Psi = 40$ degrees, but caution is required before any firm conclusion can be drawn. The curve is for one falcon during one attack on a windy day, though the stoop was head-on to the wind. While other curved flight paths were also observed, science requires that many falcons making many attacks along curved paths are observed for confirmation of deep-fovea/logarithmic spiral flight paths.

HUNTER AND HUNTED · 79

FIG 40. Peregrine mantling its prey after the successful attack depicted in Figs 38 and 39.

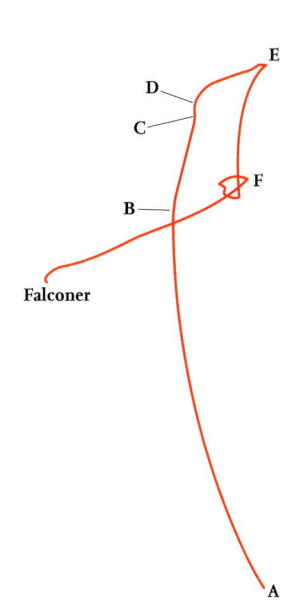

FIG 41. Plan of the attack of a Peregrine on a pair of Red Grouse. See text for an explanation of points A–F.

From the same series of flights in Scotland, one other is particularly interesting. Figure 41 shows an attack against a pair of grouse which were raised by a dog: the grouse took flight in directions separated by an angle of about 30–40 degrees. Starting its attack at a height of only 55 m above the grouse (point A) and attacking towards rising ground, the Peregrine was unable to accelerate quickly and reached a speed of only 23 m/s (83 km/h). At first the falcon followed a curved path (consistent with a logarithmic spiral), but at point B it changed to a straight path. Visually it then seemed that the falcon gave up pursuit of the grouse which was veering to the left, in favour of attacking the one which was veering right. However, the track clearly shows that the Peregrine initially set chase for the rightward travelling grouse, but then changed to the leftward prey (point C), and almost instantly changed again (point D) and returned to the rightward grouse. Whether these decisions were made as the falcon was realising its speed was inadequate to catch either grouse is impossible to say, but the momentary hesitations meant it missed both birds – though visually that always seemed the most likely outcome – and broke off the chase (point E), performing a tight circle (F) either for a last look towards the position where the grouse had been or in frustration, before returning to the falconer.

A different form of behaviour was shown in a Peregrine attack on a female Pheasant (Fig. 42). The Peregrine attacked the Pheasant from a height of only 34 m, having gently drifted down from about 50 m. Despite being at a low altitude the falcon accelerated rapidly by turning into an almost vertical stoop and hit the Pheasant at a speed of approximately 29 m/s (104 km/h) (point A). The Pheasant, stunned but alive, fell towards the ground. The Peregrine, still travelling quickly, though slowing rapidly, performed three tight left turns and approached the prey again. Though stunned, the Pheasant was presumably not badly injured and the falcon decided against locking on and taking the prey to the ground where impact and, perhaps, a lucky strike from beak or claw could cause itself injury. It therefore struck the Pheasant again at more or less the same position though closer to the ground. Once on the ground the Pheasant was still active, and the Peregrine, circling right this time, passed over it, not striking it but apparently gauging its condition. The Peregrine then circled right again and this time did make a further strike (point B) which sent the quarry off to the left. The Peregrine then made a lazier turn right, by which time the Pheasant had moved a little further (to point C), but was now injured and essentially helpless, allowing the falcon to grab it on its final attack and to dispatch it soon after. This was the only strafing attack I have observed, but apparently such a technique is often used to subdue or immobilise potentially dangerous quarry.

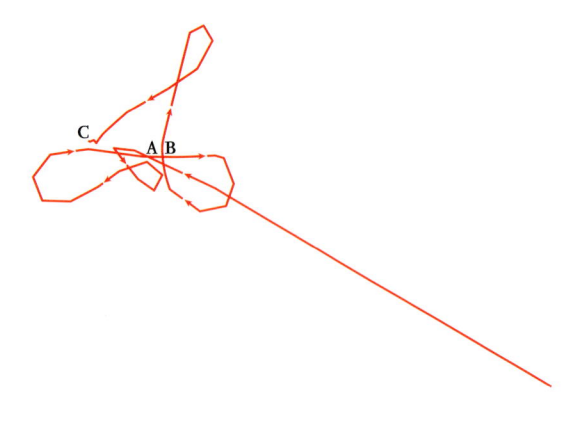

FIG 42. Plan of the strafing attack of a Peregrine on a female Pheasant. See text for an explanation of points A–C.

HUNTER AND HUNTED · 81

One further Peregrine attack is also of interest (Fig. 43). In this, in central England, a dog raised a covey of Grey Partridge (*Perdix perdix*). The Peregrine stooped, but abandoned the attack (point A) when the quarry reached shrub below a belt of trees. Making several circles, then rising over the trees, the Peregrine

FIG 43. Profile of a Peregrine flight that included an unsuccessful attack on a covey of Grey Partridge, followed by a successful attack on a Red-legged Partridge. See text for an explanation of points A–C.

FIG 44. Peregrine with a Red-legged Partridge caught after the attack that is shown in Fig. 43.

spotted a covey of Red-legged Partridge (*Alectoris rufa*) which had been raised by the falconer and his dog, who had continued into the field beyond the tree-belt. The falcon attacked and locked onto a bird after a short, very steep stoop (point C), taking it to the ground.

Kestrel

Vision

It was assumed for many years that while the vision of falcons was more acute than that of humans, they viewed the world in much the same way – in other words, that their vision encompassed the same range of wavelengths as ours does, even though it was not known if their colour vision was the same (Note 3.6).

In the 1970s it was shown that some birds could see ultraviolet (UV) light. At first UV vision was identified in very few – pigeons, chickens and hummingbirds – but the list was gradually extended. Since UV may cause retina damage, most animals, including humans, have UV-opaque structures in front of the retina to filter out much of the UV light and so minimise damage to it. The obvious question to ask is why birds may allow UV to reach the retina – what advantages accrue which compensate for the potential damage incurred? Bennett & Cuthill (1994) considered this in a seminal paper, suggesting three potential advantages: that UV vision allowed the position of the sun to be determined even if it was not visible; that UV vision allowed sexual signalling in the UV part of the spectrum, enhancing the visible-light signalling of plumage; and that UV vision aided foraging. As evidence in support of the last of these, Bennett & Cuthill noted that many fruits reflect UV whereas leaves do not, and as a consequence fruits are more conspicuous to a UV-sensitive eye.

Soon after the report by Bennett & Cuthill (1994), work in Finland by Viitala *et al.* (1995) suggested that the ability to see UV aided Kestrels in hunting, as they were able to see the urine and faeces trails left by Field Voles (*Microtus agrestis*), these trails reflecting UV light (wavelength 320–400 nm) with a particular peak at 340 nm. It was known that voles, and other small rodents, use urine and faeces to mark their trails – a form of territoriality rather than a sign of incontinence, though people whose children have pet mice often suggest the latter – and that both are visible in UV light. Viitala and colleagues therefore investigated whether this UV reflection was being used by Kestrels as a clue to areas of high vole numbers. Nineteen captured wild Kestrels were offered four laboratory areas, and the time they spent in each and the number of times they scanned an area were computed. The Kestrels were found to favour areas treated with vole urine and faeces over clean areas when each was illuminated in UV light, but showed no preference when the areas were illuminated in visible light. In the wild, areas close to 27 nest boxes erected for Kestrel occupation were then treated to create three classes: in one class artificial vole trails were formed, these being further marked by vole urine and faeces; in a second class artificial trails were formed, but were unmarked; and in the third class the areas were clean of both trails and marking. The Kestrels preferentially hunted in the Class 1 areas. (As a digression, Rough-legged Buzzards (*Buteo lagopus*) were also shown to have a preference for the Class 1 areas, a finding confirmed by a later report: Koivula & Viitala 1999.) As it was known that mouse urine fluoresces (in faint blue light) (e.g. Desjardin *et al.* 1973), Viitala *et al.* (1995) considered this as a potential clue, but considered that the fluorescence was so dim that it was readily masked in daylight and so was unlikely to be offering the Kestrels usable information. The Finnish team also dismissed olfaction as a clue, as the Kestrels had shown no interest in the vole-marked laboratory areas when they were illuminated by visible light. Later studies by the Finnish team showed that the urine of Bank Voles (*Myodes glareolus*) also reflected UV light, also with a peak at around 340 nm (Koivula *et al.* 1999a). The data of Koivula *et al.* also suggested that reflectance was strongest (the urine tracks were brightest) in mature male voles.

Although Koivula *et al.* did not investigate urination frequency and pattern, this finding of a distinction between the urine trails of dominant and other males is consistent with the findings of Desjardin *et al.* (1973), who noted that both degree and frequency of urine marking in House Mice (*Mus musculus*) depended on rank – dominant male mice urinated often and everywhere, subordinate males urinated infrequently and only in the cage corners – and also with Rozenfeld *et al.* (1987), who found similar pattern/frequency differences in Bank Voles. In later studies the Finnish team (Honkavaara *et al.* 2002) noted that the ability of Kestrels to detect the position of high vole activity would also be of assistance in areas where vole populations are subject to significant fluctuations – as they are in northern Fennoscandia.

In a further report, the Finnish team noted that Kestrels preferred the scent markings of Sibling Voles (*Microtus levis*) to those of either Bank or Field voles (with no difference in preference between the latter), and also preferred the trails of mature males to those of mature females or juveniles (Koivula *et al.* 1999b). Given that the trails of mature males were shown to glow brighter in UV, this might explain that preference, rather than that mature males were either larger or tastier (either of which could explain the preference for Sibling Voles) (Note 3.7).

Later studies have also indicated that the usage of UV clues is not confined to Kestrels and Rough-legged Buzzards, Probst *et al.* (2002) showing a similar preference in the Great Grey Shrike (*Lanius excubitor*) for the scent trails of Field

Voles, while Härmä *et al.* (2011) found the same preference in the Pygmy Owl (*Glaucidium passerinum*), a diurnal owl, for the scent trails of Bank Voles.

The fact that Kestrels were seeing vole trails captured the public's imagination, and at falcon displays the handlers could be heard explaining the idea, though rather than suggesting that the UV clue was guiding the Kestrel to an area frequented by voles, it was often suggested that the hovering Kestrel was watching a vole as it followed its trail, urinating as it went, the falcon needing only to pounce at the head of the emerging UV trail to acquire a meal, a probable over-statement.

However, while the public understanding of what hovering Kestrels might actually be looking at was on the increase, within the scientific community the use of UV signalling as a cue to hunting was coming under scrutiny. Zampiga *et al.* (2006) noted that whereas Peregrines, for instance, taught their offspring the rudiments of hunting or, at least, assisted them to learn, Kestrels did not. The researchers therefore wondered whether the use of UV clues was innate, and to test this four classes of area were set up in a laboratory. In Class 1 cardboard marked with vole urine could be viewed by the tested falcons; in Class 2 the marked cardboard could only be viewed through a UV-blocking filter; in Class 3 cardboard sprinkled with water could be viewed; and in Class 4 the water-stained cardboard could be viewed only through a UV-blocking filter. Forty-four adult and 49 juvenile Kestrels were exposed to the four areas. The result was interesting, for although the adults and juveniles both showed an increased interest in the Class 1 area, the adults flew to that area more often than the juveniles, and also showed more interest in the Class 2 area. This suggested to Zampiga and colleagues that while using UV clues was innate, the juveniles needed to learn by experience that what they were seeing was prey-related. The fact that the adults viewed the Class 2 areas as well suggested that they were picking up alternative clues, though the researchers did not suggest what these might be. It would seem most likely that the adults were either detecting faint UV clues despite the blocking filter, or that they were indeed picking up fluorescence.

The latter possibility was interesting, because other studies were suggesting that UV fluorescence might be more important to raptors, while UV reflectance was less so. Chávez *et al.* (2003) had noted that UV reflectance in the urine of three endemic Chilean rodents was similar to that of the north European rodents, but Kellie *et al.* (2004) did not find similar results in Australian rodents. The team found no reflectance peaking in the UV, but did find UV fluorescence peaking, and that this peak occurred at the wavelength (about 380 nm) which was considered to be the maximum UV sensitivity of raptors. This finding was confirmed, both for fluorescence and reflectance – the latter contradicting the earlier studies – for Field Voles in a study in Finland by Huitu *et al.* (2008), but even more interesting was that the work indicated the diet of the voles influenced the peak wavelength of the fluorescence. If fed rye grass infected by fungal endophytes, the voles lost weight, but also had the wavelength of peak fluorescence shifted so that it better aligned with the UV sensitivity of predatory raptors. Loss of weight presumably persuaded the voles to eat other vegetation – the endophytes appeared to be benefiting their host by increasing resistance to vole foraging. But the shift in UV fluorescence wavelength suggested a more profound change – that the endophytes were increasing the likelihood of foraging voles being preyed upon, a rather less subtle way of preventing the host grass from being eaten. This is similar to the suggestion that a parasite alters the behaviour of mice so that they lose their fear of cat urine and, therefore, may increase their predation risk – see Note 5.1.

These studies suggested that the original work on UV reflectance might need re-examining, and in 2013 further significant work was carried out in Sweden by Lind *et al.* (2013). The Swedish team began by considering whether UV light was actually reaching the retina of the Kestrels (and of Common Buzzards, Sparrowhawks and Red Kites). Taking raptors which had been euthanised less than an hour before, they removed an eyeball, cut an opening in the back of the eye and used a spectrometer to measure the transmission of UV from a UV source placed in front of the eye. Both eyes of a single specimen of each raptor were measured, and it was found that in each case the transmittance of UV fell off steeply as the wavelength of the light decreased below 400 nm. For Kestrels 50% transmittance was at 379 nm, and zero transmittance was reached at about 340 nm. Lind *et al.* also measured the UV reflectance of various substrates and considered that the differences between the reflectance of these and vole urine were essentially indistinguishable. They also collected urine and faeces samples from both Bank Voles and Field Voles and found that they could not replicate the data of early work on the reflectance of trail markers. In the view of Lind and colleagues, UV reflectance from vole urine/faeces was unlikely to provide a reliable clue to a hunting Kestrel – though they recognise the contradiction this raises with the earlier studies mentioned above and note that resolution of the discrepancy requires further work.

So the question of whether Kestrels are using non-visible light signals to detect voles remains open. Many workers have suggested that although fluorescence rather than reflectance seems a more likely candidate for the actual mechanism, fluorescence would be masked by sunlight and, perhaps, lost against the background of UV reflectance from plants and other substrates. But that again seems to be based on ideas of vision consistent with human vision. Perhaps Kestrels (and other raptors) really are picking up signals at frequencies and with sensitivities which are, as yet, not fully understood by ourselves (Note 3.8).

Flight

Hovering, the most familiar form of hunting employed by Kestrels, is more prosaically termed flight-hunting by falcon researchers. Kestrels have low wing loading, which improves lift, and long tails, which also aid in this form of flight. However, unlike hummingbirds, which can hover for long periods in still air, Kestrels are not adapted for the wing movements that such sustained hovering requires. Some observers consider that it is perfectly feasible for a Kestrel to hover for short periods on perfectly calm days, but in general what the hovering Kestrel is actually doing is flying into the wind at the same speed as the wind, so that it hangs effectively motionless in space. At low wind speeds this requires the wings to be flapped, wing-beats, often slow beats, being characteristic of the hovering falcon. At higher wind speeds the Kestrel can glide into the wind with outstretched wings. In a study area in southern Scotland, Village (1983a) looked at the variation of flapping and gliding flight at various wind speeds (Figs 45 & 46). Note that to avoid flapping the wind must have a vertical as well as a horizontal component, so Kestrels frequently flight-hunt above slopes which face the wind, and will also utilise the updrafts created by other obstructions to the wind's progress, such as man-made structures.

Flight-hunting is energy-intensive in comparison to perch-hunting, when, as noted in Chapter 5, the falcon watches from a perch and makes forays when prey is spotted. As a consequence, in their studies of the energetics of the Kestrel the team at Groningen

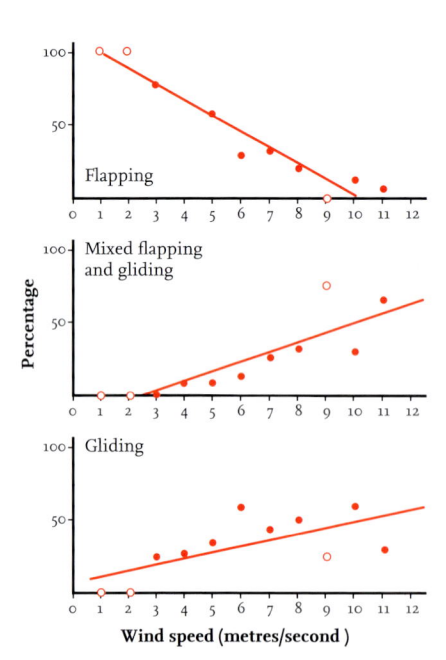

FIG 45. Variation of frequency of Kestrel flapping and gliding flight during flight-hunting with wind speed. At low wind speeds the falcon must flap more to remain static. Redrawn and rescaled from Village 1983a.

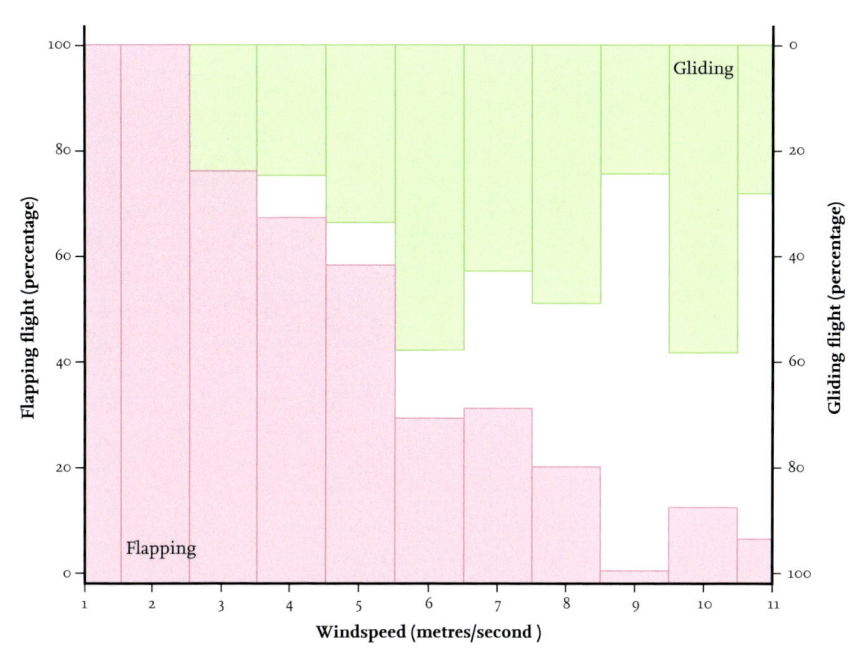

FIG 46. Histogram derived from the data of Fig. 45.

University found that Kestrels perch-hunted more frequently in winter (Masman *et al.* (1988a). In summer Masman and co-workers found that flight-hunting yielded 4.7 small mammals per hour, this falling to 2.2 per hour in winter. The figures for perch-hunting were 0.1 per hour in summer and 0.3 per hour in winter (Note 3.9). Clearly the Kestrel is opting for a low-profit, but low-cost, hunting technique in winter to minimise energy expenditure. These findings are consistent with data on Kestrels from a study area in southern Scotland – Village (1983a) (Fig. 47).

What is interesting is that Village noted that the percentage of flight-hunts increased with wind speed during spring and autumn, the possibility of glide (flap-free) hovering clearly being energy-efficient: in each case at speeds above about 5 m/s flight-hunting was the dominant hunting technique, and at about 10 m/s constituted 90–100% of all hunting. During the summer flight-hunting represented about 100% of hunting at all wind speeds, the return in terms of prey obtained outweighing energy costs when there were nestlings to feed. From Fig. 47, flight-hunting accounts for only 10–15% of hunting during the winter: though winters may be windy, convective heat losses presumably outweigh the energy gain from flight-hunting. Village (1983a) also considered

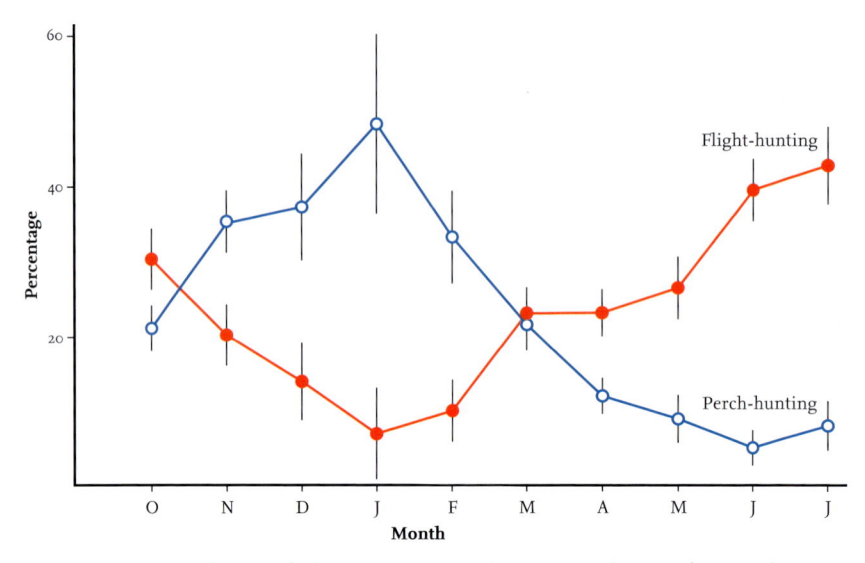

FIG 47. Variation of Kestrel flight-hunting and perch-hunting with time of year. Redrawn from Village 1983a.

the variation in usage of flight-hunting with wind speeds in spring (March/April), summer (June/July) and autumn (October/November). He noted that most flight-hunting occurred in wind speeds of 5–10 m/s in all three seasons, but that the likelihood of the hunting technique was correlated with wind speed in spring and autumn (Fig. 48).

Village does not suggest a rationale for this difference, but it seems probable that it is related to the need to provision nestlings, which requires adult Kestrels to choose the most efficient hunting technique at all times, regardless of the energy cost. Village also noted the position of the hovering Kestrels with respect to wind direction. Kestrels prefer to hover on sloping land, using windward rather than leeward slopes, and prefer the wind to be at right angles, or nearly so, to the slope direction (Fig. 49). This is a not entirely surprising result, as all who have walked on windy days will know that winds at right angles to hill slopes create significant updrafts.

However, while the data of Village suggest that Kestrels prefer windy days, both high and low winds increase the effort required to hover. In a further study by the Groningen University group (Videler *et al.* 1983), Village's data were confirmed – Kestrels predominantly flight-hunted with wind speeds between 5 m/s and 10 m/s. But above 10 m/s the time spent flight-hunting declined significantly, Videler and co-workers finding that while the Kestrels

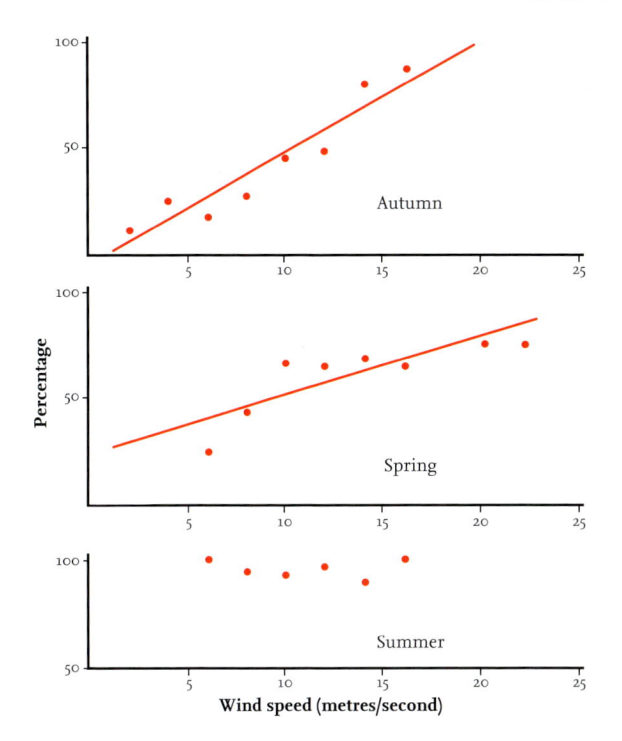

FIG 48. Variation of Kestrel flight-hunting with windspeed during three seasons. Redrawn from Village 1983a.

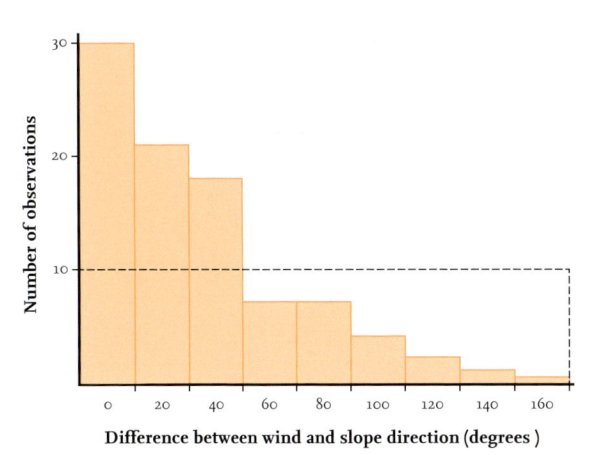

FIG 49. Slope selection by flight-hunting Kestrels. The histogram records the number of observations against the difference between wind direction and slope direction. The dotted line is the distribution that would be expected if there was no preference in wind-slope difference. Redrawn from Village 1983a.

flight-hunted for an average of 25 seconds when the wind speed was 5–10 m/s, at wind speeds above 12 m/s this fell below 15 seconds: a comparable time, about 15 seconds or less, was also observed at wind speeds below 5 m/s. The reason almost certainly involves the energy requirements of hovering at both low and high wind speeds – Videler *et al.* compared theoretical models of the energy requirements of hovering, and all predict that these rise below 5 m/s and above 10 m/s, with minimal energy costs at 7–8 m/s – but these researchers also showed that the position of the falcon's head was critical. During hovering the falcon is watching the ground below. For maximum hunting efficiency the eyes (and therefore the head, as movement of the eye itself is minimal) must remain motionless. During the gliding phase between wing-beats this can be achieved by allowing the centre of gravity of the bird to move. The centre of gravity starts close to the head, but can be allowed to move by extension of the neck. Videler *et al.* measured the potential extension on newly dead Kestrels: about 4 cm of movement could be made. So the Kestrel attains a position above the point of observation and allows its neck to extend as the wind pushes the body backwards so as to maintain the head motionless. At an extension of 4 cm the bird must then flap its wings in order to move the centre of gravity forward again (and reduce neck extension) so the process can be repeated. The head also has to remain motionless during the wing flapping which repositions the centre of gravity. To investigate this, Videler *et al.* filmed hovering Kestrels at up to 200 frames/second (fps). This showed that both vertical and lateral head movements occurred during the wing-beat, but that in neither case were head displacements greater than about 5 mm and were often less.

In order to gain further information on the Kestrel's hovering technique, I employed the IMU described above and high-speed digital video cameras to provide synchronised data between a falcon-mounted sensor and images of the position of wings. Although the cameras could operate at very high speeds they were set at only 500 fps, as the wing-beat frequency of hovering Kestrels is much lower. To synchronise the images and the output from the IMU's gyro and accelerometers, a separate time-code generator, collecting time signals from the same satellites, was used to trigger the cameras: Fig. 50 is a schematic of the set-up. In commissioning tests the internal clocks of the cameras were found to be accurate to 9 µs/s, which was acceptable for filming at 500 fps (i.e. an image every 2 ms) as the satellite time signal was used to reset the internal clocks every second. Timing data from the satellite was recorded both on the relevant frame image and on the metadata of each frame. Time was recorded in milliseconds (ms), with an accuracy of 1 ms, i.e. comparable to that of the unit's internal clock. In each case the satellite times were used to reset the camera and unit

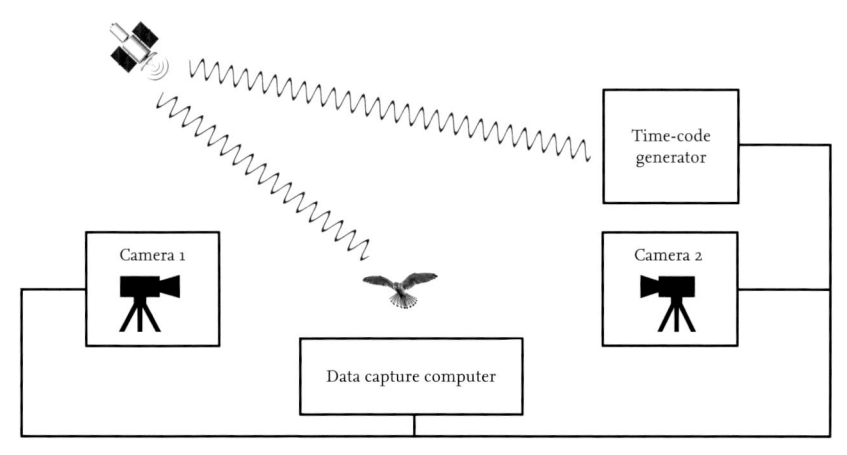

FIG 50. Schematic of equipment used to produce stereo images of a hovering Kestrel, with the falcon carrying an IMU measuring flight parameters.

times every 1 second. The Kestrel used was not a falconry bird, but a bird used extensively in filming.

In the wild, Kestrels usually hover from about 8 m up to 20 m. Shrubb (1993a) noted that the height chosen varied with the season, seemingly as a result of vegetation length, the falcons hovering above the usual range in summer when vegetation was thicker or taller. Shrubb noted in particular that in summer Kestrels were hovering high over unmown fields, but much lower as soon as these were mown, and conjectured whether the greater heights allowed a wider range of view. This would be correct if visual signals (either UV or visible light) are the primary or sole source of hunting cues, as picking up unnatural (i.e. not wind-generated) vegetation movements might be picked up over a longer distance, allowing a move to a closer vantage point for more decisive information.

Filming took place on a hillside in the Mendips south of Bristol. It was a beautiful December day, just as the weather forecasters had predicted, apart from one essential detail. Rather than the wind being 15–20 km/h (about 4–5.5 m/s), which would have been ideal for wing-beat hovering and, because of the site, the windward side of a relatively steep hill, might also have allowed periods of glide hovering, it was a disappointing 1–2 m/s – which meant that the Kestrel had to work hard to maintain position and actually lost height gradually during the hover on several occasions. The falcon was released by one handler and flew to a second handler who had positioned a lure in a grass tussock, the Kestrel hovering while searching for the lure before dropping to take the food titbit attached to it. Full analysis of the data will be reported elsewhere.

92 · FALCONS

ABOVE AND OPPOSITE: **FIG 51.** One complete wing-beat of a hovering Kestrel. The images form part of a beat filmed at 500 fps.

FIG 52. A hovering Kestrel.

FIG 53. Kestrel manoeuvring at high speed in Cornwall. (James Sellen)

Merlin

Bond (1936) noted that a falconry Merlin was twice timed over a distance of 1,542 feet (470 m), and that its speed was calculated at 29.9 miles per hour (47.8 km/h). Bond stated that by comparison to prey species Merlins 'flew faster than Quail or Meadowlarks, and more slowly, at least in a rising flight, than Horned [Shore] Larks. It could catch a shrike in a long course free from cover; it was keener after shrikes than any other bird. It could catch, bring down and kill a dove, or even a strong adult common pigeon if released within 50 feet, but was easily outdistanced by these birds after they had attained top speed.' In chasing these prey species Bond guessed the Merlin was about 50% faster than when it flew to the lure, i.e. a speed of about 70 km/h.

As shown in Table 4, Cochrane & Applegate (1986) measured Merlins in level flight travelling at speeds of 30–48 km/h. By what might best be termed a happy mistake I was also able to measure the flight speed of a female Merlin. While I was photographing a Merlin nest site from a hide, the male falcon perched conveniently close on a post with a Meadow Pipit it had captured. Previous examination had suggested that this, and one or two neighbouring posts, were used for plucking prey. Entranced by the falcon and awaiting the opportunity to film the plucking, I was caught unawares when the male called, and then picked up the prey in its bill and half-turned. Realising too late what was going to happen, I had no time to change the camera speed – and the resulting photo has the incoming female as a blur. The female was flying along the wire fence line, and by measuring the fence-wire separation close to where she was photographed, and making assumptions about the length of the bird, a speed of 31.7–36.4 km/h was calculated, in good agreement with the range observed by Cochrane & Applegate. The speed does not seem high until one remembers that the female is taking prey from the male's bill without either hauling him off the post or knocking him off with her wing: it was, in fact, a beautifully executed high-speed manoeuvre, and very likely at a speed lower (perhaps much lower) than might be expected in a high-speed chase for prey.

To test the speed of a falconry bird, the IMU described above was attached to a young male Merlin weighing about 140 g. Figure 55 is a plan of a typical flight, during which the falcon made several brief attempts (points A, B and C) to capture larks. During the illustrated flight the wind speed was reasonably constant at about 5.5 m/s from the south, explaining the rapid movement away from the falconer on release, and the curving flight back to the lure when the flight was terminated. During the flight, the fastest air speed achieved by the Merlin was during the return to the falconer, perhaps because of the enthusiasm to reach food after the abortive hunting attempts, when the falcon achieved a ground speed of 13.2 m/s more or less directly into the wind. Again allowing for the variation of wind speed with height above the ground, this

FIG 54. Male Merlin with Meadow Pipit (a). After calling, the male took the prey in his bill (b), but before I could change speed on the camera the female had taken it from him (c).

translates to an air speed of 20.9 m/s (75.2 km/h). As already noted, further details will be presented in a research report on the flight characteristics of all British falcons.

Hobby
Harpum (1983) noted a Hobby over the outskirts of Cheltenham at a time when earlier fieldwork meant he had readily to hand a clinometer and stop watch. The falcon was hunting a group of House Martins (*Delichon urbicum*) (but failed to capture one in the observed stoop). Harpum describes the Hobby's flight, which

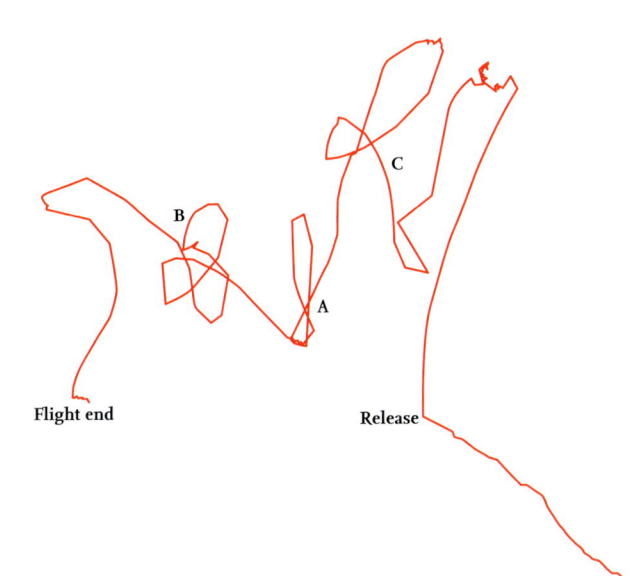

FIG 55. Plan of flight of a juvenile male Merlin. See the text for an explanation of points A–C.

FIG 56. Young male Merlin with the IMU from which the track of Fig. 55 was derived.

began with soaring at a height of about 300 m, then involved a shallow, powered dive prior to a steep stoop. Harpum had to make a guess of the Hobby's speed at the start of the stoop, suggesting this was about 80 km/h, the speed of a fast pigeon. Then using the clinometer and stopwatch, and later a theodolite to line up his data against local landmarks, Harpum calculated that at the bottom of the stoop the Hobby was travelling at 142.6 ± 8.0 km/h.

Harpum notes that the energy of the Hobby travelling at that speed is 157 J (J = joule, the SI unit of energy), which he notes is about one-tenth the energy required to dispatch a cricket ball for six. Harpum also states that the radius of the Hobby's pull-out circle at the base of the stoop was about 24 m, and so calculates the centripetal force as about 7.5 g (though this is actually the force assuming the higher speed Harpum suggests, i.e. 150.6 km/h). To actually experience that force the Hobby would have needed to maintain its speed through the pull-out arc, and the radius of the arc would really have had to be 24 m. Since the force is proportional to the square of the velocity, relatively small reductions in speed reduce the force significantly. Force is also inversely proportional to the radius of the pull-out arc, so if that were doubled, the force would be halved. Nevertheless, Harpum's observation and calculations imply that as well as being a master of fast, agile flight, Hobbies can engage in formidable stooping attacks.

The only other data located within the literature derive from the radar-tracking data of Alerstam (1987) mentioned above in the context of Peregrine stoops. Alerstam monitored two stoops of a male Hobby hunting Barn Swallows. One attack began at an altitude of 700 m with a 20–30-second period of horizontal flapping to gain speed to 23.5 m/s (84.6 km/h), and continued with an 80-second dive at an angle of no more than 9 degrees during which the falcon continued to beat its wings, gaining a top speed of 29.9 m/s (108 km/h). In the second stoop the bird did not beat its wings during a 90-second dive at an angle of 7.8 degrees with an average speed of 20.2 m/s (73 km/h). On both occasions the Hobby failed to capture the intended prey.

Unfortunately there are very few 'domestic' Hobbies in Britain, the falcons having a reputation for being difficult to train and having the far from endearing habit of often choosing to migrate rather than return to the falconer, as migration and the period allowed for hunting coincide. However, one falconer has now decided to invest time in a Hobby and has agreed to fly my IMU on the bird during 2015, so data will be available for the forthcoming research paper previously mentioned in this chapter.

CHAPTER 4

The Peregrine

PEREGRINE – FROM THE LATIN *peregrinus*, wanderer. The vernacular name, rendered in Latin, dates from the thirteenth century, though the earliest source of *Falco peregrinus* is disputed. One possible source was Albertus Magnus (Albert the Great), also known as Albert of Cologne, a Dominican Friar in Germany. Born in Bavaria sometime in the 1190s (no exact date is known, but he was over 80 when he died in 1280), he was educated at Italy's Padua University before becoming a Dominican. He lectured at Cologne, and later in Paris where one pupil was Thomas Aquinas. Albert's fame as a scholar and teacher resulted in his being made a bishop, but he resigned this position to return to monasticism. His studies and writings covered all the sciences from astronomy to zoology, and also included law, music and morality, as well as alchemy, which at the time (and for many years after his death), was considered a legitimate science. Albert produced a number of books, one of which, on falcons and falconry, was later incorporated into *De Animalibus*, a vast book on all aspects of the natural world. In his writings he refers to *Falco peregrinus*, the name being given to a large falcon, much favoured by falconers, because its nests were usually too difficult to reach so that young birds were most often captured as they 'wandered' from the eyrie, or were 'wandering' back to their breeding places in later years.

The alternative source is *De Arte Venandi cum Avibus* (The Art of Hunting with Birds) by Frederick II (1194–1250), who became King of Germany at the age of two, lost that title after one year, but was crowned King of Sicily the following year, aged four. He became King of Germany again in 1212 and Holy Roman Emperor in 1220, though his position did not prevent a series of conflicts with the Pope, one of which led him to be excommunicated. Frederick was a gifted linguist, a lover of the arts, a rationalist at a time when superstition was the norm, and a scientist, though some of his experiments on people were both deeply unpleasant and cruel. He was a gifted falconer who experimented with breeding to better understand the birds. His book is scholarly and certainly mentions the Peregrine, but experts are undecided as to whether Frederick took his lead from Albertus or vice versa, or whether both were using a name common at the time. An illustration in Frederick's book also casts doubt on the suggestion that it was the trapping of the falcon which was the basis of its name. The illustration shows a Peregrine on the stern of a ship. Was the fact that the falcon occasionally used ships as resting or staging posts during 'wandering' journeys the real reason for the name?

Whichever source for the name is correct, it pre-dates Linnaeus' *Systema Naturæ* by many centuries. What is even more surprising is that although Linnaeus included *Falco columbarius*, *Falco subbuteo* and *Falco tinnunculus* in the 1758 edition of his book, he did not include *Falco peregrinus*. That was first seen in *Ornithologia Britannica*, published in 1771 by the English ornithologist Marmaduke Tunstall. The Peregrine described by Tunstall in 1771 was British. The stuffed, mounted falcon is still held at the Natural History Museum in Tring, Hertfordshire, and is the type-specimen of the nominate (*F. p. peregrinus*). The nominate is the most widespread of the 20 potential subspecies currently under discussion (see notes to Fig. 57). Nominate Peregrines range from Ireland in the west to about 140°E (perhaps even to the Sea of Okhotsk and the Sea of Japan, though whether that is the case is contentious – Fig. 57). Nominate birds breed north of the Arctic Circle in Fennoscandia, and southward to northern Italy in Europe and to the border of North Korea in Asia. Within that vast range there are, perhaps not surprisingly, variations in plumage shade and markings which have led some to suggest further subspecies.

In Britain, according to the BOU, the vernacular name for the bird is Peregrine, the Union considering the 'international' name to be Peregrine Falcon. In the USA the Peregrine was originally called the Duck Hawk, for obvious reasons, while in Britain (where Peregrines are much less likely to kill ducks than appears the case in North America) it was often called the Blue Hawk because of the plumage colour of adults.

As with the Merlin, the collective noun for Peregrines, a cadge, derives from falconry. Cadge is a falconry term for an open square frame set on four legs on which a group of falcons can be carried. Since falconers in general use Peregrines, the term came to be applied to a group of this species.

Peregrines are found on all continents apart from Antarctica. BirdLife International (www.birdlife.org) calculates that the combined range of the

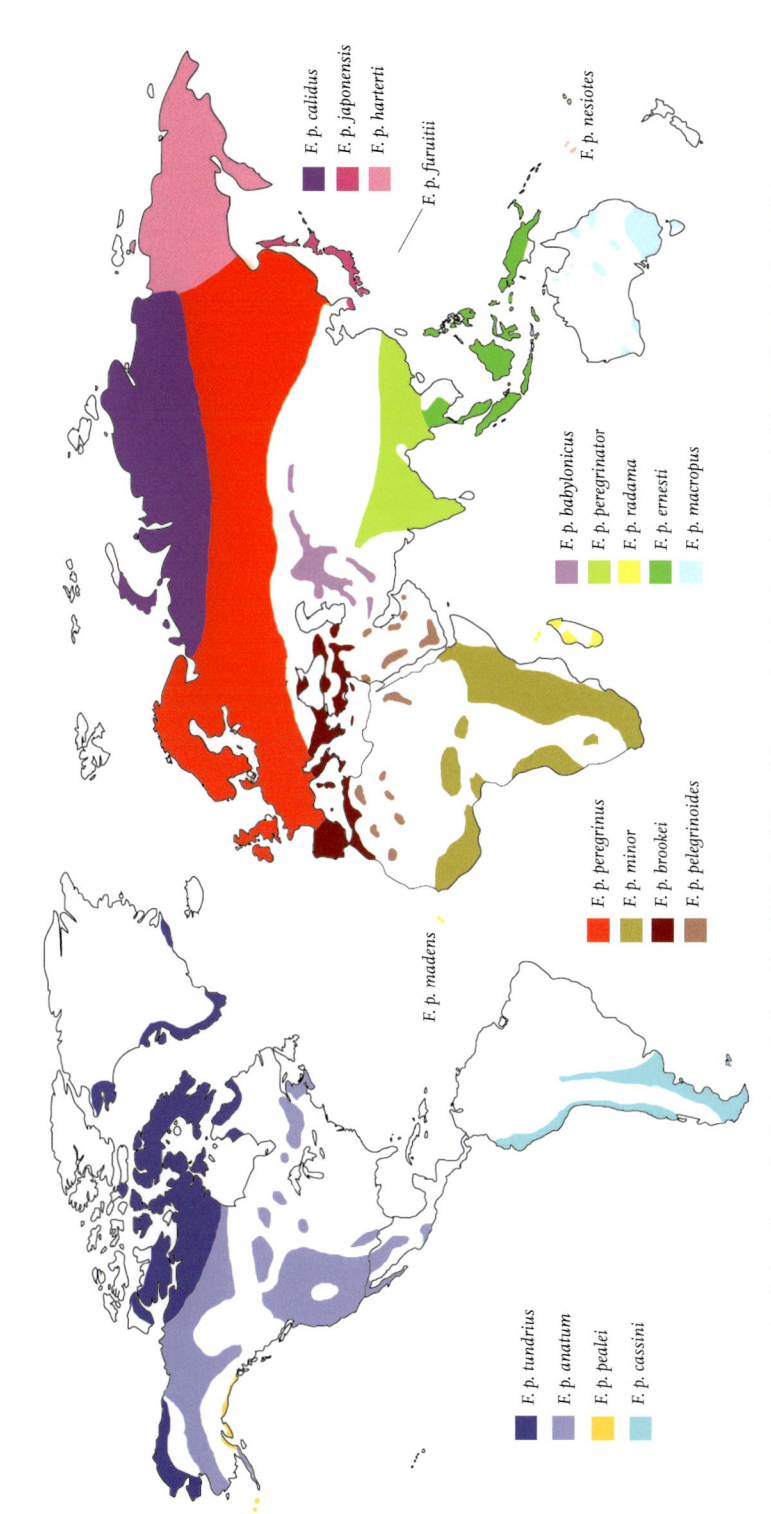

FIG 57. In their authoritative book on the Peregrine White *et al.* (2013a) list 20 potential subspecies, though this total has varied over the years and is still the subject of debate. The 20th subspecies of White *et al.* is *F. p. submelanogenys*, the Black-cheeked Peregrine of south-west Australia, which most experts believe is indistinguishable from *F. p. macropus*.

Peregrine and Barbary falcons (some experts consider the latter to be a subspecies of the former) constitutes 31% of the land surface of the Earth, an area of almost 46,500,000 km². As well as Antarctica, Peregrines are also absent from some oceanic islands, most notably Iceland, which has been colonised by both the 'cold-weather' falcons – Gyrfalcon and Merlin – but also New Zealand, and other islands that are so close to the continental mainland that the absence is curious. In their superb book on the Peregrine, White *et al.* (2013a) identify these and other islands not settled by Peregrines and consider the reasons for the falcon's absence, suggesting that the fact that it is philopatric – i.e. that it tends to return to the previous breeding places or, in the case of young birds, the neighbourhood of the birth site – militates against colonisation. However, as White *et al.* note, at some time in the past Peregrines did successfully colonise most of the world, and the reason for some islands remaining uncolonised when nearby islands or the continental mainland do have Peregrines, is enigmatic. Even more baffling is the fact that Peregrines are not found in areas of South America that appear to have the correct habitat (though much of that area comprises the Amazon Basin, and Peregrines are very definitely not forest falcons), despite these being adjacent to areas which are home to the species and over which Peregrines migrate.

The subspecies currently recognised (Fig. 57) conform, in general, to Gloger's rule (that darker subspecies inhabit areas of higher relative humidity: *F. p. ernesti* of Malaysia and Indonesia is the darkest, though the African Peregrines are also dark) and Bergmann's rule (that larger subspecies occur at higher latitudes: *F. p. pealei* of the Aleutian Islands and southern Alaskan coast is the largest, though the Nearctic and Palearctic Tundra Peregrines are almost as large).

Captive Peregrines are regularly cross-bred with other falcons, and this has caused some concern as falconry birds occasionally escape and wild Peregrines have been known to breed with them. In the USA eggs have been collected where this is known to have occurred, for fear of diluting the wild stock, but given the numbers involved and the reduced fertility often associated with hybrids, this fear is probably unfounded. Oliphant (1991) also reports hybridisation between a wild male Peregrine and a female Prairie Falcon.

In Britain the Peregrine is an iconic bird: the largest of the four British falcons, a stocky, powerful bird, seen as the epitome of the avian predator. It is a bird with a history of association with royalty, a bird of myth and legend, reputedly the fastest creature on the planet. The Peregrine's decline towards extinction in the 1960s as a result of pesticide contamination did as much as any other species to galvanise the conservation movement. One consequence was the Peregrine becoming a bird admired by, one could almost say beloved of, the public, particularly after its enthusiasm for urban living meant it became a more familiar sight, though it is still at risk from those who see it as the indiscriminate killer of domestic pigeons and game species.

Yet despite the Peregrine being one of the most famous and photographed of all British birds, studies of it and its behaviour are more limited than might be anticipated. As a consequence, some of the information set down below relies on Peregrine observations from across the world, as it is widely assumed that many behavioural traits, for instance breeding displays, are common across subspecies.

DIMENSIONS

Overall length (bill tip to tail tip) 360–500 mm – females are significantly larger than males.
Wing: male 309 ± 8 mm; female 356 ± 7 mm.
Tail: male 144 ± 5 mm; female 173 ± 4 mm.
Bill: male 20.0 ± 1.0 mm; female 24.0 ± 0.9 mm.
Tarsus: male 46.9 ± 1.1 mm; female 53.5 ± 1.5 mm.
Toe: male 47.2 ± 1.3 mm; female 53.7 ± 2.0 mm.
Claw: male 19.6 ± 0.7 mm; female 22.9 ± 0.9 mm.
Juvenile wing: female 360 ± 7 mm; male 315 ± 6 mm.
Juvenile tail: male 153 ± 4 mm; female 182 ± 5 mm.

WEIGHT

Females are about 50% heavier than males.
Male 650 ± 80g; female 1,100 ± 200g. In both cases the weight is variable throughout the year and particularly during the breeding season.

PLUMAGE

Adult male
The upperparts are blue-grey, darker, occasionally black, on the crown and paler on the tail, faintly barred darker apart from the head, which has a solid colour. The cheeks are pale cream or white, apart from dark ear coverts and a broad malar stripe. While most falcons exhibit such a stripe, the Peregrine's 'moustache' is one of its defining characteristics. The throat is white. The underparts are cream or pale cream-buff with dark spotting, heavier towards the vent, which gives the appearance of barring. The underwing is greyer, again with dark

spotting which suggests barring. The undertail is barred dark brown, the broadest bar being subterminal. The terminal bar is white. The iris is dark brown, the eye ring yellow, as is the cere. The bill base is also yellow, the remainder being slate-blue, darker (even black) at the tip. The tarsi and feet are yellow, the claws black.

Adult female

As male, but often darker above and more buff below, the markings heavier. However, differences in colour and marking overlap so that these slight plumage

FIG 58. Adult female Peregrine.

differences are not diagnostic in the field. However, when male and female are together the size difference is extremely obvious.

Juvenile
The head is dark brown, the crown feathers with cream edges, the forehead entirely cream, as are cheeks and throat. Remaining upperparts are dark brown

FIG 59. Juvenile Peregrine. (Nathan Guttridge)

with chestnut feather edges. The underparts are cream or cream/buff with dark brown arrow-like markings, these larger and denser towards the vent. The undertail is barred with brown, again the broadest bar being subterminal. The terminal bar is white/cream. The underwing is cream/buff with heavy dark barring. The iris is dark brown, the eye ring and cere pale blue or pale blue-green. The bill is blue-grey, darker at the tip. The tarsi and feet also blue or blue-green, but occasionally pale yellow.

Nestling

The first down is white/pale cream. Second down (at about 14 days) is pale grey. Feathers develop at about 17 days, with juvenile plumage complete at about 28 days. The iris is black, the cere and feet pale grey.

FIG 60. Peregrine nestling. The chick has been brought up from a cliff-ledge eyrie for ringing.

Moult

Adult Peregrines moult completely each summer. The female may start her moult at the time of laying the third egg. The male may start as soon as the eggs are hatched, despite the need to ensure good flight ability in the arduous period of provisioning himself, his mate and the brood. However, individual birds may alter the timing, some not starting the moult of flight feathers and tail until breeding is well advanced, though even in these cases body feathers may be moulted earlier. The moult begins with the primary feathers, which are moulted following the sequence 4–5–3–6–7–2–8–1–9–10. The moult of secondaries follows the sequence 5–7–4–8–3–6–9–2–10–11–1. The tail feathers are moulted sometime after P4 in the sequence 1–2–3–6–4–5, but full tail moult is often completed before the primaries. Body feathers are moulted at the same time, though a few feathers may be retained on the head and back. The full moult takes between 128 and 185 days (Mebs 1960). Northern female Peregrines are known to suspend the moult sequence during breeding, which may explain, in part, the fact that some adults complete the moult much faster than others.

Juveniles start a complete moult in the early spring of their second calendar year, though there is evidence from North American Peregrines that juveniles

FIG 61. Adult Peregrine in flight. (Nathan Guttridge)

may moult some body feathers during their first winter (Walton, in White *et al.* 2002). The juvenile moult sequence is the same as for the adults, though in general moulting of the tail starts sooner after the moult of P4 (as early as six days: Mebs 1960). However, the time to completion of the full moult to adult plumage is very individual, with some birds completing by summer, others not until the winter.

HABITAT

The Peregrine is primarily a predator of avian prey. The species therefore requires open country over which it can hunt, one irony of the Peregrine story in Britain being that it is likely that the felling of the forests which once cloaked the island and the agricultural landscape that was then created improved the country for the falcons, providing them with open country, though the later use of pesticides to aid agricultural yields was to imperil the species. As well as hunting areas the Peregrine needs adequate populations of potential prey species (though the Peregrine's plasticity in terms of diet means that the list of suitable prey is a long one), and steep, inaccessible cliffs on which it can breed. The combination is best represented by sea cliffs and inland mountain areas, and these are the principal areas in which the falcons breed in the British Isles. As a consequence there are few Peregrines in the east of the country, the flat lands of East Anglia offering no suitable breeding sites, a lack which is no compensation for the open land and copious supplies of prey. The increasing cliff heights of Britain's southern coast offer opportunities, those of Cornwall and, to a lesser extent, Devon even more. Much of the Welsh coastline is suitable Peregrine country, as are the cliffs of northwest and the very north of northeast England. Scotland's coast provides excellent opportunities, these more limited on the east coast of central Scotland. Orkney, Shetland and many of Scotland's Western Isles are also good Peregrine habitat. In Ireland the entire coastline is welcoming to the falcon. In sea-cliff areas there are colonies of gulls and other seabirds, but also pigeons – Rock Doves and the Feral Pigeons that derive from wild stock after domestication and later escape – while the immediate inland area is usually farmland well-stocked with bird species.

Away from the coast, upland areas with rocky outcrops provide a natural habitat – these very often the national parks of England and Wales, together with the Cambrian Mountains, the high spine of Wales. In Scotland the Highlands offer an obvious home: as Ratcliffe (1993) notes in his authoritative book on the species, only in the Scottish Highlands does the British Peregrine truly live in an area virtually untouched by humans. Inland Ireland is much less hospitable. Away from the national parks and wilderness Scotland, geography and humans occasionally lend a hand, Peregrines breeding in quarries, in areas such as the Avon Gorge in Bristol with its combination of natural environment and quarrying, and the entirely natural upper Clyde valley close to Glasgow. Humans have also aided the species by creating 'cliffs' on which it can breed, the immigration of Peregrines to towns and cities being one of the more intriguing aspects of the recent history of the British population. Usually using well-sited nest boxes, often set on the high towers of churches, safe from attack by terrestrial predators, and safe, too, from avian predators for whom urban areas are still off-limits, the Peregrines have been able to utilise sites that also offer the possibility

FIG 62. Juvenile Peregrine, recently fledged from an eyrie in Bristol's Avon Gorge. (Nathan Guttridge)

FIG 63. Peregrine habitat in southern Scotland. The gorse lines the top of a cliff which held the eyrie.

of educating those most relentless and fearful of terrestrial predators, humans, with video links allowing close-up views of falcon life that have endeared the bird to many. And in cities there is rarely any shortage of pigeons.

The same basic requirements of open country and inaccessible nesting areas apply through the species' vast range, despite Peregrines breeding at over 3,000 m in some places, and on oceanic islands in others. However, though the basic requirements remain fixed, the Peregrine's ability to adapt, and particularly the flexibility in its diet, means that the vision of the falcon sweeping majestically across the wilderness now needs to be augmented by the vision of it using street lights in British cities to hunt migrating shorebirds, and street lights in other cities to hunt bats, and the vision of a fortress-like eyrie on some vast cliff being set beside a box on a cathedral tower.

VOICE

Peregrines are vocal birds during the breeding season, with calls beginning in winter close to traditional eyries, but much more silent otherwise. The most common call, and one which, once heard, is never forgotten, is the alarm call, a typical falcon '*kek-kek-kek*' (often rendered as '*kak-kak-kak*', though this occasionally seems more an attempt to differentiate the Peregrine from the other British falcons by phoneme, as the main vocalisation of all four falcons is essentially similar, varying only in pitch and harmonic structure). Monneret (1974) renders the call as a suitably Gallic *kré* in a fine paper which also sets down the display flights and aggressive stances of Peregrines. The call, which is usually the only one made outside the breeding season, is a staccato series of *keks* separated by fractions of a second (on sonograms the separation is 0.1–0.2 seconds, though on occasions it can be longer, perhaps 0.5 seconds), the series being as long as the bird chooses, with frequent repetitions after periods of silence, the duration of which depend on the nature of the perceived threat. In general the female call has shorter gaps between the *keks*, so short that if the female is being very aggressive the call can become a continuous scream. The male call is higher-pitched than the female, and the call of individual birds is so regular that they can be recognised, with a high degree of accuracy, not only during a season but in subsequent years.

A second call is usually described as a wail or whine. Three forms have been described by various observers. The first is made in aggressive situations and is a variation on the standard '*kek*' call, but the individual sounds are tight together, rather in the manner of the female's continuous scream, though not as intense and usually used as a prelude to the '*kek*' call. In differentiating wail and standard alarm calls, Cade (1960) renders the male Peregrine wail as '*klee-chip*' with the emphasis on the second sound, that of the female being '*klee-chuck*', again the second sound being emphasised. Cade suggests that in each case the call is made as a precursor to conflict. A second wail is associated with the feeding of fledglings, both male and female Peregrines making the call when they are attracting the attention of the youngsters as they arrive with prey. In this case the call is less harsh. A slower, softer, higher-pitched and more drawn-out wail is also made. Both sexes use it as a way of attracting the mate's attention when they are out of sight of each other during the early breeding season. Females also use it to request food from males, as an invitation call for copulation and to suggest an incubation changeover. Males use it when arriving with food.

A third call, once memorably described as resembling a rusty hinge (and so sometimes named the 'creaking call'), is now usually described as a two syllable '*ee-chip*' or a three syllable '*ku-ee-chip*', though since it can be either two or three syllables, the call is more generally referred to as a 'chupping'. Various observers

FIG 64. Female Peregrine bullying the male off the eggs after she has returned to resume incubation.

have described subtle differences between male and female versions. Chupping may vary in intensity, tone and pitch, but is a greeting and bonding call, often used by the female to attract the male to the nesting ledge and occasionally as a copulation invitation. (Many observers consider this softer, often shorter call is a separate call – 'chittering' – rather than a chupping variant.) Females also use it when feeding young chicks, when it can bring to mind the soft clucking of a mother hen or even a cooing. Male Peregrines tend to chup when around the female: the size difference between the sexes means the female often bullies the male, particularly at the nest when she wishes to take over incubation and the male is reluctant to get off the eggs, or when demanding food, so the male frequently chups in appeasement.

Other calls have also been described, but these are all variations on those given above, most of the variation deriving from circumstance. For a comprehensive review of Peregrine vocalisations see Nelson (1970).

Carlier (1995), studying Peregrine calls in France, noted that the wail and chup calls varied in frequency for males and females through the phases of the breeding cycle: chupping was most frequent during courtship and was more or less equally used by both sexes; males chupped more frequently during incubation and used the call when delivering food once the eggs had hatched (Fig. 65)

Young Peregrines begin to chirp in the egg up to 72 hours before hatching and continue to chirp for a day or so after hatching. The chirp then alters to a

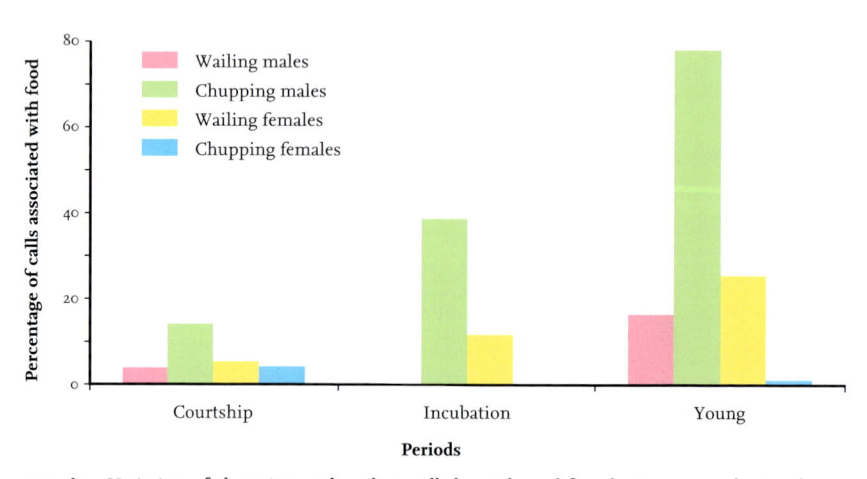

FIG 65. Variation of chupping and wailing calls by male and female Peregrines during the breeding cycle. Redrawn from Carlier 1995.

variation of the chupping call, but higher-pitched when the chicks are hungry. As they grow the nestlings develop the full range of Peregrine calls, and will make the familiar '*kek-kek-kek*' when disturbed from a young age, though when approached by, for instance, an observer from about two weeks of age, the chick will hiss loudly while lying on its back and extending its feet. However, although the calls develop as the chick ages, Peregrine chicks raised in isolation all demonstrate the complete range of calls once fledged, strongly suggesting that the vocalisations are inherent, not learned.

DIET

Prey

Not surprisingly for a species which has occupied such a vast area of Earth, even allowing for the fact that the chosen habitat across the range – open country over which to hunt – is similar, the Peregrine is flexible in terms of prey. Uttendörfer (1952) notes a total of 210 species which formed the diet of Peregrines in central Europe, a list which suggests that the falcon will take on any flying prey which it considers it has a reasonable chance of taking. However, in general, the preferred prey lies in the weight range 50–500 g, though that is a very wide band, covering a very significant number of birds. There is some evidence to suggest that Peregrines are attracted by species with conspicuous colour patterns, and to individuals with odd flight or movement patterns which might suggest they are sick or injured. In his study of Peregrines in southern Sweden, Lindberg (1983) noted that heavier prey – gulls, ducks and grouse – tended to be a greater proportion of the prey during the later breeding season when the female Peregrines joined the hunt to provide food for the nestlings. Lindberg found that the average weight of the male's prey was 188 g, that of females being 251 g. However, while this implies support for one theory of reversed sexual dimorphism (see Chapter 2), the results of a more recent study in northern Spain (Zuberogoitia *et al.* 2013) suggest that the situation is more complex.

The preferred method of attack – striking a bird in flight – allows the Peregrine to take species much larger itself. There are several records of Peregrines attacking geese as large as Greylags (*Anser anser*), males of which may weigh up to 3.5 kg (almost three times the weight of a female Peregrine), while historically falcons were frequently flown against Grey Herons, which, though of comparable weight to a female Peregrine, are very large and formidably armed. Equally formidable is the Great Black-backed Gull (*Larus marinus*), which may weigh 1.8 kg and has a reputation as a fierce predator, but which has also fallen victim to Peregrine attack.

Since there are also accounts of Peregrines taking Goldcrests, it is clear that the falcons are opportunistic hunters of any bird that comes within their territory and appears vulnerable to attack. There is, of course, a limit to the weight which a hunting Peregrine can carry back to its eyrie if it is hunting to feed chicks, this appearing to be about the weight of the falcon itself. This raises the question of why the falcon will attack prey it cannot carry away. Avian predators killing larger prey than can be carried will consume the prey at the killing site, and dismember the prey, then return at a later time to either continue eating or to carry off the now reduced-weight prey. Killing heavier prey may be a winter survival strategy if other prey is not available. It may also, of course, be that the presence of prey within the Peregrine's territory and the favourable positions of hunter and target trigger an automatic attack response in the falcon.

While the majority of prey is avian, mammals are also taken, records including Rabbits (*Oryctolagus cuniculus*), hare leverets, shrews and voles. Court (1986) found that the population of Tundra Peregrines in northern Canada increased by 30% during a year when the rodent population reached a peak, and in a study carried out subsequent to the rodent peak Bradley & Oliphant (1991) noted that mammalian prey – Northern Collared Lemming (*Dicrostonyx groenlandicus*) and young Arctic Ground Squirrels – constituted a third of the Peregrine diet by weight even though the rodent population had declined to a more normal level. Bradley & Oliphant examined pellets rather than remains at plucking posts, and suggest that this gives a better idea of the degree to which the falcons take mammalian prey, implying that it is possible that throughout the Peregrine's range, while avian prey is dominant in the diet, the mammalian fraction may be underestimated. Swann (1998) records finding an uneaten young Stoat (*Mustela erminea*) in a Peregrine nest in Scotland, while Tyler & Ormerod (1990) record the cub of a Red Fox in prey remains in Wales.

Bats are also taken: Sprunt (1951) records observing a Peregrine hunting bats in Texas, USA, stooping into the bats as they streamed out of their roost, or flying alongside the prey 'river' and then swerving sideways to grasp a nearby bat. Another account is provided by Stager (1941), who watched six Peregrines who daily waited for bats to emerge from a different cave in Texas. The falcons hunted the bats for over an hour, flying into the bats as they streamed out from the cave. Lee & Kuo (2001) observed Peregrines and Red-tailed Hawks also hunting at a cave in Texas; the hawks were better at catching the bats in the evening, the falcons better at dawn. Lee & Kuo estimated that the two raptors (an average of five of each species on the 23 days of observation) took 2,153 bats, a large number, but only 0.02% of the estimated population of 10 million Mexican Free-tailed Bats (*Tadarida brasiliensis*) at the site. In a study in France, Duquet & Nadal (2012) listed a total of 11 bat species which had been taken by avian predators, with Peregrines responsible for 29% of the total number. Bats have also been identified in the prey remains of urban Peregrines in Britain (Table 10), while Rollie & Christie (2006) record the capture of a bat in the middle of the day (12.20) in Kirkcudbrightshire. The bat – probably a Noctule (*Nyctalus noctula*) – took evasive action when approached, but the Peregrine captured it on the third attempt. The Peregrine bit the bat in flight, apparently to kill rather than consume it.

Cade (1982) records seeing a Peregrine catch an Arctic Grayling (*Thymallus arcticus*) as it broke surface in Alaska, and other attempts to catch fish. Feeding on carrion has also been observed, though this appears to be rare and seems to occur only when hunting is poor, and particularly in juvenile birds whose hunting skills are still developing: Holland (1989) observed a juvenile Peregrine one summer in California that perched near a roadkill California Ground Squirrel (*Otospermophilus beechyi*), then dragged it to the verge, mantled it and fed on it for 25 minutes. Buchanan (1991), in west Washington State, also noted juvenile Peregrines feeding on carrion during winter – a dead Guillemot (*Uria aalge*) in one case, a White-winged Scoter (*Melanitta deglandi*) in another.

From the various data on the diet of the Peregrine it is clear that the falcon is an opportunistic hunter, a behaviour which has led to occasional dismay in birdwatchers when rarities such as Wryneck (*Jynx torquilla*) are taken: Ratcliffe (1993) reports that in 1980 a juvenile Peregrine took 36 Roseate Terns (*Sterna dougallii*) at a site on Anglesey, hunting which was not likely to have endeared the youngster to local birdwatchers.

Composition of diet

While the comments above emphasise the catholic nature of the Peregrine's diet, the diet of individual falcons is usually much more restricted. The range of prey is usually a good match to the composition of local species. Thus coastal species will take a larger fraction of seabirds, moorland Peregrines may take more game birds, urban birds will take pigeons, birds wintering at estuaries will take waders. One generalisation is that pigeons, wild or feral, form a significant fraction of the diets of all Peregrines, a fact which, as we shall see when considering the British population below, has led to conflict with humans.

As for other falcons, information on diet can be obtained from an examination of feathers at plucking posts, or from an analysis of pellets. Ratcliffe (1993) collated data from several studies over a combined period covering 1904–1975 (though not continuously during that time) on the diet of Peregrines during the breeding season in four areas of Britain, and these data, with additions regarding biomass, have formed the basis of Tables 5–9.

TABLE 5 Diet of Peregrines in the Lake District.

Prey species	Percentage of total prey items	Percentage of total biomass
Feral/Domestic Pigeon	30.8	51.0
Starling	9.7	2.9
Fieldfare	9.3	4.0
Blackbird	8.5	3.0
Red Grouse	5.1	12.6
Song Thrush	4.2	1.3
Redwing	3.3	0.9
Wood Pigeon	2.7	5.1
Meadow Pipit	2.6	0.2
Golden Plover	2.4	1.8
Snipe	2.4	1.0
Lapwing	2.1	1.8
Skylark	1.8	0.3
Redshank	1.7	1.0
Curlew	1.1	3.0
Greenfinch	1.1	0.1
Mistle Thrush	1.0	0.5
Rook	1.0	1.9
Ring Ouzel	1.0	0.4
Chaffinch	0.9	<0.1
Jackdaw	0.7	0.7
Domestic Fowl	0.5	0.6
Stock Dove	0.5	0.6
Crow[1]	0.5	1.1
Cuckoo	0.4	0.3
House Sparrow	0.4	<0.1
Woodcock	0.3	0.3
Black-headed Gull	0.3	0.3
Knot	0.3	0.1
Other species[2]	3.5	3.2

1. Carrion Crows and Hooded Crows not differentiated.
2. Other species were Blue Tit (*Cyanistes caeruleus*), Bullfinch (*Pyrrhula pyrrhula*), Buzzard, Common Gull (*Larus canus*), Common Tern, Dipper (*Cinclus cinclus*), Dunlin, Green Woodpecker, Great Spotted Woodpecker (*Dendrocopos major*), Grey Partridge, Grey Wagtail (*Motacilla cinerea*), Hawfinch (*Coccothraustes coccothraustes*), House Martin, Jay (*Garrulus glandarius*), Linnet (*Carduelis cannabina*), Little Owl (*Athene noctua*), Long-eared Owl, Mallard (*Anas platyrhynchos*), Peregrine Falcon, Pheasant, Pied Wagtail (*Motacilla alba yarrellii*), Robin (*Erithacus rubecula*), Sanderling (*Calidris alba*), Snow Bunting (*Plectrophenax nivalis*), Sparrowhawk, Swift, Tawny Owl and Wheatear, together with Field Vole, Rabbit and Water Vole (*Arvicola amphibius*).

TABLE 6 Diet of Peregrines in the Southern Uplands of Scotland.

Prey species	Percentage of total prey items	Percentage of total biomass
Feral/Domestic Pigeon	49.7	66.5
Starling	7.5	1.9
Red Grouse	6.6	13.3
Blackbird	4.6	1.3
Skylark	3.4	0.4
Fieldfare	3.4	1.2
Snipe	2.8	1.0
Meadow Pipit	2.5	0.2
Golden Plover	2.4	1.4
Lapwing	2.3	1.7
Black-headed Gull	1.9	1.6
Redshank	1.7	0.8
Wood Pigeon	1.1	1.7
Song Thrush	1.0	0.3
Mistle Thrush	0.9	0.3
Ring Ouzel	0.8	0.2
Chaffinch	0.8	<0.1
Mallard	0.5	1.4
Woodcock	0.5	0.5
Redwing	0.5	0.1
Crow[1]	0.4	0.7
Jackdaw	0.4	0.3
Cuckoo	0.4	0.1
Dunlin	0.4	<0.1
Wheatear	0.4	<0.1
Others[2]	3.4	3.1

1. As in Table 5, Carrion Crows and Hooded Crows are not differentiated.
2. Other species identified were Barn Owl, Black Grouse, Bullfinch, Coal Tit (*Periparus ater*), Common Gull, Common Sandpiper (*Actitis hypoleucos*), Curlew, Dipper, Goldfinch (*Carduelis carduelis*), Goosander (*Mergus merganser*), Grey Partridge, Grey Wagtail, Jay, Kestrel, Knot (*Calidris canutus*), Linnet, Magpie, Pheasant, Pied Wagtail, Reed Bunting (*Emberiza schoeniclus*), Ringed Plover (*Charadrius hiaticula*), Robin, Stock Dove (*Columba oenas*), Stonechat (*Saxicola rubicola*), Teal (*Anas crecca*), Treecreeper (*Certhia familiaris*) and Wigeon (*Anas penelope*), together with Brown Hare (*Lepus europaeus*) leveret, Field Vole and Rabbit.

TABLE 7 Diet of Peregrines in inland Scottish Highlands.

Prey species	Percentage of total prey items	Percentage of total biomass
Red Grouse	19.4	36.4
Feral/Domestic Pigeon	17.2	21.3
Golden Plover	5.6	3.2
Ptarmigan	4.4	6.6
Snipe	4.5	1.5
Black-headed Gull	4.0	3.2
Starling	3.4	0.8
Lapwing	3.1	1.9
Blackbird	2.9	0.8
Jackdaw	2.7	2.0
Skylark	2.7	0.3
Meadow Pipit	2.3	0.1
Fieldfare	2.1	0.7
Wood Pigeon	2.0	2.8
Curlew	1.8	3.7
Cuckoo	1.8	0.6
Chaffinch	1.8	0.1
Oystercatcher	1.4	2.1
Song Thrush	1.4	0.3
Mistle Thrush	1.2	0.4
Common Gull	0.9	1.1
Rook	0.8	1.1
Greenshank	0.8	0.5
Redshank	0.8	0.4
Mallard	0.6	1.8
Teal	0.6	0.5
Woodcock	0.6	0.5
Kestrel	0.6	0.5
Other[1]	9.0	5.3

1. Other species identified were Arctic Tern (*Sterna paradisaea*), Black Grouse, Blue Tit, Brambling (*Fringilla montifringilla*), Bullfinch, Carrion Crow, Collared Dove (*Streptopelia decaocto*), Common Crossbill (*Loxia curvirostra*), Common Sandpiper, Common Tern, Dipper, Dotterel (*Charadrius morinellus*), Dunlin, Great Spotted Woodpecker, Greenfinch (*Carduelis chloris*), Grey Wagtail, Hooded Crow, Jay, Kittiwake (*Rissa tridactyla*), Lesser Black-backed Gull (*Larus fuscus*), Magpie, Manx Shearwater (*Puffinus puffinus*), Merlin, Puffin (*Fratercula arctica*), Red-breasted Merganser (*Mergus serrator*), Redwing (*Turdus iliacus*), Robin, Sanderling, Short-eared Owl, Siskin (*Carduelis spinus*), Snow Bunting, Stock Dove, Swift, Wheatear, Whimbrel (*Numenius phaeopus*), Wigeon, Wood Sandpiper (*Tringa glareola*) and Wryneck, together with Mountain Hare (*Lepus timidus*) leveret and Rabbit.

TABLE 8 Diet of Peregrines in coastal Scottish Highland sites at which there were seabird colonies.

Prey species[1]	Percentage of total prey items	Percentage of total biomass
Puffin	21.0	18.9
Rock Dove/Feral/Domestic Pigeon[2]	20.6	18.0
Fulmar	7.4	13.4
Guillemot	6.4	9.3
Kittiwake[3]	7.8	7.2
Starling	5.4	1.0
Razorbill	4.1	6.1
Lapwing	4.1	2.1
Herring Gull	3.4	8.3
Jackdaw	3.4	2.0
Arctic Tern	2.4	0.7
Unidentified auks[4]	2.0	2.4
Redshank	2.0	0.7
Black Guillemot	1.7	1.6
Other[5]	8.5	8.2

1. The diet of Peregrines at coastal Scottish Highland sites at which there are no seabird colonies is essentially similar to that given in Table 7.
2. To calculate the biomass a mean weight was calculated assuming equal numbers of Rock Doves and other pigeons.
3. In his book on Shetland wildlife Saxby (1874) states that Kittiwakes were the preferred prey of Peregrines as they were easy to catch. He tells the story of a local hunter shooting Kittiwakes (which were then retrieved by friends in a boat below the cliff) who was astonished to find that as the shot seabird was plummeting to the sea, the local Peregrine dived in to retrieve it before it hit the water and took it off to its eyrie, returning twice more to do the same thing, presumably to the annoyance of the hunter.
4. To obtain the biomass a mean body weight was calculated based on the body weights of Black Guillemot (*Cepphus grylle*), Guillemot, Puffin and Razorbill (*Alca torda*) allocated according to the numbers of prey items actually identified.
5. Other species identified were Blackbird (*Turdus merula*), Curlew, Fieldfare, Golden Plover (*Pluvialis apricaria*), Great Black-backed Gull, Hooded Crow, Oystercatcher, Red Grouse, Skylark, Snipe (*Gallinago gallinago*), Song Thrush (*Turdus philomelos*) and Wheatear.

TABLE 9 Diet of Peregrines in Snowdonia.

Prey species[1]	Percentage of total prey items	Percentage of total biomass
Feral/Domestic Pigeon	69.6	82.3
Starling	7.6	1.7
Red Grouse	2.2	3.9
Lapwing	2.2	1.3
Skylark	2.2	0.2
Chaffinch	2.2	0.1
Mallard	1.1	3.1
Curlew	1.1	2.1
Stock Dove	1.1	0.9
Other[2]	10.9	4.4

1. The species list for Snowdonia is much more limited than those for the Lake District and Scotland. The reasons for this are not clear, but it may reflect the individual Peregrine's enthusiasm for pigeons, a more limited range of prey available within the falcon's territory, a more limited collection of prey remains, or a combination of these factors. The fact that the prey included the rare Chough (*Pyrrhocorax pyrrhocorax*) will not have enhanced the Peregrine's reputation among local birdwatchers. The diet composition of Peregrines in south Wales is much more extensive, though the preponderance of pigeons remains (Richards & Shrubb 1999).
2. Other species identified were Common Tern, Chough, Cuckoo, Fieldfare, Magpie, Mistle Thrush, Redwing, Ringed Plover, Song Thrush and Woodcock (*Scolopax rusticola*).

Several things are clear from Tables 5–9. One is the importance of pigeons to the Peregrine, but also the fact that pigeons are a larger fraction of the diet outside of the Scottish Highlands. It is not clear if this is due to the availability of alternative prey, including grouse, or the relative absence of pigeons, though the latter would appear more likely given the falcon's enthusiasm for them: Ratcliffe (1993) tells an insightful story of the lighthouse keepers of Ailsa Craig, who persecuted Peregrines because they took the pigeons they used to carry messages to and from the mainland despite the fact that the rock was a vast seabird colony.

In a study to establish the diet of urban Peregrines, prey items were collected at roosting and breeding sites in Bath, Bristol and Exeter over an extended period (19 years in Exeter, seven years in Bath and Bristol) (Drewitt & Dixon 2008). A total of over 5,000 items were recovered, allowing identification of 95 prey species (Table 10).

The fraction of each species taken by the Peregrines in the three cities (Table 10) is very similar (given the small sample from Bristol), and the table again shows the importance of pigeons to the falcon. In general British cities

FIG 66. Heads of a juvenile Starling (top) and Great Spotted Woodpecker (above) found in an eyrie in southern Scotland.

have significant populations of pigeons, and this obviously contributes to their occurrence in the Peregrine diet. Pigeons also need water regularly, which takes them to drinking places, but they can be fast, agile fliers and so more difficult to catch than some other species, which raises the question of whether there is any other factor which makes them popular with Peregrines. And in a fascinating

TABLE 10 Diet of urban Peregrines. From Drewitt & Dixon (2008).

Prey species	Percentage of total prey items[1]	Percentage of total biomass[1]	Prey items as a percentage of total prey at each city[2]		
			Bath	Exeter	Bristol
Feral Pigeon	41.86	62.69	38.9	44.1	49.4
Starling	9.12	3.41	8.4	10.7	3.1
Redwing	3.94	1.23	4.2	3.7	3.1
Greenfinch	3.83	0.54	5.2	2.7	1.2
Collared Dove	3.72	3.80	3.1	4.5	3.1
Blackbird	2.98	1.52	2.2	4.1	0.9
Teal	2.39	3.88	1.8	2.2	8.6
House Sparrow	2.35	0.36	3.7	1.2	
Snipe	2.27	1.25	2.7	1.7	2.8
Woodcock	1.83	2.44	1.8	1.3	3.1
Fieldfare	1.82	0.91	1.8	1.4	5.2
Wood Pigeon	1.73	3.87	2.1	1.3	1.8
Chaffinch	1.42	0.17	1.7	1.3	
Goldfinch	1.40	0.12	2.2	0.8	
Swift	1.36	0.30	0.2	2.8	0.3
Black-headed Gull	1.33	1.99	1.8	0.5	4.0
Song Thrush	1.14	0.47	1.0	1.4	0.3
Great Spotted Woodpecker	1.12	0.47	1.4	1.0	
Lapwing	1.10	1.26	0.7	1.2	4.0
Jackdaw	0.93	1.02	1.5	0.3	0.3
Golden Plover	0.82	0.90	0.4	1.0	2.8
Pied Wagtail	0.76	0.08	1.1	0.5	
Little Grebe	0.68	0.52	0.4	0.1	1.2
Dunnock	0.63	0.06	1.0	0.3	
Skylark	0.61	0.12	1.1	0.1	0.3
Jay	0.57	0.47	0.7	0.5	
Dunlin	0.55	0.13	0.5	0.6	0.6
Moorhen	0.53	0.87	0.5	0.6	0.3
Magpie	0.53	0.60	0.5	0.6	0.3

TABLE 10 CONTINUED

1. A 0.5% cutoff was applied to the percentage of items recovered to reduce the table size (i.e. any species providing less than 0.5% of total number of recovered items is not included. As a consequence the values in these columns sum to < 100%, the difference being the percentage of prey items from all other identified species.
2. The composition of the diet was constructed from data across a number of years and so includes both breeding-season and wintering prey species. The total number of recovered prey items was 2,595 from Bath, 2,354 from Exeter and 326 from Bristol. The percentages of the diets for individual species are calculated with respect to these totals. The blank entries for Bristol arise because no items from that species were recovered.

In addition to species already noted in Tables 5–9, the following species were also identified: Avocet (*Recurvirostra avosetta*), Bar-tailed Godwit (*Limosa lapponica*), Blackcap (*Sylvia atricapilla*), Black-necked Grebe (*Podiceps nigricollis*), Black-tailed Godwit (*Limosa limosa*), Chiffchaff (*Phylloscopus collybita*), Coot (*Fulica atra*), Corncrake (*Crex crex*), Great Tit (*Parus major*), Green Sandpiper (*Tringa ochropus*), Grey Plover (*Pluvialis squatarola*), Jack Snipe (*Lymnocryptes minimus*), Kingfisher (*Alcedo atthis*), Leach's Petrel (*Oceanodroma leucorhoa*), Lesser Redpoll (*Carduelis cabaret*), Little Auk (*Alle alle*), Little Tern (*Sterna albifrons*), Quail (*Coturnix coturnix*), Ruddy Duck (*Oxyura jamaicensis*), Sandwich Tern (*Sterna sandvicensis*), Barn Swallow, Tree Pipit (*Anthus trivialis*), Turtle Dove (*Streptopelia turtur*), Water Rail (*Rallus aquaticus*), Whitethroat (*Sylvia communis*), Willow Warbler (*Phylloscopus trochilus*), Wren and Yellowhammer (*Emberiza citrinella*). In addition to these UK species, the Peregrines also captured escaped caged birds: Budgerigar (*Melopsittacus undulatus*), Canary (*Serinus canaria*), Cockatiel, and Rose-ringed Parakeet (*Psittacula krameri*). Brown Rat (*Rattus norvegicus*), Grey Squirrel (*Sciurus carolinensis*) and Noctule Bat were also identified.

FIG 67. Adult Peregrine carrying a Feral Pigeon back to its eyrie. (Nathan Guttridge)

study in California, Palleroni *et al.* (2005) sought to understand the vulnerability of pigeons to attack, assuming that this must contribute, in some way, to the high proportion of pigeons in Peregrine diets wherever they are found. Palleroni and co-workers noted that wild pigeons (Rock Doves) had a conspicuous white rump, a feature which is often absent in Feral Pigeons as a result of negative assortative mating (i.e. the feral birds do not preferentially chose mates with plumage similar to their own). The result is that over time the white patch has been lost in much of the feral stock, whose plumage patterns are now a general mix of grey, blue, and white. Palleroni *et al.* noticed that pigeons with the white rump patch were killed much less often than those with other colour patterns. To test if this was a real effect, the feathers of 756 trapped pigeons were switched, so that those without a white patch acquired one, and those with one lost theirs. The effect was dramatic, with the mortality rate of birds which had acquired a white patch dropping, and that of the birds that had lost their white patches increasing in tandem. Palleroni *et al.* conjecture that the evasive action of attacked pigeons, a roll at close approach of the falcon, causes a flash of the white patch against the more cryptic coloration of the other plumage, and that this acts to confuse the falcon, which misses the roll manoeuvre and so misses the prey. In pigeons without the patch, there is no white flash and the roll can be observed by the falcon, which can compensate for it and continue its attack. Palleroni *et al.* comment that a similar anti-predator tactic is employed by many fish species, which roll to alternate dark dorsal and white ventral surfaces. It is also speculated that the loose feathers of pigeons have evolved as a defence mechanism, the stooping Peregrine which attempts to bind to its prey occasionally catching only a foot-full of feathers while the partially disrobed pigeon makes good its escape.

While pigeons are clearly important to the Peregrine diet in Britain (and also in much of the rest of Europe), in areas where feral, domestic or wild pigeons are few or absent, such as northern Fennoscandia, Peregrines are still found, ducks or other species then predominating in the diet (see, for instance, Sulkava 1968, whose study in Finland showed that in terms of numbers taken the diet was dominated by Lapwing, Teal, Mallard and Black-headed Gull, *Choicocephalus ridibundus*).

FIG 68. Two Feral Pigeons, one showing the ancestral white rump, the other without the white patch.

Equally clear from Tables 5–10 is the plasticity of the Peregrine diet, and the fact that the diet includes both owls and other diurnal raptors, including other Peregrines, these perhaps killed during territorial disputes. We return to this again in *Friends and foes*, below

In winter many Peregrines stay close to their breeding areas, and even those that move tend to occupy similar habitats, the requirement for open country over which to hunt being paramount when the necessity for nesting cliffs has diminished. In his study in southern Scotland, Mearns (1982) noted that 86% of the inland breeding territories he visited were occupied, as were 88% of the coastal territories.

Ratcliffe (1993) noted that in the Lake District Peregrines were roosting close to their breeding sites, but while some were hunting locally, taking a greater proportion of corvids and seabirds, others were journeying to coastal sites to hunt, returning to their roosts each evening. Interestingly, despite its reputation as a solitary bird, Kelly & Thorpe (1993) reported a communal roost on the Isle of Man, with up to nine Peregrines sharing a stand of mature conifers. Even more interesting was their observation that sometimes the roost was also shared by Kestrels, Sparrowhawks, Ravens and even two Merlins on one occasion. The roost was used regularly from late August until early December and then more sporadically. The reasons for communal roosting are not obvious, and are even less so when the congregations of other raptors and Ravens are also considered.

Weir (1977) noted that in Scotland's Spey valley wintering Peregrines took advantage of migrating flocks of thrushes in autumn and spring, and hunted Red Grouse and Ptarmigan during the winter months, while Baker (1967) stated that in his study area of east central Essex (which he explored by bicycle) the diet of wintering Peregrines, which Baker assumed had immigrated from Scandinavia, comprised a mix of estuarine and farm species, the former mainly Black-headed Gull and Lapwing, the latter mainly pigeons (Table 11). However, it has to be noted that the dietary information of Baker has been called into question by some (see Note 4.1).

For the particular winter described in his book (which is thought to have been 1962/63) Baker states that the fraction of Wood Pigeons in the Peregrine diet increased to 54%, which did not surprise him as these were particularly abundant during cold weather. The remaining fraction of that winter's diet remained similar, with percentages falling approximately pro rata. The lack of feral/domestic pigeons in the diet during the harsh winter is presumably explained by the Feral Pigeons immigrating to local towns, which were warmer and offered food in the form of human-generated scraps, and by the domestic pigeons spending much more time in home lofts.

TABLE 11 Winter diet of Peregrines in east central Essex during the 1960s. From Baker (1967).

Prey species[1]	Percentage of total prey items	Percentage of total biomass
Wood Pigeon	38	48.3
Black-headed Gull	14	10.0
Lapwing	6	3.4
Wigeon	3	5.5
Partridge	3	3.1
Fieldfare	3	0.9
Moorhen	2	1.7
Curlew	2	3.7
Golden Plover	2	1.0
Rook	2	2.5
Other[2]	25	19.9

1. Baker (1967) states that his diet data were constructed from 619 prey items.
2. Baker states that the remaining 25% of the prey items after the 'top ten' had been removed included pigeons (39% of the remaining 25%), gulls (17%), waders (16%), ducks (8%), game species (5%), corvids other than Rooks (*Corvus frugilegus*) (5%), small/medium-sized passerines (5%), 'others' (5%). In view of the uncertainty in the exact composition of the 25%, the figure of 19.9% for the biomass of that fraction was calculated assuming an average body weight of 300 g.

See Note 4.1 regarding the scepticism some have for Baker's observations and data.

FIG 69. Grey Partridge, an occasional prey of Peregrines.

FIG 70. Peregrine plucking site.

Mearns (1982) studied the winter diet of Peregrines at coastal and inland sites in southern Scotland. The coastal sites were backed by farm and moorland and included estuaries within 1 km. The inland sites were sheep grazing or moorland and ranged from 250 m to 550 m in height. Prey remains were identified at plucking sites. At the inland sites passerines accounted for 47% of the diet across a four-year period (but were 71.4% of the diet in one winter: in that winter Redwings and Fieldfares constituted 44.6% of the total diet). The bulk of the remaining prey (from across the four-winter period) were pigeons (47%), waders (13%) and grouse (5%). At the coastal sites pigeons were 58% of the diet (again from across the four winters), with passerines constituting 32% and waders 7%. Interestingly in the same winter in which passerines constituted a greater fraction of the diet at inland sites, they also made up a higher fraction (47.6%) at coastal sites, though in this case Redwings and Fieldfares were only 16.5% of the total diet. Mearns also collected 91 Peregrine pellets, all but four from inland sites. The prey fractions in these were similar to those from the inland plucking sites, but included 7.1% of duck remains; duck had been absent from inland plucking sites and only formed 2% of the remains from the coastal sites. Two of the pellets also included the remains of voles. The species identified in the study of Mearns did not include any not already identified in Tables 5–10.

Other studies in Britain and North America have shown the importance of shorebirds to wintering Peregrines (e.g. Dekker 1988, Cresswell & Whitfield 1994, Cresswell 1996, Buchanan 1996: these studies are considered in the following section), while on Vancouver Island, British Columbia, Dekker (1995) noted that 88% of Peregrine prey were ducks (of five species) which were taken in flight or from land in equal percentages.

The study of the diet composition of urban Peregrines by Drewitt & Dixon (2008) covered all months across several years, and allowed the variation in species taken to be analysed (Fig. 71). The data show the importance of pigeons at all times, but of Starlings during the breeding season (with the fraction of other species taken also rising), and of Redwings wintering in Britain to the Peregrines in winter.

Interestingly, for a species which tends to form flocks, pigeons do not have an alarm call. In a neat study of their behaviour, Stephan & Bugnyar (2013) noted that individual pigeons increase their vigilance and scanning of their local environment if they either hear or see a raptor (in the case of the study, Buzzard calls or the sight of a stuffed Buzzard). Pigeons, it seems, take responsibility

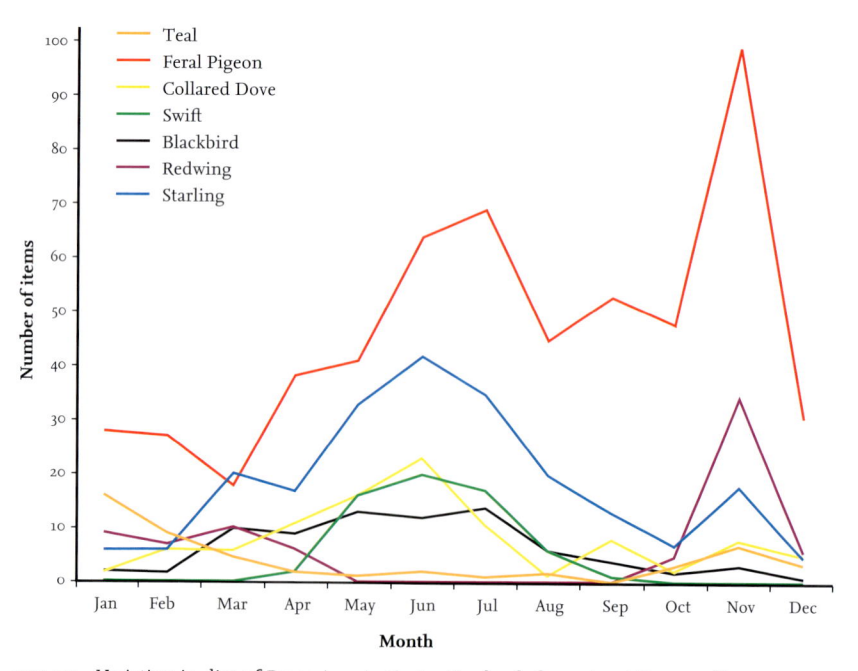

FIG 71. Variation in diet of Peregrines in Exeter, England, throughout the year (from prey items recovered 1998–2007). Redrawn from Drewitt & Dixon 2008.

for their own safety, not having evolved a system for alerting members of their flock – though of course the prompt flight of one bird will usually initiate flight behaviour in its companions.

Hunting strategy and food caching

The mathematics of the hunting techniques of Peregrines is dealt with in Chapter 3. What follows here is a more observational analysis.

Herbert & Herbert (1965) memorably suggested that the popular idea of the Peregrine was of a 'swift "engine of death" clashing and brawling about the skies with unabated fury, striking into oblivion every hapless bird of passage'. Somewhat hyperbolic, but perhaps not so very far from the truth. Rudebeck (1951) was more constrained in his description, noting that the stoop of the Peregrine gave 'an overwhelming impression of strength, vigour, and swiftness'. But although the stoop is the most spectacular of the Peregrine's hunting techniques it is not the only one. Rudebeck notes that 'sometimes birds are pursued violently in the horizontal direction, or the falcon may try to catch a bird en passant, even quite low over the ground.' Peregrines, like other predators, work with a defined programme of attacks, choosing the most appropriate for the particular occasion and executing it to the best of their abilities, not always successfully.

Peregrines mainly search for prey from a perch which allows a commanding view, though aerial searches (either by flapping flight or high soaring) are also used. The falcons will also search by walking on the ground (Dekker 1980, Rosenfield *et al.* 1995), though this seems to be a specialised behaviour for certain habitats, and will also follow humans, dogs, agricultural vehicles and the like in the hope they flush prey. Peregrines may also 'ring' prey which they find themselves initially below (see Chapter 7 for a definition of ringing flights), pursue prey in fast horizontal flight, and surprise prey by flying low and fast as they contour the landscape in an effort to flush the prey from the ground.

Stooping (high-speed diving) at prey is the most frequently used technique (but see Cresswell 1996, below), and certainly the most spectacular, but while often assumed to be fairly standard, it has many variations, the angle of attack varying from shallow, perhaps at only 30 degrees to the horizontal, to the near-vertical. Shallower angles are also seen, these hunts amounting almost to the peregrine chasing down its prey. At the end of the stoop the falcon either strikes the prey or binds on to it. The former may render the prey unconscious or semi-conscious, resulting in it plummeting to the ground where it may sustain further, perhaps fatal, injuries. As noted in Chapter 3, the Peregrine will then circle the prey to assess its capability to put up a fight, attacking in a series of loops to strike further times until the prey is no longer capable of resistance. The prey (disabled or dead) may then be retrieved or, occasionally, the falcon may circle and take it before it lands. By contrast, binding means the Peregrine clutches the prey and takes it to the ground where it is dispatched. Stoops may also end with the Peregrine diving past the prey and turning up to catch it from below. Such hunts usually end with the falcon binding on to the prey.

Baker (1967) describes the kill at the end of a long stoop based on his observation. The feet are thrust forward, the long hind toe extended so that it rips into the body of the prey at speed, causing sufficient damage to maim or kill. Saxby (1874), in his observations on Shetland, concurs, noting that on examining Peregrines shot while they were hunting, blood and prey feathers were frequently seen on the hind talon. These observations are in accord with high-speed photography (Goslow 1971). Goslow filmed strikes, but the situation was somewhat artificial – the captive falcon being freed and usually circling to a height of about 16 m, at which point a short-tethered, blindfolded pigeon was realised in front of the filming screen. Filming was at 800–1000 frames/second. While the strike speed of the falcon was clearly limited, two distinct methods of attack were seen (Fig. 72). In one the feet were extended forward, the toes stretched out, as Baker suggested. Goslow noted that the time required to deploy the talons was 60–100 ms. More recently high-speed cameras have been used to analyse binding strikes, and these confirm Goslow's findings. Kane & Zamani (2014) note the capture of a crow by a Gyr–Saker hybrid in which the falcon spread its wings and tail less than 230 ms prior to impact and extended its talons, the time to deploy the latter being 67 ms, consistent with the data of Goslow (1971). This position – tail and wings spread, talons forced forward – seemed, in Goslow's study, to be taken when there was an attempt to bind on the prey. In the second method, the toes are still open, but the body position alters (Fig. 72b). Some observers have claimed that the strike is with the toes closed, and that hind toe extends due only to its length, though Goslow (1971) suggests this is not the case. The altered body position in the strike posture would allow the falcon to better absorb the shock of contact by allowing the feet to be pushed backward, while still allowing both the impact and the claws, particularly the hind toe claw, to inflict damage. The high-speed photography suggests the toes are bunched immediately after a strike, so it may be that some birds do actually strike with a bunched foot. It is possible that the falcon's decision whether to bind or just to strike is made only immediately before the prey is reached, when the Peregrine assesses any evasive manoeuvre by the prey, and the speed differential and attack of angle this might induce, and alters its body position to compensate.

Striking, rather than binding, is clearly advantageous, as it allows a greater contact speed. If the falcon intends to bind, its speed and that of the prey need

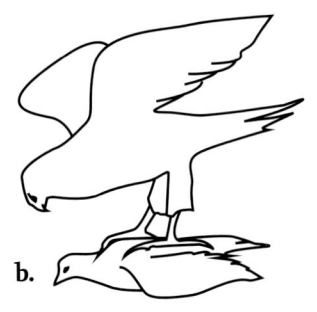

FIG 72. The position of an attacking Peregrine at point of impact with prey, when the intention is (a) to bind to the prey and (b) to strike the prey. Redrawn from Goslow 1971.

to be approximately the same. The Peregrine may also need to see its feet to coordinate the bind, which would require a significant slowing: binding without seeing the position of the feet would require great dexterity, but as the Peregrine has this in abundance perhaps visual spotting is not necessary.

But striking at speed and not retrieving before the prey hits the surface is a problem for coastal Peregrines hunting seabirds. Buchanan (1996) observed three occasions on which a Peregrine hit the water before pulling out of a stoop; he does not say whether the falcons survived, though the implication of there being no mention of the outcome is that they did. Ratcliffe (1993) also notes an attack on a Mallard on a hill loch which resulted in the Peregrine hitting the water at speed and throwing up a plume of water 3.5 m high: the duck escaped by diving, the falcon presumably escaping unhurt as again there is no contrary record. Ruthven (2013) records a pair of Peregrines retrieving a Wood Pigeon from water in Scotland which, it was assumed, had been struck. Each bird took it in turns to manoeuvre the pigeon to the shore by dragging it, the male Peregrine completing the task by swimming with its wings as it gripped the prey. The two Peregrines, presumably a bonded pair – the observation was in February – then plucked and ate the pigeon. See also the observation of Ford (2007) in *Moult*, above.

There are several observations of Peregrines collecting prey from the water surface. Fisher (1978) saw a Peregrine forced to drop prey (a pigeon) into the sea by pursuing Gulls (*Larus argentatus*) which then settled on the water around the prey, interested, but not attempting to feed. The Peregrine circled and made repeated dives, touching the prey twice before finally retrieving it and, again pursued by the gulls, flying off. One of the most extraordinary over-sea hunts was observed by Rogers & Leatherwood (1981), who were aboard one of two ships working for the US National Oceanic and Atmospheric Administration in the Pacific Ocean about 65 km from Clipperton Island, a small atoll 2,600 km west of Costa Rica and 2,400 km northwest of the Galapagos islands. For two and a half days there had been a storm with easterly winds, then conditions calmed and an Osprey and Peregrine Falcon appeared and landed on the ships. Rogers & Leatherwood noted that in competition for the highest mast perch (19 m on one ship, 25 m on the other), the Peregrine dominated the Osprey. From its high perch the Peregrine surveyed the ocean and periodically flew off to attack Leach's Petrels. Attacks were direct, with the falcon not choosing to gain height before attacking: if an attack failed the Peregrine returned to its perch rather than making a second attempted capture in the same flight. Rogers & Leatherwood saw 11 attacks, eight of which were successful, the petrels being taken as they, as usual, pattered across the water. The Osprey, which had been feeding on flying fish, stayed with the ships for four days, the Peregrine for five. Walker (1988) also observed Peregrines catching Leach's Petrels much closer to home – on the Isle of Man – and, as noted in Table 10, this species was found in the diet of a West Country urban Peregrine as well.

Voous (1961) also records a Peregrine feeding on Storm Petrels (*Hydrobates pelagicus*) caught from a ship in mid-Atlantic. Equally interesting was the behaviour of a Peregrine observed by Matsyna *et al.* (2010) in the Kuril Islands. The Peregrine had harried a flock of migrating shorebirds, one of which had dropped into the sea to escape. Unable to take off from the water, the bird had paddled its way to the shore, where it was plucked from the surf by the waiting Peregrine.

These attacks suggest surprise or (limited) pursuit hunting, and Buchanan (1996) suggests that the danger of hitting the water means that the falcons are reluctant to stoop at prey (which in Buchanan's observed cases were Dunlin) over water, particularly if the sea is rough. Buchanan did see stoop attacks that were successful when the sea was calm (and retrieval from the water's surface would have been easier). The Peregrines also used over-water horizontal pursuit of a Dunlin isolated from flocks, this technique allowing the falcon to outfly the prey and to grab it in mid-air. Ratcliffe (1993) also suggests that coastal Peregrines might wait for prey to cross from sea to land on occasions before initiating a stoop. However, while these observations show a reluctance to risk hitting water, with the inherent danger of not being able to successfully take off again (with or without the prey) the flexibility of Peregrines to local condition is indicated by their hunting of Ancient Murrelets (*Synthliboramphus antiquus*) on Langara Island, one of the Queen Charlotte Islands of British Columbia. Peregrines hunt at dawn and dusk when the auks leave for, and return from, their feeding grounds. However, Dekker & Bogaert (1997) noted that during the day Peregrines would occasionally fly out over the ocean, travelling beyond telescope range. Although

13 Peregrines returned without prey, on two occasions returning falcons were pursued by Bald Eagles: as the eagles are known to pirate prey from Peregrines it was assumed the falcons had made successful attacks far out over the ocean. No information was available on the hunting technique employed.

As already noted, Buchanan (1996) observed pursuit hunting, and Cresswell (1996) in his study of wintering Peregrines in East Lothian, Scotland, noted that a significant fraction of attacks were initiated from perches, which implies surprise and pursuit hunting. Cresswell noted 36.3% of attacks were from stoops, 36.1% were surprise, and 25.1% were 'open' attacks, in which the falcon was visible to the prey before the attack. Such open attacks conform to what Buchanan would refer to as pursuits, though, of course, a failed stoop or failed surprise attack might also lead to a chase. Cresswell noted that 2.5% of Peregrine attacks were actually 'ringing' pursuits. Most attacks were launched from the air (82.6%) rather than a perch and were directed at ground-based prey on 55.6% of occasions (airborne prey 44.4%). Prey was less than 100 m away from the falcon when an attack was launched on 39.8% of occasions, at 100–500 m on 36.7% of occasions and more than 500 m away on 23.5%. On average Peregrines made two attacks (1.8 ± 0.4) on each hunting flight: Cresswell saw one flight which involved 11 attacks. Chases were mainly single stoops of short duration (49.7% lasted less than one second), but some were longer (36.6% were 1–10 seconds, 8.9% 11–30 seconds, 2.4% 31–60 seconds and 2.4% were > 60 seconds). During his observations Cresswell found that the Peregrines' winter time budget was 72% perching, 21% flying, either moving position or hunting, and 2% feeding: the remaining 5% is not credited. Cresswell's study was of three raptors – Merlin, Peregrine and Sparrowhawk – and included measurement of the duration of hunts, and the position of the prey and raptor for the hunts. These data are presented in Chapter 7 (Tables 31 and 32).

Peregrines are also known to fly low and fast across open country areas in the manner of harriers so that prey on the ground might be flushed into the air; this technique is also used if prey has been driven into ground cover in the hope of flushing it back into the air.

In recent times there have reports of Peregrines hunting in twilight and even at night. Beebe (1960) records observations during a Peregrine study on Cox Island, one of the Scott Islands off Vancouver Island's northwest coast. The falcons were hunting Ancient Murrelets and Cassin's Auklets (*Ptychoramphus aleuticus*), both of which leave their breeding grounds before dawn (usually an hour before) to feed and arrive back after dusk (again about an hour after). Beebe notes the Peregrines hanging in the air ('as though hung on strings') at dusk when the auks were leaving the island, and stooping on the auks as they appeared 'in silhouette against the sea'. Beebe does not mention whether his observation was on moonlit nights, but from personal experience (with Ancient Murrelets), observation of the auks is best when moonlight is reflected from the water: then the birds really are silhouetted against the sea. Beebe thought the birds were catching auks, then caching them before hunting again. It is likely that the Peregrines were also hunting in similar fashion in the hour or so before dawn.

Beebe's observation is certainly of crepuscular hunting, perhaps even nocturnal, but the latter has certainly become familiar in urban settings when the Peregrines use street lighting to hunt. Many species migrate preferentially at night and are often attracted by the lights of cities, Peregrines taking advantage of the fact that the nominally cryptic plumage of shore and water birds – dark dorsally, pale ventrally – is an aid to hunting when the prey is lit from below. Such behaviour is clear from the prey composition of British urban Peregrines – see Table 10, which includes Quail, Water Rail and Woodcock – and has also been seen elsewhere (for a general review of nocturnal hunting behaviour of urban Peregrines, see Mebs 2009).

In his study at a coastal site in British Columbia, Dekker (2003) noted that Peregrines which were suffering kleptoparasitic attacks during the day often flew inland at dusk, following ducks to their roosting sites. Although he did not witness hunting directly, the inference was that the Peregrines were hunting ducks nocturnally to avoid piracy. In a later study at the same site, Dekker *et al.* (2012) noted that kleptoparasitism by both Bald Eagles and Gyrfalcons accounted for 36% of Peregrine Dunlin kills, and that the falcons had to increase their kill rate of the waders from 0.05 per hour, when the pirating birds were largely absent, to 0.30 per hour when they were present, with a corresponding effect on the Dunlin population.

Peregrine pairs will also hunt cooperatively in the breeding season, both before egg laying and when the young are approaching fledge or fledged, with some observations suggesting that one falcon will drive prey into the path of the other.

There are also numerous reports of Peregrines chasing or stooping at prey with little or no real intention of catching it, apparently either as a way of sharpening skills or in the manner of cats toying with mice. While these observations are well-attested and made by serious researchers, they are viewed with scepticism by some who consider such behaviour the preserve of 'higher' animals and note that there are also well-attested instances of Peregrines killing numerous prey and caching those they cannot immediately eat. The problem of 'dummy' attacks, whether real or not, makes assessing the hunting efficiency of Peregrines difficult: as Ratcliffe (1993) notes, assumed figures vary from 100%

success (an assumption of those who view the Peregrine as the ultimate hunter rather than a number based on observation) to much lower figures – Ratcliffe quotes the renowned Swedish ornithologist Gustaf Rudebeck as a source. Rudebeck (1951) noted 19 successes from 252 hunts, a success rate of 7.5%.

But higher percentages have been quoted, seemingly from well-observed situations. Cade (1982) quoted values for a particular Peregrine (a falconry bird named Red Baron) whose hunts could be very well observed: in 1978 the falcon was successful in 73% of 81 hunts, in 1979 in 93% of 102 hunts, and in one sequence of 68 hunts in 44 days of that year achieved 100%. However, hunts by falconry birds are artificial and so will overestimate the success rate. Falconry birds are trained to 'wait on' above the falconer and, probably, his dog, watching for the prey to be flushed, so they start with a considerable advantage over wild birds.

Watching wild falcons in southern Quebec over two breeding seasons, Bird & Aubry (1982) saw 197 hunting attempts by a male, of which 69 were successful, a success rate of 35%. Lindberg (1983) observed the same success rate (35%) in southern Sweden, and noted that the rate varied with prey species, being 55% against Starlings and thrushes but lower against heavier prey – 32% on gulls, 26% on pigeons: Lindberg considers the lower rate is compensated by the greater food resource obtained from larger prey. As an illustration, Lindberg noted that the average energy value of a Starling was 160 kcal, that of a pigeon being 600 kcal: with 100 attacks on Starlings the 'captured energy' is therefore 8,800 kcal, while for the pigeons it is 15,600 kcal. Ignoring the energy requirements of hunting and transport, Lindberg calculated that the success rate for pigeons would need to drop below 14% before they would be an unattractive target in energy terms.

Studying Peregrines in Cornwall, Treleaven (1980) claimed a success rate of 52% from 58 hunts, but considered that of these hunts only 45 were true attacks, these having a success rate of 69%. Interestingly, Treleaven timed the hunts and found that those that ended with a kill lasted less than four minutes, some less than one minute: for one Peregrine all observed hunts lasted less than one minute – at the end of that time the hunt was either successful or abandoned. These success rates seem very high, but similarly high rates were found for Peregrines hunting various species in western Japan (Yamada 2001). In over 800 observations, divided into classes according to terrain, Yamada found success rates of around 45–52%. Interestingly, the Peregrines were most successful when hunting over open water, which contradicts some of the observations noted above.

Another problem in judging hunting success is that a single flight might include several attacks. As an example, Buchanan *et al.* (1986), studying Peregrines hunting Dunlin during winter in western Washington State, noted that the success of hunting flights was 47%, but that of individual attacks was only 14.6%.

Of the attacks, 83% were directed against flocks (70% stoops plus 13% horizontal attacks), with 17% chases of individual Dunlin.

The success rate observed by Buchanan and co-workers is higher than, but comparable to, that seen for wintering Peregrines on the Firth of Forth in East Lothian by Cresswell & Whitfield (1994), though the sample size of the former was smaller. Cresswell & Whitfield noted a Peregrine success rate of 6.8%, which was lower than the rates of Sparrowhawks (11.6%) and Merlins (8.8%). In a later winter study in the same area, Cresswell (1996) noted success rates of 9.5% against Redshank (*Tringa totanus*) and 7.6% against Dunlin: there were also no successes in 21 attacks against Skylark. Cresswell noted that the Sparrowhawk success rate was higher against both Redshank and Dunlin, while the Merlin success rate was also higher for Dunlin. In a study in British Columbia, Dekker (1998) also found that the success rate of Merlins was higher than that of Peregrines, particularly for small passerines (Merlin 12.2%, Peregrine 3.8%). For waders the Peregrine's success rate improved in comparison to the smaller falcon (Merlin 12.6%, Peregrine 8.8%). In a later study, Dekker (2003) observed higher success rates, 9.1% when the falcon made open attacks on large flocks of

FIG 73. Adult female Peregrine voicing her disapproval at the author's close approach to her eyrie.

Dunlin, and 23.6% when stealth attacks were made on the flocks (Note 4.2). These higher rates are more consistent with the study of Buchanan (1996) in coastal Washington State, where success rates were 12.5% for Peregrines and 7.8% for Merlins. Arising from these studies were conclusions that were not unexpected: adult Peregrines are better hunters than juveniles, and the juveniles of prey species are more vulnerable than the adults.

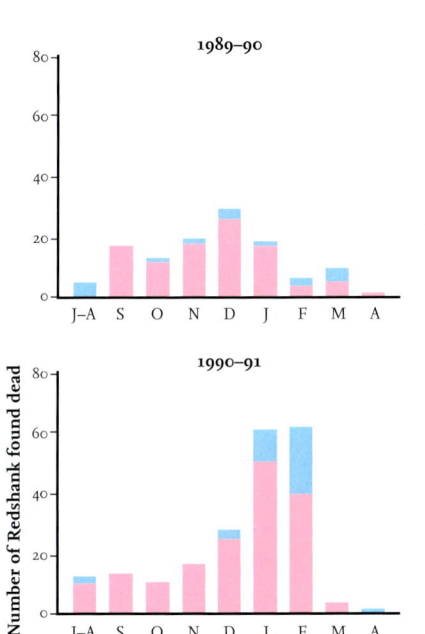

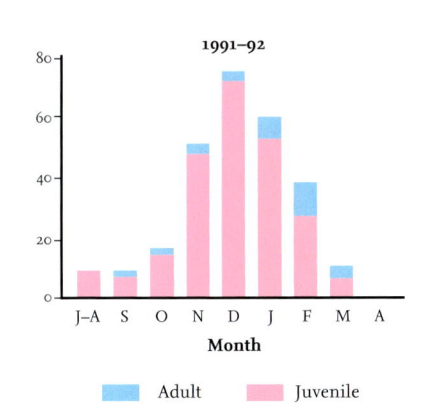

The data of Cresswell & Whitfield (1994) also noted the extreme mortality of certain prey species: Redshank mortality in three consecutive winters (1989/90, 1990/91 and 1991/92) was 31.1%, 48.5% and 57.3%, that of Snipe was 28.6%, 33.3% and 25.0%, with the attrition rate of juveniles considerably higher than that of adults (Fig. 74). Mortality rates much higher than these would have implications for the long-term survival of the species (at a local level), and so the success rates of the three predators involved could not rise significantly before the wader population crashed. It is not only direct predation which affects the prey species population. In a study in Ireland's Dublin Bay, Quinn (1997) noted that although Oystercatchers were less prone to predation than the smaller waders that shared the same habitat, the time they spent foraging (as a result of taking flight when a predator was spotted, then taking time to resettle) and the efficiency of that foraging (more time spent watching the sky and a denser aggregation of birds reducing forage area) were

FIG 74. Number of adult and juvenile Redshanks killed by raptors during successive winters at Tyninghame estuary, southeast Scotland. Redrawn from Cresswell & Whitfield 1994.

adversely affected. This is likely to be the case for the more vulnerable species as well, and for all prey species could result in a reduction of body condition.

However, there is evidence that Peregrines can have positive, as well as negative effects on prey species numbers. In a study on an island off Washington State, Paine *et al.* (1990) found that the arrival of Peregrines on the island had resulted in a reduction in numbers of the primary prey species (Cassin's Auklet and Rhinoceros Auklet, *Cerorhinca monocerata*), but an increase in population of other species. The increase was a result of the Peregrines feeding on Northwestern Crows (*Corvus caurinus*) which were a significant predator of auk, and other seabird, nests. However, there are significant differences between the two situations: in the US the Peregrines were present during the breeding season and so their attacks on crows, either killing them or curtailing their predatory behaviour, were indirectly benefiting other species, whereas the winter predation observed by Cresswell & Whitfield (1994) was a direct threat to population numbers. That said, the study of Paine *et al.* (1990) does imply, yet again, that the interaction of predator and prey is rarely as straightforward as it seems.

A lower Peregrine success rate was also observed by Dekker (1980) for migrating (both spring and autumn) Peregrines in central Alberta, Canada. Dekker observed 674 interactions with potential prey with only 52 captures, a success rate of 7.7%. Interestingly, the autumnal success rate for juvenile Peregrines was only 2.4% (42 observed hunts), consistent with the known high winter mortality of juveniles, inexperience and consequent poor hunting performance leading to starvation. In the spring migration the success rate of adult falcons was 9.8% and that of first-year falcons 7.1%, not as good, but comparable and adequate for survival. In a later study in winter in British Columbia, Dekker (1998) noted a success rate of Peregrines hunting Dunlins of 9.3%. In this study Dekker noted that during the period when their intertidal feeding grounds were under water, the Dunlins flocked over the ocean about 2 km from shore, apparently as a defence against predation.

However, while the success rates noted in his two studies were low, Dekker (1980) noted the differences in hunting that had led others (as noted above) to define 'serious' and 'non-serious' hunting. Dekker defined a 'warm-up' (or 'half-hearted') hunting phase which lasted an extended period, followed by a short burst of serious hunting, and concluded that while it was difficult to define the end of one and the start of the other, the success rate of serious hunting would be higher (though Dekker does not set down a value). It seems, therefore, that taking the various studies as a whole some Peregrines at least do indeed have an initial period where attacks are not 'real' but allow the falcon to prepare itself for true attacks, and that if only the latter are considered then high (say 30–40%) success rates are achieved.

As already noted, there is evidence that Peregrine pairs will sometimes hunt cooperatively, one falcon scattering prey while the second waits to pick up a bird which has moved into a vulnerable position as a result of panic. In his study in southern Sweden, Lindberg (1983) found such cooperation increased the success rate of hunts from 34% to 45%. However, other studies suggest cooperation is not always so successful. Dekker (1980) identified the hunting method of the Peregrines he observed, noting stoops at ground and flying targets, pursuit flights and surprise attacks. Of these, stoops at ground targets were the most successful (11.6%), though cooperative hunting by two falcons was comparable (11.1%). Low-level surprise attacks were the least successful (4.6%). Dekker also noted that the majority of captures were on targets which failed to employ the evasion tactics used by others of their species. The latter would swerve in flight and/or drop to the ground or onto water at the last moment before the attack, whereas those which were captured tended to maintain a level course and were overhauled.

While it is not easy to unpick the various quoted success rates with any degree of confidence, particularly in view of the potential for misreading some Peregrine attacks, it seems likely that Peregrines are more efficient when making stooping attacks on their primary (breeding-season) prey, rather less successful when forced to select non-optimal prey, with probable success rate varying between c.10% for the latter to, perhaps, c.20% for the former, consistent with the observations of Parker (1979) in Wales, who noted success rates of 15% (female) and 17% (male) when the Peregrines were hunting pigeons.

Dekker (1980) observed Peregrines being both the aggressor and victim of kleptoparasitic attacks in his migration-period studies in central Alberta, Canada. He saw adults taking prey from juveniles, females pirating males, and Peregrines taking prey from Merlins, Northern (Hen) Harriers and Sharp-shinned Hawks (*Accipiter striatus*), but falling victim in other attacks by the larger raptors. King (2009) saw an adult Peregrine pirating prey from a Hobby in Hampshire, while both Collar (2002) in Cambridgeshire and Rees (2009) in Pembrokeshire, both in autumn, noted piracy of Merlins. Zuberogoitia *et al.* (2002) also witnessed a Peregrine apparently successfully pirating prey from a Carrion Crow in northern Spain, but also saw 'Mediterranean gulls' (presumably Yellow-legged Gulls, *Larus michahellis*) pirating pigeons from Peregrines. One very interesting aspect of kleptoparasitism is the effect it has on the hunting rate of the Peregrines. In a winter study in British Columbia where the Peregrines had historically taken both ducks and Dunlins, an increase in Bald Eagle numbers meant the falcons tended to concentrate on Dunlin, presumably the lighter prey weight offering a greater chance of escaping piracy. When Bald Eagle numbers increased, and Gyrfalcons also started to make piratical attacks on the falcons, the Peregrine kill rate increased from 0.05 per hour to 0.18 per hour (and on one occasion to 0.30 per hour). Kleptoparasitism was therefore having a significant effect on the Dunlin population.

Some researchers have suggested that Peregrines do not hunt close to their eyries as this could identify nests to potential predators. In California, Enderson & Kirven (1983) radio-tagged a breeding pair of Peregrines in order to measure their movements from the eyrie, collecting data from 139 flights by the female and 40 by the male. In general the female remained within 1 km of the nest (74% of flights), while for the male, 65% of flights were more than 1 km and most flights were along specific corridors defined by the local topography (Fig. 75). Prey was taken in all directions and there appears to have been no evidence for

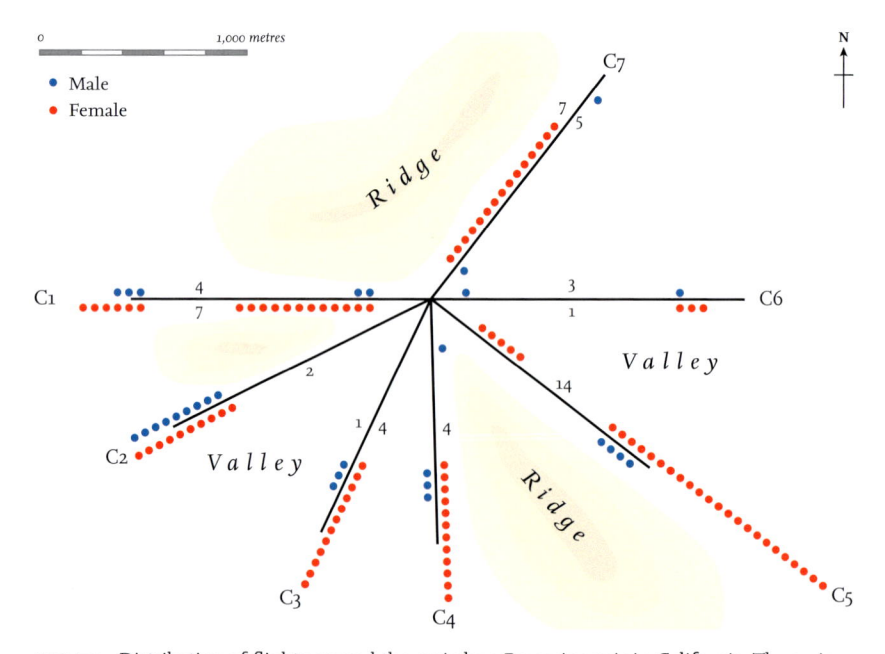

FIG 75. Distribution of flights around the eyrie by a Peregrine pair in California. The eyrie is at the focus of the lines, which represent generalised corridors used by the birds. Each dot represents a flight, with points nearer the eyrie showing flights < 1 km, and those further away showing flights > 1 km. Numbers beside the lines show flights of unknown length. Redrawn from Enderson & Kirven 1983.

hunting at distance from the eyrie. Indeed, the return flights with prey were always directly to the nest, which would seem to negate the idea that any specific attempts at avoiding eyrie detection were being made. In a separate study Enderson & Craig (1997) tracked two male and three female Peregrines (of three pairs) in Colorado. Again most flights by the five birds were within 7 km of the eyrie (Fig. 76).

However, on some flights the falcons travelled up to 43 km. On one flight a female Peregrine travelled 19 km in ten minutes, an average speed of 115 km/h. For more than half the recorded flights, the average speed of the falcons exceeded 60 km/h. Enderson & Craig's study was on *F. p. anatum*, but in a study of *F. p. minor* in South Africa Jenkins & Benn (1998) found a very similar spread of distances (Fig. 77) though with shorter distances being travelled (presumably because of higher prey densities). In each case males tended to make shorter flights. In the US study it was mainly females which made much longer flights, but this was less noticeable in South Africa as few journeys of more than 10 km were made. While these data deal with subspecies of the Peregrine which differ

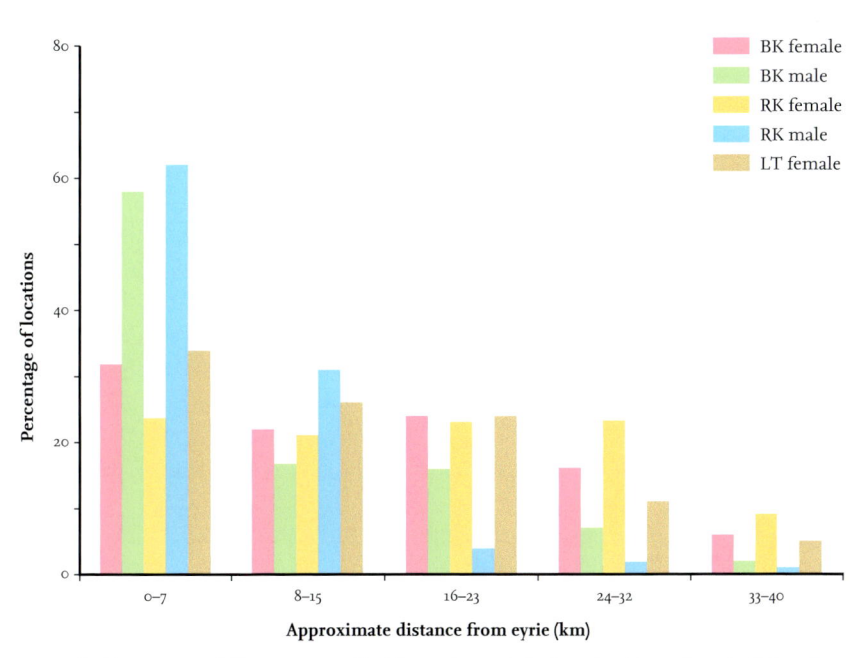

FIG 76. Percentage of distances travelled from the eyrie by hunting Peregrines in Colorado. The locations of eyries BK, RK, LT are shown in Fig. 80. Redrawn from Enderson & Craig 1997.

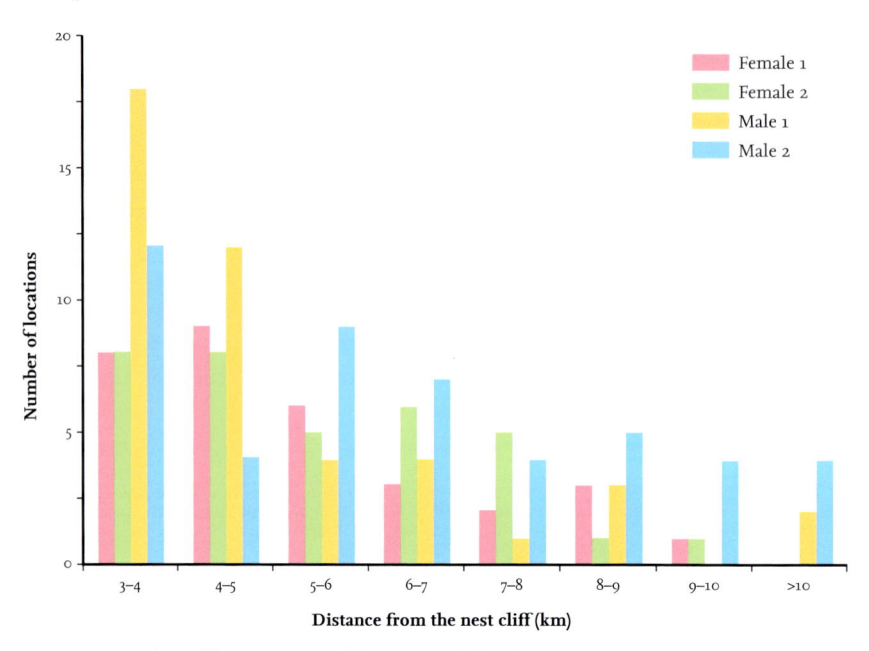

FIG 77. Number of locations visited by male and female Peregrines in relation to distance from nest cliff in South Africa. Redrawn from Jenkins & Benn 1998.

from that found in Britain, the similarity in behaviour implies that Peregrines, particularly males, tend to forage within a short distance of the nest cliff.

Whichever hunting technique is employed, Peregrines dispatch prey with a bite at the base of neck to break the spinal cord. If the prey is captured in the stoop the bite may be administered in the air. The Peregrine will usually bite the neck base of prey that has been killed by a stoop and knocked to the ground as well, suggesting that the bite is a reflex action when prey is clutched. Following the fatal bite, the prey is then taken to a perch for plucking and eating, the latter usually starting with the head, which is often consumed whole (sometimes the brain is picked out), then the breast muscles. The heart and liver are usually eaten, but the digestive tract is normally discarded. Though most food is eaten at perches there are records, few in number, of Peregrines eating on the wing. Cade (reported by Ratcliffe 1993) watched a male Peregrine kill and consume on the wing a total of seven bats during a continuous 20-minute hunt over the USA's Grand Canyon. Sprunt (1951) also records a Peregrine consuming bats on the wing, reaching forward with its feet, which clutched the bat, and down with its head, to quickly take bites while soaring. However, Stager (1941), who also watched Peregrines feeding on bats, noted that the falcons flew to nearby trees to feed, then returned to catch more. The difference could be the sheer number of bats involved in the observation of Stager: he watched six Peregrines feed on bats for an hour, suggesting that the bats represented an almost limitless supply of prey so that time was available to land, feed unhurriedly and return to the hunt.

Like the smaller falcons, Peregrines cache food, presumably for similar reasons. Ratcliffe (1993) notes that one Cornish female Peregrine killed six pigeons during a six-hour period: one was lost, one was fed to the falcon's brood and four were cached. Male Peregrines will, of course, also cache food, particularly if the day's hunting has provided a surplus. However, males in breeding pairs will also cache food for themselves: female Peregrines can aggressively take any food the male has, either for herself (during courtship) or for her brood, so that the male may cache in the hope of being able to enjoy a meal later. I have seen an urban male cache food on a building a short distance away from that on which the nesting box was situated: in this case the cache was not far enough away, as the female either saw, or was aware of the site from courtship, and robbed the male of his meal.

One additional reason for caching might be that as some prey species are large, the Peregrine is unable to consume the entire food content at one time and, once it is light enough to transport, will remove it to a suitable cache for further consumption at a later time. Cache sites are usually in fissures in cliffs. In his study of Peregrines on Langara Island, Nelson (1970) noted that the falcons frequently cached food. However, in this case, the Peregrines were feeding exclusively on Ancient Murrelets, which leave their nesting burrows before dawn and return after sunset. The Peregrines therefore had limited opportunities to hunt, these accentuated by the local weather, which was frequently bad, and so, not unreasonably, took every bird they could catch, caching to continue to hunt while prey remained available.

Food consumption and energy balance

Remarkably, very little research has been carried out on the energetics of Peregrines, and even estimates of the daily energy input are based to a large extent on data from falconers on captive birds. While the latter are obviously useful, they can only act as a pointer to the energy requirements of wild birds which do not have the benefit of being fed rather than having to hunt, and of being housed in aviaries that may also be warm and wind-free.

Woodford (1960) stated that female Peregrines require a daily average of 141 g of meat throughout the year, while males need 113 g. These values are consistent with the work of Barton & Houston (1993), who studied dietary requirements of Peregrines (and several other captive raptor species) which were fed day-old chicks (without yolk sacs or intestines), but only when the falcons were fed chicks at 20 °C. When males were fed chicks at 0 °C they required 143 g/day. The difference was due, in part, to a drop in digestive efficiency (i.e. the effectiveness of extracting energy from consumed food), but would also be influenced by heat losses. Barton & Houston found that there was a correlation between intestinal length and digestive efficiency. In general, raptors feeding on birds had short intestines and, therefore poor digestive efficiency.

These intakes are larger than, though, as a consequence of differences in the living conditions of the birds, not inconsistent with, lower figures in a study by Lindberg (1983), who measured an average food intake of 81–92 g/day fresh weight for a captive male Peregrine, and 109–112 g/day fresh weight for a captive female. While not carrying out work as extensive as that of the Groningen Kestrel team, Lindberg did make some interesting estimates of the energy balance in Peregrines.

Assuming an energy conversion of 2 kcal/g (8.36 kJ/g) wet weight, Lindberg's figures equate to a gross energy intake (GEI) of 678–770 kJ/day for the male and 911–936 kJ/day for the female. The basal metabolic rate (BMR) of the birds was calculated on the assumption of a variation with weight. The BMR for the male showed a decline in summer, but the variation through the year was small, from a minimum of about 500 kJ/day in June to about 600 kJ/day in January. The calculation for the captive female was more difficult because of breeding, which meant that for four months the falcon could not be weighed on a daily basis. However, the BMR showed a similar decline in summer (about 750 kJ/day in April and September) with respect to winter (about 860 kJ/day in January). Figure 78 shows the variation of GEI over a two-year period for the captive male. GEI is directly related to daily energy expenditure (DEE) by the falcon's metabolic efficiency, which Lindberg assumed lay between 70% and 80%. The ratio of DEE to BMR varied from about 2 in winter, when heat losses were significant, to about 1.5 in summer, and then to about 3 in late summer/autumn when the falcon was moulting. The same figures applied to both male and female. (Note that the equivalent figure to Fig. 78 for the female Peregrine is not shown, as data are missing for the breeding season.) The weight of the male bird followed a similar curve to that for GEI in Fig. 78. It is interesting to compare Fig. 78 with data from the Dutch study of breeding Kestrels (Fig. 79). In the absence of feeding duties, the male's GEI (and therefore DEE) does not show the expected sharp increase during the breeding season, the peak being displaced to autumn when the captive Peregrine moulted.

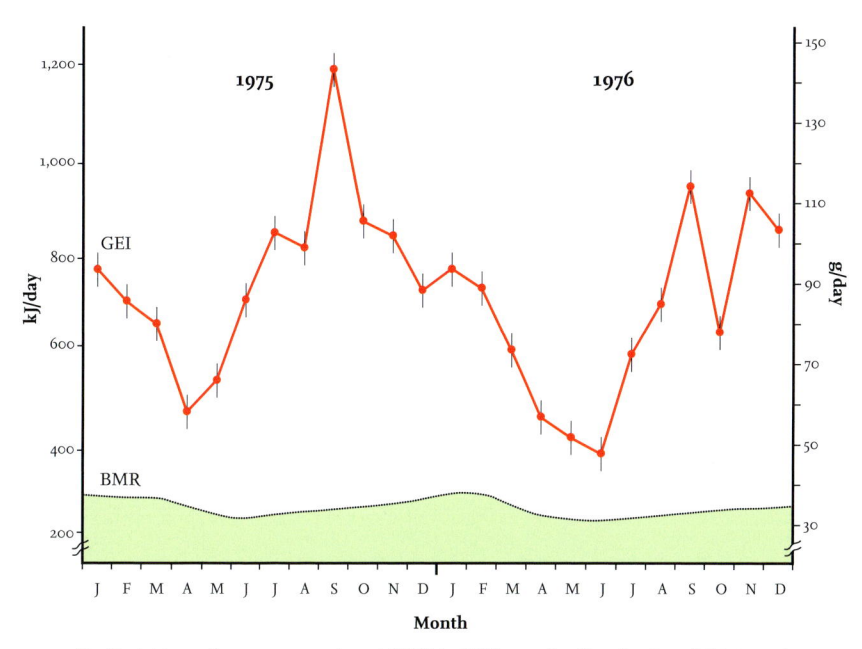

FIG 78. Variation of gross energy input (GEI) in kJ/day and g/day fresh weight, together with variation of basal metabolic rate (BMR), of a captive male Peregrine throughout the year. The falcon was kept in an outdoor aviary and not flown. The bird's moult began in May, peaked in August and ended in October in each year. Redrawn and rescaled from Lindberg 1983.

Lindberg also estimated the DEE of wild Peregrines, making the assumption that the ratio of DEE to BMR was essentially similar to that of captive birds, but allowing for the energy input of breeding (gonadal growth in males, egg production in females, etc.). From this Lindberg was able to calculate the DEE of wild birds during the breeding season for varying brood sizes (Fig. 79). The DEE in Fig. 79 is very much higher than that observed in the captive male Peregrine (Fig. 78), an indication of the energy demand of provisioning the growing brood. It is very likely that the male (and during the later days of fledging and when the fledglings are learning to fly and hunt, the female also) loses weight, just as male Kestrels do, particularly as both sexes start the moult during the time when feeding demands are greatest.

From Fig. 78, the DEE of a Peregrine pair raising four chicks is 3,782 kJ/day. This converts to 124 kg of biomass for the six-month period April–September, which equates to 476 Black-headed Gulls.

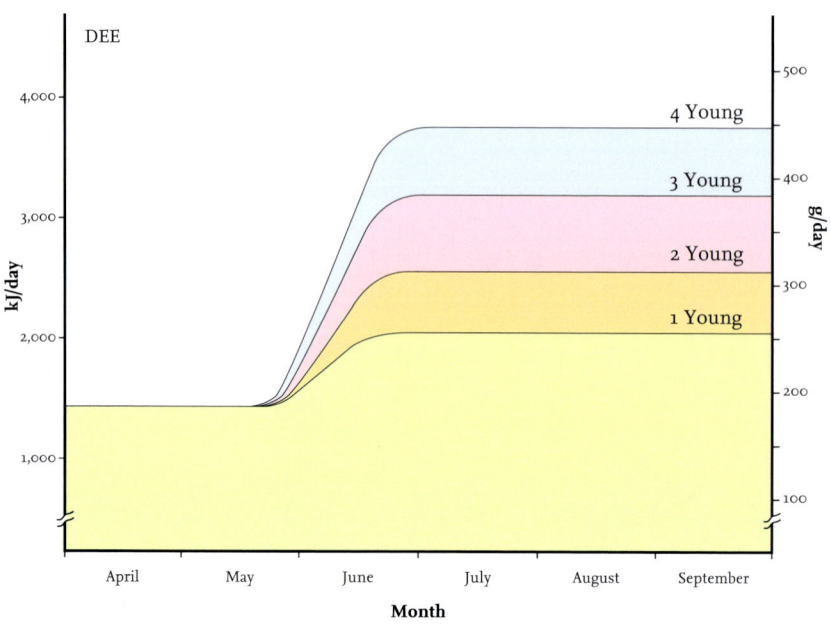

FIG 79. Variation of daily energy expenditure (DEE) in kJ/day and g/day of fresh biomass for Peregrine pairs with different brood sizes. Redrawn and rescaled from Lindberg 1983.

TERRITORY AND BREEDING DENSITY

As for other raptors, territory and hunting range differ for Peregrines, the former being a relatively small area centred on the nest site and from which intruders are usually vigorously ejected, the latter a much larger area, one whose size depends on the density of prey. In a study which involved the radio-tracking of three female and two male Peregrines from three pairs in Colorado, USA, Enderson & Craig (1997) found that the hunting ranges varied from 358 km² (a male) to 1,508 km² (the female of the same pair). There was also considerable overlap of the ranges of the three pairs despite the minimum inter-nest distance being 28 km (Fig. 80). The hunting ranges exceed those calculated in other areas of North America, and vastly exceed those estimated in Britain. Mearns (1985) used telemetry to record flights of two breeding female Peregrines in southern Scotland. The two eyries were 4.5 km apart and the data were gathered over a period of about 20 days during the breeding season, ending once the fledglings had left the nests. One female had a hunting range of 22 km², this increasing by

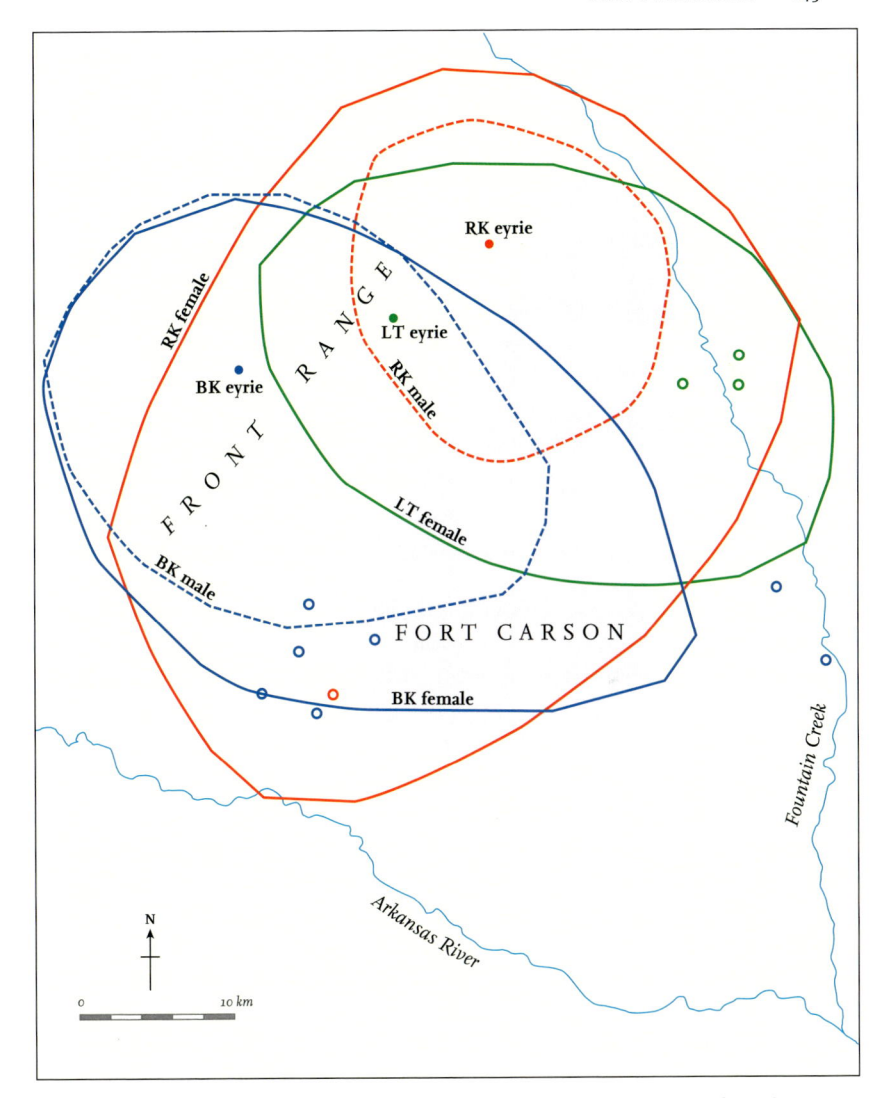

FIG 80. Estimated hunting ranges of three female and two male Peregrines from three breeding pairs in Colorado, USA. The locations of the eyries of the three pairs (BK, RK, LT) are marked. Open symbols show more outlying locations. Redrawn from Enderson & Craig 1997.

only 5% once the fledglings had left the nest ledge: this female also spent most her time (about 85%) within 2 km of the nest. The other female had a much smaller range (9 km^2) initially, and spent over 90% of her time within 2 km of the nest, but her range increased to 117 km² once the fledglings had left the nest ledge, and she spent 40% of her time further than 2 km from the nest. There was no apparent overlap of hunting range of the two females, in contrast to the findings of Enderson & Craig, though the latter does imply a willingness of Peregrines to breed where there are suitable nest sites even if prey density is low and ranges must therefore be shared with other Peregrines.

Range tolerance if circumstances require is also supported by evidence which suggests that the density of Peregrines has increased in areas with suitable nesting sites as the population has increased, in addition to the falcons finding other sites – quarries, towns – in which to breed. Beebe (1960), studying Peregrines on Langara Island, found that in one particular area there were 'never less than five, usually six and sometimes eight' breeding pairs in an area (encompassing both land and sea) of 'less than two square miles', i.e. approximately 5 km². This corresponds to a breeding density of up to 160 pairs/100 km², which is extraordinary. The Peregrines were hunting Ancient Murrelet (the main prey), Cassin's Auklet, Leach's Petrel and Fork-tailed Storm Petrel (*Oceanodroma furcata*). According to Beebe, the availability of these prey species on Langara Island could only be described as 'astronomic' and the high numbers, and density, of Peregrines 'appears to be nothing more than a response' to this. Beebe notes, for instance, that although both Fox Sparrow (*Passerella iliaca*) and Hermit Thrush (*Catharus guttatus*) were present on the island and were often observed far away from cover and therefore vulnerable, the remains of neither was found among Peregrine kills. Assuming that the Peregrines had nest sites at the centre of the 5 km² identified by Beebe, the observed density suggests an inter-nest distance of 2 km, much less than would be expected: in a study area in southwest Scotland, Mearns & Newton (1988) noted some Peregrine pairs were within 3 km of another pair, whereas other pairs were separated by up to 30 km. While the shorter distance implies a breeding density of about 3 pairs/100 km², the longer distance implies less than 1 pair/100 km².

Ratcliffe (1993) collated data from both coastal and inland Peregrine sites across Britain. For the coastal (sea cliff) areas he noted many instances where the separation was about 2 km, and several more where it was only 1 km. At inland sites, Ratcliffe noted that when nest sites were evenly distributed the Peregrine pairs tended to space themselves evenly, but where the sites were less uniformly distributed, close nesting could be seen, just as it was at coastal sites. Ratcliffe noted the mean distance to neighbours and the corresponding 'territory' size this defined, finding that historically the size varied between about 20–25 km² in some areas (north Wales, the Lake District, southern Scotland) to over 100 km² in the Scottish Highlands, with an exceptional value of about 12 km² for one small area of the Lake District. These numbers convert to breeding densities of 1–4 pairs/100 km², with the highest density being 8.5 pairs/100 km². These numbers differ markedly from the breeding density of Beebe (1960). However, observations of Peregrine behaviour in the vicinity of nests sites suggest that most birds are aggressive to intruders who stray within about 250 m of their nest, in any direction, but at greater distances are, in general, more tolerant, though some particularly belligerent falcons will attack and pursue intruders who come within 1.5–2 km. This implies that while inter-nest separations are high if circumstances allow, they could reduce if circumstances changed.

With an increase in Peregrine population it appears that the linear separation between nest sites in Britain has decreased, but the falcons have continued to maintain an approximately equal separation to neighbours in all directions, though continuing to hunt over areas which are not defined by this inter-nest separation. The breeding density of Peregrines is, it seems, defined by food resource rather than territory size, but, adopting the human maxim that high fences make good neighbours, nest separations are kept as large as

FIG 81. Landing sequence of an adult female Peregrine near her eyrie.

possible in order to minimise antagonism. This is certainly consistent with the finding of Wightman & Fuller (2006) in North America – see *Nest sites* below – that one important factor in defining 'better quality' nest sites is distance from nearest neighbour.

Mearns & Newton (1988) found no evidence to suggest that the minimal distance in their study was a factor in breeding success, but ultimately, of course, there will be a limit, one which will be defined by a combination of prey availability and the minimum tolerable distance to the adjacent Peregrine pair. Hunt (1998) investigated the way in which populations might grow, then stabilise, in an area with a defined number of available nest sites. Though highly mathematical, the investigation does shed interesting light on the influence of 'floaters' (non-breeding adults) on the approach to and achievement of population stability. In Hunt's hypothetical population, stability was achieved in 32 years (for a nominal raptor population), which is an approximation to the timescale actually seen in British Peregrine populations. Hunt's work notes that an equilibrium (and therefore limit) will be reached: that limit may (but may not) have been achieved on Langara Island, where inter-nest distances could not have been greater than about 500 m, and where the combination of nest-site availability and prey resource allowed a situation approaching the maximum achievable.

BREEDING

Some Peregrine pairs probably spend the winter months together: this is certainly true of pairs in North America, and is also known to be the case for some British urban pairs, which implies that other pairs may adopt the same lifestyle. Some birds definitely winter alone, particularly in non-breeding areas, and lone wintering may also be necessary for pairs if the food resource is insufficient to sustain both birds. There are different views on whether the male or the female of a given Peregrine pair remains at the nesting territory in order to avoid it being usurped, both sexes having been seen to do so.

The pair bond is monogamous – bigamy has been recorded, but rarely, which is consistent with the finding of only 1.3% extra-pair copulations in a Canadian Arctic population, based on DNA analysis (Johnstone 1998): the population in question was dense, which may account for the finding – and long-lasting, perhaps lifelong. Peregrines can mate in their first year, but this is uncommon in both sexes (and very uncommon in males for similar reasons to the other falcon British species – see also the comments on the breeding age difference between the sexes in Chapter 2). Wendt & Septon (1991) note that if first-year Peregrines pair they usually fail to produce eggs, and if they do hatchlings rarely survive to fledge, though they do record a pair of first-years which bred in Milwaukee, USA, in a box mounted on top of a building and raised four nestlings to fledge. However, the male then consistently attacked the fledglings when they were learning to fly, stooping at them and knocking each of the four to the ground at least once: one fledgling broke a femur on hitting the ground and died of resulting complications. Another youngster died in collision with a window, though Wendt & Septon do not say whether this accident was due to evasive action after an attack. A third fledgling was injured twice, rescued and relocated to avoid further injury. The fourth fledgling survived, but subsequently left the city. Wendt & Septon conjecture that the breeding male's youth may have resulted in this aggressive behaviour, but note that as a breeding adult the bird continued to harass his offspring when they were learning to fly, though never to the same extent.

In a study in southern Scotland, Mearns & Newton (1984) found 19 first-year females in a total of 398 territorial pairs (5%). Of these 19 only seven laid eggs, and of those seven only one raised young. The females were identified in part by trapping and in part by plumage: of six trapped males, one was a yearling male, four were two-year old birds and one was four or five years old. In a later study in the same area Mearns & Newton (1988) found only two yearling females breeding (in a sample of 62), neither of which was successful. In northern Spain Zuberogoitia *et al.* (2009), in a study over 11 years which involved ringing 426 chicks and 16 trapped adults, found no first-year breeders. 3.3% of males and 22.7% of females bred in their second year; 6.6% of males and 6.8% of females bred in their third year; with 90% of males and 70% of females breeding in their third year or later; one male did not breed until its fifth year, one female in her sixth year.

While the evidence for assortative mating on the basis of age is therefore clear, there is some evidence that size also plays a part, Olsen *et al.* (1998), in a study in Australia, finding that female Peregrines with longer wing lengths tended to mate with males with similarly long wing lengths.

If one member of a long-lasting pair dies, the widowed bird will select a new partner, though this is not necessarily always with a first-year bird as there are often non-breeding individuals in the population. In general in such cases a widowed male partner will stay on his territory and seek to attract a new female, while a female will move away to seek a new male. There is one known pairing of a female Peregrine with her two-year-old son after the death of the young male's father, and other incestuous relationships are also known. Pagel & Sipple (2011) report a case of sibling mating in California, while Bélisle *et al.* (2012) report a case involving male and female Peregrines that were the only hatchlings at an urban nest in Montreal. The latter case was very curious. The young female had a partially disabled leg, and stayed with her parents all winter. Although she could hunt, the leg disability reduced her abilities, and she begged for food from her parents and stole their cached food on occasions. The following year the juvenile female remained with her parents while they copulated and even displaced her father from incubating several times, though she showed little interest in incubating herself. Despite the juvenile's occasionally aggressive behaviour she was accepted by her parents. Three eggs hatched and one day the juvenile female grabbed a nestling from the unguarded nest and flew off, chased by the adult male. The juvenile returned without the nestling (which was not recovered) but was ignored by her parents and eventually left the area. The following year the juvenile female returned to Montreal and paired with her brother. The pair copulated and three eggs were laid, but these were lost when the nest they selected collapsed: on retrieval it was found that two of the three eggs were fertile. In general, as for other species, fledgling mortality and dispersal acts against such incestuous relationships, but the tendency of Peregrines to return to natal areas and the traditional use of nest sites may lead to more such relationships than might usually occur.

While the behaviour of the juvenile female in the study of Bélisle and co-workers was clearly aberrant, there are recorded incidents of juvenile males helping at nest sites (e.g. Monneret 1983, who reported incidents from the 1970s and 1980s with nominate Peregrines, and Kurosawa & Kurosawa 2003, who watched a juvenile male *F. p. japonensis* helping to feed chicks at the nest of an unrelated pair on Hokkaido, Japan). Spofford (1947) also saw the second female at a nest in the USA. The second bird was smaller than the mated female: the male fed his mate and ignored the smaller female. The same situation arose the following year, but this time the smaller female immediately covered the eggs when the larger female left, though she stopped incubating the moment the larger bird returned. See also the discussion of 'floaters' at nest sites in Chapter 2.

Ratcliffe (1993) records pairings in which the death of a female resulted in the male pairing with a second female who acted as foster-mother to the original brood. Ratcliffe also records one event in which an unpaired female evicted a female from her clutch, taking over not only the eggs but the male (the father of the clutch). Even more remarkably, Nelson (1970), in British Columbia, records a male pairing with a foster-mother after the loss of the female, and then the male being lost, at which point the foster-mother took a new mate, the clutch being incubated by two foster-parents.

Nest sites

Peregrines in various parts of their range occasionally utilise stick nests in trees (e.g. Buchanan *et al.* 2014, for details of incidences in North America). Such behaviour was also widespread in central-east Europe at one time, but is now concentrated in Germany as a result of Peregrine reintroduction (Langgemach *et al.* 1997).

Peregrines are, in general, cliff-breeders, eggs being laid on ledges which are large enough to accommodate four fledglings in safety. Such sites are often traditional, with usage lines going back over decades. The ledges often have sparse or short vegetation, though ledges which have formerly been used by Buzzards, crows, Golden Eagles and Ravens, and which still have the remnants of stick nests, are also used (Table 12). Of these species, Raven nests are the most often utilised. Within the nest, or in ledge soil, the female will make a scrape, usually about 20 cm in diameter and 2–4 cm deep (though some traditional sites have much deeper scrapes, these often combining soil, dead vegetation and the detritus of years of usage).

High, steep nesting cliffs are preferred, Ratcliffe (1993) noting the studies of the American Joe Hickey, who pointed out that the very best sites on such cliffs would become traditional even if there was a high rate of human killing of the adult Peregrines. Ratcliffe also states that breeding performance is improved on higher, steeper cliffs, though if a Peregrine pair were to lose a clutch, for whatever reason, they would invariably choose a different site for a repeat clutch. Ratcliffe does not suggest reasons why bigger cliffs have better reproductive success, but Wightman & Fuller (2006) suggest that this results from a despotic distribution,

TABLE 12 Nest sites used by Peregrines in Britain. From Ratcliffe (1993).

	Ledge (i.e. no nest)[1]	Raven	Buzzard	Golden Eagle	Crow
North Wales	28	3	0	0	0
Northern England	56	21	0	0	0
Southern Scotland	104	60	4	0	1
Scottish Highlands	58	18	1	1	0
Percentage of total	**69.3**	**28.7**	**1.4**	**0.3**	**0.3**

1. In a study of Peregrines in southwest Scotland over a nine-year period Mearns & Newton (1988) found that stick-nest sites had a higher success rate (in terms of number of clutches which produced fledglings) than bare ledges. They considered the likely reason was that stick-nest builders were not constrained by the need to find flat ledges and so could utilise sites which offered better shelter from the weather and were less accessible by humans.

FIG 82. Peregrine eyrie on chalk cliffs, southeast England. (James Sellen)

FIG 83. Eyrie on a cliff in southern Scotland.

FIG 84. Eyrie in a quarry, southwest England.

that is the falcons arriving first at the breeding sites occupy the higher-quality sites and act as despots in forcing late arrivals to occupy inferior sites. Despotic distribution would also imply that Peregrines of better 'quality' (Note 4.3) hold 'better' sites, with 'lesser-quality' pairs being forced to use poorer sites. Wightman & Fuller, working in central west Greenland, identified what constituted a 'better' site. They defined a series of 20 variable characteristics for nest sites. In addition to the obvious characteristics – inaccessible ledges, ledges beneath overhangs of rock which offer a degree of shelter from rain as well as better protection against potential predators – they also found that distance to nearest Peregrine neighbour was important, though this was found not to be the case in an Alpine study area covering adjacent areas of Italy and Switzerland by Brambilla et al.(2006a), even though the breeding density was low (1.43 pairs/100 km^2): in this case what appeared to be the overriding issue was the distance to urban settlements with consequent abundance of Feral Pigeons. Brambilla and co-workers categorised nest sites by similar characteristics to Wightman & Fuller (2006) and found that the same ones were critical in site selection.

At coastal sites nest ledges are usually on the upper part of tall cliffs, the better to gain protection from storm-driven waves or salty spume. At inland sites in Scotland, Peregrines nest at altitudes up to about 1,100 m, which is about as high as cliffs can be found in Britain, though in other parts of the falcon's vast range, nests are found above 3,000 m. At sea sites the Peregrines usually have little choice in terms of the direction the chosen ledge faces, but at inland sites where greater choice is available, there is no evidence for a preferred direction, though sites with an open view are usually favoured. That said, relatively tight gorges are also utilised, so the protection a ledge offers appears paramount in the selection process. Cliffs, being natural structures, do not have preferred orientation, but evidence from North America suggests that if the Peregrines have a choice they prefer a position which offers shade from the sun and may choose a ledge shaded by a boulder if that is not possible.

Having stated that British Peregrines are cliff nesters, it should be noted that instances of ground nesting are known. Though these are usually on slopes, often with broken rock outcrops and/or thick vegetation, offering a high degree of protection, they may also be on more open ground. Ratcliffe (1993) records several instances, and I have seen one site on a peat hag which qualified as an unsheltered ground nest despite the hag being on a relatively steep (though easily negotiated) slope. Ground nesting is also seen in very remote areas where human disturbance is very unlikely, for instance in Siberia where peat mounds and tussocks are found on the tundra, and where cliffs are in short supply. Mebs (2001) also notes that it is common in Finland (90% of all nests). There

FIG 85. Peregrines nesting in a box on a church tower. In (a) the female is brooding young nestlings. In (b) the sleeping chicks are nearing fledgling, while in (c) one fledgling is enjoying a meal, probably of Feral Pigeon.

have also been a handful of observations of tree nesting in Britain, though it seems this no longer occurs: the last authenticated record was in 1999 when three chicks were fledged from a clutch of four eggs in a Buzzard stick nest in Scotland (Leckie & Campbell 2000). In a study in Germany, Kirmse (2001) noted that Peregrine chicks raised in stick nests in trees may choose to use a stick nest, a cliff or a building when they begin to breed, but that chicks raised in non-tree nests had never been noted as breeding in trees. That suggests that unless chicks are placed in stick nests (as has occurred in the reintroduction programme in Pomerania, Germany), Peregrines breeding in stick nests in trees may never be seen again in Britain, though the incident in 1999 would seem to contradict this assertion.

Peregrines have also nested, though rarely, on electricity transmission towers (pylons), and more recently, of course, have adapted to urban living (Note 4.4) and also to the use of man-made structures as nest sites, sometimes using purpose-built handy ledges which may have been used previously by Ravens. Webcams have meant that urban nest sites can now be viewed easily, and with that ease has come a belief that such behaviour is modern. In fact records going back 150 years or more exist, and there were almost certainly unrecorded instances prior to those. Many sites are on churches, but other sites – factory chimneys, shipyard cranes, transmission towers (pylons) etc. – are also known. Peregrines have also nested on nuclear power stations, which probably provided the best protection against disturbance any British pairs have ever received.

Displays

Pair formation, whether the renewal of an existing bond or the beginning of a new partnership, usually begins in January or February, though earlier observations have been made. Meier *et al.* (1989) recorded courtship flight displays in autumn in two pairs (one of which comprised a juvenile male and an adult female) in Puerto Rico. The pair including the juvenile male was also observed to copulate on one occasion. Courtship behaviour, including copulation and subsequent egg laying (though the eggs were infertile) has also been seen in autumn in captive birds.

In general pair formation begins with occupation of a territory by the male, who then begins to advertise his possession (though some observers have suggested instances where female Peregrines have arrived first). A lone male will start advertising by flying about close to the nest site while chupping, increasing both the flights and the calling if a female appears. At this stage, Cade (noted in Ratcliffe 1993) considers that the occupant of a good nest site will willingly display to any passing bird of the opposite sex, being more interested in maintaining the site than in maintaining the pair bond, but that once the usual partner has arrived the pair will vigorously chase other falcons away. This seems to imply that pair bonds are not strong, though it may also mean that in pairs that do not arrive together the first arrival has to cover the possibility that his/her partner may not have survived the winter. Reunited pairs will often roost at the nest site, but in the early stages of new pairings the birds tend to find separate roosts, these becoming closer together as the bond strengthens.

The pair bond is established by courtship feeding (see Chapter 2). This is often associated with cooperative hunting, the pair choosing a target prey and assisting each other in preventing it from escaping until one or other falcon makes the kill. If the female does so, she will eat the prey; if the male kills he will present the prey to his mate. Partnership displays are, at first, aerial. In one display the male will fly fast and close along the nesting cliff, occasionally sweeping up to perform high, soaring circles above the site before swooping down to fly fast along the cliff again. This display seems to be the 'Z flight' of Monneret (1974), though Monneret emphasises that the male alters his body position so that the light underparts and dark upperparts are displayed, and

FIG 86. Food pass from male to female Peregrine. (Nathan Guttridge)

suggests the flight can be considered a territorial display as well as advertising the nest site to the female. Monneret also describes a flight by the male Peregrines in which the bird flies from the nest site and follows a horizontal figure-of-eight track. Hagar (1938) also described this flight, writing 'nosing over suddenly, he flicked his wings rapidly 15 to 20 times and fell like a thunderbolt. Wings half closed now, he shot past the north end of the cliff, described three successive loop-the-loops across its face, turning completely upside down at the top of each loop, and roared out over our heads with the wind rushing through his wings like ripping canvas.'

Some displays are silent, but occasionally the male will chup as he flies. The two birds will also fly together, making a series of loops as they make mock stoops at each other, passing very close, then separating to loop around again. Occasionally the bird being 'attacked' will roll over and extend its talons, just as an intruder would do if attacked by a territorial male: occasionally the two birds will even make talon contact. Such displays are remarkable both for their intensity and for the sheer aerobatic ability of the birds, particularly when the pair approach each other at high speed.

Although courtship feeding appears to cement the pair bond early in the breeding cycle, it becomes more important as egg laying approaches, and it forms part of the ledge displays which precede the female making the nest scrape and copulation. Wrege & Cade (1977) studied these displays in captive Peregrines, and in captive Gyrfalcons, Prairie and Lanner Falcons: the displays were essentially similar in all four species, and no differences were found across the four North American Peregrine subspecies which were observed. Wrege & Cade define 13 behaviours, but these can be usefully compressed here. The male will bow towards the female, usually bowing low into a horizontal position, though sometimes merely from the neck, as he approaches the nest scrape, often standing up on his toes (which Wrege & Cade called the 'high-step' or 'tippy-toe' gait) and chupping. The female will also bow, but hers is often a less pronounced gesture: she will also chup. The two birds will also bow and chup simultaneously, and will nibble each others' bills. As well as being an indication of bonding, head bowing can also be a threat posture (usually termed agonistic behaviour, as it rarely leads to aggression). Either sex can make this gesture, which usually follows one of the pair being startled by the other: despite the pair bond the two birds are by nature aggressive and distinctly non-gregarious, and remain wary of each other. In each case the feathers are flared, though the female's bow is usually only of the head: she may also extend her wings. To counteract the female threat the male may bow extremely low, his bill almost touching the ledge, in a gesture of appeasement. Monneret (1974) in the interesting study of Peregrine displays mentioned above also suggests that some of the aggressive displays by the female to the male are used by the former to force the latter into appeasement behaviour, leading to the male hunting for food which he brings to her.

Food transfers are another ledge display, the female usually making the wailing call as she begs for food. The male transfers food from his feet to his bill, bows several times, then uses the 'tippy-toe' walk to advance on the female. She may await his approach, or walk towards him. She then snatches the food, occasionally aggressively; the male will then leave the ledge quickly.

Copulation

A continuation of the 13 display behaviours noted by Wrege & Cade (1977) relates to copulation. Male Peregrines will raise their wings ('hitched wings') after landing on the ledge, and then bow from the neck while chupping quickly to solicit copulation: the male may also assume the hitched wing position during his flight to the ledge. The female may also solicit, making the wailing call while bowing extravagantly. Copulation follows, with, as usual, the male mounting the female and flapping his wings vigorously. The male then departs the ledge, while the female remains, fluffing her feathers. Copulation takes only a few seconds at first, but may take up to ten seconds as egg laying approaches. The rate of copulation also increases, Ratcliffe (1993) suggesting that frequencies of 3–4 per hour, or even more, have been seen. In general copulations cease after the laying of the third egg.

Egg laying

Data on the laying of the first egg by Peregrines are minimal. Ratcliffe (1993) collected what was available and found that there was consistency in the date both by area within Britain, and also within females. Ratcliffe found that the first-egg date is dependent on the temperature in February (probably because cold Februaries delay the onset of mating behaviour), latitude (though the spread of mean dates from southern England to central Scotland was only about seven days) and altitude (though again the change was small, only about three days in mean date between nests at about 200 m to those above 500 m. There was also an apparent change in first-egg date from data collected in the period 1905–1924 and that for 1925–1940 of about three days which coincided with the increase in mean annual temperatures during the 1930s. If that is indeed the case then it might be expected that as global warming continues female Peregrines will start to lay even earlier in the future, though laying dates in 2014 after the prolonged period of storms and heavy rain, and the flooding which accompanied it, were delayed. Overall, there seems to be a remarkable consistency in the first-egg date of female Peregrines, with instances of the same bird laying her first egg on the same date in successive years: Ratcliffe (1993) quotes his own experience of a female in Galloway, Scotland who laid her first egg between 3 April and 6 April in seven successive years. Captive Peregrines are also very consistent in laying dates, though in this case, of course, the vagaries of climate and food supply are largely eliminated. Mearns & Newton (1988) in their study of Peregrines in southern Scotland over a nine-year period noted that females tended to lay their first egg earlier as they aged, birds of five years or older laying an average of eight days earlier than two- year old birds, laying date having advanced 2-3 days each year. Mearns & Newton also found that the clutches of older birds were larger.

Full clutches have been seen by the end of March, but this is exceptional. More normal is for first eggs to appear in the last week of March or the first week of April.

Egg-laying intervals

Once the female has begun to lay, eggs are laid at intervals of 2–3 days (Note 4.5), though that period tends to increase after the third egg. Repeat clutches are laid if the first clutch is lost, but only if incubation is not significantly under way: if incubation has already reached 7–10 days, repeat clutches will not be laid. Repeat clutches require the breeding cycle to start again, with the full spectrum of displays, though these are significantly shortened as the repeat clutch usually starts within 14 days of the loss of the first. Instances of third clutches being laid after the loss of the first and repeat are known, but are very rare. There are no recorded instances of second clutches being laid if the first clutch is successful.

Eggs

Peregrine eggs are elliptical, measuring 47–59 mm along the major axis (mean 52 mm) and 36–45 mm along the minor axis (mean 41 mm) – all data from a sample of 300 nominate eggs; Cramp & Simmons 1980). The mean values quoted by Cramp & Simmons accord well with data in Ratcliffe (1993), who gives values of 51.5 × 40.8 mm based on measurements of 2,253 British eggs. Ratcliffe notes that while there is no significant variation of egg size within a clutch, there is a tendency for females to lay smaller eggs as they age. Though this trend is slight, Ratcliffe does quote data for one Welsh female whose eggs 'shrank' from 50.0 × 39.5 mm to 46.5 × 32.5 mm over a seven-year period. Ratcliffe also assembled egg size data by area and found no significant differences across the British Isles. In their study of egg sizes in North American Peregrines, Burnham *et al.* (1984) found significant variation in size, quoting differences of 37% in length among eggs from various sites, and 17% within clutches; and 31% in breadth (but only 0.3% in clutches). There was also a considerable variation across years – 14% in length and 48% in breadth.

Fresh eggs weigh 39–46 g (Cramp & Simmons 1980); 38.5–52.6 g, mean 45.5 g (Ratcliffe 1993), of which the shell contributes about 3.8 g. A clutch of four eggs therefore weighs 182 g, or about 17% of the weight of an average female.

The ground colour of the eggs is variable, from buff through shades of red to crimson, with blotches or speckles of red-brown to dark brown, and even with greys and shades of purple. As with other falcons, the variation in speckling is considerable both between birds and within clutches, and in general the later eggs of a clutch are the least coloured. Village (1990) suggested for Kestrels that this resulted in the depletion in protoporphyrin, the pigment which creates the speckling, and that is also likely to be the case for Peregrines.

Clutch size

Hickey & Anderson (1969) recorded a North American Peregrine laying a clutch of seven eggs (and laying a repeat clutch of six when the first clutch was lost: this seems remarkable, but it is known that if eggs are repeatedly removed from a laying female she may lay up to 16 eggs), but such clutches are rare. Ratcliffe (1993) presents data from a total of 1,920 clutches from across Britain which suggest no significant difference between regions, but do show a decline in clutch size from the period prior to 1980 to the decade after (Table 13). There is no obvious reason for this decrease, which was reflected in the data from all British regions, particularly as the health of the Peregrine population would have been expected to improve following the organochlorine contamination problems of the 1950s/1960s. Indeed, the mean clutch size during the time when shell thinning was causing egg breakage and severe depletion of the Peregrine population

TABLE 13 Clutch sizes for Peregrine clutches observed across Britain. From Ratcliffe (1993).

Period	Number of clutches	Clutch size[1] (as a percentage of total number of clutches)				Mean
		2	3	4	5	
Pre-1980	622	19 (3.1)	205 (33.0)	386 (62.1)	12 (1.9)	3.63
1980-1991	1,298	81 (6.2)	600 (46.2)	600 (46.2)	17 (1.3)	3.43

1. These data are consistent with those of Mearns & Newton (1988) who studied Peregrines in southwest Scotland over a nine-year period and found single eggs on 2.0% of occasions, with 2 eggs (4.5% of occasions), 3 eggs (34.8%), 4 eggs (56.3%) and 5 eggs (2.4%).

remained remarkably consistent with pre-contamination figures, which makes the later decline even more perplexing.

Clutches of a single egg are also seen – Mearns & Newton (1988) found five single-egg clutches in 247 observed clutches during their nine-year study period – as are clutches of six. Data collated from captive falcons suggest that females lay clutches of consistent sizes throughout their breeding years, with no decline in clutch size until they cease to breed at an age of about 20 years.

If repeat clutches are laid, these are significantly smaller than the first clutch. Ratcliffe (1993) notes that in the pre-1980 period the mean size of repeat clutches was 3.21 (cf. 3.63 for first clutches: Table 13), while in the following decade the mean declined even further, from 3.43 to 2.91.

Incubation

Incubation normally begins with the third egg, though occasionally with the fourth, so that hatching is almost synchronous. In Peregrines breeding at more northerly latitudes (e.g. *F. p. tundrius* in northern Canada) incubation may start earlier, resulting in asynchronous hatching (Court 1986, Court et al. 1988). The reasons for asynchronous hatching are not clear, and Court (1986) suggests that the studies of Tundra Peregrine do not support the brood-reduction hypothesis (i.e. that broods of mixed ages offer insurance against poor food availability, older birds out-competing younger siblings for scarce resources, so ensuring the survival of some, as synchronous hatching might result in all siblings receiving less with consequent endangering of all). Court (1986) found that 7% of all chicks died in asynchronous broods, with 50% of last-hatched chicks dying within five days. Deaths were not due to direct fratricide, though dead chicks may be fed to siblings by the female. Deaths were rather due to the inability of youngest chicks to compete with their siblings – a newly hatched chick weighing 36 g may find itself in a nest with siblings weighing up to 140 g if they are up to five days older, and may be trampled to death as a consequence – but parental effort was also involved, as all chicks in some asynchronous broods survived, and last-chick deaths were also influenced by female care in brooding and feeding. In those nests where the last-hatched chicks survived they received enough food and grew at the same rate (in terms of weight gain per day) as their older siblings (see Note 6.2)

The incubation period varies from 29 to 32 days, though there is disagreement over this figure from North American researchers, who claim that 33–35 days is more usual, based on data from Hagar (1938) and from captive falcons (White et al. 2002). In a study in southern Sweden, Lindberg (1983) found the period varying from 28 to 33 days depending on ambient temperature and the efficiency of incubation.

FIG 87. Food pass from male to female Peregrine. (Nathan Guttridge)

In his notes on Peregrines watched in Ontario, Beaupre (1922) noted, charmingly, that 'the female attends to all the domestic duties of the falcon home, but is spared the task of seeking for food. This is the duty of the male.' That division of labour seemed to fit with the lifestyle of other falcons. But for the Peregrine it is actually not entirely true. Both sexes have twin lateral brood patches, though these are less well developed in males. Females are responsible for the majority of incubation, and almost certainly sit through the night: Johnson (2011) observed a male Peregrine incubating at night at an urban (London) site, but this appears to be unusual behaviour. Ratcliffe (1993) says that in his observations (based on the number of times the male or female bird was flushed off eggs on his approach) males incubate for 12% of the time. Formon (1969) in a study in eastern France raised this fraction, noting that in his study males incubated for 16–25% of the time. In a study in North America Enderson *et al.* (1973), using time-lapse photography of Peregrines at five nests on Alaska's Yukon River and analysing the resulting 69,461 frames (which constituted 4,208 hours of filming), suggested a greater proportion of male incubation. The male incubated for periods of 2–4 hours, taking 40% of the total incubation time between 15 and 11 days from hatching, this fraction decreasing as hatching approached, though remaining at about 25% of total time. The female usually spent four hours sitting. Such fractions seem consistent with the fact that the male, being smaller, will have more problems covering the clutch, particularly if it is large, than the female, and also has less efficient brood patches. The total time when neither bird incubated was minimal (< 1% of total time, and never for more than three minutes at a time). After hatching, male brooding was minimal (< 2% of total time).

Other North American studies suggest even longer fractions of incubation by males than recorded by Enderson *et al.* (1973), with Nelson (1970) suggesting 30–50% of the total time (though a decreasing fraction as the time to hatching approached) and an extreme example of a pair of Peregrines in northern New Mexico where Clevinger (1987), observing for 202 hours over 18 days of an incubation period which lasted 33 days, noted that the male incubated for 63% of daylight hours (with a range of 27–87%). The male incubated on average for 2 hours 34 minutes, the female for 1 hour 10 minutes. Clevinger suggested that the female might have been a first-time breeder, her inexperience accounting for her reduced fraction, or that she had an abnormal lack of inclination to sit on her eggs. The latter suggestion and the data from all studies suggest that male incubation is variable, and dependent on decisions made within the Peregrine pair, but that males do spend a significant period of time incubating. During these periods, of course, the female is free to maintain her plumage, but also to hunt, reducing her dependency on the male and so maximising his energy resources for the critical time of chick feeding immediately post-hatching.

FIG 88. Incubating female Peregrine.

However, most studies indicate that the male still does a significant amount of the hunting for the female during incubation, his times for incubating usually following his arrival with food. The male will call to the female from a usual perch and transfer food when she arrives, leaving him to fly to the nest while she eats. Males will also chup, seemingly as a question to the female, asking if he may incubate: the female may or may not respond. However, if the male is incubating and the female returns and wishes to take over, the male is not asked if he wishes to depart, but ordered to do so. Nelson (1970) did observe an occasion when the female returned and the male declined to leave the eggs, the female ultimately departing: however, this seems to have been very unusual behaviour.

The incubating bird will turn the eggs at intervals using its bill, and is careful on leaving the nest, rising gently and stepping clear of the clutch to avoid moving an egg out of the scrape. Equal care is taken when taking up incubation. Nelson (1970) includes a comprehensive description of the incubating bird, covering arrival at the eggs, settling on them, the incubating bird preening, stretching, fidgeting with nest site debris, and finally dozing and sleeping; and covering brooding as well as incubating. Both activities, it would seem, would try the patience of a saintly falcon.

Chick growth

As with other species, Peregrine chicks start to cheep before hatching, usually from about 2–3 days before. Hatching takes some time – Nelson (1970) records an average of 72 hours between first starring of the eggshell and full hatching – though much of this time seems to be spent with the chick recuperating from early attempts to begin the shell-breaking process. Nelson noted the death of one chick when the shell membrane dried and the chick was unable to force a way through it, suggesting that atmospheric humidity was critical to hatching, something which has been proved in artificial incubators. Ratcliffe (1993) notes that some researchers consider that the parent birds leaving their eggs early on the morning of hatching is intentional, the eggs being exposed to the atmosphere from which they would otherwise be shielded. Nelson (1970) notes that females become more aggressive as hatching approaches, conjecturing that hearing the chicks cheeping within the shells triggers this, as the change in female behaviour does not occur if the clutch is addled.

Overall, the sex ratio of hatched chicks is 1:1. The newly hatched chick weighs 35–40 g, the egg having lost about 17% of its weight during incubation. The chick is semi-altricial and nidiculous, with a thin covering of white down. The eyes are closed, but open within a few days, occasionally as soon as the day of hatching, though in that case only as slits initially. Peregrines often neglect to remove spent eggshells from the nest area, these being trampled to join the other detritus which accumulates during the nestling stage: some parent birds will remove prey remains from the nest area when the chicks are very young, but in general once the nestlings are mobile there is little housekeeping. Brooding is mostly by the female, as the male has even more problems covering chicks than he did the eggs, particularly once the youngsters are a few days old. Brooding is more or less constant (about 90% of the time) during the early days of chick life when they are unable to thermoregulate, and is certainly most intense if there is bad weather (rain or cold), but also if there is very bright sunshine, as the lack of complete down covering means there is a risk of sunstroke. Brooding reduces after about ten days, falling more or less linearly with age to reach about 15% of total time at age 20 days, and declining to zero time at age 25 days, though there are still exceptions at times of rain or low temperatures.

FIG 89. Female Peregrine feeding young chicks at an urban site.

At that age the nestlings are also able to recognise the adults when they are still a considerable distance away. Once the chicks can be left for extended periods the female may start hunting, though the extent of her hunting varies with individual pairs: in some the male continues to do the majority of the hunting, the female merely spending time away from the nest, but still on the cliff, guarding the chicks, but in other cases, particularly with large broods and as the nestlings approach fledge, the female will take a larger share in provisioning the young.

The chicks can feed on their first day, gaping instinctively even though they may not be able to see their mother. The female feeds by taking small morsels of food from prey delivered by the male and dropping it into the open gapes. By the second day the chicks can make the chup call, though it is more of a begging whine for food, and as soon as they can see they will often nibble the female's bill to stimulate her to feed. Both male and female feed the chicks, but the female does the majority of feeding, and may even prevent the male from doing so on occasions: both Nelson (1970) and Treleaven (1977) suggest that female Peregrines are much more likely to prevent the male feeding the chicks when they are young (less than two weeks old), male feeding being more often accepted with older nestlings.

However, instances of males both feeding and brooding young chicks are known (e.g. Treleaven 1977), and there is a record of a male Peregrine successfully raising chicks to fledge after the shooting of his mate (Blezard *et al.* 1943). In a study through the whole breeding cycle in southwest France, Carlier (1993) noted the times five pairs of Peregrines were at the nest. As can be seen from Fig. 90, the percentage of total time was highest during courtship, remained high during incubation (unsurprisingly), but then declined as the nestlings grew.

The chicks beg for morsels, then consume what they are given before begging again. Nelson (1970) noted the chicks forming a neat semi-circle in front of the feeding parent, while Treleaven (1977) stated that feeding involves each chick being fed in turn until its lack of begging calls suggests satiation and the parent moves on to the next. My observations suggest that a more haphazard regime is as likely as these controlled events, with chicks making a grab for food and turning away to mantle it before siblings can take it. However, while mantling occurs, Peregrine chicks are sociable and often huddle together for warmth and mutual comfort. That said, Tordoff & Redig (1998) report an apparent case of siblicide, with three chicks seemingly pecking at a weaker one and causing its death: this behaviour might have been precipitated by hunger.

The nestlings will attempt to grab food from an early age, but are unable to feed themselves, as opposed to swallowing what they get hold of, until they are

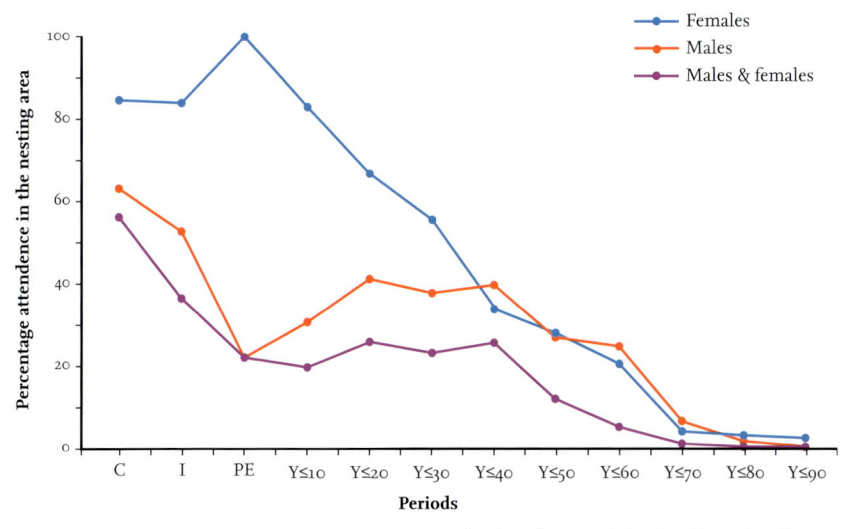

FIG 90. Fraction of time spent at the nest during the breeding cycle by female and male Peregrines, and by both birds, in the Massif Central, France. C, courtship; I, incubation; PE, eggs pipping; Y ≤ n, nestling age in days. Redrawn from Carlier 1993.

about 14 days old, or a little older, and are not fully capable of dismantling prey until they are about 25–30 days old. Once the parent birds realise the nestlings are capable of this, prey is just left for them rather than being broken up completely. Feeding frequency and the times of food delivery seem variable, but in general feeding starts very early in the day, is less frequent around midday, then increases again prior to sunset. Parker (1979), observing an eyrie on the Welsh coast, noted 4–8 feeding visits daily on average throughout the period of chick growth.

Chick growth is rapid. At 6–8 days they can preen, and stretch their infant wings and legs. The second down erupts at this time and is complete by about ten days, at which time the primary sheaths break the skin, the sheaths of the outer rectrices following a day or so later. At 12 days the chicks are able to move to the nest edge and to turn around to excrete. At 14 days the first primary (P9) emerges from its sheath. Contour feathers begin to emerge at about 17 days, and are visible beneath the down a couple of days later. By 21 days all primary and tail feathers have emerged and wing flapping begins in earnest.

Although the chicks wander about the nest ledge within a short distance of the nest scrape, they spend most of their time within it, often huddled together (as noted above), but after about day 24 they spend much more time away from the scrape and alone, frequent wing flapping removing the final down feathers.

FIG 91. This young Peregrine was about 16 days old when it was brought from a cliff eyrie for ringing. In the lower photo the primaries are emerging from their sheaths.

For the observer the nestlings are a fine sight at about day 30, with a delightful 50:50 mixture of down and juvenile feathers. At about 40 days the last traces of down are still visible, but juvenile plumage is essentially complete, though the rectrices are not fully formed. The fledgling can now fly, but not well, as some primaries and rectrices are not fully grown: Weir (1978) suggests that males fledge 1 or 2 days earlier than females. Lindberg (1983), studying Peregrines in southern Sweden, found that the age of first flight was 41 ± 3 days; in his study of *F. p. pealei*, Nelson quotes 41–44 days.

Even when they have begun to fly the young Peregrines stay close to the nest site at first, often roosting with siblings (and occasionally with adults if roosting spots are few), but eventually choosing their own roosts. The fledglings are

FIG 92. At this eyrie in southern Scotland I assumed there were only two chicks, but during the feeding a third, much smaller, chick emerged from the vegetation. Despite its calling it received no food on this occasion.

FIG 93. At the same nest site as in Fig. 92, a week after the feeding sequence there were only two near-fledglings at the eyrie, the smaller chick having clearly succumbed to starvation.

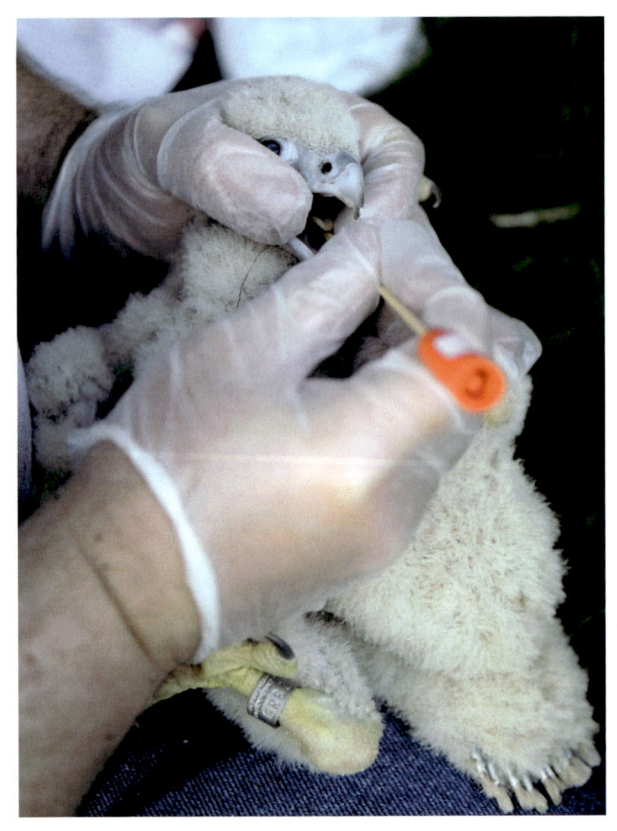

FIG 94. Taking a DNA swab sample during the ringing of Peregrine chicks in northern England. In recent years the use of DNA profiling (the use of genetic markers to allow recognition of individual birds – and to allow research into parentage and populations) has assisted in combating the crime of egg and chick stealing at Peregrine sites. For further details see Marsden (2002) and references therein.

also fed close to the nest site by the adults, though the latter begin to teach the rudiments of prey capture by making food transfers in mid-air, the youngsters catching dropped prey or taking it from the adult's talons. Prey dropping seems to occur too frequently to be a chance event rather than a deliberate strategy – see, for example, Hewitt (2013) – and can be highly entertaining for the observer. In Cheltenham, Peregrines nest on the tower of one local church. The town is also home to an annual cricket festival – and I was once told that the dropping of prey for youngsters to catch had the cricket supporters entranced, as it was much more exciting than anything happening on the field at the time.

Observers have described seeing adult Peregrines catching, then releasing, prey, the prey by now injured, for fledglings to pursue. I have also witnessed a further example of the adult birds teaching their brood. The nest site was a quarry into which the adults drove a pigeon. The two adults then circled above

FIG 95. Adult Peregrine dropping prey to a fledgling as part of the training for adult life. (Lutz Artmann)

FIG 96. Early take-off in the life of an urban Peregrine.

the quarry, preventing all attempts by the frantic, and increasingly exhausted, pigeon to escape, while the young Peregrines attacked it.

Early flights by the Peregrines also hone their hunting skills as they chase each other and also make mock attacks on any large bird which happens into the area. Most young Peregrines hunt insects at this stage, but true attacks soon start, though most of these are unsuccessful at first. By early September the fledglings have to have mastered hunting as adult feeding ceases (the period of adult feeding thus lasting about nine weeks; in migratory populations this period is much

FIG 97. One of four young Peregrines taking off at an urban site.

FIG 98. A Young Peregrine adopts a suitably angelic position on a church turret.

FIG 99. Fledgling Peregrines often crash-land on early flights, sometimes in the most curious places. This particular landing was perhaps apt, as the Peregrine was from a brood on the local church, and it is the vicar's car. (Tim Mayfield)

less, usually 5–6 weeks). Whether or not the fledglings are then driven away from the area by their parents is still debated, and evidence both for and against is available. But whether by choice or through intimidation, the young Peregrines are now ready to disperse.

Breeding success

Mearns & Newton (1988) studied the breeding ecology of Peregrines in southwest Scotland and noted both the productivity of the falcons (i.e. the number of young produced per territorial pair), a measure of the overall breeding success of the species, and the mean number of young produced per brood, a measure of the success of breeding pairs. The study area included both coastal and inland sites, which allowed a degree of comparison between them, though as the number of territories was not equal in each case direct comparison must be treated cautiously. The overall performance of the population is set down in Table 14.

In a study covering south-central Canada and the northeastern USA Gahbauer *et al.* (2015) noted that overall there was no significant difference between the breeding success of rural and urban Peregrines, but that nest sites

TABLE 14 Mean clutch size, fledglings per brood and productivity of Peregrines in southwest Scotland, 1974–1982. From Mearns & Newton (1988).

	Number of territorial pairs	Number (%) of territories at which eggs were laid	Number (%) of territories at which young were fledged	Mean clutch size	Mean number of fledglings/ brood	Mean number of fledglings/ territorial pair
Inland sites	297	246 (83)	131 (44)	3.53	2.40	1.06
Coastal sites	100	83 (83)	58 (58)	3.53	2.17	1.26
Total[1]	397	329 (83)	189 (44)	3.53	2.33	1.10

1. Coastal sites were significantly more successful than inland sites across the years of study. Mearns & Newton considered the likely cause was the accessibility of inland sites by humans. In general sites which were occupied earlier (both coastal and inland) were more successful than those occupied later. Mearns & Newton considered that this was probably because less vulnerable sites were occupied first and were more likely to be occupied by experienced Peregrine pairs (who could therefore be better hunters), the combination of these factors leading to improved success. The use of more vulnerable sites by the Peregrines resulted, in part, from the fact that the Peregrine population increased during the years of the study, which required some pairs to occupy sites on lower, and therefore more accessible, cliffs: the success rate of nest sites, measured as the percentage of nests producing young, was 42% for cliffs < 10 m high, rising to 56% for cliffs 11–20 m, 58% for cliffs 21–40 m, and 71% for cliff > 41 m. Mearns & Newton also defined three classes of cliff – those accessible without ropes, those accessible with ropes and those impossible to access. While these are subjective definitions (and climbers would likely disagree), the resulting data gave success percentages of 51%, 60% and 73% in the three classes. Interestingly, although sites below overhangs were more successful, as might be expected, those in recesses or caves were the most successful, suggesting that shelter from poor weather as well as accessibility played a part in final success. However, Mearns & Newton were not able to disassociate the influence of 'better' sites and 'better' falcons (the latter in terms of hunting skills) and so could not judge which was the most important.

with overhead cover, including human-erected boxes, had higher productivity (in terms of nestlings fledged). This result is consistent with a study in the Jura Mountains of France (Monneret et al. 2015) where the breeding success in artificial nests was 2.2 fledglings per breeding pair, compared to 1.85 on natural sites.

Mearns & Newton (1988) also investigated the cause of egg and chick loss (Table 15), and found that most chick mortality involved death soon after hatching, though some deaths did occur later, usually during spells of rain or mist when the adult birds were unable to hunt (Fig. 100). The correlation

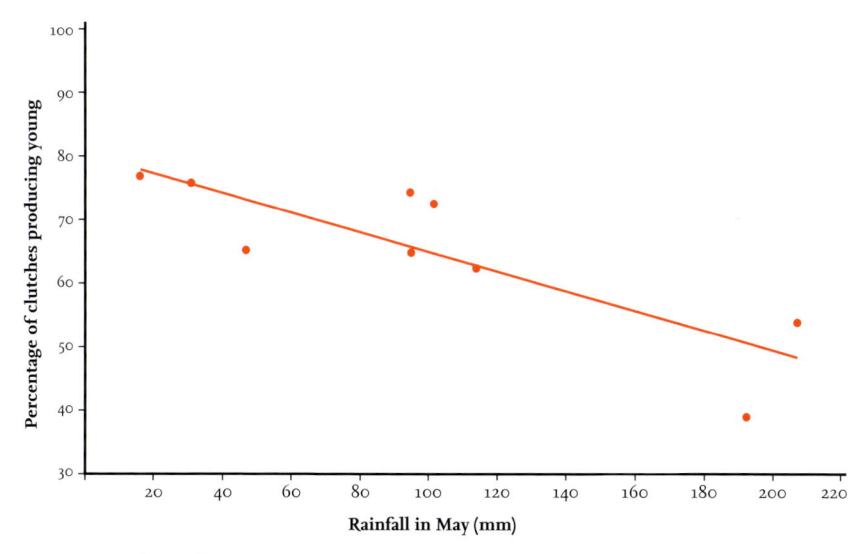

FIG 100. Relationship between percentage success of Peregrine clutches and May rainfall in successive years in south Scotland. The correlation between clutch success and May rainfall is significant at the 99% level. Redrawn from Mearns & Newton 1988.

TABLE 15 Causes of failure of eggs and chicks of Peregrine nests in southwest Scotland 1974–1982. From Mearns & Newton (1988).

Cause of failure	Number	Percentage of all failures (n = 208)	Percentage of all breeding opportunities (n = 397)
Eggs not laid	68	33	17
Eggs broken/addled	30	14	8
Eggs deserted	3	1	1
Eggs disappeared	8	4	2
Eggs robbed[1]	23	11	6
Chicks disappeared at hatch	13	6	3
Chicks died	8	4	2
Chicks disappeared	20	10	5
Chicks robbed	13	6	3
Unknown	22	11	6

1. Known to have been robbed by humans. Humans may also have been responsible for some eggs which disappeared.

FIG 101. Unusually, there was only a single chick at this eyrie in southern Scotland.

between clutch success and May rainfall illustrated in Fig. 100 is significant at the 99% level. No significant correlation was found between clutch success and rainfall over a longer period, either April–July (i.e. the entire breeding period) or May–July (i.e. the post-hatch period), indicating that rainfall in May was a critical factor in hatchling survival. In the climatically much harsher Arctic environment of Rankin Island, Canada, Bradley *et al.* (1997) found a very similar correlation between rain and breeding success, noting that success was negatively dependent on both the amount of rainfall (in millimetres) and the hours of rain. Breeding success was also negatively correlated with snowfall.

Ratcliffe (1993) gives several other examples of adverse weather affecting Peregrine breeding success, from Scotland, the Lake District and Wales, noting in particular 1981 when snow and frost in April, followed by a cold, wet May led to at least 55 pairs losing eggs or young. In a study in the Republic of Ireland, Norriss (1995) noted that the breeding range of Peregrines was limited by weather, this being seen in the interaction of cliff height and orientation, and spring rainfall. The highest (and therefore most attractive) cliffs were not occupied in high-rainfall areas or if they were orientated northwest to northeast, while lower cliffs were unoccupied in a greater range of orientations and at lower rainfalls.

The lifetime breeding success of wild Peregrines is not well documented. Hall (1955), studying the urban falcons which bred on Montreal's Sun Life building, states that the female raised 22 young over a 17-year period with three male partners. Since the female lost clutches in three of those years, and did not breed in each of her first two years, her breeding period was 12 years. However, in a study of captive Peregrines, Clum (1995) investigated female reproduction as measured by six factors indicative of reproductive success – clutch size, egg fertility, 'hatchability' (i.e. the likelihood that a fertile egg will hatch), brood size at hatching, survival of nestlings and brood size at fledging. For the experiment 21 female Peregrines were kept year-round with males chosen on management considerations. Egg production was maximised by removing eggs to induce re-laying; the females incubated their eggs for seven days, then the eggs were removed and artificially incubated; chicks were hand-raised until they were 7–14 days old, then returned to falcons (not necessarily their parents) for raising to fledge. Of the 21 females, nine had mates that remained with them constantly through life, eight had one mate change and four had two changes of mate. Changes were due to male deaths (five occasions) or management decision. The results of the experiment are shown in Figs 102 and 103.

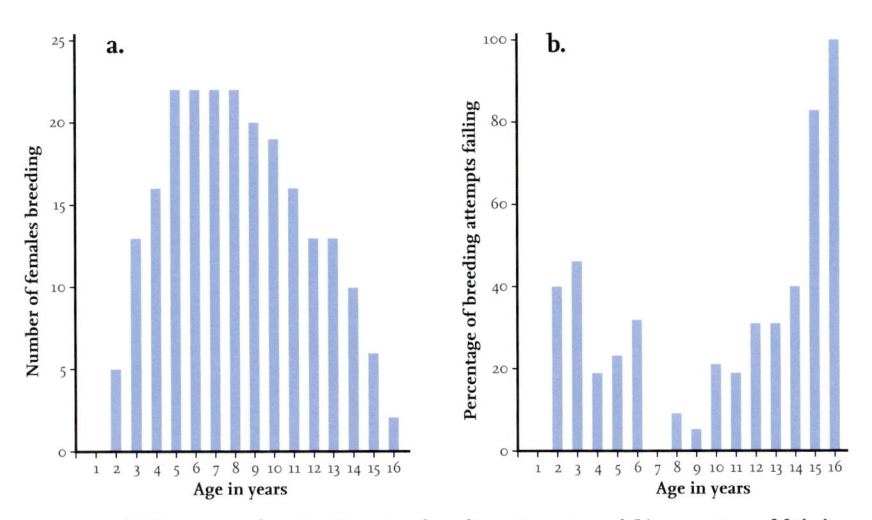

FIG 102. (a) Frequency of captive Peregrine breeding attempts, and (b) proportion of failed breeding attempts, both in relation to female age. Failures tended to be due to infertility in the female's first two years and from age 10 years onwards; and to embryo or nestling death during years 3–9. Redrawn from Clum 1995.

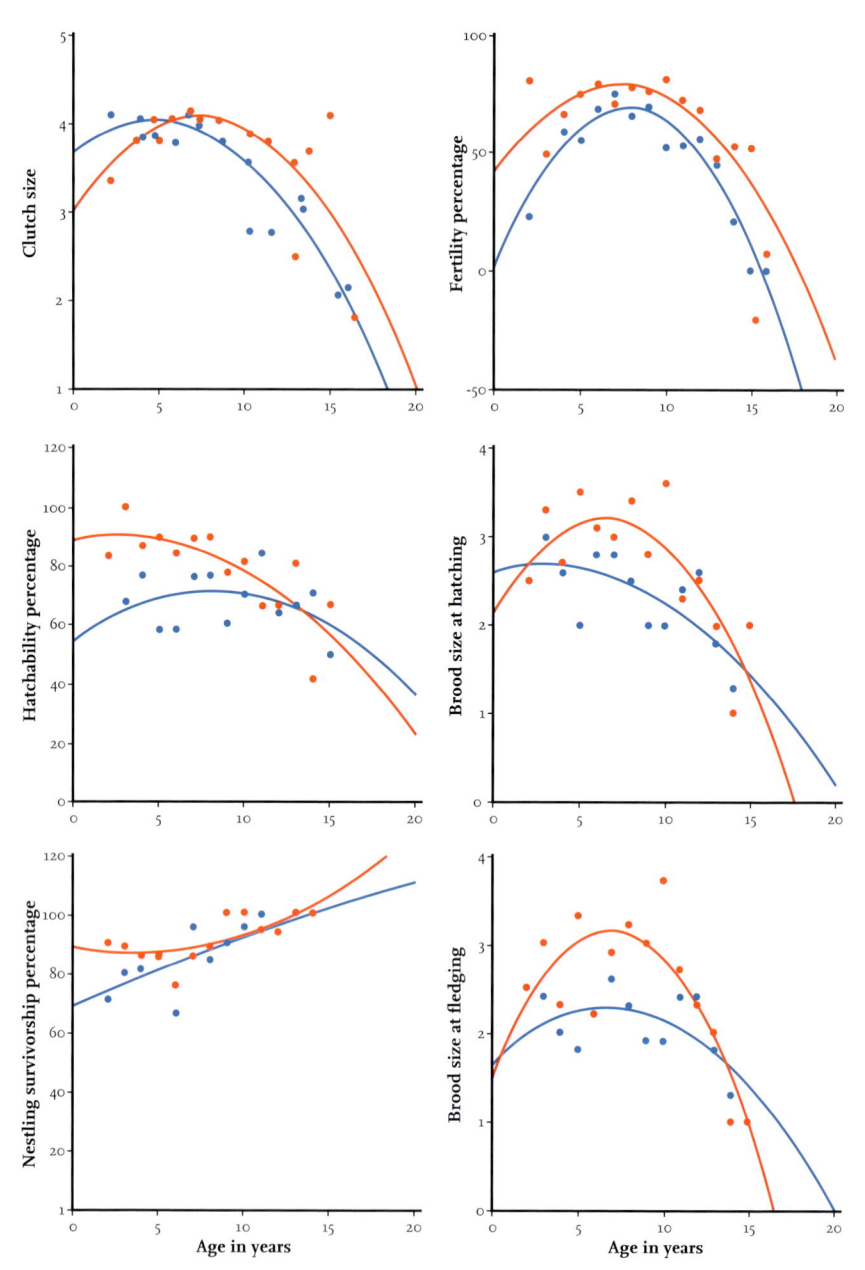

FIG 103. Variation of the six measures of reproductive success with female age, in a study of captive Peregrines. In all cases apart from nestling survival the plotted data follow a quadratic form, with a marked tendency for success to increase with age to about age seven years, then to decline. Red points and lines are females retaining the same mate throughout their breeding life; blue points and lines are females experiencing at least one mate change. Redrawn from Clum 1995.

From Figs 102 and 103 it can be seen that all measures of reproductive success except nestling survival peaked at female age seven years, and then declined. Nestling survival is curious: in the wild it is usually assumed that experienced parents are more likely to have hatchlings which survive, and this factor would not therefore decrease with female age. However, in this experiment hatchlings were not necessarily raised by their parents. The result therefore is either spurious, or suggests that experienced females produce hatchlings which are intrinsically more likely to survive.

Clum was able to conclude that birds with prior breeding experience had higher productivity than those of the same age which had not previously bred, and that increased experience resulted in increased productivity. By moving the pairs Clum was able to show that productivity was not affected by such movements. However, changing mates did affect productivity, causing a 53% fall in the change year, though there was an increase in subsequent years. The results of Clum were not entirely borne out in a study of wild Peregrines in Spain's Basque Country by Zabala & Zuberogoita (2015), who studied 37 breeding territories over a 16-year period. They found that breeding performance stabilised once the falcons had acquired adult plumage (in their third calendar year), though age did eventually mean a fall-off in performance. Zabala & Zuberogoita did note that the performance of yearling breeders was poorer than that of adults, but considered this was due to a lack of maturity, as the performance of inexperienced breeders did not differ from that of experienced adults. Zabala & Zuberogoita consider that the differences between their study and that of Clum might be associated with wild birds being able to choose partners rather than having them assigned. This suggestion has implications for breeding fidelity which are considered in the following section.

Nest-site, territory and mate fidelity

In a study in southern Scotland, Mearns & Newton (1984) found that during a five-year period (1977–1981) 60 females were retrapped on the same territory as the previous year, while six had moved territory. Of eight retrapped males, six were on the same territory. Mearns & Newton also looked at the dispersal of ringed nestlings, finding that females had moved further (an average of 68 km, maximum 185 km) than males (an average of 20 km, maximum 75 km). See Note 6.9 for thoughts on the sex differences in site fidelity.

Site fidelity is in the interests of the Peregrine, as secure nest sites are essential for breeding success, and moving away means the possibility that on return in the spring the territory will have been claimed by another pair. As a consequence, if pairs are able to stay, sufficient food resources being available, then they will. Juveniles also tend to stay within a short distance of their natal site if territories are available, moving to coastal sites where they can feed on waders if they are not or if prey resources are inadequate. These birds, assuming they survive the winter, will then move back towards their natal sites unless they have moved to areas where territories and nest sites prove attractive.

Breeding success underpins site fidelity, and mate fidelity is presumably similarly predicated, given that both sexes would be inclined to stay on a good territory, and, as we have seen above, the work of Clum (1995) indicates that pairs with prior breeding experience together have a higher productivity (in terms of fledglings raised per breeding cycle) than newly paired birds. While evidence from captive birds cannot be considered conclusive, this strongly suggests that mate fidelity is actually an important criterion.

The critical nature of nest site fidelity in the breeding success of Peregrines can be gauged by the fact that the highly migratory Tundra Peregrines of North America show a similar degree of fidelity to the sedentary British population. In a study in Canada's Northwest Territories over a seven-year period (Court *et al.* 1989), mortality appeared to account for virtually all the observed changes in male territory holdings. There were changes by females, but these were few, and chiefly associated with nest failures.

One interesting example of nest-area fidelity which did not involve nest-site fidelity was reported by Ponton (1983) studying Peregrines in northern New Mexico, where the falcons were nesting in eroded potholes in volcanic tuff (ash) along a 1 km cliff. The female of one pair at the cliff used ten different potholes in ten consecutive years. After the female failed to lay during the next two years a new female continued the process by changing potholes in consecutive years. Interestingly, the latter female laid two repeat clutches and in each case she laid the second clutch in the pothole used (successfully) in the previous year, a process which Ponton referred to as 'fall-back-one' behaviour.

Also interesting was the experience of Wimsatt (1940) in Pennsylvania. Wimsatt removed an incubating female from a clutch of four eggs, hooded her and took her to Cornell University, 100 km away, where the bird was kept in darkness. He then returned to see if the male would continue to incubate. He did, but only for a few days before deserting. Wimsatt therefore removed the clutch, and then released the female. The bird headed off in the direction of the nest site. Four days later Wimsatt found the female at a new nest site 3 m from the old one: she had already laid an egg and would go on to complete a new clutch of four, three of which hatched. Wimsatt has no information on whether the male bird responsible for the second clutch was the original partner.

MOVEMENTS AND WINTER DENSITY

As we have seen (see *Hunting strategy and food caching*, above), the ships carrying Rogers & Leatherwood (1981) were temporary home to a Peregrine over 2,000 km from South America, and Voous (1961) records another which joined a ship for two days in the Atlantic Ocean, arriving when it was 1,300 km west of Africa, and leaving when it was still 1,100 km from South America. Such journeys indicate a willingness to move if circumstances require, though true Peregrine migration is mainly restricted to the northern subspecies, where the Arctic winter means prey availability is severely reduced, while the accompanying period of darkness restricts hunting on what little prey remains. The Peregrines of the Nearctic tundra (*F. p. tundrius*) probably make the longest migratory flights, travelling from breeding grounds as far north as the southern islands of Canada's Arctic archipelago to Mexico and the Florida Keys. Satellite tracking suggests the falcons rarely stop to rest and feed, making their long flights in a single passage which includes flying through the night (Note 4.6). Kerlinger *et al.* (1983) studied data on autumn migration of raptors observed from cruise ships in the waters off northeastern North America, from Nova Scotia south to Cape Hatteras, North Carolina. While in general Ospreys were seen further from land than other raptors, there were sightings of Peregrine Falcons at distances which meant that the birds were not able to see either the coastline to the west or the coast in the direction in which they were heading. Given the sightings already noted of Peregrines over 1,000 km from land, migration flights across water out of sight of land are not surprising, but are a further indication of the flying ability of the species. The Siberian tundra Peregrine (*F. p. calidus*) has similarly long migration flights to its Nearctic cousins, falcons from Yamal flying as far as Spain (see Ganusevich *et al.* 2004 for details of satellite-tracked falcons reaching southern Spain) and Sudan, those from Taimyr and the Lena delta region reaching Pakistan and India, and east Siberian falcons reaching Thailand and southern China.

Wheeler (2003) notes that for migrating Tundra Peregrines in North America, in general adults leave before juveniles, confirming a result from a study involving the trapping of 23,000 raptors of ten species at Cedar Grove, Wisconsin, between 1953 and 1996. There, Mueller *et al.* (2000) also noted that there was no difference in the timing of male and female migration, though the sample sizes for adult males and females were too small for this to be definitive. A similar result regarding adult migration prior to that of juveniles was also found for Peregrines observed migrating at Falsterbo, Sweden, by Kjellén (1992) (Fig. 104).

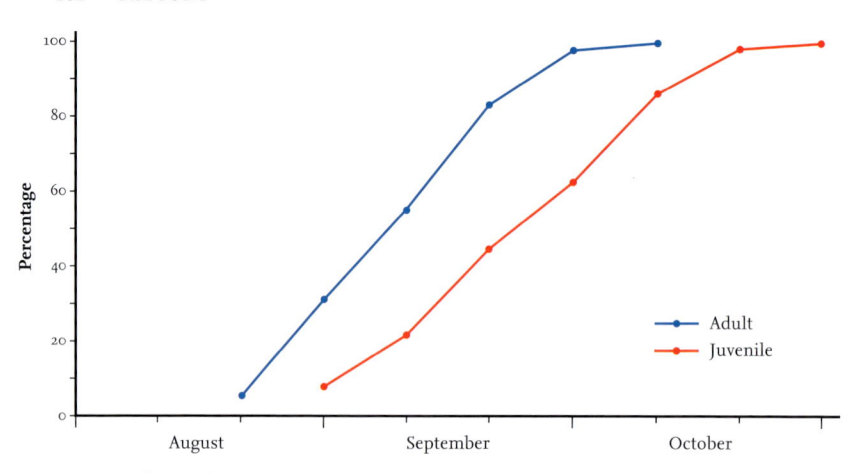

FIG 104. Differential autumnal migration of adult and juvenile Peregrines observed in the period 1986–1990 at Falsterbo Peninsula, southern Sweden. The curves show the cumulative percentage of birds that had migrated at a certain date. Redrawn from Kjellén 1992.

British Peregrines are much more sedentary. As already noted, Mearns (1982) found over 80% of both coastal and inland breeding territories were occupied in winter in southern Scotland. He also noted that the coastal Peregrines had a smaller hunting range than inland falcons, presumably because of the availability of seabirds and waders. Data on the recovery of ringed Peregrines indicate that most were found close to where they had been ringed: of 554 recovered birds the median distance travelled was only 45 km, with 55% travelling less than 50 km, and 78% less than 100 km (Ratcliffe in Wernham *et al.* 2002). Only 6.7% of the recovered birds had travelled more than 200 km. Of the long-distance travellers, i.e. those travelling more than 200 km, most were falcons moving from Scotland to England or Wales, or northern England to southern England or Ireland. The Peregrines in northern Scotland make the longest journeys and are the most migratory of the British population, those at coastal sites lacking prey once the seabird colonies that are their main resource disperse, as local estuaries hold smaller populations of waders and the inland moorlands are equally devoid of potential prey: this movement is clearly indicated in the species' wintering map (Lack 1986).

In the data of Ratcliffe (in Wernham *et al.* 2002) only two falcons were recovered outside Britain, one bird ringed in Pembrokeshire being recovered in Brittany, while the other, a first-year bird ringed in Northern Ireland, was recovered in Portugal. The data showed that females travelled a little further than males (about 12 km) on average, but that the wintering grounds of both sexes were similar. The data also showed that contrary to earlier studies which had implied that first-year birds travelled further than older falcons, there was no significant difference in the distances travelled. The data on the movement of male and female Peregrines are also consistent with the findings of Mearns &Newton (1984) from a study in southern Scotland, though in that case the distances moved by males (an average of 20 km) were much less than those travelled by females (68 km), though the sample size was much smaller. The sample was also of first-year birds ringed as nestlings and then trapped. Trapping of older birds indicated that the distance travelled by first-year falcons was greater than of older birds, leading Mearns & Newton to conclude that Peregrines make their longest movements during their first year, but remain faithful to territories thereafter.

The data also showed that Norwegian and Swedish birds were crossing the North Sea to reach Britain, a general direction of travel being southwest, in keeping with the data from eastern Palearctic Peregrines in general. However, one bird from southern Sweden was recovered on Shetland, having travelled a little north of due west. The earliest date at which one of these Scandinavian birds reached Britain was 22 October (Mead 1993). It will be recalled that the famous book on Peregrines by Baker (1967) was devoted to the study of falcons wintering in Essex, and these birds were probably Scandinavian immigrants. Ratcliffe (1993) notes that the collapse of the Scandinavian Peregrine population due to organochlorine contamination was due to migrating birds feeding in parts of Europe where pesticide use was prevalent.

As a consequence of the minimal movements of adult Peregrines, the winter density of the birds is comparable with the breeding density, and is just as lacking in uniformity. Juvenile Peregrines move out of their natal sites unless they are able to secure suitable (i.e. vacant) territories, or to establish themselves between existing territories (see *Territory and breeding density*, above), and are chiefly to be found in lowland coastal sites where prey availability in the form of wintering waders, particularly at estuaries, is high. They will also, of course, be joined by older falcons whose breeding grounds do not hold a sufficiently high prey density to allow overwintering. However, it is worth noting again that prey density is critical in defining the wintering ranges of Peregrines, just as it is during the breeding season. In Mexico, at coastal sites on the Gulf of Mexico McGrady *et al.* (2002) measured the hunting ranges of 12 wintering adult Peregrines fitted with PTT satellite trackers. The ranges varied from 17 km^2 to 700 km^2 with a mean of 83 km^2, giving an indication of the effect of prey density as the primary prey, shorebirds, were dependent on feeding grounds (mudflats) which were distributed and varied in size, and were subject to tidal inundation.

FIG 105. Adult female Peregrine.

Finally, it is worth noting one aspect of urban living which has altered Peregrine wintering, at least in one female. Hatched in an urban nest, this female moved to a local quarry to breed, but habitually returned to her natal town during the winter to take advantage of the higher temperatures and the abundance of Feral Pigeons. It will be interesting to see if this form of commuting catches on.

SURVIVAL

Annual mortality can only be assessed from recovered ringed birds whose birth date is known with certainty. For the Peregrine such data are in short supply, but using data from sources outside Britain allows an estimate to be derived (Table 16).

The data trend of Table 16 is consistent with that for other raptors. The mortality of first-year birds is high, the rigours of a first winter testing their hunting experience to, and beyond, its limits. The lower mortality in later years calculated from the study by Mearns & Newton (1984) in southern Scotland, where birds were trapped so that their ages could be determined from leg rings,

TABLE 16 Mortality of Peregrines not surviving until spring of year following birth year, and of adult birds in the second and subsequent years until six years of age.

Country	Mortality of first-year birds (%)	Annual mortality of adult birds (%)	Source
North America[1]	70	25	Enderson (1969)
Finland	71	19	Mebs (1971)
Sweden	59	32	Lindberg (1977)
Germany	56	28	Mebs (1971)
Scotland	46	11	Mearns & Newton (1984)

1. The first-year mortality is consistent with the data of Faccio et al. (2013) for the reintroduced population of New England, where 68% of falcons did not survive their first year. Faccio et al. also noted that 11% of second-year birds died.

is consistent with data from North America for Peregrines in temperate zones. Tundra Peregrines have lower survival: Court et al. (1989) found mortality to be 15% for adult males, 19% for adult females at Rankin Inlet in Arctic Canada, while 23% was estimated for adult females in Alaska (Ambrose & Riddle 1988). However, in all cases the number of falcons involved was relatively small and so all figures are probably subject to significant uncertainty, though it is clear from all the studies that the mortality of first-year birds is high. A figure of 46% is currently stated by the British Trust for Ornithology (BTO) as first-year mortality.

The data that exist from ringed-bird recoveries in Britain suggest that life expectancy for Peregrines is of order 6–7 years, though one recovery was a male which died of natural causes at just over 17 years of age. The female breeding on the Sun Life building in Montreal was at least 18 years old (Hall 1955), and a female in Alaska was trapped alive (and released) 19 years after ringing as a nestling. Several falconry birds are known to have reached 20–25 years of age. However, in the wild few birds are likely to reach double-figure ages.

One aspect of adult mortality which has been investigated, but with mixed results, is whether brood size influences adult survival, both of males (because of the stresses of hunting to provision the brood) and of females (because of the stresses of egg production, incubation and nest defence). Nelson (1988) found that on Langara Island adult survival was halved if the falcons had three chicks rather than one or two (though, curiously, was only marginally increased for broods of four), while data from an Arctic study (*F. p. tundrius*) suggested lower mortality for higher broods, perhaps implying that healthy, more efficient adults have higher broods and are better able to cope with the additional stresses. Further studies are clearly required before a definitive understanding of this can be reached.

Ratcliffe (in Wernham *et al.* 2002) presents data on the causes of death of recovered ringed Peregrines, but the analysis allows only a very broad-brush assessment of causes, with 21% taken by humans, 30% human-related (which would encompass collisions with man-made structures), 29% of natural illness, and 20% 'other'. Hager (2009), in a study of the causes of death of urban raptors in the USA (where the number of birds of all species which die annually as a result of anthropogenic causes is estimated at 1,000,000,000), found that falcons (all urban species) were susceptible to injury caused by collisions and electrocution, with vehicle collisions and window strikes accounting for 39% and 12% respectively of all deaths. In an earlier study in the USA, Sweeney *et al.* (1997) found that 81% of 168 Peregrines brought to a veterinary care centre had sustained collision injuries, and in a similar study of 107 known causes of death (of 149 mortalities) 61% of the birds had died from collisions (Gahbauer *et al.* 2015). In each case many of the falcons were first-year birds. Sadly, in the study of Sweeney *et al.* (1997) 45% of the birds died or were euthanized, but 41% were successfully treated and released.

In none of the three studies above are details of the 'other' causes of death given, but historically such a designation often means that the bird is so emaciated that no cause can be ascertained, starvation being the likely cause, though invariably this will have been itself caused by an underlying illness or injury. While the data are not entirely helpful, the categories are broadly in line with those for other raptors.

While starvation will lead to the falcon being emaciated, it is possible that there are underlying problems which contribute to ill health and the bird's inability to hunt. One possible explanation would be a contaminant burden. Even though the levels of organochlorines in Peregrines fell significantly following the problems in the 1960s (see Chapter 8), the persistence of the contaminants means that residues continue to be found in the species. Newton *et al.* (1989) considered the levels were no longer causing shell-thickness reductions and consequent reduction in brood sizes, but they did find levels of mercury (partly naturally occurring, but also derived from industrial sources and alkyl-mercury pesticides) which may have been responsible for reduced brood sizes.

In the latest of a series of reports on studies into environmental pollutants in the eggs of birds of prey in Norway – a work programme which became part of the *Program for Terrestrisk naturovervåking (TOV)* (Programme for Terrestrial Monitoring) in 1992 – Nygård & Polder (2012) used data gathered over the previous 40–50 years to produce long-term trends in pollutants. The study showed that the levels of legacy pollutants continue to decline, and that the majority of eggs show concentrations below the believed critical levels, but that levels of PCBs have stabilised in some species. In the eggs of Peregrines, Merlins and White-tailed Eagles the by-products of DDT, particularly DDE, and the persistent organic compounds PCB and HCB, are still the dominant pollutants. Figure 106 shows the variation of some of these persistent contaminants, and also of mercury in the eggs of Peregrines over the period 1975–2010. Peregrines, Merlins and White-tailed Eagles also have the highest levels of mercury (see Chapter 7 for details regarding Merlin). A study in Nevada in which the mercury contamination of Peregrines was assessed from feathers indicated a much wider range of mercury levels, and also some significantly higher values (Barnes & Gerstenberger 2015). The study also showed that the higher levels were associated with the falcons taking aquatic avian prey, the mercury levels in a large lake being high, presumably as a result of organomercury runoff, causing consequent high levels in waterfowl and waders.

More worrying, as it took many years for the effect of organochlorine contamination to be understood, both brominated flame retardants and perfluorinatedalkyl compounds are now being seen in raptor eggs. Levels are small, but little is known about the biological effects of these compounds, particularly in the longer term. Similar concerns have also recently been raised about the use of neonicotinoids, as outlined in Chapter 2.

Another contaminant which has caused concern over many years is lead, with waterfowl in particular ingesting spent lead pellets, surviving being shot but having lead pellets embedded within them, or not being retrieved by shooters. Raptors subsequently eating lead-carrying birds then build up lead concentrations within their own bodies. Pain et al. (1995) measured lead levels in the livers of 424 British raptors of 16 species found dead in the 1980s and early 1990s. They found concentrations associated with lead-based mortality (> 20 ppm dry liver weight) in only one (of 25) Peregrines and one (of 50) Buzzards, but elevated levels in other specimens, including one other bird of each species with a concentration of 15–20 ppm. Pain and co-workers concluded that both the Peregrine and the Buzzard probably died of lead poisoning. In 1999 the African-Eurasian Waterbird Agreement introduced a ban on lead shot for hunting shorebirds, ducks and geese. Although the agreement was binding across the UK, implementation was left to the devolved governments, the regulations coming into force in England immediately, in Wales in 2002, in Scotland in 2005 and in Northern Ireland in 2009. Shooting groups are opposed to the ban and have made efforts to have the restrictions lifted (or, in the case of the Republic of Ireland, for the implementation of the

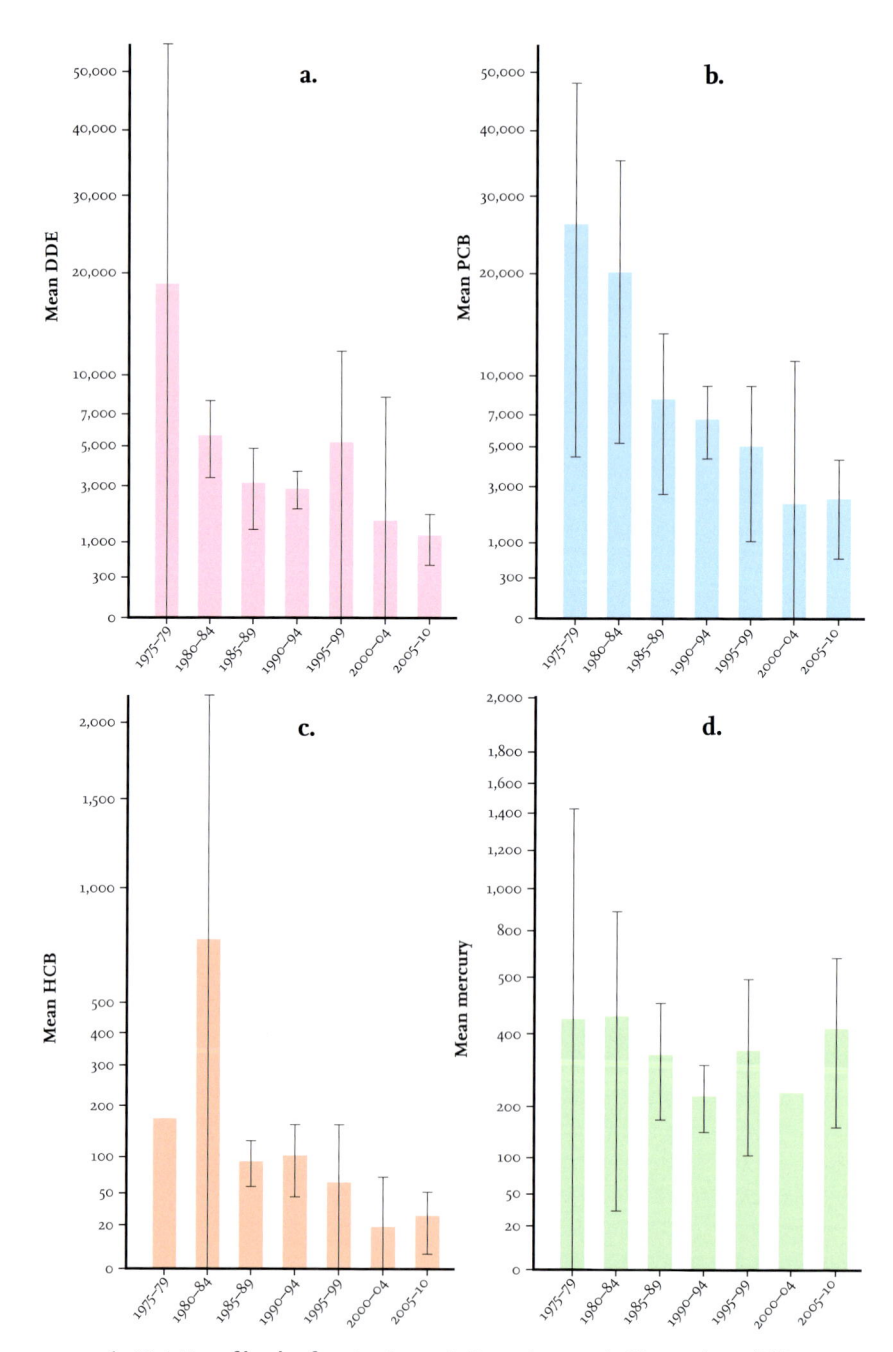

FIG 106. Variation of levels of contaminants in Peregrine eggs in Norway (parts/billion fresh weight) for: (a) DDE (to be absolutely accurate, p', p' DDE); (b) PCB; (c) HCB; (d) mercury. Redrawn from Nygård & Polder 2012.

agreement to be delayed). The ban does not, however, apply to ammunition used against species other than wildfowl, and so lead shot continues to be used for grouse, Pheasant and other game birds. Fragments of lead slough off shot which passes through or is embedded in a game bird, and these may be difficult to detect. Consequently the lead content of consumed game birds may be higher than the levels permitted in sheep meat, pork and beef. Despite this, game which is shot rather than farmed is exempt from lead level regulations, and in 2012 the Food Standards Agency issued advice to game consumers to limit their intake (http://www.food.gov.uk/science/advice-to-frequent-eaters-of-game-shot-with-lead). It is estimated that 6000 tonnes of lead is fired each year, of which 2000 tonnes remain in the soil and so may be ingested by feeding birds. Despite a recommendation to ban lead shot it appears (February 2016) that the UK government is set to bow to the wishes of the shooting fraternity.

Parasite burden may also reduce a falcon's ability to hunt effectively. Body parasites in falcons include screw-worm flies, chewing bird lice and louse flies (Hippoboscidae), many forms of which are associated with falcons (Maa 1969). In a study of raptor nests as a habitat for invertebrates, Philips & Dindal (1977) noted that nests are a potential home to parasites which may infect adult birds and nestlings, as well as animal saprovores (invertebrates which feed on carrion, excreta, pellets etc.), and humus fauna (invertebrates which feed on nest material). Philips & Dindal noted 22 species of arthropods from 15 families which have been found in North American Peregrine nests (though they did not specifically name them), as well as listing the insects commonly found in raptor nests. It is probable that the nests of British Peregrines will also carry a significant burden of parasites.

Internal parasites can also infect Peregrines, with known conditions including trichomoniasis, caused by *Trichomonas gallinae*, a motile single-celled protozoan which lives in the mouth, throat and crop and causes 'frounce' or 'canker', which can be fatal; coccidiosis, caused by a parasitic protozoan of the intestinal tract; the fungal infection aspergillosis; filariasis, caused by roundworms; and myiasis, caused by fly maggots growing beneath the skin. Krone (2007) provides details of the protozoan endoparasites known to infest raptors. While the potentially harmful effects of internal parasites are obviously significant, Barton & Houston (2001), in a post-mortem study of 379 birds of six raptor species, including 23 Peregrines, found that only 20% of the specimens had one or more internal parasites present.

Trainer (1969) gives brief details of the diseases of raptors and a list of the bacterial, viral and parasitic infections which may be found in Peregrines. Bacterial infections include fowl cholera, tuberculosis and salmonellosis, while viral infections include ornithosis, viral encephalitis and fowl pox. Trainer's list of parasites is as above, with further additions such as tapeworm. Cooper (1993) also gives a brief résumé of diseases which are known to affect captive Peregrines and may therefore be found in wild falcons. Cooper et al. (1980) also note that *Corynebacterium xerosis, Enterobacter cloaca, Escherichia coli, Staphylococcus aureus, Streptococcus* sp. and *Proteus* sp. were isolated in swabs taken from the pharynx and cloaca of wild nestling Peregrines at the time of ringing: swabs were also taken from seven captive falcons. Each of the identified organisms is associated with avian disease. *Staphylococcus aureus*, which can cause 'bumblefoot', was only found in the captive falcons, suggesting that humans might have been the vector, though *S. epidermidis* was found in the wild birds. *Pasteurella* (now *Riemerella*) *anatipestifer* is associated with diseases in waterfowl which the adult Peregrines were hunting.

FRIENDS AND FOES

There are many instances of small birds nesting close to breeding Peregrines, too many it would seem for all to be chance, the inference being that the small birds gain a degree of protection from potential egg and chick predators which the Peregrine will not tolerate. In exchange it is possible that the Peregrines benefit from the alarm calls of the other species acting as an early warning of approaching danger. One suggestion was that the smaller birds gained protection by the reluctance of the Peregrine to hunt close to its nest for fear of giving away its position, but the many observations of the falcons hunting in close proximity to their sites means that this theory is now largely discounted. In Britain instances of Wrens, Twites and even species as large as Ring Ouzels (much more likely to be potential prey to the falcon than the smaller birds) are known to nest close to Peregrines, though such commensal nesting seems more common in the Arctic, perhaps because both Peregrines and other species are more likely to be forced into using nest sites vulnerable to terrestrial predators, much of the Arctic being short of cliffs or large rock outcrops. In the Nearctic, Canada Geese (*Branta canadensis*) have been seen to nest close to Peregrines and other raptors, while the association of Red-breasted Geese with not only Peregrines, but also Snowy Owls and Rough-legged Buzzards in Siberia is one of the best-known examples of such behaviour (e.g. Quinn et al. 2003). One interesting aspect of these associations is that geese tend to land away from, and walk to, their nest sites rather than flying in, probably a useful precaution against attack, though in general the Peregrines seem to ignore these neighbours, even when the chicks are hatched. In their study of Peregrines nesting near Sondre Stromfjord in western Greenland, Meese & Fuller (1989) found no evidence that the falcons were preferentially hunting local prey.

However, Meese & Fuller did find that, contrary to the general view regarding such nesting, most prey species had lower nest densities near the Peregrine nests: while Snow Buntings were found in relative abundance, the nesting populations of the Greenlandic subspecies of the Common Redpoll (*Carduelis flammea*), Lapland Bunting (*Calcarius lapponicus*) and Wheatear had lower than average abundance. Because Meese & Fuller did not see preferential falcon hunting close to their eyries, they assumed that such hunting, prior to their study, was not the cause of the lower prey densities. As well as seeing lower prey densities, Meese & Fuller questioned the hypothesis that Peregrines offer enhanced protection of local passerines by attacking Arctic Foxes (*Vulpes lagopus*) searching for eggs and nestlings, as they could find no evidence for this happening (though Quinn et al. 2003 definitely suggest that both Snowy Owls and Peregrines offered enhanced protection against the same predator in their study in Siberia). More interestingly, Meese & Fuller (1989) noted that Snow Buntings nested in crevices in the same cliffs on which the Peregrines nested, but used crevices which were too small for an Arctic Fox to enter. The buntings were therefore gaining protection from fox predation irrespective of any attacks by the Peregrines. As Meese & Fuller note, the possible reasons why the behaviour seen elsewhere in the Arctic is not seen in the Peregrines they studied is both interesting and worthy of further study.

Peregrines at coastal sites sometimes nest within colonies of their prey species, but this close proximity seems to arise rather less from symbiosis than from necessity, as the seabird colonies are densely packed, occupying almost every available ledge space. There is also little to be gained by either side, as the likelihood of predation by the falcons at such sites is minimal (for an individual bird) and the protection offered by the falcons in seeing off potential nest thieves seems equally small. At some sites the Peregrines may also be at risk from their neighbours. If Fulmars are disturbed at their nest sites they defend themselves by vomiting the contents of their stomachs at whoever approaches. Having suffered such attacks while rock climbing, I can report that the only good news is that the Fulmars' aim is poor, the vomiting being initiated by the disturbance and going in the direction the bird happens to be facing at the time rather than being directed at the intruder. But some vomits hit: the sticky, fishy mess of stomach oil being both foul and difficult to remove. Ratcliffe (1993) notes that an examination of four dead Peregrines showed conclusively that they had died as a consequence of Fulmar oiling. The oil clogs the feathers, reducing insulating properties, affecting the ability to fly and reducing waterproofing, all of which will, in time (and the oil is persistent as well as difficult to remove) cause the affected bird's health to decline. In addition to the four deaths noted by Ratcliffe, there are other observations of Peregrines being fouled by Fulmar stomach oil (e.g. Mearns 1983; Dennis 1970 also notes the death of a White-tailed Eagle on Fair Isle and a Honey-buzzard (*Pernis apivorus*) on Orkney due to Fulmar oiling).

As noted in Chapter 5, there are several instances of Peregrines raising Kestrel chicks, though whether the larger falcon supplanting the smaller one by force to commandeer rights to the chicks can be classified as friendship, rather than kidnapping, probably induced by the Peregrines losing their own clutch or brood, is a matter of debate. The same can also be said of the report by Ellis & Groat (1982), who observed a fledgling Prairie Falcon intruding into a Peregrine eyrie and being fed by the adult Peregrines. It seemed that the adult Peregrines were aware of the intruder and occasionally stooped at the eyrie entrance, causing it to scuttle away from the edge. However, no concerted effort to remove the Prairie Falcon was made, and it fed on three delivered prey items. The Peregrine nestlings seemed unperturbed. Given the fact that Peregrines have preyed upon Prairie Falcons (see below), it is surprising that this very bold (or very foolish) behaviour was tolerated. In similar fashion, Johnson (2008) noted Kestrels and Peregrines nesting within 6 m on a Devon sea cliff (see Chapter 5 for further details).

Not surprisingly, Peregrines and Ravens share nesting areas: Nethersole-Thompson (1931a) records an instance where the two had nests only 5 m apart, while Ratcliffe (1993) notes a separation of 10 m at one site, a buttress of rock shielding direct viewing between the nests and so allowing the two pairs to maintain a (presumably uneasy) truce. Relationships between the two species are poor, the falcons usually being the aggressor, and there are instances in which Ravens have been not only 'buzzed' but struck, and occasionally killed. Ravens have also been found in Peregrine prey remains, though this is more likely to have occurred when the corvids were killed in territorial disputes than actually hunted. However, battles between the two species do not always go the falcon's way, and there have been instances of the Raven turning onto its back in mid-air as an attack is made and using its bill and/or talons to inflict damage on the attacker, with records existing of Peregrine deaths as a consequence.

The likely reason for the antagonism existing between Peregrines and Ravens is that the latter are potential predators of the falcon's eggs and young. Peregrines will also attack other corvids, probably for similar reasons. Corvids will also mob Peregrines, and Cocker (2007) records an interesting observation in which a juvenile female Peregrine on prey was surrounded by 18 Carrion Crows which seemed intent on pirating the prey, to the extent of pulling at tail and wings as the falcon mantled her catch. Eventually the Peregrine took off, and many of the crows pursued her. However, far from fleeing the scene (and the prey) the Peregrine stooped on the remaining crows, who all took off in alarm. The crows then dispersed, and the Peregrine returned to the prey. Interestingly, after Cocker's note had been published, Combridge (2008) reported a similar incident in which the Peregrine (an adult?) took no notice of 12 encircling Carrion Crows and finished its meal before flying off with the remaining carcass.

Unlike Ravens, Buzzards have a common diet with Peregrines, which may be a factor in the antagonism between them. There are known instances of Peregrines killing Buzzards, which have then formed part of the falcon's diet. Peregrines are also known to have killed (and consumed) Sparrowhawks, Merlins, Kestrels and other Peregrines. While the latter may have been killed in territorial disputes, it is more likely that the smaller raptors were deliberately targeted as prey. All five British owls are also known to have been killed and eaten by Peregrines. However, the Peregrine does not have it all its own way. In Europe Eagle Owls predate both Peregrine chicks and adults (Mikkola 1983), while the same is true for Great Horned Owls (*Bubo virginianus*) in North America (though in that case falcons killing owls is also known). However, while the proximity of owls might therefore be expected to influence Peregrine breeding sites, particularly as the owls are prey competitors, Brambilla *et al.* (2006a) found no evidence that distance to owl nests influenced falcon nest selection, but the same authors did find that proximity to an owl nest lowered Peregrine productivity, though it was not clear whether this was due to predation of falcon chicks, or because nest sites near owls are obviously poor quality and therefore likely to occupied by suboptimal falcon pairs (Brambilla *et al.* 2006b).

Peregrines will attack other Peregrines intruding on their nest area, or even during territorial disputes prior to breeding. Tordoff & Redig (1999) report two disputes which resulted in death for one combatant. In one case a female Peregrine was discovered dead after flying into a building, either having been driven into it or hitting it while fleeing, probably after a fight with her half-sister; in the second case a female died from injuries sustained in a prolonged battle (two hours) with another female. Hall (1955) also records a territorial dispute which led to death in the saga of the Sun Life building Peregrines living in Montreal.

Peregrines will also harass Golden Eagles on rare occasions. The eagles and falcons rarely interact, as their ranges do not have a significant overlap, but where they do it is clear that the eagles are dominant, particularly when it comes to nest-site selection. MacNally (1979) found the plucked, partially eaten carcass of a Peregrine at a Golden Eagle feeding perch, the talon marks to the falcon suggesting capture rather than carrion feeding.

Hunt et al. (1992) noted many instances of Peregrines harassing Bald Eagles (weighing about 4.7 kg) in Arizona, USA. In one case a falcon was believed to have chased an eagle which flew into power lines and was killed, and in another a falcon hit an eagle in the head. The eagle subsequently behaved erratically, indicating a brain injury, and was found dead a month a later apparently from the injury it sustained. The falcon attack was not thought to be on prey, but part of the general antagonism between the two species during the breeding season. Hays (1987) also recorded an attack by a Peregrine pair on a Golden Eagle in Colorado, USA, which caused the eagle to collide with a cliff. Now disorientated, the eagle was struck in the head by the stooping male Peregrine. The eagle fell, with no attempt to fly, over 180 m into the forest below. Though the eagle was not recovered, it was not seen again and survival seems very unlikely. Beebe (1960) recorded Peregrines mobbing Bald Eagles on Langara Island, British Columbia, when they were out over the ocean away from the nesting cliffs, the eagles ignoring them, but more intensive attacks when the eagles came closer to the nest sites. The eagles would roll over and show their talons, but some attacks by the falcon pair would result in hits by one bird while the other distracted the eagle. Beebe also saw an eagle attack a Peregrine which strayed too close to the eagle's nest. In this attack the falcon was lucky to escape with its life. Also on Langara Island, Nelson (1970) considered that Bald Eagle interference with nesting falcons caused a delay in the fledging of the young Peregrines: Nelson saw four unsuccessful attempts by the eagles to pirate Peregrine prey, from which it can perhaps be concluded that further attempts might have been successful.

In the USA Peregrines are also known to usurp Prairie Falcon nests and even to kill the falcons, even though the two species are comparable in size. In the North American Arctic I have seen Gyrfalcons and Peregrines nesting in close proximity, and while in general the two ignored each other, aerial conflicts were seen, though none which involved contact. However, Gyrfalcons have been known to pirate Peregrine prey (Dekker 1995), and Gyrfalcons predating Peregrines has been surmised. Booms & Fuller (2003) found traces (< 1% of total remains) of Peregrine in Gyrfalcon pellets in Greenland, but this does not necessarily imply predation rather than feeding on a carcass. Lindberg (1983) found no evidence of Peregrine in the diet of Swedish Gyrfalcons. However, Pokrovsky et al. (2010) report a case in which an immature Gyrfalcon had apparently taken a fledgling Peregrine from close to the nest and then, while eating it, had been attacked and killed by an adult Peregrine.

FIG 107. A notice in Bristol's Avon Gorge asks climbers to stay away from the portion of the cliffs where Peregrines regularly nest.

At coastal sites Peregrines will also attack, and potentially kill and consume, both Long-tailed Skuas (*Stercorarius longicaudus*) and Arctic Skuas (*S. parasiticus*), each of which is a predator in its own right and, as noted in the section on diet, Great Black-backed Gulls.

Both Arctic and Red foxes have been known to take Peregrine chicks, and other terrestrial predators would almost certainly do so opportunistically, but the combination of the inaccessibility of nest sites and the fierce defence of the parent falcons is a strong deterrent. However, all records suggest that humans are the most persistent and dangerous mammalian predators of the falcons. In Britain it is likely that at most nest sites humans are the greatest potential threat to Peregrines. Since rock climbing increased in popularity as a sport the potential for human disturbance of Peregrine sites has also increased. An evolution in climbing techniques and equipment has allowed steeper cliffs to become accessible, while competition between adherents has meant that cliffs that had long been ignored have become popular. Persistent disturbance stresses the birds, Brambilla *et al.* (2004), in a study in northern Italy and southern Switzerland, noting that the productivity of falcons nesting on cliffs popular with climbers had declined, some pairs raising no chicks. In Britain, sensible cooperation between the climbing fraternity and bird enthusiasts has resulted in restrictions being put in place which limit access to certain parts or entire cliffs for the duration of the breeding season. In all cases, and particularly at remote cliffs, continued goodwill is required to ensure disturbance is eliminated.

In a study of North American raptors, Morrison *et al.* (2006) classified Peregrines as Category 4 in terms of nest defence. This, the highest category, means very aggressive defence, and the recorded aggression was against any intruder, not only humans. Similar aggression has been seen in Britain, and there are records of attacks against humans, though individual falcons react in different ways, these varying from high circling of one or both parent birds, each of which will make repeated alarm calls, through dummy stoops that pass close by, to strikes, though the last have to date been reported only in the USA.

CHAPTER 5

The Kestrel

KESTREL – PROBABLY FROM MEDIEVAL French, either *quercerelle*, ratchet, or *crécelle*, rattle, both arising because of the bird's main call. The French was transposed into the medieval English *castrell*, which became *kestrel* when spellings were regularised. The second part of the species' scientific name, *Falco tinnunculus*, derives from the Latin *tinnulus*, ringing or tinkling (which is also the root of tinnitus), probably because of the shrill nature of the bird's call. The old English name for the species, Windhover, deriving from its characteristic hovering flight during searches for prey, is occasionally still heard in country areas. For presumably obvious reasons, the collective noun for Kestrels is a hover.

In his excellent book on the (Eurasian or Common) Kestrel, Village (1990), having listed the world's kestrel species, attempts to enumerate the characteristics which define a 'kestrel'. The obvious one, hovering, which would be chosen as diagnostic by most observers in Britain, fails when it is noted that almost half the species defined as kestrels in Chapter 1 hover rarely if at all: while a hovering falcon will be a kestrel, a kestrel does not have to hover. Plumage colour, again so diagnostic for observers in Britain, also fails, for while most kestrel species have upperparts which are chestnut/rufous or mainly so, in contrast to most other Falconiformes, and are more definitely patterned than other *Falcos*, three forms (Grey, Dickinson's and Madagascan Banded) are grey. And while sexual dimorphism in plumage is uncommon among the True Falcons other than kestrels, only half of kestrel species exhibit the characteristic. As Village (1990) concludes, it is easier to define what a kestrel is not than what it is.

Falco tinnunculus, the Eurasian Kestrel, is the most widespread of the kestrel group, ranging from western Europe to Japan, breeding north of the Arctic

FIG 108. Distribution of Kestrel species and subspecies of *Falco tinnunculus*.

Subspecies

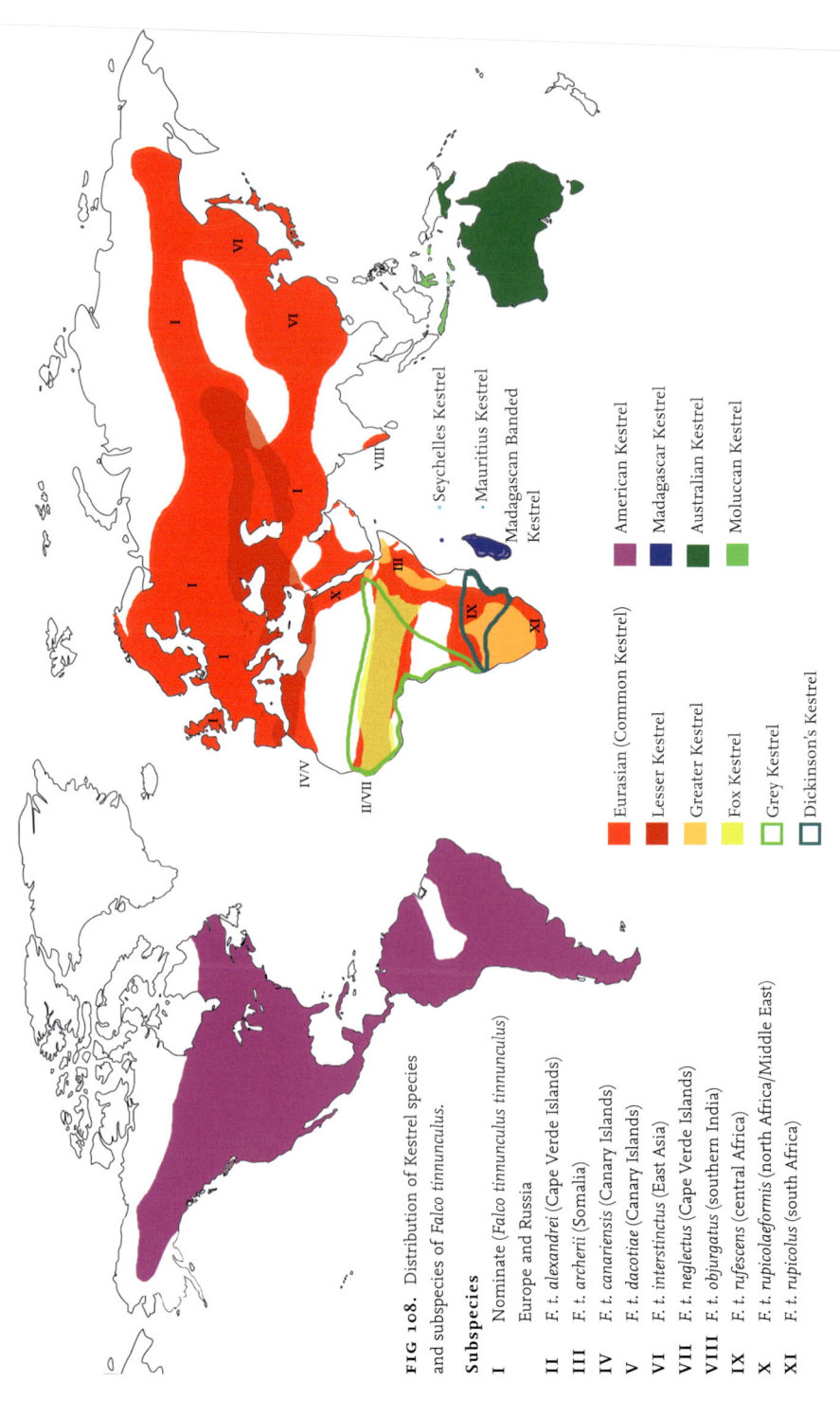

I   Nominate (*Falco timnunculus tinnunculus*) Europe and Russia
II *F. t. alexandrei* (Cape Verde Islands)
III *F. t. archerii* (Somalia)
IV *F. t. canariensis* (Canary Islands)
V   *F. t. dacotiae* (Canary Islands)
VI *F. t. interstinctus* (East Asia)
VII *F. t. neglectus* (Cape Verde Islands)
VIII *F. t. objurgatus* (southern India)
IX *F. t. rufescens* (central Africa)
X   *F. t. rupicolaeformis* (north Africa/Middle East)
XI *F. t. rupicolus* (south Africa)

The range areas are approximate, as all raptors may be found outside their normal range if prey is plentiful elsewhere. For information on the genetic variation of Kestrel subspecies see Li Zhang *et al.* (2008).

Circle in Scandinavia and close to the Cape of Good Hope in South Africa, where the species is often called the Rock Kestrel to distinguish it from the Lesser and Greater Kestrels. The Eurasian Kestrel is a chestnut falcon, a little larger than the Hobby, more significantly larger than the Merlin. Kestrels prey primarily on rodents (Note 5.1), taking them after a short flight from a perch or by dropping on them from hovering flight (see Chapter 3), but will also take a very wide range of other prey. This flexibility in diet has allowed the species to adapt to a variety of habitats. It is the most numerous Old World falcon, though perhaps not the most numerous worldwide, that distinction likely belonging to the American Kestrel. Until the early years of the new century Kestrels were probably the most numerous of British raptors, but a decline in population – which we will return to later in the chapter – coupled with an increase in Common Buzzard numbers, means the species is perhaps no longer the nation's most numerous diurnal raptor, and may also be outnumbered by the Tawny Owl. However, if not the most numerous, the Kestrel is arguably the best known, its habit of hovering over the central reservations and verges of motorways and other roads having brought it to the attention of, and endeared it to, millions.

At present 11 subspecies of the Kestrel are recognised (Fig. 108), of which the nominate (that found in Britain) has the most extensive range. Gray (1958) records a presumed natural hybrid between a male Merlin and a female Eurasian Kestrel, but no verified hybridisation records have been identified.

DIMENSIONS

Overall length (bill tip to tail tip) 320–350 mm.
Wing: male 246 ± 6 mm; female 256 ± 8 mm.
Tail: male 163 ± 6 mm; female 171 ± 7 mm.
Bill: male 13.9 ± 0.6 mm; female 15.0 ± 0.9 mm.
Tarsus: male 39.6 ± 0.9 mm; female 39.6 ± 1.2 mm.
Toe: male 26.5 ± 0.8 mm; female 27.0 ± 1.0 mm.
Claw: male 11.4 ± 0.3 mm; female 11.9 ± 0.5 mm.
Juvenile wing: male 240 ± 12 mm; female 249 ± 14 mm.
Juvenile tail: male 157 ± 12 mm; female 165 ± 13 mm.
Female slightly larger than male. Eurasian Kestrels (and, in general, all kestrels) have tails that are long in proportion to wing length, which is an aid to their hunting techniques.

WEIGHT

Male 210 ± 20g; female 250 ± 30g. In both cases the weight is variable throughout the year and particularly during the breeding season. The changes in weight, and the reasons for these changes, are discussed below in the section on breeding.

PLUMAGE

Adult male

Chestnut back and wing coverts spotted with teardrop/arrowhead black spots. Primaries dark brown/black, paler or buff-edged, this being noticeable on the

FIG 109. Adult male Kestrel. (James Sellen)

perched bird or the flying/hovering bird if viewed from above. Slate-grey head with darker moustachial stripe and pale buff/cream throat: the contrast between moustache and throat becomes more pronounced with age. Tail blue-grey with broad black subterminal and narrow white terminal band. Underparts buff-spotted with dark teardrops. Underwing coverts paler buff/cream, much paler on the undertail and vent. Underside of primaries pale grey/cream with dark brown/black tips and bars. Iris dark brown, bill blue-grey with darker tip, cere yellow, tarsi and feet yellow, claws black.

Adult female
Upperparts, including head and nape, chestnut with more abundant, darker spotting than on the male. Moustachial stripe and throat as male, though stripe usually much less well defined. Primaries as male. Tail chestnut with darker barring continuously along the length, but with broad dark subterminal and pale buff terminal band. Underparts darker buff than male, with more spotting. Undertail continuously darker barred, as is the underwing. Iris dark brown, bill blue-grey with darker tip, cere yellow, legs/feet yellow, claws black.

FIG 110. Adult female Kestrel.

It is often suggested that the unbarred grey tail of the male can be used to distinguish the sexes if the male's head is not seen, but some males show pale banding, and in some it is very distinctive, while some females have grey, not chestnut tails. The easier distinguishing feature is the richer coloration of the female's back and upper wings, with heavier spotting and barring on the secondary coverts.

Juvenile
Resembles adult female, but usually paler with heavier streaking and barring on upper and underparts, and buff fringing to primaries. Iris dark brown, bill blue-grey with darker tip, cere pale yellow, legs/feet yellow, claws black. In the section below on breeding an interesting study by Finnish researchers (Hakkarainen *et al.* 1993) on the possible reason for juvenile male Kestrels having adult female-like plumage is discussed. Historically juveniles were considered extremely difficult to sex accurately (e.g. Village 1990), but Dijkstra *et al.* (1990a) were 99% accurate in the sexing of 193 nestlings using the tail coverts, which were grey in males, with narrow, pointed crossbars, but brown in females.

FIG 111. Juvenile Kestrel.

Nestling

First down is sparse and white. Second down (at about 8 days) is buff/grey on upperparts, paler on underparts. Feathers appear at about 14 days. Down almost gone and all feathers full grown apart from primaries and tail at 28 days.

FIG 112. Nestling Kestrel, brought from an urban nest site for ringing.

Moult

Adult Kestrels moult from May onwards. Females moult earlier than males, beginning a few days after laying the first egg, with first-year females starting a few days earlier than older females (Village 1990). However, as first-year females lay their first egg later than adult females, this means that moulting starts at about the same time for both groups. As Village notes, this phenomenon cannot be associated with moulting starting on or close to a given calendar date (i.e. at a time defined by sunrise or position of the sun in the sky) as earlier moulting is also noted in non-breeding first-year females. The feathers of a female Kestrel weigh 21–24 g (while those of a male weigh 16–18.5 g – both weights from Dietz et al. 1992). The energy required to synthesise feathers is approximately 106 kJ/g (dry weight) (Dietz et al. 1992), to which must be added the energy equivalent of the feathers themselves (23 kJ/g) to produce an overall cost of moulting of 129 kJ/g (dry weight). Moulting increases the basal metabolic rate (BMR – the minimum rate needed to sustain life assuming an organism in an ambient temperature equal to body temperature) of the female by up to 30% (Masman 1986). Egg laying is also energy-intensive, and so it is clear why females would wait until after laying had begun, suggesting that the more experienced females also wait until incubation is under way before moulting.

On average the male's moult starts about 15 days later than his mate's, delayed by the necessity of hunting to provide food for both the female and the hatchlings, which reduces or eliminates the energy available for feather synthesis. Both males and females end the moult at about the same time, so males moult faster than females. Both males and females may exhibit an arrested moult, i.e. they may halt the moult, the likely cause being a shortage of prey during the chick-rearing phase – both parent birds hunt once the chicks are ten days old and are able to regulate their own body temperature – so that increased energy is required in hunting.

Adult moulting starts with the upper tail coverts and rump, followed by the wing coverts and underside, then the back and head. Moulting of the primary feathers follows the sequence 4–5–6–3–7–8–2–9–10–1, with two or three feathers in moult simultaneously, while that for the tail is 1–6–2–3–4–5. Moulting is usually symmetrical on both wings and both sides of the tail. During the moult, 'flight-hunting' is considerably reduced, as hovering is much more difficult if there are gaps in either the flight or tail feathers – though Shrubb (1993a) notes that some flight-hunting Kestrels exhibit a remarkable degree of feather loss or damage, but are still able to function. The moult sequence of both wing and tail might imply an evolutionary advantage for a hovering species, but in fact the sequence is standard for falcons. The duration of a full moult is about 180 days in total, though the main moult phase, when the primaries and tail feathers are moulted, takes 136 days in females and 122 days in males (Village 1990). Village also considered that the growth rate for an individual primary feather was about 25 days.

Juveniles moult to adult plumage during the winter; work on trapped birds by Village (1990) showing that although some birds began their moult as early as August, most did not start until October and the majority were moulting during the coldest months (Fig. 113). Since loss of feathers increases body heat loss, this seems a potentially dangerous strategy, but is perhaps required if the juvenile is hoping to breed during the coming spring. In support of this argument, neither

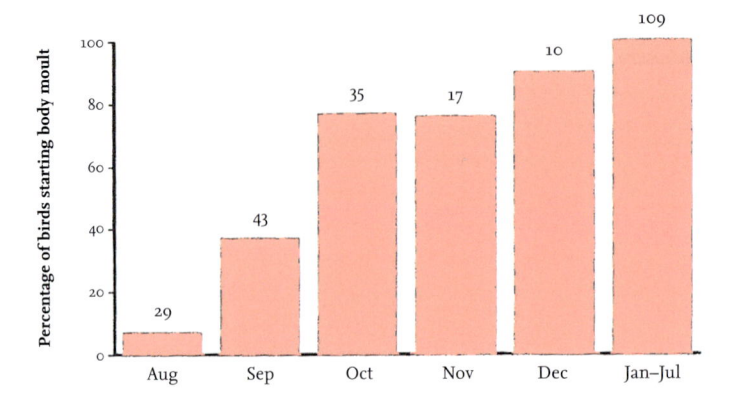

FIG 113. Start of body feather moult in first-year Kestrels. Histogram indicates proportion of birds that had replaced at least one feather on head, back, rump or upper tail coverts by indicated month. Figures above each bar indicate sample size. Redrawn from Village 1990.

the primary nor tail feathers are moulted during the winter, so hunting is not compromised. The primaries and tail feathers are moulted at the same time as in adult birds. At that time the juvenile feathers match the size of those of adults, the first juvenile flight plumage showing shorter wings and tails. The implication of this is that the wing loading of juveniles differs from that of adults, presumably an evolutionary tactic to aid the young birds when they are learning to hunt their own prey. During the primary and tail feather moult the juveniles finally acquire the characteristic plumage of the adults.

HABITAT

Kestrels are primarily birds of open country – farmland, heath, grassland, scrub and low-lying moorland, as well as features such as riverbanks and woodland edges – but also do well in cities, taking advantage of any open area which might offer the possibility of rodent prey, or taking city-dwelling passerines. They also frequent other human-defined landscapes such as road verges, railway embankments, canal edges, and areas of felled forestry, where they hunt rodents in the newly created scrub before new tree growth closes out the area as a hunting ground. Despite the extensive range of the species they do not inhabit tundra, forest-tundra or taiga. While in parts of their range Kestrels are found at considerable heights (up to 3000 m or higher in the Caucasus), in Britain they rarely breed above about 500 m. However, while Kestrels as a species show a high degree of flexibility as regards habitat, Avilés *et al.* (2001) showed that clutch size and breeding success of Kestrels in southwest Spain were higher in pasture than in cereal cropland. This finding was echoed in a study in England which found that Kestrels preferred recently cut grassland for hunting (Garratt *et al.* 2011). The study found that grass cut within the last two weeks (grass blades less than 5 cm in length) was preferentially chosen, and that such grassland resulted in a higher take of mammalian prey (4.36 mammals to every invertebrate), uncut grassland reducing the ratio to 1.73:1. This finding echoed results from Switzerland (Aschwanden *et al.* 2005), where the authors studied the results of conservation measures put in place after a reduction in the vole population had led to a decline in both Kestrel and Long-eared Owl populations. The Swiss scheme required the creation of ecological compensation areas (constituting 7% of the farmland) which were not mown. It was found that the vole population density in such areas was eight times that of 'standard' fields and grassland. However, both the Kestrels and the owls preferred to hunt new-mown grass despite voles being scarcer, the benefit of the compensation areas being in the overall ecology of a site and in providing a winter source of food when the vegetation was less dense.

Garratt *et al.* (2011) also measured the time spent by hunting kestrels across a spectrum of habitats (Figs 114 & 115). A similar study, but encompassing a

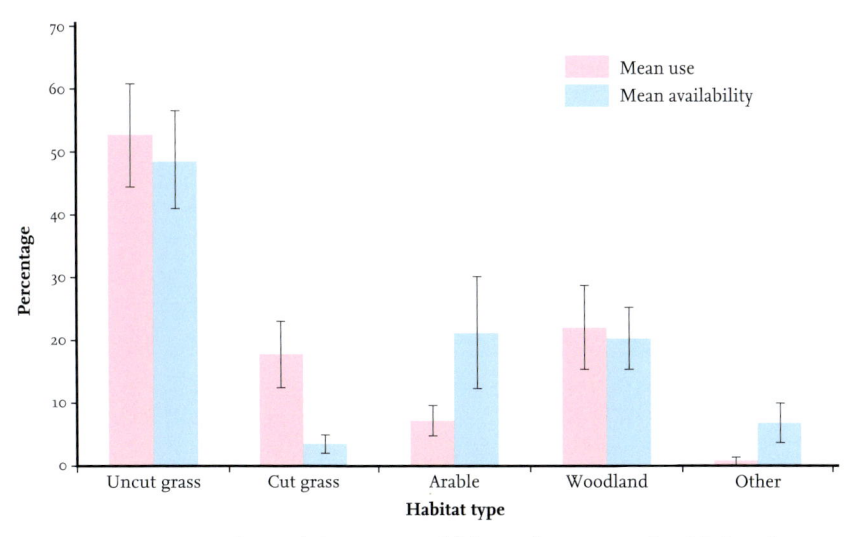

FIG 114. Comparison of mean habitat type availability and mean use of each habitat by hunting Kestrels (e.g. for uncut grass the habitat was 48% available, 56% utilised). Data averaged across seven pairs of Kestrels. Redrawn from Garratt *et al.* 2011.

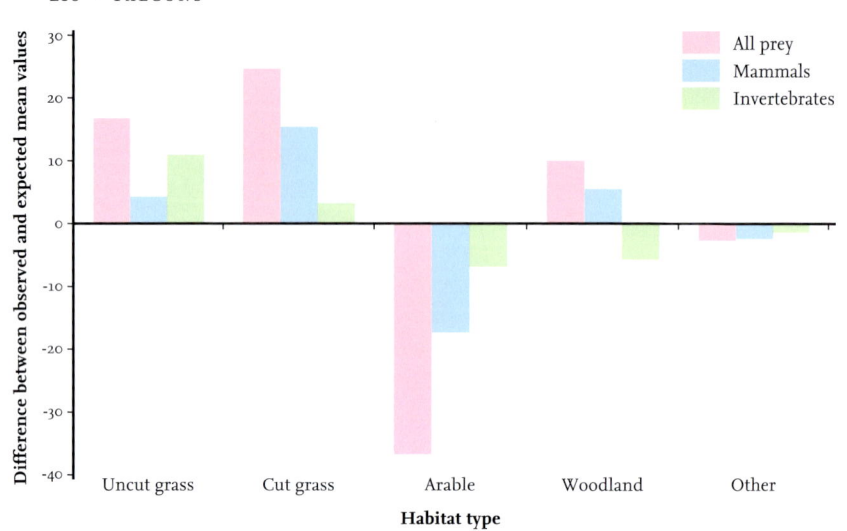

FIG 115. Difference between expected and observed prey captures by Kestrels across the habitats of Fig. 114. A positive value indicates greater habitat usage than expected (e.g. if 100 mammals were taken in total and habitat A represented 10% of total, then 10 mammals would be expected if habitat usage was by chance). Birds are included in 'all prey', as too few birds were taken to differentiate them in a meaningful way. Redrawn from Garratt *et al.* 2011.

larger number of Kestrel territories (461–462) over a period of years (1997–2002), also identified a spectrum of habitats in Wales, covering coastal sites (91 or 92 territories), farmland (127), hill grazing (100), forest (5) and urban/industrial areas (21) (Shrubb 2003).

VOICE

Kestrels are vocal birds, particularly during the breeding season, but personal experience suggests Walpole-Bond (1938) was incorrect in suggesting that the species was mute during November and December, though calls are more rarely heard in those months. The most common call, the alarm call, is usually described as '*kik-kik-kik*' or '*kee-kee-kee*'. The Kestrel's voice was most famously described by Tinbergen (1940), in a paper which also described the courtship and territorial displays of the species. The call, used by both males and females, is most often heard if the birds are disturbed at the nest or if the nest is approached, but the birds also use it during any aggressive event, such as when harassing another raptor or trespassing corvid. The number of syllables is usually 2–4, but is variable, with longer calls being heard. With these longer calls, usually uttered when the bird is more aggressive, the pitch rises, the call becoming much shriller. Occasionally a single '*kee*' is heard, particularly from fledglings exercising wings and voice at the same time.

The common call is the Kestrel's communication with the wider world, but a second call is more private, a gentler, trilling '*wheee*' heard when the Kestrel pair is together and when they greet each other at the nest. The female also uses it when begging for food from the male, the call then being more of a nasal whine. A shorter, higher-pitched, more clipped version, usually written '*clip*', '*kit*' or '*tsick*', is also used by the female when feeding her brood and also by the male when he arrives at the nest with food.

The calls of nestlings are variations on adult calls, but they also have a plaintive '*cheep*' most often heard during the first days after hatching when they are cold and in need of brooding, or later when they are hungry. In a study of American Kestrels, Smallwood *et al.* (2003) found a number of different calls of nestlings, but were unable to use voice as a means of distinguishing nestling sex. The authors noted that by the age of 16 days the chicks were producing calls similar to those of adults. It is likely that vocal development in the Eurasian Kestrel follows a similar path.

Kochanek (1984) analysed the calls of three pairs of wild Kestrels, both adults and young, by sonogram and concluded that females made 11 different calls, males nine calls and young Kestrels five. While these were all variants on the basic calls noted above, Kochanek's work does suggest that the bird-to-bird communication of the Kestrel is rather more complex than it first appears.

DIET

Prey

Though, as noted above, Kestrels are flexible in their diet, they are primarily predators of *Microtus* voles and other rodents. In the absence of voles or mice, the birds will feed on anything readily available on the ground (Shrubb 1993a, Village 1990). Ground prey covers a substantial array of mammals including shrews (Kestrels apparently not being put off by the foul taste of shrews, as most mammal predators are), young Rabbits, leverets, the young of rats and squirrels, and Weasels. Village (1990) reports seeing a male Kestrel attacking a leveret, being able to hold it, but unable to kill it. The female of the pair arrived and dispatched the hare with several bites at the base of the neck. However, the female was barely

FIG 116. Bank Vole (left) and Wood Mouse (right). Both species are on the prey list for Kestrels. How did the mouse work out that there was a bird feeder over 2 m up in a tree?

able to take off with her kill and Village (displaying an admirable enthusiasm for science, if unchivalrously depriving the falcon of her meal) forced her to leave it: he measured it at 120 g – about half the likely weight of the female of about 230 g. Moles have also been found – both as remains, in pellets, and as prey items at nests – these invariably having been taken after periods of heavy rain when the animals had been forced to abandon waterlogged burrows.

Once taken, prey is dispatched with the standard bite at the base of the neck or on the head. In a somewhat gruesome experiment in northern Italy Csermely

FIG 117. Body of a Common Shrew found in a nest box occupied by Kestrels. The intact body suggests that shrews are not eaten if more palatable prey is available.

et al. (2009) offered mice (in an enclosure which simulated the local environment: the rodents contained within the enclosure, but not tethered) to both captive and wild Kestrels. In all cases the falcon took a short exploratory flight above the victim, presumably assessing capture possibilities, before swooping to capture. The only difference between the two cohorts was that wild Kestrels flew away with their prey, taking it to a perch where it was killed and consumed, whereas the captive Kestrels killed and ate the mouse at the point of capture.

Kestrels will also prey on non-flying insects, both larger beetles and much smaller insects (e.g. ants), these sometimes being taken by ground foraging after either a successful or an unsuccessful rodent kill: grasshoppers may also be taken during ground foraging. In a study in the Alto Palancia region of Valencia (east-central Spain) grasshoppers actually formed the bulk (83%) of the diet of nestling Kestrels (Gil-Delgado *et al.* 1995). Dragonflies are also recorded as having been taken, but in general Kestrels lack the aerial agility of Hobbies and do not

FIG 118. A female Kestrel brings a Viviparous Lizard (*Lacerta vivipara*) to a brood hatched in an old metal basket.

take these or other fast-flying insects often, though Kestrels in Africa take newly emerged swarming termites.

In warmer parts of the species' range, lizards may form the main vertebrate prey but, even in Britain, lizards are taken, as are Slow Worms (*Anguis fragilis*) and, though much more rarely, snakes. Amphibian prey includes newts and frogs (Deane 1962), while Village (1990) records seeing a Kestrel feeding on a Common Toad (*Bufo bufo*): as the toad was 'road kill' Village believes the bird was able to bypass the poisonous skin to reach the harmless flesh beneath. Earthworms are frequently eaten, and slugs are also consumed, while rarer menu items include fish and crabs (Village 1990 and references therein). Perhaps the most unusual dietary addition is that observed by Rejt (2005) while studying urban-nesting Kestrels in Warsaw. Rejt noted that unhatched eggs disappeared from the nest as soon as the last chick had hatched, and that continuous video monitoring of one nest showed that an adult took an unhatched egg and cached it, then fed the contents to the hatched chicks a few hours later. The observation implies that infertile eggs may be routinely fed to nestlings.

Aerial prey is also taken. Kestrels are not adept bird hunters, but will take both adult birds and chicks, and these may even form a significant part of the diet of fledging Kestrels. The birds taken are species which share the Kestrel's preferred habitat – in open-country Meadow Pipit, Skylark and Starling; in urban environments House Sparrow and other town passerines – though many other species have also been noted, including waders and the young of much bigger species such as ducks and gulls. Village (1990) records a male Kestrel killing a Turtle Dove and then flying off with it in a series of short, presumably

FIG 119. Bird remains, probably a juvenile Robin, in a nest box occupied by Kestrels.

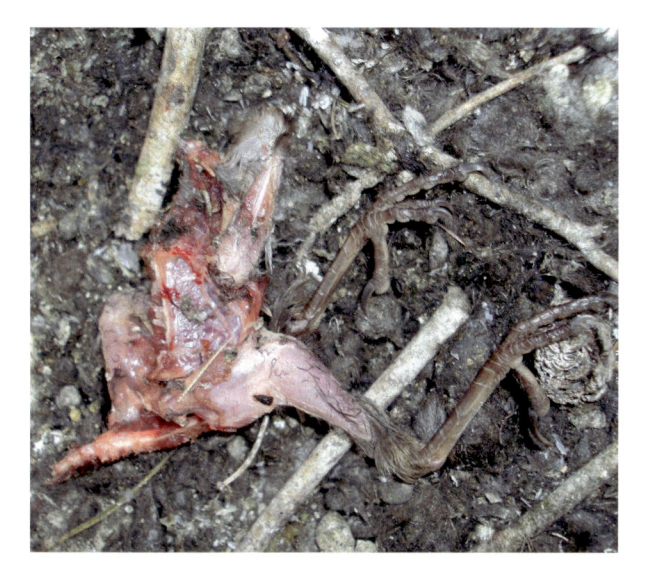

FIG 120. Bird remains in another Kestrel nest box. The long back claw suggests a juvenile Meadow Pipit.

FIG 121. Remains of a Long-eared Owl fledgling found beneath a stick nest that was occupied by Kestrels.

exhausting, flights. Given that the falcon may have weighed only about 140 g, while the dove was likely to be around 120 g if a juvenile (the kill was in July) or more if an adult, this shows both remarkable strength and determination by the Kestrel. Further evidence of Kestrel's determination is not lacking: Gentle et al. (2013) record a (failed) attempt at predation of House Sparrow nestlings from a nesting box, while Ponting (2002) reported seeing a Kestrel grab a Canary through the bars of a cage suspended on the outside of an apartment block on Tenerife. The Kestrel held the bird in one talon and plucked it through the bars, eventually letting go of the dead bird and flying to perch on another cage. In this case the Canary's owner appeared and scared off the Kestrel before it could add another Canary to its feast. To complete the picture of predation of typical caged birds, Riddle (2011) records finding feathers at one site which could only have come from an escaped Budgerigar.

Shrubb (1993a) notes that Kestrel prey has included Collared Dove, Stock Dove and adult Lapwing, while other records include Snipe, all of which would have been a handful (as it were) for the predatory Kestrel. Mead & Pepler (1975) recorded Kestrels at a Sand Martin colony, but noted that the falcon was not especially skilled at taking the martins, those that were taken probably being juveniles. Riddle also mentions an incident on a North Sea oil platform where a Kestrel, having consumed a good fraction of the small birds taking refuge, retrieved a Goldcrest which had dropped onto the water, and later retrieved several bodies of recently drowned passerines in similar fashion. Messenger et al. (1988) also recorded a Kestrel at Seaforth, Merseyside, that attacked a group of Leach's Petrels, catching one about 15 cm above the water.

In a study of urban Kestrels in a town in northeast Slovakia Mikula et al. (2013) noted the birds taking Swifts. The technique the Kestrels used was to wait close to, or at the mouth of, ventilation shafts in the hope of catching the Swifts as they emerged from roosting. The authors suggest 'sit-and-wait' as a new technique to be added to the hunting repertoire of Kestrels. Riddle (2011) also records the attempted taking of Hobby chicks, the Kestrel being fought off by the adult Hobby, the two raptors eventually locking talons as they fought.

Before leaving avian prey it is worth noting a fascinating study in Finland by Huhta et al. (1998) which showed, by artificially dulling the plumage of some Great Tits using a black marker pen (!), that hungry Kestrels were no more attracted to the unmarked, bright tits than to the duller ones, which, if they were able to understand, would doubtless be of some comfort to our more colourful small passerines.

Being crepuscular as well as diurnal, Kestrels also take bats. Negro et al. (1992) note predation of Pipistrelles (*Pipistrellus pipistrellus*), the Kestrels hunting these in winter, preferentially choosing fine weather, when the bats emerged from their roosts earlier and in greater numbers, by circling above them and diving on an individual, or by perch-hunting. One radio-tracked male was found to have a diet comprising 30–60% of bats over a nine-day period. Mikula *et al.* (2013) noted that Kestrels used the same 'sit-and-wait' technique to catch bats that used the same shafts for daytime roosting as those used by Swifts at night. In a study in France, Duquet & Nadal (2012) listed a total of 11 bats taken by avian predators. Although Hobbies took the highest percentage (39%), Kestrels were responsible for 20% of identified bat kills.

In general Kestrels do not take carrion, but records of them doing so exist (e.g. Dickson & Dickson 1993), and it may be that for some individuals or in some circumstances it is a more common behaviour than most observers consider. Kestrels also exhibit kleptoparasitism, the pirating of prey, of other raptors such as Sparrowhawks, other Kestrels, or other species such as Magpies: both Village (1990) and Korpimäki (1984a) note that Short-eared Owls are frequent victims of piratical attacks, probably because the two species are diurnal vole hunters and so more likely to share hunting areas. Interestingly, in a study in western France Fritz (1998) noted that kleptoparasitism of Short-eared Owls was more prevalent when the wind was lighter and so unfavourable for flight-hunting, stronger winds allowing hovering with a much reduced energy expenditure. Piratical attacks on Barn Owls are also known, while Shrubb (1993a) notes that Kestrel attempts to steal prey from Weasels have also been recorded. However, Kestrels may also be the victims of piracy, Combridge & Combridge (1992) noting a male Red-footed Falcon forcing breeding Kestrels to give up prey destined for their nestlings. Kettle (1990) also records a Red-footed Falcon attacking a juvenile Kestrel which had caught a vole, dropping onto the back of the juvenile and sinking its talons into it. In the fight that followed the Red-footed seems to have been lucky to survive, but actually took the vole when the Kestrel flew off. Both *et al.* (2013) also recorded a curious incident in the Netherlands where a Peregrine took prey from a Kestrel in the air and landed with it, only to then discard it; the prey item was a Common Vole (*Microtus arvalis*). Piratical attacks by Hobbies on Kestrels are noted in Chapter 6.

Composition of diet

Analysis of Kestrel pellets, which measure 20–30 mm in length, 12–17 mm in diameter (Village 1990), or 20–40 mm × 10–25 mm (quoted by Riddle 2011 in his absorbing book on his own experiences with Kestrels), has allowed a reasonably accurate examination of the diet of the birds across a range of British habitats, though the poor survival of feathers and the difficulty of identifying skeletal remains of birds may mean that unless claws or bills are found the bird content of the pellet may be underestimated. Pellets are usually pale grey when dry, rounded at one end and pointed at the other. When cast they are slimy with mucus, which often means they adhere to branches close to nest sites. Pellet analysis has shown that more than 20 mammal species are taken by Kestrels, the majority, as expected, being small mammals (mice, voles and shrews) or the young of larger mammals.

Village (1990) notes that most studies of Kestrel diet in temperate regions indicate that *Microtus* voles are the most important prey. In his own studies (1976–1980), undertaken in a grassland area near Eskdalemuir, Scotland, and in mixed and arable farmland areas in east central England, Field Voles (*Microtus agrestis* – also known as the Short-tailed Vole, a name favoured by Village) were the most common prey species, occurring in over 90% of the pellets collected in Scotland and around 75% of English pellets. Shrubb (1993a), collating data from studies in both Britain and Scandinavia, noted that overall for those countries vertebrate prey accounted for 56% of the total diet (75% being mammal, 22% bird, and 3% reptile or amphibian): voles comprised 45% of the mammalian prey. It therefore seems probable that voles form the greater part of the Kestrel diet where they are abundant, and this was certainly borne out in a study in the Netherlands where voles (in this case the Common Vole) contributed over 90% of the Kestrel diet in all months except June, when the Common Shrew (*Sorex araneus*) formed about 10% of the diet (shrews being more active on the surface at that time), and December, when songbirds formed about 10% (Masman et al. 1988b) (Note 5.2). These data are consistent with those of Cavé (1967) and Shrubb (1993a). Shrubb also collated data from studies in Mediterranean Europe, noting that vertebrate prey constituted only 14% of the Kestrel diet (voles being 15% of this vertebrate fraction), with invertebrate prey comprising the remaining 86%.

Studies in Finland (Korpimäki 1985a, 1985b) have confirmed that Kestrels are primarily a mammal predator, but have also revealed some interesting aspects of the species' diet. The earlier work (Korpimäki 1985b) noted that Finnish Kestrels hunted in different habitats when seeking avian rather than rodent prey, 71% of avian prey being forest species, implying that Kestrels find forested areas an easier environment for hunting birds. Korpimäki (1986b) also noted that the dietary width (i.e. the number of prey species appearing in the diet) of breeding Kestrels increased as summer progressed. Korpimäki conjectured that this increase was influenced by several factors. One was a change in local environment, with voles, the primary prey, became less accessible as vegetation cover increased. Another factor was the increased food requirements of the

Kestrel nestlings, while a third was the availability of fledglings of other species, young rodents and insects.

In the data of Village (1990), the variation in the percentage of pellets containing vole remains in Scotland through the year was minimal, as it was in the English mixed farmland, though the percentage dropped in the English arable farmland area from midsummer, reaching about 55% in midwinter before rising again as spring approached. Interestingly, in the Scottish study area around 50% of pellets (on average) during the five-year period contained only vole remains, that percentage dropping to only about 10% in the farmland study areas, reflecting the larger number of habitats in the latter and, hence, the greater number of rodent species. Also of interest was the fact that Wood Mice (*Apodemus sylvaticus*) were entirely absent from the Scottish pellets, but were found in the English farmland in summer. As Wood Mice are nocturnal their absence from Scottish pellets is understandable; their presence in English pellets indicates that the mice move into arable fields as crops become available and are then more easily discovered in summer, and particularly during harvest when machinery disturbs them, making them visible to waiting Kestrels (personal communications with Gloucestershire farmers). In Ireland, where there are no Field Voles, Kestrels prey mostly on birds, as well as taking Wood Mice (Fairley & McLean 1965, Fairley 1973). In his study of Kestrel diet in English farmland, Village (1990) noted that there was some suggestion that Kestrels took voles when both voles and mice were available, but he did not consider that the evidence was sufficient to imply genuine selectivity. In general, the results of his study indicated that prey selection relied primarily on prey abundance.

By contrast to the essentially constant fraction of voles in the pellets, the occurrence of bird remains was seasonal, peaking in June/July, the time when broods were fledging and so reflecting the relative ease with which Kestrels could catch young, inexperienced birds. Beetle remains were found in 50–60% of farmland pellets but, not surprisingly, in a smaller fraction of Scottish grassland pellets: in each case the percentage of pellets containing insect remains increased during the summer, before falling off as winter approached. The earthworm content of pellets was surprisingly high, the annual average for the farmland study area being around 50%. Less surprisingly the percentage was much lower (a few per cent only) in the Scottish grassland. In each case the percentage was higher in the late winter/early spring period, reflecting the likelihood of unfrozen but waterlogged ground forcing worms to the surface. In the farmland area, the percentage then fell, before rising again in autumn, with its attendant higher rainfall (Fig. 122).

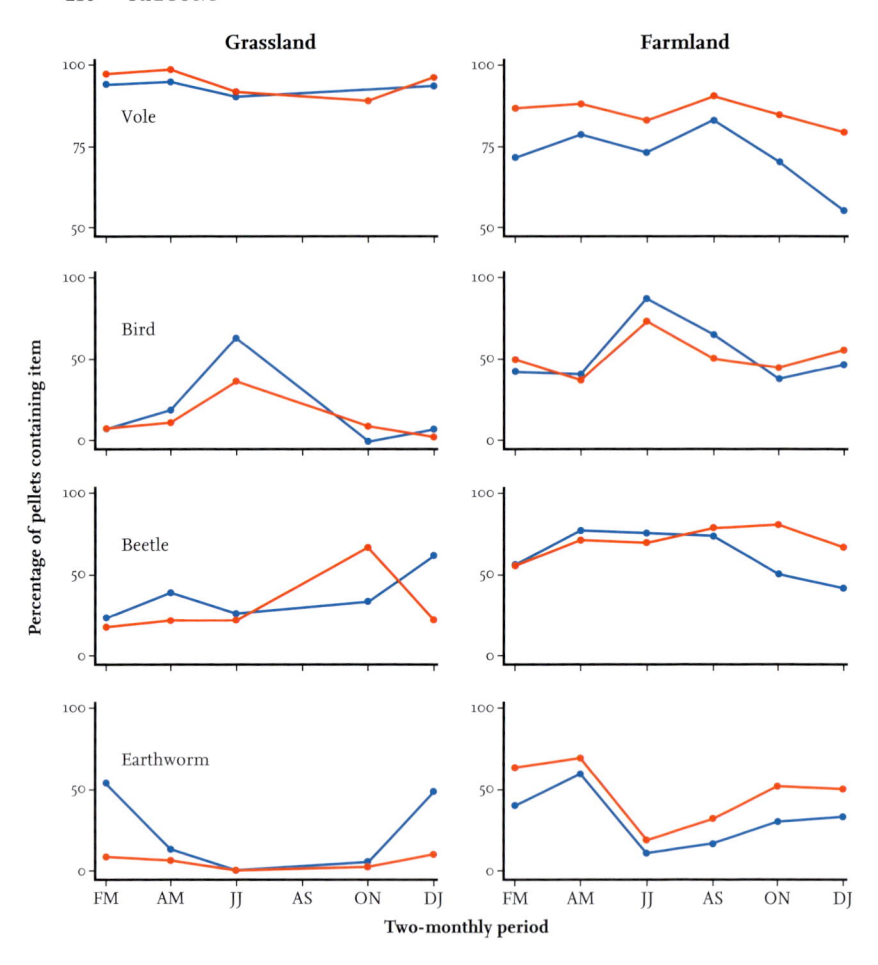

FIG 122. Seasonal variation in diet of Kestrels on grassland (1975–1979) – red data from young plantations, blue data from sheepwalk – and on farmland (1980–1985) – red data from mixed farmland, blue data from arable farmland.

The data shown in Fig. 139 are consistent with those of Shrubb (2003) for Kestrels in Wales, and with Shrubb (1993a), but the latter adds interesting data on the variation of mammalian prey during the year, noting that Bank Voles, Harvest Mice and Wood Mice were taken more often in winter when they became less predominantly nocturnal, while rats were more frequently taken in spring and autumn as they moved to and from the fields. Figure 139 is also consistent with data from a study in a boreal area of Norway in which video monitoring of 55

FIG 123. Kestrel in flight in Cornwall. (James Sellen)

nests sites allowed the composition of prey delivered to nestlings to be analysed (Steen *et al.* 2011). Steen and colleagues noted that 60% (by number) of prey items were voles, with birds (14%), shrews (12%), lizards (9%), insects (3%), frogs (0.4%) and unidentified prey forming the remainder of the diet.

Shrubb (1993a) also noted the difference in diet between male and female Kestrels: males took about twice the fraction of insect prey that females secured, but this was reversed for earthworms; males took more birds than females (though this, perhaps, may have been accounted for by the number of chicks taken by a male feeding a female and nestlings), but it was invariably the female Kestrel that took reptiles. These data are consistent with that of Village (1990).

Village (1990) also compared the diet of adult and juvenile Kestrels (Fig. 124), noting that the fraction of avian prey in the pellets of the younger birds was

218 · FALCONS

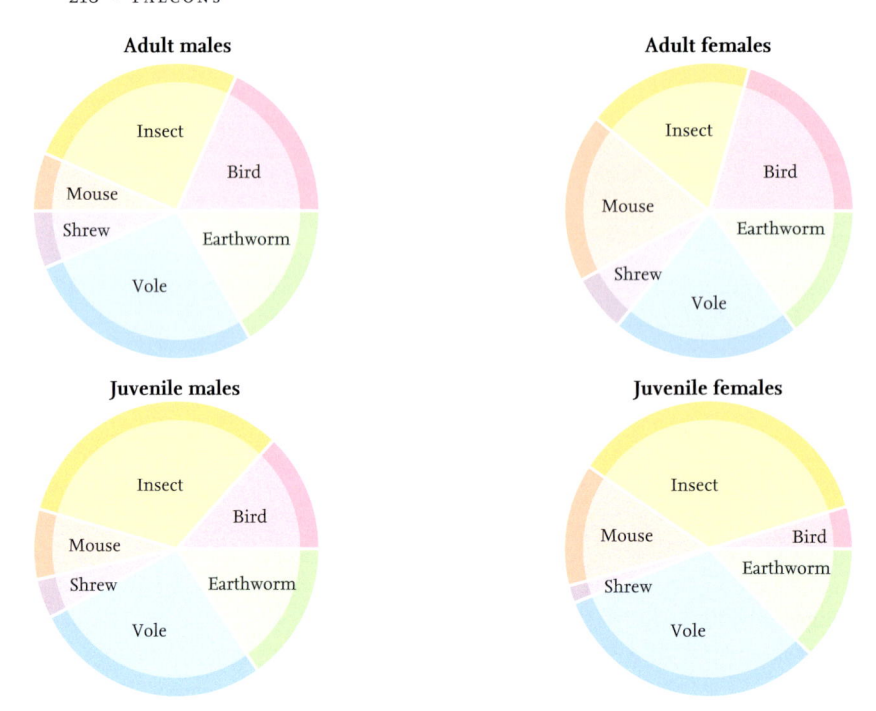

Adult males **Adult females**

Juvenile males **Juvenile females**

FIG 124. Diet by age and sex of Kestrels in English farmland. Juveniles of both sexes ate more invertebrates and fewer birds than did adults. Redrawn from Village 1990.

reduced, while that of insects increased, clearly indicating the relative ease of capture of insects. Interestingly, the fraction of voles in the pellets was similar for adults and juveniles, supporting the intuitive suggestion that the skills required to catch voles are less demanding than those required to catch birds.

Yalden (1980) studied the diet of urban Kestrels in Manchester, noting that it chiefly comprised passerines (58% by number, 64% by weight) of which the majority (about 90%) were House Sparrows. The next largest fraction was pigeons (4% by number, 10% by weight). Goldfinch, Dunnock (*Prunella modularis*), Starling, Blue Tit and Pied Wagtail were also found, though in all cases Yalden was cautious to claim certainty of identification because of the difficulty of identifying bird remains in pellets. The rest were rodent species. Overall the urban Kestrel diet consisted of birds (76% by weight) and mammals (22%) with traces of insects and earthworms. More recent studies of urban diet have been made by Romanowski (1996) in Warsaw. Romanowski studied two urban sites, one close to the centre of the city, an open area with parkland, the other a heavily built-up area where the Kestrels nested on the flat roofs of houses. In the central area birds accounted for only 12% of the breeding season diet, House Sparrows being the major prey species, with mammals forming the bulk (79%) and insects the remaining 9%. However, in the built-up area birds comprised the majority of the diet (57%), with mammals 38% and insects 5%, consistent with the Yalden data. The difference seen in Warsaw between the 'true' urban and 'open' urban areas was well illustrated in a study in Berlin, where Kübler et al. (2005) studied the dietary differences between Kestrels breeding in areas of differing housing structure and building density, and land utilisation and vegetation cover. The differences in diet are shown in Fig. 125. As can be seen, Kestrels have the flexibility to switch prey if their territory does not provide adequate numbers of their preference (i.e. rodents) but will always take a higher fraction of rodents if a full spectrum of prey is available. A similar result to that of Kübler and co-workers was found by Boratyński & Kasprzyk (2005) in north-central Poland. In this case the authors had assumed that they would find a preponderance of avian prey in the diet of urban Kestrels, but were surprised to find that mammals comprised the overwhelming bulk. It was only when they observed the hunting range of the Kestrels that this apparent anomaly was explained, the Kestrel's range taking in a large area outside the town limits which allowed the birds to take their preferred prey.

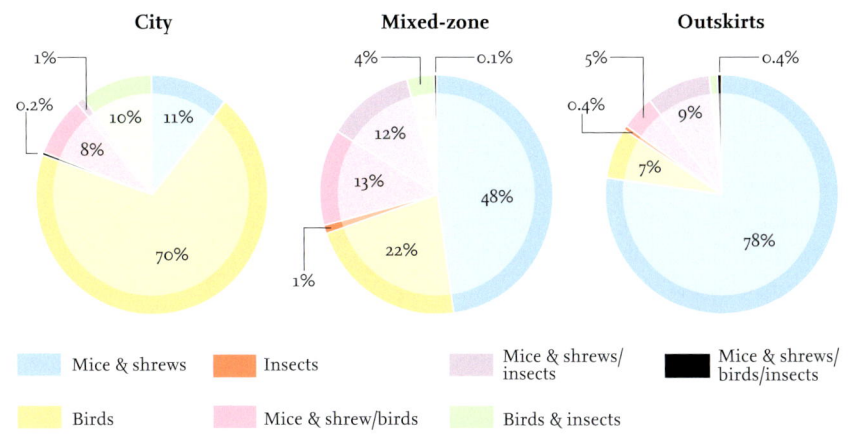

FIG 125. Variation of diet for urban/suburban Kestrels. 'City' refers to an area with 75–95% of buildings within a 3 km² Kestrel hunting range. For the 'mixed zone' this percentage reduces to 45–60%, the remaining area being urban green, fallow land or garden. For the 'outskirts' the percentage of buildings is 25–40%, with increased urban green and fallow land, and the huge gardens of villa-type accommodation. Redrawn from Kübler et al. 2005.

Hunting strategy and food caching

Kestrel hunting techniques are dealt with in detail in Chapter 3. Although well known for their use of hovering as a hunting technique, Kestrels also hunt from perches, choosing a perch at a height which allows a wide scanning area and watching for movement on the ground. Once prey is detected the Kestrel will then fly directly to it or may hover above it briefly. In general in perch-hunting the falcon will move position every few minutes, taking up a new perch. Kestrels will also soar, but this not a frequently used technique as it requires specific weather conditions, rising thermals that do not carry the bird too high or too fast, as either would (presumably) make spotting small rodents more difficult. Kestrels will occasionally use a combination of soaring and hovering to move across the landscape, the hovering pauses allowing a better scan of likely-looking areas.

Like all raptors, Kestrels will also hunt opportunistically. As noted in Chapter 6, Trollope (2012) reported seeing Hobbies following a steam train which was flushing dragonflies from track-side ditches. Walker (2012) picked up on this observation to note that his father regularly saw Kestrels following trains in the 1960s as the trains of the day, hauled by steam locomotives, regular shot jets of steam into track-side vegetation which would flush prey.

To the surprise of few, and of no surprise at all to those who have, for instance, visited the feeding stations set up for Red Kites after the conservation effort to boost numbers of the species in Britain, such stations are known to influence the raptors' behaviour, large numbers of birds congregating at the same time each day. Feeding time becomes such a part of the birds' daily time budget that the human feeders have to adjust times to allow for changes to/from British Summer Time, the birds (unsurprisingly) having little concept of the decision to alter the clocks. It is therefore no surprise to know that birds are able to comprehend the feeding times of their prey. In a study in the Netherlands the researchers noted that the voles emerged from their burrows to feed in two-hour cycles, and that the arrival of Kestrels to hunt corresponded with these probable emergence times (RUG/RIJP 1982). The number of Kestrels hunting decreased over the two-hour feeding time as a successful bird would catch prey and fly off to consume it, perhaps not returning until the next vole feeding period (Fig. 126). The Dutch team noted that Hen Harriers saved about 90 minutes of flight-hunting daily by adopting this temporally linked behaviour (corresponding to about 12% of their daily energy intake). It must be assumed that Kestrels benefit from a similar reduction.

My own observations also suggest, as seems intuitively obvious, that Kestrels not only know the favourable times to hunt, but also the most favourable locations within their territory, and adjust their hunting behaviour accordingly.

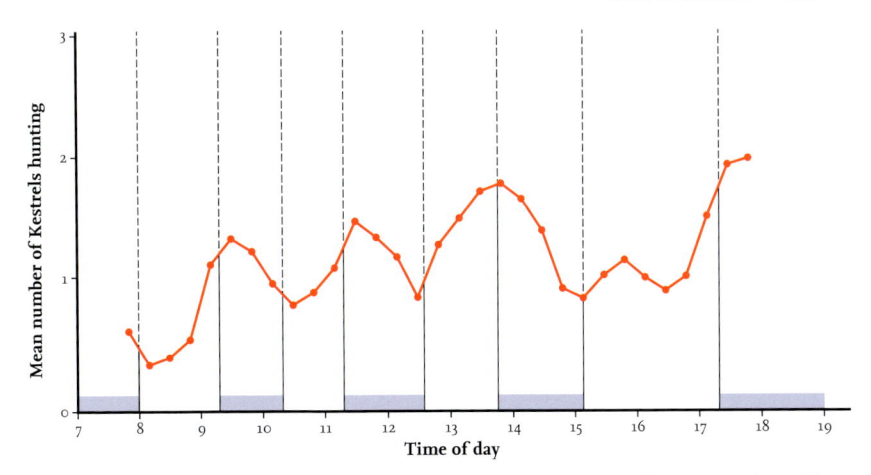

FIG 126. Number of Kestrels flight-hunting a field in Holland averaged over a number of days in February 1982. The shaded areas are the times of vole surface activity. Points are three-point running means of average numbers for each 20-minute period. Redrawn from RUG/RIJP 1982.

For the bird enthusiast, watching hunting behaviour of the species over a relatively short period will therefore allow the observer to identify favoured positions and so increase the likelihood of seeing hunting.

Kestrels usually consume invertebrate prey on the ground, though larger insects may be lifted into the air, and even partially consumed in the manner of Hobbies while flying to a nearby perch. Mammals and birds are taken to a perch: birds are plucked before the meat is taken in a succession of torn-off morsels; mammals are eaten in similar fashion, usually after an attempt to remove the fur. Hungry Kestrels will consume all of their prey, but the internal organs are often discarded by well-fed birds, the grass-filled stomachs of voles seeming to be especially distasteful (or pointless in view of the available energy content). Kestrels will also cache food, tending to cache larger prey items, particularly if smaller items have already been consumed. Masman *et al.* (1986) provide interesting data on the weights of voles (in this case Common Voles, as the study was carried out in the Netherlands) eaten, fed to chicks or cached, which indicates that adult birds tend to consume smaller voles, feeding larger specimens to the chicks and caching the largest (Fig. 127). In their study of the energy intake of Kestrels (see below) Masman *et al.* (1986) noted that it was clear that the birds were heavily dependent on cached food during days when the weather prevented hunting, a fact which probably explains why it is the larger prey that are cached.

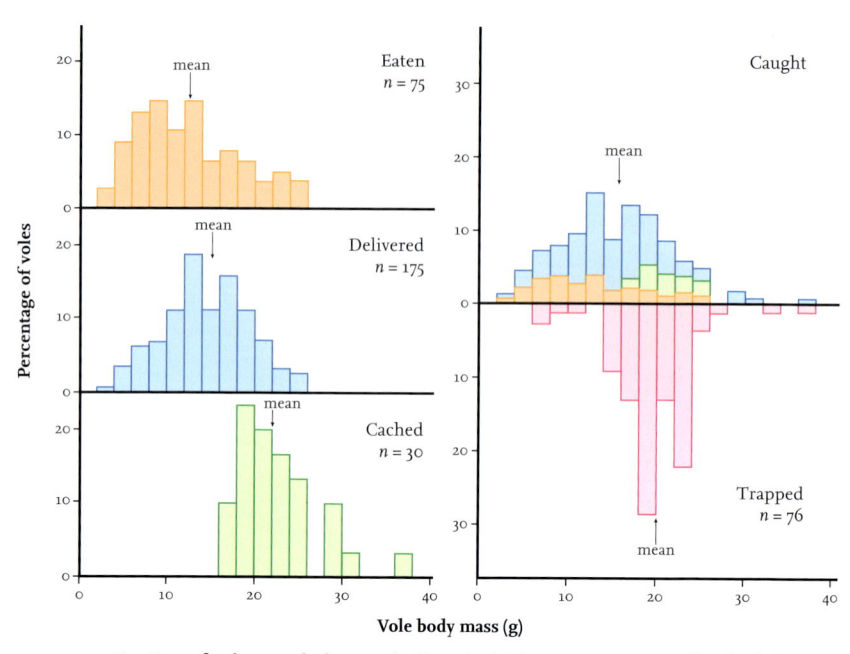

FIG 127. Fraction of voles caught by a male Kestrel which were eaten immediately, fed to the female/nestlings or cached. Clearly the male is making decisions by assessing the mass of the prey. In the right-hand histogram the distribution of mass of total voles caught by the male is compared to the distribution of vole masses trapped by the Dutch experimenters. The histograms imply that the male Kestrel is preferentially taking lighter voles, but the researchers note that biases in both samples may account for the difference and no firm conclusion can be drawn. Redrawn from Masman *et al.* 1986.

There is very limited information on the success rate of hunting Kestrels. Steen *et al.* (2012) give figures for the mass delivery rate of various prey types – voles, shrews, lizards and birds – during chick raising, but conversion of this to hunting success is too complex for a definitive estimate. I once photographed six prey deliveries (four rodents, one lizard and one bird) to a brood of five 14-day old chicks during a period of 2 hours 8 minutes. The female Kestrel stood guard for some, but not all of the time, so it is not clear what the total hunting time of the pair was, but there were five prey captures in the total time, i.e. one every 25 minutes including time to and from the hunt site and, on occasions, prey passes from male to female.

Caching is most likely to occur if conditions allow significant hunting success. Village (1990) reports two occasions on which Kestrels discovered young

FIG 128. Flight-hunting (hovering) Kestrel. (James Sellen)

rats, as a result of nest disturbance by harvesting on one occasion, juveniles making early explorations from the nest on the other: the Kestrels were able to take five or six in the space of a few minutes, caching them all. Such caching would be particularly useful if there are chicks to feed, but is also a useful insurance against tomorrow's hunting being less successful for any of a number of reasons. Despite the fact that it appears to invite theft by scavengers, most caches are on the ground (Table 17). This is perhaps because invariably Kestrels

TABLE 17 Kestrel food cache sites. Data from Village 1990.

Cache position	Percentages of 45 identified caches
On the ground	
– at base of post, pole or tree stump	22
– tuft of grass or straw	33
– clod of earth	16
– stone	2
Total percentage on the ground	**73**
Above ground	
– on buildings	5
– on fence posts	5
– on straw stacks	11
– in trees or shrubs	6
Total percentage above ground	**27**

are hunting on open ground with few possible above-ground cache sites, but might also be because cached food is most frequently retrieved on the same day or early the following day, so the likelihood of theft is reduced. Caches are usually on a prominent tussock or at the base of a post, but despite the bird retrieving the prey within a relatively short period, Kestrels seems to lack the legendary memories of corvids (particularly Jays) and may fail to find their caches.

While caching obviously has benefits in times of prey abundance, it is also seen in winter, when it appears to function as a means of allowing the bird to eat an evening meal. Rijnsdorp *et al.* (1981) suggested that this behaviour allows the bird to hunt more efficiently by reducing body weight during the day, quoting a figure of 7% of daily energy expenditure, if a 22 g vole was consumed just before nightfall. However, the researchers' observation was based on a single male Kestrel eating during summer evenings and so may be explained by the need to feed chicks during the day. In winter a more logical explanation would seem to be that for a falcon having to endure the long, cold hours of darkness with no opportunity to hunt, eating an evening meal is a survival strategy.

Food consumption and energy balance
As already noted, the Raptor Group at Groningen University has produced a remarkable body of work on Kestrels, which includes an accurate study of the energy intake and expenditure of free-living Kestrels, research in the field backed up by some excellent laboratory experiments. In the field Kestrels were observed on 375 days over a seven-year period (Masman *et al.* 1986), the birds consuming 1,944 prey items. By weighing, then replacing, 43 cached items which were later retrieved and eaten by the birds, the time taken to consume a prey item of known species and a given weight was calculated, and this time was used to estimate the weight of prey of the same species observed to be eaten on other occasions. For other species, average weights were taken from snap-trap specimens (mammals) or estimated (birds). The data were then used to assess the energy intake throughout the year for both male and female birds. Figure 129 indicates that energy intake was highest during the breeding season (April–July) and lowest during the moult (August, September) for both sexes.

The peak intake rate for the female corresponded to the period of egg laying, while for the male it corresponded to the period of chick feeding. What is striking is the sharp 50% fall in female energy intake during the first ten post-hatching days. During that period the female consumes very little of the prey delivered by the male, taking only small amounts of skin and the intestines, the latter probably mainly to provide water. However, it must be remembered that during this period her energy requirements are at a minimum, as she is largely inactive. In terms

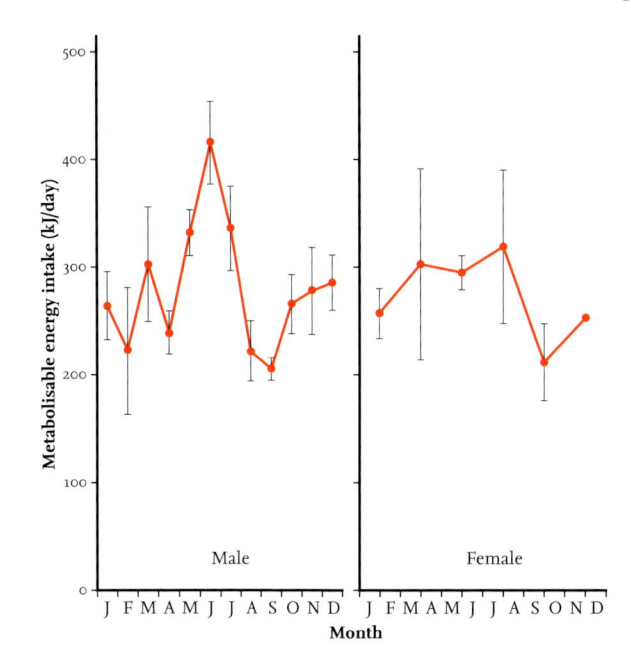

FIG 129. Monthly mean daily metabolisable energy intake for male Kestrels and bimonthly mean for female Kestrels throughout the year, together with standard errors on each mean value. Redrawn from Masman *et al.* 1986.

of vole consumption, the daily average throughout the year of both male and female is about four rodents, the male requiring a further eight rodents per day to satisfy the energy requirements of brood feeding, the female six rodents per day during egg laying. The mean intake during winter was similar for both males and females, reflecting the limited sexual dimorphism in the Kestrel.

Having established the energy intake of Kestrels, what was required next was an estimate of energy expenditure. Historically this has been calculated by using a 'time budget', that is observing the activity of a bird during a day – the time spent flying, preening, loafing etc. – coupled with an understanding of the energy required for the bird to fuel its vital processes and to feed, and estimating total energy expenditure for each. This requires knowledge of the energy requirements of each activity, particularly of flying, which is clearly the most energy-intensive.

The Dutch team (Masman *et al.* 1988b) then calculated total energy expenditure (E) by adding the components of this equation:

$$E = B + T + A + H + S \text{ (kJ/day)}$$

where

B is a basal component, the energy required to keep a thermoneutral fasting bird alive

T is the energy required for thermoregulation (i.e. to overcome heat loss). The Dutch team actually calculated not only heat loss for a fully fledged bird, but also the additional heat loss by a bird in moult (T_r) as feather loss increases heat loss

A is the energy required for activity, which was subdivided as A_b (activities other than flying), A_f (flight) and A_h (flight-hunting)

H is the energy required for feeding (i.e. digestion)

S is the energy required for tissue synthesis (e.g. feather synthesis during moulting)

Some of the above components can be estimated using standard laboratory methods, such as calorimetry, but others required more ingenious methods. To calculate *T* the researchers used, among other things, a heated taxidermic Kestrel mounted on the roof of their building and calculated the heat loss in various weather conditions. Even more ingenious was the use of a bird trained to fly along the corridors of the university building between two handlers in exchange for a food titbit (Masman & Klaassen 1987). If the bird was weighed prior to the testing, and the titbits were organised to maintain body weight, this allowed the energy input for a given flight mileage to be calculated (allowing for the energy requirements of the less energetic activities between flights which could be more easily measured). The trained bird was persuaded to fly up to 20 km during the study. The results on the trained bird were partially checked with tests on captured live birds which were injected with heavy water (Note 5.3).

The results of the Dutch study (Fig. 130) indicate that flying is energy-intensive, Masman *et al.* (1988b) calculating that it requires about 62 W/kg, though interestingly they found that the costs of directional flying and flight-hunting were similar. When flying, Kestrels therefore compare favourably with the sprinter Usain Bolt, who, when winning his 2012 Olympic gold medal developed a maximum power output of 2,619.5 W or 29.1 W/kg, as he weighs 90 kg. Since flying is usually more sustained than sprinting, a more reasonable comparison might be with the power output of Chris Froome during a climb on one stage of the 2015 Tour de France, a ride which led to intense speculation about his performance. During the 41.5-minute climb Froome generated an average of 414 W, yielding a power/weight ratio of 5.78 W/kg, since he is lighter than Bolt at 67.5 kg (sprint cyclists generate outputs closer to that of Bolt). In more recent tests carried out under scientific conditions (see the *Guardian* newspaper 4 December 2015 – a more complete report of the tests was given in the January/February 2016 edition of *Esquire* magazine) Froome generated 6.25 W/kg over a sustained period. Of course Kestrels are a better aerodynamic shape for flying than Usain Bolt is for running or Chris Froome is for cycling – the best estimate being that Bolt uses 92% of his energy output to overcome drag, a rather smaller percentage being

THE KESTREL · 227

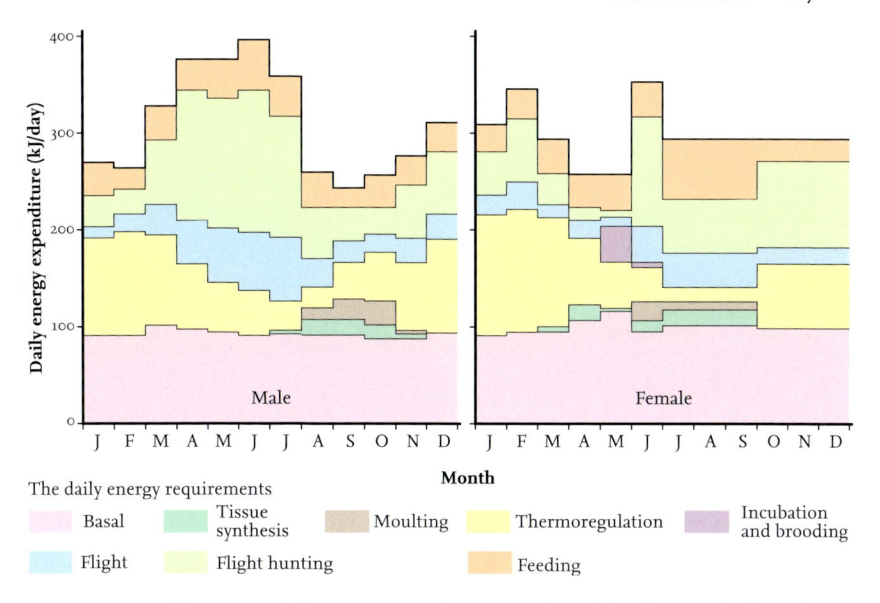

FIG 130. Monthly average daily energy expenditure in male and female Kestrels throughout the year. Redrawn from Masman *et al.* 1988b.

required by the cyclist. But despite Kestrels (and other birds) being both built for it, and good at it, flying is hard work.

Having now calculated both energy input and energy expenditure, the Groningen team could compare the two (Fig. 131). The differences between energy

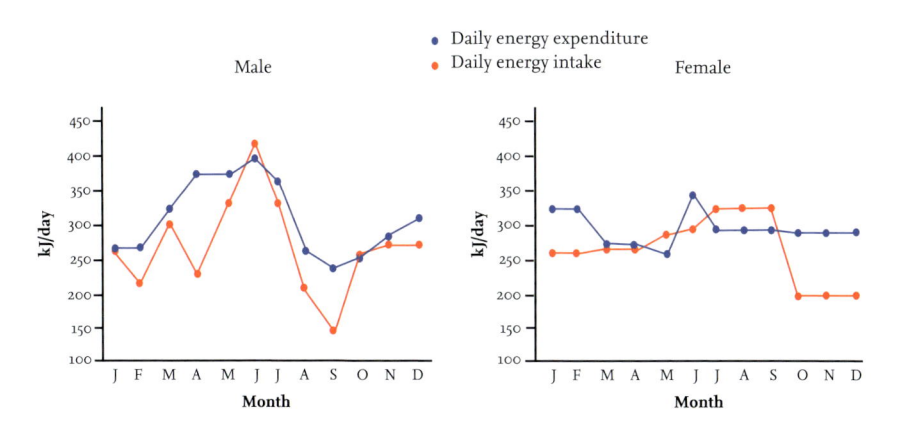

FIG 131. Variation of daily energy intake and expenditure in male and female Kestrels throughout the year. Redrawn from data in Masman *et al.* 1988b.

input and output is most instructively considered in terms of the variation in body weight of male and female Kestrels, and by considering the changes not by time of year but by the phase of the birds' life during the breeding and non-breeding periods of the year (Fig. 132).

Figure 132 again indicates that for females, energy expenditure is at a minimum during the courtship feeding stage (see Chapter 2), when much of her food is provided by the male. In this phase she is able to store body reserves in readiness for egg laying. With egg laying, her body weight reduces, and reduces further once the eggs hatch as she is unable to hunt to feed herself and the majority of the food

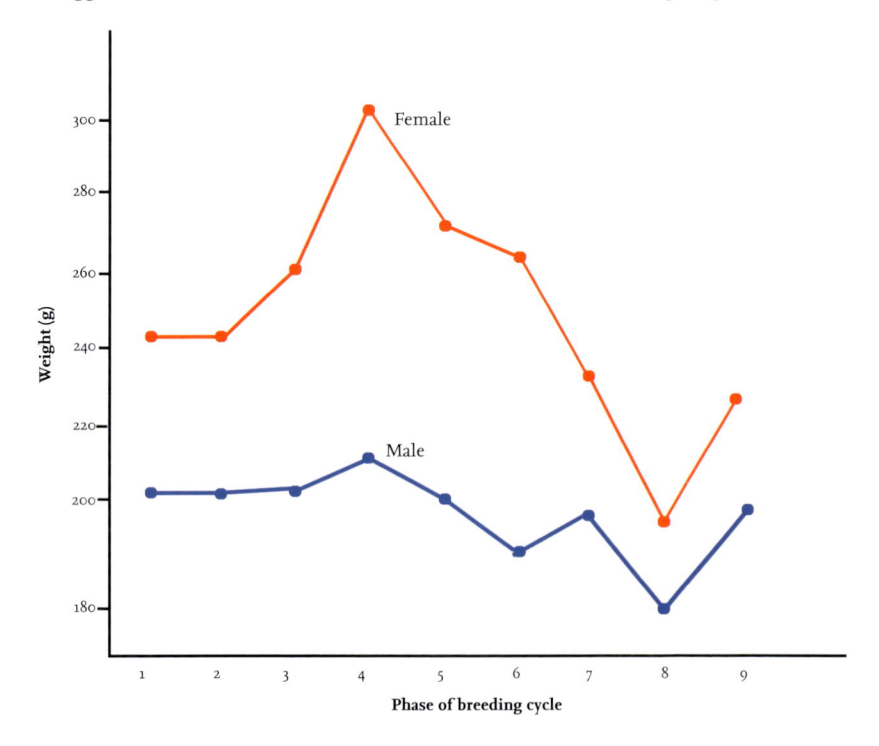

FIG 132. Variation of body weight in male and female Kestrels by phase of the annual cycle. Phases are:

1. Wintering unpaired
2. Wintering paired
3. Courtship feeding
4. Egg laying
5. Incubation
6. Nestlings below the age of 10 days
7. Nestlings above the age of 10 days
8. Dependent juveniles
9. Post reproductive moult

Redrawn from data in Masman *et al.* 1986.

provided by the male is given to the chicks to aid rapid growth. Even after the female is able to hunt, her body weight still declines because of the demands of the nestlings. Only when these become independent is the female able to replenish body reserves. By contrast, the male's energy expenditure remains high throughout the breeding phase, the need to feed both the female and, later, the chicks requiring him to hunt for prolonged periods (Fig. 133).

The Dutch study also indicated another aspect of the male's energy requirements during the period of intensive feeding of hatched young (the first ten days). During this period the male is providing food for the chicks, for the female and for himself, as he must fuel the exertions of hunting. What Masman *et al.* (1986) found was that if the male spent less than about 4.6 hours of flight-hunting his food consumption was adequate in supplying the energy requirements of hunting. But beyond 4.6 hours the male was unable to process food into energy fast enough to equate the energy outlay in hunting and despite consuming perhaps half his body weight in voles, he would lose weight. While the value of 4.6 hours is obviously specific to a given male, the spread of male body weights implies that for most male Kestrels, flight-hunting for more than 5 hours will involve a loss of body weight.

One final but equally fascinating aspect of the work of the Dutch group was in their compilation of the way in which male and female Kestrels spend their time during the day for each month of the year, or phase of their breeding/non-breeding cycle, and of how the activities which form their time budget vary with environmental conditions. This is shown in Figs 134 and 135. What is clear from

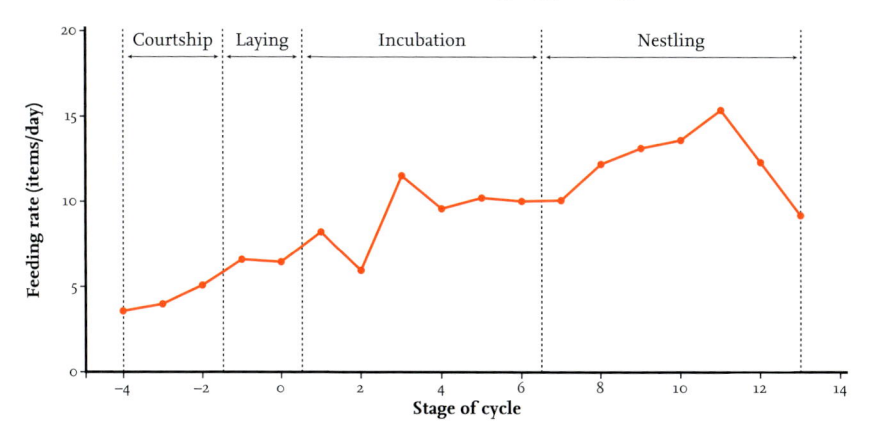

FIG 133. Rate of delivery of prey during the breeding cycle by a male Kestrel. Each point is the mean of five nests over a five-day period. The horizontal axis is in weeks, with 'o' being the time the clutch was completed. Redrawn from data in Tinbergen 1940.

230 · FALCONS

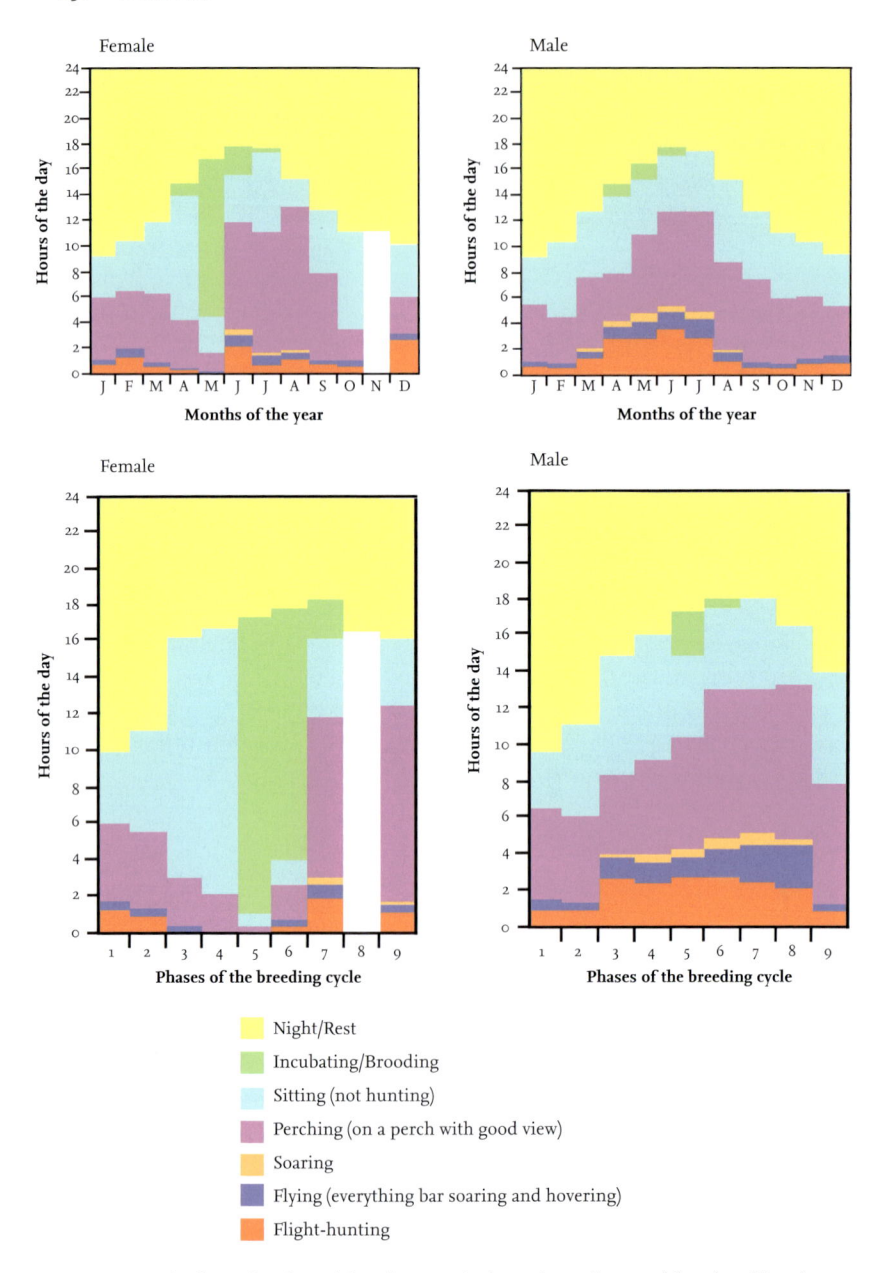

- Night/Rest
- Incubating/Brooding
- Sitting (not hunting)
- Perching (on a perch with good view)
- Soaring
- Flying (everything bar soaring and hovering)
- Flight-hunting

FIG 134. Time budget of male and female Kestrels throughout the year (above) and by phase of the breeding cycle (below). Phases of the breeding cycle are as for Fig. 132. Perching means the bird was perch-hunting, whereas sitting means the bird was sitting on the ground, or sheltering. Redrawn from Masman *et al.* 1988a.

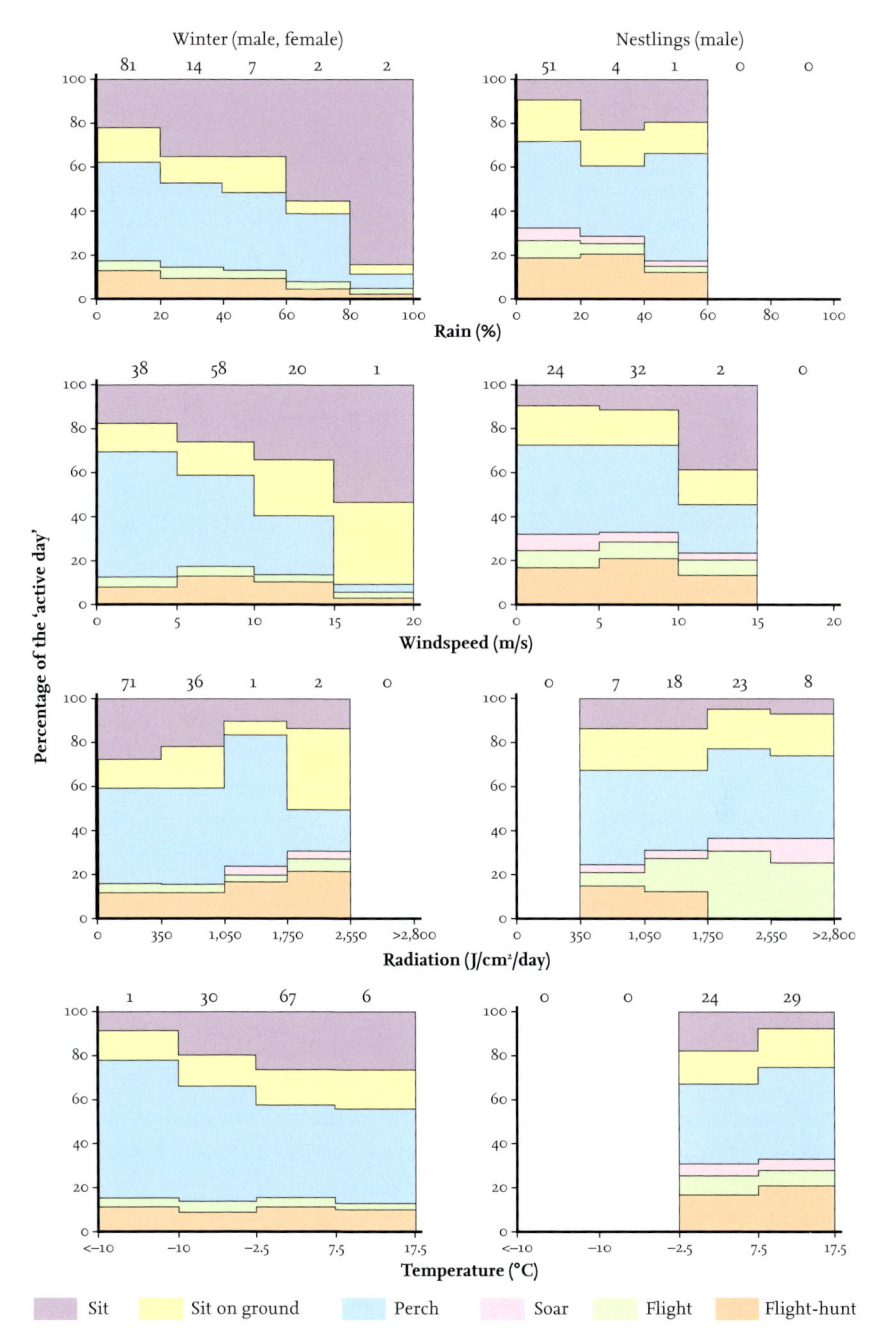

FIG 135. Time budget, expressed as percentage of active day, of adult Kestrels during the winter, and of male Kestrels during the nestling phase of breeding, plotted against a range of environmental factors. Rainfall percentages are defined by hours of the day in which rain ≥ 2 mm fell. Sample sizes shown at top of each graph. Redrawn from Masman *et al.* 1988a.

these figures, and is succinctly set down in another report by the Dutch group (Masman *et al.* 1988a), is that during the summer Kestrels maximise their daily energy gain in order to maximise their reproductive output, while in winter they minimise their energy expenditure in order to minimise their daily energy requirements.

TERRITORY

Village (1990) differentiates between a Kestrel's territory and its home range, the former being the area around the bird's nest from which it excludes conspecifics and competitors, whereas the latter is the area over which it hunts. As Village notes, the home range can be larger than the territory, but never smaller.

Village observed that in his Scottish study area non-breeding ranges were initially smaller than summer ranges, but that as the population declined, birds migrating away from their breeding territories, range sizes increased. He also noted that the ranges were defended, so that winter ranges became territories, probably as a consequence of the reduction in prey numbers, vole breeding ceasing at the approach of winter: with a diminishing vole population, a bird's interest in increasing its hunting range and in maintaining it against competitors increased. Territories were also held primarily by single birds. In England the winter situation was different, as the Kestrel population was more stable, migration being reduced and breeding pairs often staying together and maintaining much the same range during the non-breeding season.

The change in population in Village's less productive Scottish study area also produced a more noticeable change in ranges during spring and summer. With the requirement to feed chicks, the Kestrels needed a larger range over which to hunt, particularly as the ranges were shared with adjacent breeding pairs. Initially, birds holding winter territories into which newcomers were seeking to advance attempted to hold on to their territories with displays and conflicts, but ultimately pressure from incoming pairs forced territory sizes to diminish. However, at the same time, home ranges increased, and significant range overlaps occurred. Within the areas of overlap, hunting male Kestrels will occasionally have aerial jousts, but these are invariably short-lived, and apparently inconclusive, as both birds go back to hunting when they are concluded. It is possible that males adjust their hunting times to avoid being in the same area as another, but as we have already noted, since the males hunt when they know their prey is most likely to be active, the more likely pattern is mutual tolerance in a situation of prey abundance (vole populations tending to increase during the summer), after a brief display to ensure that neither bird is willing to be driven away. In times of prey shortage, mutual tolerance becomes a less attractive option, and in a study of Kestrels and Long-eared Owls Korpimäki (1987) noted that at such times 'competition theory', the idea that the overlap of diet in neighbouring pairs of a species will reduce, apparently holds.

In his English study areas, Village (1990) noted that although the influx of newcomers was reduced in comparison to his Scottish area, so that territory sizes remained much the same, a similar increase in range size and bird behaviour was observed. Within their territory, male behaviour was very different to within their ranges, the intrusion of other males not being tolerated as the territory holders protected their females. In an experiment in which wild breeding Kestrels were presented with an adult caged Kestrel, Wiklund & Village (1992) noted that the male of the breeding pair always responded aggressively to a male intruder, but a third of males displayed to an intruder female. Females were aggressive to female intruders before laying had commenced and after the eggs had hatched, but less so between these periods, as might be expected, as it in the interests of the female to keep her mate away from other females at these times. Wiklund & Village considered that the relative lack of female aggression during the egg-laying period was explained by the female's increased body weight at this time, which reduces her flying ability and therefore increases the risks of combat. Once the eggs had hatched, female aggressiveness to a female intruder increased with brood size. Again this is a natural response to the need to keep her mate away from other females during a period when he is sole provider of food for herself and her brood, and larger broods require more intensive hunting. By contrast, females actually solicited male intruders during the courtship period, though they were more aggressive once eggs had hatched.

Shrubb (1993a) notes that although attacks by the defending bird do occasionally result in physical contact this is rare. If it does occur, the birds may lock talons in the air, and may even fight on the ground, such fights occasionally ending in injury or death. However, a perched bird attacked by a territory owner usually flies off, while the attacker of a flying intruder will position itself beneath the offender, fan its tail and force the offender upwards and away. Often during this manoeuvre the territory holder will perform the 'shivering' flight (see *Displays*, below). Shrubb also noted a seasonality to territorial displays, these peaking in early spring when the imperative was to secure a breeding territory, nest site and mate; during June when the need to feed growing chicks requires control of a hunting range; and in autumn when the dispersal of juveniles increases the pressure on available hunting land.

The overall pattern of behaviour – smaller summer territories, with larger home ranges, followed by winter territories which correspond to home ranges, so that territories increased in size in winter, while ranges decreased – has been noted elsewhere (Cavé 1967, Shrubb 1993a) – and so is likely to be replicated across the species' range, with winter territory defence being driven by the need to protect food supplies, and summer territory defence by the need to protect females from the attentions of other males.

The fact that territories and home ranges differ in summer, and that winter territories are dependent on prey availability makes defining the size of each difficult, but in general it seems that the summer territory of a Kestrel pair is 1–2 km^2, while the home range is usually 2–3 times as large (but may be up to 5 times larger). In winter, territories/ranges in areas of stable population may increase to 2–3 km^2, but may be larger (perhaps 5 km^2) in areas in which the summer population decreases (data from Shrubb 1993a and Village 1990). In all cases the variation in range size is dependent on vole population: Village (1982) noted a clear inverse correlation between size and vole density in his study areas at all times of year.

BREEDING

Kestrels are essentially monogamous, though polygynous males have been recorded. Korpimäki (1988) hypothesised that polygyny in raptors was dependent on several factors, and considered it would be higher in rodent-eating than in bird-eating species, as rodent populations were more subject to cyclic fluctuations that saw relatively frequent higher densities. He noted that a consequence of this would be greater polygyny in northern rodent-eating raptors, as the peak population densities of rodents tended to be higher in northern latitudes; and that polygyny would be more frequently seen in species in which pair bonding was annual rather than longer-term, as the latter favoured both strong bonding and strongly held territories. As the Kestrel was a northern, rodent-eating, annual-bonding species Korpimäki anticipated seeing polygyny expressed in good rodent years, and that is indeed what he saw, 1985 and 1986 being peak rodent years, with 4% and 10% polygyny. Village (1990), from his own study and other studies in the Netherlands, suggests a lower figure of 1–2% of pairings in areas which do not see such exaggerated rodent peaks as occur in Fennoscandia. In either case, the low incidence is consistent with the view that it represents non-standard mating behaviour which arises only when conditions offer the opportunity. Shrubb

(1993a) observed one such opportunity. He noticed a female soliciting the male of an established pair with clear mating display flights over the pair's nest site, and also at a second potential nest site some distance away. The male seemed intent on driving the second female off – as, occasionally, did his mate – but she persisted. Ultimately the male seemed to accept the second female, though his mate still attempted to drive her away. Shrubb then found the first female dead at the nest, sitting on four now chilled eggs: she had apparently been poisoned. He then discovered that the second female was incubating her own clutch, and from the timing it was clear that the male had mated with the second female while his first mate was alive and incubating.

Glutz von Blotzheim et al. (1971) claimed that polygyny also occurred in colonial nesting situations, but this is much more difficult to prove without DNA analysis and so is conjectural, though it is obviously true that opportunities for male infidelity would be increased. Polyandry is also claimed by Glutz von Blotzheim et al., and by Packham (1985a). In each case the behaviour could only be inferred by observation of two males feeding a single female, but the use of DNA has allowed a more definitive study. Korpimäki et al. (1996) carried out DNA analysis of Kestrel egg clutches during the years 1990–1992, and found that during 1990 and 1992, when vole numbers were low, there was no evidence of the paternity of a clutch being shared by more than one male, but in 1991, when vole numbers were high, 7% of 27 broods (5% of 112 chicks) showed evidence of extra-pair copulation by the female. This suggests that when conditions allow, both male and female Kestrels may explore the option of extra-pair copulation to enhance the chances of passing on their genes. For female Kestrels, other than chasing away females potentially soliciting their mates, there is little that they can do to prevent the male from mating with other females, and policing other females becomes increasingly difficult once incubation has begun. Their own behaviour in terms of extra-pair mating may also be regulated by the need to maintain male care, both for themselves and for their brood, such care being potentially jeopardised by infidelity. For the male Kestrel, strategies for protecting his own interests are available, and I will examine these when dealing with copulation behaviour below.

Pair formation depends, in part, on the population of a given area. In areas where the winter population of birds is relatively stable, some pairs may stay together through the winter and will remain paired for the new spring. In cases where there are males and females in the area who have not remained paired, the birds may start courtship behaviour during the late winter. Any remaining unpaired birds will then pair with migrants arriving as spring approaches, the migrants then pairing with other migrants once the surplus of wintering birds has been exhausted. In more northerly areas of the UK where few birds overwinter, the bulk of the population arriving in early spring, the early arrivals tend to pair up with resident birds, taking advantage of formed territories and the understanding of feeding areas to take potentially better mates. In his study areas Village (1990) noted that in general adult birds paired with other adults, with first-year birds – both male and female Kestrels can mate in their first year – tending to pair with other first-years. Cross-pairing by age did occur, but this was almost exclusively adult males with first-year females. It seems that adult females have a very marked preference for adult males, presumably working on the principle that adult birds, being likely to have been through the breeding cycle before, know the ropes, as it were, and so are more dependable sources of food, as well as their survival being an indication of good genes. Males seem much more likely to take the risk that a first-year female will be as dependable an incubator and chick rearer. In his studies Village (1990) noted the formation of 358 Kestrel pairs and found that 71% were adult–adult, 9% were first-year pairings, 17% were adult male–first-year female, with only 3% of adult females mating with first-year males. The proportion of birds apparently fit and able to breed, but not breeding, were adult males 25%, adult females 21%, first-year males 67%, first-year females 34%. (See also the comments on the breeding age difference between the sexes in Chapter 2.)

As noted when discussing the plumage of juvenile birds, both male and female juveniles look similar to adult females. In a study in Finland Hakkarainen *et al.* (1993) considered why juvenile male Kestrels have female-like plumage. They noted that this phenomenon is found in many dichromatic species during their first potential breeding year, and that two hypotheses have been put forward as an explanation. In the *female-mimicry* hypothesis it is conjectured that the mimicry aids the juvenile males to mate by deceiving adult males into believing that they are females, and therefore not competitors for mates. In the *status-signalling* hypothesis the mimicry allows adult males to differentiate low-status males, again reducing competition. This second hypothesis assumes that adult male Kestrels can distinguish sex. The Finnish team noted that juvenile males tended to choose breeding sites closer to adult males, and that this increased both their mating success and the outcome success of the breeding, particularly if they mated with adult females. This suggested that plumage mimicry was an adaptive feature to enhance breeding potential, but still did not differentiate between the two hypotheses. To aid in distinguishing the two options, the Finnish team showed captive adult male Kestrels both adult female and female-like juvenile males. If the two were shown simultaneously the adult males preferred the females, but if the two were shown separately the adult males were unable to distinguish them. This strongly suggests that adult male

Kestrels are not good at distinguishing sex, providing evidence for the female-mimicry hypothesis.

With the proviso that mate choice follows the statistics of Village (1990) as set down above, mate selection seems random. In a study of American Kestrels, Duncan & Bird (1989) found that females did not discriminate against male siblings in their choice of mate, though they did prefer males who displayed more actively. The authors suggest that high mortality and the limited number of nest sites available may mean that incest is rare in the wild and so may not influence mate selection. Since the Common Kestrel is subject to similar conditions, this lack of an apparently evolutionarily advantageous strategy may also be seen in the UK population, and it is known that incestuous relationships exist in other UK falcons. However, as the females in the Duncan & Bird study were captive it might be argued that they had little choice in mates and so might have exhibited behaviour which was rarer in the wild.

In a study of wild birds, Palokangas et al. (1994) noted that female Kestrels preferentially chose males with bright plumage (as measured in visible light). Zampiga et al. (2008) extended this by looking at the potential influence of ultraviolet (UV) signalling by male Kestrels, allowing captive females to view two males, one in front of, and one behind, a filter which blocked UV light. The females preferred the male with the UV-reflecting plumage, as measured by the time they spent closer to the male without the filter. These studies suggest that plumage may be a good indicator of male quality, and more recently Piault et al. (2012) have suggested that plumage, specifically the subterminal band, of juvenile birds may differ, depending on the condition of the bird. In a separate study Hakkarainen et al. (1996) trapped Kestrels (12 males and 14 females) in central Finland and kept them in aviaries so that light and diet could be controlled. The body mass, wing and tarsus length of the male Kestrels was measured. In early spring the 'daylight' was increased suddenly from 7 to 20 hours day, and the female diet was increased to advance their sexual activity. The females were then shown the male Kestrels in a controlled way so their preferences could be registered. The males were also tested for hunting success by introducing rodents to their enclosures and measuring the success rate of attacks on them. The Finnish team found that the female Kestrels preferred males with a smaller body mass and smaller tarsus, but did not seem to express any preference by wing length. However, the preference for smaller males and smaller tarsus was weak and apparent only when the difference in each was (relatively) large. When hunting success was assessed, it did not accord precisely with the weak female preference, as smaller, shorter-winged males were more successful than heavier, longer-winged males, but tarsus length seemed unrelated to hunting success.

The Finnish study concluded that female Kestrels may be biased towards smaller males, as such a size bias implies superior hunting success and, hence, improves the likelihood of breeding success. The study also provides some support for the idea that reversed sexual dimorphism in falcons (see Chapter 2) is related to breeding protocol.

The work of Village (1990) also suggests that mate selection is not random, reporting instances where pairs seen early in the breeding season were later observed to have not bred. In each case the male had remained on his territory and bred with another female. Village conjectured that in some cases the first female had died, but noted a small number of cases in which the first female left and bred with another male. In these latter cases it appears that the first female was ousted by the second, implying that some females select mates other than by chance encounter.

Each of these studies suggests that female Kestrels respond to plumage signals which indicate male quality and the likelihood of breeding success.

Displays
In the most frequently described displays, the two falcons soar and circle at a considerable height, frequently with fanned tails. During these flights the male (much more rarely the female) will often exhibiting a rocking (e.g. Village 1990, Shrubb 1993a) or rolling (e.g. Glutz von Blotzheim *et al.* 1971) flight in which he moves horizontally with jerking wing-beats, occasionally rocking (or rolling) from side to side so as to flash his underwings. Village (1990) considers this to be most often seen when there is intrusion into the male's territory, which would see the display as a territorial, as much as a courtship, display, but Shrubb (1993a) considers it much more a mating display. What Village (1990) does not note is a display mentioned by both Walpole-Bond (1938) and Glutz von Blotzheim *et al.* (1971) in which the male makes mock attacks on the female, occasionally brushing her with his wings as she evades his approach. Shrubb (1993a) also remarks on this display, noting that occasionally a male will stoop so close to a perched female that she flinches away, and that if this is performed when the female is in flight she will roll so as to point her talons at the approaching male.

The V-flight is another courtship display, the male soliciting the female by pointing out a suitable nesting site, the name deriving from the male holding his wings in a V-shape as he does so. Village (1990) states that the V-flight is invariably performed at speed, but others have suggested a more leisurely approach to the nest site by the male: the difference appears to derive from the start position of the birds – if the pair are in the soaring flight, then the approach is rapid, while if the pair are at a lower altitude the approach is slower. Females can also perform the V-flight, sometimes as a prelude to potential nest inspection, but also as an invitation to copulate. Shrubb (1993a) also notes that while the male V-flight seems primarily employed during mate attraction or nest selection, the female V-flight is more closely associated with territorial defence, the female often performing the flight while the male is seeing off the intruder.

The final common display is a 'winnowing' (Village 1990) or 'shivering' (Shrubb 1993a) flight, called the *Zitterflug* – trembling flight – by Tinbergen (1940), in which either the male or female flies close to the nest, travelling slowly with wings that vibrate quickly. Winnowing is seen as a prelude to, or following, copulation, but may also be used to see off intruders. Juvenile birds also winnow when soliciting food from adults.

Shrubb also mentions two further displays, each of which he saw rarely and only performed by female Kestrels. The first was a slow flight with exaggerated wing-beats, similar to that seen in hawks and buzzards, the other a parachuting flight with legs dangling, again in the manner of buzzards. Shrubb also considers that perching may be a territorial display. He notes that during the winter Kestrels will often sit in prominent positions in poor weather, when seeking shelter would appear a better alternative, and considers that such behaviour must therefore have an ulterior motive, with territory defence being the obvious candidate.

Although most courtship displays are aerial (and certainly most of the observed displaying is aerial), a Kestrel pair may also indulge in perched displays, such a bowing and bill nibbling; the female may also beg for food.

Courtship may start early for pairs which have overwintered at breeding sites, in which case the courtship period may be lengthy. For birds arriving late at breeding grounds, courtship must be curtailed if egg laying is not to be delayed. In his work at his Scottish study area Village (1990) noted a linear relationship between length of courtship, measured as pair formation to first egg laying, and date of pairing (Fig. 136).

The male starts to feed the female during courtship, the female ceasing to hunt and not resuming until the hatchlings are about ten days old. That the female's hunting cessation allows a decrease in energy expenditure as a prelude to egg laying, which is intuitively obvious, is borne out by a study by Meijer (1988), who noted a correlation between the start of courtship feeding and the laying of the first egg. And while the female is reducing her energy expenditure the male is increasing his (see Fig. 130), catering not only for the food requirements of the female, but also his own in policing his territory. Village (1983b) measured body weight in both males and females during the courtship/egg-laying/incubation period, his data indicating that the male body weight decreases slowly during the

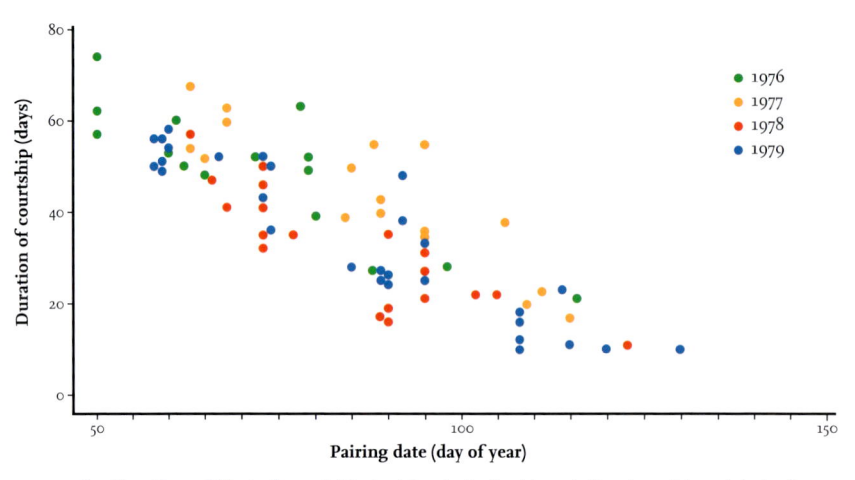

FIG 136. Duration of Kestrel courtship (pairing to laying) in relation to pairing date in four successive years in southern Scotland. Redrawn from Village 1990.

period, while that of the female increases during the courtship phase, decreasing rather more sharply after egg laying has begun, confirming the data from the Dutch study of Kestrel energetics (see Fig. 132).

In the early stages of courtship, food passes may be aerial, the female rolling to one side so as to grab the offered prey from the male's talons. However, most food passes, particularly once the female has stopped hunting as a prelude to egg laying, are at a perch, and this is invariably the case once incubation has started. To signal his intention of passing food, the male will take a favourite perch and give the '*clip*' call. This usually summons the female immediately, though several, increasingly insistent, calls may be needed. When the female arrives the male may offer her the prey, or she may take it from his foot. The female usually gives the '*clip*' call, reinforcing the pair bond. When the female is incubating she may take the food back to the nest.

Nest sites

Mester (1980) and Piechocki (1982) considered that male Kestrels choose nest sites, and while not endorsing this view Village (1990) does note his observation of a male Kestrel systematically searching the canopy of an area of woodland clearly looking for old nests. Village also notes that males make a great deal of noise at nest sites, which could be interpreted as attempts to persuade the female that a good site has been located. Shrubb (1993a) is less confident that males are wholly responsible for nest selection, his observations suggesting that both sexes are involved, having seen females examining nest sites as well as being shown potential sites by the male. Overall, while available evidence is not conclusive, it seems that males are at the very least involved in nest selection, but that the final decision rests with the female.

Kestrels are eclectic in their choice of nest sites, a fact which, added to their dietary flexibility, has been a factor in their success as a species, particularly after humans began to drastically modify the environment. Prior to human influence, Kestrels were restricted to the use of stick nests of other species, and ledges on cliff faces, but the fact that nests can also be found in tree holes and surprisingly narrow rock clefts/caves indicates that the birds were long capable of adapting to circumstance. It is likely that ever since people began to construct buildings which have all the attributes of cliffs, offering convenient ledges and protection from mammalian predators, these have been used, and Kestrels have more recently become one of the more frequent users of large nesting boxes.

Stick nests are most often those of corvids, particularly Carrion Crows. In an analysis of BTO nest records over a 50-year period from 1937 to 1987, Shrubb (1993b) noted that 83% of stick nests were of that species, the next

FIG 137. Kestrel nest in an open box.

FIG 138. Male Kestrel emerging from a closed nest box, having delivered prey to the incubating female.

BELOW: **FIG 139.** Four well-fledged chicks in a closed box.

highest percentage being Magpie at 11%. Sparrowhawk and Common Buzzard contributed 2% each, while the remaining nests were of Raven, Wood Pigeon, Jay, Rook and Grey Heron. Old squirrel dreys may also be used, the Kestrels scraping a hollow in the top. In Shrubb's study two Grey Squirrel dreys were reported from a total of 556 stick nests. Shrubb also analysed the trees in which the stick nests were found, noting 45% in pine species, though many types of tree, both coniferous and deciduous, had been utilised by the original nest builders.

THE KESTREL · 243

FIG 140. Kestrel chicks in a wicker basket.

FIG 141. A well-fledged Kestrel chick, one of five, peers over the edge of a Carrion Crow stick nest.

In general Kestrels avoid stick nests close to the ground and prefer trees which stand with others rather than alone.

Usually stick nests are one year old, as many do not survive to be used again. However, some are reused, and an extreme example was observed in Russia's Tuva Republic (close to Mongolia's northwestern border), where a Magpie nest was used in consecutive years in 2004 and 2005, and was then used again in 2010, when the male of the pair had been hatched in the same nest in 2004 (Karyakin & Nikolenko 2010). If a suitable remnant lining exists in a stick nest, this will be used as a substrate, the female Kestrel laying directly onto it, but if the nest cup has collapsed, a scrape in the remaining material may be made before laying. Occasionally female Kestrels will remove old nest lining material or, more unusually, may add material if the nest is messy. Instances of Kestrels using newly constructed nests if their builders have abandoned the site are known, and historically it is known that the larger falcons have evicted corvids from recently constructed nests, though this behaviour, once thought to be relatively common, is now considered very rare.

As well as using stick nests in trees, Kestrels also utilise tree holes, choosing anything which will accommodate the female, but avoiding deep holes. In most cases such holes occur naturally, but holes excavated by Green Woodpeckers which then begin to rot and expand will also be used. There is no evidence that Kestrels prefer one tree species to another, choice being solely on the basis of nest-site availability. In tree holes the female will often not make any scrape, accepting the hole base as she finds it, rejecting the hole if the base is not suitable for eggs. Interestingly, Kestrels will actually share a hollow tree with other species: in a trawl of BTO nest records Shrubb (1993a) noted 13 instances of sharing with Barn Owls, seven with Jackdaws (*Corvus monedula*), six with Stock Doves, four with Shelduck (*Tadorna tadorna*), three with Little Owls, two with Tawny Owls and once with a Black Redstart (*Phoenicurus ochruros*). While in most cases the entrance to the tree was not shared, it definitely was in the case of one Barn Owl and the Black Redstart. Given the fact that some of these species are predators of Kestrels or eggs, while others are potential prey of Kestrels, this information is fascinating.

In the absence of trees, Kestrels will nest on the ground, Balfour (1955) reporting the use of tunnels in heather and Rabbit burrows in a well-known paper on breeding Kestrel in the Orkneys (the Orkney Vole, *Microtus arvalis orcadensis*, being a prey species). In 1991 Riddle (2011) visited the area and found Kestrels still using ground nests, though by then the annual number had dropped from Balfour's 19 to just four. Another example of ground nesting was reported in Austria, where, from the photograph that accompanied the report, the nest appeared to be among the debris from a small fire lit in an area of open fields

FIG 142. Young Kestrel chicks snuggling together in a cleft in a rock face. (Mike Price)

BELOW: **FIG 143.** Kestrel nest on a cliff ledge.

(Wassmann 1993). It is usually assumed that Kestrels avoid ground nesting in other areas because of the possibility of predation, but as Merlins and harriers regularly nest on the ground this would only be true if there was some reason why the nests of Kestrels were more likely to be discovered, which seems unlikely. More likely is that the areas used by, for instance, Merlins, are not suitable as hunting grounds for Kestrels, despite their dietary flexibility.

In his analysis of 50 years of BTO nest records Shrubb (1993b) noted 27% of nests on rock ledges, 20% in tree holes, 17% in stick nests, 16% on buildings

FIG 144. Young Kestrels on a vegetated ledge halfway up a steep hillside.

and 15% in nest boxes. The remaining 5% included 3% where the nest site was not adequately described, and 2% which comprised tree forks, ground nesting (mostly in Orkney), Rabbit burrows and ledges on steep banks. Doubtless over the 25 years since that survey the number of building and box nests has gone up, while the use of stick nests has declined. Shrubb noted marked regional variations in the percentages for each site type, attributing these, at least in part, to the likelihood of local predation.

The Kestrel's enthusiasm for nesting on buildings is responsible for its German name (*Turmfalke* – tower falcon). The birds will take any structure on offer – old barns, high-rise housing or office blocks, church towers, bridges and the like. Pike (1981) tells an engaging story of a Kestrel pair nesting in a box section (measuring 142 mm wide, 355 mm high, 370 mm deep) of a normally inaccessible girder in a Birmingham brewery. During repair work the girder was inspected and two eggs were found. The workman carefully removed these as he needed to paint the box section. After painting he returned the eggs. A few days

FIG 145. Two Kestrel chicks from a brood of four reared on the window ledge of a city church. The lens above them formed part of a system to monitor their progress using CCTV.

later he noted that the female had laid three more eggs, and incubated the clutch despite the frequent noisy comings-and-goings of bricklayers and painters. All five chicks hatched and fledged successfully, aided, in part, by a management decision to minimise disturbance once the young were learning to fly.

Today the use of man-made structures by Kestrels includes occupation of purpose-built nest boxes. While most of these are erected on trees or outbuildings, some are attached to the window boxes of high-rise flats, offering the occupants of the flats a grandstand view of chick incubation and rearing. Village (1990) notes that some human occupants of such flats find that opening their windows causes the Kestrels, who have clearly lost their fear of humans, to aggressively defend their territories. So familiar are Kestrels with the concept of box nesting that they will take boxes even in rural areas, while their enthusiasm for boxes is sometimes surprising: on one occasion I saw Kestrels nesting in a box less than 40 m from nesting Merlins (the latter in a basket), and once, having erected a box in a tree in the hope of encouraging an owl to take up residence, I was surprised to find the first tenants were a pair of Kestrels, who successfully raised three chicks.

There is conflicting evidence regarding the breeding success of Kestrels in urban environments. Sumasgutner *et al.* (2014a) claim, from a study in Vienna, that reproductive success was lowest in the city centre, where breeding density was highest due to the relative abundance of nest sites, as a consequence of limited rodent availability and competition for avian prey. However, other studies (e.g. Pikula *et al.* 1984, Salvati 2002) claimed higher reproductive rates, while others (e.g. Charter *et al.* 2007) suggest that the differences seen arise not from the environment, but from the nest site. Charter *et al.* (2007), following a study in Israel, claim that Kestrels nesting in rock cavities or in the closed nest sites on buildings show higher breeding success than those in more open sites such as stick nests and open nest boxes, and that it is the reduction in predation in closed sites which accounts for the increased success. This suggestion is in accord with earlier work in which the breeding success of Kestrels in Spain was computed for a range of different nest sites, both nest boxes and natural sites, the latter including stick nests in trees and on pylons, and building cavities (Fargallo *et al.* 2001). Fargallo and co-workers noted that the population of Kestrels increased after the introduction of nest boxes, and that falcon pairs in nest boxes began laying earlier and had higher breeding success in terms of the number of fledglings raised. They considered that the latter effect was due to lower predation in nest boxes, but cautioned against assuming that the earlier laying was due to nest-box usage, as it might also have due to nest-site quality. However, in later work in Finland it was found that Kestrel pairs using nest boxes which had been left uncleaned from the previous year nested earlier than those in nest boxes which had been cleaned, and it was conjectured that prey remains and pellets from previous occupation might indicate 'public information' which was used in the following year to indicate advantageous sites (Sumasgutner *et al.* 2014b). These researchers found no difference in the breeding success of Kestrels in cleaned or uncleaned boxes, but confirmed the Spanish finding that predation was lower in nest boxes than in natural sites. There was, however, a difference in the ectoparasite burden of chicks, and we return to that issue when considering chick hatching, under *Incubation* below.

Perhaps more interesting than the discussion of whether the breeding success of urban Kestrels is higher or lower than that of their rural cousins is the suggestion in the work by Rejt *et al.* (2004) that urban Kestrels may be in the process of becoming both genetically and ethologically separate from rural ones. In a study in Warsaw, Rejt *et al.* found that the urban birds had lower genetic variability, perhaps as a result of isolation and subsequent inbreeding. As the urban Kestrels showed a marked increase in nest-site fidelity, the differences in diet and nest-site preference between them and the surrounding rural Kestrel population could ultimately result in the creation of an isolated subpopulation. However, as Rejt *et al.* note, further work is required before definite conclusions can be reached. A later study has indeed been made, in the Czech Republic, but Riegert *et al.* (2010) did not support the idea of genetic separation between urban and nearby rural Kestrel populations, though they did confirm the idea of more interbreeding in urban populations. The study also failed to confirm any ethological difference, but did note that urban female Kestrels tended to be heavier than their rural cousins.

Breeding density

Measuring the breeding density of any species has inherent difficulties similar to those of assessing overall population. Some birds may not find partners and so will not breed, while other pairs may mate but fail to breed. Assessing the density of those that do breed requires identifying viable nests, and while Kestrels breeding in boxes and on buildings may be relatively easy to spot, those using old stick nests and tree holes, which are scattered across the countryside, are more difficult to find. Village (1990) noted that the problem of finding nests means that the larger the area searched the more nests are likely to be missed, so that many quoted breeding densities, which rely on relatively small areas, may overestimate the true overall density. Village considers that choosing areas of approximately 80–200 km^2 gives the best estimate of breeding density. In support of this claim, he notes that in a study by Parr (1967) a breeding density of 1,797 pairs/100 km^2 was established for one 7 km^2 area, and 203 pairs/100 km^2 for another 10 km^2 site, while in an area of 14,000 km^2 of Finland Kuusela (1979) found a density of only 3 pairs/100 km^2. On the basis that a study area of 80–200 km^2 smooths out such anomalies, Village cites densities of 12 pairs/100 km^2 for arable farmland, rising to 20 pairs/100 km^2 for mixed farmland, and 30 pairs/100 km^2 for grassland. However, he notes that these approximate values are subject to a high degree of change depending on prey population and weather conditions. The density for mixed farmland agrees reasonably well with data from Germany, where Kostrzewa & Kostrzewa (1991) noted densities of 6–15 breeding pairs/100 km^2 depending on conditions the previous winter: as the mean winter temperature declined from 6 °C to −1 °C the number of territorial pairs fell from 18 to 8 pairs/100 km^2.

Intuitively, the number of breeding Kestrel pairs in a given area would depend on local survival over the previous winter and the food supply in spring, and this was confirmed by Village (1985) in a study of British Kestrels. A similar mechanism operated in a farmland population near Cologne, Germany

(Kostrzewa & Kostrzewa 1991), where, as noted above, Kestrel density in spring was positively correlated with temperature in the previous winter. Kostrzewa & Kostrzewa (1990) also examined the effect of spring and summer temperatures and rainfall on Kestrels at the same study area and found that the density of breeding pairs was dependent on spring rainfall, confirming an earlier result of Cavé (1967) – see below.

The relationship between food supply and breeding density is borne out by the correlation between predator and prey numbers, this occasionally being seen in spectacular fashion. The instances usually quoted are between avian predator numbers and lemming density in Arctic areas, where peak lemming years are accompanied by an increase, for example, in the breeding density of Snowy Owls – e.g. Potapov & Sale (2012). In the case of Snowy Owls the female can lay anything from 2 to 14 eggs, raising nestling numbers in accord with the lemming population, and the latter population can reach staggeringly high densities, much greater than is seen in vole populations. As we shall see, Kestrels are limited in the number of eggs they can lay (six is the maximum number the female can incubate, though larger clutches have been claimed – see *Clutch size*, below), but they can take advantage of increased vole numbers by raising more nestlings to fledge, and the breeding density can also be raised. In Britain, and in many other areas throughout its range, the Kestrel population is essentially sedentary, and such populations do not easily respond to increases in prey abundance, but this is not the case for Kestrel populations which are partially migratory, and the studies of Korpimäki (1984b, 1985c, 1994), and Norrdahl & Korpimäki (1996) on Kestrels in Scandinavia clearly show that at times of increased vole population additional falcon pairs can rapidly arrive in, settle in, and breed in an area of abundance. The study of Korpimäki (1984b) shows both the reduction in breeding pairs of Kestrels during a crash in the population of *Microtus* species and the subsequent recovery in breeding pairs when the vole population recovered, together with population increases for Bank Voles and *Sorex* species. Those populations in Britain which are partially migratory show a similar pattern on the few instances where the vole population reaches epidemic levels. Adair (1891, 1893) reported a sharp increase in numbers of both Kestrels and Short-eared Owls during a vole plague which afflicted the Scottish Borders, and the subsequent decline in both when the vole population collapsed (Note 5.4). Riddle (2011) plots the mean clutch size of Kestrel pairs with time in his Ayrshire study area over the period 1986–2009 and notes the position of good vole years (Fig. 146), clearly indicating a correlation. Interestingly, Riddle notes that Kestrel numbers peaked in the years of high vole population, then declined, whereas the population of Barn Owls peaked the year after a high vole population, and then declined.

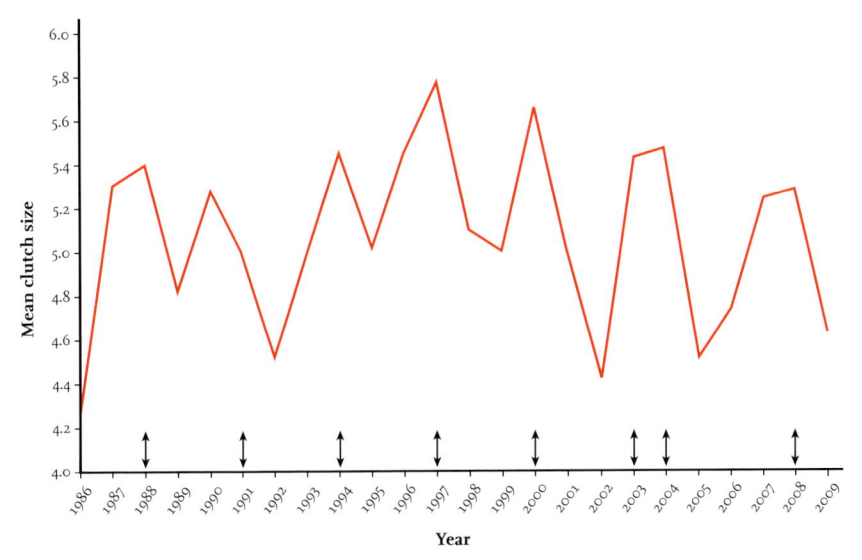

FIG 146. Variation of mean Kestrel clutch size during the period 1986–2009 in southwest Scotland. The good vole years are indicated by the arrowheads. Redrawn from Riddle 2011.

However, the relationship between breeding Kestrels and the availability of prey is not quite what it seems, as food resources are not the only factor influencing Kestrel breeding, a study of Kestrels on reclaimed Dutch polders suggesting that more subtle influences were at work (Cavé 1967). In particular the breeding density was negatively correlated with rainfall, especially in spring, and positively correlated with temperature. Rainfall was considered significant because it impeded hunting and reduced the above-ground activity of the voles that were the main prey of the Kestrels. This effect was most apparent in spring, as later in the year there were more hours of daylight, to the advantage of both species, and a reduced food intake in spring affected the ability of the female Kestrels to breed. Temperature was considered to have an effect because higher temperatures reduced the energy expenditure in thermoregulation. Counterintuitively, the breeding density appeared to be independent of vole population density, but here too there are several factors which have to be considered. If voles are scarce, adult Kestrels can switch prey – in the case of the Cavé study to young Starlings – but there was also evidence that male chicks weighed less than in years of more abundant voles, apparently because they were losing out in competition to their female siblings (which did not show a weight reduction), and that the rate of brood desertion was higher. Such factors would mean that provided the vole population density varied within a 'normal' range, the Kestrel breeding density was (relatively) insensitive to it, steep rises or falls in bird breeding being seen only when the vole population altered spectacularly. The data that Village (1990) collected over a four-year period in his Scottish study area supports this (though the sample is too small for a statistically significant result). What Village discovered was that in his farmland study areas, where the Kestrel breeding density was lower because the vole habitat was reduced, winter temperature had a much larger effect. As lower temperatures meant an increased likelihood of snow, which adversely affected the birds' ability to catch voles, there was a significant reduction in breeding density as mean temperature decreased.

Kestrel breeding density is also dependent on the availability of nest sites, and it is clear that the increased availability of nest boxes in areas with poor natural sites over recent years has been a factor in the increased breeding density in those areas. In a study in southern Scotland, Village (1983c) noted that while some areas had an excess of usable nests, the erection of artificial nests allowed some pairs of Kestrels to breed that would otherwise not have done so. Some pairs of Kestrels were therefore inhibited from breeding either by lack of nests or by the territorial behaviour of some breeding pairs who prevented use of available nests nearby. However, sometimes breeding pairs are unable to prevent the use of nearby nests, and nest availability may create close nesting. Village (1990) quotes one case where two nests were 40 m apart and the male of one of the pairs was the two-year-old son of the other male, but notes that there is no evidence that the close positioning of nests always implies some relationship between member(s) of the pairs.

There are several studies which indicate that urban Kestrels tend to nest close together (e.g. Salvati 2001, who found large numbers of Kestrels nesting semi-colonially in scaffolding holes in ruins and medieval towers in Rome) and there is ample evidence that in certain circumstances close nesting forms what might be termed true colonies of birds. Piechocki (1982) records a colony of 15 pairs in an abandoned rookery in Germany, and 7–9 pairs nesting on the same gasometer near Leipzig. In the latter case there were around 100 identical cavities and some females were laying single eggs in several of these, having apparently forgotten where they had laid previously. Piechocki also references an account of more than ten nests in a small wood on the Russian steppe. In another case near Jena, Germany, Peter & Zaumseil (1982) noted a colony of up to 28 pairs of Kestrels inhabiting a 400 m long motorway bridge, while in an abandoned sandstone quarry in Spain measuring 20 m in height and about 200 m in width, Bustamante (1994) found 12–15 pairs of Kestrels in a colony with a number of Lesser Kestrels. There is also information on a colony of 17 Kestrel pairs (*F. t. interstinctus*) on a natural cliff face in Japan (Hyuga 1955). During the vole plague in the Scottish

Borders mentioned above, Adair (1891, 1893) recorded six nests in one wood: this colony seems to have been caused by prey abundance, and there is some evidence to suggest that other colonies may similarly relate to available food resources. In his study of colonial nesting in Rome, Salvati (2001) found that the reproductive success of a pair was low if the breeding density was high, reflecting the idea that overlap of hunting ranges limited the access to food when the number of hunting Kestrels rose.

Copulation

Copulation starts significantly before egg laying – Dickson (1987) recorded it in November, while Masman *et al.* (1988a) recorded it as occurring in January – and can therefore be considered part of pair bonding. The female solicits copulation

FIG 147. Mating Kestrels. (Nathan Guttridge)

by making the '*clip*' signal call. She bends forward, fans her wings and raises her tail, moving it to one side when the male mounts her. The male beats his wings rapidly and fans his tail to maintain position and gives the '*kik-kik-kik*' alarm call, the female responding with '*clip*' calls. Copulation takes a few seconds only, the pair then separating and spending time preening. Copulations increase in frequency as egg laying is approached, reaching a peak during egg laying when the birds copulate 7–8 times daily (Masman *et al.* 1988b, Korpimäki *et al.* 1996, the latter giving an average time between copulations during the day of 42 minutes, consistent with the 45 minutes quoted by Riddle 2011), more frequently in the early morning than at other times. Copulation usually occurs close to the nest, sometimes within it.

Copulation rates have been seen to increase in years when rodent numbers were high (Korpimäki *et al.* 1996). These authors suggest that this increased rate, together with a noted increase in the time the male spent guarding his mate, is a means of avoiding extra-pair copulation by the female and so protecting his investment in his brood. Of course both activities also mean the male has less time for an infidelity of his own.

Egg laying
In order to accumulate the energy reserves required for egg production the female reduces, then ceases, the time spent hunting, eventually relying entirely on food supplied by her mate. In Britain, where the majority of Kestrels do not migrate, this usually means the female stops hunting 2–4 weeks before the first egg is laid. However, in Scandinavia where the population is entirely migratory, females cannot afford the luxury of such a period of hunting abstinence, needing to replenish the energy reserves drained by migration as well as preparing for egg production, and Korpimäki (1985b) noted that in southern Finland the females were fed by their mates only for one week prior to laying. During the period when the male is provisioning his mate Shrubb (1993a) noted that males fed their mates every 2–3 hours, suggesting 4–6 meals daily. Usually the feeding follows a set pattern, occurring at regular times during the day, the male's approach being stealthy, especially during incubation, in an effort to minimise the detection of the nest site by potential predators.

The female spends an increasing amount of time on or near the nest as egg development begins. From the work of Cavé (1967) and Meijer (1988), egg development in the ovary begins during the winter, the eggs reaching about 20% of final yolk size a few weeks before laying. Then, a week or so before laying, the egg grows rapidly, with albumen and shell formation occurring just two days before the egg is laid. This rapid development means that the female will, at the point of lay of the first egg, hold the entire clutch, each egg at a slightly different stage.

While the preparation of the first, and subsequent, eggs is well understood, the actual timing of the laying of the first egg is much more fluid. The breeding season for the species as a whole is remarkably mutable, the birds of northern Europe commencing breeding in April and May; those of southern Europe, north Africa and the Indian subcontinent a month or so earlier; those of equatorial Africa in October and November (the dry season); and those of South Africa in September–November, the southern spring. But even this apparently clear pattern is overwritten by curiosities, such as the earlier breeding season of the birds of southern India than those of nearby Sri Lanka, and the birds of the Horn of Africa choosing to breed during the rainy season. Table 18 indicates the mean laying dates from various countries of northern Europe.

TABLE 18 Variation of Kestrel laying dates in northern Europe

Country	Latitude °N	Laying dates Good vole year	Laying dates Poor vole year	Laying dates All years	Number of nests	Source
Finland	61			13 May[1]	136	Korpimäki 1986b
	63			7 May[1]	131	Korpimäki 1986b
Sweden	57			1 May[2]	37	Wallin et al. 1987
Scotland	55	28 April	11 May	3 May	127	Village 1990
	55	18 April	8 May	29 April[1]	142	Riddle 1987
England	53	4 May	17 May	12 May	263	Village 1990
Netherlands	53	16 April	24 May	27 April	705	Meijer 1988
Germany	48–55			29 April	1,197	Kostrzewa & Kostrzewa 1997
Czech Republic urban	49			26 April	44	Pikula et al. 1984
rural	49			2 May	252	Pikula et al. 1984
Bohemia	49	19 April	4 May	27 April	238	Plesník & Dusík 1994
France	47	22 April	11 May	3 May	82	Bonin & Strenna 1986
Switzerland	47			30 April	237	Schmid 1990

1. These dates are median, i.e. the date on which half the females had started laying.
2. Calculated by assuming first lay was 36 days prior to hatching.

Note also that the datasets summarised in the table represent a sample which includes the date of the first egg laid in years of differing vole populations, in habitats which are comparable to Britain. For a very much more comprehensive list of mean laying date with geographical position, hours of daylight and clutch size see Carrillo & González-Dávila (2010), which tabulates data from about 20 studies across Europe and north Africa, from the Canary Islands to Finland (28°N – 65°N) and altitudes from sea level to 1,300 m; and Zellweger-Fischer *et al.* (2011), which provides updated data for Switzerland. In their study Carrillo & González-Dávila (2010) conclude that photo-period and both winter and spring weather affect laying date.

The data shown in Table 18 suggest that there is little correlation between laying date and latitude, as might have been expected intuitively, with factors such as habitat and weather conditions clearly being the prime drivers. This is perhaps clearest in the case of Finland, where the Kestrels begin their breeding cycle before the last snows have melted, an indication that increased day length compensates, at least in part, for lower temperatures. In his studies Village (1990) noted that laying in Scotland began earlier than in England despite the fact that the Scottish study area was 300 km further north. We return to this apparent contradiction below. The histograms of first-egg dates are also interesting (Fig. 148). Whereas the histogram of English dates is symmetrical, as might be anticipated, that of the Scottish Kestrels is skewed towards the earlier first-egg date. Village explored this, and found a correlation between mean first-egg date and the laying of the first egg, but no correlation between the mean and either the last laying or the duration of the laying season. In other words, the end of the laying season was more or less constant in all years; birds

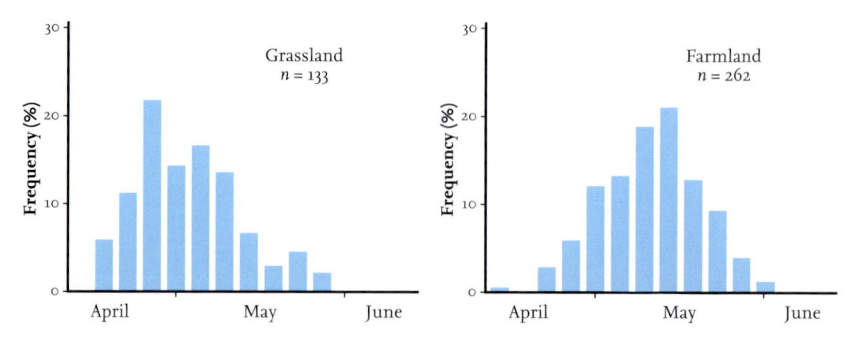

FIG 148. First-egg dates in five-day periods for Kestrels breeding on grassland in southern Scotland and farmland in east-central England. The mean first-egg date is earlier in Scotland despite the breeding area being 300 km further north. Redrawn from Village 1990.

may start to lay early if conditions allow, but the early laying of some birds lengthens the laying season rather than moving the entire season forwards in time.

While there are several drivers influencing the start of the Kestrel breeding season, the main driver is the availability of prey. That this is the case was shown by Masman (1986). Without the constraints imposed by the physiology of males and females, a pair of animals could breed at any time when the availability of food allowed the female to successfully overcome the energy expenditure of reproduction and the pair could provide sufficient food to raise the resulting offspring. In practice, most animals are 'programmed' to breed at a specific time, the time being defined by the availability of food resources, since these are usually not available consistently. Masman (1986) calculated the daily energy expenditure of male Kestrels during the year (Fig. 149), and found that from August to mid-January the shorter northern day meant that the male did not have the time to catch the food required to feed a female and brood as well as feeding himself. In principle Kestrels could breed in the autumn when the vole population is comparable to that of spring, but the male is then constrained by hunting time. To prove the point, Karyakin (2005) discovered three juvenile Kestrels during the first week of December at a site in southwestern Russia and

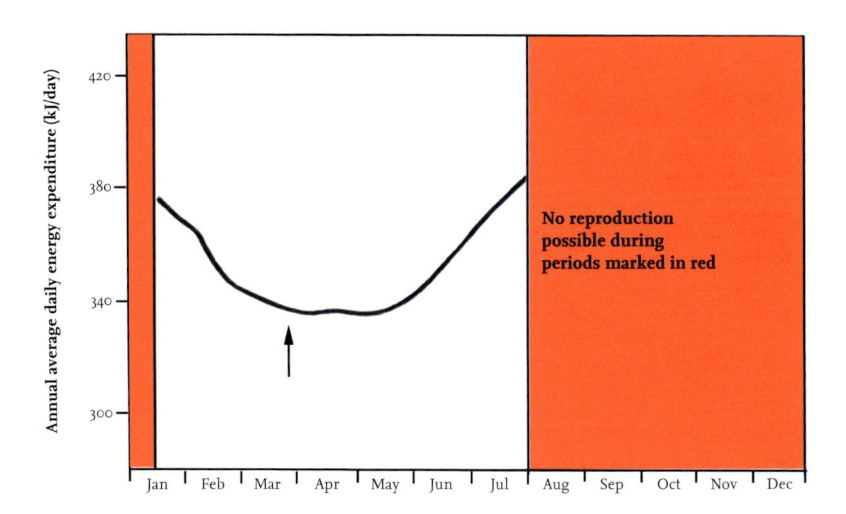

FIG 149. Estimated daily energy expenditure of a male Kestrel throughout the year, assuming breeding starts at that time. The data derives from a study in the Netherlands. The arrow indicates the average start of courtship. The red area indicates the periods when breeding is not possible because daylight constrains hunting time. Redrawn from Masman 1986.

speculated that they were from an autumnal brood with breeding prompted by a very high vole population density in the area. Karyakin does not record whether the juveniles survived the winter, but as he refers to them as juveniles rather than nestlings, they had clearly fledged.

While the window for breeding opens, as far as the male Kestrel is concerned, during the early days of spring, another mechanism is required to ensure that female Kestrels are also ready to reproduce. From the work of Bird *et al.* (1980), it is the start of the longer days of spring that triggers the female to prepare for breeding. Bird and colleagues experimented with captive American Kestrels, exposing them to artificially shortened days during October, then to artificially longer days in November. As a consequence six of ten pairs bred in January at a time when, in the wild, the probability of raising young was vanishingly small. A similar result was shown in the Eurasian Kestrel by the work of the group at Groningen University (Meijer 1988, 1989): Meijer showed that not only breeding but moult could be triggered early by artificially controlling the 'daylight' hours the birds experienced.

So as the days lengthen into spring the male Kestrel's daily energy expenditure reduces and he is able to fend for his female and, later, his brood, while the lengthening days ready the female for breeding. What now triggers the laying of the first egg?

As noted above, at the study area of Village (1990) in Scotland the Kestrels laid earlier than their English cousins despite being 300 km further north. Village hypothesised that this was due to the Scottish study area being better vole habitat and so, all other conditions being the same, allowing the birds an enhanced possibility of catching prey. As already noted, it is also clear that rainfall and temperature affect Kestrel hunting, and these factors will influence the onset of laying on an annual basis. Meijer (1988) also noted that a female's first egg was laid 2–3 weeks after she had begun to be fed by her mate. This evidence all points to the onset of laying being related primarily to the availability of food.

Confirmation can be found in the work of Cavé (1967) and Dijkstra *et al.* (1982). Cavé took two groups of female Kestrels, giving one group more food than the other. The ovaries of birds were then examined post-mortem at regular intervals, with the better-fed birds exhibiting a more advanced state of development than those with poorer rations. In the work of Dijkstra *et al.*, dead rodents were placed in the nest boxes of some pairs of wild Kestrels, but not in the boxes of others. In this case the pairs that had the benefit of extra rations bred earlier than the unfed pairs. The period by which laying was advanced in the fed birds was as much as three weeks in poor vole years, but less in good vole years, when the ration difference between the fed and unfed birds was less stark.

The increase in body weight by the females in each study indicates that the accumulation of body reserves is important in the timing of laying. This result was confirmed by Meijer *et al.* (1988). However, this later work showed that while the effect of artificially increasing the food supply of a female Kestrel was to advance the laying of the first egg, it had little effect on the number of eggs laid. In years of high vole population density, the advance in laying date was minimal and there was no increase in clutch size (as measured by observing the clutch size in control nests which had similar laying dates). In years of low vole population the advance in laying date was significant, but the increase in clutch size was not. Meijer *et al.* (1988) also artificially fed female Kestrels who had not begun to lay late in the season to see if this could either advance their laying date or increase their clutch size. In this case there was a statistically significant advance in laying date and in clutch size (though in the case of the latter, the increase was from 4.4 to 4.8 eggs per clutch, the increase of 0.4 eggs being within the standard deviation of the mean). The results of the Dutch experiments with the provision of supplementary food were confirmed by a study in Finland which also showed that the supplemental feeding increased the number of fledglings surviving in a given brood (Wiehn & Korpimäki 1997). This increase was shown to occur in both poor and good vole years, the authors noting that this implies that the reproductive output of Kestrels is food-limited whatever the abundance of prey.

The idea that the date of laying of the first egg by any female Kestrel is dependent on food supply seems entirely reasonable, but the fact that there is a difference in laying date between individual females in a given study has been the subject of considerable debate in academic circles, and has resulted in the development of two hypotheses. In an ideal situation a pair of birds will time their breeding so that the peak food requirement of hatchlings corresponds to the maximum available food resource. The first hypothesis, the *constraint* hypothesis, posits that the optimal laying date is the same for all pairs in a population, but that not all females are able to take advantage of it because of differences in their condition or in the territory of the pair. Since the female's condition is defined by resource availability, they may be ready to breed only after the optimal laying date has passed, resources representing a constraint on breeding. The second hypothesis, *individual optimisation*, contends that the lay date is adaptive and depends on parental quality so that each individual female begins egg laying on her own optimal laying date. Numerous papers have been produced which deal with these hypotheses, and the various experiments which have been carried out to test them (e.g. Daan *et al.* 1988, 1990, Aparicio 1994a, 1994b, 1998). Though the issue is still debated, the general consensus is that the quality of the Kestrel pair, in terms of the hunting ability of the male and the initial body weight of the female – i.e. individual optimisation – is critical in determining both laying date and clutch size. A further complication was added by the suggestion of Tomás (2014) – for all avian species rather than specifically for falcons – that it is hatching date rather than laying date which is critical, as greater information on food availability is more clearly available as egg development proceeds and the female can adjust the timing of hatching by intensity of incubation, though in the particular case of falcons the variation in observed incubation periods suggests that the female's ability to hold back hatching is severely limited. While the debate between the various theories will continue, what is clear from the many studies of breeding Kestrels is that clutch size declines with the progression of first egg laying: in other words, the later the first egg is laid, the smaller the clutch, as we shall see below.

Egg-laying intervals

Once the first egg has been laid the female usually produces eggs every other day: Village (1990) estimated a two-day interval, having decided not to risk extreme disturbance of the female by seeking a more accurate number; Hasenclever *et al.* (1989) calculated a mean of 2.03 days from a total of 57 eggs; and Aparicio (1994a) calculated 2.12 days ($n = 66$). However, Aparicio's study included some pairs which were given supplementary food in order to assess the effect on laying interval, the 2.12-day interval being an amalgam of pairs which received extra food (mean laying interval 2.04 days) and a control group which were not fed (mean interval 2.50 days). This study sought to understand the effect of female energy (i.e. food) intake on clutch size, and concluded that food intake was more important than the start of laying in determining clutch size. However, as we have seen above, this conclusion is not as straightforward as it might at first appear.

In other observations, some females have been noted as extending the laying interval to three or four days, and Hasenclever *et al.* (1989) noted females laying the last egg of a clutch five days after the penultimate egg.

Eggs

Each egg is elliptical and measures 34–47 mm along the major axis and 27–39 mm along the minor axis (Village 1990 and references therein, Boileau & Hoede 2009). The larger egg sizes noted by Village (1990) were from a study in Germany and Poland with a small dataset, whereas the study of British eggs indicated 35–45 × 29–35 with a sample size of 306. In a study by Aparicio (1999) in central Spain, the diet of some female Kestrels was supplemented, while that of a control group was not. In the control group the size of eggs laid increased from the first to the penultimate, the final egg being smaller, while in the fed females egg size decreased from the first to the last. Aparicio's study was attempting to provide evidence for the suggestion that larger egg size was positively correlated with hatching success and nestling survival. However, the noted differences in egg size, while significant, were within the normal scatter of egg sizes, and the effect on nestling survival could not be distinguished from the effect of hatch date.

When first laid, the eggs weigh about 20 g. In a study of six eggs by Meijer *et al.* (1989) the mean weight was 21.5 ± 1.8 g, made up of shell (2.1 ± 0.2 g), albumen (14.8 ± 1.5g) and yolk (4.6 ± 0.4 g). For a female of average weight (250 g) a clutch of four eggs therefore represents almost 35% of body weight, though as the eggs are formed on a conveyor belt this is not a fair assessment of the bird's input to the process. Meijer *et al.* (1989) also calculated the caloric value of each egg as 99.70 kJ. When this energy is apportioned to the production process of a clutch of four eggs, it represents an energy requirement of 72 kJ/day. As the daily energy intake of a female was calculated as 388 kJ, egg formation actually requires the female to devote 19% of her energy input to egg production during the egg formation and laying phase. In order to prepare for the energy expenditure of egg production, Meijer *et al.* (1989) found that female Kestrels increased their body weight by about 70 g (from about 230 g to about 300 g depending on individual birds). Of this weight gain 64% was accumulation of body reserves, the remainder being the development of oviducts and eggs.

The ground colour of the eggs is white/pale buff, with heavy speckling, usually of red-brown, but varying to darker brown. Village (1990) notes that the variability of speckling is considerable, some eggs being almost plain white with a few brown spots. There is also variability within a clutch, and in general the last egg is the least coloured, Village suggesting that this results from the depletion in protoporphyrin, the pigment which creates the speckling.

Clutch size

The usual clutch size is 4–6. Single eggs and clutches of seven have been recorded, though these represent less than 1% of all clutches; clutches of one and two are also rare, and may actually result from partial predation rather than being full clutches. Records of clutches greater than seven exist, but Village (1990) considers these probably arise from two females laying in the same nest. However, Heukelen & Heukelen (2011) record a nest (on a haystack within a barn in the Netherlands) with a clutch of ten eggs which they consider had been laid by the same female rather than involving egg dumping. As evidence they claim that a second female was never seen in the vicinity, and the large number of unconsumed carcasses suggested a bumper vole year: at least nine of the eggs hatched and eight chicks fledged. Considering the difficulty female Kestrels have in covering much smaller

FIG 150. Female Kestrel having difficulty in brooding a large and lively collection of youngsters – there are five chicks in this brood.

broods, the female had performed a remarkable job of keeping the total brood warm, while the male's hunting achievement was equally remarkable.

Shrubb (2003) collected data on clutch sizes from 83 Kestrel nests in Wales in the period 1997–2002 and found that clutches showed considerable annual variation, with a mean of 3.00 in 2001 compared to a mean of 5.00 in 1999.

In a study of Dutch Kestrels by Dijkstra *et al.* (1990b) in which the brood size of Kestrel pairs was manipulated, the results indicated that Kestrels are capable of raising larger clutches to fledge than are actually seen (in all but exceptional circumstances) in the wild. Using nests with, on average, five eggs, two extra eggs were placed in some, while two eggs were removed from others. The parent birds fed and raised the manipulated broods, but both the male and the female flight times were affected by brood size. The male flight time increased by 26% when the brood was enlarged (energy expenditure rising by 18%), but fell by 18% when the brood was reduced (energy expenditure falling by 6%). In the enlarged broods hatchling mortality was about 20%, compared to under 2% in reduced and control broods, but once the brood size had been reduced by nestling deaths, the offspring were successfully raised, an average of one extra chick being raised over the control broods. This implies that Kestrel pairs could lay larger clutches and increase the number of fledged young (though at the expense of nestling deaths). The answer to why this is not seen lies in the effect of the enlarged broods on the parent birds.

The findings of Dijkstra *et al.* (1990b) confirmed early work by the Dutch group (Masman *et al.* 1989) who had shown that male Kestrels were able to provide substantially more food to their broods than was necessary, and therefore could, in principle, have raised more nestlings to fledge. They did this by repeatedly removing prey delivered to the nests of wild Kestrels in order to ensure that the nestlings consistently showed signs of hunger, which, in turn, stimulated the male to hunt and deliver more food. While the average time spent hunting in a brood of 'normal' size was 4.46 hours per day, this was artificially increased to 8.41 hours per day. As we have already seen, such an increase in workload results in the male losing weight and clearly cannot be sustained indefinitely: in the Dutch experiment the males were able to sustain the increase in hunting effort for 11 days.

However, the increased provisioning required by a large brood does not come without cost, and Dijkstra *et al.* (1990b) showed that the mortality of parent birds was significantly influenced by brood size, a result which was confirmed in a later study by Deerenberg *et al.* (1995). Although these two studies defined mortality as the female not reappearing to breed the following year, which is an indirect indicator that could be influenced by other factors, Daan *et al.* (1996) were able to show that parent bird mortality had actually increased, by recovering and examining birds which had died subsequent to brood manipulation experiments. It would appear that for female birds there is a 'cliff-edge' effect in terms of clutch size, below which the likelihood of surviving to breed again is not significantly altered, but above which it is reduced. This would certainly influence clutch size.

For the male the situation is different, survival to breed again being affected almost linearly with increasing clutch size. In males it would seem that the seasonal imperative to breed and to produce many offspring takes precedence over the possibility of producing fewer offspring this year and being in good condition to breed again next year. But while these findings seem clear-cut, a study of brood manipulation in Finland adds a further complication (Korpimäki & Rita 1996). In their study these authors found no increased mortality in broods which had been artificially increased. However, they did find that the parent birds did not raise all the chicks to fledge even if the vole population was high and they would have been able to do so. Korpimäki & Rita explained this apparent contradiction by noting that the Dutch and Finnish birds were breeding in areas where the vole population followed a different cycle. In the Netherlands the vole population was essentially stable, so the parent birds considered that attempting to raise more chicks in a given year enhanced the possibility of their gene survival even if their own lives might be shortened (the so-called *intra-individual strategy*, where the trade-off is between current parental effort and future adult survival). In Finland, the cyclic fluctuations in vole population meant that the best strategy for the parent birds was to maximise their own survival (the so-called *inter-generational strategy*, where the trade-off links current parental effort with the number and size of offspring, which thus affects offspring reproductive value).

As noted above, from many studies of breeding Kestrels it is clear that the earlier a clutch is started the larger it may be (Fig. 151). The decline in clutch size is almost certainly controlled by hormonal changes, these defining an egg-laying period with a start point defined by the laying of the first egg and an end point defined by hormone levels, consistent with the finding of Village (1990), as noted above, that the end of the laying period is the same for all females irrespective of the first-egg date.

As part of the work on Kestrels by the group at the University of Groningen, Beukeboom *et al.* (1988) manipulated the clutches of wild Kestrels breeding in nest boxes in two areas of the Netherlands, adding (13 nests) or removing eggs (18 nests) in order to analyse when clutch size was fixed by the female. At the nests, a thermistor placed in the nest substrate measured the air temperature close to the eggs, giving an indication of when the female was incubating. The study showed that in nests where four eggs were added the day before the first egg was due to be laid (a date which could be accurately predicted by the team by careful observation of female behaviour and abdomen shape) the female reduced her clutch from the predicted number by about one egg. However, if four eggs were added to a nest which already had two eggs, the females consistently produced expected clutch sizes: thus if the first-egg laying time suggested a six-egg clutch,

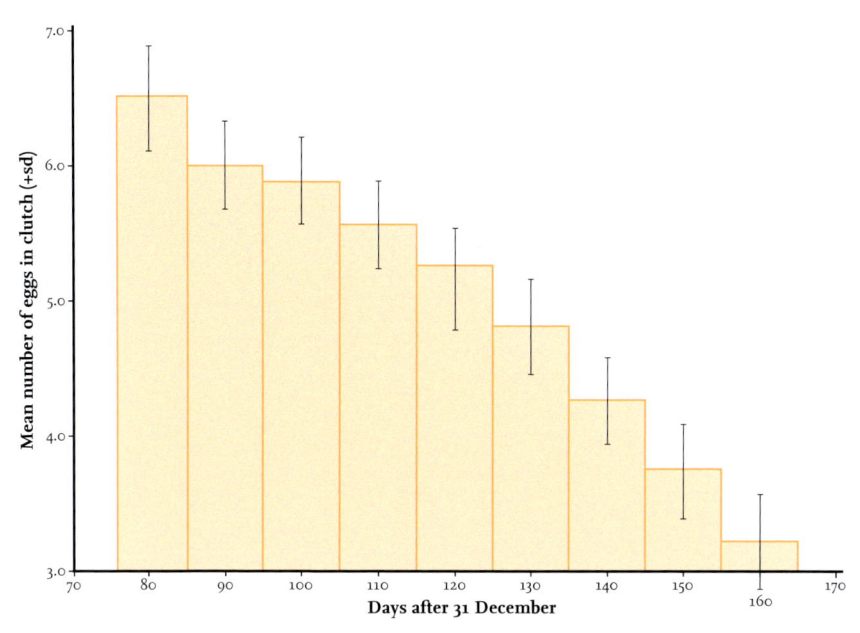

FIG 151. Variation of Kestrel clutch size with laying of first egg. Redrawn from data in Beukeboom *et al.* 1988.

but four eggs were added, the female finished with ten eggs in the nest. If eggs were removed, the female either produced more eggs so that her expected clutch was laid (i.e. she actually laid eight eggs if two were removed from an expected clutch of six), or laid only the expected clutch (i.e. if six eggs were expected then six were laid, leaving four if two were removed).

Having installed a thermistor in the nest, Beukeboom *et al.* (1988) were also able to observe incubation behaviour. They found that females with clutches of three or four eggs began purposeful incubation earlier than those with clutches of six, the start of incubation in earnest being predicated on cessation of laying. In a continuation of the work, it was hypothesised that control of clutch size was associated with the point at which the female spends 50% of her time incubating ('50% incubation': Fig. 152) (Meijer 1988, Meijer *et al.* 1990). Those females which lay early in the season have a low tendency to incubate and may lay four eggs before this point is reached; a late-laying female will reach 50% incubation after only two eggs. From experiments with egg removals and additions, the Dutch group suggest that the decision of the female to stop laying and to resorb developing follicles occurs approximately four days before the laying of the last egg. In each case this means that only two further eggs will be laid, resulting in a clutch of six for the early female and a clutch of four for the later bird (Fig. 153).

It is usually considered that Kestrels lay a single clutch, but evidence from a montane population of Kestrels in central Spain suggests that in certain circumstances second clutches may be laid (Fargallo *et al.* 1996). The researchers noted that three of 11 pairs of Kestrels began second clutches after the chicks of the first clutch had fledged. These pairs had laid their first clutches earlier than single-clutch pairs. The second clutches were of one, three and four eggs, and all

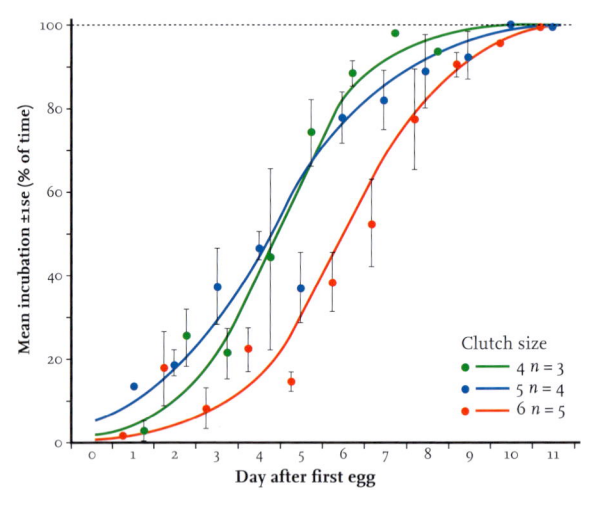

FIG 152. Development of incubation by female Kestrels in the Netherlands with differing clutches. Redrawn from Beukeboom *et al.* 1988.

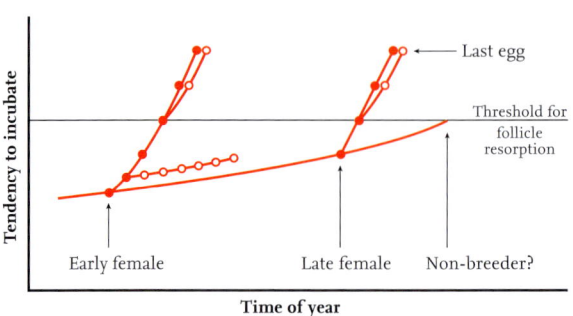

FIG 153. Proximate model for the seasonal control of clutch size in the Kestrel. The laying of a clutch of six eggs by an early-laying female, and of a clutch of four eggs by a late-laying female, are indicated. Egg removal is indicated by o–o–o. What the experiment showed was that egg removal (from the second egg) interrupted the feedback loop between laying and incubation, causing larger clutches in early-laying females, but not in late-laying females. Once the female has reached the threshold for follicle resorption, the number of eggs she will lay is fixed and egg removal has no effect. Redrawn from Meijer 1988.

were incubated, but only the clutch with three eggs hatched; in that nest all three second-clutch chicks fledged successfully. Fargallo *et al.* believe that the southerly position of the site (40°N) and the high availability of prey were the explanation for the double clutches. Santing (2010) recorded the laying of a second clutch of three eggs in the same nest box in the Netherlands in which a Kestrel pair had raised four fledglings from six eggs. While the timing of the second clutch was consistent with a double clutch, Santing was unable to positively confirm that the same pair was responsible.

While double clutches are rare, females may lay a second clutch if disturbed during laying or incubation, with eggs either being taken by predators or chilling due to lack of incubation. Village (1990) noted that in 60% of cases of egg chilling the repeat clutch was laid in the same nest, the female then incubating all the eggs though only the later eggs would hatch. As Village notes, the female would only lay her repeat clutch in the same nest if there were few eggs remaining from the first clutch, as she would need to ensure she was able to cover the entire number during incubation. Females may also abandon clutches due to food shortages or the death of the male. In such cases repeat clutches may also be laid if better food resources become available or a new mate is found.

In the case of one bird of a pair dying, the remaining bird may take a new partner, and this newly formed pair may take over the clutch or brood, or may start the breeding process again. The fact that there are 'spare' birds available for pairing requires that there are non-breeding birds in the population, and in his work Village (1990) found this was the case. Village noted that the number of breeding pairs in an area was always less than the theoretical number (i.e. half the total population, assuming a sex ratio of 1:1): Village estimated that about a third of birds present in an area were non-breeding. When Village's estimate that 6–13% of breeding pairs failed to produce eggs is added to this estimate of non-breeding birds, it can be seen that the Kestrel is not as successful a breeding entity as might be assumed.

While the reasons for nest failure are clear, the obvious question therefore arises of why some Kestrels do not breed. The first possibility is that there are just not enough available nest sites for the number of potential Kestrel pairs to utilise, and evidence for the species being nest-site limited was provided by Piechocki (1982), who noted that after the Rooks at one rookery had been subject to a cull late in the breeding season, several now empty nests were occupied by Kestrel pairs. An experiment by Village (1990) showed similar results: in his Scottish study area, where there were few natural nest sites, or where possible sites (such as stick nests in patches of woodland) were unusable because they lay within the territories of other Kestrel pairs, the erection of artificial nests late in the breeding season saw half the sites being utilised, while in his English study area, where natural nest sites were readily available, and Kestrel territories smaller so that few sites were denied to others by the aggressiveness of territory holders, none of the artificial sites were occupied. Village also experimented by removing one bird of a pair and watching the response. In three of four nests in his Scottish study area the removed bird was replaced, while in 25 nests in his English study area, 11 birds were replaced. Of the 25 English removals, 13 were male, 12 were female, but there were more female replacements (8 of 11, 72%) than male (3 of 11, 27%); in all three cases the replacement males failed to breed, but four of the replacement females bred successfully, in addition to one who took over the clutch of her predecessor. The implication of the failure to breed of all three replacement males is that they were poor hunters: two of the three were first-year males, which might suggest this was the case, as an ability to survive your first winter does not necessarily mean you are up the task of supporting a female (and, perhaps in her eyes, a brood). In the English study area, one removed male bred again with his original partner when he was released. Some other removed/released birds bred the following year, occasionally with their original mate. However, nine removed birds were not seen again after release. The experiments suggest that many non-breeding Kestrels are such because they lack territory, or a mate, or both.

Incubation

The female's brood patch develops prior to laying, feathers of the belly and lower chest area being lost to expose an area of richly vascularised skin, blood heat being transferred to the eggs. The stimulus for female birds to begin incubation may be visual or tactile. The tactile stimulus would be contact between the brood patch and an area/volume of eggs which would depend, in the Kestrel's case, on final clutch size. In the study of Beukeboom *et al.* (1988) – see *Clutch size* – it was concluded that the eggs both stimulated incubation and fixed clutch size by follicle suppression, though whether the stimulus was visual or tactile or both could not be differentiated.

During incubation the female will periodically turn the eggs: she will also give a soft call to initiate a response, reassuring herself that her mate is present. Male Eurasian Kestrels do not develop brood patches (whereas their American cousins do) or incubate, though they do sit on the eggs for short periods while the female feeds, preens or bathes. Packham (1985b) observed a male which not only showed a brood patch but took turns to incubate, and gave references for others who had seen males incubating. However, the report of a male brood patch is anomalous and in general males do not incubate.

Females avoid defecating at the nest: they usually break from incubating for no more than 20–30 minutes, during which time they not only defecate, but preen and stretch. But while the female is fastidious in terms of defecation, she will cast pellets at the nest, these occasionally accumulating around the eggs during incubation and forming part of the substrate for the hatchlings. Incubating females may sit tight if approached – to the point of allowing the observer to catch them: Village (1990) claims 10% of his catches were made this way – or may fly off immediately on approach. As a panicky escape may result in eggs or chicks being thrown out of the nest, any approach should be made with the utmost caution.

Because incubation does not begin once the first egg of the clutch has been laid, and because the brood may take several days to hatch, defining the incubation period precisely is difficult. Village (1990) notes periods from 26 to 34 days, with a mean of 30.8 days. Although there is a spread in hatching dates, several eggs usually hatch on the same day because of the delayed start to incubation: occasionally the entire clutch may hatch on the same day, though it has been known for hatching to take 4–5 days to complete.

The advantages and disadvantages of synchronous and asynchronous hatching have been debated for many years, and evidence from the field is not conclusive. In a study in Finland Wiebe *et al.* (1998) noted that synchronous hatching resulted in better fledgling survival in times of food scarcity, though the authors noted that the difference was not clear-cut and that other factors needed to be investigated before a final conclusion could be reached. But in another Finnish study (Wiebe *et al.* 2000) it was noted that the time female Kestrels spent away from the nest (and therefore not incubating) was not spent hunting as had been assumed, indicating that the female was actually delaying incubation in an effort to enhance the survival rate of an asynchronously hatched brood. Interestingly, although the observed females were nesting in boxes, and could therefore have taken advantage of the shelter afforded by the box by staying within it, sitting beside the eggs, the females chose to leave the box even though they were not hunting. This could, perhaps, imply that the sight of the clutch was a stimulant to incubation and so was being avoided. In Britain one female Kestrel stopped incubating during a period of very cold weather with snow, covering the eggs long enough to avoid chilling, apparently delaying hatching until the male was able to hunt (C. Dobbs, personal communication).

One factor potentially influencing the Finnish studies (Wiebe *et al.* 2000) is the cyclic nature of the vole population, with well-defined peaks and troughs. However, in another study in Finland Massemin *et al.* (2002) found that while early growth rates of late-hatched chicks in asynchronous broods were slower, by the age of 26 days these chicks had attained the weights of their siblings, while in Spain, an area where the vole population is more stable, Martínez-Padilla & Viñuela (2011) found that asynchronous hatching did not lead to a higher rate of chick survival. However, the Spanish team did suggest that in their studies (which involved injecting nestlings with a lectin to induce an immune response) nestlings of asynchronous broods had an enhanced immune response which could imply a better 'quality' of nestling. To add further confusion, this finding appears in conflict with early work in Switzerland which looked at the parasite burden of chicks from asynchronously hatched broods of several species, including Kestrels (Roulin *et al.* 2003). The aim of the study was to test the captivatingly named 'tasty chick hypothesis' (TCH), which suggests that chicks hatched later in asynchronous broods are more attractive to ectoparasites. Chick hatch rank was identified in such broods and the chicks were checked for immune response and number of parasites. The results showed that immune response was greater in earlier-hatched chicks of Barn Owls, but not in Great Tits: the burden of the tick *Ixodes ricinus* was random across hatchlings; and the louse fly *Crataerina melbae* infested older rather than younger hatchlings in the Alpine Swift (*Apus melba*). These results do not support TCH as a global hypothesis, but the burden of the fly *Carnus haemapterus* was greater in late-hatched chicks in both Barn Owls and Kestrels, which does imply that Kestrels produce tasty chicks. As noted above, the introduction of nest boxes has led to Kestrel population increases in some areas, but studies have shown that nest-box usage has also resulted in an increase in chick ectoparasite burden: for example, Fargallo *et al.* (2001) noted an increase in chick infestation with *Carnus haemapterus* in nest boxes, the average fly count being five times higher than for chicks in natural nests. However, while Sumasgutner *et al.* (2014b) found a similar increase in the burden of the same fly in nest boxes which had not been cleaned compared with boxes which had been cleaned, the parasites had no effect on breeding success.

Village (1990) observes that the chick can be heard calling a day or so before hatching, but notes that it is not known if this is to alert the female or to an attempt to synchronise hatching. Hatching is slow and exhausting, the chick chipping away at the shell for up to 24 hours with its egg tooth before being completely free. Some chicks are so exhausted by the hatching process that they do not survive. The egg tooth disappears a week or so after hatching.

Chick growth
On hatching, the chicks are semi-altricial and nidicolous, and weigh 14–18 g. They are covered in white down which dries quickly under the brooding female. Though initially blind (the eyes are fully open by the third or fourth day after hatching), the chicks are able to lift their heads to call for food. They are voracious when it comes to food intake. Though the female is careful to provide, bill to bill, pieces which can be easily swallowed, a chick will readily take any item of food

it can reach irrespective of its size and attempt to swallow it. Village (1990) notes that this occasionally results in chicks with prey items – legs, wings – sticking out of their bills, these having to be retrieved by the female if they are not ultimately swallowed. The wonder of it is that more chicks do not die as a consequence of choking. Since most chicks which die do so of starvation, competition between siblings does appear to involve survival of the fittest, but Shrubb (1993a) observed some females carefully ensuring that all chicks received food: he suggests that such behaviour is likely to be more common when food is plentiful, competition and starvation resulting when food becomes scarce – see Note 6.2.

The ravenous hunger which drives them to take any available food item means the chicks grow quickly (Figs 154 & 155), the parent birds

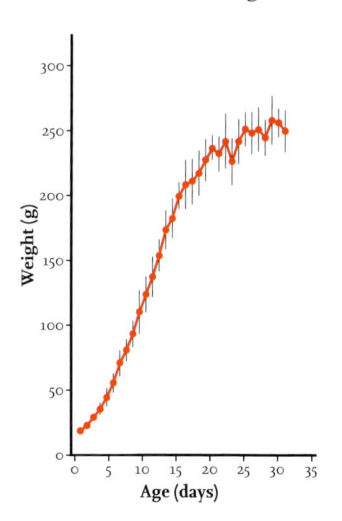

FIG 154. Growth rate of 17 Kestrel chicks from five broods in southern Scotland. The S-shaped curve is approximately the same for all species of bird and does not depend on the initial state of the hatchling, i.e. whether altricial or precocial. For more information on the growth of chicks see, for instance, Ricklefs (1968, 1973). For further information on altricial nestlings see Ricklefs (1969). In general the weight of all chicks peaks prior to fledging, then decreases. The reasons for this are debated. Redrawn from Village 1990.

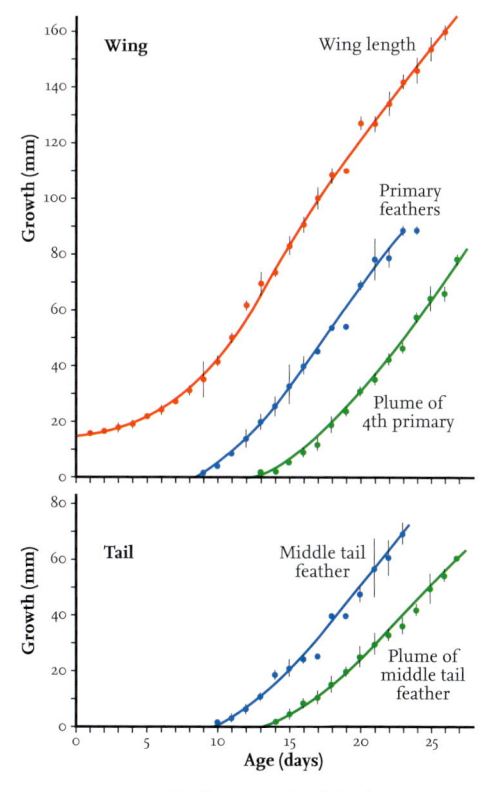

FIG 155. Growth of wing and tail feathers in a Kestrel nestling near Cologne. Redrawn from Kostrzewa & Kostrzewa 1993.

FIG 156. Kestrel chicks in a basket nest in southern Scotland watch expectantly (a) as the female brings in a vole. Because of the position of the camera only the vole can be seen, the female being out of shot. In (b), the female Kestrel has begun to feed the vole to the chicks.

adjusting food delivery to suit chick demand (Steen *et al.* 2012). Chick weight doubles within two days of hatching, and rises steadily over the next 12–14 days, so that at about 15 days the chick is at 80–85% of adult weight. Weight gain then slows, the chick reaching 90% of adult weight at about three weeks of age.

The overall sex ratio of the chicks is 1:1, but Dijkstra *et al.* (1990a) noted significant variations in the ratio dependent on both the sequence of eggs and the date of laying of the clutch. In early clutches males dominated (being about 58% of nestlings) whereas in later ones the number of males declined (to about 32%). In early clutches eggs which would develop into male birds tended to be laid early in the clutch (eggs 1–3), while in later clutches 'male' eggs were laid later (eggs > 4) (Fig. 157). Given that in general eggs laid early hatch first, and early chicks may out-compete their later-hatched siblings and consequently have a higher inherent survival rate, this predominance of males over females in early clutches and of females over males in later ones accords with the breeding behaviour of yearling Kestrels. The probability of a yearling male breeding declines with its birth date, whereas that of a yearling female does not, so by producing males early and female late, a female Kestrel is maximising the potential of passing her genes to the third generation. This effect was modelled by Daan *et al.* (1996), who showed good agreement with the data of Dijkstra *et al.* (1990a). Daan and colleagues therefore concluded that the observed preponderance of male chicks born early and female chick is born late was in line with the evolutionary hypothesis that early breeding parents are usually in the best condition and habitat, and will therefore produce an excess of the gender which profits most from an early birth date.

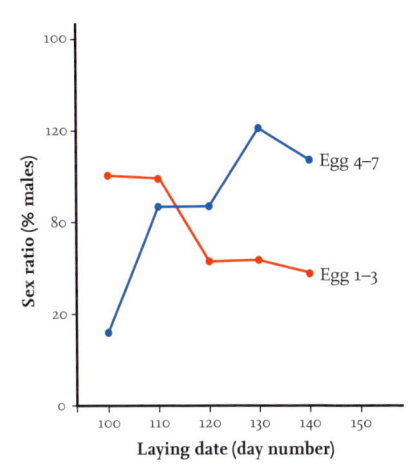

FIG 157. Seasonal change in the sex ratio of 265 Kestrel eggs in the Netherlands of known laying order. Redrawn from Dijkstra *et al.* 1990a.

The chicks are brooded more or less continuously by the female for about ten days. In a study of hand-reared Kestrel chicks, Kirkwood (1981) noted that the chicks were largely inactive and produced little heat during the early period after hatching, almost all food intake being converted into growth, the lack of heat production meaning that the chicks are unable to regulate their body temperature until they are ten days old. Weight gain predominates during this early period of growth, plumage development being relatively

274 · FALCONS

slow – which, of course, exacerbates heat loss unless the chicks are brooded. During the initial ten-day period the female must be in constant attendance at the nest, leaving only to receive food from the male. The female usually feeds the meat of prey items to the chicks, contenting herself with the entrails and

FIG 158. Another feed arrives at the Kestrel basket nest in southern Scotland.

skin that remains, and so loses weight unless the male brings a surplus of food. During this ten-day period the male Kestrel does not cover the chicks, as he occasionally did the eggs. Once the chicks are ten days old the females spends progressively less time brooding, preferring to stand guard from a nearby perch, though she may brood for long periods if the weather is wet or cold. Once she has reduced her brooding time the female starts to hunt, for herself and the chicks, and the male starts to deliver prey directly to the nest. Riddle (2011) records that at one nest where the female was injured, probably in a fight with a Tawny Owl, and had to be destroyed, the male bird continued to feed the chicks and successfully reared them to fledge and dispersal.

In a study in Czechoslovakia (as it then was) Pikula *et al.* (1984) noted that prey was delivered at fairly regular intervals during the day, though with a slackening towards evening. In another interesting study by the Groningen University team, nest boxes were organised so that the comings and goings of the male Kestrel could be observed (Masman *et al.* 1988a). The researchers then varied the number of nestlings in the nest. Adding more chicks had little effect on male prey deliveries when the chicks were less than ten days old, but once they were older and the male was delivering prey directly to the nest, the rate of prey delivery increased, presumably because the male was able to judge the hunger of the chicks. What was clear from the study was that the male could not differentiate his own chicks from those added to the nest. When the chicks in a brood were given extra food by the Dutch team, the male reduced prey deliveries, reinforcing the idea that he could gauge chick hunger and alter his hunting behaviour appropriately. It must, of course, be the case that there is a limit to what the male is able to do, and in times of prey scarcity he might be unable to increase his delivery rate.

The initial white down of the chicks is replaced by a coarser grey down eight days after hatching. At about the same time the sheaths of the primaries emerge (growth is highly asymmetric, the legs and feet being near adult size before the flight feathers emerge), followed by those of the tail 2–3 days later. The primaries erupt from their sheaths on day 13, by which time the chicks take food from the adult's feet and eat it themselves (Village 1990). However, although the chicks grab at food in order to forestall attempts by siblings, it is not until day 20 that the characteristic mantling of obtained food to preclude its being stolen is seen. During periods when they are not eating or competing for food the chicks exercise their wings and practise their killing skills with attacks on remnant prey items. They also stare from the nest site, seemingly taking in the local area as though composing a mental map: if that is the case then it is likely to be time well spent when the time to leave the nest and start exploratory hunting arrives.

276 · FALCONS

As the chicks age they become more aggressive to the parent birds bringing food, the parents no longer attempting any feeding but, rather, spending minimal time at the nest, apparently so as to avoid injury.

In addition to the female's cast pellets which accumulate at the nest, the chicks also produce pellets as soon as they are feeding themselves, as they ingest fur and feathers as well as meat. Once they are mobile, the chicks move to the edge of the nest to excrete, but their aim is not always true. With prey items

FIG 159. The first of five eggs hatching in a clutch laid in a Carrion Crow nest.

FIG 160. The chicks at the same nest aged 6 days.

THE KESTREL · 277

FIG 161. The five chicks in the crow stick nest are now 16 days old.

FIG 162. The chicks at 23 days old.

FIG 163. The chicks at 28 days old.

FIG 164. At 28 days old the chicks were large and aggressive and the female was reluctant to land on the nest in case she was injured in the pandemonium that erupted on her arrival. In this shot she barely touches the nest edge as she throws a rodent into the chaotic mass of feathers ahead of her.

FIG 165. By contrast the male Kestrel was less fearful of the chicks, and would stand at the nest edge after delivering prey. In this shot the chick facing the camera has taken the rodent while its siblings surround the male to see if he has anything else.

occasionally being cached, or left uneaten, over time the nest, particularly the periphery, becomes somewhat rank.

By day 26 down feathers are being lost and juvenile feathers are emerging, the young birds being fledged at about 35 days, at which time they leave the nest (though in some studies chicks as young as 28 days have been seen to leave the nest). When they leave, young Kestrels are heavier than adult birds, but usually a little lighter in weight than a maximum achieved a couple of days before leaving. In most observations the young stay close to the nest after first leaving it, often for 2–3 weeks, but in a study of colonial breeding in Spain, Bustamante (1994) noted that the young infrequently returned to the nest area once they had left it, perching on ledges or the top of the colonial cliffs and sometimes gathering in groups of unrelated birds. It is not clear whether this behaviour is specific to colonial nesting. In the UK it is usual for the young to stay reasonably close to the nest while they are being fed by the adult birds. During this period the young birds practise flying – they begin to practise flight-hunting about ten days after leaving the nest (Bustamante 1994), and may also practise hunting techniques, either on inanimate objects or on insects. They may also engage in high-spirited play with their siblings. When delivering food to young that have left the nest the adults call as they arrive, prompting reply calls that direct them to where the chicks are sitting. As soon as their flying techniques allow, the chicks will fly up to meet the returning adults, allowing them to gain an advantage over their siblings as in those circumstances the adults give food on a first-come basis. To obtain the food the young bird flies to the adult, then rolls sideways to take the prey from the adult's talons.

The period over which the juveniles require food from the adults (or over which the adults continue to provide it, as the two periods may not necessarily be the same) varies considerably, Masman (1988a) noting times from 18 to 32 days. In western France, Boileau & Bretagnolle (2014) also found a range of dependence periods, but varying from 3 to 31 days with a mean of 18 days. They also noted that the majority of the feeding was by the male, females stopping their contribution after only three days, a finding which is at variance with other studies. Interestingly, Boileau & Bretagnolle noted that there was a positive correlation between the body condition of the youngsters (as measured by wing length and weight of the chicks at age 31 days) and the time of continued feeding – the male bird was preferentially feeding those birds which appeared to have a better chance of survival. The decision by the male to continue feeding an individual did not appear to be influenced by the hatching order of the chicks, and Boileau & Bretagnolle commented that the positive correlation with body condition recalled previous work on Kestrels. In a study in Spain Vergara &

FIG 166. Kestrel chick removed to the ground for ringing.

FIG 167. Tail and wing feather growth in a young Kestrel.

Fargallo (2008) had noted that sibling rivalry for food in the post-fledging period differed from that between nestlings, with male chicks tending to obtain the larger prey items delivered by their parents, as these were left on the ground for the fledglings to retrieve and males had superior flight abilities. In addition, males with rumps which were greyer did better, in terms of larger prey, than

FIG 168. Early flight by a fledgling Kestrel (a). The early flight ended with a crash-landing onto a steep roof ridge (b), the young falcon having to immediately take off again when it failed to cling on.

male siblings with browner rumps. Vergara & Fargallo suggested that grey rumps are an indication of better body condition, and that this enables the grey-rumped youngsters to out-compete brown-rumped siblings, but it might also explain the finding of Boileau & Bretagnolle (2014), as coloration would allow male falcons to distinguish better-quality offspring.

In a further study in Spain Vergara *et al.* (2010) again showed the importance of male fledgling coloration in the post-fledge period, but also noted that the 'quality' of the parent birds was important in defining the post-fledge feeding period. Particularly in scarce prey years, better parents feed post-fledge youngsters for longer, though even then better juveniles are fed preferentially.

During the post-fledge period the juveniles begin to learn the art of catching prey. Initially, starting about ten days after leaving the nest, this will be insect prey caught on the ground. The juveniles then graduate to catching flying insects. At about 20 days from the nest they start to flight-hunt, early attempts being close to the ground and often unstable. They become proficient at about four weeks from the nest. The juveniles also play, with sticks of feathers, using these as proxy prey which are duly 'killed'. Shrubb (1993a) reports an observation from Gwent, Wales in which the adult birds spent about 20 minutes dropping sticks and balls of sheep's wool for their youngsters to chase and catch (see Hewitt 2013 for more general thoughts on prey dropping). Bustamante (1994) studied the behaviour of fledglings in a colonial nest site in Spain and saw the play noted above, but also saw the birds involved in apparently social behaviour with not only siblings but the youngsters of other broods. In general a fledgling from one nest would perch closer to fledglings from another nest than it would to either its siblings or its own nest. Bustamante also noted that the fledglings would chase each other or would carry out mock attacks on perched birds, causing them to fly off, but that the roles would often be reversed, implying social behaviour rather than aggression. I have also observed one boisterous youngster stooping repeatedly on another perched fledgling (it was not clear whether the perched bird was a sibling or from another nest), one mock stoop getting out of control and involving the youngster in a very precarious slowing manoeuvre, after which the mock stoops ceased. Similar mock (or assumed mock) attacks by a juvenile on an adult female have also been observed (Oakley-Martin 2008).

Breeding success

Studies of the breeding success of Kestrel pairs show that multiple factors are involved in determining whether the path from pair formation to fledged young is a smooth one. One interesting factor is whether the Kestrel population of a

FIG 169. One fledgling Kestrel had managed to land higher up a building than a sibling. Diving down with the apparent intention of terrifying its sibling all went well in a stoop at first (a) but soon the young bird lost control (b) and seemed lucky to have pulled out of the dive before catastrophe overtook it.

given area is sedentary or migratory. In England (Village 1990) and Germany (Kostrzewa & Kostrzewa 1997), where the population is sedentary, the number of territorial pairs which failed to lay eggs was high (13%), while in the partially migrant population of Scotland it was lower (6%: Village 1990; 7%: Riddle 1987), and in the completely migrant population of Finland it was lower still (3%: Korpimäki & Norrdahl 1991). To examine what lies behind this variation in failure rate it is necessary to consider several potential inputs.

The influence of winter weather on the number of breeding pairs in a given area has already been mentioned with reference to the study of Kostrzewa & Kostrzewa (1991). That study also indicated that while the territorial density of Kestrels was independent of 'vole rank' (an indication of the population density of voles) the breeding density did depend on vole population. Kostrzewa & Kostrzewa (1990) also studied the effect of spring and summer weather, confirming the results of Cavé (1967) – already noted previously in relation to breeding density – that spring rainfall had a negative effect on Kestrel breeding, while fledging success was very positively correlated with the temperature in May and June, the number of successful fledglings per Kestrel pair rising from 3.5 if the mean May–June temperature was 13 °C, to 5.1 if it was 16 °C. In particular, the temperature during the hatching period and for the subsequent two weeks was critical. As would be expected, the number of fledged chicks from a Kestrel pair was also dependent on the vole population.

From the work of Village (1990) there is also a relationship between the laying date of the first egg and the success of the pair in fledging young (i.e. of breeding success) and the number of fledged young (Fig. 170). As has already been discussed, the timing of the first egg laying and subsequent clutch size is a subject of debate, but there is little doubt that parental quality is influential, as evidenced by Village's studies, which suggest that poor quality of either or both parents may influence the success of the pair in producing any chicks, and in nurturing those chicks that do hatch through to fledging. Overall, Village's work showed that 30% of Kestrel pairs failed after laying eggs and that 32% of successful pairs lost either eggs or chicks.

Village (1990) found that complete breeding failure was more frequent during incubation than after chicks had hatched, and that the most likely reason was nest desertion, accounting for over 50% of failures in each of

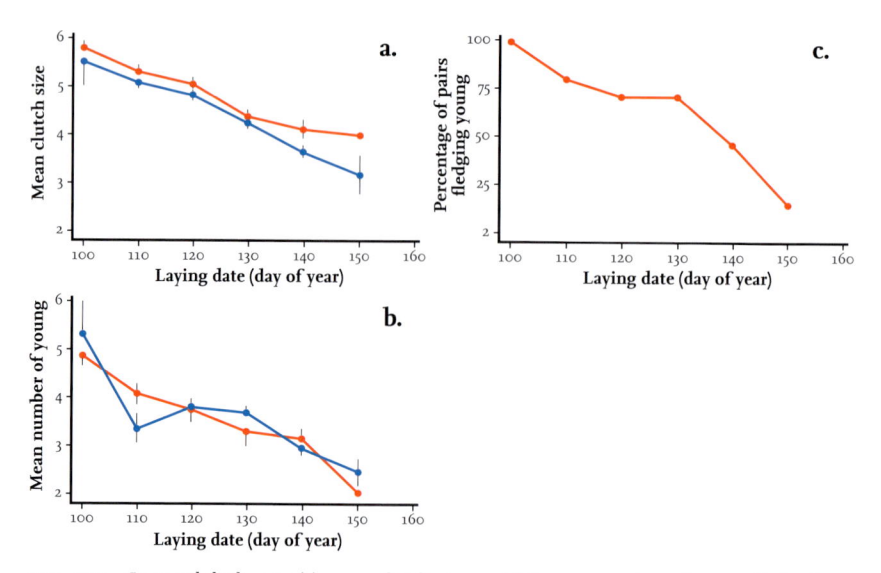

FIG 170. Seasonal decline in (a) mean clutch size and (b) mean number of young fledged per laying pair, laying in a ten-day period: data from southern Scotland grassland (red) and east-central England farmland (blue). Seasonal decline in (c) percentage of pairs fledging young, also laying in a ten-day period: data combined for Scottish and English sites. Redrawn from Village 1990.

his English study areas, and over 70% in his Scottish study area. The most probable cause of desertion is that the female has to abandon the nest as she is receiving inadequate food from the male. From the work of Cavé (1967) this is most likely due to the male being unable to catch sufficient prey in poor prey years, or being unable to hunt in poor weather. However, the fact that nest failure is positively correlated with time of laying indicates that parental quality is also a contributory factor. Human interference and predation are also likely contributors, while historically, egg addling and breakages due to organochlorines were undoubtedly significant factors.

Village (1990) states that overall about 50% of eggs laid failed to produce fledged young, with the bulk of failures (about 70%) being due to failure at the egg stage. Egg failures were due in the main to eggs not hatching (76%), though there were losses from broken eggs (9%) or eggs falling from the nest (5%) – in 10% of cases the cause of egg failure was not ascertained. Losses among chicks were 28% at hatch, 5% in falls from the nest and 55% where the probable cause was starvation – in 13% of cases the cause was not ascertained. (In the case of unknown chick loss Village notes that these losses were usually within ten days of hatch, and that dead chicks were likely to have been eaten by siblings or parents, a rather sad and macabre occurrence.) The statistics of Village are in reasonable accord with those of Shrubb (1993a), who studied the records of Kestrel nesting in Britain during the period 1950–1987, a total of 1,350 eggs in 308 nests. Shrubb found 48% of eggs laid failed to produce fledged young, with 64% of the failures occurring at the egg stage. Shrubb's analysis also confirmed that the bulk of egg losses were due to the eggs not hatching, because they were either infertile or had been deserted. However, Shrubb also found that the taking of Kestrel eggs by humans was a significant cause of failure. Humans taking chicks was also significant, Shrubb quoting the analysis of Mather (1986), who pointed out that the number of hatchlings removed from the nest by would-be falconers had increased dramatically when the film *Kes* was released (in 1969).

One interesting aspect of Village's study of English and Scottish breeding areas was that the productivity of the Kestrels – i.e. the number of chicks raised per unit area of countryside – was positively correlated with breeding density, the number of fledged young/100 km^2 rising logarithmically with breeding density. This implies that when conditions are good, i.e. the vole population is high, more Kestrel pairs can breed early, clutches are larger and the survival rate of chicks is high. Of course this relationship cannot continue indefinitely, but the Kestrel breeding density in the UK is relatively low so population dynamics of predators similar to those seen in areas such as Fennoscandia, where the lemming population cycles through peaks and troughs, will probably never occur. However, even at low breeding densities, an effect might be expected within nests if direct competition between siblings led to higher chick mortality – but Village did not see this, and neither did Cavé (1967) in his study of brood survival rates in the Netherlands.

A final factor in the survival of chicks is the experience of the adult pair, and here Village's (1990) data showed a clear effect both in terms of the age of the pair, and whether they were newcomers to an area or had bred there previously. As might be expected, older adults and pairs who had previously bred together in the same area bred earlier than other pairs, first-year male and first-year female partnerships bred later, and pairs new to the area also bred later. As earlier breeding leads to higher clutches and better chick survival rates, the best that a Kestrel chick can do is to ensure that his or her parents are older birds, at home in the area and with each other. Bad news for the chick is a pair of first-year birds who have just moved in. Sadly, of course, Kestrel chicks find choosing their parentage no easier than the rest of us.

Nest-site, territory and mate fidelity

In his study of Scottish and English populations, Village (1990) was able to identify specific factors which influenced the fidelity of Kestrels, both to nest area and to mate. In his Scottish study area most of the Kestrels were migratory, only 11% being resident, and 66% were summer-only visitors; there were no winter visitors. However, in the English study area 52% of the birds were resident, the area attracting fewer summer-only and more winter-only visitors than in Scotland, numbers which are in keeping with what would be expected, given that the migratory pattern of UK Kestrels is dominated by movements of northern birds. A consequence of the relative state of flux of the Scottish birds was that most individuals bred only once (70% of males, 80% of females), though Village did see a small number of birds which bred in successive springs. In England, with its higher resident population, the number breeding once was lower, around 50% of males and 60% of females. In the English populations males bred in up to six successive seasons, and females up to seven (in a seven-year study). The corollary of this information on successive breeding was that many more of the breeding birds in Village's Scottish study area were new to the area than in his English area. In general, those birds which successfully bred were more likely to return to the area, a feature which was equally likely for both sexes in Scotland, but more likely for males in England. It would therefore seem that the more likely a bird was to remain in a breeding area, the more likely it was to be breed there (illustrating territorial and, perhaps, nest fidelity, and, though less likely, mate fidelity).

For Scottish birds, with over 70% of birds in pairs migrating, it was much less likely that either would return, and much less likely that they would mate again if they did. However, in Village's English study area, where many more birds were resident, the percentage of birds mating again with the same partner was not significantly different, suggesting that migration did not influence mate fidelity to any great degree. More significant was the success of the previous year's breeding. This was particularly the case for English birds, though, as Village points out, this result may have been due to the much smaller dataset for the Scottish area masking a similar effect. We can therefore conclude, with some confidence, that if a Kestrel pair are successful in breeding in a given spring, then provided that both birds meet again the following spring they are more likely to remain together than not. In his study of Kestrels in Ayrshire in 1980–1992, Riddle (2011) noted that at one site, one female returned in three successive years, while another returned three times in four years. However, in general he found females returned no more than twice, and often did not return at all. These data are consistent with Riddle's view that the life expectancy of adult Kestrels is four years.

Village (1990) also considered movements of birds – wing-tagged for ease of identification – between nest sites in successive breeding seasons (Fig. 171). He found that such movements averaged 0.7 km for males and 1.0 km for females (combining data from both his Scottish and English sites, which showed similar results). With data relating to birds that used the same nest site in successive

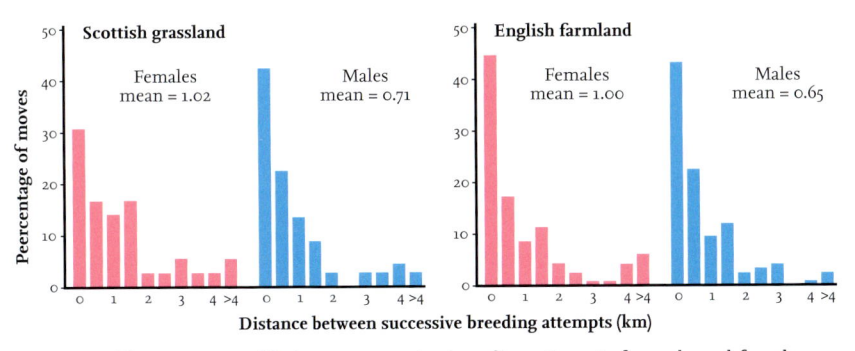

FIG 171. Distances moved between successive breeding attempts for male and female Kestrels in southern Scottish grassland and east-central English farmland. The distances moved were similar for each area, but in general females moved further than males. Redrawn from Village 1990.

years excluded, movements rose to 1.1 km for males and 1.6 km for females. Older birds were less likely to move between breeding attempts, especially females, where 47% moved after their first breeding season, but only 29% after subsequent ones. These percentages imply a high degree of fidelity not only to a nest site territory, but to a particular nest site. While for some pairs this may be a result of the limited number of available sites, personal observation suggests that fidelity to a particular nest box, rock cleft and even stick nest, if it remains serviceable, is high. We have already noted the nest-site fidelity of urban Kestrels. That this is, in part, a territorial fidelity was illustrated by a study of Kestrels in a town in the Czech Republic (Riegert & Fuchs 2011). There, snow cover in winter made predation of rodents more difficult, but some male Kestrels did not migrate, choosing to stay in the town, supplementing their diet with birds and insects, and roosting near the nest sites used during the previous breeding season. This behaviour allowed the males to be in a good position to defend territories and so acquire mates early in the following breeding season. In Britain one particular urban nest site, a church window ledge, is known to have been in used over a period of at least 40 years (C Dobbs, personal communication).

MOVEMENTS AND WINTER DENSITY

Once the adult birds have stopped feeding their offspring – there is no concrete evidence to indicate that parent birds engage in active, aggressive attempts to expel their brood, though Shrubb (1993a) does suggest that adults occasionally steal from their young and move them away from preferred hunting areas, either of which would encourage the juveniles to seek their own space – the young Kestrels disperse, usually taking up residence close to the breeding territory of their parents. Riddle (2011) reports several observations of Kestrels being seen in congregations, citing records of 15–25, of 30, and even of 40 on one occasion. These aggregations seem to have been in highly prized prey areas and must be considered unusual.

In a tabulation of data on recovered, ringed young accumulated over a 70-year period to 1984, Village (1990) found that in the first month after dispersal 74% of birds had moved less than 25 km from the natal territory. However, some had moved greater distances, 4% exceeding 150 km. Village's own observations included one Scottish bird which had flown over 300 km from the parental breeding territory in only 24 days, but this pales in comparison to one of Riddle's (2011) Ayrshire birds which was ringed on 19 June and died after flying into a pylon on Tenerife, 3,076 km away, on 11 October. That represents a daily flight of 27 km if it is assumed the bird died on the day of arrival and it could, of course, have arrived some time earlier. Such distances and times are in keeping with the observations of Adriaensen *et al.* (1997) on the recoveries of ringed Kestrels in Belgium, which indicated that Kestrels are strong fliers. Shrubb (1993a) also notes one bird which moved from a nest area in Shropshire to Northern Ireland, a journey which involved a significant sea crossing, and notes another juvenile which was ringed in Luxembourg in June 1983 and recovered in County Clare in August of the same year. Many Dutch-ringed birds also turn up in southern England, which again involves a sea crossing, but in general sea crossings are rare rather than the norm.

As time from cessation of feeding increases, the fraction of birds travelling greater distances increases – as winter approaches only 20–25% of young are still within 25 km of the natal territory. In sedentary populations these birds, together with those that have travelled greater distances, say up to 100 km, will have found territories which they will maintain for the winter. In migratory or partially migratory populations, the distances travelled by young birds as winter approaches may indicate migration rather dispersal, particularly as early dispersal directions tend to be random, whereas later migration routes are southwest.

Young Kestrels fledged from early nests disperse sooner and tend to stay closer to their natal territories than fledglings from later nests. This is not a great surprise, as later birds searching for a territory are moving through areas which are more likely to be occupied. But the requirement to move further usually means that the establishment of a territory is delayed. That, in turn, is reflected in both winter survival rates and in the ability of the young birds to breed in the following spring. The work of Adriaensen *et al.* (1998) on Belgian Kestrels also shows that young birds are driven to move further from the natal territory if prey is in short supply when they become independent. Using the energy content of the seeds (acorns and beech nuts) from the previous winter as an indicator of probable rodent population, the researchers showed a linear relationship between this measure of prey availability and the average distance travelled from the natal territory by young birds. Again, extra distance travelled will be reflected in winter mortality and spring breeding rates. In both the work in the UK by Village (1990), and in work on Dutch Kestrels (Dijkstra 1988), it was found that birds fledging early were five times more likely to breed in their first year than were those that fledged later. In his Kestrel studies, Village (1990) found no correlation between the distances travelled by dispersing siblings, but a significant correlation in the direction of travel. He also found some evidence of siblings travelling together, though this does not appear to be a general rule.

True migrations for most populations in Europe begin in September and October, and are usually complete by November. The general direction of travel is northeast to southwest, at least initially, the birds heading towards southern France and Spain. Birds reaching Spain may cross the Straits of Gibraltar to enter north Africa, then make their way south to west Africa. In Britain, the sedentary population is joined by birds arriving from Scandinavia, these birds often being seen resting on North Sea oil platforms en route. All populations of Kestrels in northeastern and eastern Europe that breed in areas with permanent winter snow cover are migratory, taking routes which cross southern Europe to reach Spain, then crossing to north Africa and heading south to west Africa or the coastal belt from Liberia to Nigeria; or crossing the Adriatic, Italy and the Mediterranean to north Africa and then heading south across the Sahara to west Africa. Although data are scant, it seems Kestrels from south-central Asia take a route though Arabia to reach east Africa (Wernham *et al.* 2002).

Few British Kestrels migrate, and those that do largely come from Scotland and northern England. This raises the obvious question of why some birds migrate and others from the same area do not. Those that remain in an area risk bad weather with its inherent risk of starvation: snow cover reduces the availability of voles and Britain is unpredictable in terms of snow duration, explaining why Kestrels breeding in areas of northern and eastern Europe where snow cover is both more certain and lasts predictably longer are entirely migratory. But remaining in an area means being able to maintain a territory and even perhaps a mate, and so enhances the chances of early breeding when spring arrives. Migration reduces the rigours of winter, but the trade-off is a potentially dangerous journey which must be accomplished twice, the need to find a winter territory and, possibly, problems with finding a suitable spring territory after the return journey and, potentially, a later breeding date as a consequence. Village (1990) found no evidence of migrants becoming residents during later winters, or of residents choosing to become migrants. This implies that once a pattern of behaviour is chosen by an individual bird the pattern is maintained through life.

Most migrating British Kestrels travel much smaller distances than their northern and eastern European cousins, reaching only central or southern England, though some British birds do reach Spain and Africa. In a study in Sweden, Wallin *et al.* (1987) found that Kestrels from the north of the country migrated twice the distance of those from the south, but took the same time to complete their migration. As the migration route of the southern Kestrels lay entirely within that of the northern birds, this meant that those from the north were moving at twice the speed. However, Wallin and his co-workers found that during the return journey, the northern birds travelled at the same speed, and so reached their breeding grounds later, the more leisurely journey reflecting the fact that snow cover in the north took longer to clear. One interesting aspect of this leapfrogging is that most of the Kestrels which migrate south of the Sahara are from the populations of northeastern and eastern Europe. There is no evidence of a similar leapfrogging in migrating British Kestrels. During long migrations, Kestrels use flapping flight rather than the soaring flight associated with many other raptors. For this reason Kestrels rarely figure among the spectacular concentrations of migrating raptors seen at various famous points adjacent to sea crossings.

In many species of raptors, males migrate further than females (Newton, 2008), but this is not the case in Kestrels. Not only do females travel further than males, but they migrate earlier than males, and the fraction of females migrating is greater than in males (Wallin *et al.* 1987, Village 1990, Kjellén 1992, 1994). In his study of migrating birds at Falsterbo in Sweden, Kjellén (1992) noted that both females and juveniles migrated earlier than males (Fig. 172). The reasons for differential migration are still discussed. Kjellén (1992) considers that the most likely explanation involves the timing of the moult, with females having completed the moult during incubation and so being in a better position to migrate than males who must wait to moult as they are the primary suppliers of food to the nestlings. The moult hypothesis does not contradict the migration

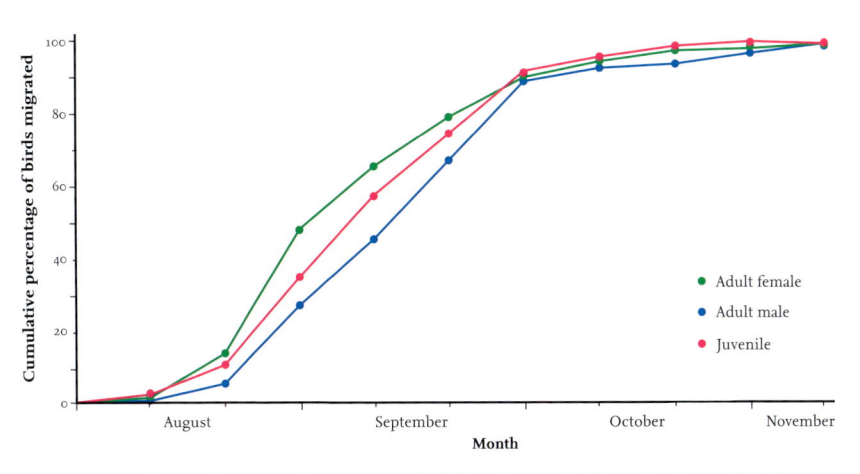

FIG 172. Differential autumnal migration of adult and juvenile Kestrels observed in the period 1986–1990 at Falsterbo Peninsula, southern Sweden. The curves show the cumulative percentage of birds that had migrated at a certain date. Redrawn from Kjellén 1992.

FIG 173. Wintering Kestrel in southern England. The bird was roosting in a barn and using all available daylight to hunt on days when hunting was possible.

pattern seen in those falcon species in which the males and females depart at the same time, as these birds are long-distance migrants and arrest the moult in autumn prior to migration, completing it at the winter quarters.

The likely reason for males to stay on the wintering grounds, if staying is an option, is to occupy or protect a territory and so be in a position to mate and breed early when females return. For similar reasons, males tend to return earlier in the spring. For British migrants Village (1985) notes not only that males arrive earlier than females at the breeding grounds, but that adults arrive earlier than first-year birds.

Village (1990) notes a degree of winter site fidelity in migrants, pointing out that such behaviour is to be expected, since a bird finding available resources to sustain it over winter would likely head for the same area rather than seek out a new area unless the latter was identified by chance.

The spring migration may start as early as February, though is mainly seen in March and April, with some birds, those likely to be heading for northern Scandinavia, not leaving until early May. For British birds migrating short distances and therefore staying within the country, mild winters may mean an earlier return to their breeding grounds. Further evidence that Kestrels are strong fliers is given by the fact that some returning long-distance migrants, birds ringed at Cape Bon, Tunisia, and then recovered in Europe a few days later, had travelled over 200 km/day (Dejonghe 1989). The routes followed by spring migrants do not follow the exact line of their outward journeys, wind direction altering the points at which coastlines are crossed. Though the tendency is for birds to return to, or close to, former breeding grounds or to where they were born, birds ringed in other European countries have been recovered in Britain, and vice versa. As Village (1990) notes, while rare, this genetic exchange seems sufficient to have prevented the development of subspecies within Europe, as has happened in the extremely sedentary, and therefore isolated, subspecies on the Canary and Cape Verde islands.

The density of wintering Kestrels depends on where the observer sits, as it varies from zero birds in areas where the entire population migrates, to a density significantly larger than the summer density in areas where the migratory arrivals outnumber the local population. In Britain the density at the start of winter may be larger than the spring density: juvenile birds add to the breeding plus non-breeding population and, in southern areas, northern birds arrive as winter visitors, the total influx usually outnumbering those migrating away. Then, as winter deepens, the population and density decrease as birds, particularly juveniles, die.

Village (1990) noted the change in density of the Kestrels in his Scottish study area following the expected pattern, the density in autumn being much the same as that during the breeding season as some local juveniles stayed and were joined by juveniles from elsewhere, this influx outnumbering the breeding birds which migrated. Then as winter began, immigration ceased and the Kestrel density fell as birds died or migrated to search for better resources. The population and density then rose again in the spring as migrants returned. In midwinter, the Kestrel density had fallen to 20–25% of the breeding density. By contrast, in both his English study areas, Village (1990) found that the winter Kestrel density exceeded the breeding density, significantly so in the arable farmland area, where the peak population could be twice that recorded in spring (Fig. 174). In his mixed farmland area, Village saw a decrease in density in midwinter, though this was much less apparent in the arable farmland area. The most obvious factor influencing the winter density of Kestrels is food supply, but while Village was able to show a positive correlation between Kestrel and vole numbers (as might be expected) in his mixed farmland area, there was no such correlation with vole numbers in the arable study area, and only a marginally significant correlation with mouse numbers. While this is strange, and counterintuitive – though as Village notes, his study did not note the relative importance of non-rodent prey (birds, invertebrates) in the Kestrel diet – the general conclusion must be that the winter density of Kestrels is primarily influenced by food supply, together with weather conditions, which make hunting more or less difficult.

During winter Kestrels choose roosts which offer shelter against the elements, using barns and ruins, rock clefts in natural or quarried cliffs, tree holes etc. Such roosts may also be used during the day if rain, snow or fog

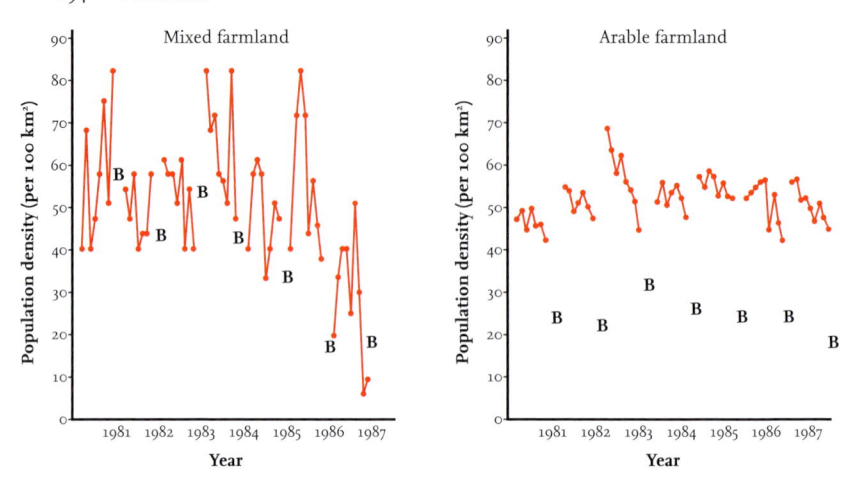

FIG 174. Monthly estimates of Kestrel population density across the years 1980–1987 on differing habitats in southeast England. B is the density of breeding birds. Density in both habitats decreased as winter progressed. While spring density and breeding density were similar in mixed farmland, in the arable study area the breeding density was much lower. Redrawn from Village 1990.

make hunting impossible. Shrubb (1993a) observed Kestrels sharing barn roosts with Barn and Little owls, which – given that both predate the falcons – is an indication of the greater necessity to escape exposure. Shrubb noted that winter roosts may be traditional, telling the story of Kestrels which used a barn for 20 years until it was pulled down, but then using the one erected in its stead. He also noted that Kestrels are stealthy in the approach to roosts, pausing occasionally on a devious route to watch for danger, and that their preferred roosts in buildings were on or close to doors and windows which offered ease of escape. More interestingly, he noted that on doors or beams the birds would usually roost, not across the beam as would be expected during the day, but along it, in the manner of a Nightjar (*Caprimulgus europaeus*), this allowing the bird to have its body against a wall, which aided it in keeping warm. The birds also take up positions offering protection against rain and the prevailing wind.

SURVIVAL

The age of Kestrels at the time of their death can only be ascertained with any certainty for ringed birds, and use of those data has both advantages and disadvantages. The advantage is that age is known with certainty for birds ringed as nestlings. The major disadvantage is that 90% of ringed birds are never recovered, so that information for the total population has to be inferred from a small sample. A second disadvantage is that recovered birds are likely to have died close to, or as a consequence of, human activity, which means that birds dying as a result of 'natural' causes – i.e. not being hit by a vehicle, flying into windows or other unforgiving structures, or being shot – are less likely to be recovered. Birds dying of starvation and/or disease may be recovered if they drop near human habitation, but otherwise are unlikely to be spotted, while the victims of predation are very unlikely to be recovered (though the finding of leg bones with rings attached in the nest of raptors is not unheard of).

Using data from 665 ring recoveries between 1912 and 1972, Village (1990) estimated the survival rates of juvenile Kestrels at 40% (i.e. 60% did not reach their first birthday), with 66% of second-year birds and 69% of third-year birds surviving. In a study of 2,121 nestlings ringed from 1911 to 1976 in the Netherlands Daan & Dijkstra (1988) calculated similar fractions, finding survivals of 51%, 58% and 63%. While the survival rates of older Dutch birds are similar to those of British Kestrels, that of juveniles is markedly better. However, Village (1990) notes that this difference arises largely from the choice of birth date, although, as we see below, vole population density may also have influenced the data. The Dutch study also allowed data on the survival prospects of an egg, in terms of fledging, surviving until the following year and breeding in the following year. Figure 175 illustrates these survival rates, plotted against the laying date of the egg. What is

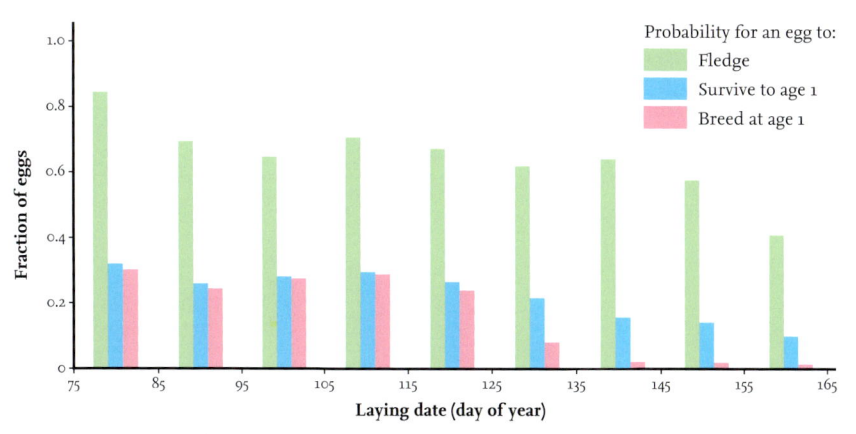

FIG 175. Fraction of Kestrel eggs from different laying dates in the Netherlands which survive to fledging, survive to 1 June of the following year, and which breed in the following year. Redrawn from Dijkstra 1988.

clear from the data in each of these studies is that the attrition rate of juvenile Kestrels is very high. But it is not uniquely so, being similar to that found in the American Kestrel (Henny 1972) and the Sparrowhawk (Newton *et al.* 1983) and, as we shall see, other British falcons.

Kestrels also survive their second winter less well than older birds: but having survived two winters, adult birds are better able to survive a third. This was confirmed in his study of Dutch Kestrels by Dijkstra (1988), who plotted annual adult survival rates as a function of vole population. From Fig. 176 it can be seen that Kestrel survival is better for Kestrels of all ages in good vole years. This effect is most noticeable for juvenile Kestrels, as might be expected, but what is notable is the significant difference in juvenile survival rates between good and poor vole population levels: juvenile survival in poor vole years was very low, consistent with spot survival percentages noted by Village (1990), who found only 21% survival in his English arable farmland study area in 1984/85 and 38% in his English mixed farmland area in 1980–1984. Using data from his own study areas, Village also calculated that the annual survival rate of male Kestrels was 74%, while that of females was 67%. The difference is not statistically significant at a high level, but the data consistently showed that female survival was lower than male.

Presumably old age starts to lower survival rates eventually: one British Kestrel is known to have lived 15 years, while in the study of Daan & Dijkstra (1988) one ringed bird, recovered freshly dead, was aged 14.6 years. In addition to collecting data on the age of death of birds over the period 1911–1976, Daan

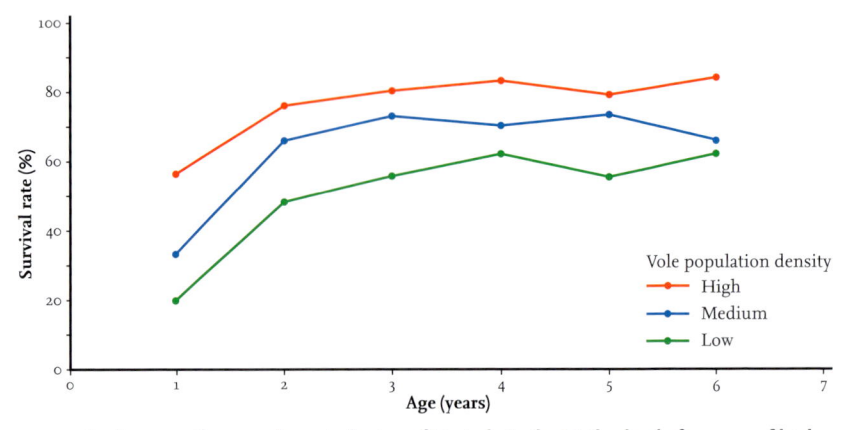

FIG 176. Age-specific annual survival rates of Kestrels in the Netherlands for years of high, medium and low vole population densities. Redrawn from Daan and Dijkstra 1988.

& Dijkstra were able to do a more detailed study on the survival of birds in the period 1967–1973 (Fig. 177). Calculating an average age at death for a Kestrel from the data of Fig. 177 is difficult, as both the mean and the median suggest Kestrels do not live beyond two years. However, allowing for the fact that first-year birds have a very low survival rate, and that survival of second-year birds is also relatively poor, the data imply that the average life span of a Kestrel is 4–5 years and that birds rarely survive to achieve ages in double figures.

While winter sees a rise in Kestrel deaths for all age groups, it is most noticeable for juveniles, adult birds showing a much more even death rate during the year (Fig. 176). Starvation is the most likely cause of death of recovered Kestrels, and this is particularly true of juveniles, many of which, it can be assumed, have failed to acquire the experience and life skills, and body reserves, necessary to survive winter, given its inherent cold, the possibility of bad weather, and reduced daylight hours for hunting. It is also likely that juvenile birds have

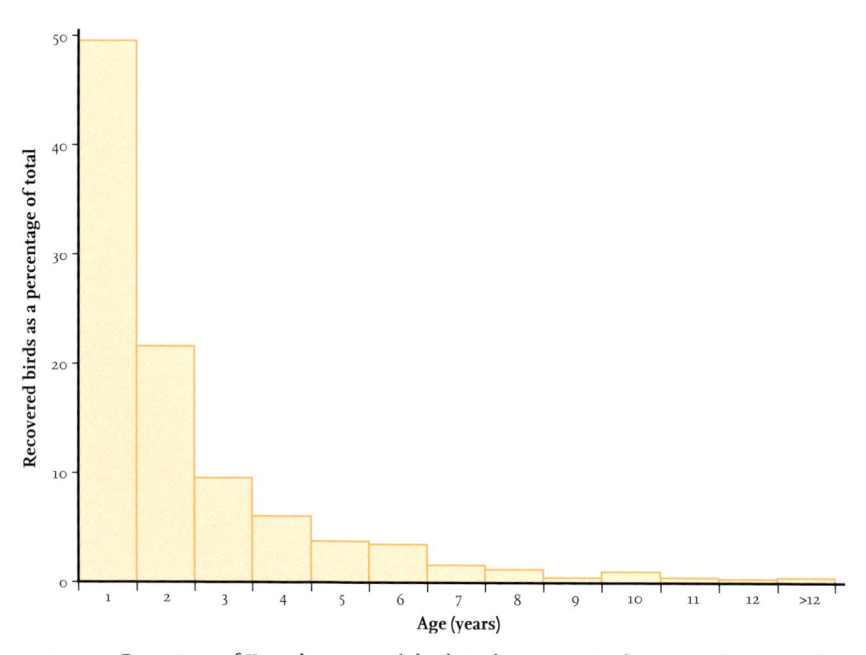

FIG 177. Percentage of Kestrels recovered dead at a known age in the years 1967–1973 in the Netherlands. Within each histogram the recovered birds were no older than the age on the horizontal axis, i.e. 49.8% of recovered birds were less than 1 year old, etc. In the study period only one bird was recovered with an age greater than 11 years. That bird was 14.6 years old. Redrawn from data in Daan and Dijkstra 1988.

more problems finding and defending territories, and that the territories they do acquire are likely to be less productive than those of adults.

If lack of experience is a factor in juvenile winter deaths then it would be expected that youngsters that fledge early should have a better chance of survival. And such is the case, this having been first identified by Cavé (1967), who noted that while 47% of young Kestrels fledged before 30 June survived their first winter, only 35% of those fledged later did so. Village (1990) noted the same effect of early fledging. He divided his year up into four fledging periods (prior to 15 June, 15–21 June, 22–30 June and after 30 June), and then considered the recoveries made prior to 1 October, from 1 October to 31 December, and from 1 January to 31 July. While the mortality increased in birds from all four fledging periods as winter progressed, youngsters fledging after 30 June were 55% more likely to die than those fledged before 15 June. The work of Dijkstra (1988) in the Netherlands confirmed Village's analysis. Village also plotted survival rates against mean winter temperature and vole index (an indication of vole population), and noted that for adults, survival was only minimally dependent on either, but for juveniles, survival was positively correlated with both (Fig. 178). However, since vole population is itself correlated to winter temperature, the exact relationship between juvenile survival, vole numbers and temperature is more complex than first sight suggests. Low temperatures indicate the possibility of snow cover, which makes catching voles more difficult and may force the juvenile Kestrels

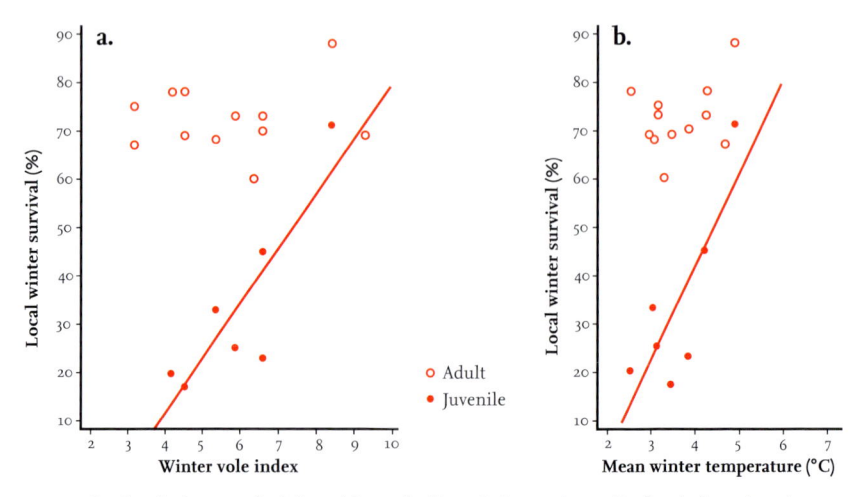

FIG 178. Survival rates of adult and juvenile Kestrels in southeast England plotted against (a) winter vole index (a measure of vole population density) and (b) mean winter temperature. Redrawn from Village 1990.

to catch birds, which are a more difficult prey, particularly for an inexperienced bird, increasing the risk of starvation.

Starvation may also lead to death by other causes. Weak birds may be less able to avoid traffic accidents, either because they are distracted by the possibility of food or because their reactions or flight capabilities are impaired. Newton (1986) also noted that in Sparrowhawks the use of fat reserves to counteract starvation releases accumulated pesticides into the bird's bloodstream, adding another potential contributory cause of death, even if lethal doses are not created.

Kestrel contamination by organochlorines is much lower than that seen in raptors favouring avian prey. This was recently confirmed by Nygård & Polder (2012) (see Chapters 4 and 7 for further details), but that work indicated that mercury in Kestrels had risen from a not discernible level prior to 1989 to levels of order 200 ppb by 2005–2010. As well as being subject to 'collateral damage' from the use of pesticides, raptors may also be deliberately killed by the laying of poisoned bait, but because Kestrels rarely consume carrion they are again at a lower risk than some other species.

As noted in Chapter 2, Kestrels were as vulnerable as other raptors to the indiscriminate killing of landowners and their agents until the passing of the Protection of Birds Act 1954. Prior to the Act shooting was a significant cause of death in recovered Kestrels, amounting to 50% of the total, but contributing a diminishing fraction in subsequent decades, about 27% in the 1950s, 10% in the 1960s, and less than 5% by the 1980s. In a study of Kestrel deaths from 1962 to 1997 (1,483 birds) Newton *et al.* (1999a) found that only 1.8% had died as a result of shooting. But as deaths by shooting decreased, deaths by collision with vehicles increased: having been non-existent as a cause in the years before 1950, the fraction leapt up after the 1960s, and was 20% in the 1980s; in their study, Newton *et al.* found 34.9% of Kestrels were road casualties, implying that the number dying in collisions had risen again in the 1990s. In a study in Campo de Gibraltar in southern Spain, Barrios & Rodríguez (2004) found that the death rate of Kestrels near onshore windfarms was higher than for any other species. The Kestrel death rate was 0.19 deaths/turbine/year, most deaths occurring in summer when the local population was maximal; the next highest death rate (0.12/turbine/year) was for the resident Griffon Vultures (*Gyps fulvus*), these mainly occurring during the autumn and winter when the absence of thermals meant the vultures used slopes for lift. The high death rate among Kestrels was due to the local area around the turbines being a favoured hunting habitat. In a study of the causes of windfarm collisions, and potential mitigating strategies, Marques *et al.* (2014) speculate that hovering birds might lose sight of the turbines, or might be pushed towards the blades by unexpected gusts. While there is currently no evidence to support the contention that windfarms are resulting in higher death rates in the UK Kestrel population, it is noted that the population decline in Britain has coincided with an increase in onshore windfarms, though it must be pointed out that other factors may also be involved and may be much more significant (see Chapter 8).

Disease is likely to be a significant killer of Kestrels, but may be more often a proximate factor, as the likelihood of a bird succumbing to disease increases if it is starving and/or suffering the exposure effects of prolonged inclement weather. Newton *et al.* (1999a) found that 46.2% of their 1,483 had died from natural causes, but attributed most of these to starvation (86%, i.e. 39.8% of total deaths), and only 11.2% (i.e. 5.2% of total deaths) to disease. Smit *et al.* (1987) reported that 67% of 481 dead Kestrels had died as a result of 'non-infectious diseases', a heading which included flying into structures, being shot and 'exhaustion'. The last of these, which probably included many cases of starvation (as emaciated birds are often considered to have died of exhaustion when the underlying cause is actually starvation), contributed 39% of this category of deaths (26% of the total). However, 33% of the examined birds died of other causes. Of this total (159 birds), 39% died of bacterial infections: 19 cases of avian tuberculosis, 32 of 'local inflammation' and 11 labelled 'diverse'. In the remaining 61% (20% of the total) the cause of death was parasites. Of these the major cause was coccidiosis (67%), with other worm infestations contributing 27%, the remainder being labelled 'diverse'. *Caryospora* species have also been found in free-living Kestrels (Martínez-Padilla & Millán 2007) and *Caryospora* infection was certainly implicated in the death of a juvenile Kestrel captured when sick in Berlin (Krone 2002).

Kestrels also carry other parasites – Trematoda flukes, Cestoda tapeworms and nematodes have been found in Slovenian birds (Šumrada & Hanžel 2012 and references therein; see also Krone 2007) – which, though not necessarily fatal, may contribute to a weakening of the bird and accelerate death from other causes. While the potentially harmful effects of internal parasites are obviously significant, Barton & Houston (2001) in a post-mortem study of 379 birds of six raptor species including 76 Kestrels, found that only 20% of the specimens had one or more internal parasites.

Kestrels may also carry parasitic louse flies, several species of which were found in a study of birds close to Moscow (Matyukhin *et al.* 2012), and other body parasites are also probable. A study of invertebrates in North American raptor nests found eight species of arthropods from six families in the nests of American Kestrels (Philips & Dindal 1977). There is no reason to believe that British Kestrel nests will not also carry a burden of potential parasites.

FRIENDS AND FOES

A study in Finland has shown that the siting of Kestrel nests can influence the breeding decisions of of other bird species. Norrdahl *et al.* (1995), in a study area in western Finland, noted that the nests of Curlews were closer to Kestrel nests than a random scatter would indicate. The Kestrels took 5.5% of Curlew chicks, but in control areas the Curlews lost 9% of their chicks to corvids. The Kestrels' enthusiasm for ridding their territory of corvids was thus responsible for an increase in Curlew fledglings. While such commensal behaviour has been noted before, most famously between goose species and Snowy Owls (see Potapov & Sale 2012, and references therein), this seems the only confirmed example of the behaviour with regard to Kestrels.

FIG 179. There is evidence to suggest that Curlews preferentially nest close to Kestrels, trading losses to the falcons against protection against other predators.

Much stranger stories of inter-species friendship have also been noted. Kupko & Kübler (2007) were watching Kestrel and Peregrine pairs nesting on a tower in Berlin. The female Peregrine had a single nestling and abandoned it in favour of chasing away the Kestrels and adopting their five nestlings. The male Peregrine continued to feed his single chick, raising it to fledge, while the female Peregrine successfully raised three of the five Kestrel nestlings. The authors noted that after the fledglings had left the breeding site one young Kestrel was found, minus its head, close to the site, though there was no indication of how or by what it had been decapitated. While the raising of both Peregrine and Kestrel chicks is rare, other instances of Peregrines incubating Kestrel eggs and raising Kestrel chicks are known. Ratcliffe (1962) records seeing a female Peregrine incubating Kestrel eggs. He believed the female had likely lost her clutch but, feeling the urge to incubate, had dispossessed a female Kestrel. Ratcliffe was not able to return to the nest to see if the Peregrine had successfully raised the Kestrel brood. He did, however, see another Peregrine female which had taken over a Kestrel clutch, and in this case the Peregrine pair had raised Kestrels to fledge (Ratcliffe 1963). It is worth noting that Ratcliffe's observations were carried out at a time when organochlorine pesticides were causing breakages of Peregrine eggs, and it may well be that these female Peregrines had lost clutches to this cause and so were inclined to seek alternatives which they otherwise might not have sought.

FIG 180. Flight-hunting Kestrel. The hunting technique makes the falcon vulnerable to attack by Goshawks, and perhaps other raptors. (James Sellen)

Semi-adoption of Kestrel youngsters by adult Peregrines was also witnessed by Johnson (2008) at a coastal site in Devon. Peregrines and Kestrels were nesting on a cliff ledge 6 m apart, though not visible to each other, and when the fledglings were able to move about the ledge the two broods (five Kestrels, who were older than the two Peregrines) met. The two broods tolerated each other, and when the young Kestrels begged for food from the returning adult Peregrines they were fed apparently without distinction. Close nesting of Kestrels and Peregrines on the chimney of a working mill has also been reported (Smith 1992).

Kestrel and Barn Owl pairs took up residence in the same nesting box in Austria, both females laying full clutches (six owl eggs and four Kestrel eggs). The Kestrels then abandoned their clutch, which the observers (Waba & Grüll 2009) removed. The owl chicks hatched, but the parent birds then deserted the brood, four of the six hatchlings rapidly succumbing to starvation. At that point the female Kestrel returned and began to feed the remaining two owl chicks. Assisted by the male she raised the chicks to fledge, both apparently leaving the box independently. The sharing of nest boxes by Kestrels and Barn Owls has also been noted in Britain (Tempest 2009, Riddle 2011), though the outcome for each species is unclear.

Such 'friendly' relations are, however, a rarity. As we have already noted, Kestrels defend their territories and hunting ranges strenuously both against other adults during the breeding season and also against juvenile birds when the latter are attempting to consolidate territories for winter. Kestrels will also attack other birds which encroach on their territories, hassling raptors and owls as well as attacking other trespassers if the female is incubating or there are chicks in the nest. Shrubb (1993a) records attacks on Great Black-backed Gull, which is not really surprising given the marauding reputation of that species, but also, more surprisingly, on a Pheasant. Coath (1992) records a Kestrel and a first-summer Red-footed Falcon locking talons and tumbling out of the sky over Essex, which must have been memorable for several reasons. Corvids are also attacked more or less on sight, Kestrels showing a particular dislike for Magpies. As Hasenclever *et al.* (1989) record that in their study in Westphalia Magpies were the primary culprits in cases of Kestrel chick predation, this is perhaps not surprising.

Shrubb (1993a) catalogued attacks by Kestrels on other diurnal raptors and noted that the Common Buzzard was the victim in the great majority of these. He noted that this was explained by the similar hunting techniques of both (flight-hunting and perched hunting) and the overlap of their prey, Buzzards taking voles and earthworms as well as larger prey. Shrubb noted that often he would see Buzzards hovering below Kestrels, a classic manoeuvre to move the higher bird away from an area – and a technique utilised by Kestrels for the same purpose. Often, it would therefore appear, the Buzzard did move the Kestrel away from what was presumably a good hunting area. As we note below, the Kestrel is a declining species in Britain, and it has been proposed that the increase in Buzzard numbers may be one reason for the decline.

The behaviour of fledgling Kestrels at a colonial nest site in Spain observed by Bustamante (1994) has already been mentioned. The site was occupied by both Common and Lesser Kestrels, and Bustamante noted that the adults of both species were aggressive towards each other and also towards the fledglings of the other species. One adult male Common Kestrel attacked a female Lesser Kestrel after he had witnessed the female's attack on a Common fledgling.

FIG 181. Young Buzzard. There is evidence to suggest that the reduction in Kestrel numbers is correlated to the increase in the Buzzard population.

As well as attacking raptors which stray too close to their nests, Kestrels also suffer reciprocal attacks, Gamble (1992) and Ristow (2006), for example, reporting attacks by Hobbies on Kestrels, while Kestrels have been observed attempting to predate Hobby chicks (Nicholson 2010), suggesting perhaps that predation by both species on the chicks of the other may occur. Adult Kestrels may also suffer direct predation from raptors. Direct predation by Buzzards seems limited, but Kestrels are preyed upon by other larger raptors – Golden Eagles, Goshawks and Peregrines, as well as Sparrowhawks and Tawny Owls. Shrubb (1993a) noted one very interesting piece of information regarding flight-hunting Kestrels in his Welsh study area. The flight-hunting times were reduced compared with those at his study area in Sussex, and the birds could be seen extending their necks to look behind them. A hovering Kestrel, intent on observing the ground below, is certainly vulnerable to attack from above, and Shrubb considers that although the altered behaviour may reduce the risk of attack, predation by Goshawks and Peregrines may be a contributory factor to the decline in Kestrels in Wales. In Europe, Mikkola (1983) found that Eagle Owls were significant predators of Kestrels, accounting for 91% of the Kestrels taken by owls. The remaining 9% were taken by Barn (1%), Tawny (7%) and Little (1%) owls. Although Mikkola noted owls being taken by Eleonora's, Gyr, Peregrine and Lanner falcons, he reported no observation of owl predation by a Kestrel. Foxes are also known to have eaten Kestrels.

Kestrels react to human intruders into their nest areas in a range of ways. Females will occasionally sit tight on eggs, moving only when actually forced to do so. Other females will vacate the nest and fly away. More frequently females will sit nearby and sound the alarm call, alerting the male, and also warning the intruding human to move away or risk attack. Attacks rarely occur, but have been known, with close passes and even occasional soft touches.

FIG 182. Black-headed Gull attacking a recently fledged Kestrel. The previous day an adult Kestrel had taken a chick from a gull nest, and it was difficult not to see the attack – one of several observed – as retaliation by the gulls.

CHAPTER 6

The Hobby

Hobby – very likely from the medieval French *hobé* or *hobet*, derived from *hober* – to move or stir – probably because of the falcon's agile flight, which is still the basis of the French name for the species, *Hoberau*. While the French and English have maintained the old name, other languages have adopted a name which describes other distinguishing features of the species. In German the Hobby is the *Baumfalke*, in the Netherlands the *Boomvalke*, in each case the 'tree falcon', as the species invariably breeds in stick nests in trees, while in Scandinavia it is the *Lærkefalk* (Denmark), the *Lerkefalk* (Norway) and the *Lärkfalk* (Sweden) – in each case the 'lark falcon', because of the species' enthusiasm for hunting larks, though in Swedish *lärka* is lark and *lärk* is larch, the one name neatly capturing both the tree-nesting and dietary preference of the species.

The second part of the species' scientific name, *Falco subbuteo*, was first assigned to it by Linnaeus (1746) in a work in which the description included a reference to the falcon's *femora ferruginea* – rust-coloured thighs – the 'red trousers' that are the Hobby's most defining characteristic. *Subbuteo* translates as 'below a buzzard' or 'smaller than a buzzard': Linnaeus' name for the Buzzard was *Falco buteo*, so he was placing the Buzzard (*Buteo buteo*) in the same genus as the Hobby, an attribution he confirmed in his later *Systema Naturæ* (Note 6.1).

Apart from the somewhat bizarre association of the falcon with the Buzzard, the scientific name is now equally bizarrely more likely to be associated in the mind of the general public with the table football game invented by Peter Adolph (1916–1994) who attempted to trademark his game as Hobby (rumour has it that Adolph was a bird enthusiast and the falcon was his favourite bird, but another rumour suggests a more prosaic explanation, that he hoped his 'hobby' would

306 · FALCONS

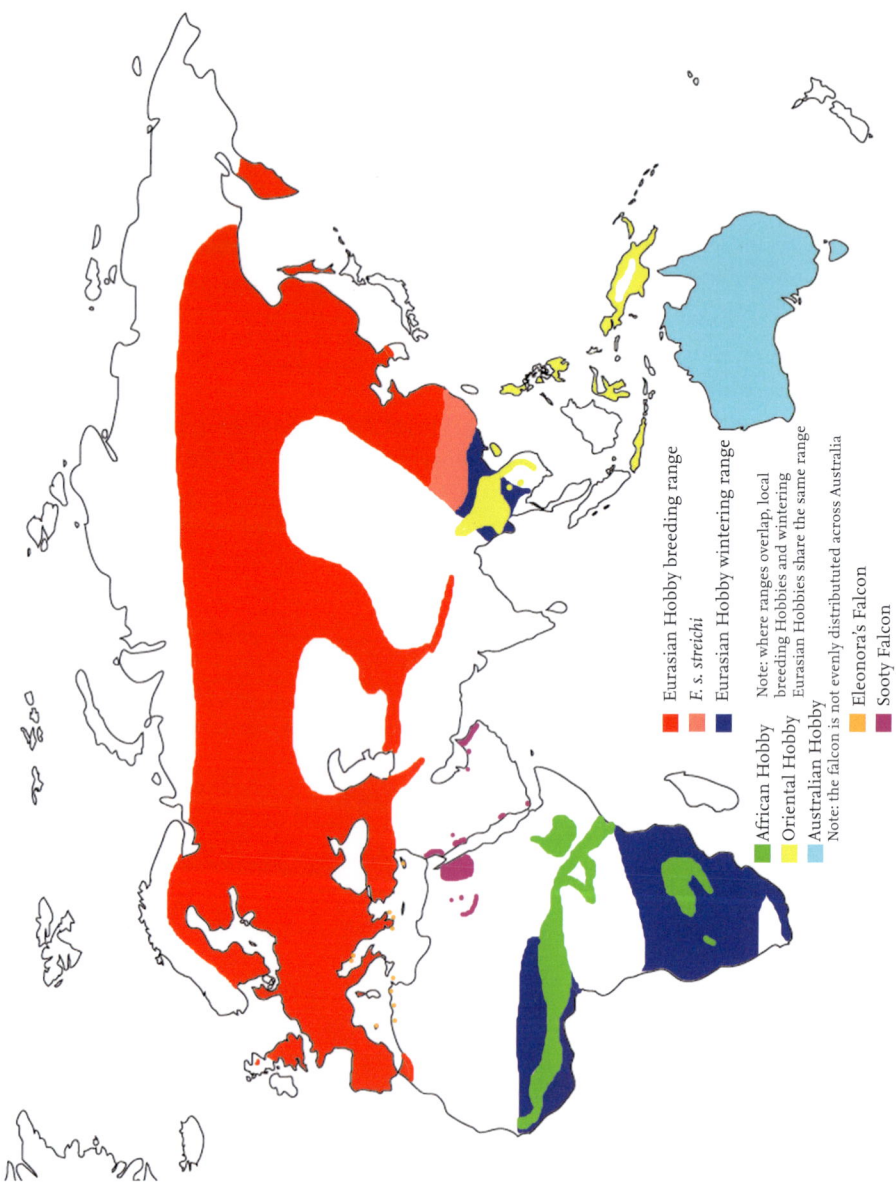

FIG 183. Distribution and wintering range of the Eurasian Hobby and subspecies *F. s. streichi*, together with ranges of other Hobbies and Sooty and Eleonora's falcons.

become the hobby of choice of young Britons), but chose the second part of the falcon's binomial name when his attempt was refused.

Equally curious is the collective noun for the falcon – a nest of Hobbies. 'Nest' has been used as a collective name for several species, notably Pheasants, which tend to congregate, as Hobbies do in Britain when they first arrive, large numbers often being seen hunting insects above marshland, this tendency presumably being the basis of the choice of the noun.

The Eurasian Hobby is the most widespread of the four 'true' Hobbies, breeding from Portugal in the west to the shores of the Pacific Ocean in China and to the southern Kamchatka Peninsula (Fig. 183). Hobbies breed at least as far north as 67°N in Finland and European Russia (i.e. north of the Arctic Circle), and as far south as 32°S. So vast a range might suggest numerous subspecies, but in fact there are only two, the nominate *F. s. subbuteo*, which breeds across most of the range, and *F. s. streichi*, a smaller non-migrant form that breeds in China.

Though a breeding species, the Hobby is not resident in the British Isles (or in Europe), wintering in Africa. Hobbies also differ from the other British falcons in being primarily insect feeders. Avian prey is taken during the breeding season, but this seems largely a result of the sheer number of insects that would need to be taken (primarily by the male) to provide the biomass necessary to provision the female and chicks. Hobbies are also late breeders, having chicks in the nest much later than the other British falcons and, indeed, the greater majority of other British birds. Hobbies are therefore timing their breeding to coincide with the fledgling phase of their main avian prey species.

DIMENSIONS

The Hobby is larger than the Merlin. It is comparable to the Kestrel (though usually smaller), but has a shorter tail.

Overall length (bill tip to tail tip): 300–360 mm.
Wing: male 256 ± 9 mm; female 268 ± 8 mm.
Tail: male 130 ± 5 mm; female 135 ± 5 mm.
Bill: male 12.6 ± 0.5 mm; female 14.0 ± 0.8 mm.
Tarsus: male 33.2 ± 0.9 mm; female 34.8 ± 0.8 mm.
Toe: male 31.5 ± 1.2 mm; female 32.9 ± 1.2 mm.
Claw: male 10.3 ± 0.4 mm; female 11.3 ± 0.4 mm.
Juvenile wing: male 252 ± 4 mm; female 256 ± 11 mm.
Juvenile tail: male 127 ± 2 mm; female 128 ± 5 mm.

The female is larger than the male, but not significantly so, usually by only about 10%.
F. s. *streichi* is smaller than the nominate: female wing 253 cm; male wing 243 cm (though the range of sizes of nominates of both sexes includes that of F. s. *streichi*).

The comparison of middle toe size in Hobby and Kestrel is an indication of the difference in preferred prey. The Kestrel has a smaller toe (27 mm for the female), the length sufficient for dropping on to prey, while the longer toe of the Hobby (33 mm) is effective in grasping prey in flight, particularly small (insect) prey which must then be retained for in-flight dining.

WEIGHT

Male 180 ± 50g; female 240 ± 100g. In both cases the weight is variable throughout the year and particularly during the breeding season.

PLUMAGE

Adult male
Dark blue-grey or slate-grey upperbody, including crown and 'moustache'. There is a cream superciliary stripe, but this may be difficult to see other than at close quarters. The cheeks and throat are cream, often with a buff tinge. The underbody is also cream, but heavily streaked dark brown. The thighs and undertail coverts (vent) are rusty-red. The uppertail is not as dark as the upperbody, and often tinged dark brown. The undertail is pale grey with darker barring. The underwings are also pale grey with heavy barring. The iris is dark brown, the cere and eye ring are yellow. The bill is blue-grey with a darker tip. Tarsus and foot are yellow, the claws black.

Adult female
As adult male, but thighs and vent usually richer red.

Juvenile
Head as adults, but upperparts are browner, and with buff feather edges which give a scalloped appearance. Underparts similarly streaked dark brown, but base colour is cream-buff. Lacks the rusty thighs and vent, these being buff-brown. The tail has a red-brown terminal band. Iris and bill as adult. Cere and eye blue-grey or green-grey. Tarsus and foot paler yellow. As has been noted on occasions (e.g. Small 1992), Hobbies in their first summer are similar to yearling

FIG 184. Adult Hobby. (Torsten Pröhl)

female Red-footed Falcons, which can cause confusion now that the latter are more commonly seen in southern England. As Small notes, shape – the long pointed wings of the Hobby versus the shorter, broader blunt wing of the Red-footed – and behaviour – the fast, agile flight and aerial capture of prey versus the hunting from perch or hovering technique favoured by the Red-footed – are usually diagnostic.

FIG 185. Female Hobby feeding a single chick. The photo illustrates that the falcons not only have red 'trousers' but red vents.

FIG 186. Juvenile Hobbies lack the characteristic red 'trousers' of adults.

Nestling

First down is long and thick, cream on the upperbody, white on the underbody. The second down, at about seven days, is coarser and darker. The legs and feet are pale green.

Variation

In recent years there has been correspondence in the scientific journals on the possibility that a darker version of the Hobby might occur, specifically in the Sila Mountains of Calabria, southern Italy. These were first described by Corso & Montrosso (2000), who saw the falcons in family groups with others of 'normal' plumage. The darker birds were a uniform dark brown apart from paler fringes on the feathers of the upper wing, and more extensive paler fringing on the underwing. Corso & Montrosso pointed out the similarity to Eleonora's Falcon, but noted that the latter was much darker and had much less, or absent, paler fringing, and considered that the dark birds they had observed were either melanistic Hobbies or had aberrant plumage. The interpretation was challenged by Ristow (2004), who wondered if the dark birds were actually Eleonora's Falcons, noting that if this was the case the interaction of the two falcon species was of itself a very interesting development. Corso & Montrosso (2004) responded by confirming their view that the dark falcons they had observed were indeed Hobbies, and that they were continuing with their studies of a potentially new form. The falcons, if they were indeed Hobbies, seem to be concentrated in southern Italy and are few in number. However, Zuberogoitia *et al.* (2008) reported seeing a dark Hobby in northern Spain where there are no Eleonora's Falcons. In this instance it was a single bird among over 100 which

FIG 187.
Hobby chick.

were examined in the field or in the hand (nestlings). While such a small sample suggests an aberrant plumage, the existence of dark birds in well-separated parts of the range (assuming the Italian birds are dark Hobbies) raises the possibility that such dark plumage is genetic in origin.

Moult

There is confusion over the moulting of Hobbies, in part because Fiuczynski & Sömmer (2011) have queried the data of Stresemann & Stresemann (1960) who stated that adult birds moulted only primary P4 and occasionally P5 during the breeding season. This observation is at odds with Dement'ev & Gladkov (1966), who claim that it is P9, P10 and even P8 which may be moulted at that time. A further complication is that on examining the data on which Stresemann & Stresemann (1960) based their conclusion, Fiuczynski & Sömmer (2011) considered that it applied to yearling birds (second-calendar-year birds only), that not all in this cohort moulted, and that adult birds (i.e. third calendar year or older) did not replace primary feathers in the breeding season, though there was some evidence that a small number of females might moult a single primary. It is therefore generally accepted that adult birds do not moult during the breeding season. The replacement of primaries is anticipated during the breeding season, but is interrupted if not completed before the autumn migration. This lack of moulting means that adult birds make two complete migration flights with no primaries in moult, and that yearling birds may actually make three migration flights before most, or any, primaries are moulted. These data are consistent with information from captive birds, and also with observations in Africa (Bijlsma *et al.* 1994a).

Juvenile birds moult some or all of their contour feathers during the breeding season. The mix of new, dark slate, and older, browner, body feathers and missing primaries may therefore be diagnostic of juveniles.

The full moult is completed in wintering quarters in the sequence 4–5–3–6–7–8–9–10–1. Depending on whether a primary is moulted early, the full moult may therefore take from August/September to February.

HABITAT

The Hobby is a bird of open woodland, both coniferous and deciduous. The falcons avoid dense forests, but will breed at forest edges, and on agricultural land which offers rows or clumps of trees. Isolated trees may be used for nesting, but invariably these are found on agricultural land which also has other trees set among hedgerows. Open areas are essential for hunting, and marshland, rivers

FIG 188. Typical Hobby habitat for the hunting of chafers and dragonflies. The photograph was taken at Shapwick Heath, Somerset.

and farmland are preferred, both for the insects that form a significant part of the diet, and for the sparrows, finches, larks, Swifts and hirundines which form the remainder. In a study in southern England, Parr (1985) found a preference for there being uncultivated, wet ground in the nest area, and for arable farmland on chalk downland. However, in river valleys, the Hobbies preferred pasture, perhaps because this includes a high percentage of flood-plain grassland.

The Hobby's enthusiasm for hunting Barn Swallows, House Martins and Swifts means that farmhouses, villages and other urban settings may also form part of its territory. In general the falcons avoid being too close to human habitation, preferring to fly further in order to avoid the disturbance that often results from human presence. In their ten-year study in Derbyshire, Messenger & Roome (2007) found only five nests (4.7% of the total) within 200 m of a farmhouse; four of these were successful. As with other species, the falcons were seemingly less perturbed by vehicles and the noise they produce. Though most nests were at a distance from roads, some were close to busy roads, two being within 100 m of a slip road for a dual carriageway; both were successful. However, by 2012, with the Derbyshire population of Hobbies having increased significantly (see Chapter 8), Messenger (personal communication) noted one nest only 240 m from a housing estate within the Derby city boundary and several hundred metres from a busy shopping mall.

The Hobby's habitat also requires a supply of corvid nests (chiefly Carrion Crows). The requirement for corvid nests and a prey which may be urban-based

FIG 189. Typical Hobby breeding habitat, English Midlands.

has allowed Hobbies to colonise towns, or rather suburbs. While this is not common, it has been seen over many years in Europe, such as in cemeteries and large gardens in Berlin (Fiuczynski & Sömmer 2011) and in several cities/towns in the Netherlands, including The Hague (Izaaks 2007) and Utrecht (Nus 2003). Though instances are not yet reported in Britain, several observers have noted Hobbies hunting close to towns. In mainland Europe Hobbies are now frequently using corvid nests on electricity transmission towers (more familiarly known as 'pylons', a name which will therefore be used in what follows), presumably without realising the impressive security such sites offer. Pylon nests have been noted in Britain, but usage is not yet as frequent as is seen, for instance, in Germany.

In Britain, Hobbies are a lowland species, but in other parts of their range they breed at much higher altitudes. Berezovikov & Zinchenko (1988) record Hobbies breeding at 1,900–2,000 m in the southern Altai Mountains, while Fiuczynski & Sömmer (2011 and references therein) note similar altitudes in France's Alpes-Maritimes, as well as altitudes to 1,800 m in Morocco, at over 3,000 m in Georgia, and up to 4,000 m in the Himalayas. In all cases the Hobbies are breeding below, or at, the tree limit because of their dependence on stick nests, and choosing areas with a biodiversity which will sustain the flying insects, and insect feeders, that form the bulk of their diet. However, suitable nest sites in areas of lower prey density can be utilised, as Hobbies often roam far from their nest sites when hunting.

VOICE

Hobbies are relatively silent birds, making few if any calls during winter, and for much of the breeding season, though courtship and chick feeding are much noisier times. The most commonly heard call is '*kee-kee-kee*', a multi-syllable repetition, in one sense a typical falcon alarm call, but much less coarse. The male call is higher-pitched than that of the female, and individual birds of both sexes have calls which may be so distinctive that they can be identified by voice in successive seasons. The similarity between the male Hobby's call and that of the male Wryneck has been mentioned many times, but is no less true because of this repetition.

The primary call has several forms. Shrill and harsh, it is an alarm call, most often heard by humans if they approach a nest, but also heard if the resident Hobby pair spot an avian intruder. A much gentler form, the syllables often extended, this slowing adding to the general calmness of the call, is used between male and female, both as a greeting and also by the male when he delivers food. During courtship this softer call is heard when the birds are inspecting nest sites, and may then be a duet. Fiuczynski & Sömmer (2011) note that such a duet is both tender and beautiful.

The gentler primary call is also heard when either bird is soliciting copulation. Fledglings may also use this form when they are hungry, particularly after they have left the nest but are still in its vicinity, and have spotted an adult approaching. The same call, but delivered in an even softer, quieter form, is also used by the female when she is feeding the young.

Other calls have been identified. Fiuczynski & Sömmer (2011) note a soft '*pik*' call used by the female when feeding the young, and by the male when calling an incubating female to feed. They also describe a '*pittzjirrr*', the '*rrr*' being rolled so that the call extends, as the specific call by one of a pair when another Hobby is seen intruding on the nest territory. Others have suggested that in this event the intruding bird may call '*keer*' by way of appeasement to avoid conflict. This call is also used during aerial food passes. Walpole-Bond (1931/1932) identified a series of nine separate calls, though these are mostly variations of the 'standard' calls heard in different situations.

Nestlings cheep from a young age when they are left unattended, perhaps as a comforting sound among siblings, though the same call, now rapid and louder, is made when food arrives (Note 6.2). From about 20 days of age the nestlings can make the adult alarm call in its several forms, and use these as appropriate to the situation – alarm, begging for food, between siblings. The call is also used by fledglings when they are exercising their wings.

DIET

Prey

Hobbies feed mainly on insects and birds, but will also take bats, rodents, reptiles and amphibians. They are primarily diurnal, but have been seen hunting by the light of a full moon (Slijper 1946), and hunt both bats and insects in twilight. Insect prey includes a very wide range of species. Chapman (1999a), Dronneau & Wassmer (2008) and Fiuczynski & Sömmer (2011) include lists of the insects identified in the prey remains during their studies or research. Dronneau & Wassmer, who studied Hobbies breeding in agrarian Alsace, France during the period 1982–2000, identified over 700 invertebrates from 33 differing families in food remains and in pellets. Other studies have identified various moths, flying ants, beetles and, of course, dragonflies. In England, Cramp & Simmons (1980) note that the remains of Emperor Moth (*Saturnia pavonia*), Fox Moth (*Macrothylacia rubi*), Oak Eggar Moth (*Lasiocampa quercus*), Cockchafer (*Melolontha melolontha*), Violet Ground-beetle (*Carabus violaceus*), Dor-beetle (*Geotrupes stercorarius*) and bumble bees (*Bombus* spp.), as well as dragonflies (one species mentioned being the Golden-ringed Dragonfly (*Cordulegaster boltonii*), were found in Hobby pellets. Frost (1983) also recorded Hobbies feeding almost exclusively on Northern Eggar Moths (*Lasiocampa quercus callunae*) when these were abundant on Derbyshire moorland. Insects are usually eaten in the air, the wings having first been discarded.

FIG 190. Southern Hawker (*Aeshna cyanea*), a typical Hobby insect prey. (Nathan Guttridge)

When hunting avian prey Hobbies prefer open-country species – hirundines, larks, pipits, small waders, wagtails, finches and Starlings – but will take available small passerines, including both Goldcrest and Wren, and there are numerous examples of Budgerigars successfully escaping captivity but failing to escape the clutches of hunting Hobbies (Note 6.3). Larks and pipits are often taken during their high song flights. Perhaps the most curious prey item to have been recorded (though it was actually a failed attack) was that of Gricks (2007) who observed a first-summer Hobby repeatedly stooping in pursuit of a European Storm Petrel. The Hobby had arrived on a drilling rig some 100 km northwest of Lewis in the Outer Hebrides and attacked the petrel from the rig. The petrel repeatedly dived into the sea to avoid capture, and after about 30 attempts over a period of around three minutes the Hobby returned to the rig exhausted. As interesting as the information of a Hobby hunting pelagic avian prey is the fact that a Hobby was observed over the Atlantic Ocean 100 km from land at such a latitude. There are also records of Hobbies in Iceland, 17 having been observed between 1970 and 2006 (https://notendur.hi.is/yannk/status_falsub.html, retrieved 9 August 2014). These falcons were seen from April to July and in late September/early October, and were recorded in increasing numbers in later years. Although seen primarily on the east coast, they were also recorded in the northeast and southwest of the island.

FIG 191. Barn Swallow. Hirundines are a favoured prey of adult breeding Hobbies.

Vagrant Hobbies have also been seen in Alaska (presumably arriving from Siberia) and Newfoundland (presumably after crossing the Atlantic via Iceland?).

Urban Hobbies in Berlin take House Sparrows (Fiuczynski & Sömmer 2011). Hobbies breeding close to the coast will take small waders: in southern Spain, Morata (1971) noted that the Hobby diet included Little Terns. Birds taken in flight are occasionally eaten on the wing (e.g. Beven 1945, Martin *et al.* 1988), but more often are taken to perches for plucking and consuming. Plucking has been observed in an old crow nest (Baker 1982) rather than the more conventional post or branch. While most avian prey is small, larger birds are also occasionally taken: in Georgia, Abuladze (2013) notes Magpies (weight up to 240 g) and Jays (up to 170 g) in the diet, while Witherby *et al.* (1939) recorded a Woodcock (up to 280g) being taken by a British Hobby.

In autumn, in the days before migrating, Hobbies will hunt at the roosts of hirundines gathering prior to migration. Glue (1968) also noted Hobbies taking Starlings at a roost near the New Forest which numbered 200,000 adults and juveniles, and taking wagtails and waders at a nearby estuary: Pied Wagtail, Yellow Wagtail (*Motacilla flava*), Dunlin and Ringed Plover were all taken. Similar behaviour was noted by Faulkner *et al.* (1968) at a Starling roost (100,000–120,000 birds) in Wiltshire during late August/early September in successive years. In this case the Hobbies were occasionally, it seemed, hunting cooperatively, two falcons causing small groups of Starlings to break off from the main body of birds. Such small groups would then be attacked by the Hobbies operating singly.

FIG 192. From the hide where I watched the female arriving to feed her chicks I saw a tug of war between the female and one chick. The tree camera recorded that one chick pulled the head off the prey (probably a House Martin), the female being left with a bill full of feathers and the remains of the prey in her talons.

Ground mammals are also taken. While these are usually rodents (voles and mice) and shrews, Tinbergen (1932) found the remains of six Moles in Hobby pellets in the Netherlands, while Cramp & Simmons (1980) mention young Rabbits in the British Hobby diet, and Dement'ev & Gladkov (1966) noted Hobbies taking pika (most likely Northern Pika, *Ochotona hyperborea*) in Russia's Ural Mountains; Berezovikov & Zinchenko (1988) record a single instance of a Hobby taking an Alpine Pika (*O. alpina*) in the southern Altai Mountains. Bats are also taken: Insley & Holland (1975) recorded finding the remains of Noctules in Hobby nests, while Haverschmidt (1948) and van Manen (1995) noted both Noctules and Serotines (*Eptesicus serotinus*) in the diet of Dutch Hobbies. In a study in France, Duquet & Nadal (2012) found 11 species of bat in the diet of diurnal raptors, with the majority (38%) taken by Hobbies. The species taken were primarily Noctules, pipistrelles (*Pipistrellus* sp.) and Serotines, but the remains of

FIG 193. Bat remains found in a Hobby nest in Germany.

Lesser Horseshoes (*Rhinolophus hipposideros*), Daubenton's (*Myotis daubentonii*) and Brown Long-eareds (*Plecotus auritus*) were also found. Most bats were taken in late summer and autumn. The hunting of bats is not confined to the breeding season, Jaarsveld (1988) recording wintering Hobbies hunting bats in South Africa's Kruger National Park. When captured, bats may be eaten in flight.

In other parts of the Hobby's range reptiles also form part of the diet. Roberts (1991) reports that in Pakistan one Hobby had learned to take Large-scaled Rock Agamas (*Laudakia nupta*). These are large lizards that can grow up to 30 cm in length, Roberts reporting that the Hobby held the reptile with both feet and carried it in the manner of an Osprey carrying a fish. Fiuczynski & Sömmer (2011) also note the hunting of lizards in Morocco, and that in the valley of the Syrdarya River (which rises in the mountains of Tajikistan and flows through Uzbekistan and Kazakhstan to reach the Aral Sea) at some sites Hobby nestlings were being fed a diet the main feature of which was Zarudny's Bent-toed Gecko (*Cyrtopodion russowii*) (Note 6.4). Reptiles are also mentioned in the diet of Hobbies closer to home, Dronneau & Wassmer (2008) noting remains of two lizards (*Lacerta* spp.) among 1,685 Hobby vertebrate prey remains in France. Hudec & Cerny (1977) also mention a frog among prey in Czechoslovakia (as it then was).

Hobbies will make kleptoparasitic attacks on Kestrels, Tinbergen (1932) noting that the Hobby will fly at speed and take a rodent from the foot of a Kestrel after it has made a kill. Similar attacks on Kestrels have also been reported by others, such as Fritzsche & Weisse (1963), who claimed that it was more prevalent when the Hobbies were feeding young, and Bednarek (1986), who claimed that Hobbies were successful in nine of 12 attacks, which meant that kleptoparasitism of Kestrels was a more successful way of obtaining food than attacking birds. Some observers suggest that a Hobby harrying a Kestrel into dropping its prey was also successful on occasions. However, the reverse situation is also observed, Huitzing (2002) noting a piratical attack of a Kestrel on a juvenile Hobby. Chapman (1999a) also notes Hobby piracy of Montagu's Harrier and Red-footed Falcon and, more interestingly, of Common Tern. However, Hobbies also suffer piratical attacks, King (2009) noting a Peregrine catching a prey-carrying Hobby from behind and below, and rolling onto its back so that its talons were extended towards the smaller falcon. Perhaps in surprise or, as King surmises, because it was intimidated, the Hobby dropped the prey, which the Peregrine caught neatly, in the manner of a standard aerial food pass.

Composition of diet

The diet of Hobbies at four differing habitats – cultivated chalk downland, river-valley farmland, the New Forest, and heathland in Surrey – was investigated by Parr (1985), the results being tabulated in Tables 19 and 20.

TABLE 19 Diet of Hobbies during the nestling phase of breeding in southern England. From Parr (1985).

Prey species	Habitat			
	Downland	Farmland	New Forest	Heath
Swift	–	–	58 (35)	46 (10)
Barn Swallow[1]	17 (17)	18 (14)	19 (7)	4 (3)
House Martin[1]	27 (22)	4 (4)	12 (7)	14 (6)
Skylark	–	–	3	6
Tit spp.	–	–	7	1
Pipits/wagtails	2	–	2	2
Finches/buntings	2	–	–	1
Sparrows	3	3	1	5
Other	1	–	1	1

All Notes from Table 20 apply to Table 19.
1. The prey remains also included a further eight unidentified hirundines.

TABLE 20 Diet of Hobbies during the incubation phase of breeding in southern England. From Parr (1985).

Prey species	Habitat[1]			
	Downland	Farmland	New Forest	Heath
Swift	6	–	3	8
Barn Swallow	1	–	–	2
House Martin	9 (4)[2]	–	–	8
Skylark	5	–	–	3
Tit spp.[3]	3	1	10 (5)	2
Pipits/wagtails[4]	–	–	3	–
Finches/buntings[5]	6	7	6	3
Sparrows[6]	–	–	5 (1)	6 (1)
Other[7]	–	–	1	2

1. The study covered three Hobby pairs in the downland area, one in the farmland area, five in the New Forest and two on heathland in Surrey.
2. Figures in parenthesis are the number of juvenile birds in the total number.
3. Tit species were Blue Tit, Great Tit, Marsh Tit (*Poecile palustris*) and Willow Tit (*P. montanus*).
4. Pipit/wagtail species were Meadow Pipit, Tree Pipit and Pied Wagtail.
5. Finches/buntings were Chaffinch (*Fringilla coelebs*), Corn Bunting (*Emberiza calandra*), Greenfinch and Reed Bunting.
6. Sparrows were House Sparrow and Tree Sparrow (*Passer montanus*).
7. Other species were Dunnock, Stonechat and Whinchat (*Saxicola rubetra*).

In addition to the data in Tables 19 and 20, Parr (1985) also collected prey remains during the post-fledgling period. During that period the downland Hobby remains revealed a single Skylark; the farmland remains included 21 Barn Swallows, all of them juveniles; the New Forest remains included 22 Barn Swallows (17 juveniles) and one Skylark; and the heathland remains included nine Barn Swallows (seven juveniles), one House Martin and one sparrow (unspecified, but in the nestling phase both House and Tree Sparrows were taken).

Overall 50% of the Hobby prey across the four study areas were juvenile birds, with hirundines accounting for the bulk of prey at the downland and farmland sites (around 70%), but Swifts being more important than hirundines in the New Forest and on the heathland area. Similar data have been obtained in studies of Hobbies in other European countries (e.g. Fiuczynski & Sömmer 2011).

The data above indicate the adults' preference for feeding chicks on avian prey because of its large biomass (in southern Spain, Morata 1971 noted that

FIG 194. Female Hobby delivering House Martin prey to a brood of three chicks.

while insects formed 97% of the Hobby diet by prey number, they provided only 3% by biomass). Some male Hobbies are specialist avian feeders, particularly of hirundines, and Cramp & Simmons (1980) noted that in this case the advantage in terms of biomass may be outweighed by the accumulation of ectoparasites from the prey species: they reported one case where the infestation of Hobby chicks with ectoparasites of Swifts probably resulted in brood death. Though avian prey certainly reduces the workload of the male Hobby, feeding on insect prey has been observed. Schuyl *et al.* (1936) noted one case in Germany in which the decision to feed chicks an insect diet required the adults to feed every three and a half minutes during a four-hour observation period; Tinbergen (1932) noted a similar delivery rate for insects fed to Dutch Hobby chicks. In a study in the southern Altai Mountains of Russia, Berezovikov & Zinchenko (1988) noted that when feeding a brood with insect food, adults visited the nest 120–170 times each day. But if avian prey is usually critical for chick growth, insects are an important part of the diet of young Hobbies, just as they are for adults. Nestlings

FIG 195. The same female brings another House Martin to her brood.

will eat ants and other insects opportunistically, and the catching of flying insects is important in the honing of flying skills as well as supplementing the diet of fledglings.

During migration there is good evidence to suggest that Hobbies time their flights to coincide with migrating Barn Swallows, so that food can be readily sourced. However, the countries through which the falcons pass have resident populations of finches and other small birds which can also be utilised. In winter, the diet appears to consist mainly of insects. Brown (1976) notes that just as the Hobby diet during breeding in Europe comprises mainly birds, so does that of the African Hobby. Eurasian Hobbies migrating into Africa therefore have less competition from local birds for the insects which form the majority of the winter diet. Brown notes that when rain is followed by swarming termites (*Isoptera* spp.), Hobbies will collect these in great numbers, both along the migration route and at winter quarters. To such an extent is this the case, Brown writes, that Hobbies will appear where there are thunderstorms 'as if by magic'. Brown recalls seeing a flock of 200 Hobbies feeding on flying termites in east Africa, and another occasion when he was 'lounging at dusk, enjoying a sundowner outside my tent' as 'a flock of Hobbies streamed overhead for ten or fifteen minutes going to roost on a steep hillside above me.' Brown estimates that there were at least 200–300 falcons, and that they had been feeding on termites after a local rainstorm. Brown notes that the Hobbies feed in light rain, pausing occasionally to shake their feathers. Chapman (1999a), quoting a Kenyan resident, confirms the suggestion of rainstorms attracting Hobbies, noting that the falcons arrive at new locations with feathers still wet from the last feed/rainstorm. Reynolds (1973) suggests that Hobbies are attracted to bush fires, which result in swarms of insects taking to the air: a Hobby following the advancing fire front would be guaranteed a ready supply of insects.

The forested areas where the Hobbies reside in winter are rich in insect life, and it is reasonable to assume that insects form the basis of the winter diet, with termites, grasshoppers and locusts forming the bulk of the consumed biomass, though as the falcons are opportunistic hunters they will also take local avian, mammal and reptile prey. Pepler (1991) records the diet of Hobbies near Stellenbosch, Cape Province, South Africa. While insects (crickets, dragonflies, termites) were eaten, so were local birds. Interestingly, Barn Swallows that had migrated from Europe formed the largest fraction of the avian prey (41 of 121 prey items (34%) collected) though local species, Cape Canary (*Serinus canicollis*) at 24% and Little Swift (*Apus affinus*) at 19% also formed substantial fractions. In the more common area for wintering Hobbies (central southern Africa: see *Movements and wintering quarters*, below) the falcons probably supplement their diet of termites and other insects with local species such as pipits and wagtails, Barn Swallows and local hirundines, bats and small mammals. They will also feed on the vast Barn Swallow flocks which assemble in some areas.

Bijlsma *et al.* (1994b) noted the predation of large Barn Swallow roosts in Botswana by six raptor species and, in a later report, Bijlsma & Brink (2005) reported that in Botswana such roosts could hold as many as 2,700,000 birds, and that the number of species preying on the swallows had risen to ten, these including the Hobby as well as the Barn Owl. The study of Bijlsma & Brink was of the African Hobby, but it is likely that the same general rules apply to predation by the Eurasian Hobby. The African Hobbies would arrive at the roost a few minutes before the swallows departed in the morning and arrived in the evening, preferentially attacking flocks of less than 50 swallows with a success rate of 38%. The swallows responded to predation by departing or arriving en masse and making synchronised ascents and descents in an effort to confuse the predators (and to minimise an individual's predation risk) and also by maintaining a low body mass until a short time before the spring migration commenced, to maximise flight abilities.

Hunting strategy

Hobbies have a fast and agile flight, their repertoire being a masterly ensemble of rolls, twists, stoops and climbs which have entranced many. A stooping Hobby would be able to turn some of the stoop speed into horizontal speed if it was forced to chase prey; whether it would then be able to outfly a Swift is open to debate, though anecdotal information suggests that it may do so on occasions. Henningsson *et al.* (2010) used two high-speed (200 fps) cameras mounted 1.4 m apart on a rigid beam to make calculations on Swifts flying in 'screaming parties' close to the ground near breeding sites. The system was calibrated using stakes in the ground across the chosen field of view (which was close to a breeding area). Wind speed was estimated in a delightful fashion, by tying a piece of string to a stick and measuring the angle at which it flew, then calibrating angle against wind speed in a wind tunnel. The data collected showed that the mean Swift horizontal speed during fast flights was 75.2 ± 18.4 km/h, the measured top speed being 112.0 km/h. The Swifts were also measured in vertical flight. Here the speed dropped dramatically, being an average of 14.4 ± 10.1 km/h. Wing-beat frequency varied linearly with horizontal velocity, the fastest flier beating its wings 12.5 times per second. Since most attacks on Swifts are surprise attacks or stoops, the Hobby does not have to match these horizontal speeds. However, Kirmse (1989) records seeing a Hobby chase (but fail to catch) a Swift for four minutes over a distance of about 3.5 km. If both time and distance are correct then the average speed of the two birds was 'only' about 53 km/h, but as time is much easier to define accurately than distance for the stationary observer it is likely that Kirmse underestimated the distance travelled. The observation was in May, so the swift was an adult, and life-and-death pursuit by a falcon is likely to induce fast flight every bit as much as a 'screaming party', so a speed of 100 km/h can probably be assumed.

The falcon takes prey in level flight or following short stoops, occasionally swinging up at the end of a stoop to make the capture. This latter technique is often seen when hunting dragonflies over water and during evening hunts, probably because it allows the Hobby to see the prey silhouetted against the sky rather than the dark background of the ground or water surface. Mead & Pepler (1975) noted the same technique – stoop and upswing – in the hunting of Sand Martins in southern England. Mead & Pepler claimed a 100% success rate for the technique against martins, but with a low sample size (11 attacks). Many of

FIG 196. Adult Hobby about to grasp a Summer Chafer (*Amphimallon solstitialis*). (Dave Soons)

the falcon's prey are insects taken above water, its formidable agility meaning that it rarely fails to lock on to its chosen victim, which makes two observations particularly interesting. Hamlett (1984) saw Hobbies picking up insects from the water surface, while Gamble (1990) noticed a Hobby hovering above a dark object on a reservoir in Leicestershire. Although mobbed by Lapwings and Black-headed Gulls, the Hobby persisted and eventually flew down and retrieved the object, which turned out to be a Barn Swallow, presumably knocked into the water rather than locked on to by the Hobby some time earlier.

Hobbies will hunt from a perch, making a short fast flight to surprise their prey. Hunting from a perch allows the Hobby to spot ground mammals, which are then attacked in a quick pounce. Pouncing is also seen occasionally when the Hobby is quartering in an attempt to flush avian prey into the air. Robertson (1977) noted a Hobby hovering at a height of about 20 m then dropping onto the ground, presumably to catch insects. In this observation Robertson noted that the Hobby hung in a light breeze, its wings slightly folded rather than fanned as a Kestrel would hover, though the tail was fanned. Hovering was soon reported by others (Harding 1978, Mills 1980), but despite these observations hovering seems to be a relatively uncommon hunting technique, though presumably one that a Hobby could use to pounce on mammals. Hayman (1979) recorded a Hobby hanging in a 'stiff' wind so that the falcon was actually moving slowly backwards. Milsom (1987) also noted occasions on which Hobbies used the wind to rise along an upslope to gain height, before diving down the slope to attack prey.

Watson (1982) recorded a Hobby making a 'ringing' capture of a House Martin, the two birds rising in tightening circles to a height of 300 m or so. Such ringing flights are usually thought to be the preserve of Merlins; the general view of observers and the falconry community is that Hobbies do not engage in long pursuit flights, suggesting that the hunt seen by Watson (like that observed by Kirmse 1989) was very rare. Cade (1982) points out that the Hobby's wing loading (0.21–0.25 g/cm^2) implies buoyancy rather than fast flight, and speculates, following Michell (1900) (Note 6.5), whether Hobbies might, in fact, not be powerful fliers. Given the extremely long migration flights of the falcons this suggestion seems curious, but evidence from migratory flights is not clear-cut. As noted below, migration flights seem to be carried out at altitude, which implies soaring and gliding. However, Hobbies do not cross water at the points favoured by true soarers (such as Buzzards), taking such hazards head-on, as it were, which does imply flight stamina.

Interestingly, the enthusiasm of Hobbies for hunting hirundines seems to have led Barn Swallows to develop a specific call to warn conspecifics of the approach of the falcon. Atherton (1997), working in Warwickshire, noted that on the appearance of a Hobby, Barn Swallows gave a specific, 'low-pitched, quiet, slurred double note' call which was very different from the alarm call when Sparrowhawks and Kestrels approached. Once the Hobbies had departed, the swallows would sing briefly, seemingly as an 'all clear'. Chapman (1999b) concurs with this Hobby-alarm call of the Barn Swallow, rendering it '*phoo-it*' and also noting that Barn Swallows have a different call for the Sparrowhawk, while Edwards (1999) agrees, though considers that 'quiet' is not an appropriate term for the call, and suggests that House Martins have different alarm calls for the Hobby, though in this case it is the degree of urgency of the standard call, the falcon eliciting a panic in the call rather than the 'standard' call which is heard for Kestrels or cats.

The falcons will hunt opportunistically, both Parker (1982) and Billett & Rees (1984) noting Hobbies catching prey which were flushed by Montagu's Harriers,

FIG 197. Adult Hobby closing in on a Summer Chafer.

while Trollope (2012) notes that the falcons will use trains for the same purpose. Over a number of years Trollope watched Hobbies following a steam train in Kent which, he assumed, was travelling slowly enough for the Hobby to follow comfortably, and across marshland so that it flushed dragonflies from ditches on either side of the line. Hobbies also occasionally hunt cooperatively, several observations having been made of Hobby pairs hunting hirundines together. More interestingly, Robertson (2012) reports a Hobby using mimicry to gain prey. Robertson had several times seen a Sparrowhawk apparently mimicking the flight pattern of a Mistle Thrush to get close to hirundines before accelerating and capturing one, but then saw an immature Hobby making a similar approach to a flock of Barn Swallows. Later Robertson saw two Hobbies which mimicked the flight pattern of swallows themselves to place themselves inside a flock. Once established there, with the swallows taking no notice of the interloper, presumably its size and coloration being obscured by the scurrying mass of hirundines, the Hobby turned against the flow of the flock and grabbed a swallow.

Pepler (1993) noted cooperative hunting at wintering quarters in urban Stellenbosch, South Africa, noting two Hobbies pursuing and catching a Little Swift, and also noting one occasion on which a third Hobby attempted to pirate the prey after two falcons had successfully captured a swift. However, Pepler was not able to say whether the two cooperative hunters were a pair, or whether they shared the prey that one of the two had captured. It is therefore unclear whether this was genuine cooperative hunting or whether one Hobby was taking advantage of the attack of another.

Milsom (1987) studied the effect of temperature and wind speed on Hobbies hunting insects. In this study, carried out in the New Forest, Milsom noted

FIG 198. This female Hobby has just received a plucked prey from her mate and will soon be feeding her chicks.

that the Hobbies did not hunt until the temperature had risen above 13 °C, and so hunted (in June) between 09.30 and 14.25, the warmest part of the day. On the warmest days the Hobbies would remain airborne for long periods, hunting continuously while rising air currents provided lift. The capture rate of insects increased with temperature, finally reaching 12.8 captures per minute. Milsom noted that this rate was much as observed by Parr (1985), who recorded a maximum of 12 captures per minute, and conjectured that the rate might represent the maximum possible. The effect of temperature is twofold. Milsom noted that the frequency of flapping flight by the falcons increased as the temperature, and therefore thermal lift, fell. The availability of insects will fall with declining temperature so that ultimately (Milsom's study would suggest at about 13 °C) the energy obtained from captured insects drops below that required for hunting. The Hobbies are then forced to hunt alternative prey or to wait for better hunting days. Milsom's finding that Hobbies preferentially hunt insects during the heat of the day was confirmed by a study over a ten-year period in Alsace, France, by Dronneau & Wassmer (2008) (Fig. 199). Dronneau & Wassmer also noted the heights at which the Hobbies hunted for insects over both water and trees (Fig. 200).

However, while it might be generally true that Hobbies preferentially hunt insects during the warmest part of the day, they will also hunt in the early morning and at dusk, not only changing their prey to bats and/or birds, but continuing to hunt insects if conditions allow: Fiuczynski & Sömmer (2011)

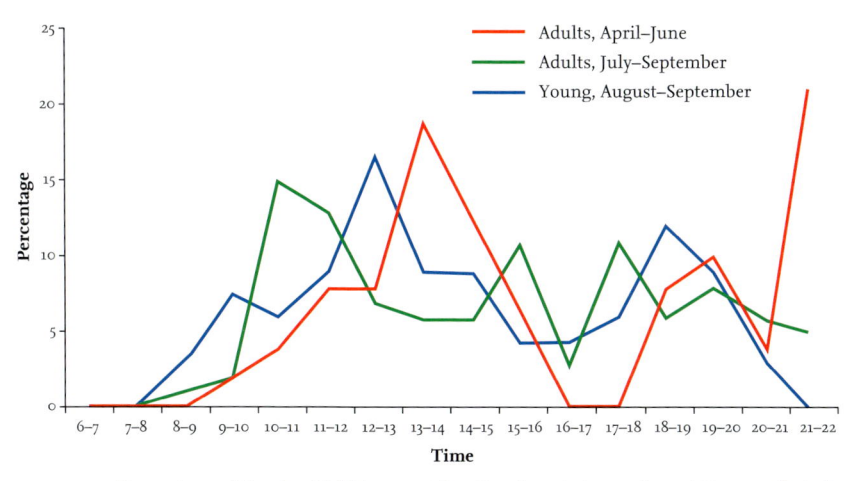

FIG 199. Percentage of the day Hobbies spent hunting insects in north-east France, plotted against time of day. Redrawn from Dronneau & Wassmer 2008.

330 · FALCONS

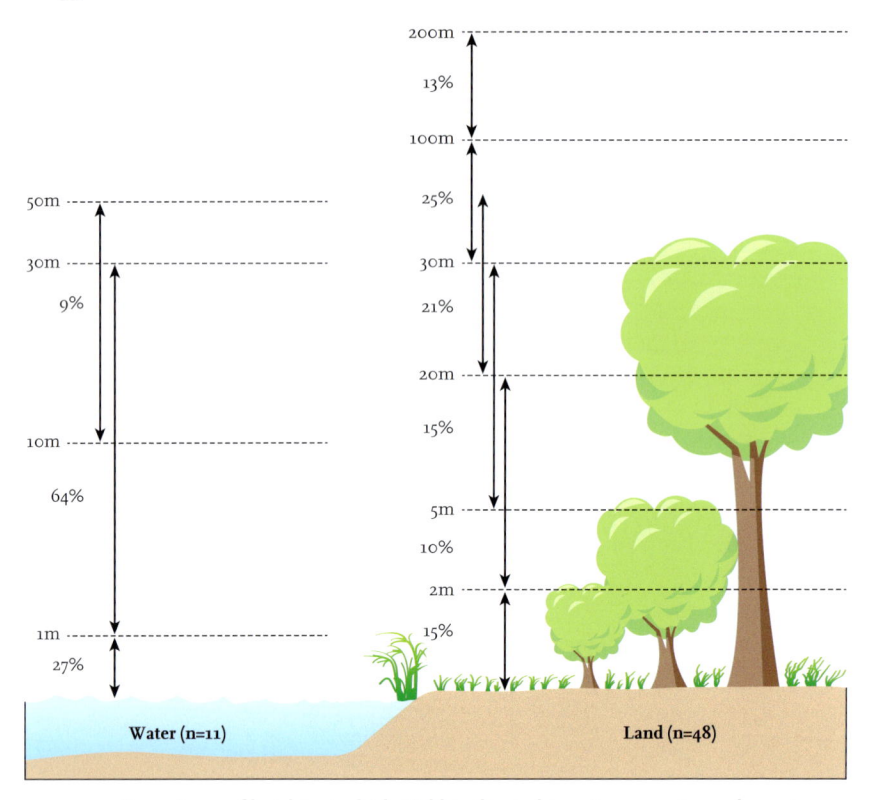

FIG 200. Percentages of heights at which Hobbies hunted insects over water and over trees on land in north-east France. In brackets is the number of Hobbies observed. Redrawn from Dronneau & Wassmer 2008.

record four Hobbies hunting at a Berlin dump at dusk, each flying only 2–3 m above the ground before turning upwards to catch House Crickets (*Acheta domesticus*), seemingly observing them against the lighter sky. Chapman (1999a) notes the hunting of Summer Chafers (*Amphimallon solstitialis*) at up to 47 minutes after sunset, presumably again seeing the insects against the pale sky. The study of Szép & Barta (1992) also suggests that Hobbies are most active early and late in the day when they are hunting avian prey.

While in Britain Barn Swallows are often solitary nesters, in continental Europe they nest colonially, one suggestion being that such colonies are a defence mechanism against Hobby predation, an idea consistent with the fact that until recent times Hobbies have been uncommon in Britain: it will be interesting to see if swallows modify their nesting behaviour when the risks of

Hobby predation rise significantly. In their study in northeastern Hungary, Szép & Barta (1992) studied predation at a Barn Swallow colony on the Tisza River where around 2,000 pairs nested annually during the three years of study. While Hobby attacks were made at any time during the day, the attacks peaked in early morning and late afternoon (Fig. 201).

Figure 201 also shows a clear difference between the number of attacks in June and July. In June the nestling swallows were pre-fledge, while in July of both years they had fledged: the Hobbies were preferentially hunting inexperienced, poor-flying juveniles. While the study in Hungary was of attacks on Barn Swallows, in Britain Hobbies hunt Sand Martins, which also breed colonially, and observations suggest that the same pattern, both of hunting activity through the day and of the increased number of attacks once the young martins have fledged, is maintained.

In the Hungarian study, a single pair of Hobbies was attacking the large Barn Swallow colony. In the studies of wintering Hobbies in Africa noted above, the falcons were content to share the sky with both conspecifics and other species – see also the comments of Brown (1976) on winter flocking, below. When feeding on insects in Britain early in the breeding season Hobbies will also readily tolerate the presence of conspecifics, with 'flocks' of up to 100 occasionally being seen as well as other species such as gulls and Common Terns.

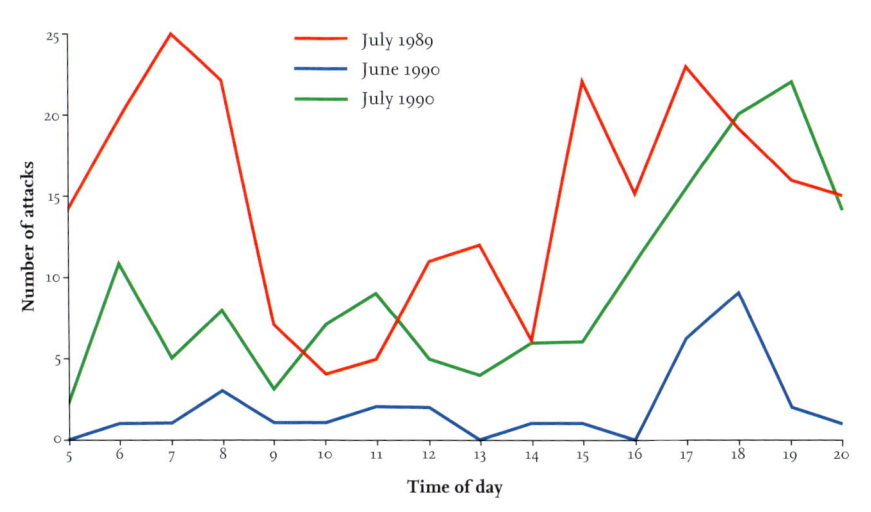

FIG 201. Number of Hobby attacks on a Barn Swallow colony in Hungary against time of day for two consecutive years of study. See text for an explanation of the reduced number of attacks in June 1990. Redrawn from Szép & Barta 1992.

Pepler (1993) describes the hunting strategies of Hobbies in their winter quarters in urban Stellenbosch, South Africa. There, hunting for avian prey began before sunrise and ceased at sunrise, then commenced again in late afternoon. During the early-morning period the falcons would not take any insect prey, hunting avian prey only. The Hobbies would leave the town before sunrise, circling to heights of up to 800 m, presumably taking advantage of rising air currents, and fly off to a nearby mountain area where they would hunt different avian prey, but also insects, particularly dragonflies and butterflies. When hunting birds in town in the early morning, the falcons would make attacks over open land from trees or buildings, but would also make fast flights over rooftops, taking Little Swifts by surprise as they flew from nests under the eaves. During the evening, perch-hunting was common, though the prey differed, comprising chiefly wintering Barn Swallows. The Hobbies also stooped in the crowns of trees, made vertical pounces on prey within tree crowns, and attacked flocks of wintering Starlings which were returning to roost. They also hunted Common Garden Crickets (*Gryllus bimaculatus*) which swarmed on warm evenings, taking 1–2 per minute, and bats.

Food caching

Food caching is a common feature of the British falcons, all engaging in the practice when conditions are good as a hedge against poor hunting times. In his study of Hobbies in southern England, Parr (1985) noted that of 93 food passes from the male Hobby, the female immediately plucked 84 (90.3%) and fed them to her brood. On the other nine occasions the female cached the food item. Caches were within 50 m of the nest site. Two cache site types were observed, the top of a dead Silver Birch (*Betula pendula*) stump, and within a clump of pine needles in a Scots Pine (*Pinus sylvestris*). The female attacked Green Woodpeckers, Jays and Magpies which flew close to her caches. Of the nine cached prey items, the female retrieved six within three hours of caching. Parr also reported that on a previous occasion another observer had seen a juvenile Hobby retrieving cached food.

Food consumption and energy balance

Very little is known of the food requirements of wild Hobbies. Brown (1976) assumes daily consumption is 20% of body weight, which corresponds to 35–50 g (the lower figure for males, the higher figure for females, but in each case there is a spread of body weights which mean there will be overlap). Brown notes that this requirement would be satisfied by one lark or starling, or a great number of insects. Brown's estimate is consistent with that of Dement'ev & Gladkov (1966), who note that Hobby food requirements are 'slight', and state a daily need of

25–30 g of meat, but offer no supporting evidence, or comment on the difference between prey weight and 'meat'. Fiuczynski & Sömmer (2011) suggest a figure of 40–50 g as the food requirement of a captive Hobby, though this appears to have been, at least in part, in the form of complete mice or passerines and so is comparable with the figure of Dement'ev & Gladkov (1966) if an allowance is made for the 'meat' content of prey.

However, while both direct (i.e. from wild birds) and experimental evidence is scant, Clarke *et al.* (1996) have carried out interesting work on the energy content of dragonflies and have made an estimate of the energy requirements of a juvenile Hobby which they were then able to convert into the number of insects the falcon would need to catch each day. Clarke and co-workers netted Azure Damselfly (*Coenagrion puella*), Common Darter (*Sympetrum striolatum*), Brown Hawker (*Aeshna grandis*), Migrant Hawker (*A. mixta*) and Southern Hawker (*A. cyanea*) dragonflies/damselflies and measured their energy content (kJ/g) from the carbon content. The energy content was essentially constant across the species at 24.6 kJ/g, the energy value of individual insects varying, of course, with size, from 0.8 kJ for the smallest (Azure Damselfly) to 9.4 kJ for the hawkers.

In order to estimate the insect catch necessary to sustain life, Clarke and co-workers assumed that the energy requirements of a juvenile Hobby could be estimated by scaling those of a Kestrel, and so used the work of the group at Groningen (see Chapter 5) to arrive at an energy requirement of a juvenile Hobby. The derived figure was 250–300 kJ/day. As already noted, in the absence of their parents, juvenile Hobbies satisfy their food requirements by hunting insects, Clarke *et al.* noting that to sustain life the juvenile would therefore need to catch and consume 200–250 Common Darters or 75–90 Migrant Hawkers each day. Such predation rates seem extreme, but dragonfly numbers can also be extreme, as can capture rates: in a two-week period during one summer in Cambridgeshire it was estimated that 10,000 Black-tailed Skimmers (*Orthetrum cancellatum*) were taken by falcons (Kestrels, Hobbies and Red-footed Falcons) (Parslow 1992). In the Netherlands, Bijlsma & Beunder (2007) observed one second-year Hobby female capturing 66–89 large dragonflies per day over a three-day period, with a capture rate of 6.5–7.4 per hour.

The assumption that the Groningen data on Kestrels can be used as the basis for calculating energy needs of Hobbies seems reasonable, given the similarity of size of the two falcons and the essential equivalence of the energy content of their prey. It is therefore also reasonable to assume that the weight variations through the breeding season noted in Kestrels, particularly the male, will apply to Hobbies, as provisioning rates are comparable in the two cases. Parr (1985) noted that during the pre-laying phase of the breeding cycle, a male Hobby was seen to deliver an average of 2.3 prey items per day to his female, this rising to 2.6 per day during the incubation phase and to 5.9 per day during the nestling phase (the brood was three chicks). However, in each case there was a significant range in the number of deliveries, for instance between 2.3 per day and 11.4 per day in the nestling phase. Provisioning the female and chicks is hard work for the male and it is likely that, as with male Kestrels, this will be reflected in weight loss.

TERRITORY AND BREEDING DENSITY

As with other falcons, Hobbies are usually highly territorial with regard to nesting areas, but more relaxed in terms of hunting ranges. In general males arrive at breeding grounds ahead of females, and displays and conflicts are then seen between adjacent males as they seek to establish territories (Note 6.6). Some nest areas may be isolated from other Hobby pairs, but nest clustering is often seen, with nest separations down to 100 m having been reported. Much greater distances are much more usual: in a study in southern England Parr (1985) found closest neighbours to be at distances of about 4–5 km, while Messenger (personal communication) noted separations of less than 3 km after the Hobby population had increased in Derbyshire. In some areas where they occur, clusters may involve several nests, suggesting a loose association, this idea being supported by the occasional report of tolerance being shown to adjacent pairs and even intruder birds. Most hunting activity is away from the nest area, favoured hunting sites often being at a distance of several kilometres: data in Chapman (1999a) suggest that distances of about 6 km are the limit of the Hobby's hunting range, as at greater distances the falcon is unlikely to be able to carry prey of significant weight back to the nest. However, Fiuczynski & Sömmer (2011) note one Hobby which hunted in the centre of Berlin, where prey was abundant, at a distance of 17 km from its pylon nest: at that stage the young had fledged, so it is not clear if this extreme travelling distance to hunt involved carrying prey back to the nest.

Given the nest separations seen in Britain, hunting distances of up to 6 km may mean that several Hobbies hunt in the same range, implying that the mutual tolerance very frequently seen in Hobbies hunting insect swarms may be carried over (though to a lesser extent) to avian hunting. It is also the case that there are examples of 'third party' birds (see *Breeding*, below) which are accepted at nest sites. But these, usually yearling birds which do not offer a mating threat to established pairs, are exceptions, and Hobbies are strongly protective of their nest areas against other adults. The protected area extends to about 200 m around the nest site (see, for instance, Parr 1985 and references therein) and any adult

FIG 202. Adult Hobby, showing the distinctive coloration of the upperparts. (James Sellen)

Hobby straying into this area will be driven off. If an adult is spotted at about 500 m the breeding pair will take a horizontal position and stretch their legs to show their red trousers. The bird(s) will also make the alarm call. If the intruder comes closer the male Hobby will attack. This usually results in the intruder flying off, but talon grappling may occur. Fiuczynski & Sömmer (2011) consider that to avoid such conflicts in pairs which are relatively close, different flight routes to hunting areas will be used: in their study, in the woodland around Berlin, Fiuczynski & Sömmer found some nest sites which were only 100 m apart, making the formalising of intrusion policy a necessity in order to avoid almost constant antagonism which would have been detrimental to breeding success.

Because of the occasionally observed proximity of neighbouring nests, Hobby breeding densities can be very high: Bogliani *et al.* (1992) recorded densities of 25.8–29.0 breeding pairs/100 km^2 in their study of Hobbies in poplar wood lots in northern Italy. The 29.0/100 km^2 figure of Bogliani *et al.* is the highest given in the review of breeding densities across the western Palearctic by Sergio *et al.* (2001), who tabulate data with a range of 1–29 pairs/100 km^2.

In southern England, Parr (1985) measured densities of 4.8 pairs/100 km^2 in the New Forest, 2.8/100 km^2 in farmland and 1.6–3.5/100 km^2 on chalk downland. However, these densities do not imply territory sizes, as Parr measured the areas of breeding activity shown by Hobby pairs. These areas included several potential nest sites, usually including the site used in the previous year, and covered an average of 7.5 km^2 in the New Forest (with a range of 3.4–16 km^2) and 6.6 km^2 on chalk downland (2.5–9 km^2). Within these areas there were an average of 3.8 possible nests for the New Forest, 3.6 for the downland. For Hobbies it therefore seems that 'territory' has two meanings, one early in the breeding season when the pair may well defend a relatively large area before deciding which of several potential nest sites will be used (Fuller *et al.* 1985 refer to this area as the 'nesting range', an area which is regularly used, but within which only one pair of Hobbies is found, a definition which has been taken up by later researchers), and a smaller area around that chosen site once it is selected. Parr's breeding density is at the upper end of that measured in Britain, Prince & Clark (1993) measuring 1.3 pairs/100 km^2 in Cambridgeshire, Fuller *et al.* (1985) measuring 3.8 and 4.8 pairs/100 km^2 in two study areas of undulating farmland between the Cotswolds and Chilterns, and Messenger & Roome (2007) measuring 3.1 pairs/100 km^2 in lowland, mixed farmland in Derbyshire across a ten-year period, with a range of 1.7–4.4 pairs/100 km² in individual years. However, as the population increased, the breeding density of Hobbies in Derbyshire increased. In an updated study Messenger (personal communication, 2014) noted that in a core area of 100 km² of the 412 km² area used as the basis of the earlier study, the breeding density had increased from 3.0 pairs/100 km² in 1992–1994 to 3.67 in 1999–2001 and then to 8.67 in 2010–2012. The mean nearest-neighbour distance had decreased from 5.6 km (1992–1994) to 4.4 km (1999–2001) and to 2.92 km (2010–2012).

A similar increase in breeding density as a consequence of the increase in the British Hobby population was noted by Clements & Everett (2012). Their study covered six areas of Bedfordshire, Hertfordshire and Kent, each of which comprised a high proportion (about 75%) of open habitat (farmland, grassland and orchards), with smaller fractions of woodland and urban land. Within their study areas Clements & Everett identified the number of different pairs of Hobbies and attempted to discover if each pair was breeding. The number of identified pairs ranged from 9.0 to 15.0/100 km², with a mean of 12.0 ± 2.4 pairs/100 km². If the urban land was removed from the land area of each study area on the reasonable assumption that it offered no possibility of breeding to a Hobby pair, then the density of identified pairs rose to 10.1–17.3/100 km² with a mean of 14.6 ± 2.8 pairs/100 km². However, not all identified pairs were confirmed as breeding. If only breeding pairs were included then the breeding density across the study areas (ignoring one area in Kent where none of 12 identified pairs was confirmed as breeding) varied from 5.5 to 14.6/100 km², with a mean of 10.0 ± 3.7 pairs/100 km². Again if the urban land is removed from the calculations (and the area with no confirmed breeding pairs excluded) then the range of breeding densities is 12.1 ± 3.7 pairs/100 km². In reality there is a high probability that some pairs not confirmed as breeding did breed – as Clements & Everett note, Hobbies are not an easy subject for study, as they are particularly elusive in the area close to their nests – so the breeding density across the study areas lies between 12.1 and 14.6 pairs/100 km², a much higher density than any previously confirmed in Britain.

A consequence of the high breeding densities noted by Clements & Everett was a reduction in nearest-neighbour distance to 2.1 ± 0.6 km, with a range of 1.8–2.8 km. In one case, a Hobby nest outside the study area was found to be within 1 km of a nest inside the area. A similar reduction was observed in Derbyshire by Messenger (2012), the breeding density in a 100 km² study area increasing from 3.0 to 8.67 between 1992/94 and 2010/12, and the mean nearest-neighbour distances falling from 5.60 km to 2.92 km. The potential implications of such reductions are considered in Chapter 8.

BREEDING

Hobbies are monogamous and pairs may be maintained in successive breeding seasons, with some observers suggesting that pairs will remain together until one partner is lost. Schuyl *et al.* (1936) suggest the evidence for pairs to be maintained during winter is scant, but there are cases of pairs arriving together at breeding sites, which implies pair formation during winter, or pairing during migration. However, in most cases males arrive at the breeding areas first, the females a few days later. As there are many examples of pairs being maintained in successive seasons, such staggered arrival does imply that pairs may not winter together, as does the fact that lone males may display to any passing female, though the arrival of the previous year's mate ends such indiscriminate behaviour. Because a returning female will be familiar with the territory, which other females will not be, she will presumably behave differently, although of course it may also be the case that mates recognise each other when they meet.

Female Hobbies may be able to breed in their first year, but such behaviour seems rare, with some yearling females which do mate failing to produce eggs or laying small clutches. Males may also be able to breed in their first year, but no evidence of yearling males breeding has been identified, and in general it is assumed that males do not breed until they are two years old (see the comments on the breeding age difference between the sexes in Chapter 2). There are many examples of extra birds assisting at the nests of breeding pairs, both males and females, and these are assumed to be yearling birds gaining experience: 'third party' males have been observed to provide food for females, and 'third party' females have been observed to feed nestlings when the 'true' female has been away for a time (see discussion of 'floaters' in Chapter 2). Zuberogoitia *et al.* (2003) record two instances which appear to have been of yearling males assisting an older pair of birds, both in feeding of the female and in nest defence.

As with the other British falcons (and falcons in general) the male provides the majority of the food for the female during egg laying and incubation, and for the family during the early phase of chick growth.

Displays

Hobbies are more elusive than the other British falcons, their displays less noticeable. Displays are also less frequent, particularly if the pair bond is already well established before the birds reach the breeding area. Males arriving before females will establish ownership of a territory by making both low and high circling flights, calling loudly. The high circling flights may involve the male turning frequently, almost as though corkscrewing through the air. These flights continue when the female arrives and she may join in once the pair bond is established (or re-established). Hobbies are noisy at dawn and at dusk, and either period can assist the observer in locating breeding areas, though early-morning calling is often masked by the dawn chorus, whereas late-calling birds have the auditorium to themselves.

Male courtship flights consist of a fast horizontal flight with periods of gliding on raised wings, rather as pigeons glide. The flapping flight between the gliding sections involves rapid wing-beats and the male corkscrewing. As with the corkscrewing during high flights, the overall appearance seems to suggest that the male is advertising his abilities at the rapid, agile flight that will be essential in provisioning his mate and brood. The male will also dive quickly at

FIG 203. Adult Hobby, showing the distinctive patterning of the underwing and body. (Dave Soons)

either the female or the nest site. During these dives he makes a drumming noise reminiscent of the Snipe. When describing this phenomenon, Pounds (1948) considered the sound to have been produced by a controlled vibration of the primaries or secondaries rather than of the outer tail feathers as it is in the wader. If the female is in flight when the male dives at her, she may turn onto her back as he approaches and call loudly.

Once the breeding territory has been established, the Hobby pair is then seen only rarely during the period prior to egg laying. Nethersole-Thompson (1931b, 1931c) considered that during this period the pair frequently soar high above the nest site, reinforcing their territorial rights, but in a discreet fashion. The pair also roost separately during this time, usually at a distance from the nest site.

The territory occupied by the male will have several potential nest sites, these perhaps including nests previously used, if the site is traditional. The male will indicate the sites by landing beside them, taking up a horizontal position to display his red thighs, calling and then standing in the nest. Eventually the female will make a decision. She also then takes up a horizontal posture at the site, her legs stretched to display her red thighs, and gives the 'keer' call. This female nest display excites the male, who will make figure-of-eight flights around the site and finally perch beside her. The pair may then perform a mutual display flight, with various fast loops while calling loudly.

As well as display flights, courtship feeding occurs. In the early stages the feeding is ritualised. If the prey is exchanged on a perch, the male will call the female and then transfer the prey from talons to bill. When the female arrives he will advance towards her making the 'keer' call softly. The two birds will bow towards each other, their legs stiff to reveal their red thigh feathering. The female will then take the prey and fly to another perch to feed. Aerial food passes are also used in this breeding phase. These may take several forms: the male may stoop towards the female then turn sharply upwards, dropping the food for her to catch; he may fly horizontally, the female approaching him at speed and taking the prey from him as she turns and extends her feet; or the two may lock talons on the prey and tumble through the air before the male releases the prey. Later, when incubation has begun, or when the chicks are young, the passes are less spectacular, the male calling the female to a perch where she takes the prey from him immediately: before taking the prey she may adopt the juvenile begging position, her bill half-open and her extended wings quivering. These food passes usually occur away from the nest, the occurrence increasing in the time immediately before egg laying. Once incubation begins, food passes are much closer to the nest so that the time the female is away from the eggs is minimised, and on occasion the male may actually deliver plucked prey to the female at the nest.

Nest sites

Hobbies nest in stick nests, usually of Carrion Crows, but also those of other corvids, other raptors such as Buzzard, Goshawk and Sparrowhawk, Grey Herons and Wood Pigeons. Squirrel dreys have also been used. In their study in England's southern Midlands Fuller *et al.* (1985) found all 57 pairs of breeding Hobbies were in Carrion Crow nests; in Derbyshire, Messenger & Roome (2007) found 103 of 106 were in Carrion Crow nests (the others were in Rook nests in small rookeries); while in an analysis of 278 nests (Fiuczynski & Nethersole-Thompson 1980) those of Carrion Crows had been used on 251 occasions (90.3%), indicating a clear preference. However, as both Chapman (1999a) and Messenger & Roome (2007) note, the enthusiasm of crows for adding polypropylene baling twine to their nest structures has occasionally resulted in both adult and nestling Hobbies becoming entangled. Messenger & Roome note one dead Hobby found hanging with twine around its legs and feet and three nestlings saved from a similar fate (see also Fig. 227).

The chosen nest will sometimes have been constructed during the same breeding season, and there are many stories of Hobbies standing on the edges of occupied crow nests staring at the nestlings, not with an eye to predation, but apparently to assess when the nest might become available for new tenants. Bergmann (1952) wrote that on one occasion he saw Hobbies taking control of a Raven nest just minutes after the fledgling corvids had left it. However, older nests are used, and the same nest may be occupied in successive seasons, though as Hobbies do not make repairs, winter weather may mean that stick nests do not survive long enough to become traditional. In Britain the chosen nest may be in a variety of trees, both coniferous and deciduous. Across the Hobby's range the choice of trees varies, though in general Scots Pine is preferred where it is available (Fiuczynski & Sömmer 2011: data from Germany and the Netherlands). In their study of English Hobbies, Fiuczynski & Nethersole-Thompson (1980) noted that 227 of 281 nests were in Scots Pine – though, of course, it is largely the nest-building crows that are expressing this preference rather than the Hobbies themselves. Across the falcon's range some two dozen tree species have been found to accommodate Hobbies (and their nest-building antecedents). Of deciduous tree species, most British nests are to be found in oaks, a preference which seems to have been forced upon the crow nest builders as prior to the arrival of Dutch elm disease to Britain, the English Elm (*Ulmus minor*) was the most common deciduous tree in which to find the falcons. The height of nest chosen by Hobbies in Britain varied from 4 m to 28 m in a study of 140 nests by Fiuczynski & Nethersole-Thompson 1980. In a study in southern England, Parr (1985) found a range of 8–29 m. In their study of 35 nests in Derbyshire,

Messenger & Roome (1994) noted 10–30 m, with most nests at heights of 13–18 m, while in a later study in the same area, nest heights were 7.5–30 m with a mean height of 14.1 m (Messenger & Roome 2007). These British data are consistent with studies across the falcon's range.

Messenger & Roome (2007) identified the trees for 106 Hobby nests over their ten-year study period and found that 84 (79%) were in oak, with 9 (8%) in Ash (*Fraxinus excelsior*) and the remainder in Alder (*Alnus glutinosa*, 3 nests), Norway Spruce (*Picea abies*, 2 nests), willow (*Salix* spp., 2 nests) and single nests in Beech (*Fagus sylvatica*), Common Lime (*Tilia europaea*), Scots Pine and Sycamore (*Acer pseudoplatanus*). The remaining two nests were on pylons.

Cliff sites are rarely used. Dement'ev & Gladkov (1966) mention cliff-top sites in the mountains of what is now Kyrgyzstan, and Roberts (1991) noted a breeding pair of Hobbies in a treeless valley in Pakistan and so surmised cliff breeding. Fiuczynski & Sömmer (2011) cite one example of ground nesting in Kazakhstan. Over recent times in continental Europe there has been a marked trend towards the use of corvid nests on pylons (Note 6.7). Nests on pylons have no protection against bad weather, and offer easy access to predators, which militates against their use, and may explain why Devrient & Wohlgemuth (1992) observed young hobbies which had fledged from a pylon nest spending the night in trees, as did the adults.

However, while it is unlikely to have been a significant factor in the Hobbies' choice, such sites have the advantage of being safe from interference by humans. Since interference is known to be a cause of both egg and chick failures, this positive effect might outweigh the negatives mentioned above, and this was indeed found to be the case in a study in France where Dronneau & Wassmer (1986) noted that the success rate of pylon-nesting Hobbies was 2.83 fledglings per breeding pair whereas that of falcons breeding in 'conventional' sites was 2.38. Whether this is also the case in Britain, where the climate is less stable, has yet to be tested.

Pylon-nesting Hobbies are now a feature of the landscape of many countries, both in Europe and elsewhere across the falcon's range. The first recorded use of a pylon nest in Britain was by Trodd (1993), who in Bedfordshire in 1988 noted Hobbies using an old Carrion Crow nest. Three young were successfully fledged from the nest: pylons were also used as look-out posts and plucking posts by the Hobby pair, and by two other pairs nesting within 3 km. Catley (1994) noted another pylon nest in Lincolnshire the following year.

Hobbies will also use artificial nests if crow nests are not available, Fiuczynski (1986) noting that in the pine forests around Berlin the falcons actually used the artificial sites (baskets) in preference to crow nests that could have been utilised. This was advantageous, as nestlings were much less likely to fall from the baskets.

Dement'ev & Gladkov (1966) mention an apparent observation of a colony of nesting Hobbies ('4–5 pairs near Kiev') but dismiss this as dubious. No other record of colonial nesting has been found.

Copulation

Hobby copulation is much more discreet than that of many other birds, but follows the same general pattern. The female usually initiates copulation by calling softly, either the '*kew-kew-kew*' or '*keer*' call. She will then stretch forward,

FIG 204.
Mating Hobbies.
(Torsten Pröhl)

raising her wings slightly and her tail. The male makes a short approach flight, sometimes looping over before hovering above her and gently landing on her back, maintaining position by fluttering his wings. After copulation the two birds may call softly to each other, or more loudly as they move away. Witherby et al. (1939) observed an attempted copulation in the air, the female flying on decurved wings while the male landed on her back. Since many copulations occur prior to egg laying, it was obviously not possible to say if the copulation was successful or even if it actually occurred, and, as Cade (1982) has noted, the interpretation of aerial contact between mates needs very careful assessment. However, given the extraordinary flying abilities of Hobbies, such aerial copulation could be possible, and while anthropomorphism is to be avoided it is difficult to escape the idea that such behaviour smacks of showing off.

While normally copulation ceases after the onset of egg laying, Ganzeboom (2014a) noted a breeding pair of Hobbies copulating (a single occasion, lasting only about three seconds) about two weeks after egg laying had been completed.

Egg laying
The female's decision on nest site is usually made after inspection of several potential sites: Parr (1985) noted that Hobby pairs would prospect 5–8 nests before a decision was made. In each nest the female will sit and turn around, presumably checking the viewing angle and take-off options from the nest as well as its suitability as an egg platform. While the degree of camouflage offered by tree foliage might be assumed to be a factor in choice, Hobby nests can be both well-hidden in tree crowns and on (relatively) bare and isolated branches: clearly a balance between hiding the nest from potential predators and offering a wide view and easy exit has to be struck. Once the site is selected the female may spend long periods occupying the nest before she commences laying: Berezovikov & Zinchenko (1988) reported a case in which the female sat in the nest for more than a month before she began to lay, though such a timescale is abnormal. In a study in Derbyshire across the years 1992–2001 Messenger & Roome (2007) noted that the mean laying date for the first egg of a clutch was 12 June. This mean date was remarkably stable, varying only from 11 to 13 June across the ten years of study. However, within a given year there was a range of dates for individual females which showed a greater disparity, the earliest date being 3 June, the latest 26 June. Within a given year, the range of first-egg dates was much tighter than these extreme dates suggest, varying from only 4 days to a maximum of 17 days: the mean range was 10.8 days. Later nesting has been noted, Potters (1998) recording first-egg dates of 4 July and 9 July for clutches which were not considered to be repeats. Both nests were successful.

Egg-laying intervals

On average females lay one egg every two days, but this interval may be as short as 36 hours, or as long as three days. As a consequence of this variation in laying interval there is no set time during the day for the female to lay.

As with other falcon species the onset of laying varies, and the reasons for this are no better understood for Hobbies than they are for the Kestrels, for which much more intensive investigations have been carried out. As with the Kestrels, the general view is that a combination of female condition, spring food resource and weather are likely causes of delays in egg laying. For the Hobby, food resource availability during winter is more stable because of the long-distance migration, but the migration flight itself will potentially affect the female's condition if difficult weather en route saps energy, or food is scarce. Spring weather in Britain can affect insect numbers, which may also affect the time taken to build up the reserves required for egg production. Weather conditions may be beneficial if they result in copious supplies of insects, and this may result in egg laying occurring earlier, or may delay laying if conditions are poor and insects scarce. In Britain, Chapman (1999a) noted that a study of nesting records for the period 1896–1976 showed the date of completion of clutches varying from 29 May to 2 July, with a mean data of 15 June; almost 50% of clutches were completed between 13 and 17 June. These dates are consistent with data from Germany and the Netherlands. Chapman noted that laying appeared synchronous between Hobby pairs in a given area, which implies that weather and/or food resource are the dominant factors in the timing of the first egg. However, as noted above, the reasons for the spread in first egg laying dates are still debated.

Eggs

Each egg is elliptical, measuring 37–47 mm along the major axis and 30–36 mm along the minor axis (Schönwetter 1967, from a sample of 150 eggs which indicated no geographical variation; later data do not amend these figures – Sergio *et al.* 2001). The eggs weigh 22–28 g. The ground colour of the eggs is pale yellow-brown. Usually there is heavy red-brown spotting, but spotting may be much sparser. As with other species, later eggs are usually paler than earlier ones, and have sparser markings (as in Kestrels: see Chapter 5). The colour of the eggs also fades with incubation, the base colour becoming more yellow.

Clutch size

Cramp & Simmons (1980) state that of 271 clutches from English nests 85% had three eggs, with 11% having two, and only 4% four. Single eggs are also rare. The mean clutch size across the sample of Cramp & Simmons was 2.93. Brown (1976) states that although clutches vary from one to four eggs, the norm is for two or three (Note 6.8): in a sample of 35 clutches Brown found a mean of 2.8. Messenger & Roome (2007) found a mean clutch of 2.96 from 126 breeding pairs across a ten-year period. Such average clutch sizes are replicated across the Hobby's range, Chapman (1999a) presenting data from Germany, Italy, the Netherlands and Spain which suggested mean clutches in the range 2.6–3.1. In a study in Italy over an nine-year period Sergio & Bogliani (1999) found a mean clutch size of 2.65 from 89 nests, with a variation of 2.40–2.88 across the years of study. In Britain clutches of four eggs are so comparatively rare that the discovery of Hobby pairs which fledge four young may make news (e.g. Combridge & King 2007). The small number of clutches with four eggs is also mirrored in other countries: in Germany Fiuczynski & Sömmer (2011) found the percentage varying from 0% to 11% across several years, while in Italy Sergio & Bogliani (1999) found 7.1% of clutches had four eggs. Interestingly, in the environs of Berlin after an influx of Goshawks had significantly reduced the breeding success of Hobbies the number of clutches with four eggs increased (K. D. Fiuczynski, personal communication to A. Messenger).

In general the same female will lay the same clutch size in successive years. In their study of Hobbies in both England and Germany, Fiuczynski & Nethersole-Thompson (1980) noted one female laying three eggs in three successive years; one laying 2, 2, 3, 3, 3; another laying 4, 4, 4, 3; and a fourth laying 3, 4, 4, 3.

A replacement clutch is laid if the first clutch is lost early in incubation. Replacement clutches are smaller than first clutches: Cramp & Simmons (1980) state that replacement clutches were laid on 45% of occasions, and that of a sample of 20 such clutches 40% had three eggs, 40% had two, and 20% had a single egg for an average of 2.2. In general repeat clutches are laid in a different nest, though one within a short distance of the original. In their study in Derbyshire, Messenger & Roome (2007) noted 12 nest failures (nine failed clutches, one failed brood, a failure at an unknown stage and a replacement clutch which also failed). Five replacement clutches were laid, one of which, as noted, also failed.

Those pairs which lose clutches to predation and in which the female does not lay a replacement clutch, or which lose a brood, may behave in different ways. Some apparently migrate early, while others continue to occupy the territory. If the female has not laid eggs, the pair may continue with courtship behaviour into August before finally abandoning the idea of breeding. In pairs where addled eggs have been laid, the female may continue to incubate for many weeks, but the male ultimately loses interest and stops bringing in food, causing his mate to abandon the clutch.

Incubation

The female starts to incubate after laying the second egg and does the majority of the incubation herself, though the male does sit if the female is away from the nest. Dement'ev & Gladkov (1966) state that the male has a brood patch, but Fiuczynski & Sömmer (2011) query whether this is the case. If male Hobbies lack a brood patch then their egg covering is probably more an insulation against heat loss than incubation, the latter being entirely the work of the female. However, Parr (1985) records a male Hobby sharing sitting for an average of 1.3 hours each time over an eight-day period. Such extended periods suggest incubation rather than merely protecting the eggs from chilling.

During incubation food passes are inconspicuous, with little calling. The male will land close to the nest and make the soft '*pik*' call to summon the female. The female will go to him and take the prey. If the male has plucked the prey she will eat, otherwise she will pluck it herself and eat. She then defecates, sometimes preens quickly, and returns to the nest. During her feeding the male will stand guard or cover/incubate the eggs.

The incubation period is 28–32 days, the work of Bijlsma (1980) in the Netherlands suggesting that the exact period depends on clutch size, a single egg requiring 28 days, two eggs 30 days, three eggs 31 days and four eggs 32 days. Because of the early incubation most hatchings are asynchronous, though not usually by more than 1–2 days. Spent eggshells may be removed from the nest, eaten by the female or left in situ, where, over time, they become an addition to the general detritus of the nest area.

Chick growth

On hatching, the chicks are semi-altricial and nidicolous, and weigh about 17 g. They are covered in white down and are initially blind, the eyes being fully open 2–3 days from hatching. They are brooded by the female more or less continuously for the first 8–12 days, even in good weather, then only at night for a few days (and during heavy rain) before, finally, the female stops brooding in favour of standing guard either within the nest tree or close by.

The male initially provides all the food for the female and brood, the female feeding the chicks bill-to-bill at first. Once the female has stopped brooding and begun only to guard she will occasionally leave to hunt insects if they are swarming close to the nest; often the male will take over guarding during these hunting periods. Later the female may also hunt for the nestlings as well as for herself. In other cases the male may continue to feed the female for a time post-brood, as well as provisioning the chicks. If the male brings insects he may take these directly to the nest and feed the chicks, but in general avian prey is still passed to the female. Tinbergen (1932), in a study of Hobbies in the Netherlands, noted that in the early stages of chick feeding the male delivered plucked prey, but as the demands on him rose he delivered unplucked prey, the female plucking and feeding. Tinbergen noted that the male delivered food 4–5 times daily at first (i.e. about every 3–4 hours), but this increased

FIG 205. The 'standard' clutch size for Hobbies is three. Single eggs (and therefore chicks) are rare. In the shots here an adult female (rather than a first-year female) has apparently laid a single egg in an old Carrion Crow stick nest. The female dutifully tended the single chick, which was successfully raised to fledge.

to 8–10 prey deliveries daily and feeds every 1.5 hours, though other studies imply somewhat lower delivery figures. Chapman (1999a) quotes data from a study in the English Midlands in which prey was delivered four times daily, rising to seven times. However, while these provisioning rates differ, it should be noted that exact nestling ages and brood sizes, and the weight of prey delivered, were not routinely noted, and that prey deliveries may be influenced by weather conditions. The exact number of deliveries should therefore be treated with caution. Messenger & Roome (2007) conducted three all-day (dawn to dusk) watches on Hobby nests to count prey deliveries. While the female was incubating, the male delivered four items in the day, at 05.00, 09.00, 17.00 and 21.00 (times are nearest hour). When the chicks were newly hatched (1–2 days old) eight items were delivered, at 06.00, two items at 09.00, 13.00, 14.00, 15.00, 19.00 and 20.00. When the chicks were 25–27 days old 12 prey items were provided, at 05.00, 06.00, two at 07.00, 08.00, 10.00, 12.00, 15.00, 16.00, 18.00, 20.00 and 21.00.

Parr (1985) sets down the average number of deliveries observed in a study of a Hobby nest with three chicks in Surrey (Table 21).

Once the eggs hatch, food deliveries must increase, the chicks' appetites being seemingly insatiable as they put on weight and grow feathers. Figure 206 illustrates the change in weight of a Hobby chick: the increase in weight follows a standard S-curve. After fledgling the weight drops to 220 g which then remains constant through life, with fluctuations during periods of high activity demand, such as when breeding.

From six days of age the second, greyish down emerges and the sheaths of the primary and tail feathers are apparent. At about ten days the sheaths of the contour feathers appear, initially on the back. Primary and tail feathers emerge

TABLE 21 Prey deliveries to a Hobby nest with three eggs/nestlings. From Parr (1985).

Breeding phase/period	Total hours of observation	Prey deliveries	Deliveries/day[1] Mean	Range
Pre-laying (mid-May – 10 June)	138	20	2.30.3	0–4.0
Incubation (11 June – 7 July)	207	33	2.60.3	0–4.6
Nestling (8 July – 14 August)	251	93	5.90.5	2.3–11.4

1. In calculating daily deliveries Parr assumed a 16-hour hunting day. The range of deliveries may indicate the possibility of reduced hunting due to weather conditions and/or the possible use of food caches, depending on prey size.

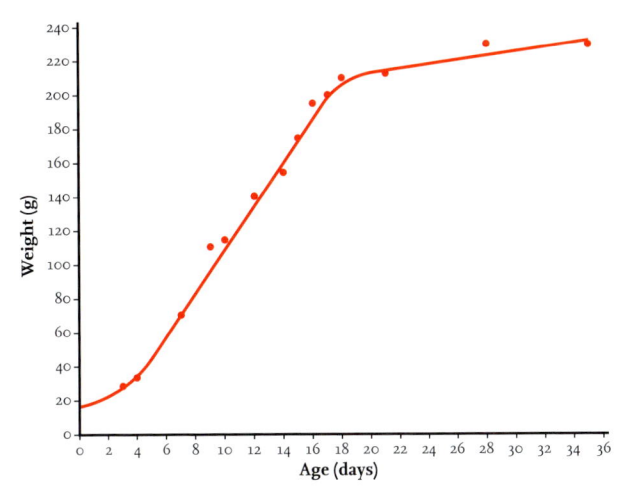

FIG 206. Variation of weight (g) of a hand-reared (assumed male) Hobby chick with age (days). Redrawn from data in Heinroth & Heinroth 1927.

at 12–15 days. During this phase of feather development the chicks preen often: Fiuczynski & Sömmer (2011) note an instance where a chick with a lame left leg developed feathers only on the right side of its head, suggesting that preening is important to feather development. When the chicks are about 14 days old they can stand and begin attempts to take prey from the female's talons when she arrives, though they are still not capable of dismembering it themselves. This behaviour becomes increasingly aggressive, and after another few days the female ceases to attempt to feed, dropping unplucked prey into the nest, even though the youngsters continue to beg. The young then tear up the prey and mantle their share to avoid sibling piracy. By 19–20 days of age the juvenile plumage is apparent, though down remains over most of the body. Wing exercises begin at about 21 days. At 27 days the nestlings may leave the nest and stand on nearby branches, though they do not move very far at first. The nestlings fledge after 28–34 days. Synchronously hatched broods may actually fly on the same day, though some observers consider males fly earlier than females. Figure 208 illustrates chick development: the data, from a study by Morata (1971), involved measurements on two Hobby chicks in a nest in the Doñana National Park, Andalusia, Spain. Morata considered that the two chicks were male and female, as one was smaller than the other. Figure 208 indicates that tarsus growth is rapid in comparison to body and feather growth, full size being attained at an age of about 15 days. Wing and feather length were measured only to 25 days and indicate that significant further growth occurs before fledgling.

FIG 207. When the single chick shown in Fig. 205 had grown it became very protective of its food, snatching it from the female when she arrived and immediately turning and mantling it. The female looked on, apparently bemused, for several minutes each time before flying away.

Hobbies often leave the nest before their first flight and climb about in local branches. The excursions can be abruptly interrupted when the female arrives with food, all the youngsters hurrying back to the nest, each calling loudly to be first to be fed. At this stage the young Hobbies' wings are up to 4 cm shorter than adult wings, and this may add to the clumsiness of first flights, which are usually short and end with awkward, panicky landings, though these are never on the ground, a distinct contrast to fledgling Peregrines which often do so.

THE HOBBY · 351

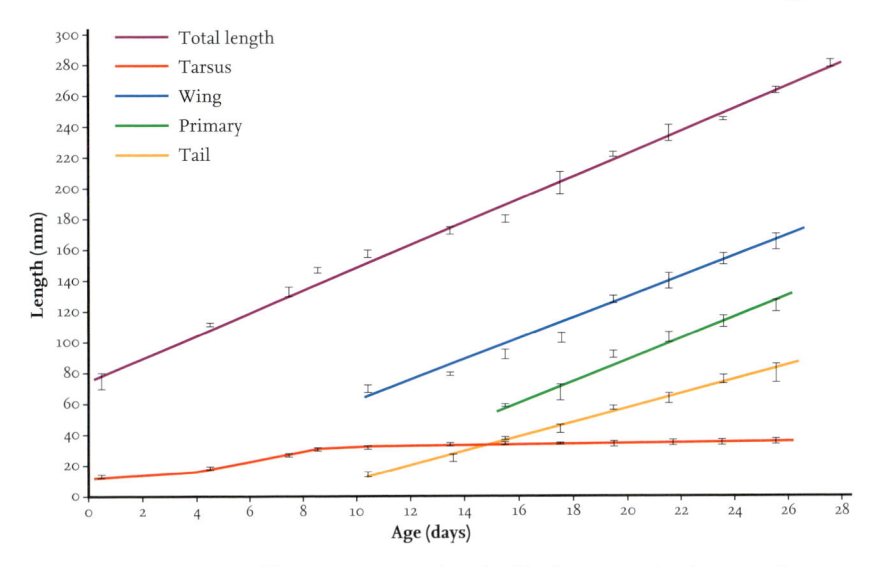

FIG 208. Variation in Hobby measurements: length of body, tarsus, wing, longest primary feather and longest tail feather. Redrawn from data in Morata 1971.

FIG 209. Single Hobby chick at 1 or 2 days old.

FIG 210. Single Hobby chick aged 7 days.

FIG 211. Single Hobby chick aged 11 days.

However, there are few such flights at first, Dronneau & Wassmer (2005) noting that for the first three weeks after fledging the juveniles spend 80% of their time resting and preening and rarely move more than a kilometre from the nest site, returning to it after flight attempts in order to rest. The juveniles may even roost in, or very close to, the nest. Juveniles engage in mock hunting with siblings to

FIG 212. Single Hobby chick aged 22 days.

improve their flying and hunting techniques, and on some early flights they may accompany the adults on avian hunting trips, learning the techniques necessary for taking larger prey.

Begging for food (with loud calling and shivering wings) continues after fledging, with the juveniles begging not only from their parents but also from

FIG 213. Recently fledged Hobby. Note the buff rather than red thighs.

FIG 214. Early take-off by a juvenile Hobby.

each other, from any other Hobby intruding on the nest area, and also from other species, observers having noted begging from both Kestrels and Wood Pigeons, and that juveniles will join younger fledglings of nearby broods so as to fed by 'foster-parents'. Hie (2014) records a Hobby raised by humans after seemingly being abandoned which, when released close to three recently fledged juveniles, was seen in their company, having apparently been accepted by the three siblings. It is not clear if the parent birds fed the new juvenile, though Hie considers this doubtful. The released juvenile was about a week younger than the three sibling falcons and although it hunted insects with them, it did not leave when the older birds did, remaining in the area for several more days.

Juveniles learn to take aerial food passes from the male soon after making their first flights, their first efforts being poor, with failures to catch dropped items. They soon learn, however, and will also attempt to pirate food from a sibling successful at a food pass. The attacked sibling will resist by mantling and will confront the pirate by assuming a threat posture, standing tall with raised wings and calling loudly: despite this, some attempts succeed. Though such attacks indicate a fierce rivalry for food items, the relationship between siblings is actually peaceful, with none of the overt competition, even siblicide and cannibalism, that is seen in some other species.

The male may deliver prey to the youngster, or the female may take it from him and deliver it herself: the female may also hunt and deliver captured prey directly to the juveniles. The adults do not pluck or tear up the delivered prey, the juveniles now doing this for themselves. Some females have been observed to pluck prey in front of juveniles, apparently to teach the techniques, but as

FIG 215. In this action sequence a juvenile Hobby approaches a male carrying a Barn Swallow, but the female Hobby then arrives, also intent on taking the prey. However, the juvenile, showing neat flying abilities, performs a back-flip and takes the prey. (Harry Albrecht)

most females deliver unplucked prey to the nest in the later stages of fledging most youngsters presumably learn how to dismember prey by trial and error. Both adults also continue to protect the prey, mobbing any raptor that comes too close. After about 7–10 days of trial flights, the juveniles start to hunt insects for themselves, the males seemingly out-competing their female siblings at this stage. Initially the fledglings take slower insects such as Dor-beetles, but their flying skills soon allow them to take more taxing prey such as dragonflies. They may also attempt to catch bats. However, most food is still provided by the adults, and this continues for about 20 days after fledging. Dronneau & Wassmer (2005) noted that the education of the young is rapid: they receive food on branches for the first three days after fledging, but by day 4–7 can take prey in aerial passes; from day 4–7 they are hunting insects, their success rate suggesting they are fast learners; they can pluck their own food by day 8–10; and they are hunting avian prey and bats, and attacking crows, a few days later.

Dronneau & Wassmer also noted that helpers – third birds at a nest site – would provision the juveniles on occasion, and that the fostering of juveniles by other adults sometimes occurred. The latter seemed specific to the timing of migration and is mentioned again in that context (see *Movements and wintering quarters*, below). However, the existence of third birds at nests is not always as useful as in the examples in each of the papers of Dronneau & Wassmer. In Germany, Devrient & Wohlgemuth (1992) noted a Hobby nest at which a third bird – indeed several different third birds – was present. When the (two) chicks were about 12 days old the male Hobby disappeared, presumably preyed upon or killed. The female then attempted to provision the youngsters, but received no help from the third bird; ultimately the chicks died.

Juveniles do not start to hunt birds until the days immediately prior to migration, and they are not very successful, Dronneau & Wassmer (1987) recorded hunting of, but failure to catch, a Barn Swallow and several Noctules: it seems likely that before and during migration, juveniles feed mainly on insects. Dronneau & Wassmer suggested that bat hunting was infrequent in young Hobbies, implying that it might be a learned behaviour by fledglings which accompanied their parents on hunting trips – though they also proposed that the erratic, seemingly clumsy flight pattern of bats might encourage juvenile Hobbies into considering them an easy vertebrate target. In recent years bat hunting by Hobbies has been shown to be a much more widespread behaviour, in both summer and winter quarters. But the hunting abilities of juvenile falcons seem much as Dronneau & Wassmer found it, with the young birds mostly feeding on insects once they are independent

FIG 216. After feeding, juveniles will often lie along horizontal branches in the manner of a Nightjar.

of their parents. As the energy return from insect hunting is low, the inability to catch avian prey might involve the juveniles losing condition during the long migration flight, which is a possible reason for the mortality rate during the Sahara Desert crossing (see *Movements and wintering quarters*, below).

Breeding success

Brown (1976) states that success in terms of the hatching of eggs is 80%, the main cause of loss being infertility, though predation by crows also occurs. However, Parr (1985) noted that in his study in southern England in all but one case the loss of clutches at the egg stage was due to human interference. In their study in Derbyshire, Messenger & Roome (2007) found 12 nest failures. Of these five were due to human activity (three being unintentional disturbance by farmers), three to predation by Carrion Crows, two to predation by Grey Squirrels and two from unknown causes. The overall failure rate was 9.2%, i.e. a success rate of 90.8%.

These success rates are consistent with the data of Cramp & Simmons (1980), who quote 88.4% success based on 138 eggs laid in 47 nests producing 122 nestlings, and also consistent with data from other countries. Even higher hatching success rates have been observed in other countries: 90.5% of 676 eggs over the period 1956–1972 in Germany (Fiuczynski & Sömmer 2011) and 91.8% of 134 eggs in the Netherlands (Bijlsma 1980).

Brown (1976) quotes data on the fate of 35 chicks, of which 19 (54%) fledged. Of the 16 which did not survive, seven were lost to unknown causes, two were preyed upon by a Tawny Owl, one died of anaemia, and six died as a consequence of human action (a clutch of three starved after the female was shot, and another three died after a heath fire). Waddell (1978a) also records circumstantial evidence which points to Tawny Owl predation of Hobby chicks. Cramp & Simmons (1980) state a higher fraction of chicks fledging, with 109 fledglings from 122 hatchings (89%): this success rate corresponds to an average of 2.3 fledglings per nest. Cramp & Simmons also quote a German study in which 666 chicks fledged from 277 successful nests (2.4 fledglings per nest). However, in the German study the 277 successful nests were from a total sample of 358 Hobby pairs. Allowing for the pairs which produced no fledglings, the overall success rate was therefore 1.86 fledglings per breeding pair. In their study in Derbyshire, Messenger & Roome (2007) found a much higher success rate in overall terms, with 119 successes (defined as at least one fledgling) from 131 breeding pairs, i.e. 90.8%. Only 126 of the 131 pairs produced clutches, so the success rate measured against clutches laid was 94.4%. Messenger & Roome noted a mean of 2.44 fledglings from their 119 successful nests. Given their mean clutch size of 2.96, the mean number of fledglings represents a success rate of 82.4% in terms of fledglings per egg laid. Other studies from Europe suggest comparable success rates: for example, a mean of 2.2 fledglings from a mean clutch of 2.7 in northern Italy (81.5%) (Bogliani *et al.* 1994), means of 2.06 and 2.41 fledglings from a mean clutches of 2.7 (76% and 89.3% from two areas near Berlin (Fiuczynski & Nethersole-Thompson 1980), and a mean of 2.7 fledglings from a mean clutch of 3.1 from the Dutch Wadden Sea islands (Bijlsma & Diermen 1986).

These figures indicate remarkably low chick mortality. Parr (1985) recorded no nestling deaths at 15 nests in southern England. Bijlsma (1980), in the Netherlands, recorded a mortality rate of only 2.3%, while Fiuczynski & Sömmer (2011) recorded a figure of 2.6% (of 684 nestlings in the period 1956–1972). However, with an increase in the Goshawk population in the latter's study area (around Berlin) the mortality rate of Hobby fledglings rose, from 5.7% in 1976 to 10.3% in 2010. Such mortality as does occur may be due to bad weather, to human interference or to predation. In their study over a nine-year period in Italy, Sergio & Bogliani (1999) noted that breeding failures during incubation accounted for 83% of all failures (i.e. 17% of failures occurred during the nestling/fledgling phase). During incubation most failures were from unknown causes, but human activities – forestry and shepherds with their flocks – accounted for about 20%. During the nestling phase, all failures were due to forestry activities. Young birds may also fall from the nest: Waddell (1978b) noted the finding of a Hobby nest in a precarious state, and attempted to secure it with string to protect the two eggs it contained. Returning some days later he discovered the nest gone, presumably collapsed, and both adults on the ground beneath the tree, one apparently brooding a chick which seemed no more than three days old but was clearly in good health. Waddell does not record the fate of the chick, but given that it would be another 30 days or so before the chick would fledge, it is unlikely that it survived. Fiuczynski & Sömmer (2011) report ground feeding of a near-fledged nestling which had apparently jumped from the nest. From the whitewash marks Fiuczynski & Sömmer consider the youngster had been there for a couple of days and was obviously being well fed by the adults, one of which was seen in attendance. On finding the Hobby's nest apparently preyed upon by a Pine Marten (*Martes martes*), the two researchers replaced the youngster in a nearby Black Kite (*Milvus migrans*) nest. Grünhagen (1978b) also records finding a near-fledged Hobby chick on the ground which was apparently being reared, speculating that it had attempted to fly and failed, after seeing two siblings being more successful. In this case Grünhagen left the chick, but noted it had successfully fledged when he returned later.

As noted below (see *Friends and foes*), there is good evidence that Wood Pigeons nest in close proximity to Hobbies in order to gain protection against predation. The value of this to the pigeons was studied in northern Italy by Bogliani *et al.* (1999), and Sergio & Bogliani (2001) considered nest defence by Hobbies as a tactic which might enhance the falcons' own breeding success. The nest defence of 42 male and 43 female Hobbies was assessed on a scale of 0 to 7, where 0 signified the adult Hobby flying away on the approach of a human, and 7 where the falcon stooped close to the intruder. Dummy nests containing domestic Quail (*Coturnix japonica*) eggs were then set up at distances up to 100 m from Hobby nests and survival of the eggs in these was correlated against intensity of nest-defence aggression. The intensity of defence increased as the breeding season progressed, though this was more pronounced for females (Fig. 217), and the intensity for female falcons increased with clutch size (Fig. 218).

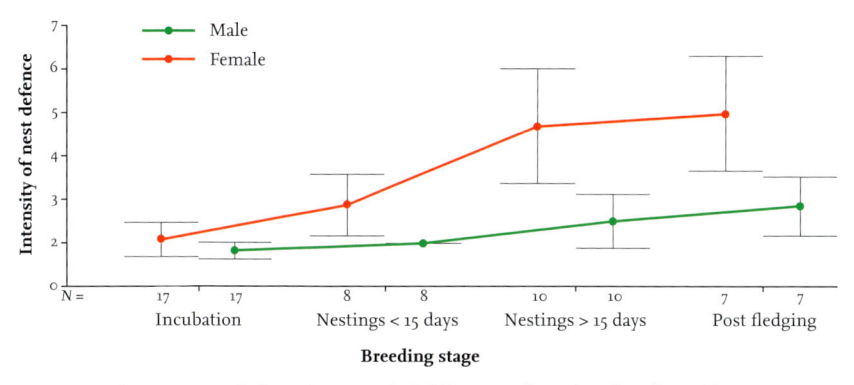

FIG 217. Average nest-defence intensity (± SE) for 42 male and 42 female Hobbies in northern Italy against phase of the breeding cycle. Scale on y-axis runs from 0 (flies away) to 7 (stoops at intruder). Redrawn from Sergio & Bogliani 2001.

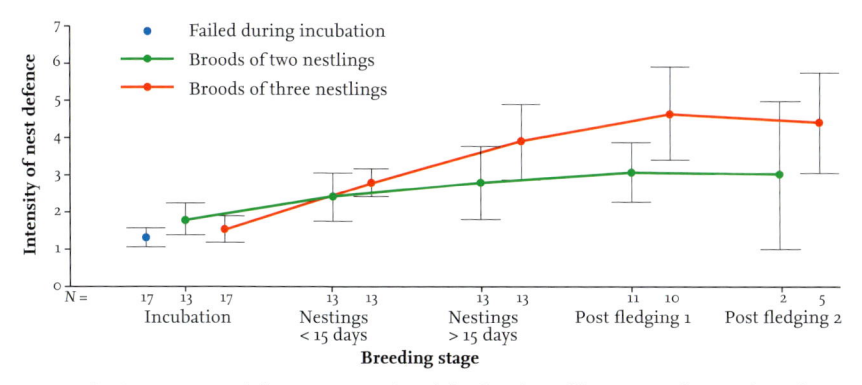

FIG 218. Average nest-defence intensity (± SE) for female Hobbies in northern Italy, with nests that failed during incubation, and with broods of two or three. Scale on y-axis runs from 0 (flies away) to 7 (stoops at intruder). Redrawn from Sergio & Bogliani 2001.

The results conform to the parental-investment hypothesis, i.e. that the closer the young are to adulthood the greater their reproductive value, and that the risks of nest defence therefore become increasingly worthwhile: for further details see Andersson et al. (1980), who derived a model for optimal parental defence against a predator, trading risk to the adult against security for nestlings by studying Fieldfares. But the results also suggest, as does the enthusiasm for Wood Pigeons nesting close to Hobbies, that the falcons are aggressive parents, behaviour which underpins the known low mortality of nestlings.

Nest-site, territory and mate fidelity

Sergio & Bogliani (1999) noted in their study of Hobbies in northern Italy over a nine-year period that nest-area fidelity was high. By nest area the Italian researchers meant an area which represented the territory of a male bird within which there might be several suitable nests, any of which might be chosen in a given year. Sergio & Bogliani noted that occupancy was positively correlated with breeding success, and that while some nest areas were occupied in successive years, other areas which appeared to offer similar nesting potential were not occupied (Table 22). This implies 'traditional' nest sites, but since stick nests have a finite lifetime, calling such nesting areas 'traditional' means that they are within the same area of the country; the nests themselves might lie within 100 m of earlier nests, but might be much further away (2–3 km).

From Table 22 it can be seen that the 'quality' of a nest area, measured by the success of breeding, is positively correlated with the occupancy of that site. Indeed, this idea that occupancy can be used as a measure of territorial quality

TABLE 22 Occupancy and breeding success of Hobby nests in a study area in northern Italy. From Sergio & Bogliani (1999).

Occupation rate[1]	Nests	Laying date in June (± SE)[2]	Clutch size (± SE)	% of nests failing during incubation	% of eggs hatched	Fledged young (± SE)	% Successful nests
0–25%	3	–	–	100	0	0	0
25–50%	5	19.5 ± 0.5	2	60	66	0.80 ± 0.49	40
50–75%	7	18.5 ± 3.5	2.6 ± 0.5	43	69	1.57 ± 0.57	57
75–100%	37	16.9 ± 1.4	2.8 ± 0.1	14	83	2.00 ± 0.17	82

1. Occupancy defined as percentage of years of study in which an area was occupied.
2. In general earlier laying leads to greater breeding success.

has been extended to other species. Sergio & Newton (2003) found that for Black Kites nesting in Switzerland, site occupancy was not only positively correlated with breeding success but negatively with mortality risk as measured by the proximity of the nearest Eagle Owl. In a study in southern England, Parr (1985) noted 17 of 21 nest-site areas being reoccupied in the following year; of those that were reoccupied only one pair used the same stick nest again, all other cases involving movements of less than 1.5 km. In a study in England's southern Midlands, Fuller *et al.* (1985) found that 8 of 21 Hobbies which returned to the same nest area (38%) were in the same tree or an adjacent one within 100 m, with a further 29% within 1 km; only 5% of Hobbies had moved more than 2 km from the previous year's nest site. In Derbyshire, Messenger & Roome (2007) found that of 106 nests identified over a ten-year period, eight nests used in the previous year were reused the following year; in two cases a nest was used, then not used the next year, but used again in the year after; and in two cases a nest was used again after not being used during the intervening two years. Messenger & Roome found one nest in which chicks were successfully fledged in three successive

FIG 219. Clutch of three (with one egg apparently addled) in a crow nest which was many years old and had been used on several previous occasions. (Mike Price)

years. They also found that changes in nest-site location were comparable to those of Fuller et al. (1985), with 48% pairs moving less than 600 m and only 19% moving more than 1 km. Fiuczynski & Sömmer (2011) record several instances of nest areas being used, though not necessarily in all years, over very long periods, in one case for over 40 years, implying true 'tradition' as the nest sites must have outlived several pairs of Hobbies.

Such nest-site fidelity is also reflected in the dispersal of juvenile Hobbies, as reflected in the distance they are to be found from their natal site when they return to breed. For Hobbies this distance is small. Galushin (1974), using all available data, including ringing data from within what was then the USSR, derived a mean figure of 39 ± 14 km, the lowest of any of the 11 raptors for which data were collected. Interestingly, Galushin proposed that raptors showing such small juvenile dispersal distances were those whose populations showed limited fluctuations. Galushin considered that species that preyed on birds fell into this category, while predators on mammals, particularly those whose main prey (e.g. rodents) were species whose populations showed significant fluctuations, showed much longer dispersal distances. The suggestion seemed to hold for Kestrels and Rough-legged Buzzards, particularly as the data were biased towards the USSR and therefore included lemmings, a significant prey for each species, but one which undergoes very significant population fluctuations. However, one of the largest dispersals was for the Honey-buzzard, which is not a significant mammal feeder.

Glutz von Blotzheim (1971) records male Hobby site fidelity as 75%, while that of females is only 11%, based on studies in Germany, and Fiuczynski (1978) found similar return frequencies (84.8% for males, 10.9% for females) in his studies around Berlin. However, these data refer to yearling birds returning to natal sites and so imply only that yearling female Hobbies disperse further than males (Note 6.9).

Although it can be difficult to be definitive about Hobby pairs, such studies as have been made, involving trapping, the identification of coloured rings and, in some cases, by the recognition of individual voices (since, as mentioned under *Voice*, above, these are so distinctive as to allow birds to be distinguished), suggest that Hobby pairs are long-lived, usually ending only with the loss of one of the pair.

Pairs do not, however, appear to remain together over winter, which is perhaps not surprising given that females tend to migrate earlier than males and the wintering ranges of Hobbies can be very large (see the following section). Schuyl et al. (1936) cite a single instance, but the fact that it remains the only instance reinforces the view that such winter pairing is rare.

MOVEMENTS AND WINTERING QUARTERS

Hobbies are summer visitors to Britain: indeed, they are summer visitors to all northern latitudes, though wintering specimens are known. Cramp & Simmons (1980) record German-ringed birds being recovered in Italy and the Netherlands in December, and in Belgium in January, and another falcon recovered in what was then Yugoslavia in January, while Pyman (1954) records observations of a Hobby in Essex several times between November 1953 and January 1954. The editors of *British Birds*, in which Pyman's observation was published, noted that the winter of 1953/54 was particularly mild, with some species being seen on nests as late as early December. However, Fiuczynski & Sömmer (2011) consider that most of these observations are dubious and probably relate to escapees, falcons handicapped in some way, or misidentification (e.g. with Merlins).

But, excepting these few possible examples, the entire nominate Hobby breeding (or potential breeding) population across a range from the Atlantic to the Pacific migrates, the European population heading south or southwest to Africa, the eastern (Russian Asia) population south and southwest to the Indian subcontinent and southeast Asia. At some longitude, Hobbies must choose to head for Africa or India, but recoveries of ringed birds to date do not allow such a precise drawing of migration routes or where the breeding populations differentiate between them. In a study which combined birdwatching and Himalayan trekking in an enviable manner, Dutch ornithologist Rob Bijlsma noted single Hobbies migrating south along the valley of the Kali Gandaki river in Nepal, and a group of six falcons, behaving as though they were a pair with young, at Birethanti (Bijlsma 1991). Bijlsma also noted more than 20 other species, mainly raptors.

Recoveries of juveniles ringed in Britain and Scandinavia show a distinct southwesterly route, implying a crossing of the Mediterranean at Gibraltar and wintering in western or southwestern Africa (Chapman, in Wernham *et al.* 2002). Observations suggest that European Hobbies (which may include some from eastern Britain if they fly south rather than southwest) may cross the Alps (being seen at altitudes to 2,000 m at passes well known as migrant routes) and fly south through Italy, crossing to Sicily and continuing to Malta and the African coast. The few sightings of Hobbies suggest both that they migrate on a relatively broad front and that they migrate at high altitude, being spotted only if weather conditions force them down to levels at which they become visible. Brown (1976) recorded having seen Eurasian Hobbies in east Africa which soared up to the base of thunderclouds, at about 600 m, then disappeared within the cloud. He conjectured that thermals within the cloud could have taken the falcons up another 3,000 m and wondered if such a strategy might be an aid to migration flights. Such behaviour would also account for why Hobbies, which are regularly seen at some northern migration 'hot spots' such as Falsterbo in Sweden and the French Alps, are less often seen at more southerly points unless bad weather forces them to lower altitudes.

While the above assumptions were based on ringed bird recoveries and observations of migrating birds, and were therefore reasonable, a degree of proof only became available in the current century when researchers in Scotland, Sweden and Germany fitted Hobbies with platform transmitter terminal (PTT) satellite transmitters (Note 6.10) to investigate migration routes. In the Swedish study, four adult Hobbies were captured (one female in 2005, two females in 2006 and one male in 2007) in southern Sweden, fitted with the transmitters and released (Strandberg & Olofsson 2007, Strandberg *et al.* 2009a, 2009b). The device of one 2006 female ceased transmission before the bird had reached the assumed winter grounds. All four birds headed southwest at first, then turned south. Three birds crossed Italy, Sicily and Malta to reach the north African coast, while the fourth flew southwest across France (to avoid the Alps which the other birds crossed?) then crossed the Mediterranean further west by way of the Balearic Islands (Fig. 220). That bird, the female trapped in 2005, then stayed to the west, traversing the western Sahara Desert before turning east. As a consequence this female had the longest journey, travelling 11,226 km in 62 days (which involved 43 days of flying). A second female, trapped in 2006, travelled 8,540 km in 59 days (38 days flying). The male Hobby travelled 9,139 km in 61 days (37 days flying). The female whose transmitter failed had travelled 7,987 km in 54 days (37 days flying) by the time of failure.

The routes taken by the birds differ from what might be considered to be ideal, i.e. a straight line from start point to destination (but allowing for the fact that the falcons are traversing a spheroid, not a two-dimensional plane, so that the shortest distance is actually along a great circle). In part this can be explained by the prevailing easterly winds across the Sahara, which either caused the birds to drift west or was exploited by the birds to aid flying in a southwesterly direction. Individual birds also took differing routes, both in southern Europe and, more significantly so, in northern Africa, for unknown (and probably unknowable) reasons. However, what is very clear is the convergence of the four routes once the equatorial rainforest was approached (Fig. 221).

From Fig. 221 it can be clearly seen that the falcons chose to cross the rainforest, which is an obvious environmental barrier, though not as severe a barrier as the Sahara, by choosing a narrow belt of intact forest to the north and south of which are areas of degraded forest and agricultural land. Use

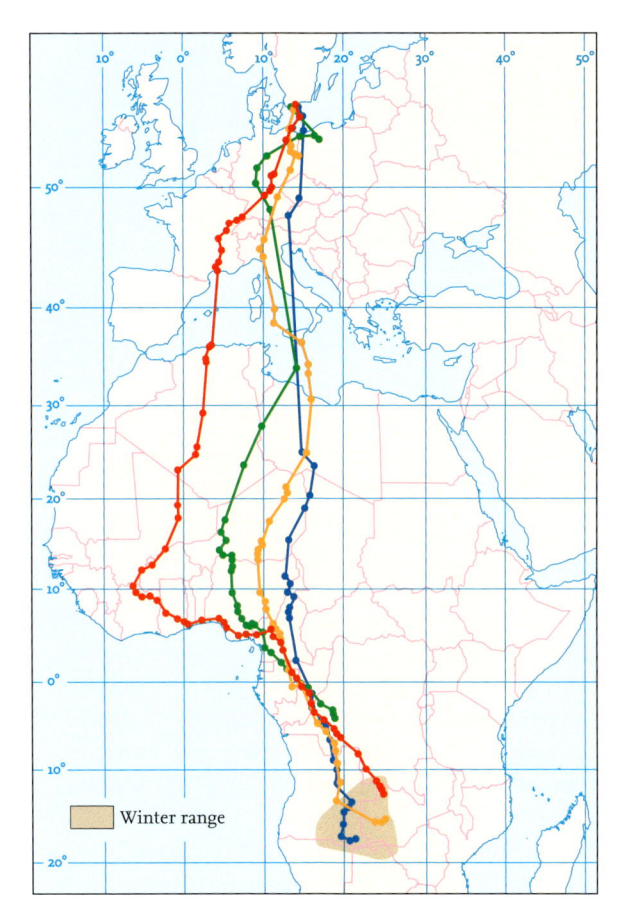

FIG 220. The autumn migration routes of four Hobbies (three females and one male) in 2005–2007. Redrawn from Strandberg *et al.* 2009a.

of this restricted belt reduced the forested area which had to be crossed by approximately 50% (to 450–600 km). Strandberg *et al.* (2009a) considered how the Hobbies might have located the particular corridor they all took, but dismissed use of the coastline (too far to the west), areas of high ground (the entire area is essentially a level plateau), and geomagnetism (no obvious anomalies). The Swedish team noted that other species also take the corridor route, which might explain the Hobbies' decision as they migrate at the same time as hirundines and Swifts, their principal food. However that only transfers the mystery of how the corridor is located to other species. Presumably the answer lies in the existence of factors, maybe visible or olfactory, which are not currently understood.

In a separate article Strandberg *et al.* (2009b) noted that the Hobbies all increased their flight speed and the average daily flight times while crossing the

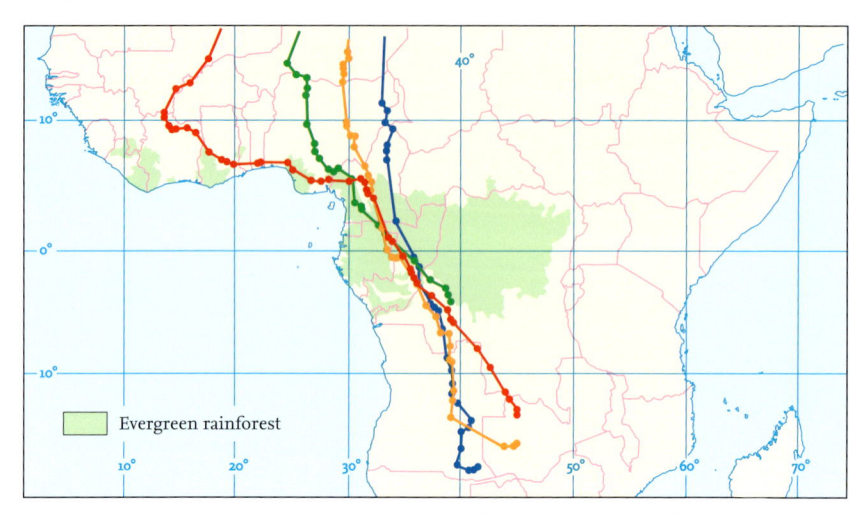

FIG 221. Convergence of the migratory routes of all four satellite-tracked Hobbies close to the equator. Redrawn from Strandberg *et al.* 2009a.

Sahara Desert in comparison to that both north and south of the obstacle, and also exceeded the speed associated with soaring flight: that is, they were using powered flight to minimise crossing time. On average the Hobbies travelled 189 km/day in Europe and 200 km/day in tropical Africa, but 391 km/day while crossing the Sahara. The mean speeds were also significantly different between the three sectors –23.8 km/h above Europe, 19.9 km/h above tropical Africa, 33.4 km/h above the Sahara.

However, the expectation that the Hobbies would make significant journeys by night was not fulfilled, the migration flights being essentially diurnal (about 10% only during night hours). In Europe the falcons flew an average of 10.5 hours per day, while above the Sahara the daily average was 12.3 hours per day and in tropical Africa it was 13 hours per day. Daytime flying allows birds to take advantage of the thermal effects of solar heating of the atmosphere, though this needs to be balanced against greater turbulence. Water losses are higher during the day, with an incumbent earlier onset of dehydration, and predation risks are also higher, each being minimised by nocturnal flying. Nocturnal flying allows daytime hunting, which is likely to be more efficient. Strandberg *et al.* (2009b) found it difficult to understand why the Hobbies did not use nocturnal flying to reduce the time for the Sahara, as do many songbirds, particularly as the Hobbies flew during both the periods before and after the maximum thermal time window (09.00–17.00) which is used by migrating soaring birds. One possible explanation for this might be that for Hobbies the balance between diurnal and nocturnal flying favours daytime migration because their ability to forage for insects on the wing means hunting and migration are not necessarily mutually exclusive.

The Scottish study involved fitting 5 g PTT transmitters to two juvenile Hobbies hatched at Speyside (www.raptortrack.org, retrieved 6 August 2014). One, a large female chick which weighed 283 g, named Aeshna after her favourite food, departed Scotland around mid-September 2010. Signals from her were spasmodic, but it is known she crossed the Straits of Gibraltar into north Africa about a week later, then travelled southwest to Senegal. She crossed The Gambia and Guinea-Bissau to Guinea, and travelled on to Sierra Leone, then east to Ivory Coast and Ghana, where she arrived in early December. Aeshna stayed around Lake Volta, Ghana, until early April, when she started her return journey, retracing her outward journey to Senegal. But the journey was not smooth, and she returned to Guinea and The Gambia before heading north across the Sahara to Morocco, flying 848 km in two days in mid-May. Progress then slowed, and ceased around 25 May. Signals continued to be received through to early July, but they indicated no further movement, implying the falcon had died.

The second Scottish bird was a young male, named Sylvestris, presumably after the Scots Pine in which its nest was found. Sylvestris migrated south along the Pennines then through Hampshire to the Isle of Wight, and across the Channel to Jersey and on to France. The falcon flew through Brittany to a point close to Nantes where the signal was lost.

In the German study, a single adult female Hobby was trapped after raising two chicks in a nest in northwest Berlin and fitted with a PTT satellite transmitter (Meyburg *et al.* 2011a, 2011b). In this case data on both autumn and spring migrations were collected over two complete cycles (2008–2010) (Fig. 222). As can be seen, the two autumn migrations covered similar routes, the Hobby crossing from Sardinia to Malta and on to the north African coast in 2008, but taking a more direct line from Sardinia to Africa in 2009. However, the return (spring) routes were substantially different, that of 2009 being a similar line to the autumn routes, though more westerly, but that in 2010 being a meandering route which took the falcon through Niger, Mali, Mauritania, Algeria and Morocco and across the Gibraltar Strait (a crossing accomplished at night) to Spain and France: the journey also began with flights through Angola, the two Congolese countries, Gabon, Cameroon, and Nigeria – countries which were common to all inward and outward journeys. Meyburg *et al.* (2011a, 2011b) found no evidence for weather changes which might have initiated a more westerly

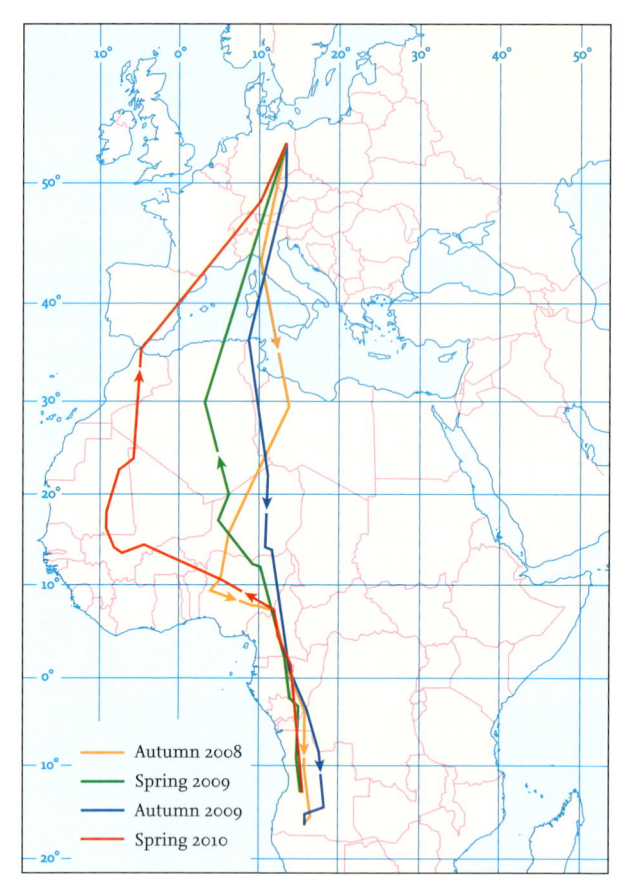

FIG 222. The autumn and spring migration routes of a female Hobby in 2008/09 and 2009/10. Redrawn from Meyburg *et al.* 2011a.

route, and surmise that it may have been taken because the hirundines and Swifts whose route the Hobby was sharing had themselves taken a different route for some unknown reason. Such a different route raises other questions about whether the birds carry a world map and, if so, how the information is gathered.

The 2010 spring route took the western edge of the Sahara Desert rather than the more direct line across it followed on the previous three journeys. The autumn 2008 migration covered 8,525 km in 49 days; the autumn 2009 journey was 7,793 km accomplished in 42 days. The spring 2009 return route was 7,640 km and took 35 days; that in 2010 was 8,678 km and took 38 days. In 2010 the Hobby reached southern Germany, but then slowed dramatically prior to the signal being lost.

FIG 223. Patrick Olofsson releases one of the Hobbies fitted with a PTT in the Swedish study.

The autumn journeys were not continuous: in 2008 the bird stayed on the island of Elba for seven days; in 2009 she rested for seven days near the Tunisia–Algeria border. Crossing the Sahara Desert, a journey of about 2,000 km, took four to four and a half days, but again the African equatorial rainforest was an equivalent barrier: on each of these crossings the bird flew fast and also flew partially at night, though the actual daily flying record was achieved in Mali/Morocco when she flew 1,243 km in two days. Apart from these long flight days, and the desert and rainforest crossings where feeding possibilities were limited or non-existent, the bird's progress indicated a strategy that, not surprisingly, included short-distance days, presumably when hunting/feeding/resting dominated, and longer-flight days when the imperative of reaching winter quarters dictated performance. As with the Swedish study, the German Hobby showed a convergence of all four journeys to take advantage of the corridor which offered crossing of a restricted belt of rainforest.

Interestingly, when the falcon had reached winter quarters she did not reduce her flying (Fig. 224). The winter range was huge, covering 406,000 km² in 2008/09 and 461,000 km² in 2009/10, ranges which are vast in comparison to the hunting range during the breeding season: can this huge size be entirely explained by the Hobby's enthusiasm for seeking out termite swarms? In both 2008/09 and 2009/10 the range was centred on Angola, but the falcon also visited Namibia, Botswana and Zimbabwe. The huge wintering range involved significant flying, the Hobby travelling over 9,000 km in total during 2008/09 and over 6,400 km in 2009/10. When combined with the migration journeys these data mean that in each 12-month period the Hobby was flying not less than 22,000 km and perhaps in excess of 25,000 km. Overall, the Hobby spent 65% of her time in Africa and 35% in Europe, with 18% of her time spent travelling between breeding and wintering quarters, most of that time being spent in Africa. These figures imply that the European Hobby is actually an African bird.

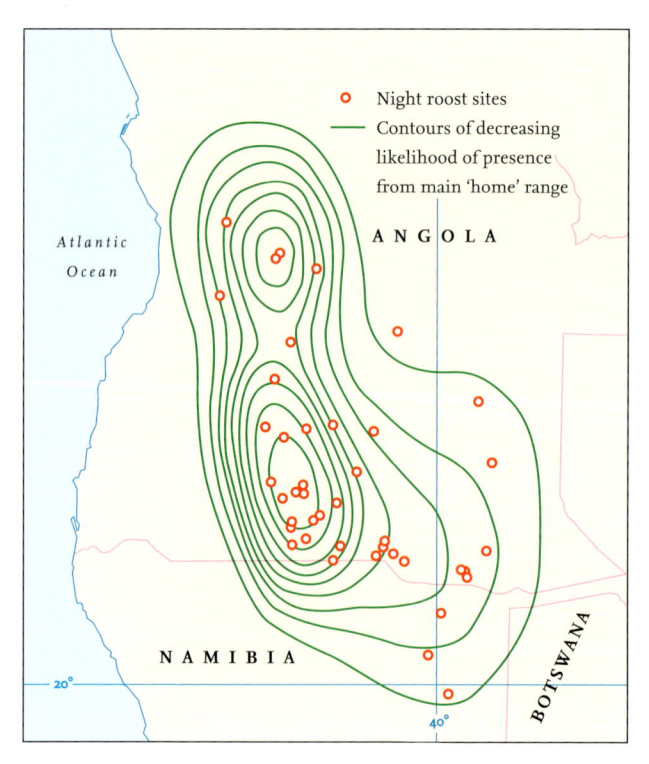

FIG 224. The estimated pattern of activity of a female Hobby during the winter of 2008/09. The assumed flight paths do not include a known 2,785 km excursion from 25 December 2008 to 12 January 2009 when the falcon flew from Angola to Zimbabwe, then returned via Botswana. The data for the winter of 2009/10 were essentially similar. Redrawn from Meyburg *et al.* 2011a.

The obvious hazard presented to the migrating falcons by the Sahara Desert was considered in a further study by the Swedish group (Strandberg et al. 2010), with data gathered from satellite-tracked Honey-buzzards, Marsh Harriers (*Circus aeruginosus*) and Ospreys, as well as Hobbies: the Hobbies included two juvenile birds, data from which were not included in the two articles published in 2009. Strandberg and co-workers defined five categories of 'aberrant behaviour' on the desert crossing – distinct course change, slow speed, interruption of migration, aborted crossing/retreat, and failed crossing/death. Of 63 autumn migrations 40% showed some aberrant signs (chiefly course change, slow speed or interruption, though there were three retreats and four deaths, all of juvenile birds – one Osprey, one Marsh Harrier and both Hobbies). Of 32 spring migrations, again 40% showed aberrant signs, with two retreats and two deaths (two adult Marsh Harriers). While an aberrant crossing slows the arrival of the bird at its wintering quarters, this time loss could be made up, though at a cost of loss of condition due to malnourishment. However, the loss of four juveniles from a pool of 13 across the four raptor species, a mortality rate of 31%, suggests that the desert crossing is a significant cause of juvenile deaths. For spring migrants loss of time means arrival at the breeding grounds late, and Strandberg and co-workers were able to show that these birds had a breeding success rate of only 10% compared to 53% for conspecifics that did not show aberrant crossings. While these data apply to Ospreys and Marsh Harriers only, as no Hobbies were recorded on spring migration, there is no reason to believe the same would not be true for the falcons. The Sahara Desert is, therefore, a significant threat to Hobbies (and to other raptors).

The observations of Thake (1977/1978) at Buskett, Malta, suggest that the route through Italy and Malta is favoured by Hobbies from eastern Europe, though as we have seen above it may also be used by western European falcons. In Malta, observations are usually of single birds, though groups of five or so are occasionally seen. The falcons that are seen tend to arrive in the afternoon, with few seen after 16.00 local time, suggesting that the crossing from Sicily is undertaken early in the day. Thake's observations of Hobby numbers are consistent with the intuitively obvious idea that the falcons choose to migrate during stable weather. Unfortunately, those Hobbies which are driven to low altitudes in Malta may find themselves within range of the hunters for which the island is infamous, though the numbers of Hobbies quoted by Thake compare with those observed in more recent years by Sammut & Bonavia (2004) covering 1998–2002 and Sammut et al. (2013) for the period 2005–2012. (The latter observations were made from Misrah Ghar il-Kbir, known to the local birdwatchers as 'Clapham Junction', which is about 0.5 km from Buskett.) While stable migration numbers imply hunting losses are not population threatening, and progress in protecting raptors from annual persecution has been made (particularly at Buskett), hunting in Malta and in Italy takes a toll of Hobbies which appears comparable to that of the Sahara Desert crossing. Also of concern is the recent finding by an Australian, British and American team that only 9% of the 1451 migratory birds are adequately covered by protected areas across all stages of their migration (Runge *et al.* 2015). Of the migration 'black spots' the team identified much of Asia and significant parts of South America and Africa. In Africa the areas of least protection cover significant sections of the migration routes of the Hobby.

The autumn migration in Britain and northern Europe begins in August and is completed, or largely so, by September, though Messenger & Roome (2007) found one juvenile Hobby roosting within 50 m of its nest on 16 October 1995. In Germany communal roosting was noted in the pre-migration period (Klammer, quoted by Fiuczynski & Sömmer 2011). Klammer noted that Hobbies were roosting on three adjacent pylons and would arrive about 15 minutes after sunset, aerial displays and calling seemingly establishing contact before the birds settled in groups – some of only adult falcons, some of only juveniles, but some mixed – on the pylons. Klammer saw the birds over a period of seven days, with numbers as high as 17 individuals. The falcons would depart about 30 minutes after sunrise.

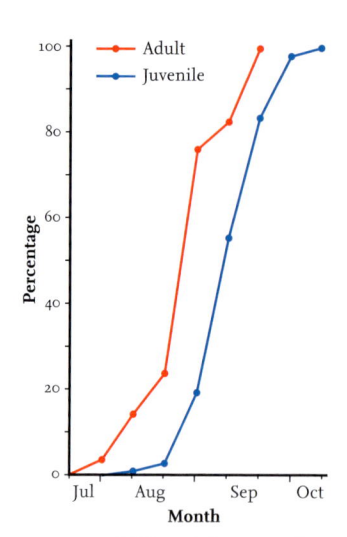

Kjellén (1992), counting migrating birds at Falsterbo in southern Sweden, noted adults making the crossing to Denmark significantly earlier (of order 14 days) than juveniles (Fig. 225). However, the total number of birds counted by Kjellén was small, and the number which could be positively assigned to an age category inevitably smaller still, so the conclusion must be treated with caution. That said, the conclusion is consistent with Kjellén's finding for Kestrel, Merlin and Peregrine (though for Kestrels differential migration was much less marked). Merlin also show a marked differential between the migration times for

FIG 225. Differential autumnal migration of adult and juvenile Hobbies observed in the period 1986–1990 at Falsterbo Peninsula, southern Sweden. The curves show the cumulative percentage of birds that had migrated at a certain date. Redrawn from Kjellén 1992.

males and females (see Fig. 276) and it is possible that Hobbies could show a similar trend. However, while the behaviour of other falcons may imply that Kjellén's observation is correct, evidence from other sources (albeit limited) is less conclusive. Dronneau & Wassmer (1989) recorded an interesting case in France in which two Hobby nests were set 1.5 km apart, but one brood was later than the other. Late in the season, Dronneau & Wassmer noted that rather than two broods of two and three fledglings, one adult pair was now successfully provisioning five juveniles, the second adult pair having migrated. Ultimately the remaining adults and five juveniles all departed, though the timing of the adoptive parents leaving was not noted. Dronneau & Wassmer noted six similar cases of adoption/fostering among 40 Hobby pairs in the area. These observations certainly imply that adults migrate before juveniles, but Fiuczynski & Sömmer (2011) noted that in their studies in Germany the male Hobby of a breeding pair was invariably the last bird to be seen, and in the satellite-tracking experiment on the adult female Hobby she left Berlin on 28 August, but the male continued to feed the young until 18 September; four days later both male and young had departed (Meyburg et al. 2011a, 2011b). While it is not clear if the male and youngsters migrate together, they do apparently leave at more or less the same time.

The exact wintering area of British Hobbies is unclear. The Scottish juvenile female wintered in Ghana, while the Swedish and German birds went further south to Angola. Presumably the birds observed in South Africa (see *Diet*, above) had bred in Europe, and so it is possible that British birds could travel that far south. There is also evidence that some Hobbies may actually winter north of the Sahara, in Tunisia, Algeria and Morocco, these birds perhaps being from the group which migrated through Italy and across Malta and then found favourable overwintering conditions along the African coast. Thiollay (1989) notes observations of wintering Hobbies from Ivory Coast westwards through Togo to Cameroon, while others have observed falcons in Senegal, The Gambia, Chad, Mali and Niger. However, in all cases the numbers were small in comparison to the estimated European population which would migrate to west Africa and it was not always clear if the falcons observed were wintering or passage migrants. It is therefore assumed that many Hobbies continue south to winter on the savannahs of southern Africa. That supposition is consistent with the weather in southern Africa where rain fronts of the Intertropical Convergence Zone (Note 6.11) move south during the austral summer, the rains resulting in the swarms of insects on which the Hobbies feed. It is likely that British Hobbies are among the migrants to these southern regions, joined there by their European cousins and perhaps even by some Hobbies from as far east as central Asia. Migrating Hobbies actually reach the southern tip of Africa: Cruickshank (1980) in discussing the finding of an emaciated Hobby in Cape Province, South Africa, noted that a specimen in Cape Town Museum which had been collected in 1894 was actually collected in Wynberg, a district of Cape Town itself, just a few miles from the Cape of Good Hope. Pepler (1991) has already been noted as observing Hobbies in Stellenbosch, and Martin *et al.* (1988) also record seeing a group of up to six Hobbies in the town, the falcons being seen hunting for both birds and insects above the central part of the town where they seemed to be using buildings to conceal their approach, suddenly appearing from behind one to catch their prey off-guard.

However, most Hobbies do not find their way this far south, the greatest abundance appearing to spend the winter in the eastern part of an area encompassing northern Botswana, Zimbabwe and Zambia, though with some in western Mozambique and Malawi. This area lies entirely south of the equator, the Hobby being one of six bird species which migrate to Africa whose usual wintering range lies entirely south of the equator (Newton 1995 – the other five species are the Red-footed, Amur and Sooty falcons, all of which are predominantly insect feeders, the Lesser Grey Shrike (*Lanius minor*) and the Icterine Warbler (*Hippolais icterina*), which are also insectivorous). Newton calculates that the range of the Hobby in Africa is three times smaller than its Palearctic breeding range, which is an indication of the available food resources in the two areas.

The return migration begins in March, though the exact timing is, of course, dependent on where in Africa the British migrants have wintered and so may be earlier. The Hobbies are therefore migrating at the same time as Swifts and hirundines, which provide dietary biomass during the long flights if insect food is not readily available. It is interesting that none of the satellite-tracked Hobbies in the Swedish and German studies migrated back into Europe in the spring from Cap Bon in Tunisia (a famous migration viewing point where Hobbies have often been seen (e.g. Thiollay 1977, Corso 2001), though not in the numbers seen of other raptors. It is, though, worth noting that Thiollay (1977) recorded almost three times as many Hobbies crossing at Gibraltar as at Cap Bon. Hobbies arrive in Britain as early as April, though pairs do not actively begin their breeding cycle for another month or so.

SURVIVAL

Fiuczynski & Sömmer (2011) provide data on the survival of Hobbies during the first year of life. As already noted (see *Breeding success*), from data on German Hobbies, survival during the nestling phase is very high, with only

2.6% mortality. However, Fiuczynski & Sömmer note that based on their observations in Germany, juvenile Hobby, survival is much less assured, with only 33% of Hobbies surviving to celebrate their first birthday, i.e. a 67% mortality rate. Excluding the deaths of nestlings, the mortality rate of juveniles is about 65%, and Fiuczynski & Sömmer consider the largest contribution is failure to survive migration and wintering: this period accounts for 59% of overall mortality. Thus, of 100 hatched Hobbies, 97 will fledge, 92 will migrate, but only 41 will return to Europe. The German data imply a higher mortality than that quoted by Cramp & Simmons (1980), who suggest first year mortality is 55%.

Fiuczynski & Sömmer (2011) also consider the annual mortality of Hobbies which do survive beyond their first birthday, and suggest that for males it is 17–27%, while for females it is about 20%, though it is possible that mortality is higher in earlier years than in later years. Fiuczynski & Sömmer also present data on the age distribution of the breeding population, based on data presented by Fiuczynski in an earlier version of the same book (Fig. 226).

Rather than relying on ringing recoveries, the data quoted by Fiuczynski & Sömmer (2011) were compiled by ringing nestlings with coloured leg rings, the colour indicating the natal year, and then observing these rings on breeding birds in later years. From these data the authors were able to calculate that the life expectancy of a hatched male Hobby was 3.3–5.4 years, but if the bird survived its first winter this would rise to 4.8–6.9 years. Life expectancy for females is comparable, but probably at the higher end of the range. This is consistent with the calculation of Fiuczynski & Nethersole-Thompson (1980)

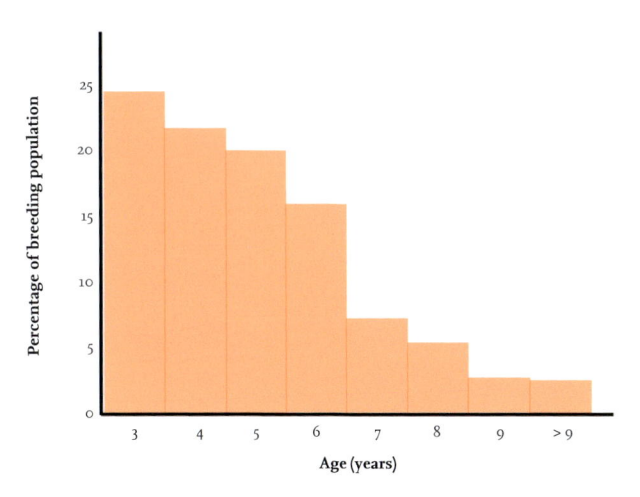

FIG 226. Age distribution of Hobby breeding population, based on studies near Berlin. Drawn from tabulated data in Fiuczynski & Sömmer 2011.

FIG 227. During observations of a Hobby nest in Wales two fledglings were observed, each exercising its wings vigorously. One was perched on a branch close to the nest, while the second was still within the nest. Later just one juvenile was observed with the adult birds. On subsequently visiting the nest I found one dead juvenile and an unhatched egg (a). The dead bird had both legs completely enmeshed in bailing twine used by the original nest builders (b). The fledgling 'exercising' its wings had actually been frantically attempting to free itself. In its efforts it had actually severed one leg completely (c) and must have died a hideous death.

FIG 228. Juvenile Hobby. Studies show that the winter mortality of young Hobbies is 55–65%.

that the average breeding life of the female Hobbies that they studied in England and Germany was 2.6 years. In their study around Berlin, Fiuczynski & Sömmer (2011) found one male which had been colour-coded in 1966 and, having bred successfully in 1980, left on its autumn migration but did not return. They also report two other 14-year-old birds, one shot on autumn migration in Sicily, the other found in a poor state of health in Germany. They also report one of the satellite-tracked females which was aged 11 years when she bred successfully, but from which the signal was subsequently lost in the Sahara Desert in 2009.

Data in Wernham *et al.* (2002) from Hobbies ringed in Britain and recovered there, and from a small number of foreign-ringed falcons recovered in Britain, suggest that 62% of Hobby deaths are either deliberately related to human activity (e.g. shooting) or consequent upon it (e.g. collisions). Of the other 38%

FIG 229. Ringing a nestling Hobby. The ringing is being carried out by Dr Klaus-Dietrich Fiuczynski, whose death in 2014 robbed the world of one of the foremost experts on the species.

of deaths, 61% were due to natural causes, i.e. disease or, in the case of juveniles, starvation. The remaining deaths are listed as arising from 'other causes'. Data from the recovery of Hobbies ringed in the Netherlands suggest similar causes of death, with 65% shot, 17% caused by collisions with structures, 14% by collisions with vehicles, 2% by electrocution and 2% listed as exhaustion (i.e. starvation and disease) (Sergio *et al.* 2001). As Fiuczynski & Sömmer (2011) note, the migration routes of Hobbies cross countries where the hunting (involving indiscriminate shooting) of birds is an established tradition, and Hobbies will therefore inevitably fall victim. They point out that all recoveries from northern/central Italy were of birds on autumn migration, and all of them were shot or captured.

No specific study of the diseases of Hobbies has been identified, but there is no reason to suppose that they are not susceptible to the diseases found in, and the parasites which infest, the other three British falcons. Like the other species, they probably carry parasitic louse flies, though Matyukhin *et al.* (2012) found only one species, *Ornithomya frigillina*, on Hobbies.

FRIENDS AND FOES

Müller & Rohde (1993) record a curious assembly of nesting raptors on the Danube Delta in Romania, with Hobby nests within 100 m of Red-footed Falcon nests and Kestrels nesting in the same area. With the three falcons being tolerant of each other and conspecifics, Müller & Rohde suggested a loose colonial structure. Dement'ev & Gladkov (1966) also note a Hobby breeding in the same tree as a Black Kite, a Kestrel, a Lesser Grey Shrike and a Magpie, an ensemble which shows a remarkable degree of tolerance (as well as being the answer to many a bird photographer's dreams).

The presence of potential prey species nesting in (relatively) close proximity to falcons has been mentioned in previous chapters. Hobbies also have a 'friend' species, though in this case it seems a more curious association, as it is the Wood Pigeon, a species which does not show a similar relationship with Kestrels – which are comparable in size and so just as unlikely to be a threat. The association between Wood Pigeons and Hobbies has been known for many years. Ashley (1918) noted them nesting in the same tree, and there is an even older report from Germany (Naumann & Naumann 1905) which commented not only on the frequent proximity of the two species, but that noting where Wood Pigeons are nesting is a good way of finding Hobbies. Naumann & Naumann suggested the reason for the association is the falcon's aggressiveness to crows, which are predators of Wood Pigeon eggs and chicks: Hobbies defend their nests fiercely against crows, as they also predate Hobby eggs. Collar (1978) gives several examples of Wood Pigeons and Hobbies nesting within a few metres of each other, as well as multiple Wood Pigeon nests near a Hobby nest. Examples are even cited of a female Hobby allowing a pigeon to within 60 cm of its nest, and of two fighting pigeons forcing a male Hobby to leave its perch. Collar also notes that similar associations have been seen not only in Britain and Germany, but in the Netherlands (Tinbergen 1932) and Spain (Morata 1971), implying that it probably occurs across all of the falcon's range where the two species are found in close proximity.

Bijlsma (1984) studied the association between the two species in the Netherlands, noting that while most Wood Pigeons were nesting in August and September in order to take advantage of spilled grain for brood rearing, some were nesting earlier, timing their nesting to that of Hobbies. The pigeons waited until the Hobbies had chosen their nest sites and begun laying, then nested, the speed required in nest building so that the incubation and nestling phases could be synchronised being clear from the unusually flimsy pigeon nests. Pigeon nests were constructed close to the Hobby nests, occasionally in the same tree and on one occasion within 1 m, and there was a distinct drop-off in the number of pigeon nests with distance from the falcon nest (Fig. 230).

Equally interesting was the number of pigeon nests which were associated with each Hobby nest (Fig. 231). While it would be assumed that only one or two pigeons would nest close to one falcon nest, the population of pigeons relative to that of Hobbies meant that on average each falcon nest had 5.4 pigeon

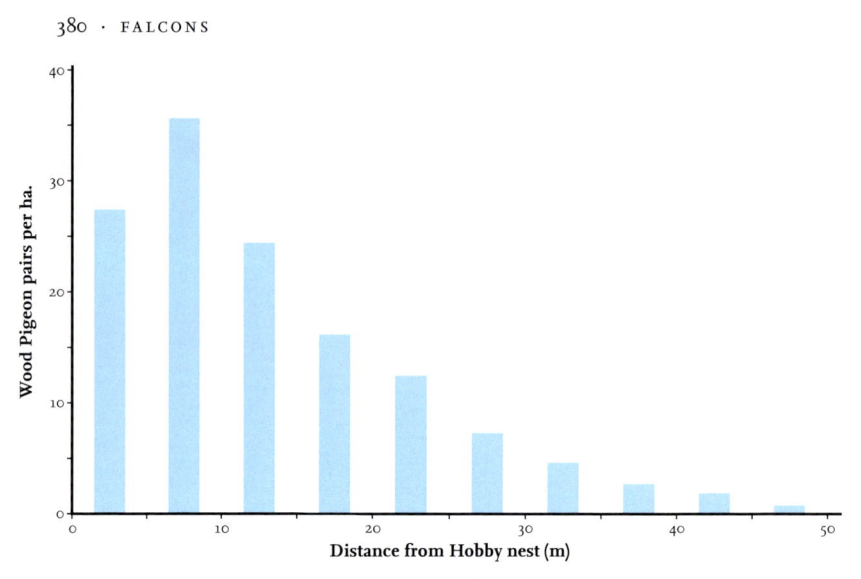

FIG 230. Breeding density of Wood Pigeons (pairs/ha) in 5 m intervals from Hobby nests. Redrawn from Bijlsma 1984.

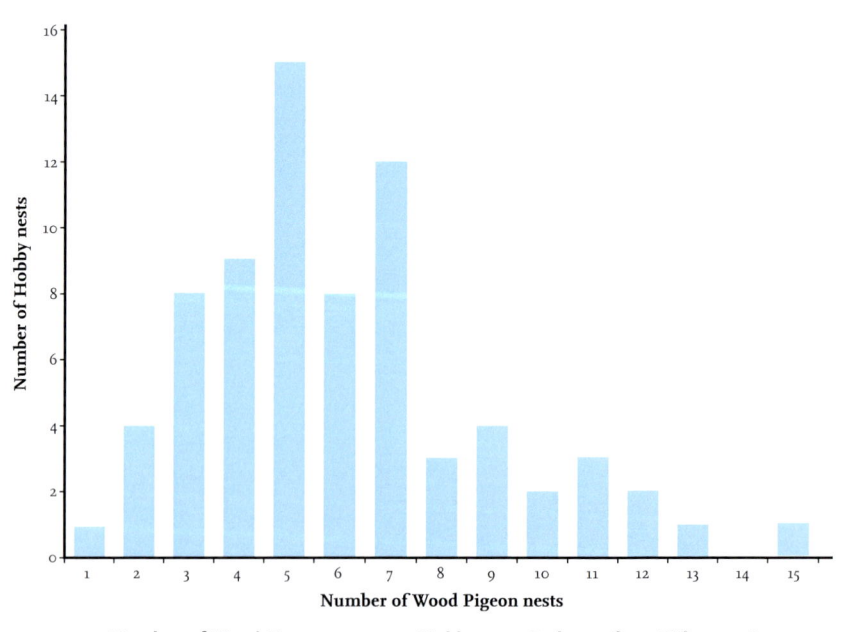

FIG 231. Number of Wood Pigeon nests per Hobby nest. Redrawn from Bijlsma 1984.

nests close to it: one falcon nest had 15 nearby pigeon nests. Bijlsma examined the breeding success of the pigeons associated with the Hobbies and found a significant difference to those pigeons which nested later than the Hobbies – 86.7% of pigeons synchronised with Hobby breeding were successful, in terms of fledglings raised from eggs laid, while only 25% of nests in which eggs were laid after the Hobbies had bred were successful.

Further work on the association was carried out in a 62 km² study area on the Po plain, northern Italy (Bogliani *et al.* 1992). The area included 20 km² of cultivated poplar (*Populus* spp.) coverage distributed as discrete 'woodlots'. Of over 200 of these lots, 77 had Hobby nests (all in Hooded Crow nests), while 50 had Wood Pigeon nests. However, 47 of the 50 pigeon nests were within lots which had a Hobby nest, indicating a high degree of association between the species. Figure 232 indicates the distance between a pigeon nest and that of a Hobby based on groupings centred at 20 m intervals, and the availability of poplars within the same-distance groups.

Figure 232 indicates that most pigeon nests were within 40 m of a Hobby nest: the shortest inter-nest distance was 5 m. That the pigeons were apparently preferentially seeking to nest close to the falcons was indicated by the finding that the pigeons started nesting after the Hobbies had done so. Hooded Crows were common in the poplar lots and are a known predator of both Wood Pigeon and Hobby nests, and Bogliani *et al.* noted that the falcons were particularly aggressive to the crows, behaviour which was clearly advantageous to the pigeons.

To further their understanding of the association between the pigeons and falcons, in follow-up work at the same study area, dummy Wood Pigeon nests were placed near Hobby nests (Bogliani *et al.* 1999). At 20 Hobby nest sites, five dummy nests were placed within 50 m of the falcon nest, with five more at more than 100 m. Two domestic Quail eggs, treated so as to resemble pigeon eggs, were placed in each dummy nest. The dummy nests were then examined for predation at intervals, and the experiment was

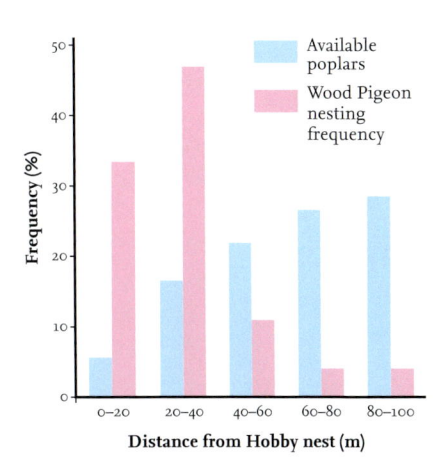

FIG 232. Distance of nesting Wood Pigeons from nesting Hobbies as a fraction of total nests identified and the distribution of available poplars within the same distance groupings. Redrawn from Bogliani *et al.* 1992.

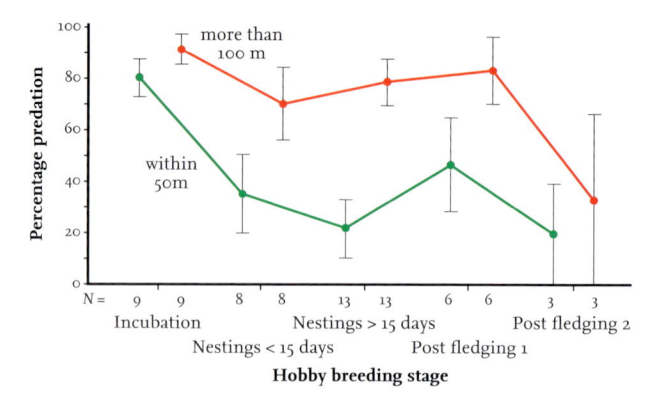

FIG 233. Percentage of dummy Wood Pigeon nests preyed upon (± SE) for nests within 50 m of a Hobby nest and more than 100 m from a Hobby nest during different phases of the Hobby breeding cycle. Redrawn from Bogliani et al. 1999.

replicated 15 days later. Bogliani and co-workers also assessed the nesting female Hobbies for aggressiveness, classifying them on the basis of their reaction to a human intruder – did the female sit tight, did she flush and disappear, did she stoop at the intruder, etc.? The rate of predation of the dummy pigeon nests varied with the phase of the Hobby breeding cycle, but was always greater in the nests further than 100 m from the falcon nests (Fig. 233), though the difference was only statistically significant at the 99% level when the Hobby chicks were older than 15 days (but had not fledged). There was no statistically significant difference in predation rates for dummy nests greater than 100 m from a Hobby nest at any time during the Hobby breeding phase (though, as with the difference between < 50 m and > 100 m dummy nests, the sample sizes were small).

Dummy nest predation was also negatively correlated with Hobby aggressiveness, the latter also varying with phase of the breeding cycle. An attempt to rule out the possibility that both species, pigeons and falcons, preferentially chose tree lots where Hooded Crow predation rates were low was made by varying the choice of lots during the experiment. Although this possibility could not be entirely excluded, Bogliani *et al.* consider it to be unlikely.

Overall, therefore, Wood Pigeons were best protected by nesting close to an aggressive Hobby pair, and timing their reproduction so that their nests were most vulnerable when the Hobby chicks were between 15 days old and fledging. While proximity to a Hobby nest is easy for the pigeons to judge, they are also, of course, able to assess falcon aggressiveness and the age of chicks by direct observation: in a sample of 24 pigeon nests for which laying dates could be established, 71% of clutches were begun when the associated Hobbies were incubating, 25% when the Hobbies had chicks less than 15 days old. Bogliani *et al.* were not able to judge whether the Hobbies gained from the association by benefiting from early warning of intruders by the pigeons (i.e. whether the relationship was truly commensal).

Collar (1978) notes that the association between Wood Pigeons and Hobbies is not without its problems for the pigeons, for Hobbies are occasionally aggressive towards them. Bijlsma (1984) found that nine of 82 Hobby nests were not surrounded by Wood Pigeons nests, suggesting that those Hobbies (11% of the total) were intolerant of the pigeons. However, Bogliani *et al.* (1992) noted that Wood Pigeon feathers were found in only two of 46 examined Hobby nests, while Bogliani *et al.* (1999) found that of 317 Hobby prey remains Wood Pigeons formed 1.6% by number (five instances), 15% by biomass. (Overall, 15 prey species were found, with 53% by number (46% biomass) being Swifts, and 25% by number (13% biomass) sparrows – Italian House Sparrow (*Passer domesticus italiae*) and Tree Sparrow.) The cost to the pigeons was therefore minimal (though, of course, fatal to the five Wood Pigeons which fell prey to the falcons), and the relationship was beneficial as the pigeons offered no defence against crow predation themselves. Bogliani *et al.* (1992) noted that Buzzards were also nesting in the poplar lots, but that there was no similar association between pigeons and Buzzards, probably because, unlike Hobbies, Buzzards regularly take the pigeons as prey so that the benefits of enhanced breeding success would be outweighed by the risk of direct predation from Buzzards.

Of other species, Hobbies seem particularly exercised by the presence of Green Woodpeckers, several accounts existing of the falcons attacking the woodpeckers apparently with a view to frightening them rather than killing them (Clifford 1947, Goater 1948), though in each case the woodpeckers sustained injury or lost feathers.

Corvids will take Hobby eggs, and since Ravens are known to predate Peregrine nestlings (Monneret *et al.* 2009) it can be assumed they would also take Hobby nestlings if the opportunity arose. Hobbies therefore react aggressively to all corvids: Mayo (1953) records seeing two Magpies in Switzerland standing on either side of a Hobby nest attacking the resident female in turn and forcing her to counter-attack, the second Magpie sneaking into the nest in her absence. Ultimately the Hobby flew off and the Magpies entered the nest, though it is not clear if they made off with eggs.

Hobbies will also see off many other species, including large raptors, having been recorded as attacking Black Kites, Buzzards, and Ospreys, as well as other large birds such as Herons, Herring Gulls and Ravens. Goshawks are also vigorously attacked, but with rather more reason as they are a danger to Hobby nestlings – as already noted (see *Breeding success*), the hawks were responsible for a doubling of the mortality of Hobby chicks in the neighbourhood of Berlin when hawk numbers increased – as well as to the adults. Müller & Rohde (1993) note that Hobbies will pursue Goshawks for up to 1 km, so fierce is the falcon's enthusiasm for ridding its nest area of the predator. Sadly the Hobby is not always successful in its quest, Fiuczynski & Sömmer (2011) recording an observation by Nikolaas Tinbergen of a Goshawk being pursued by a Hobby which suddenly turned upside down and caught its assailant.

Kestrels may also be attacked, Hayhow (1988) noting two Hobbies chasing a male Kestrel, and one of the Hobbies locking talons with the Kestrel so that the pair tumbled to the ground. Once separated the Kestrel was again pursued. The observation was in Greece in late April, which suggests the Kestrel had intruded on a Hobby pair's breeding territory. Boer & Hut (1997) also record attacks on Kestrels. They were observing a single Hobby nest in a poplar set in open farmland and saw three Kestrels, two Buzzards, two Goshawks and a Sparrowhawk in the vicinity. The Hobby pair chased any of these which came within 200 m of the nest. Boer & Hut noted a particular attack on a juvenile female Goshawk which forced the hawk to take cover in nearby woodland and then to leave the area.

Tawny Owls will also predate Hobby chicks. Waddell (1978a) reports circumstantial evidence of predation of chicks, while Roberts & Lewis (1992) present evidence for the killing of an incubating female during the night by a Tawny Owl, the skin, skull and body feathers alone being found. Roberts & Lewis suggest a night-time killing, as the clutch of three eggs remained intact, indicating that there was no fight between the birds; the male Hobby remained in the area, but the eggs were later preyed upon by a Carrion Crow. Mikkola (1983) notes that adult Hobbies have been killed and eaten by Eagle Owls. Peregrines also predate Hobbies. In a study of the diet of Peregrines on the Biscay coast of northern Spain, Zuberogoitia *et al.* (2013) found the remains of 19 Hobbies among 2,832 prey items, this figure representing 0.67% by prey item and 1.06% by biomass. While the number of Hobbies is small in relation to the numbers of other species taken by the larger falcons, it is higher than would be expected and suggests that the Peregrines might be taking advantage of Hobbies on spring migration. Fiuczynski & Sömmer (2011) note that a Buzzard has been seen to kill an incubating Hobby female, and that Buzzards are also probably responsible for some Hobby nestling losses. Most surprising of the species known to consume Hobbies is the Lammergeier (*Gypaetus barbatus*),

FIG 234. Hobby being seen off by a Black-headed Gull. Both species were hunting insects above a large body of water. However, the gulls did not always win territorial battles. (Dave Soons)

Thibault *et al.* (1993) finding feathers of a Hobby in a Lammergeier nest in Corsica. Given both the normal diet and the foraging strategy of these large vultures, it is much more likely that the Hobby was picked up dead rather than preyed upon.

Mammals may predate Hobby eggs and chicks. Fiuczynski & Nethersole-Thompson (1980) note that Pine Martens were responsible for 22.5% of all nest failures in the Berlin area, and that Red Squirrels (*Sciurus vulgaris*) had destroyed two nests in England. Humans are another threat to Hobbies, both by deliberate acts (shooting, egg collection etc.) and because many falcons are killed in collisions with buildings and vehicles. Wind turbines are also a threat: Fiuczynski & Sömmer (2011) note that deaths of both adults and juveniles have occurred in several European countries, though the skilful flight abilities of the Hobbies means that risk is perhaps less than for other species. However, the risk might be higher in places where pylons are associated with wind turbine 'parks', bringing nesting possibilities and hazards close together.

When humans approach the nest the female may, if she is incubating or has newly hatched chicks, attempt a distraction flight, fluttering towards the ground or using a laboured flight pattern to suggest injury before making her escape. However, some females sit tight, almost to the point of their being able to be taken by hand, whereas others may quietly fly away, perhaps hoping that their unseen departure will not reveal the nest site. Once it is clear the intruder has discovered the nest, some females will circle above the area persistently making the '*kee-kee-kee*' alarm call: Ashley (1918) noted that he 'had remained in the vicinity of a nest when the birds have had incubated eggs or young, until the constant "Greek, greek, greek" has almost got on my nerves.' Some Hobbies will boldly attack a human, flying quite close and making the drumming noise with their wings which is a feature of breeding displays. Nethersole-Thompson (1931b) records someone being struck repeatedly when attempting to take photographs, and also that he had to duck to avoid being struck himself. In another record (Nethersole-Thompson 1931c) he says that a female Hobby flew within three feet of him (though he may actually be describing the same incident in the two reports). However, as noted above (see *Breeding success*) Sergio & Bogliani (2001) were able to define nest defence aggressiveness on a scale of 1 to 8, varying from the adults disappearing to attacks such as those described by Nethersole-Thompson. Females may also take little notice of intruders – Orr (1996) noting an adult continuing to feed nestlings during the construction of a photographic tower about 5 m from the nest – though such behaviour is rare.

CHAPTER 7

The Merlin

MERLIN – PROBABLY FROM THE old French *esmerillon*, a small artillery piece, perhaps alluding to the bird's fast attack on prey. However, the root is the Germanic *esmeril*, from which the Old French *esmerillonné* – quick or sprightly – and *esmerveillé* – marvellous, wonderful – also derive, so the name could allude to the falcon's ability to chase down prey. Another view is that the original French word derives from 'stone-falcon', used to describe the species' habitat of rocky uplands. Though this derivation has less support, the name 'stone falcon' was that given to the bird by Shetland islanders, who also noted its preference for boulder-strewn hillsides; Merlins were once relatively common on Shetland, several place names deriving from *smyril*, the old Norse name for the falcon. *Smyril* is still the Icelandic name, though in Sweden the name is *stenfalk* (stone falcon) and in Norway it is *dvergfalk* (dwarf falcon).

Whatever the derivation, the French evolved into the Anglo-Norman *merlun* and the present name. The second part of the bird's scientific name, *Falco columbarius*, is from the Latin for dove, and the old American name for the species is Pigeon Hawk. The natural assumption that the bird is named for its common prey is erroneous, as Merlins rarely take species as large as pigeons: the name is actually from the similarity of the Merlin to a pigeon in size and flight pattern. The Americans also occasionally call the Merlin the Bullet Hawk, for much more obvious reasons. In Ireland the falcon was, and occasionally still is, called Snipe Hawk or Bog Hawk because of its partiality to prey and habitat.

The collective noun for Merlins is a cast. As well as being an alternative to pellet for the mass of indigestible feather, fur, bone etc. which a falcon regurgitates, this term is also applied to a group of hunting falconry birds released as a group. In the USA this method of hunting was usually associated

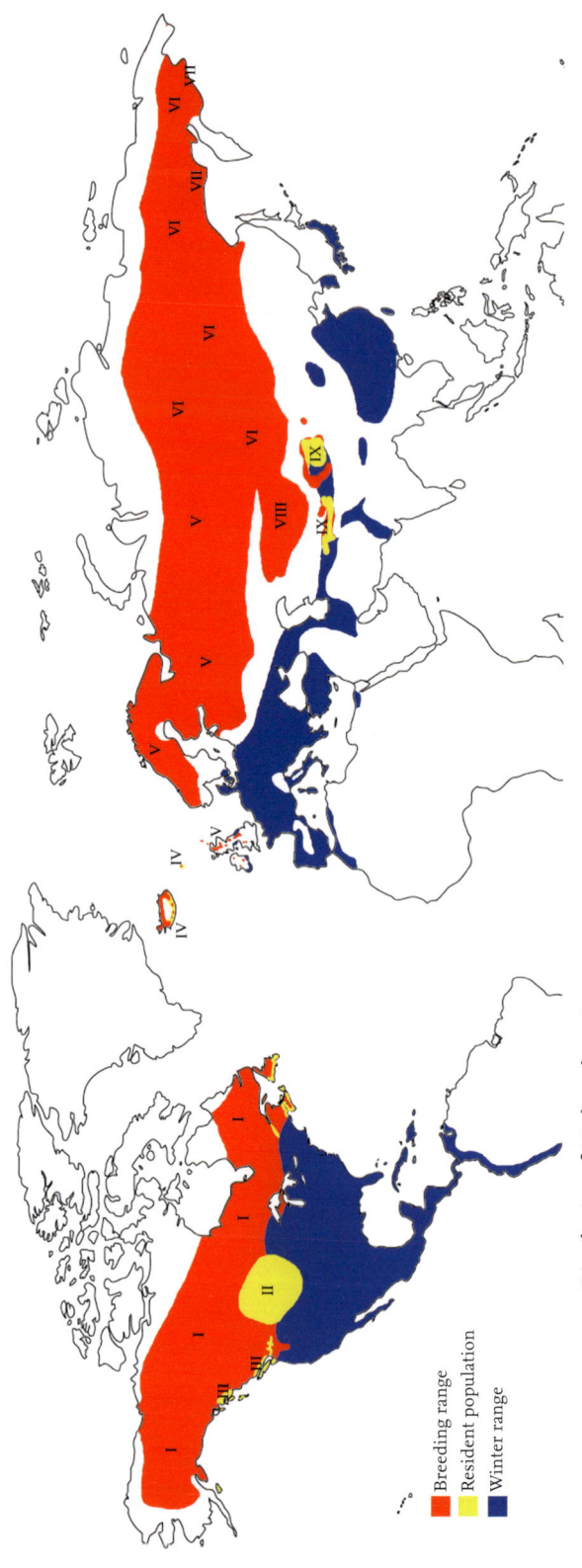

FIG 235. Distribution of Merlin subspecies:

(a) North America
I Taiga Merlin (*Falco columbarius columbarius*)   II Prairie Merlin (*F. c. richarsonii*)   III Black Merlin (*F. c. suckleyi*)
IV Icelandic (*F. c. subaesalon*)   V Eurasian Merlin (*F. c. aesalon*)   VI East Siberian Merlin (*F. c. insignis*)
(b) Eurasia
VII Pacific Merlin (*F. c. pacificus*)   VIII Steppe Merlin (*F. c. pallidus*)   IX Central Asian Merlin (*F. c. lymani*)
Note: the populations of Iceland and the Faroes are largely migratory.

Breeding range
Resident population
Winter range

with Harris Hawks (*Parabuteo unicinctus*), but the word is used as the collective term for 'hawks' in general. In Britain it is generally associated with Merlins.

As noted in Chapter 1, as a species the Merlin is a curiosity, standing outside the defined groups of falcons and inhabiting a part of the world which makes it a specialist in an environment which is shared by only two other falcons, both much larger and with a less specialised diet. Merlins have a circumpolar distribution, being found in all the nations which border the Arctic Ocean, and in Iceland, though absent from Greenland and the Svalbard archipelago (Fig. 235). They breed as far north as the Arctic coast of northern Fennoscandia and western Russia, throughout Iceland, and almost to the Arctic Ocean coast in North America (Sale 2006), though are uncommon in all areas. In Britain Merlins are confined to the upland moors of Wales, northern England and Scotland. They were formerly found in very small numbers (2–3 pairs during this century) on the moors of the Southwest Peninsula, but there has been no confirmed breeding since 2010.

Merlins are small, but stocky, falcons with pointed wings which are relatively short in comparison to those of other small falcons, a long tail, and a small bill. When perched, the wings are clearly shorter than the tail, reaching about 75% of tail length. Merlins are sexually dimorphic, males 25–30% smaller than females. They hunt avian prey with fast, chasing flights achieved by rapid, powerful wing-beats. In poor light Merlins may be confused with Sparrowhawks, and also with racing pigeons, as the flight pattern is similar. For more information on Merlins, including further data from North America, Iceland, Scandinavia and Russia, see Sale (2015).

Currently nine subspecies of Merlin are recognised, three being found in North America (one being the nominate), one in Iceland and five in Eurasia (Fig. 235). Whether the Icelandic race is actually different from that found in Britain is the subject of ongoing debate, as the DNA studies of Marsden (2002) indicated that genetic data did not support a difference between the two races, though Marsden suggested caution, and that further analysis was required before a conclusion could be reached. For further details of the subspecies see Sale (2015).

Gray (1958) records two instances of presumed natural hybrids between male Merlins and female Eurasian (Common) Kestrels, each dating to the 1890s. In captive (falconry) birds, hybrids are common, one of the more popular being the Peregrine × Merlin or Perlin.

DIMENSIONS

Overall length (bill tip to tail tip) of male 272.0 ± 6.8 mm; female 302.6 ± 8.1 mm.
Wing: male 199.4 ± 4.0 mm; female 221.9 ± 4.0 mm.

TABLE 23. Measurements of adult Merlins trapped in northern England. From Wright (2005).

Attribute	Male		Female	
	Mean	Range (sample size)	Mean	Range (sample size)
Wing length (mm)	199	193–205 (12)	222	206–231 (45)
Tail length (mm)	120	117–124 (9)	133	120–142 (42)
Culmen (mm)	13.7	12.5–13.8 (8)	15.0	14.1–17.0 (38)
Tarsus width (mm)	3.1	3.0–3.3 (10)	3.6	3.2–3.9 (44)
Tarsus depth (mm)	4.2	3.7–4.7 (10)	4.9	4.4–5.5 (44)
Tarsus length (mm)	36.5	33.5–38.0 (10)	38.5	36.0–38.5 (44)
Mid toe (mm)	28.2	25.0–30.5 (10)	32.5	29.3–31.9 (44)
Weight (g)	174	163–188 (13)	247	227–277 (46)

Tail: male 121.6 ± 2.6 mm; female 136 ± 3.4 mm.
Bill: male 12.4 ± 0.4 mm; female 13.8 ± 0.6 mm.
Claw: male 10.8 ± 0.3 mm; female 11.8 ± 0.4 mm.

Further details from northern England are given in Table 23. On Orkney, Picozzi (1983) measured some of the physical data noted in Table 23 for fledglings no older than five days from fledge and noted that on average the male tarsus width, depth and length were 3.4 mm and 5.0 mm and 35.1 mm respectively, with females measuring 4.2 mm, 5.9 mm and 38.0 mm. The mean mid toe was longer than in northern England, measuring 34.3 mm in males and 37.4 mm in females. Picozzi also measured the hind claw, his sample of newly fledged birds having a mean length of 10.4 mm (male) and 11.4 mm (female).

F. c. subaesalon, the Icelandic subspecies, is bigger, with male wing 208.0 ± 4.7 mm, female wing 227.0 ± 2.6 mm; male tail 122.0 ± 3.4 mm, female tail 134 ± 2.6 mm.

WEIGHT

Male 166.9 ± 11.1 g; female 255.5 ± 17.1 g. *F. c. subaesalon* on average 30 g heavier.

In all cases the weight is variable throughout the year and particularly during the breeding season. The changes in weight, and the reasons for these changes, are discussed below under *Breeding*.

PLUMAGE

Merlins show a greater degree of plumage dimorphism than any other falcons apart from kestrels.

Adult male

Head has blue-grey crown and auriculars, and an often indistinct white supercilium. No distinct head pattern, but a weakly defined malar 'moustache' is sometimes visible. Blue-grey back, scapulars and rump. Throat is white, the rest of the underside pale rufous-brown with dark brown streaking. Upperwing is blue-grey, the primaries darker, with black streaking. Underwing primary and secondary feathers are blue-grey, the coverts brown. All these feathers are heavily white-spotted, which gives the impression of a pale underwing with heavy dark barring in a bird overhead. Uppertail is dark blue-grey, with broad black subterminal, then pale terminal, band. Undertail is black with several narrow pale bands. Cere and orbital skin are yellow, tarsi and feet are yellow.

FIG 236. Adult male Merlin with Meadow Pipit.

Adult female

Head has dark brown crown and auriculars, with pale brown supercilium. Nape is paler mottled. Malar stripe more prominent than in male. Upperparts are dark brown with sparse black streaking. Throat is cream, as is the remaining underside, and with prominent darker streaks. Upperwing is dark brown with darker primaries and paler feather fringes. Underwing is similar to male. Uppertail is brown or dark brown with several narrow, paler bands. Undertail is dark brown with several paler narrow bands. Cere and orbital skin are yellow, tarsi and feet are yellow.

Juvenile

Both male and female juveniles resemble the adult female and are not easily distinguished at a distance. Males tend to have less brown on the head, which is also difficult to distinguish at a distance. Juveniles attain full adult plumage during their second year, though some adult females take longer to attain full adult colour on rump and upper tail coverts.

FIG 237. Juvenile Merlin. This back-lit bird left the nest on the day of the photograph, but could not yet fly, needing to jump and climb back to the nest for food.

FIG 238. Merlin chick, about 15 days of age.

Nestling

The first down is sparse, cream/white. Second down (4–8 days) is longer and more complete, pale brown/grey on the upper body, pale grey and white below. The cere and feet are yellow, the bill blue.

Moult

In general the moult begins in June for both male and female, females usually beginning earlier, and is completed in the autumn. The moult pattern of the primaries is not fixed, and may start 4–5–6, 5–4–6 or 6–5–4, but is usually completed as 3–7–8–2–9–1–10. However, Morozov *et al.* (2013) state that for Steppe Merlin the sequence is 6–7–5 (or 7–6–5) 8–4–3–9–2–10–1, but provide no data for the sequence in the other three Asian subspecies. The tail feathers are moulted from the centre outwards.

In a study of moulting in urban-breeding Merlins in Saskatoon, Canada, Espie *et al.* (1996) noted that the timing of the male moult depends on the quality of his territory: if prey resources are good the male may start to moult earlier. The start of the male moult was also found to be correlated with hatch date. Espie and co-workers found that moult suspension was significantly more likely in males than females, and that 48% of males had suspended their moult, an indication of the energetic overload of hunting in the breeding season, but also of the flexibility in moult which allows the male to divert energy away from moulting to feeding his offspring if that is required. For female Merlins Espie *et al.* found that those birds which did not arrest the moult had significantly smaller broods than those that did.

In general, juveniles partially moult body feathers and tail feathers (occasionally only the central pair) early in their first spring, with other feathers at the same time as the adults so that full adult plumage is acquired late in the second calendar year. In a study of the number of first-year birds moulting during the winter/early spring period, Pyle (2005) found that only 4% of the birds were moulting in September–November, and that these were replacing only 5% of their feathers. In December–February, a third of birds were moulting, replacing 15% of their feathers. By March–May all birds were moulting, with 50% replacement.

HABITAT

At present European Merlins are confined to remote undeveloped areas of rough grazing or moorland, with some agricultural areas. Rebecca (2011) identified the habitat types across Britain based on the principal habitat found within 1 km of the falcon's nest area, noting that dry heather moor was most common in Britain as a whole, with mixed dry and wet moorland the next most common. Only southwest Scotland and Wales, where Merlins were more likely to be found in coniferous woodland, were exceptions, though even there dry moorland was the 'second favourite' habitat.

During migration the birds are usually found on farmland, particularly arable land. Newton *et al.* (1978) studied Merlins nesting in Northumberland, an area which includes the large Kielder Forest which then measured 30 × 20 km. No nests were discovered deeper than 1 km from the forest edge, emphasising the importance of open land to the species for hunting. The birds also ignored clear-felled areas if these were deep within the forest.

Studies over long periods indicate that even if the Merlins at a particular nest site have been killed, the site is very likely to be reoccupied. Rowan (1921–1922 part I) gives two remarkable examples from a time when the killing of raptors on land reserved for game shooting was common and indiscriminate. In one case both birds of a pair of Merlins were trapped and killed every year from 1898 to 1916 at the same nest site in northern England, despite the fact that no adult bird escaped killing and no egg was hatched. In his other case Rowan reports a similar story over a 12-year period. These examples indicate the importance of both habitat and nest site to the species, but, as Rowan notes, they do raise the question of where the continuous supply of new Merlin pairs came from. In a separate study of Merlins in northern England, Newton *et al.* (1978) noted that

FIG 239. Typical Merlin breeding habitat in northeast England.

of 37 areas known to have been used in the period 1880–1940 at least 25 were still in use in their study period 1971–1976. Of the 12 that were not used, five were no longer suitable for Merlins as a consequence of change in land usage or increased human presence. This site fidelity is not restricted to British Merlins, Trimble (1975) noting that a ground nest site in Newfoundland had been used continuously for 23 years. However, it is important to distinguish between the fidelity of Merlin as a species to specific requirements in terms of nest site and territory and the fidelity of individual birds. The latter is discussed under *Nest-site, territory and mate fidelity*, below.

This section began with 'at present', the reason being that in recent years the habitat preferences of the species have evolved to include urban areas, at least in North America. James (1988) notes that prior to 1971 such urban dwelling/breeding was unknown (or, at least, unrecorded). In that year a pair of Merlins bred in Saskatoon: by 1987 the population had increased to 27 pairs. James puts the appearance and increase in Merlins down to the increase in American Crows and Black-billed Magpies. Being omnivorous and opportunistic, the corvids had invaded urban North America once trees planted there had matured sufficiently to provide good sites for stick nests, the Merlins taking advantage of the nests in later years. Within urban areas Merlins are able to take advantage of flocks of

House Sparrows as prey, the fact the passerines are available year-round allowing some Merlins to overwinter in towns and cities despite temperatures regularly reaching −35 °C. In winter the Merlins roost in conifer stands, which give some protection against night-time temperatures. Within the urban environment, the Merlins hunt in gardens, parks and cemeteries (Sodhi & Oliphant 1992). It will be interesting to see if British Merlins ever emulate their North American cousins and develop a taste for urban living.

VOICE

Merlins are very vocal during the breeding season, but much quieter at other times. The alarm call, usually written *'kee-kee-kee'*, is made by both male and female, the male voice higher-pitched and more rapid. However, I do not consider the call to be harsh enough to be written with a *'k'*, as it has a softer first sound, *'hwee-hwee-hwee'*, though in what follows the more general construction is used. The call is reminiscent of that of the Kestrel, but the delivery is much faster. Craighead & Craighead (1940) commented that if the birds were highly excited their call ended with a piercing *'ki-ki-ki-ki-kieeee'* or guttural *'kac kac kac'* (and said that 'once heard it can hardly be mistaken'). Occasionally a bird will intersperse single *'kee'* calls between full alarm calls. In North America, Feldsine & Oliphant (1985) identified the common alarm call, but also three others, these having also been described for British birds. One call is a *'chip'*, made by both males and females during courtship, which is also often heard from females if the male is not in sight. The male *'chip'* is again higher-pitched and more rapid. A *'chrrr'* is made by males seeking copulation, both in pairs and by non-paired males who are intruding on a territory. Finally there is a whining call used by females begging for food from their mate. The same call may be made by hungry nestlings, but is then more urgent. Nestlings will make the same sound if they see an aerial predator, probably in an effort to alert an adult. Females will also make a sharp *'tick tick'* when they are feeding nestlings, presumably to reassure the youngsters, but seemingly as an indication of contentment.

DIET

Prey
Merlins are essentially predators of aerial species, taking birds (typically weighing less than 40 g, but as we shall see not restricted to such smaller prey), but also

flying insects and bats (Duquet & Nadal 2012). Merlins will take terrestrial mammals, though these usually form a small fraction of the diet. During a huge increase in the vole population of the Scottish borders in the early years of the 1890s, a witness to the commission set up to investigate the causes and effects of the 'vole plague', as it was termed, claimed that Merlins did not prey on voles, and by implication any terrestrial mammal, but this was contrary to the evidence provided by Laidlaw (1893) which showed clearly that they did. (It is probable that the rodent responsible for the plague was the Field Vole, though at the time 'voles' and 'mice' were commonly interchanged in reports so there is no absolute certainty.) Rudebeck (1951) states that from his observations in Scandinavia Merlins were able to subsist on a diet composed mainly of lemmings when they were abundant, but notes that this was exceptional and that avian species were invariably the main prey, while Wiklund (2001) in a study in two Arctic-fringe national parks in Sweden also provides evidence that the diet of Merlins includes rodents (voles and Norwegian Lemming, *Lemmus lemmus*) even though the primary prey remained avian species.

Studies on North American Merlins have shown that terrestrial mammals and insects form a small fraction of the diet: the suggestion has been made that juvenile Merlins may take these in the early days of independent hunting as they are easier to catch. Insect prey being part of the juvenile diet is also consistent with British studies. North American Merlins seem to be rather more eclectic in their diet, Palmer (1988) stating that unusual prey items include lizards, garter snakes, 'horned toads' (*Phrynosoma* spp.), toads, crayfish, scorpions and spiders. Bibby (1987) also found remains of a Vivaparous Lizard (*Lacerta vivipara*) in Merlin prey remains in Wales.

While the above information makes it clear that Merlins will take rodent prey, it is equally clear from Iceland, where there are few rodents (all of which have been introduced by human settlers and are almost exclusively found in or close to human habitation) that Merlins can exist entirely (or almost entirely) on a diet of birds.

Equally unusual, to judge by the absence of reports in the literature, is the taking of carrion. There are some reports from North America, and in Scotland Thomas (1992) noted a Merlin feeding on a fresh roadkill Rabbit. Wright (2005) also noted that Merlin nestlings which died, through sickness or injury, were invariably eaten, though Wright does not specify whether this was by siblings or parents. However, Dickson (1998a) definitely records young Merlin consuming a dead sibling.

In Britain avian prey includes Meadow Pipits, Wheatears, Starlings and Skylarks, in addition to finches and waders. But records also include other, surprising, species – see Chapter 2. Such large prey is exceptional, though Merlins will take adults of larger bird species opportunistically, as well as the nestlings of larger birds. In Finland, Bergman (1961) recorded a Merlin taking all 12 chicks of a brood of Grey Partridge. British records also include a number of day-flying moth species – particularly the Emperor and the Northern Eggar – as well as dragonflies and beetles.

FIG 240. Typical Merlin prey species: Meadow Pipit (a), Northern Wheatear (b) and female Snow Bunting (c).

Several observers have reported finding the remains of the chicks of prey species in the nests of Merlins: Sperber & Sperber (1963) noted nestlings of Brambling in a study in Norway, and McElheron (2005) found that feathers of unfledged nestlings outnumbered those of adults by 2 to 1 in late summer at the plucking post in his study in Ireland. However, see Table 29, which is based on data from Northumberland where Newton *et al.* (1984) found that even when the percentage of fledglings in the diet was at its highest, fledglings still constituted only about a quarter of the Merlin diet.

Intuition would suggest that the composition of the Merlin diet would reflect the relative abundance of prey species, assuming that all available species were of more or less equal merit as prey, and more or less equally easy to catch. But the assumptions involved in equating abundance and likelihood of capture mean that intuition is not a good judge of the subtleties of prey selection. In a study in Wales, involving analysis of 6,366 avian remains recovered from Merlin plucking sites, Baker & Bibby (1987) found that Merlin prey reflected the local abundance of prey species, but that the falcons were (very slightly) more likely to catch prey which was conspicuously coloured (Note 7.1). In a study of urban Merlins in Canada, Sodhi & Oliphant (1993) noted that the falcons were also less likely to capture cryptically coloured House Wrens (*Troglodytes aedon*), but noted that House Sparrows and Shore Larks (*Eremophila alpestris*) were taken more frequently than expected, implying that the Merlins were selecting their prey rather than merely responding to abundance. In their study, Sodhi & Oliphant noted that the two preferred species were more likely to leave cover than other species, and were therefore more vulnerable, and that their mass was in the range 21–40 g, which was the preferred mass of the Merlins (based on the observed prey mass spectrum) (Fig. 241).

Composition of diet

The composition of the Merlin diet can be ascertained in two ways. The simplest is to observe the feathers or skeletal remains (sternum, pectoral girdle, synacrum, legs) at plucking posts or the remains at nest sites in order to identify prey species and the number of each. But this method has several drawbacks, as Newton *et al.* (1984) note. Firstly, the feathers of large, pale birds are more easily seen than those of small, dark birds. Secondly, the adult Merlins may consume larger prey away from the nest, as these are difficult to carry, so remains at the nest may not correctly represent the diet. The adults may also consume smaller prey, such as moths, themselves and so these, too, may be under-represented in nest remains. Thirdly, the birds may entirely consume some small prey items, which would therefore leave no remains.

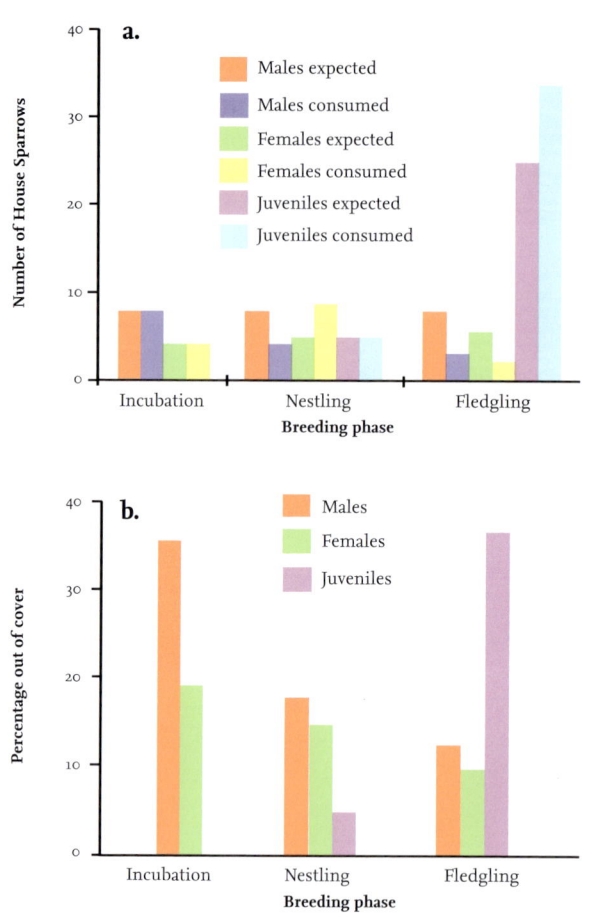

FIG 241. (a) Consumption of House Sparrows by adult Merlins from an urban-breeding Canadian population at various phases of the breeding cycle. (b) Percentage of time spent out of cover by adult and juvenile House Sparrows during phases of the Merlin breeding cycle. Redrawn from Sodhi & Oliphant 1993.

An alternative to collecting remains at plucking posts or nests is to use pellet analysis. It is generally assumed that pellet analysis is a more accurate method of defining diet, particularly if small mammals are a significant fraction of the total prey, but in a study of the diet of Irish Merlins, Fernández-Bellon & Lusby (2011a) found there was no significant difference in the two methods for Merlins, probably because they almost exclusively consume avian prey. A combination of the two methods is, of course, also possible.

Dickson (1999) collected both summer and winter Merlin pellets in southwest Scotland. The summer pellets had a mean length of 29.3 ± 8.8 mm (range 12.5–53 mm, $n = 76$) and mean width (at the widest point) of 11.6 ± 2.1 mm (range 8.0–16.5 mm). In

FIG 242. Males do little of the feeding in most Merlin pairs, but as these photos indicate males do feed younger nestlings on occasion. This Merlin brood, in southern Scotland, was raised in an old metal basket which had originally been installed in a Scots Pine in the hope of attracting Long-eared Owls.

winter the pellets were smaller, mean length 23.6 ± 6.7 mm (range 12–41 mm, $n = 88$), mean width 11.3 ± 1.9 mm (range 6–16 mm).

In a study of Merlins in Northumberland, Newton et al. (1984) derived the prey species data shown in Table 24. The data were derived from over 1,800 prey items recovered from close to nests or at plucking sites. Although most prey items weighed 10–40 g, some were 100 g. Newton et al. (1978) also looked at the variation of the diet with local land usage (Table 25). Rebecca (2006) collected a total of 11,225 prey items over the period 1980–2003 to explore the diet of Merlins in northeast Scotland (Table 26).

Table 26 includes some unusual species, although others have also been noted, Weir (2013) noted Bluethroats in the diet. As these are rare arrivals from Scandinavia – only about four are seen each year (Rebecca et al. 1987) – for local birdwatchers this was an unfortunate choice by the Merlins, though Bluethroats are regularly taken in Scandinavia. The choice of a Wryneck was equally unfortunate. Rebecca (2006) also found the remains of a single Budgerigar, the remains of 547 moths (314 Northern Eggar, 232 Emperor and a Kentish Glory, *Endromis versicolora*), two Small Tortoiseshell butterflies (*Aglais urticae*), and several unidentified dragonflies/beetles, two Field Voles, a shrew, other unidentified mammals, and a single Common Frog (*Rana temporaria*).

Heavisides (1995) studied the diet of Merlin in the Lammermuir Hills, southern Scotland, during 1984–1994 by collecting 2,040 prey remains from plucking posts, and found that Meadow Pipits constituted 62.9% of the diet by number and 37.7% by biomass. Other significant prey species were Skylark (9.3%, 10.8%), Wheatear (6.2%, 4.7%) and Chaffinch (4.5%, 3.3%). In addition to the items in Table 26 Heavisides also found the remains of Woodcock.

Weir (2013) examined the diet of Merlins in Speyside, central Scotland, during the period 1964–1984 from the remains of 656 prey items found in three differing habitats (open moor, birch moor and pine moor). In this study Meadow Pipits formed 80.8% of the prey (by number), with Wheatears forming 6.6%, Skylarks 3.4% and Chaffinches 3.1%. Mammalian prey included voles and a Pygmy Shrew (*Sorex minutus*). In addition to vertebrate prey, Weir found the remains of various moths, beetles and dragonflies. The fractions of prey taken by the Merlins in the three habitats were approximately the same. Weir also found that one Merlin had an enthusiasm for newly hatched Lapwing chicks, eight pairs of legs being found.

In a study in Orkney, Meek (1988) noted that Meadow Pipits comprised 38.9% of the diet by number (25.5% by biomass) with Skylarks 20.5% by number (24.8% by biomass) and House Sparrows 17.9% by number (17% by biomass). The remaining diet comprised species already identified with the addition of Garden Warbler (*Sylvia borin*), Ringed Plover, Rock Dove and Twite.

TABLE 24 Diet of Merlins in Northumberland. From Newton et al. (1978).

Prey species[1]	Percentage of total prey items	Percentage of total biomass
Meadow Pipit[2]	55.8	36.8
Skylark	11.8	15.6
Chaffinch	5.8	4.6
Starling	3.6	8.9
Wheatear	2.0	2.0
Fieldfare	1.8	6.5
Song Thrush	1.5	3.2
Willow Warbler	1.2	0.4
Goldcrest	1.1	0.2
Snipe	1.1	3.8
Whinchat	1.0	0.6
Lesser Redpoll	0.6	0.2
Ring Ouzel	0.6	2.0
Robin	0.6	0.3
Pied Wagtail	0.5	0.4
Redshank	0.4	1.7
Blackbird	0.4	1.3
Mistle Thrush	0.3	0.9
Golden Plover	0.3	2.0
Lapwing	0.2	0.7
juvenile Red Grouse	0.2	1.3
Feral Pigeon	0.1	0.7
Stock Dove	0.1	0.5

1. As well as the tabulated bird species, the following species were found in prey remains, though in no case did these account for either 0.5% by number or by biomass: Blue Tit, Brambling, Bullfinch, Coal Tit, Common Crossbill, Cuckoo, juvenile Curlew, Dunlin, Dunnock, juvenile Kestrel, Goldfinch, Greenfinch, juvenile Grey Partridge, House Martin, House Sparrow, Linnet, Long-tailed Tit (*Aegithalos caudatus*), Redwing, Reed Bunting, Sand Martin, Siskin, Snow Bunting, Barn Swallow, Tree Pipit, Treecreeper, Willow Tit and Wren.

    Other prey items included Common Shrew, beetles, caterpillars, Fox Moth and Peacock Butterfly (*Inachis io*). An earlier study of Merlin diet, in what is now the Lake District National Park, Brown (1935) also noted the remains of Long-tailed Field-Mouse (now more commonly called the Wood Mouse) and 'Short-tailed Field-Mouse'. It is not clear what species Brown meant by the latter, but it is likely he meant the Short-tailed Vole (now more commonly called the Field Vole).

2. In a study of Merlins in southeast Yorkshire during the period 1983–2002, which collected feathers from plucking posts and remains at nest sites, Wright (2005) found that Meadow Pipits comprised 50.9% of the Merlin diet, with a 29.7% contribution from Starlings. The next most popular prey species was the Wheatear, with 4% of the diet. Wright found that 17 species comprised the total diet.

TABLE 25 Diet of Merlins in Northumberland defined by land usage within 1 km of nest sites. From Newton et al. (1978).

Prey species	Sheep grazing areas	Heather moorland	Mix of forestry and open land	Forest	All areas
Meadow Pipit	10	101	24	109	244 (48%)
Skylark	7	25	10	20	62 (12%)
Starling	8	8	3	3	22 (4%)
Fieldfare	4	12	2	1	19 (4%)
Wheatear	0	7	2	3	12 (2%)
Other songbirds[1]	4	10	4	6	24 (5%)
Snipe	0	13	2	1	16 (3%)
Other waders[2]	1	4	2	1	8 (2%)
Other birds[3]	0	3	0	2	5 (1%)
Total of open-country birds	34 (85%)	183 (85%)	49 (79%)	146 (81%)	412 (83%)
Chaffinch	2	5	0	15	22 (4%)
Goldcrest	1	3	6	3	13 (3%)
Song Thrush	2	3	0	4	9 (2%)
Other songbirds[4]	1	22	7	13	43 (9%)
Total of woodland birds	6 (15%)	33 (15%)	13 (21%)	35 (19%)	87 (17%)

1. Included House Martin, Tree Pipit, Pied Wagtail, Whinchat, Ring Ouzel, Mistle Thrush, Linnet, Snow Bunting and Reed Bunting.
2. Included Eurasian Golden Plover, juvenile Lapwing, Dunlin and Redshank.
3. Included fledgling Kestrel, adult and young Red Grouse, feral Rock Dove and small white doves (*Streptopelia* spp.).
4. Included Wren, Dunnock, Robin, Blackbird (*Turdus merula*), Redwing, Chiffchaff, Willow Warbler, Long-tailed Tit, Marsh Tit, Great Tit, Treecreeper, Greenfinch, Goldfinch, Lesser Redpoll, Common Crossbill and Bullfinch.

In a study in Galloway, Orchel (1992) noted that Meadow Pipits were 65.5% of the Merlin diet by number, with Wheatears providing a further 10.0%, Skylarks 8.2% and Chaffinches 3.7%. The remaining diet comprised species already noted.

In a study on peatlands of the Isle of Lewis, Rae (2010a) noted that while Meadow Pipit still formed the basis of the Merlin diet (54.3% in 2003, 37.4% in 2005), waders were also significant prey items, with Dunlin comprising 10.8% of prey in 2003, 5.9% in 2005, and Ringed Plover and Turnstone (*Arenaria interpres*) also being taken. In 2005 many more insects were taken, Lepidoptera forming

TABLE 26 Diet of Merlins in northeast Scotland. From Rebecca (2006).

Prey species[1]	Percentage of total prey items	Percentage of total biomass
Meadow Pipit	65.5	52.4
Wheatear	6.7	8.2
Chaffinch	6.0	6.1
Starling	2.4	8.9
Skylark	2.3	3.9
Goldcrest	2.1	0.6
Barn Swallow	2.0	1.8
Pied Wagtail	1.5	1.4
Whinchat	1.2	1.0
Linnet	1.1	1.0
Siskin	1.1	0.8
Willow Warbler	1.1	0.5
juvenile Red Grouse	0.7	2.2
Greenfinch	0.6	0.8
Yellowhammer	0.5	0.6
Wren	0.5	0.2
Blue Tit	0.4	0.2
Robin	0.3	0.3
Snipe	0.2	1.2
Song Thrush	0.2	0.7
Mistle Thrush	0.1	0.8

1. In addition to the above, other species contributing less than 0.1% by number were juvenile Black Grouse, Bluethroat (*Luscinia svecica*), Brambling, Bullfinch, Coal Tit, Lesser Redpoll, Common Sandpiper, Common Crossbill, Cuckoo, juvenile Curlew, Dipper, Dunnock, Fieldfare, Golden Plover, Goldfinch, Great Tit, Grey Partridge, Grey Wagtail, House Martin, House Sparrow, Lapwing, Long-tailed Tit, Oystercatcher, feral Rock Dove, Reed Bunting, Redshank, Redstart (*Phoenicurus phoenicurus*), Redwing, Ring Ouzel, Sand Martin, Snow Bunting, Spotted Flycatcher (*Muscicapa striata*), Stock Dove, Stonechat, Treecreeper and Wryneck.

25.7% of the diet by number. Rae could not tell if this was because of a significant increase in insect numbers, or a fall in the number of avian prey species.

The high predation rate on Meadow Pipits indicated by the above studies may have an impact on local populations. In a study of the impact of raptors on prey species populations in southern Scotland, Amar *et al.* (2008) noted that Meadow

Pipits had declined in number by 60% over a seven-year period during which the Hen Harrier breeding pairs had doubled from 10 to 20 within the study area: there were also 10 breeding pairs of Merlin. About 60% of the diet of both raptors comprised Meadow Pipits, Amar and colleagues estimating that one falcon pair would consume 91 pipits during the breeding season, so that in their study area the 10 falcon pairs would take over 900 pipits, about 18% of the population.

Dickson (1995), observing six nests in Scotland, calculated that 0.26 prey items per hour were delivered by the male during a 47-hour period of observation in the pre-laying phase of breeding (with seven deliveries in the morning, four in the afternoon and one in the evening), this falling to 0.15 per hour during 71 hours of observed incubation (deliveries also altering to two in the morning, four in the afternoon and five in the evening), then rising to 0.54 per hour (69 hours of observation: 7 morning, 18 afternoon, 12 evening) when nestlings were being fed. During the post-fledging phase, 0.49 items per hour were delivered to the chicks over a 79-hour period (7 morning, 11 afternoon, 21 evening).

Bibby (1987) examined the diet of Merlins in Wales by collecting 6,366 prey items from plucking posts across the Principality (Table 27).

In Ireland, Fernández-Bellon & Lusby (2011a) studied the diet of Merlins at ten sites in the counties of Donegal, Galway and Wicklow by a combination of collecting remains at plucking posts and analysing pellets. They found that 69.5% of prey items were birds, with 33.1% being moths and 1.0% dragonflies. Meadow Pipit and Skylark were the main avian prey, though the percentages in the diet were much lower than those in Table 24, with 22.9% and 8.9% respectively (17.0% and 13.2% by biomass). Irish Merlins also took more Barn Swallows (4.7% by occurrence, 3.9% by biomass) and many more Snipe (3.9%, 17.4%) and Mistle Thrush (2.9%, 14.9%). No species other than those already noted in the data above were taken. The moth fraction in the diet was very high by occurrence, but contributed only 3.2% by biomass. The most frequently taken species were Fox Moth, Emperor Moth and Northern Eggar, as was the case in Britain. In a study of Merlins that breed on the lower slopes of the Wicklow Mountains to the south of Dublin, a range which reaches 925m, McElheron (2005) found that in spring the birds supplemented their diet of local species with Barn Swallows arriving exhausted after their long flight from Africa, while in summer a diet of Chaffinches was extended to include nestlings.

Newton *et al.* (1984) looked at the variation of prey species through the Merlin breeding season. Dividing the prey into woodland and open-country species, the researchers noted that the former dominated the Merlin diet early in the season, the latter at later stages of the breeding cycle (Table 28), which they considered was due to the availability of open-country prey early in the season. This was

TABLE 27 Prey of Merlins in Wales. From Bibby (1987).

Prey Species[1]	Percentage of total prey items	Percentage of total biomass
Meadow Pipit	60.5	52.1
Chaffinch	8.4	7.2
Wheatear	4.5	5.1
Whinchat	3.0	1.7
Skylark	2.8	4.5
Starling	2.5	9.0
Barn Swallow	2.3	1.8
House Sparrow	1.9	2.2
Blue Tit	1.9	1.1
Great Tit	1.7	1.4
Pied Wagtail	1.3	1.2
Goldcrest	1.2	0.3
Fieldfare	1.0	4.8
Linnet	0.9	0.6
Willow Warbler	0.9	0.3
Coal Tit	0.5	0.2
Redwing	0.3	0.8
juvenile Red Grouse	0.3	0.8
Greenfinch	0.3	0.3
Bullfinch	0.3	0.3
Robin	0.3	0.2
Song Thrush	0.2	0.7
Redstart	0.2	0.1
Yellowhammer	0.2	0.3
Goldfinch	0.2	0.1
Others[2]	2.2	2.9

1. Bibby also noted that as the proportion of farmland within 4 km of the Merlin nest site increased, so did the diversity of the prey taken (Fig. 257). Prey diversity was also reflected in the egg size of the falcons (see *Eggs*).
2. Other species identified were Blackbird, Brambling, Chiffchaff, Lesser Redpoll, Common Sandpiper, Cuckoo, juvenile Curlew, Dunnock, Garden Warbler, Grey Wagtail, House Martin, Lapwing, Long-tailed Tit, Marsh Tit, Mistle Thrush, Nuthatch (*Sitta europaea*), juvenile Pheasant, Pied Flycatcher (*Ficedula hypoleuca*), Reed Bunting, Ring Ouzel, Sand Martin, Siskin, Snipe, Spotted Flycatcher, Stonechat, Swift, Treecreeper, Wood Warbler (*Phylloscopus sibilatrix*) and Wren. Bibby also identified the remains of a single Viviparous Lizard, Emperor, Fox and Northern Eggar moths, and Golden-ringed Dragonfly (*Cordulegaster boltonii*).

TABLE 28 Percentages of open-country and woodland species in the Merlin diet through the breeding season. From Newton et al. (1984).

	April[3]	May	June	July
	N (%)	N (%)	N (%)	N (%)
Open country species	270 (76.9)	548 (81.4)	537 (90.7)	358 (93.0)
Woodland species[1,2]	81 (23.1)	125 (18.6)	55 (9.3)	27 (7.0)

1. Woodland species include scrub and woodland edge.
2. In their study of Merlins breeding on moorland in northeast Wales, Roberts & Jones (1999) noted that while the percentage of moorland birds increased as Newton et al. (1984) found in their study, the importance of House Sparrows (from June onwards) and Starlings (from July) increased so that non-moorland species were contributing 39% of the diet in July and August. Both House Sparrows and Starlings are considered 'urban' species, and it is therefore significant that none of the Merlin nest sites in the Roberts & Jones study was more than 4 km from the nearest hamlet or village. Roberts & Jones also recorded a decline in the fraction of these urban species in the Merlin diet from 1983 when the British population of both declined.
3. The variation between different months is statistically significant at the 99.9% level. The data are also consistent with that of Bibby (1987), who noted that April diet of Welsh Merlins comprised chiefly resident species – Chaffinch, other finches, tits etc. – with migratory species and those whose juveniles were available when the Merlins had nestlings, particularly Meadow Pipit and Skylark, dominating in summer. The data are also consistent with a later study (in northeast Wales) by Roberts & Jones (1999).

confirmed by Petty et al. (1995), who recorded a similar trend in the Merlin diet from woodland to open-country species, noting that Meadow Pipits, the main prey of Merlins in northern England, were absent from the Merlin breeding habitat in winter and did not return to the moorland on which they bred until the Merlins had returned and established territories.

The variation in proportion of the two classes of prey species reflects the availability of prey through the season, with the 'preferred' open-country species being scarce in the spring because they are migratory. A similar change in the ratio of woodland to open-country prey as the breeding season progresses has been seen in studies in other parts of Great Britain, as well as in Irish Merlins (Clarke & Scott 1994 for Northern Ireland, Fernández-Bellon & Lusby 2011a for the Republic of Ireland).

Newton et al. (1984) confirmed findings from North America that the number of fledglings (defined as birds with incompletely developed flight or tail feathers) in the diet increases during the time the Merlin pair are feeding their own nestlings (Table 29). Table 29 clearly demonstrates the vulnerability of inexperienced fledglings to attack. However, what is equally striking is that the Merlin diet still consists largely of full-grown birds even at this time.

TABLE 29 Percentage of fledglings in the Merlin diet as the breeding season progresses. From Newton et al. (1984).

	April	May	June	July
	n (%)	n (%)	n (%)	n (%)
Full-grown birds[1]	229 (100)	483 (98.8)	367 (80.8)	181 (72.4)
Fledglings[2]	0 (0)	6 (1.2)	87 (19.2)	69 (27.6)

1. Includes both adults and full-grown juveniles.
2. Includes 12 nestlings and two downy chicks of Eurasian Golden Plover and Red Grouse.

Newton et al. (1984) also investigated the dietary difference between male and female Merlins, that there is such a difference being one of the theories regarding the distinct reversed sexual dimorphism of the species (and other falcons). The investigation was not straightforward, as it was not possible to differentiate between prey remains which had been brought to the nest by males and females, but Newton and his co-workers were able to infer the difference by grouping the prey items recovered from plucking posts and nests into pre-laying, incubation/young chicks, and late nestling/post-fledge periods, as during the incubation/young chick phase only the male hunted. Within the groups which represent phases of the breeding cycle, the prey items were then divided into classes by weight. These data are shown in Table 30, from which it is clear that male Merlins primarily take prey weighing up to 40 g (98% of all prey), with only one heavier prey item (a Fieldfare, about 100 g) being taken during the incubation

TABLE 30 Weight classes of prey taken by Merlins during three phases of the breeding season. From Newton et al. (1984).

	Number (percentage) of items in each weight class						
Breeding phase	≤10 g	11–20 g	21–30 g	31–40 g	61–80 g	81–100 g	>100 g
Pre-laying	24 (7)	190 (55)	31 (9)	34 (10)	17 (5)	8 (2)	43 (12)
Incubation/ young chick	12 (4)	243 (72)	22 (7)	51 (15)	8 (2)	0	1 (<1)
Late nestling/ post-fledge	1 (<1)	210 (53)	15 (4)	56 (14)	102 (26)	2 (<1)	13 (3)

There were few birds in the weight class 41–60g in the study area and the remains of none were found among prey items.

phase. By contrast, when the female Merlins were hunting, the balance of prey weights shifted, with 19% above 40 g in the pre-lay phase and 29% in the late nestling/post-fledge phase. Newton *et al.* (1984) note that these differences must have been due to differences in the prey of the sexes, as they could not be entirely explained by seasonal changes in prey availability.

In the study of Newton *et al.* (1978) on only three occasions were the wings of moths discovered, on one occasion the remains of a vole, and on one other the remains of a bat. This low fraction of terrestrial mammal prey is consistent with other studies in Britain, and also with studies in North America. However, Wiklund (2001) found significant numbers of rodents in the diet of Merlins in northern Sweden and considers that a possible reason for the disparity is that British studies of the species' diet tended to collect remains at plucking posts, a technique which could seriously underestimate the number of rodents killed.

Winter diet

Prey during migration and at wintering sites is not well documented, though as it is clear that resident Merlins continue to take local, i.e. available, prey, it can be assumed that the eclectic nature of the Merlin breeding-season prey means that the falcons will take whatever is available during migration flights and in their winter quarters.

Dickson (1988) studied wintering Merlins over a 19-year period (1965–1984) in Galloway, southwest Scotland, where the falcons were hunting an area comprising moorland, lowland cultivated land and coastal sites. In this study the Merlins were primarily hunting Skylark and finches (including Lesser Redpoll, Greenfinch, Linnet and Twite), but also waders (Dunlin, Lapwing, Redshank, Ringed Plover and Turnstone), as well as Blackbird, Pied Wagtail, Redwing and Reed Bunting. Dickson also monitored the number of times male and female Merlins attacked prey, and the success rate of attacks. The success rates of males and females were the same, at about 10%. (Dickson defined 'blue' and 'brown' Merlins, and I assume that the colours were sex-related, i.e. male = blue, female = brown: Dickson noted that brown Merlins were more likely to attack larger birds, and since the possibility of adult males taking smaller prey than first-year (brown) males is minimal, the colour/sex assumption seems reasonable, as Dickson himself agrees.) In a further analysis, Dickson (2000) extended his analysis of the Merlin winter diet by another eight years (1992–2000). In those years 'blue' Merlins preferentially attacked Linnets and Twites (64.7% of attacks) and Chaffinches (17.6% of attacks), with Skylarks being the target on only 8.9% of occasions. This differs markedly from the earlier data (Dickson 1988) in which the combined finch fraction was 31.6%, with Skylarks accounting for 21%. For 'brown' Merlins the rate of attacks on

FIG 243. First-winter Merlins of both sexes are 'brown', i.e. they have brown backs, while adult males are 'blue'. The colour difference of the upper body of the two sexes (and first-winter birds) is shown here: male (a), female (b).

Linnet and Twite had also increased (58.6%, cf. 11.6% for all finches in the earlier study), though in this case the Skylark fraction had also increased (32.9%, cf. 21%).

Studies of the diet of migrating Merlins are few, but those that exist, chiefly from North America, suggest that the falcons exploit both those species which are migrating at the same time, and local species. This willingness to hunt any species which is both available and within the weight spectrum capability of the falcon can also be seen in some winter observations. Odin (1992) watched Merlins (a total of 34 observations in a 57-day period) hunting passerines above the sea off Dungeness, Kent. Odin considered the Merlins were not returning migrants, but falcons wintering locally: it was not clear whether the captured passerines were migrants, though the observations (from late February to mid-April) suggest that is possible. The Merlins were often successful in their hunting, suggesting they were taking advantage of the lack of cover available to the passerines (and, potentially, their exhausted state). Equally interesting is the observation of Dean (1988), who saw a wintering juvenile Merlin returning from the sea off the Cumbrian coast clearing flying with difficulty because of the prey it was carrying. Dean believes the Merlin was first seen over 1 km from shore. When it arrived at the beach it was seen to be carrying a Leach's Petrel. The Merlin ate for 30 minutes, then departed leaving only the petrel's wings, legs and upper mandible.

Food caching

The reasons for prey caching appear straightforward – it provides a larder for food caught in abundance when conditions or prey availability are favourable, to be used when the weather prevents hunting, or when prey density declines. But studies carried out on other species suggest that more subtle reasoning is at work. In the Netherlands, adult Kestrels tended to consume smaller voles, feeding larger specimens to the chicks and caching the largest, and it was clear that the birds were heavily dependent on cached food during days when the weather prevented hunting, (Masman *et al.* 1986; see Chapter 5). No similar studies appear to have been carried out for Merlins, but the similarity of size of the two small falcons, the food intake requirements of their nestlings, and weight spectrum of their respective prey allow the contention that a similar strategy may well be at work in Merlins.

Merlins are known to cache prey both during the breeding season and in winter. Greaves (1968) observed the caching of a Meadow Pipit by a female Merlin in northeast Scotland in August ('about 50 feet from the spot, lying in a sleeping bag wrapped in a mudstained green fly-sheet (having spent the night there)'), and another instance of similar behaviour in Ireland seen by another observer, also in August. Greaves records another observer watching a female Merlin leaving the chicks she was brooding to retrieve cached prey after her partner had not provided fresh food for about two hours. Sperber & Sperber (1963) also noted instances where a female Merlin in Norway received food from her mate, but did not take it to the nest, returning to her brood without food, then later leaving the nest again and returning with food even though there had been no prey delivery by the male. Clearly the female was caching food and then retrieving it later, presumably gauging chick hunger in order to decide on feeding times. In a study of urban-dwelling Merlins in Saskatoon, Oliphant & Thompson (1976) noted that food caching occurred at all times of day apart from the early morning, suggesting that females were hungriest at that time and consumed any prey the male delivered. In the study Oliphant & Thompson noted that the Merlins tended to use different trees rather than a particular one for caching, and that the falcons used elms less often than spruce once the former had started to shed their leaves: concealment was clearly an issue. In the Canadian study all caches were in trees, but British caching records suggest that ground caches are also used. Oliphant & Thompson (1976) observed occasions on which a Merlin searched for cached food, including one search which began at the top of a tree and continued with the falcon hopping purposefully down from branch to branch, searching until it reached the ground. Such search patterns suggest Merlins are not good at recalling the position of caches.

In his study of ground-nesting (and ground-caching) Merlins in southeast Yorkshire, Wright (2005) notes that females occasionally retrieved prey from where their mates had cached it, even if the female had not been present or

FIG 244. This Goldcrest had been cached by a Merlin in southern Scotland. See also Fig. 14, which shows a Meadow Pipit cached by a Merlin. After the photograph had been taken the bird was returned to the cache, care being taken not to contaminate it with human scent.

nearby when the male had secreted it. This suggests either the use of preferred sites, or that female Merlins, perhaps away from the nest to hunt or to preen, had actually observed the caching, but from such a distance that the human observer was unaware, and so was amazed by her apparently telepathic abilities.

Prey caching also occurs in winter, and an interesting observation by Warkentin & Oliphant (1985) was of one Canadian Merlin hunting immediately after having cached food. Winter nights in Saskatoon are long and cold, and this behaviour seems to indicate a deliberate strategy of preparing food either for later the same day (i.e. before nightfall) or for early-morning consumption (i.e. the following day). Winter caching would appear to allow the bird to profit from an evening meal at a time when the long, cold hours of darkness must be endured with no opportunity to hunt. Coupled with the possibility of poor weather the next day, which might make hunting difficult, this would make winter caching a survival strategy.

Hunting strategies

After observing Merlins at Falsterbo in Sweden, Rudebeck (1951) wrote:

> The flight seems wild and vigorous although the bird is so small. The Merlin possesses an extraordinary capacity to turn round and make sudden zig-zags at great speed. It reacts with the utmost swiftness and is full of vitality: it may almost seem to have a nervous vibration in its movements. The latter is sometimes so pronounced that one has the impression of an entirely new flying technique, and the bird takes on a changed appearance. The tips of the wings are directed backwards, the 'wing knuckles' [i.e. the carpal joints] become still more pronounced and lie close to the sides of the body. The wings are thus not fully extended but are moved in a similar way to that of small passerine birds. The wing-beats become trembling and extremely rapid. Gliding on outspread wings is of course impossible in this position, but the wings can be kept still for short moments during which the bird glides ahead by its own momentum as many small birds do. The tail is narrowed and closed.

Its size and flying ability made the Merlin popular as a falconry bird – not necessarily only with ladies, despite what the *Book of St Albans* (see Chapter 1) claims, though there is no doubt that ladies of the European court did favour the birds. The preferred sport was the 'ringing' flight used to catch larks. In this, the Merlin was released in pursuit of a lark which had been startled into flight by the falconer or his dog. If the lark was far from cover, then being slower than the Merlin in level flight it would fly upwards as it could gain height faster. In classic flights the lark would make tight circles (rings) as it climbed, the Merlin following, usually on a wider circle to contain the prey, until, occasionally, both birds were out of sight having climbed several hundred metres. The Merlin would then return with or without its quarry. Successful ringing attacks involved the Merlin outflying the prey, either closing in on and ultimately catching the tiring prey from below, or managing to climb above the exhausted lark and stooping onto it. Merlins were usually successful against juvenile birds, but against adults the falcon might well become exhausted first and return to the falconer empty-taloned.

However, although ringing flights are seen in the wild, they are not the usual hunting technique. Merlins usually hunt from a perch, chosen to offer a wide view across the hunting range, though the bird will quarter the ground, making fast flights either close to the ground, following its undulations, in open country, or below the tree tops in more wooded areas in the hope of being able to make a surprise attack.

Merlins will also stoop in the manner of Peregrines. Long stoops are rare, though a series of short stoops may be utilised, seemingly as a way of gathering speed or adding surprise to an attack on prey which is proving difficult to overhaul in straight flight. In his study in east Scotland, Cresswell (1996) noted that in winter hunts the Merlins used surprise attacks 62.2% of the time, with ringing flights 29.9% of the time, but noted that ringing often followed a surprise attack which failed to take the prey. Surprise attacks were mainly launched from a perch (83.3% of all attacks) at prey which was usually on the ground (78.3%) and close to the Merlin (60.2% were at < 100 m, 37.0% at 101–500 m). Overall Merlins spent 83% of their time perched and 7% feeding, the remaining time hunting.

One surprise attack which did not result in a ringing flight was seen in Scotland by MacIntyre (1936), who watched a Merlin chase a lark (MacIntyre does not say which species, but probably a Skylark, though at the time Meadow Pipits were often called larks) which chose not to try outclimbing the falcon, but dived beneath a cow, circled over the cow's back and dived beneath the cow again. The Merlin followed, but could not keep up on the second circuit and rose in the air. The lark, now with a little time, settled close the cow's hoof, where it was safe from attack. A similar escape strategy was observed by Boyle (1991), who had a Skylark dive under his car, brushing his leg as it passed, to escape a pursuing Merlin.

Sodhi *et al.* (1991b) record forms of both the main 'open-country' techniques being utilised by urban-dwelling Merlins in Saskatoon. Attacks from perches represented 58% of summer attacks and 95% of those in winter: the winter data are consistent with those of Cresswell (1996) and suggest that Merlins are organising their time budget to minimise energy expenditure at a time when bodily heat loss is maximal, though in a study of wintering Merlins in southwest Scotland, Dickson (1988) found that the falcons hunted primarily by 'low flight' in which the falcon flew fast over the ground at a height of about 1 m in an effort to surprise prey into the air. This mode, which is a high-energy hunt, represented 49% of observed hunts. Dickson also noted perch-hunting (32% of total hunts), the remaining 19% of hunts being higher flights in which the falcon searched the ground for prey. In a separate study, Dickson (1996) again mentions low flying as a hunting technique, but as a form of perch-hunting, implying that such flights are against a predetermined prey observed from a distance of 50–300 m – which, from a point of view of the bird's winter energetics, would make more sense. Dickson (1996) also mentions 'bounce tactics' in which the Merlin makes a downward thrust towards avian prey which has crouched on the ground as a means of defence, the 'bounce' being a technique to force the prey into the air. In addition, Dickson (1996) notes that Merlins will occasionally stalk prey, walking across the ground using vegetation as cover until close enough to pounce. Dickson says his stalking observations represented only 1% of hunts and involved stalks of only 2 m or so, but Fleet (1993) observed a Merlin walk and hop over 30 m in a ground stalk of a Dunlin flock. The Merlin then took to the air for the last 30 m to the flock, where it successfully caught a bird. As strange as stalking on foot is the record of Craib (1994), who looked over a wall to catch a glimpse of a Merlin landing on the ground. Craib saw nothing until the falcon emerged from a Rabbit burrow and flew away after catching sight of him. A few seconds later a juvenile Starling, which the Merlin had clearly pursued into the burrow, emerged. Though apparently carrying a wing injury the Starling flew off. Craib looked into the burrow and was surprised to see a second Starling, which he retrieved by hand, and which flew off uninjured.

One interesting outcome of a study of Merlins in Scotland (Rebecca *et al.* 1990) arose from the collection of leg rings of Golden Plover and Lapwing chicks from three nests (of five under study during 1986–1988) which had been preyed upon by Merlins and fed to their brood. The chicks were aged 4–32 days (with a mean age of 10.3 ± 7.1 days). The mean distance the Merlins flew to take the chicks was 3.4 ± 1.1 km (range 2.0–5.6 km). This is in accord with studies of urban Merlins in Canada which also found that male Merlins did not hunt close to their nests. However, Dickson (2005) observed a female Merlin hunting when the nestlings were 14–15 days old: she caught a Meadow Pipit and fed it to the young. The male brought six prey items in the next three hours and the female cached two of these. Overall the male seemed a good provider, so the reason for the female to hunt was not clear. The female always hunted within 100–200 m of the nest and continued to hunt through to the time the young fledged, often giving her catch to the young, but occasionally taking moths which she consumed. The reason for this behaviour is not apparent, though the fact that the female ate the insects herself suggests she was supplementing her own diet as well as that of her brood.

Another hunting 'technique' must also be mentioned. Uttendörfer (1952) notes that a Merlin will occasionally mimic the flight pattern of its prey in order to close in on it before launching an attack. Rudebeck (1951), whose observations of hunting Merlins include excellent descriptions of the flight pattern (as noted above), mentions a falcon which was flying 'with half folded wings and very rapidly vibrating wing-beats. In flight it resembled a swallow and a thrush.' Rudebeck goes on to say of one hunting Merlin that 'in a quite remarkable way it resembled a swallow, in outline as well as in behaviour. Nearby and at a somewhat lower altitude there were several swallows: they kept quiet and silent and apparently did not recognize the Merlin as a source of danger.' Rudebeck then quotes another observer who twice noted a Merlin 'flying in a very peculiar manner in the midst of a flock of swallows which showed no fear at all'. On each occasion the Merlin was able to take a swallow. This clearly leaves a question – does the flight pattern of the Merlin resemble that of its occasional prey, or does the Merlin deliberately mimic flight patterns in order to get close to prey?

In a study of Merlins wintering near the Tyninghame estuary in East Lothian, Scotland, Cresswell (1996) noted that the Merlins mainly used surprise attacks. Cresswell's study was of three raptors that worked the Scottish site, Merlin, Sparrowhawk and Peregrine, and the differences between them are interesting. He considered the position of the raptor when an attack started (Table 31). For the Peregrine, the falcon was usually in the air when it started an attack (80% of all attacks), whereas Merlins started 82% of attacks from a perch or the ground. (The starting position of the Sparrowhawk was rarely seen and so was not given.) For the Peregrine, in 60% of attacks the prey was not in flight (perched or on the ground) at the start of the attack, while for the Merlin the prey was not in flight for over 80% of attacks, and for the Sparrowhawk the prey was not flying at the start of over 95% of attacks. Cresswell also noted that the start position of both the raptor and the prey differed with different prey species.

Cresswell (1996) found that 50% of Merlin attacks lasted less than one minute (Table 32). Though the hunt durations of the three species are significantly different, with those of the Sparrowhawk being substantially shorter on average,

TABLE 31 Position of raptor and prey at the start of an attack. From Cresswell (1996) for raptor attacks in east Scotland.

Raptor	Prey species	Raptor position		Prey position	
		Air	Perched/ground	Air	Perched/ground
Sparrowhawk	Redshank	–	–	13	464
	Dunlin	–	–	6	74
	Skylark	–	–	14	92
Peregrine	Redshank	108	18	14	105
	Dunlin	42	13	35	28
	Skylark	11	8	17	2
Merlin	Redshank	11	27	2	44
	Dunlin	24	90	13	108
	Skylark	30	178	60	172

TABLE 32 Duration of hunts for three raptors in east Scotland. From Cresswell (1996).

Raptor	<1	1–2	2–3	3–4	>4
			Hunt duration (minutes)		
Sparrowhawk	634	100	22	10	1
Peregrine	83	45	15	9	40
Merlin	171	75	44	17	33

most attacks for all raptors lasted less than one minute. The longest recorded hunts were those of Merlin on Skylarks. Cresswell considered that shorter hunting flights reduced energy input and the risk of injury during the winter season, and hence improved the chances of survival to breed again. Within the one-minute hunt, Cresswell (1996) broke down the actual timings of observed attacks on Skylarks and found that the attack itself lasted less than one second in 41.4% of attacks. For the remaining attacks, the initial surprise failed, and a chase ensued, these lasting 1–10 seconds on 25.4% of occasions, 11–30 seconds on 9.5%, 31–60 seconds on 6.3%, and more than 60 seconds on 17.4% of occasions. Cresswell noted that many of the attacks involved no final stoop, but that longer, ringing flights ended with stoops on 50% of occasions. While it might be assumed that these would be single stoops, which either succeeded or failed, the hunt terminating at that point, Cresswell found that only 38.1% of ringing flights which ended with a stoop involved a single stoop, 30.2% involving 2–5 stoops and 31.8% involving six or more stoops.

The data of Table 32 are consistent with Fig. 245, which derives from the study of Buchanan *et al.* (1988) of Merlins hunting Dunlin in western Washington State.

Overall, Cresswell noted that the Merlin success rate was 10.7%, though the individual rates for different prey differed: Merlins were more successful against Dunlin (14.2%) than Skylarks (12.1%) but had no successes in 48 attacks against Redshank. Cresswell also noted that not all attacks in which the Merlin captured the prey led to a kill, 2 of 19 captured Dunlin and 1 of 31 captured Skylarks escaping; both captured Redshanks got away. The Merlin's overall success rate compares well with that of the other two raptors – Sparrowhawk 10.7%, Peregrine 8.7% (as might be expected, the larger falcon being less able to capture smaller, more agile prey) – but both falcons had a better record of turning captures into kills than the Sparrowhawk, which lost 10 of 75 captured Redshanks (though only 1 of 12 captured Dunlin and none of 3 captured Skylarks).

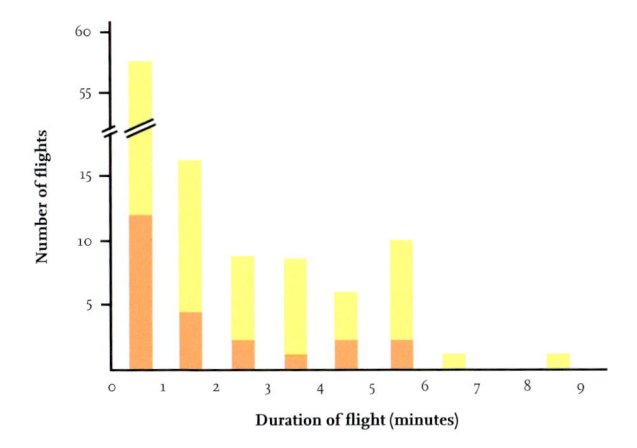

FIG 245. Duration of hunting flights by Merlins in pursuit of Dunlin at an estuary in west Washington State, USA. Red bars represent successful hunts. Note that these data do not differentiate between the various hunting techniques adopted by the Merlins, a hunting flight being defined solely as one which involved an attempt, or several attempts, at capture of one or more prey individuals. Redrawn from Buchanan *et al.* 1988.

The successes rate noted by Cresswell (1996) compared well with an earlier study at the same site (Cresswell & Whitfield 1994) which noted 8.8% success for Merlins, 11.6% for Sparrowhawks and 6.8% for Peregrines averaged across three winters (Note 7.2). What was striking about the earlier study was the damage inflicted on the local wader population. In the winter of 1991/92 Dunlin mortality was 21.2% of the population, Snipe mortality was 25.0%, while the Redshank population was reduced by 57.3%. Most of the waders killed were juveniles, Cresswell & Whitfield suggesting that this was, in part, due to their exclusion from low-risk feeding areas: around 90% of the juvenile Redshank population was killed during the 1991/92 winter. Cresswell & Whitfield suggested that the high mortality figures were due, in part, to kleptoparasitism of the raptors by Carrion Crows. Overall the crows took 24.5% of all kills: Sparrowhawks were the most sorely affected, with Cresswell & Whitfield suggesting that an individual raptor might need to catch 50% more prey than necessary for survival as a consequence of crow piracy.

These Scottish success rates for Merlins are consistent with those measured in North America (see Sale 2015 and references therein). One interesting outcome of North American studies was the observation by Dekker (1988) that male Merlins were more successful hunters than females.

The low success rate implies good defence mechanisms by the potential quarry. One obvious defence is flocking. Buchanan *et al.* (1988) noted three

420 · FALCONS

FIG 246. Evidence of Merlin prey plucking below a fence post (a) and on a moorland boulder (b). In each case the victim was a Meadow Pipit.

flocking defence techniques of Dunlin. In flashing flight the Dunlin changed direction or tilted their bodies synchronously so that the dark upper and pale lower side were flashed successively. In rippling flight the body movements were not synchronous, a wave of movement passing through the flock. Finally, in columnar flight the flock rose in a 'tornado-like vertical column'. Combinations of the techniques also occurred: in all cases both flashing and rippling might be observed. The various techniques presumably confuse the predator, and each seems successful: flashing, which was used in 64% of attacks, had an 85% success rate at avoiding a Merlin attack; flashing and rippling occurred in 28% of attacks and had a 91% success rate; a combination of columnar flight, flashing and rippling occurred in 8% of attacks and had a success rate of 71%. Boyce (1985), in a winter study at Humboldt Bay, California, added a further dimension to anti-predator tactics of flocks. He noted that often a Merlin would knock a prey individual (Dunlin was again the main target) into the water rather than capturing it, or occasionally the Dunlin would deliberately dive into the water to escape capture. If the Dunlin survived being hit and could still dive as the Merlin came around in an effort to catch it, the wader might survive, and on occasions Boyce saw a Dunlin dive to escape capture, and as the Merlin slowed in order to return to seize the wader from the surface, the flock wheeled around and positioned itself over the water-bound bird, shielding it from the Merlin and giving it a chance to return to the flock. Often this tactic succeeded, though if the downed bird was injured it obviously did not. In other circumstances, Merlins have been observed taking prey from the water: Duncan (1990) reports a Merlin capturing a Dipper 30 m from shore above a Scottish loch, then (accidentally) dropping the prey and circling to retrieve it from the water surface.

Other defensive tactics by potential prey have also been observed. Both Buchanan (1996) and Dekker (1998) in North America noted that Dunlin remained airborne when their intertidal feeding grounds were underwater. Buchanan (1996) also noted that when at sea the Dunlin engaged in synchronised flights in the troughs between waves. Prey also seem to be least vulnerable when they are feeding at low tides – many eyes to watch for predators – and most vulnerable when roosting – fewer eyes watching – and when the tide begins to ebb. In a study in North America, Dekker & Ydenburg (2004) noted that the kill rate of Dunlins was highest at this time, the waders returning to feed then being closest to shoreline vegetation and so most vulnerable to surprise attack.

If flocks are such a successful anti-predation strategy, then it would be anticipated that Merlin attacks on flocking birds would be limited, but in his Scottish studies Cresswell (1996) found that all three raptors attacked larger flocks of Dunlin more frequently than would have been expected by chance (Fig. 247). This suggests that although a large flock enhances the chance of an individual bird surviving a raptor attack, it also improves the raptor's chance of a kill. But Cresswell's data did not support the idea that the raptor's chances of a kill were improved, as for both Merlins and Sparrowhawks the attack success rate was better against small flocks (defined as 1–10 birds) than against larger ones (11–200 birds); for Peregrines the success rate was similar. However, the difference in capture rates for the two smaller raptors between small and large flocks was not significant, so the result is not counterintuitive (i.e. it does not necessarily imply that raptors appear to consider that having more targets improves the likelihood of a kill even though defence strategies by flocks are successful, an idea which

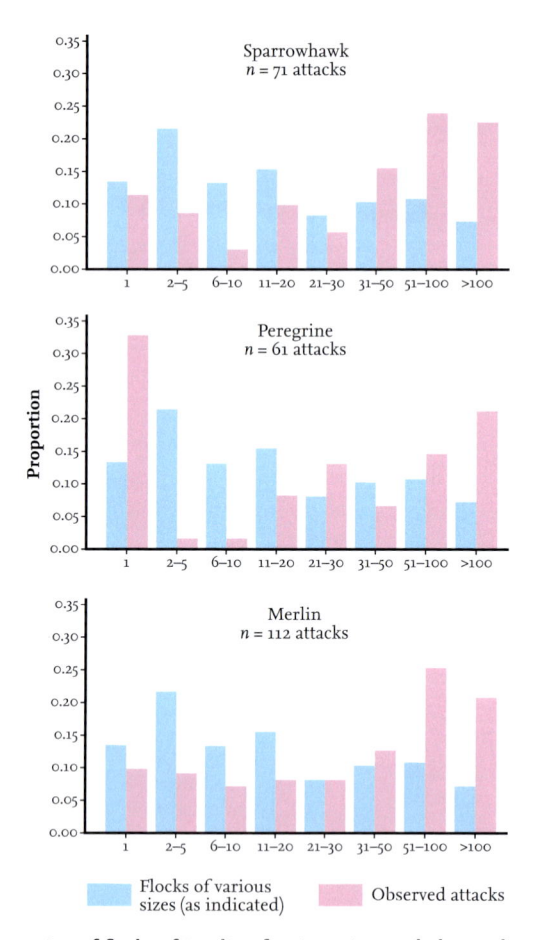

FIG 247. Proportion of flocks of Dunlin of various sizes and observed attacks for three raptors in east Scotland. The data for attacks on Skylarks (Cresswell 1994) followed the same general pattern, though Skylark flocks tended to be very much smaller. Redrawn from Cresswell 1996.

would imply that raptor attack strategies are not influenced by experience). The more likely explanations are that raptors attack larger flocks because this increases their chances of spotting a weak bird, and that flocking as a defence has its limitations, particularly for species such as Dunlin which are less successful at maintaining close separation and the cooperation needed for complete safety. Invariably some birds are left at the periphery of the flock where they are vulnerable to attack.

Attacking wintering wader flocks has other drawbacks. Buchanan (1996) observed three occasions on which Merlins hit the water before pulling out of a stoop, as did three Peregrines: Buchanan does not say whether the falcons survived, though the implication of there being no mention of the outcome is that all six birds did.

Flocking is one form of defence against predation, but prey species have other alternatives. One obvious one is that they can seek cover, either by crouching on the ground or, for waders, by diving. Cresswell (1993) noted these strategies, as well as outflying the predator, by observing the escape responses of Redshanks under attack by Merlins, Peregrines and Sparrowhawks in eastern Scotland. He noted that 22% of Redshanks which crouched were captured by attacking Merlins, while all waders which flew or dived escaped capture. For the other two predators the figures were 8% capture if flying, 20% if diving and 91% if crouching (Sparrowhawk), and 14% flying, 2% crouching or diving (Peregrine). However, it should be noted that very many more Sparrowhawk attacks than either Peregrine or Merlin attacks were observed – for instance, over 500 Redshank responses to Sparrowhawk attacks were observed, compared to about 150 for Peregrines and only about 50 for Merlins. What was clear, however, despite the difference in numbers of observed attacks, was that the Redshanks were altering their escape behaviour dependent on which predator attacked: the risk of capture in crouching when under attack by Sparrowhawks meant that 86% of attacked Redshanks flew, only 4% crouching. For Peregrine attacks the higher risk of aerial capture meant that over 60% of Redshanks chose to crouch or dive. Similarly, most Redshanks attacked by Merlins flew rather than crouching. Another escape strategy noted by Cresswell in a separate study was the use of song as an indication to the predator that the individual prey bird is in good condition, presumably in the hope that the predator will become disheartened and give up the pursuit (Cresswell 1994). Cresswell studied the interaction of Merlins and Skylarks during winters on the Tyninghame estuary in East Lothian, Scotland. When attacked, a Skylark might not sing, sing poorly, or sing well. Cresswell's data show that both the Merlin's chase time of a prey bird and the capture rate varied significantly depending on the Skylark's singing behaviour (Fig. 248).

Note that although Fig. 248a implies that Merlins preferentially attack a birds which can sing, either well or poorly, the Skylark will not start to sing until it is attacked, so the Merlin has no prior knowledge of the singing abilities of the bird until it attacks it, as Skylarks are normally silent in winter. The relative frequencies of attack are therefore more a measure of the overall condition of local Skylarks than of the Merlin's ability to choose its victim, particularly as Cresswell found no apparent difference in the flocking ability of Skylarks

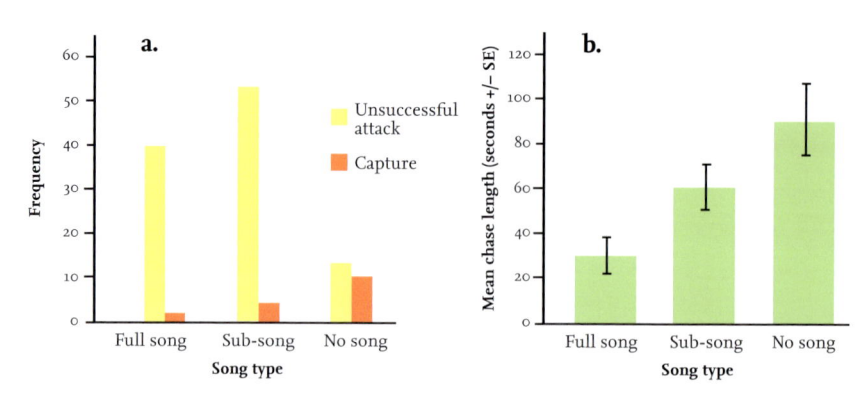

FIG 248. (a) Frequency of capture by Merlins of Skylarks with differing song types. (b) Length of time of Merlin chases of Skylarks with different song types. Redrawn from Cresswell 1994.

based on their ability to sing. That singing is an anti-predation strategy was apparent not only from the statistics of Merlin attacks (i.e. that they were less likely to pursue a singing Skylark) but from the deployment of singing against differing predators. Skylarks do not sing when attacked by Sparrowhawks. The Sparrowhawks have broader, shorter wings, a shape which is most efficient at lower speeds. In contrast, the Merlin wing is better adapted to both faster and more sustained flight. If chased by a Sparrowhawk, the Skylark's best defence is therefore to save its energy and to outfly the raptor, but when pursued by a Merlin, it is better to try to persuade the raptor to give up.

If the Merlin attacked a flock several birds might sing, but by that time the Merlin would have chosen its intended victim, usually a bird, or one of several, marginally detached from the flock. Once attacked, the Skylark would start to sing (if it was going to sing) when the Merlin was within about 10 m. While singing is not overly energy-intensive, singing while being pursued will inevitably result in the bird either slowing or becoming exhausted sooner, either of which enhances the likelihood of capture and so is a dangerous strategy. A bird which can therefore sing, and especially one which can sing a full territory-claim song, is clearly signalling its condition – I have energy to spare, chase someone else: Cresswell's data show that Merlins respond by calling off the chase of full-singing birds early.

Concerned that other variables might be affecting the Skylark's decision to sing or not, Cresswell looked at the effect of ambient temperature on Skylark response to Merlin attack. He found that in November, a mild month, 20% of Skylarks were caught on the ground, but that this rate rose to 60% in the colder months of December and January. As lower temperatures were likely to affect the condition of the Skylarks, this marked difference implies that singing is indeed a defence strategy, as any bird which could sing would prefer to risk the chase than to rely on cryptic plumage.

In his study of Merlin, Peregrine and Sparrowhawk attacks in east Scotland Cresswell (1996) also noted the behaviour of the three raptors in attempts to capture prey by surprise. If an attack fails, the raptors have two choices as a consequence of the failed attempt having alerted the local prey to danger: either moving to another area or waiting until the vigilance of the prey has declined to a point where surprise becomes a possibility again. Cresswell found that, in general, within 3–5 minutes Redshank had relaxed to the point where a renewed attack would have the same element of surprise as an initial attack. In addition, because Merlins (and Sparrowhawks) are relatively small raptors with limited hunting ranges (in comparison to Peregrines, which fly greater distances in search of prey) they needed to move only about 100–200 m in order to reach an area where they could mount a surprise attack on a different prey population, one not spooked into extra vigilance by an earlier attack. The Merlins could therefore choose to wait a short time, or move a short distance. However, either strategy only works if there is no other Merlin in the area, and Cresswell noted during his study that on 97% of the occasions he saw two Merlins, one was chasing the other, apparently confirming the idea that to maintain surprise a Merlin must attempt to preserve sole hunting rights to a wintering area.

Once captured, the standard way for falcons to dispatch prey is with a bite to the back of the neck. Limited observation of Merlins suggests that this is the technique employed against smaller prey. However, a famous English book on falconry (Salvin & Brodrick 1855) suggests that for larger birds the Merlin clutches the prey's throat, killing by suffocation.

Food consumption and energy balance

Although studies comparable to those undertaken on Kestrels at the University of Groningen have not been carried out on Merlins, the urban Merlins of Saskatoon have been the subject of some fine experimental work (Warkentin & West 1990). Nine captive Merlins (five males and four females) were subjected to tests to establish the metabolic rates of resting, preening and other activities, while nine wild Merlins (six females and three males) were captured and radio-tagged so that their daily time budget could be computed. The caloric value of the prey both sets of falcons were consuming was also measured by calorimeter analysis of specimens. The time budget for the wild falcons is shown in Table 33. Warkentin & West calculated the basal metabolic rate (BMR) of a thermoneutral falcon and

TABLE 33 Time budget of wintering Merlins in Saskatoon. From Warkentin & West (1990).

	Resting at perch: mean (range)	Alert at perch: mean (range)	Eating: mean (range)	Preening: mean (range)	Flight: mean (range)
Female Merlins					
(a) as % of 24-hour day	60.5 (51.6–65.5)	34.2 (32.9–35.6)	3.1 (1.5–4.0)	1.3 (1.0–1.9)	0.9 (0.6–1.5)
(b) as % of active phases	0.0	86.5 (83.3–90.0)	7.9 (3.7–10.2)	3.3 (2.6–4.8)	2.3 (1.4–3.9)
Male Merlins					
(a) as % of 24-hour day	59.6 (54.6–64.5)	34.1 (31.2–38.3)	2.4 (0.6–4.8)	2.7 (1.1–3.0)	1.2 (0.4–1.8)
(b) as % of active phases	0.0	84.4 (77.3–94.7)	5.9 (1.6–12.0)	6.6 (2.6–7.5)	3.1 (1.1–4.5)

1. Figures in parentheses below each mean value are the range of observed percentages. Ranges are wider for male birds because of the smaller sample size.
2. The percentages of active phases are very similar for male and female Merlins, and are not statistically different, apart from the larger time fraction spent in body care by male Merlins. This could imply that male birds are more fastidious, but is more likely to arise from the small male sample group.
3. It is not correct to assume that during the resting phase the falcons are idle. Warkentin & West found it took a Merlin about 30 minutes to ingest a House Sparrow and another 45–60 minutes to empty the crop, so much of the resting phase is actually digestion. As the experiments were carried out in winter it is, however, also the case that the birds were minimising energy expenditure.

the energy costs of the various activities in Table 33. They calculated that flight required 7.4 times the BMR.

Warkentin & West were also able to estimate the prey consumption required to keep Saskatoon's resident Merlins – 38 at the time of the experiments – alive during the harsh winters experienced by the city: during the 120-day winter period the researchers calculated that if the falcons consumed only House Sparrows they would need to catch 7,524. They also found that on days of extreme cold (down to –30 °C on occasions) the city's Merlins were needing to catch and eat as many sparrows as they could, given the time required for flying, consuming and digesting: the falcons were essentially living at their ambient temperature limit.

In a separate experiment on the Saskatoon Merlins, Sodhi (1993) trapped wild males and radio-tagged them to assess the hours they spent flying during the breeding season (Fig. 249). As the breeding season advances, the male's duty increases, as seen by the increase in percentage time spent flying. What is interesting from Fig. 283 is that as the duration of hunting trips increases through the phases of breeding, the number of hunting trips rises from the incubation to the nestling phase, but then falls – longer hunting flights mean fewer can be made. In another study, the fraction of time the male spent flying in the phases of breeding was computed: 30.9 ± 2.3% of daylight hours during the incubation phase of breeding, rising to 57.5 ± 4.3% during the nestling phase, and to 70.8 ± 3.9% during the fledgling phase (Sodhi *et al.* 2005). It was noted that males in prey-rich territories spent fewer hours flying, confirming the idea that territory ownership is critical.

The energy consumption data of Merlins calculated by Warkentin & West (1990) and the flight data from the reports of Sodhi (1993, Sodhi *et al.* 2005) are

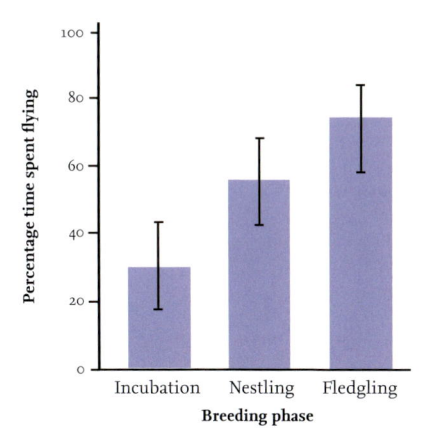

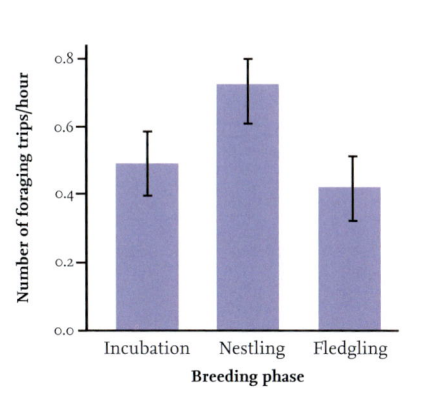

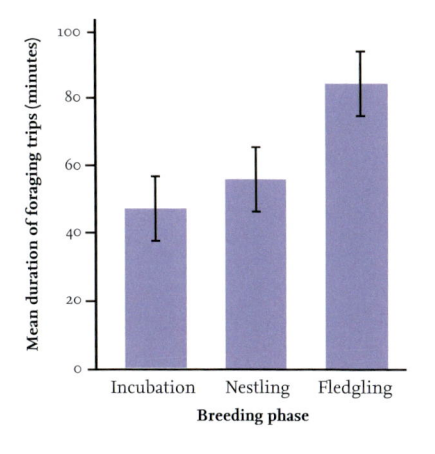

FIG 249. Hunting flights by male urban-breeding Merlins in Canada through the phases of the breeding season. Each bar of the histograms represents the mean for all males observed during each phase, together with standard errors. Redrawn from Sodhi 1993.

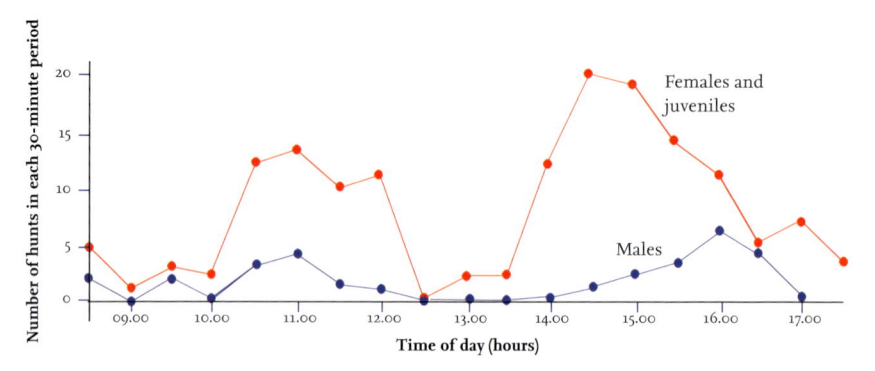

FIG 250. Hunting times of Merlins wintering in Galloway. Redrawn from Dickson 1993.

comparable to those found by the Groningen group for Kestrels. It is therefore reasonable to assume that weight changes similar to those experienced by Kestrels (see Fig. 132) will also be experienced by Merlins.

Research on the Saskatoon Merlins also found that wintering falcons preferentially hunted early in the morning and late in the afternoon, as might be expected by birds needing to prepare for a long, cold night and to replenish energy levels after experiencing one. A similar hunting pattern was noted by Dickson (1993) for Merlins wintering in Galloway (Fig. 250).

TERRITORY

As with many raptors, there is a difference between a pair's territory and their hunting range, the latter often being larger (sometimes much larger), though never smaller. In their study of Asian Merlins, Morozov *et al.* (2013) explicitly point out the difference between the two, noting that in their studies Merlins had an area around their nests which was rigorously defended, and within which an intruder would always be attacked. Normally this area would be 200–300 m in all directions, but could be as little as 50 m in some cases. However, defining territory solely on the basis of intruder distance probably underestimates the actual size, as Merlins will pursue intruders to boundary edges they perceive around their nests and will also attack intruders at greater distances if they come within these boundaries, so that while there may well be a reduced area around the nest in which defensive action is heightened, there will be a wider area over which defence is maintained. Defining territory can also be complicated by other factors. For instance, in studies of the urban Merlins of Saskatoon, it was found that there were fewer conflicts between adjacent males than had been anticipated (Sodhi & Oliphant 1992), which the researchers considered was due to three factors. Firstly, the high breeding density of the urban falcons may have made range defence costly in terms of time and energy expenditure; secondly, local prey was abundant and its population was stable, reducing the potential benefits of exclusivity; and thirdly, the prey (small birds) was mobile and mostly taken in surprise attacks, which meant that defending a particular area was not worthwhile.

In their study of Merlins in northern England, Newton et al. (1978) noted that Merlins frequently flew further to hunt than the minimum distance between nests, while in a study in two Swedish national parks (Padjelanta and Stora Sjöfallet), Wiklund & Larsson (1994) found that hunting ranges could be twice the pair's territory, the latter averaging about 2 km^2. The latter figure is significantly larger than that quoted by Morozov et al. (2013), but this could arise as a result of the differing definitions of territory. The Swedish data also suggest a very good hunting area, and in general hunting ranges and territories are likely to be larger in most areas. In a study in southwest Scotland, Orchel (1992) calculated the minimum area of grass and heather moorland required to support a breeding pair of Merlins as 20 km^2, a figure which is comparable to those derived for rural areas of North America.

BREEDING

Pair formation
Merlins are considered to be monogamous, or largely so, though both Newton (1979) and Cosnette (1991) in Britain and Sodhi (1989) in North America present data suggesting that polygyny occurs. Newton (1979) reports the observation of another who saw a male Merlin visiting more than one nest site with no other male apparently present while Cosnette (1991) saw two females with nests close together with only one male Merlin apparently in the area. Later a 'combined' group of three juveniles was seen together, one about eight days younger than the other two, which were being fed by both females with no signs of aggression between them: the single male was seen passing prey to one of the females. In a study of urban-dwelling Merlins in Saskatoon, Sodhi (1989) watched a male Merlin (colour-marked so there was no doubting that it was the same bird) maintain two nest sites 450 m apart, making prey transfers to each and copulating with the females at the different sites. However, the attempt to raise two families failed: the male apparently deserted one nest,

and the female deserted a few days later. At the other nest four chicks were successfully raised. There is also evidence of extra-pair copulation (See *Copulation*, below).

Both first-year male and female Merlins can breed, but in a study in northeast Scotland using DNA profiling to identify individual falcons, Marsden (2002) found that while females often did breed in their first year, males did not. Marsden recorded the average age of first breeding as 1.3 ± 0.1 years for females and 2.3 ± 0.1 years for males. These figures are consistent with those from a study of urban Merlins in Saskatoon, where Lieske *et al.* (1997) calculated that the average age of Merlins at first breeding was 1.3 ± 0.6 years for females and 1.9 ± 0.7 years for males. As fractions of the population, they found that 27–37% of males bred in their first year, but almost all had bred by their second year; about 80% of females bred in their first year. The percentage of males breeding in their first year is surprisingly high in comparison to other falcon species, and also in comparison to data from Northumberland, where Newton *et al.* (1986) found 18% of pairs including a first-year female in a study which lasted across nine years, while only 8–9% of pairs included a first-year male over the same period. Lieske *et al.* (1997) found no evidence that first-year breeders were less successful than older falcons, which is surprising when viewed against data from other falcon species. There is, though, evidence of third birds assisting at nests, which many interpret as males gaining the experience necessary for successful breeding (see also the comments on the breeding age difference between the sexes in Chapter 2).

Before leaving mate selection, it is worth recalling that juvenile male Merlins are very similar to females in plumage, a trait which is mirrored, for instance, in the Kestrel and which has led to a discussion of whether the coloration endows the young male with a reproductive advantage – see the work of Hakkarainen *et al.* (1993), discussed in Chapter 5.

Displays

More display flights have been identified in North American Merlins than in those of Eurasia. Indeed, the work of Feldsine & Oliphant (1985), based on observations in Saskatoon, Canada, is unsympathetic towards the comment by Cramp & Simmons (1980) that display flights (of Eurasian Merlins) are 'rather inconspicuous and rarely observed', noting that 'the Merlins we observed regularly performed complex aerial displays that were nothing short of awesome.' Working on urban-dwelling Merlins in Saskatoon, Feldsine & Oliphant noted a whole series of display flights, many of which (though not all) I have seen myself, not only in North America but in Iceland, Britain and Fennoscandia.

At the start of the breeding season, male display flights are used to define and advertise their territory, both to rival males and potential mates. The main display flight used by the male at this time is a fast flight with strong wing-beats during which he rocks from side to side in order to flash his underwings, while making occasional '*chip*' calls. Feldsine & Oliphant (1985) call this power flying. During the display the male may also dive steeply and quickly, pulling out of the dive in a sharp upward turn. Feldsine & Oliphant call this power diving, and also note a rocking glide, similar to power flying but without the strong wing-beats.

Once a female has become interested, the male makes conspicuous short flights from perch to perch around his territory making the '*kee-kee-kee*' call frequently, presumably advertising that he possesses a territory of sufficient size and prey potential to be worth considering. The male may also make flights in the direction of possible nest sites, often hovering above the site or making slow circles above it. Once a female has shown an interest the two birds may chase each other around the territory, taking turns at chasing and being chased. In a communal winter roost in Scotland, Dickson (1973) noted that two or three birds, usually a male with one or two females or juveniles, would frequently engage in aerial chases soon after leaving the roost, or in the evening before returning to the roost. Keeping close together, the birds would climb high, then dive through the wooded roost thicket, before repeating the performance, all the time calling loudly. Occasionally, at the top of a climb, two birds would stall and briefly touch talons. The display lasted anything from a minute or two to almost 30 minutes. Dickson, almost certainly correctly, considered the activity an exercise in pair bonding.

Once the pair is formed, the two birds perform the main courtship display, which is similar to that of other small falcons, the two birds circling high above the proposed nest site with a specific wing action similar to the *Zitterflug* of the Kestrel (see Chapter 5). The male usually interrupts the shivering wing-beats with slower beats and makes the '*chip*' call, the female often replying with the standard '*kee-kee-kee*', but sometimes making a curious whistling call.

The passing of food between male and female is the final stage of pair formation, the female makes the begging call to her mate to initiate food passes. Food passes may take place in the air, but more frequently are made at a perch, usually foot to foot, but occasionally bill to bill. Nest-site selection now follows. Simms (1975) reported seeing male and female Merlins touching talons during what he had assumed were to be food passes because of prior calling, but in which no food was passed. This behaviour, which Simms observed several times over a period of years, suggests that the birds may use 'food passing' close approaches to reinforce the pair bond even if no food is actually involved. (Simms also saw a close approach between two male Merlins which might have involved talon-locking: if so, this would appear to have been extreme aggression in territory defence.)

Although the male clearly prospects suitable nest sites and invites the female to view them, it is not clear that he actually chooses the site rather than making suggestions. Nest viewing is usually accompanied by a great deal of calling by both birds. Often the female will take the brooding position at several sites (Nethersole-Thompson & Nethersole-Thompson 1943) before a final decision is made, that decision seemingly being the female's alone. Once the decision is made, the pair may then reinforce their bond by making displays at the nest, the male making the '*chip*' call while standing at the nest with a fanned tail and drooping wings. The birds may also bow to each other at the nest site or engage in bill nibbling.

Nest sites

Across their range Merlins breed in stick nests (usually of corvids), tree holes, old buildings, on cliff ledges and on the ground. In Britain, Merlins utilise old stick nests, isolated boulders and cliff ledges, but despite the existence of terrestrial predators – Red Fox, Badger (*Meles meles*) and various mustelids – most nests are on the ground, usually a scrape made in the soil amongst thick vegetation on sloping ground, particularly towards the head of a small valley, which allows the incubating bird an open view. The female will occasionally collect small pieces of vegetation to form a sparse lining. One fascinating variation occurs in Shetland. There Hooded Crows occasionally build stick nests on the ground, the islands being free of mammalian predators (apart from feral cats, domestic dogs, Brown Rat – found on all inhabited islands – Hedgehogs (*Erinaceus europaeus*) – introduced in the nineteenth century and now relatively common on inhabited islands – Stoats – introduced to Mainland in the seventeenth century – and the occasional Otter (*Lutra lutra*)), and Merlins have been known to use these stick nests, a combination of stick nest and ground nesting that appears unique to the islands. Formerly in Wales, Merlins nested on coastal sand dunes at the base of Marram Grass (*Ammophila arenaria*) tussocks: such nests were relatively common at one time but are infrequent or no longer found there now.

Across most of Britain, nests are on upland moor. In a study in Northumberland, Newton *et al.* (1978) found that of 91 observed nests 25.3% were in trees, 6.6% on crag or boulder tops, 3.3% on cliff ledges and 64.8% on the ground, where nests were concealed among the abundant Heather (*Calluna vulgaris*): Merlins avoid nesting among Bracken (*Pteridium aquilinum*). Of the ground sites, 83% were on sloping ground. Newton and co-workers noted that 94% of tree nests and 75% of boulder-top nests fledged at least one nestling. Among ground nests, success was 68% for sloping ground, 78% for flat ground. However, data from Wales are at variance with these data, Williams & Parr (1995) finding that the breeding success of ground nests was higher than that of tree nests. In 1993 ground nests had a mean clutch of 4.3 ± 0.5 eggs, which produced a mean brood size of 3.3 ± 0.7 nestlings and 2.0 ± 1.0 fledglings. The figures for tree nests were 3.9 ± 0.7 eggs producing 3.2 ± 1.0 nestlings and 1.5 ± 0.5 fledglings. Though the reason for either complete or partial nest failure was not known in the majority of cases, where it was known (30%) predation was the cause. Four ground nests were preyed upon by Foxes, one by an avian predator, but while no tree nests succumbed to a Fox, six fell to avian predators, principally Goshawk and Tawny Owl.

The ground-nest success data are curious, as it would be assumed that ground sites are more vulnerable to all predators, but as many Merlins nest on moorland managed for grouse shooting, terrestrial predators are controlled and so have lower population densities and, consequently, pose a lower risk.

FIG 251. Chicks at a Merlin ground nest in northeast England.

FIG 252. Well-feathered Merlin nestlings in a basket nest in southern Scotland. This is the same basket as in Fig. 242. The nestlings were now occasionally leaving the basket to 'branch-walk', but always returned for feeding.

However, it is not all good news: control of raptors by shooting or poisoning is illegal, but sadly it does continue and Merlins are likely to suffer as a consequence, although in reality the risk Merlins pose to adult game birds is minimal, and while they do take chicks if the opportunity arises, the numbers involved are probably small.

Ground nests are, however, at risk of predation and may also be trampled by sheep, though the protection offered by thick vegetation, which means the nests are well-hidden, and by the remoteness of sites, goes some way to offsetting this vulnerability. But despite the risks Merlins continue to prefer ground nesting. In a study of 717 nest sites from across Britain in 1993–1994, Rebecca (2011) found 78% were on the ground, with 20% in stick nests in trees and 2% on rock outcrops. Of the stick nests, almost all were in tall conifers. More recently Merlins have been using artificial nests placed in trees. Rebecca's numbers would suggest Merlins are preferentially choosing ground nest sites in Britain rather than having ground nesting imposed on them by the lack of available trees in preferred hunting areas. However, in his work in southwest Scotland, Orchel (1992) noted that conifer planting had altered the nesting habits of the Merlins

FIG 253. Merlin chicks in a stick nest constructed by Buzzards.

there. In the period 1960–1976, 30 of 31 Merlin nests were on the ground (97%), but as planting accelerated the percentage changed. In 1977–1985, 71% were on the ground, the remainder in trees, and by 1986–1987 only 15% were on the ground, with 85% in trees.

Wright (2005) found that most of his nest sites in Yorkshire were at altitudes of 300–350 m, but some were above 500 m, which in British terms is high, and none were below about 200 m. In Wales some Merlins nest to 650 m (Williams & Parr 1995), while the falcons have nested up to 800 m in the Grampian peaks of northeast Scotland (Rebecca *et al.* 1992). In a study of nest sites across Britain in 1993–1994, Rebecca (2011) found that Merlins nested across an altitudinal range of 10–650 m, both the highest and lowest nests being found in Scotland.

Ireland's Merlins show a similar elevation ceiling. In the Wicklow Mountains McElheron (2005) found nest sites from about 220 m to just over 500 m. The Merlins were almost exclusively utilising the nests of Hooded Crows, which preferentially build in oaks or Scots Pine in mixed woodland, or Sitka Spruce (*Picea sitchensis*) in conifer plantations. Ground nesting sites were known, but were in a minority (< 10%).

Breeding density

In Northumberland, Newton et al. (1978) measured average inter-nest distances of 1.0–1.6 km, though with some up to 4.8 km apart, and noted that in the greater nest separations the intervening land had no suitable alternative sites. It therefore appears that breeding density is influenced by nest-site availability. In studies of the urban-dwelling Merlins of Saskatoon, Sodhi et al. (1992) noted that the Merlin population in the city had initially increased exponentially after the first arrivals, then slowed and finally stopped at 31 pairs. As the city was well endowed with available corvid nest sites, it seems that prey availability had become limiting. Merlin breeding may therefore be limited by the availability of both nest sites and prey. In his study of Merlins in southeast Yorkshire, Wright (2005) measured the closest separation at 350 m, with the furthest separation 4.74 km and a mean of 1.75 ± 1.07 km.

Wright (2005) also measured the orientation of the nests in his study areas. Orientation in this context was defined by the most open aspect of a nest placed on a slope. In several of the study areas the local topography meant that most sites were orientated to the south. However, in an area in which the topography allowed the Merlins a choice of either a north- or south-facing site, the chosen sites showed an equal number in each direction. This strongly suggests that the bird chooses a nest site with reference only to the openness of the view from it, rather than for any reason based on wind direction or sun position. In Northumberland, Newton et al. (1978) calculated densities of 3–13 pairs/100 km^2 over the years of study (1974–1978) with a mean of about 8 pairs/100 km^2, while the average breeding density measured across the study areas of Wright (2005) over the 18-year period 1983–2002 (excluding 2001, when access to the areas was prohibited because of an outbreak of foot-and-mouth disease) was 10 pairs/100 km^2. However, the two areas covered by these studies were 'prime' Merlin habitat. Another 'prime' Merlin area is the Isle of Lewis in the Hebrides, off Scotland's west coast, where there are no terrestrial predators to worry the ground-nesting falcons. In a study of Merlins there in 2003 and 2005 Rae (2010b) found a breeding density of 6 pairs/100 km^2, the nest sites being spaced at a mean distance of 2.4 km (range 1.4–5.8 km). At a 'prime' site in Wales (moorland in the northeast of the Principality) Roberts & Jones (1999) found a density of 5 pairs/100 km^2 over the period 1983–1997.

In a study of Britain as a whole, Bibby & Nattrass (1986) concluded that a breeding density as high as 5–10 pairs/100 km^2 was seen in areas of suitable habitat, but these were rarely extensive, so overall densities were lower: as an example they quoted a value of 1.7–2.2 pairs/100 km^2 for the central Highlands of Scotland, a figure which accords well with the 2.3 pairs/100 km^2 calculated for the moorland of the north of England as a whole (Nattrass et al. 1993). In a study across Ireland covering the period 1986–1992, Norriss et al. (2010) found breeding densities varying from 1.22 to 5.89 pairs/100 km².

These densities are consistent with those seen in Iceland, over much of the Eurasian range of the falcon, and in non-urban North America, but higher densities are seen. In their study of Merlins in two Swedish national parks (Padjelanta and Stora Sjöfallet), Wiklund & Larsson (1994) found an area of 12 km × 5 km in a valley which held 15 breeding pairs, implying a breeding density of 25 pairs/100 km² and suggesting a habitat that was extremely rich in prey resource; considering the entire area of the parks, Wiklund (1995) found an average breeding density of 4.75 pairs/100 km². In rural Alberta, Canada, Smith (1978) found a breeding density of 20 pairs/100 km², while Sodhi et al. (1992) found 25.4 pairs/100 km² for the urban Merlins of Saskatoon.

Copulation

Copulation often follows a food pass and may be initiated by either bird. The male may show his enthusiasm by staring at the female and, once he has her attention, bowing, fanning his tail and making the '*chip*' call. Alternatively, the female may show her readiness by bowing and fanning her tail to the male. Feldsine & Oliphant (1985) note that the male may also perch close to the female and make the '*kee-kee-kee*' call or a single '*chip*', and that during a bout of staring at the female may make the '*chrrr*' call, then 'flutter fly' towards her.

In one British pair of Merlins, Stubbert (1943) noted that the two birds chased each other up and down a tree branch for ten minutes, each moving sideways with down-spread tails, occasionally jumping up and fluttering on partly raised wings ('in the manner of cocks fighting') before eventually copulating.

Once copulation has been agreed, the female bends forward, fans her wings and raises her tail, moving it to one side as the male mounts her. The male beats his wings rapidly and fans his tail to maintain position and usually gives the '*kee-kee-kee*' call, the female responding with '*chip*' calls. Copulation takes 5–10 seconds and is repeated throughout the breeding season. In a study of Merlins in southwest Scotland, Dickson (1994) noted only three of 22 copulations (13.6%) occurring after a food pass, but ten of the 22 (45.5%) occurred before or after a nest visit by either sex. This suggests that one theory of sex in falcons, the *copulation trading* hypothesis, which posits that males feed females to stop them going to other males, and females offer copulation in exchange, does not apply to Merlins, but rather supports the *social bond* hypothesis which sees sex as a pair-bonding strategy. Support for this comes from studies of the urban Merlin population in Saskatoon, where copulation was also seen during winter, seemingly acting as cement to the pair bond of birds which wintered together. For further information on the hypotheses relating to Merlin copulation see Sale (2015).

After copulation, the birds observed by Stubbert (1943) flew up, with wings almost touching, to a height of 150–180 m, then turned simultaneously and swooped down, one above the other at great speed to tree-top level before turning upwards again and repeating the performance; the total post-copulation display lasted about an hour. However, while Stubbert's display must have been a joy to behold, most observers must be content with the birds enjoying a post-coital preening session.

Extra-pair copulations, or attempted copulations, were observed by Sodhi (1991) in the urban-dwelling Merlins of Saskatoon. However, Marsden (2002) found no evidence of polygyny in a study in northeast Scotland by DNA sampling. In another study in Saskatoon, Warkentin *et al.* (1994) also found no evidence of extra-pair fertilisation, nor any evidence of intraspecific brood parasitism, i.e. the dumping of eggs by one female Merlin into the nest of another female.

Egg laying

With such a large range, in terms of both circumpolar distribution and latitude, and therefore differences in climatic conditions, it is not surprising that the date of laying of the first egg varies across the globe, from mid/late April through to late May. However, in studies in southeast Yorkshire, England from 1983 to 2002, Wright (2005) recorded first-egg dates between 21 April and 6 June (Fig. 254), a variation which virtually covers the entire global range of observed first-egg dates.

In a study by Espie *et al.* (2000) of the urban-dwelling Merlins of Saskatoon, it was noted that hatching date was positively correlated with the age of both male and female parents (Fig. 255). The advantages of early egg laying, and consequently early hatching, are clear. Merlins time their breeding so that juvenile birds of

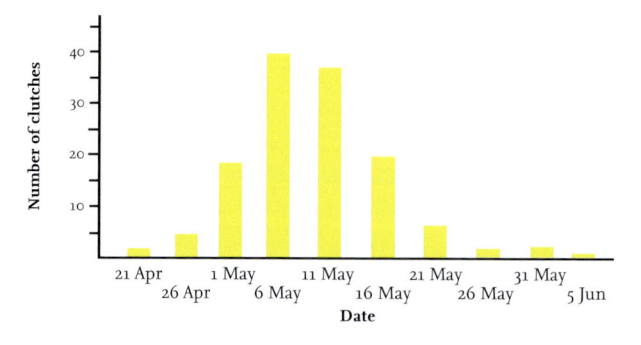

FIG 254. Variation of laying date in Merlin: first-egg dates in a study area in southeast Yorkshire from 1983–2002. Redrawn from Wright 2005.

prey species are abundant during the late nestling/fledging phase of their own cycle. This has two advantages: it maximises hunting efficiency, as the juvenile prey are more vulnerable than their experienced parents and so easier to catch, and the adult Merlins commence the moult at this time so both they and their brood benefit. The fledglings also benefit by gaining time to hone their hunting skills, both in terms of the possibility of easier prey, and in terms of maximising the number of 'training days' before the onset of winter. However, as noted in the case of the Kestrel (Chapter 5), the date of first egg laying cannot be as easily manipulated as might be imagined, with the availability of prey, the effect of the increase in daylight hours on the female reproductive cycle, and the 'quality' of the birds all influencing the date.

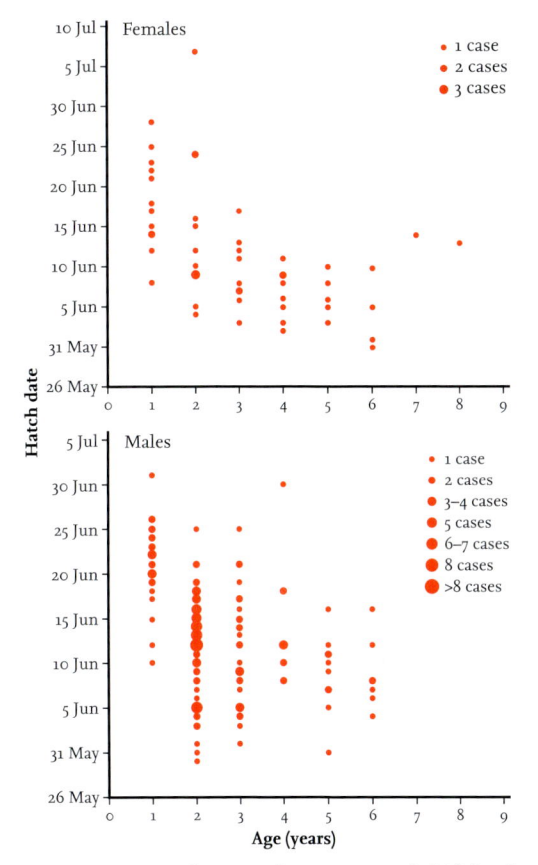

FIG 255. Scatter diagram of parent age and chick hatch date for male and female urban-breeding Merlins in Canada. Redrawn from Espie *et al.* 2000.

Once established, the Merlin pair divides the workload between them in the standard format for northern-hemisphere falcons. For a period before the female commences laying the male feeds her, allowing her to build up the resources necessary for the production of a clutch of eggs. The male continues to feed his female during egg laying and incubation, and for the first days after the chicks have hatched. The male also brings food for the chicks during this time. Sodhi *et al.* (1992) tabulated the division of labour in Merlin pairs nesting in urban Saskatoon (Table 34).

TABLE 34 Division of parental care by male and female Merlins. From Sodhi et al. (1992).

Phase of breeding	Contribution of male (%)	Contribution of female (%)
Deliver food		
– during incubation	100	0
– during nestling period	96.6	3.4
– during fledgling period	65.0	35.0
Incubation	7.2	91.8[1]
Brooding	0	100
Nestling feeding	Only when female absent	Almost always
Nest defence	57.6	32.9[2]

1. The eggs were left unattended for 1% of the time.
2. 9.5% of attacks were initiated by male and female simultaneously.

Eggs

Once egg laying has begun, eggs are laid, on average, every two days (Palmer 1988) – Ivanovski (2003) suggests 36–48 hours from his study of Merlins in Belarus – though the last egg may be laid up to seven days after the penultimate. In Ivanovski's study, each egg measured 33–43 mm along the major axis and 28–33 mm along the minor axis, consistent with the data of Sodhi et al. (2005) from the three North American subspecies. Ivanovski (2003) notes one egg which measured 44.5 mm in length, and that length is also noted for some North American eggs (Trimble 1975). In his study of eggs Schönwetter (1967) considered there was no discernible difference in the size of Merlin eggs across both its geographical range and the various subspecies, an opinion consistent with the data of Morozov et al. (2013).

Using the formula $V = 0.51LB^2$, where V is the volume of an egg, L its length and B its breadth (Hoyt 1979), Rebecca (2006) calculated a mean volume of $20.1 \pm 1.3 cm^3$ for eggs in his study area (Note 7.3).

In a study in Wales, Bibby (1987) found that the volume of Merlin eggs increased with the diversity of the diet of the falcons (i.e. the number of species in the diet). Figure 256 plots prey diversity against the proportion of farmland within 2–4 km of the nest site, and Fig. 257 indicates the variation in egg volume with diet diversity. While the variation in diversity in Fig. 256 is not surprising (farmland offering a habitat for a wider range of species), the effect on egg volume is much more so. But, interestingly, egg volume was not correlated to breeding success: Merlin females which laid eggs with larger volumes neither produced

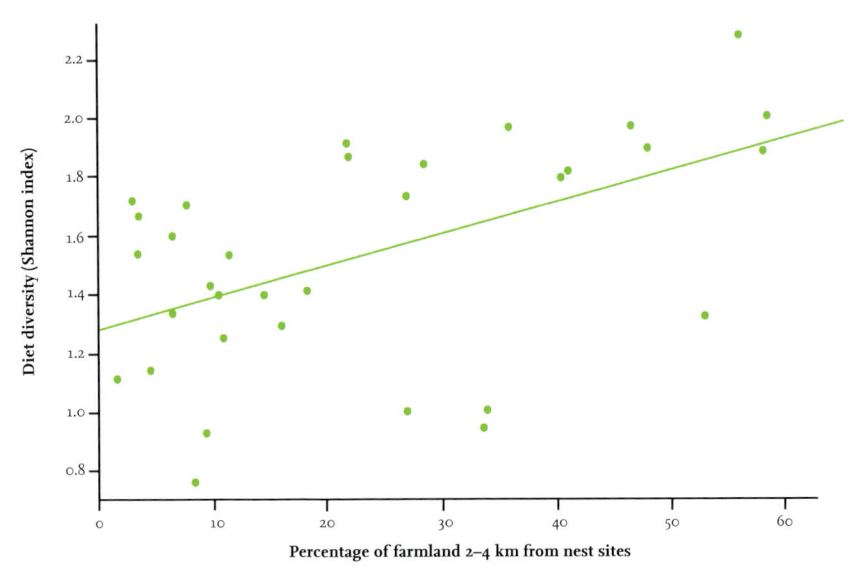

FIG 256. Variation in diversity of the Merlin diet in Wales with the percentage of farmland at 2–4 km from the nest site. Diet diversity is defined by the Shannon index, which is calculated by relating the number of species to their importance (e.g. biomass). Redrawn from Bibby 1987.

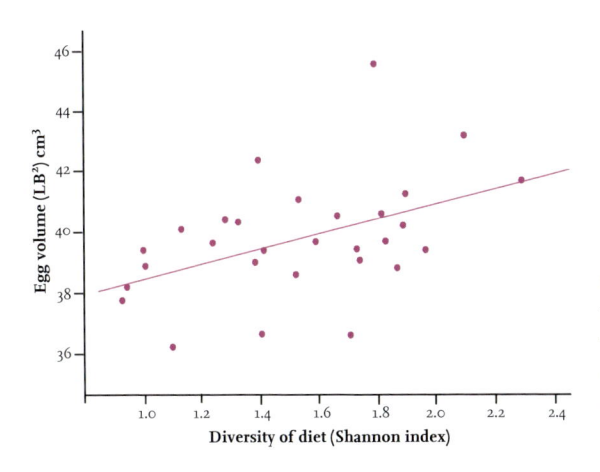

FIG 257. Variation in volume of Merlin eggs in Wales with diversity of the falcon diet. Diet diversity is defined by the Shannon index, as above.

larger clutches (though the sample size was probably too small for a correlation to have been identified) nor produced a greater number of fledglings. However, as the latter was significantly affected by nest failures any correlation might have been masked.

Wright (2005) calculated a mean weight of 21.5 g, with a range of 20–24 g, from a sample of 145 eggs in Yorkshire. Wright also noted that the average egg weight at hatching was 17.9 g (the egg losing weight as the chick develops). Again there seems no difference in the range of egg weights across the subspecies.

The base colour of the eggs is pale buff, this overlaid with blotches and spots of dark red-brown. However, there is a spread of egg coloration, with some having few dark markings, others having a base colour which is richer, this occasionally due to heavy spotting of dark ochre.

Clutch size

Clutches are normally 3–5 eggs, with a range of 1–7; Sodhi et al. (1992) recorded a clutch of eight in their study of the urban-breeding Merlins of Saskatoon, but there was a possibility that the eggs had been laid by two females. Table 35 indicates the variation of clutch sizes in studies of European Merlins.

TABLE 35 Variation of clutch sizes in European Merlins.

\multicolumn{6}{c	}{*Percentage of clutches with various numbers of eggs*}		
1	2	3	4	5	6[2]	Mean[3]	Study[1]
0	2.1	9.8	52.1	35.1	1.0	4.2	Newton et al. 1986
0	0.7	11.8	53.5	34.0	0	4.21	Wright 2005
0	0	14.9	51.1	31.9	2.1	4.2	Nielsen 1986
0	3	11	52	31	3	4.2	Ivanovski 2003
2	0	6	59	30	3	4.25	Hagen 1952
2	1	20	41	35	1	3.96	Brown 1976
1.4	0	8.3	54.2	36.1	0	4.24	Roberts & Jones 1999

1. Newton et al. (1986) sampled 194 clutches in Northumberland, England. Wright (2005) sampled 144 clutches in Yorkshire, England. Nielsen (1986) sampled 47 clutches in northeast Iceland. Ivanovski (2003) sampled 35 clutches in northern Belarus. Hagen (1952) sampled 63 clutches in Norway. Brown (1976) sampled 109 clutches across Britain; this work was carried out at a time when the Merlin population was recovering from the effects of organochlorine contamination, which likely explains the lower mean in comparison to that of Hagen, which preceded use of the pesticides, and that of Newton et al., which was made substantially after usage had ceased. Roberts & Jones (1999) sampled 72 clutches in Wales; their study covered 1964–1997 and so included both a period when organochlorine contamination was high and the period when the population was recovering.
2. Seven eggs are rarely seen, but have been observed in Fennoscandia in 'peak lemming' years (e.g. Jourdain 1938). As noted in the text, Sodhi et al. (1992) recorded a possible clutch of eight.
3. In a study of the variation of clutch size across Britain, Rebecca (2006) found variations from 3.2-4.9 in 1993 with a mean of 4.3 across 249 nests; and 3.7-4.9 with a mean of 4.2 across 259 nests in 1994.

The mean clutches are consistent with the data of Nattrass *et al.* (1993), who calculated a mean of 4.2 (range 3.7–4.4) when studying data from seven regions across England. Rebecca (2011) found means of 4.2 and 4.3 in successive years (1993 and 1994) for clutches in nests across Britain.

There are no recorded instances of Merlins breeding twice in the same season. Jourdain (1938), discussing the Eurasian Merlin subspecies, refers to 'second layings' but it is assumed by most experts that the reference is to replacement clutches which are known to have been laid. Data from various studies across the Merlin range suggest there is no significant difference in clutch size between first and replacement clutches. Replacement clutches are usually laid close to, but not in, the original nest. In Scotland, Cosnette (1984) noted a male mating with a second female after his first mate had been killed (probably by a mammalian predator which had also eaten the eggs). The second female nested less than 25 m from the first nest and hatched three eggs.

Incubation

Although incubation is begun by the female, the male Merlin also incubates, though in general contributes a smaller fraction of the total incubation time. Newton *et al.* (1978) considered the fraction to be about 34%, obtaining this figure by observing which of the pair of Merlins was flushed from the nest on approach. In a later study Newton *et al.* (1986) flushed males on 65 of 230 nest visits (28.3%). In his Yorkshire studies, Wright (2005) said that females sit for periods of 2–4 hours and males for about half this time, and considered that females incubated for about 60% of the total time (i.e. males incubating for about 40%), in general agreement with both reports by Newton and colleagues. In their studies of Asian Merlins, Morozov *et al.* (2013) found male incubation times varied from 8.7% to 35%. Some North American studies suggest similar fractions to the British data, but the studies of urban Merlins in Saskatoon indicated a lower fraction, as shown in Table 34.

Rowan (1921–1922 part II) noted that incubation periods were 1–2 hours for each bird of the pair in turn, which would imply a higher fraction of total incubation by the male if he also shared night-time duties. Rowan noted one occasion when the male incubated through the night. However, as he pointed out, this was the only time he kept night-time watch on a Merlin nest and so was unable to decide whether this was standard behaviour, peculiar to that night, or the idiosyncrasy of the individual bird. Most male incubation periods occur after he has delivered food to the female. When arriving with food the male makes the 'kee-kee-kee' call and the females goes to him to receive the prey. She then flies to a convenient place, rarely out of sight of the nest and usually within about 150 m, where she feeds, then preens. Occasionally the female will hunt for herself so that the male's turn at incubation lasts longer. Otherwise she calls to her mate and returns to the nest, perching nearby and waiting until he vacates so she can resume incubation.

The exact time of the start of incubation is still debated. Ruttledge (1985), who studied the breeding habits of captive Merlins, states that partial incubation begins once the third egg of a clutch of five has been laid and that continuous incubation begins only a day prior to the laying of the last egg. As most clutches appear to hatch synchronously, or nearly so, this seems the likely pattern, though asynchronous hatching has been recorded, implying that some females begin full incubation early.

During incubation the female will periodically turn the eggs: she will also give a soft call to initiate a response, reassuring herself that her mate is present. Rowan (1921–1922 part II) noted that the female's habit of tucking her feet under the clutch meant that on occasions when she left a ground nest one egg would be disturbed a small distance from the clutch and she would recover it when she returned. On one occasion an egg rolled 30 cm and resisted attempts at return as it had become trapped in its new position. After several attempts the female gave up and began to incubate the single egg, and then the remaining three eggs of the clutch, in turn. Finally she made one further attempt to dislodge the single egg and successfully managed to return it to the clutch. Rowan also noted that it was fortunate that the eggshells were strong, as one female had the habit of landing on the clutch.

Because of the difficulty of deciding precisely when incubation starts, the exact duration is not known, but lies within the range 28–32 days (Cramp & Simmons 1980). Mention must also be made of the extraordinary record of Ingram (1920), who found, in south Wales, a female Merlin sitting on three Grey Partridge eggs which had presumably been used as a replacement when her own eggs had been stolen. Ingram did not note the outcome of this situation but wondered, as will all others on hearing the information, what happened when the Partridge chicks hatched – were they preyed upon when, being precocial and essentially self-feeding, they left the nest, or did the female Merlin attempt to brood them and raise them on a diet of fresh meat?

Chick growth

Hatching takes about 24 hours, the emerging chick being semi-altricial and nidicolous. The chick weighs an average of 16.3 g (range 13.0–17.5 g) (Wright 2005) and is exhausted by the process of escaping from the shell. The chick's eyes are closed, opening after a few days. The female removes and discards, or occasionally eats, the eggshell.

FIG 258. Female Merlin arriving with prey to feed a brood of four chicks raised in an old Buzzard nest.

Though essentially helpless, the chick can raise its head and will call softly for food. The chicks are brooded more or less continuously until they can thermoregulate at about ten days. Morozov *et al.* (2013) state that the period of intense brooding is longer for Merlins in the extreme north of their Asian range, noting brooding for 73–84% of the time for chicks 11–13 days old and 67% of the time at 14 days old. Not until the chicks were 21 days old did brooding cease.

During the period of intense brooding, Wright (2005) notes that in some pairs if the male brings food to the nest rather than landing nearby and calling to the female, she may be aggressive towards him, forcing him away. However, Wright also saw chick feeding by some males and, on one occasion, chick brooding. Newton *et al.* (1986) noted males brooding on only three occasions in 80 nest visits during the early stages of chick growth. The three occasions were when the chicks were one, five and ten days old, i.e. during the period when they were unable to thermoregulate, or shortly after they had become able to.

Rowan (1921–1922 part III) maintained that at the nest he observed the nestlings were not brooded at all after the first, critical, period. In a wonderfully evocative passage which says as much about the weather he was forced to endure as the chick-rearing habits of Merlins, he wrote that 'from beginning to end I never saw the mother attempt to brood her young. No matter whether it thundered and poured in buckets, day and night they were left to themselves.

FIG 259. Female Merlin arriving with prey at a basket nest.

At such times when quite young, they would huddle together, all four quite symmetrically arranged, breast to breast, four doleful little heads making a dome at the top of which the rain coursed down their backs in little runnels through the matted down.' If left alone, the nestlings freeze at the base of the nest if an adult gives the alarm call, so as to avoid aerial predators.

The nestlings are voracious and will make attempts to grab food from the female even when they are not old enough to cope with the prey themselves. Because of their enthusiasm for eating, the chicks grow quickly, growth rates differing for males and females. Picozzi (1983) measured the increase in weight of 17 chicks in six broods on Orkney (Fig. 261), and noted that nestlings fell into two classes, those that attained a maximum weight of 225 g and those whose weight did not exceed 210 g: he correctly assumed that the first class were females (nine chicks) and the second were males (eight chicks). The variation in length of the outer (10th) primary with weight of chicks on the Southern Uplands (chiefly the Lammermuir Hills) of southeastern Scotland is shown in Fig. 262. The data, obtained from 154 male and 125 female Merlin chicks (for primary length) and 55 chicks for age, are consistent with Picozzi's from the 17 Orkney chicks. The weight curve for the chicks follows the familiar

FIG 260. Female Merlin feeding her brood in an old Buzzard nest. Interestingly, each time the female visited the nest she landed on the open side, away from the camera, but walked around so as to stand with her back to the main tree trunk, presumably to gain its protection.

sigmoid curve, and indicates that the period of maximum growth is between days 5 and 15 from hatching. The weight data are consistent with those of Wright (2005) in Yorkshire.

Oliphant & Tessaro (1985) measured the food intake of a pair of urban Merlin chicks hatched in the laboratory from eggs taken from nests. Figure 263 indicates

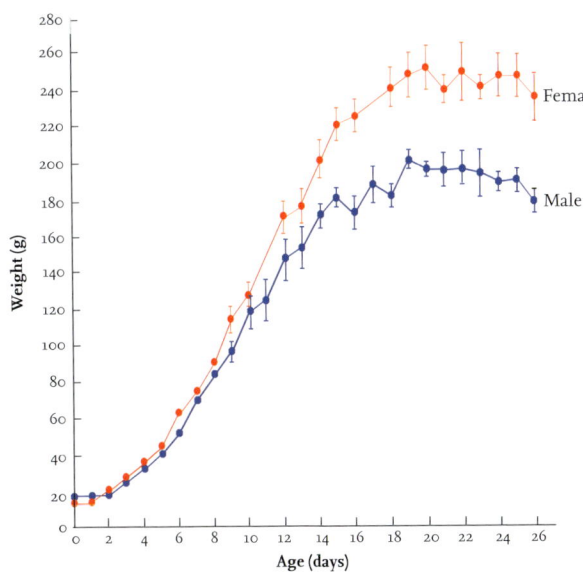

FIG 261. Mean weight gain of eight male and nine female Merlin nestlings on Orkney. Drawn from data provided by Nick Picozzi. For full details see Picozzi 1983.

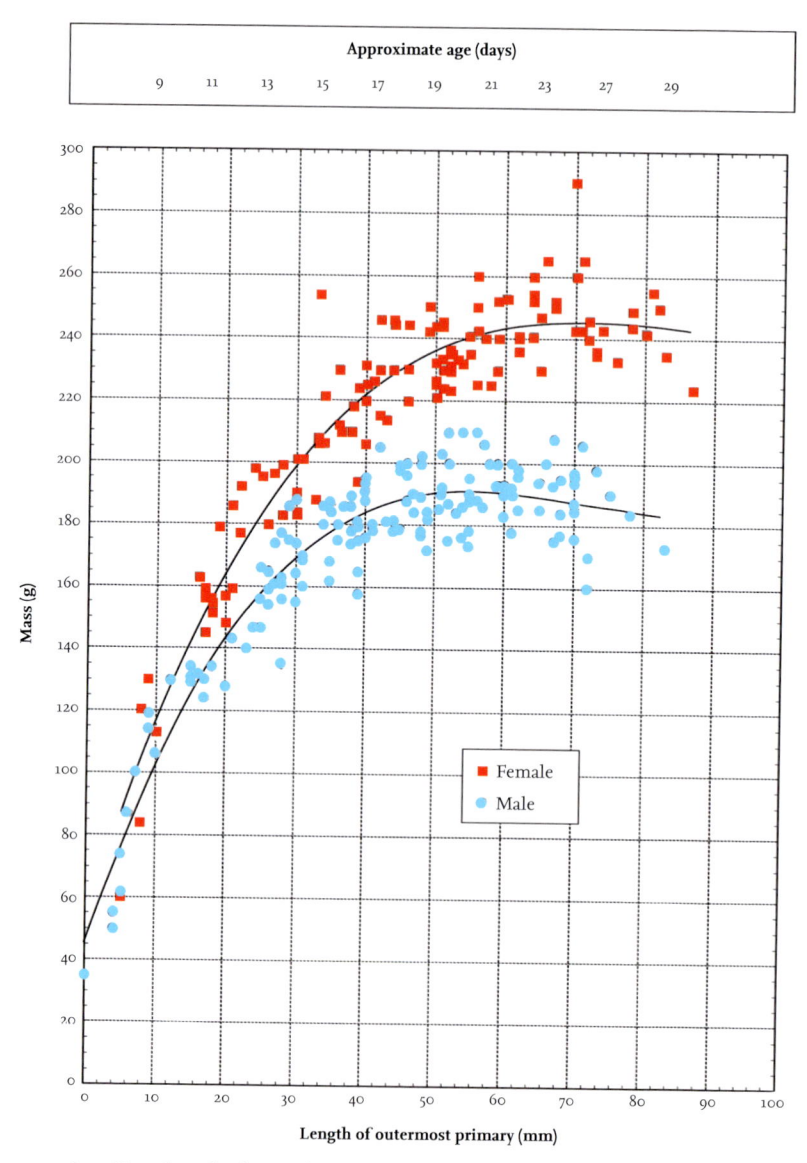

FIG 262. Mean length of outer (10th) primary for male and female Merlin nestlings. The data on primary length were obtained from 154 male and 125 female nestlings from 70 broods over a 15-year period in the Southern Uplands of southeast Scotland. The age data were obtained from 55 nestlings of known age. (Unpublished data of Ian Poxton and Alan Heavisides, by kind permission of Alan Heavisides.)

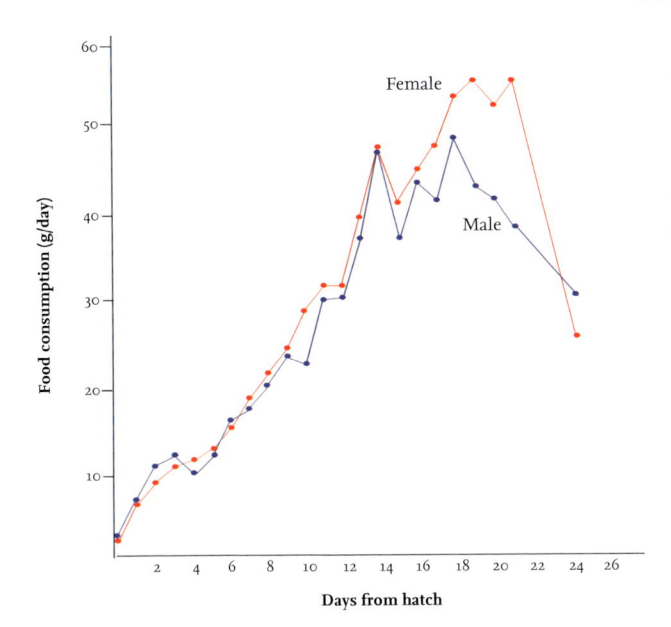

FIG 263. Food consumption by male and female Merlin chicks as a function of time from hatching. Redrawn from Oliphant & Tessaro 1985.

an essentially linear increase from hatch to day 14, with the male chick taking 40.0 g/day and the female 46.1 g/day. Table 36 indicates the development of young Merlins.

In general the male plucks the prey before delivery, using a favoured plucking perch which often lies within 150–200 m of the nest. Usually the head and wings of the prey will be removed, as well as the feathers. For ground-nesting birds the

TABLE 36 Development of young North American Merlins. From Oliphant & Tessaro (1985), with minor amendments from other sources.

Day from hatching	Status of development
1	Eyes closed, down wet, but dries quickly
3	Eyes open
4–8	Second down develops
9–11	Sheathed contour feathers appear Can sit erect on tarsi Wing flapping commences
12–14	Primaries break from sheaths First cast

continued overleaf

TABLE 36 *continued.*

Day from hatching	Status of development
15–17	Secondaries emerge
	Retrices break from sheaths
	Egg tooth lost
	Stands upright[1]
18–21	Head and body feathers develop
	Flight feathers develop rapidly
	Holds food with feet
	Wing flapping increases
	Weight gain and food consumption level off
22–28	Maximum weight attained
	Down replaced by contour feathers (down only visible on head at 28 days)
	Makes short jump flights
29–34	Fledges and makes short flights[2]
35–40	Long flights made
	Notices prey and makes first attempt at pursuit
40–50	Begins to hunt and kills first prey (usually insect)
	Feather growth complete
50–60	Becomes independent and disperses[3]

1. While feather development moves quickly, the birds locomotive skills lag behind, nestling Merlins being unable to stand upright until they are 15–17 days old, and unable to hold food in their feet until they are 18–21 days old. Remarkably, the day after being able to successfully hold food in their feet some birds take their first flight, though some nestlings will be 28 days old before they are fully fledged. The young of ground-nesting Merlins usually abandon the nest and disperse among the surrounding Heather once they can walk easily, though they do not move far and can therefore reach the female quickly if she arrives with food. The dispersal aids both camouflage and sanitary conditions at the nest, the chicks being unable to avoid nest spoiling by defecating over the nest edge as those in stick nests do.
2. Studies of British Merlins state that fledging is complete at 28–32 days.
3. Once fledged, the juvenile birds stay in the vicinity of the nest and continue to be fed by their parents, which pass food either aerially or at perches. Aerial passes seem to be a method of improving the juvenile's flying skills as well as their hunting skills. The juveniles also hone their hunting skills by chasing feathers, leaves or thistledown, and also by chasing insects, quickly developing the agility that is a characteristic of the species. The juveniles become independent of parental care 2–4 weeks after fledging. From personal experience Merlin fledglings are remarkably quick learners, moving from branch-walking to early flights, and then to longer flights, in a matter of very few days. Fledglings have been seen to chase the adults for food with good flight capability and at distance from the nest only a day or two after taking their first branch-walks.

THE MERLIN · 451

FIG 264. The first Merlin chick of a clutch of four hatches in a basket nest in southern Scotland.

FIG 265. A brood of four Merlins aged about 7 days nestle together in an old Buzzard nest in southern Scotland.

452 · FALCONS

FIG 266. A brood of five Merlin chicks in a ground nest in northeast England. The chicks are about 15 days old.

BELOW: **FIG 267.** Merlin chick brought to the ground from a stick nest for ringing. The chick is well-feathered and aged about 21 days.

FIG 268. A female Merlin arrives with prey (a), and leaves after feeding her brood (b) in an old Buzzard nest.

plucking 'post' may be an area of bare ground among the vegetation, but is more usually a nearby boulder, which becomes conspicuously covered in whitewash from the bird's defecation as the season lengthens, as well as with discarded prey detritus. Usually the boulder will be in direct line of sight of the nest, often on the opposite side of the valley. Boulders are also commonly used as plucking posts if the nest is in an isolated tree, but a nearby tree is used if the nest is within a wooded area.

Once the food is delivered to the female, she will initially break off small sections of the prey and feed each chick bill to bill, but soon the chicks are snatching at any available morsel and attempting to swallow it whole. Craighead & Craighead (1940) tell a story of a female engaged in a tug-of-war with four nestlings which successfully pulled prey away from her only to discover they were completely unable to dismember it and had to wait until the female regained possession and had torn off pieces they could cope with. With the meal

FIG 269. A female Merlin feeds a brood of five in an old Buzzard nest in southern Scotland.

completed, one nestling grabbed the remains of the prey and mantled it, despite being unable to either swallow it or tear lumps from it. A sibling then grabbed it, with the same outcome. As Craighead & Craighead note, 'the remains of the [prey] went the rounds: none could swallow it and all were too young to tear it up.' Once they are old enough to manage their own food, taking any larger piece they are able to grab, the nestlings will mantle the food to avoid their siblings from taking it.

Female hunting during the nestling phase seems to be individual, with some females hunting when the young are only seven or so days old, while others do not hunt almost until they are fledged.

Breeding success
In the study by Newton *et al.* (1978) in northern England it was found that about 37% of nest areas which were occupied by Merlins at the start of the breeding season did not result in nests with eggs, so that the breeding attempts of over one-third of apparently paired birds failed before the egg-laying stage, a failure rate at that stage comparable to that of Hodson (1976) in North America. Newton *et al.* noted that if breeding failed then both birds tended to leave the nest area within a few days. In their study of Merlins in Ireland, Norriss *et al.* (2010) found comparable figures, with 33% of pairs deserting their nests before eggs were laid. Norriss *et al.* also found that 90% of nest desertions occurred during the pre-hatching phase, the only exceptions being two broods of chicks less than ten days old which failed during prolonged heavy rain; no mortality of older nestlings was observed.

Newton *et al.* (1978) also looked at the success rate, in terms of the number of eggs laid which resulted in hatched chicks, for those pairs which did lay, and identified the causes of egg failure in clutches which were entirely lost (Table 37). As can be seen from this table, predation of eggs and nestlings is a major source of loss from Merlin nests.

Converting the data from Table 37 into overall mortality, but only for the period 1971–1976 so as to eliminate, as far as possible, the effect of organochlorine contamination, Newton *et al.* (1978) concluded that losses at the egg stage from all causes were responsible for the loss of 1.5 chicks per brood. By contrast, losses at the nestling stage were minimal (Table 38).

The fate of young which die in the nest is unclear. Temple (2008) found all five nestlings from one nest had been plucked, four in or close to the nest, one at a plucking post about 100 m away; the latter had been partially eaten. Temple believes the chicks had died following several days of continuous rain and had been eaten by the adults. Whether dead chicks are consumed by siblings in other instances, as is the case in some species, is not known.

TABLE 37 Causes of complete Merlin nest failure in the period 1961–1976 in northern England. From Newton et al. (1978).

Period	Eggs not laid	Eggs broken by parent or predator[1]	Eggs taken	Eggs deserted	Eggs addled[2]	Eggs trampled	Nestlings taken by human or predator	Female died	Unknown[3]
1961–1970	1	3	1	0	4	1	0	1	7
1971–1973	4	6	2	0	1	0	5	0	2
1974–1976	1	7	13	1	0	0	2	0	(1)

1. It was not possible to determine any significant differences as a result of a decline in eggshell thinning during the period, because of the difficulty of assigning egg breakages to specific causes. However, as the number of nestlings successfully fledged during the period increased and the number of instances of addled eggs declined, this implies that overall egg failures resulting from organochlorine contamination declined.
2. Egg addling, along with eggshell thinning, is a known effect of organochlorine contamination.
3. It is notable that Newton et al. (1978) do not specifically note the loss of clutches as a result of adverse weather (though 'unknown' may include this).

TABLE 38 Brood losses of Merlins at the nestling stage. From Newton et al. (1978).

	Number of broods	Mean number of nestlings lost[1]
All nestlings fledged	59	0
Nestling mortality	6	1.2
Early loss[2]	13	1.0

1. The data on nestling losses are consistent with those of Roberts & Jones (1999) in northeast Wales, where a mean clutch size of 4.24 eggs produced a mean of 3.1 fledglings in the period 1964–1974, 3.7 fledglings in 1975–1982, but then 2.9 fledglings in 1983–1997; and with those of Rebecca (2011), who found 3.1 fledglings from a mean clutch of 4.3 eggs in 1993 and 3.5 fledglings from a mean clutch of 4.2 eggs in 1994 from nests across Britain.
2. It was unclear in these cases whether the loss was at the egg stage or when the chick was very young. However, hatching is exhausting for young birds and losses at that stage are known in comparable species. It is also the case that some hatchlings suffer developmental abnormalities that may result in death at an early stage, or after fledging when the juveniles are unable to fend for themselves. While rare, such cases are known. Cooper (1984) records a case of a three-week old male Merlin taken from the nest with the third and fourth digits of the right foot fused. The digits were separated under anaesthetic and the bird recovered, but then, sadly, died of Dieldrin poisoning.

Newton et al. (1986) continued the study of Merlins in Northumberland through to 1983 and were therefore able to update the information of nest failures and breeding success. At the time the population of Merlins was in decline in the area. Combining data from the earlier study with the new work to

FIG 270. Pre-fledge Merlin chicks peer over the edge of their nesting basket.

allow a ten-year period (1974–1983) showed a decline in observations of activity in potential nest areas from around 60% of sites in 1974 to about 25% in 1983, and a decline in nests found from about 38% in 1974 to about 20% in 1983. Newton *et al.* repeated their analysis of the causes of complete failure of nests over the ten-year period (Table 39).

In total 370 sites with signs of activity were observed in April, but only 230 nests were found, so 38% of apparent breeding activity did not result in eggs being laid, in agreement with the earlier study (Newton *et al.* 1978). Of the nests found, 217 had eggs, and of these chicks were fledged in 143. What is clear from Table 39 is that predation of both eggs and nestlings is the most significant reason for breeding failure.

These studies suggest that the overall success per pair is low. Merlin breeding also seems susceptible to weather conditions, perhaps not surprisingly given the relatively weatherswept nature of their preferred habitat. In other studies the weather has been responsible for breeding failure: for example, Hodson (1976) noted in a study on the Canadian prairies that after a storm that lasted two days and which included winds to 80 km/h, over 10 cm of rain and a fall of 17 °C in

TABLE 39 Causes of complete Merlin nest failure in 1974–1983. From Newton et al. (1986).

	Eggs not laid[1]	Eggs broken by parent or predator[2]	Eggs taken[3]	Eggs deserted[4]	Collapse of tree	Nestlings taken by human or predator[5]	Female died[6]
Total failures	13	21	46	13	2	25	2
Percentage of total failures	10.7	17.2	37.7	10.7	1.6	20.5	1.6

1. Includes a female taken by a Peregrine Falcon in 1981.
2. Includes one nest trampled in 1982.
3. Includes six definitely taken by humans.
4. Includes two addled clutches.
5. Includes seven taken by humans and seven definitely taken by natural predator as remains were discovered.
6. Includes a female shot in 1978.

ambient temperature, the number of active Merlin nests had fallen from 26 to 15, a 42% loss. Of the 11 inactive nests, one had two dead nestlings, six had cold, dead eggs, two were empty, and two had eggshell remains – in one case with the shells found some 6 m beyond the nest, which had itself been blown 5 m out of the tree in which it had stood. Hodson considered that the shell remains were likely the result of crow predation. Of the still active nests, dead nestlings were found in two. Other species nesting in the same study area also suffered losses. In Iceland

FIG 271. A juvenile Merlin pursues the adult female in the hope of being fed.

Nielsen (1986) found that in 1981 when spring was cold only 71% of occupied nests produced young, this figure rising to 84% in years where the spring climate was more amenable. In one of Nielsen's study years only six nestlings died, four in one severe rainstorm.

However, once Merlins have a clutch of eggs the situation improves. Note 1 of Table 38 indicates the success in producing fledglings from eggs, and that has also been borne out in studies across the falcon's range: among the urban-dwelling Merlins of Saskatoon, Sodhi *et al.* (1992) found that in only 4% of nests (10 of 256 nests observed between 1971 and 1990) did no eggs hatch, and in those that did an average of 4.2 ± 0.04 eggs produced 3.8 ± 0.03 chicks, a success rate of 90.5%, comparable with British studies. Once a clutch is produced, Merlins are consistent, and consistently good, parents, though both age and experience improve success. In other studies on Saskatoon's urban Merlins, Sodhi *et al.* (1992) noted that the earlier the pair bred the more likely they were to lay a larger clutch and to produce fledglings, clutches in which the first egg was laid in April yielding 4.4 fledglings from 4.7 eggs, compared to 3.8 fledglings from 4.3 eggs for nests where the first egg was laid in May. (The standard deviation in both cases is 0.1, and the differences in both egg and fledgling numbers are statistically significant at the 99% level.) Early breeding tends to be by older, more experienced birds, and Espie *et al.* (2000) also found that the breeding success of Merlins improved with age. In females this was due to higher mortality of less successful breeders rather than any specific change in individual birds (though, of course, the gathering of experience cannot be detrimental), while changes in male breeding performance with age were largely due to experience gained in the first two or three years of life. In essence the results of Espie and co-workers mean that if a falcon of either sex survives from one year to the next its breeding performance will improve, until the natural deterioration of age forces a decline.

As noted above, predation is a significant risk to Merlin eggs and chicks. To assess the effect of possible predation on Merlin behaviour, Wiklund (1990a), in a study in Sweden, observed the reaction of male and female falcons when a stuffed Raven was placed close to their nest during the time of egg laying and after hatching. The results (Fig. 272a) indicated that during the egg-laying phase males attacked more frequently than females, and the frequency of attacks made by the male was positively correlated to clutch size, while the female attack frequency was negatively correlated with clutch size, the two frequencies effectively cancelling so that the overall number of attacks was not correlated to clutch size.

When the chicks had hatched, the female attack frequency increased, but there was no difference in the behaviour of males (Fig. 272b). Overall the number

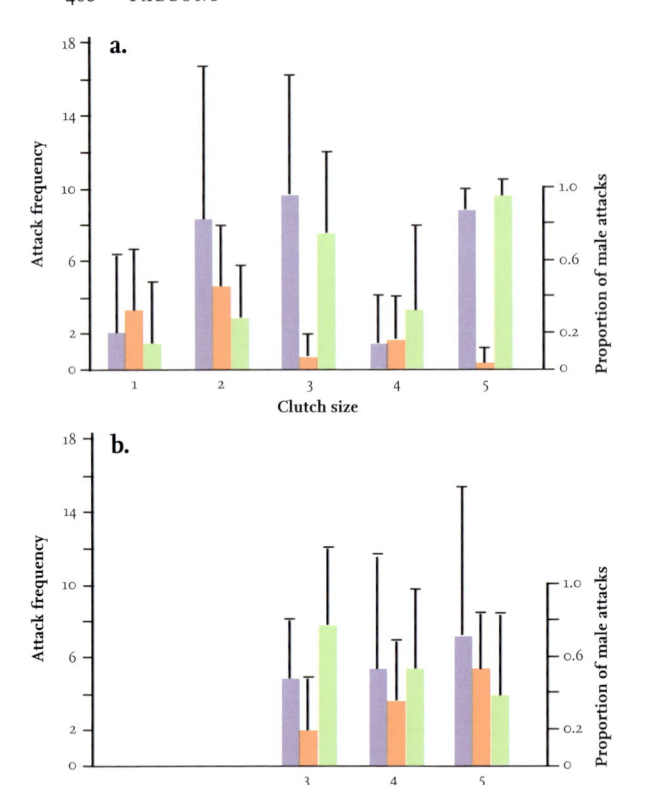

FIG 272. Attack frequency on a potential predator by breeding male (blue bars) and female (red bars) Merlins: (a) variation with clutch size; (b) variation with brood size. Green bars indicate the proportion of attacks made by the male. Redrawn from Wiklund 1990a.

of attacks increased with brood size as a consequence of the positive correlation of female attacks with brood size. These findings suggest that male Merlins assess the value of nest defence by the size of the clutch, but it is the female, who does most, often all, of the feeding of chicks who is able to assess their value, in terms of fitness to survive. Male attacks were the likely reason for females not to desert clutches: females heavy with eggs are less agile than males, so attacks on predators are more risky. In situations in which the male is not pulling his weight the female therefore has a decision to make: does she make attacks, and if so at what frequency? At a high frequency she risks injury or death, while at a lower frequency the likelihood of egg predation increases. Or does she abandon the breeding attempt while there is still time to lay a replacement clutch and so attempt to salvage something from the breeding season? In a second study Wiklund (1990b) used the same stuffed Raven, but manipulated brood size, taking chicks from some nests and placing them in others. When brood size

FIG 273. When you cannot yet fly, branch-walking has its perils, requiring wings and legs to maintain balance.

was increased, females attacked more often, when brood size was decreased they attacked less often: though Wiklund is cautious when assessing these findings, as some females did not react in this way, it does seem that some female Merlins are assessing the likely reproductive success of their broods and adjusting their behaviour accordingly. This seems to be borne out by Wiklund's observation that female predator attack behaviour declines in replacement clutches, and the fact that it is known that the survival rate for chicks that fledge late in the breeding season is reduced.

Predation is also critical to the lifetime reproductive success (LRS) of female Merlins. In a further study Wiklund (1995) noted that it accounted for 31.1% of the variance of LRS: only breeding lifetime (inevitably) accounted for a greater fraction. Wiklund (2001) noted that on average Merlin predation losses were 33.6%, but that the range was 16–48% over a seven-year study period. That range means that in the worst year almost half of nests were lost to predation. While all of Wiklund's work was carried out in Sweden, Table 39 suggests comparable predation losses in British nests, which implies that behavioural trends are likely to be replicated.

Nest-site, territory and mate fidelity
It has already been noted (see *Habitat*, above) that there is strong fidelity to nest areas in Merlins as a species, but this fidelity is not necessarily reflected in the fidelity of individual birds. Wright (2005) captured six male and ten female Merlins that had rings which enabled their nest of origin to be established. Only

one of the males, and none of the females, had been hatched close to where they were recaptured; on average the females had travelled 58.1 km from their natal area (range 18.9–105.0 km), males travelling an average of 30.6 km (range 2.7–63.3 km). Wright also recorded the number of times birds were recorded returning to their breeding sites. Over a ten-year period (1993–2002) only two of 11 males (18%) were discovered to have returned in successive years. In each case they occupied the same territory in those years, though the nest sites used had moved (by 360 m and 700 m). Female Merlins seemed more likely to return to areas where they had successfully bred. Four of 33 females were recorded in successive years, though in each case they had moved to adjacent territories. Two of the 33 were recorded three times, one using the same territory in successive years, then moving to a territory 4 km away, the other using adjacent territories on three occasions in four years, being absent from the area for one year. Two females used the same territory in four successive years, while a third used two territories, breeding in each for two successive years. Finally, one female was

FIG 274. Two well-feathered Merlin chicks in an old Buzzard nest. There were three siblings who had branch-walked away from the nest. All five had been recently fed, the two in the photo having very full crops.

recorded in two successive years, was then absent for a year, then returned, could not be assessed in the next year when access to the moor was stopped due an outbreak of foot-and-mouth disease, but was recorded again in the sixth year. Over the years of recording, this female used three adjacent territories.

In a study of Merlins in northeast Scotland, Marsden (2002), using DNA profiling based on the extraction of DNA from feathers found at nest sites, noted that of 185 females 82% bred in a particular nest area once only, 10% twice, 5% three times, 2% four times and 1% five times. Data for 96 males found 74% breeding in the same nest area once only, with 19% twice, 5% three times, 1% four times and 1% five times. Marsden also found that if a female returned to a nest area she would mate with the same male on 39% of occasions, with a different male on 11% of occasions; on the remaining occasions the same male would mate with a different female (22%) or both male and female would have changed (29%).

These data from Britain are consistent in studies in Iceland (Nielsen 1986) and Sweden (Wiklund 1996), and with studies in North America, which also show that dispersal distances from natal areas are higher in females than in males, but that breeding birds often return to the areas in which they have bred successfully. Wiklund also found that male site fidelity was comparable to that seen by Wright (2005), with seven of 49 males (14%) breeding in the same area throughout their breeding life (of 2–4 years); only one female of 45 showed similar behaviour. For urban Merlins, Warkentin *et al.* (1991) recorded one male returning to the same nest-site area for four consecutive years, and one female for five consecutive years. These figures suggest not only site fidelity in both sexes (though to a much lesser degree in females – see Note 6.9 for a comment on female falcon dispersal as a means of avoiding the incestuous relationships which might arise if both male and female nest-site fidelity was high) but also that Merlins might be exhibiting mate fidelity. Nielsen (1986) found that one pair which had bred successfully in one year mated again the following year, but on a territory which was 2 km away; their original territory was occupied by a new pair. Another pair which had bred successfully also occupied the same territory again. In Sweden, Wiklund (1996) noted nine males and ten females who retained mates during two or three consecutive years: one male bred with one female for two consecutive years, then with a different female for three consecutive years. While Wiklund's study involved a total of 220 birds, suggesting that 19 is a small sample, the number which bred on two occasions was lower, at 94, and the number that bred in three years lower still at 46, so the same-mate data do imply a degree of mate fidelity. However, for the urban Merlins, Warkentin *et al.* (1991) found that, although one Merlin pair that stayed together in successive years actually moved nest site, a result which could be construed as implying mate fidelity, overall the probability of males and females mating with the same partner in successive years was no better than chance would suggest, reinforcing the view that mating in the species is random. The researchers also measured the productivity of the Merlin pairs and found no significant difference between that of the same pair breeding in successive years, and no significant difference in pairs which changed mates in successive years.

MOVEMENTS AND WINTERING QUARTERS

Most ringed British birds have been recovered within Britain, suggesting that British Merlins that are not resident move relatively short distances (an average of about 100 km), chiefly to lower elevations and coastal areas, particularly estuaries, where personal observation suggests their presence usually causes panic and chaos among populations of waterfowl as well as shorebirds (the most likely prey). However, some British birds have been recovered from continental Europe. The recovery of ringed birds has also shown shipboard curiosities: on ships near Norway, north of the Faroes and south of Ireland. Wright (2005) records the recovery of only three adult birds ringed at his breeding sites during the period 1987–2002. One male travelled 264 km, while two females travelled 196 km and 287 km. In addition, 21 of 267 ringed chicks were recovered. The average distance travelled between fledging and recovery was 119.2 km (range 2.5–224.0 km) for males and 76.5 km (6.5–119.0 km) for females, though the latter excluded a single female which travelled 1,239 km (from northern England to Navarra in northern Spain) in 91 days. Movements in Britain begin in September, with birds returning to their breeding areas in April. Interestingly, while the first arrival dates of Hobbies have been earlier in recent years (see Chapter 8 and Fig. 298), those of returning Merlins have not (Fig. 275), though the limited number of migratory Merlins may mean that a change is being masked.

In general, the recovered birds in Wright's study had travelled south, though some had travelled east or west to reach the coast. This is consistent with the finding of Newton *et al.* (1978) in a study in which 394 hatched Merlins were ringed as nestlings. Of these, 19 were recovered before the onset of winter and, of these 19, all but one had moved less than 100 km from their nest site, but in random directions, initial dispersion seemingly a search for an available hunting range rather than any early migration.

In one of the series of studies on the urban-dwelling Merlins of Saskatoon, Warkentin *et al.* (1990) noted that in addition to its resident population the city had a large wintering population. The aim of the wintering study was to shed

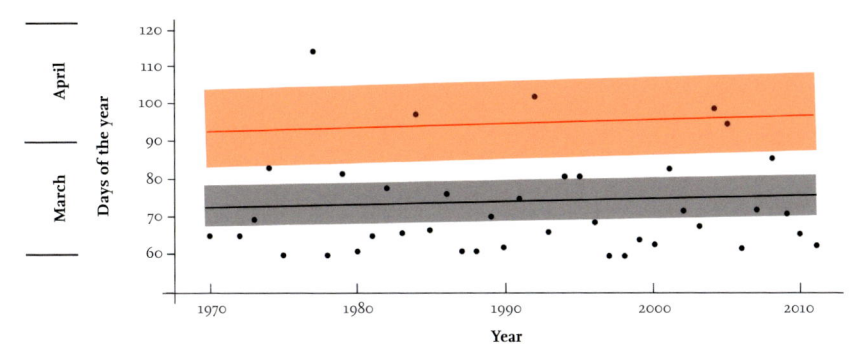

FIG 275. First arrival date for Merlins, as recorded by the Portland Bird Observatory, Dorset, for the years 1970–2011 inclusive. Note that a small number of years have been excluded because no falcons were observed. The y axis is the number of days of the year, with 1 January = 1, with allowance for leap years. The black line is a least squares fit to the first arrival date data, with the shaded block representing one standard deviation on the inter-year data. The red line is the least squares fit to the mean annual date, again with the shaded block at one standard deviation on the inter-year data. (With thanks to Dr Anne Goodenough of the University of Gloucestershire and Martin Cade of the Portland Bird Observatory.)

light on the four hypotheses that have been put forward to explain why such partial migration might develop. Briefly the hypotheses are: *body size*, which proposes that smaller birds migrate, as those with larger bodies can endure the lack of food that residing in the breeding area demands; *dominance*, which suggests that the population hierarchy means that dominant birds can out-compete subordinate birds, forcing them to move to avoid starvation; *arrival time*, which maintains that breeding birds obtain better territories by arriving first in breeding areas, and the most efficient way of doing so is not to leave; and *genetic*, which argues that the migrate/stay decision is genetic.

In their study Warkentin and co-workers found no significant body-size differences in the population of wintering Merlins. Furthermore, the age structure and sex ratio of the trapped Merlins did not support the dominance hypothesis, while the age structure did not support the arrival-time hypothesis. However, it was found that 19 of 20 birds trapped in winter had at least one parent that had also been captured in the city in winter, while only 4 of 13 birds which were hatched in the city, returned to breed there the following year and were trapped during the winter had at least one overwintering parent. The research team also considered that this fraction (31%) could have been an overestimate because of detection rates. While further work is obviously necessary before final conclusions can be reached, the results of this elegant study would appear to confirm that the decision of a bird to migrate or remain is genetic in origin.

The female of Wright (2005) which travelled over 1,000 km is not unique. Other long-distance travellers (Heavisides 1987) include an adult male ringed on Fair Isle, which was trapped alive in France having travelled 1,767 km in just 23 days, and a bird ringed as a nestling in Cumbria, on 2 July 1938 and shot in France on 20 October 1938 after travelling 1,178 km in around 100 days (the age of the bird at ringing is not given so it is not clear when it fledged).

One interesting aspect of Merlin migration is the finding by Kjellén (1992), who observed migrating raptors at the famous viewpoint of Falsterbo, southern Sweden, and found that, as with Kestrels, adult females migrated first, juvenile birds of both sexes migrating later and adult males migrating even later (Fig. 276). The difference in median dates of migration for the three groups were statistically significant. As noted in Chapter 5, Kjellén considered the most likely explanation for differential migration to be the timing of the moult. However, Mueller *et al.* (2000) have questioned Kjellén's data. They trapped 23,000 raptors of ten species between 1953 and 1996 at Cedar Grove, Wisconsin, the trapping allowing the aging and sexing of the birds to be reliably accomplished. Their data suggested that adult male Merlins older than two years migrated later than older adult females, but that there was no significant difference in timing between the sexes for two-year-old adults. Adults migrated later than first-year birds, and first-year males migrated later than first-year females. The criticism of Kjellén by Mueller *et al.* rests on the ability of the former to distinguish females and juvenile birds adequately in flight, which throws into doubt Kjellén's contention that females precede juveniles, though it does not contradict Kjellén's view of the validity of the moult hypothesis, as the sample size of Mueller and co-workers for two-year-old adults, particularly females, was small.

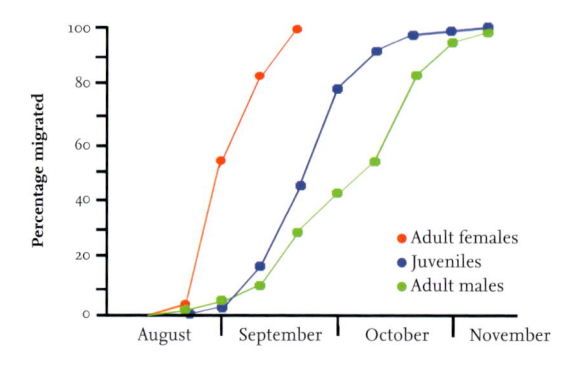

FIG 276. Differential autumnal migration of adult and juvenile Merlins observed in the period 1986–1990 at Falsterbo Peninsula, southern Sweden. The curves show the cumulative percentage of birds that had migrated at a certain date. Redrawn from Kjellén 1992.

Merlins which vacate their summer territories are mostly found on estuaries or other coastal regions, with a spread of observations that covers most of the British coastline. The wintering density of Merlins has not been measured in Britain, though it is usually assumed that the winter population is higher than the breeding population because the influx of Icelandic birds outweighs the migration of British birds. Cramp & Simmons (1980) state that winter ranges are 'restricted', leading to marked aggression towards other species. However, Dickson (1989) states that in his experience this is not the case, and he saw only one Merlin with a well-defined hunting range during a study period of 1965–1984. In this case a female Merlin occupied a hunting range of about 0.3 km^2 comprising rough pasture and a stubble field which was home to a flock of more than 300 Skylarks. The restricted range did appear to result in aggression, Dickson reporting four attacks on Hen Harriers, three on Peregrines and one on a Sparrowhawk. Dickson speculates that the selection of a specific hunting range might have been due, in part, to the winter being exceptionally cold, the permanent Skylark flock representing readily available prey, and the fact that the range lay only about 2 km from a communal Merlin roost which the female apparently shared.

In a study of wintering Merlins in Northumberland, Kerr (1989) noted that the assumption that most Merlins move from the relatively elevated moorland breeding grounds to coastal areas seemed valid, though with the proviso that there are many more observers in coastal areas than on the moorland in winter, which has the potential to influence the result of falcon counts. Over the course of two winters (1986/87 and 1987/88) 295 Merlins were observed, 211 at or within 3 km of the coast, and only 84 inland. Only 26 of the coastal birds were positively identified as male, while 32 inland birds were definitely male. This accords with the idea that male Merlins prefer to stay close to breeding territories in winter if that is a possibility so as to be in a good position to obtain mates and to breed the following spring. Of the 32 inland males, 18 were within short distances of known breeding sites. Kerr commented that as the average breeding population of Merlins in Northumberland in the decade prior to the winter study was 18 pairs, this observation was further proof of the reluctance of male Merlins to move any further from breeding sites than was absolutely necessary to find enough prey to survive the winter: although on the high moorlands of the area prey is very scarce in winter, Chaffinches, House Sparrows and Starlings were available in the valleys which run down from the moors, and the Merlins were taking advantage of these species.

Scott (1968) also noted an association between Merlins and Starlings, though in this case the Merlins appeared to be sharing a Starling willow-copse roost (at which several other species, including pigeons and Magpies, were also present), and although Scott noticed the consternation among the Starlings when the Merlins (there were up to four falcons) arrived he saw neither an attack by the falcons nor a Merlin eating a roosting companion. However, once the Starlings left, the Merlins also left. This is curious behaviour, perhaps best explained by the Merlins hunting the Starlings at certain times of day which happened to coincide with Scott's absence, though that would suggest the Starlings chose to stay at the roost despite the risks.

British Merlins are also known to roost on the ground amongst dense vegetation or on low branches in woodland thickets during the winter. Merlin pairs have been seen to winter together, and communal roosting has also been reported in Britain. In Scotland MacIntyre (1936) recorded a communal tree roost which had been used continuously for at least 40 years in which up to eight Merlins had been seen, and Dickson (1973) reported another observed in three consecutive winters. The roost was in an extensive area of willow trees which grew in waterlogged ground close to the coast, and up to five birds were seen in residence. The Merlins arrived around sunset (birds arriving both before and up to half an hour after) and would usually be gone before sunrise, up to 50 minutes before. Both 'blue' (male) and 'brown' (female or juvenile) birds used the roost and occasionally, either in the evening or the morning, the birds would engage in spectacular aerial chases. Kelly & Thorpe (1993) also noted a communal roost of Peregrines on the Isle of Man, off England's west central coast which was usually shared by Kestrels, Sparrowhawks, Ravens, and occasionally by one or two Merlins.

SURVIVAL

In a study of data on recovered Merlins ringed as nestlings in Britain, Heavisides (1987) listed the ages of 242 birds found dead or so sick that they did not recover (Fig. 277). The birds found dead by the end of August of the year in which they were hatched represent 17.4% of the total recoveries. Newton *et al.* (1978) continued to observe Merlin nest-site areas during the period in which the juveniles were wholly or partially dependent on their parents for food and noted that the loss rate was 7–15%. The wide range of the estimate was due to the difficulty of knowing with certainty whether a juvenile had been lost as a consequence of starvation due to not developing adequate hunting techniques at a time when parental feeding had been reduced, as a result of predation, or as a consequence of early dispersion from the nest area. However, the data do

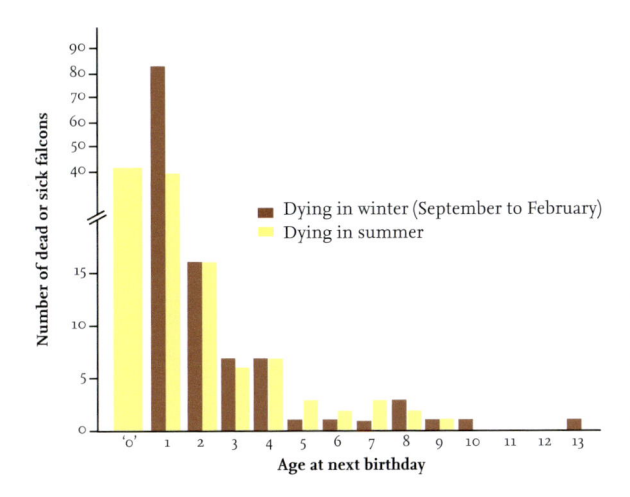

FIG 277. Age distribution of Merlins recovered dead or terminally sick with rings which allowed their ages to be determined. In general the sex of the recovered bird was not noted by the finder and no attempt has therefore been made to separate the recoveries into male and female. Redrawn from data in Heavisides 1987.

suggest that perhaps 10% of Merlin nestlings do not survive until the start of their first winter.

Once the adult birds have stopped feeding their offspring – there is no concrete evidence to indicate that parent Merlins engage in active attempts to expel their brood, though in other falcons, such as the Kestrel, it appears parent birds may move youngsters away from preferred hunting areas – the juveniles must rapidly acquire the hunting skills necessary to feed themselves. As most Merlin populations are partially migratory, the juveniles must then transfer these skills to a new area, and also cope with weather conditions that are usually poorer, and potentially with a reduced prey population as well. The combination means that many starve, or are unable to fight disease or parasitism because hunger has reduced their overall condition. Figure 277 reflects this higher death rate in first-year birds during the winter, with 82 of 121 (67.8%) of recovered yearlings being found dead in winter. Excluding deaths of fledglings, the deaths of first-year birds represent 60.5% (121 of 200) of recovered birds. The first year of a Merlin's life is hazardous, the first winter the most hazardous part of it. While the skew towards first-year birds makes the calculation of mean life span difficult, it appears that most Merlins that survive their first winter live 3–5 years, with very few reaching an age in double figures. The data of Heavisides (1987) shows only two birds living to their tenth year, one dying at age ten, the other in its 13th year: from various studies the latter can be considered to have been a very old small falcon indeed. The 13-year-old bird, a male, was ringed in County Down, Northern Ireland, on 21 June 1959, and recovered on 1 January 1972, only 35 km from where it had been ringed (Heavisides 1987).

The mean life of a Merlin suggested by the data (3–5 years) above is consistent with the finding of Marsden (2002) in the DNA profiling study of Merlins breeding in northeast Scotland. Marsden found that the typical breeding life of a Merlin was just one or two seasons (giving mean lives of both sexes of 3–4 years), though two females which were at least nine years old and a male of seven were noted. A 3- to 5-year mean life is also consistent with data from Espie *et al.* (2000), who studied the effect of age on the breeding performance of the urban Merlins of Saskatoon. That study allowed the age profile of breeding birds in Saskatoon to be established (Fig. 278) for 53 female and 105 male Merlins of known age. From these data the mean life spans of the two sexes were calculated as 3.15 ± 1.91 years for females and 2.67 ± 1.51 years for males. In northern Sweden, Wiklund (1995, 1996) calculated a mean life span of 2.2 ± 1.4 years for 92 females, and 4.0 ± 2.1

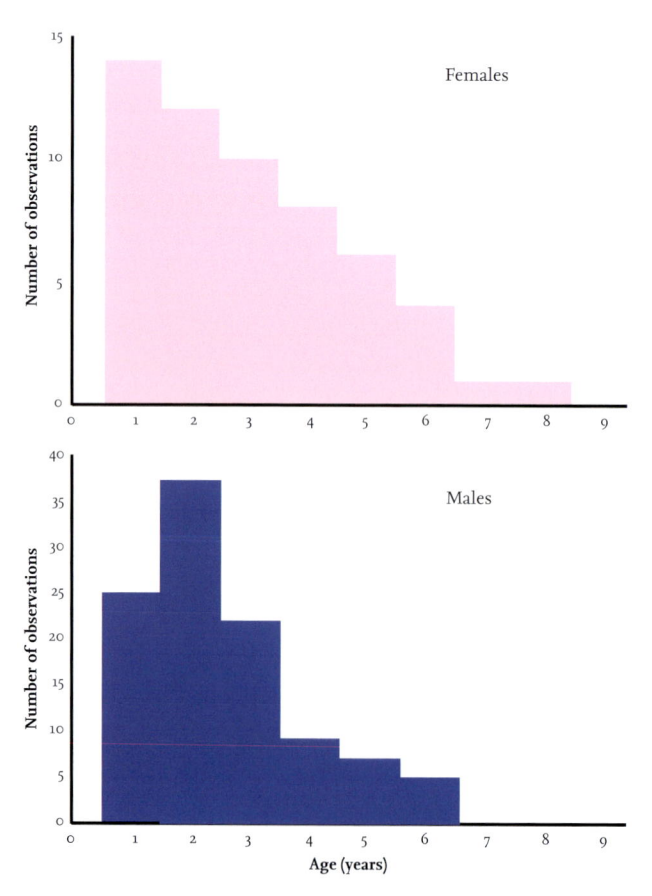

FIG 278. Age distribution of breeding male and female urban-dwelling Merlins in Canada, for 53 females and 105 males of known age. Redrawn from Espie *et al.* 2000.

years for 55 males. Espie and co-workers also investigated the LRS of male and female Merlins (see *Age of first breeding* in Chapter 2, and Figure Ch2_1).

Causes of death
The effects of organochlorine contamination on the Merlin population are considered in Chapter 8. But while that specific problem has been overcome, it is worth noting that other man-made contaminants, including those which derive from industrial and agricultural processes, are still widespread in the natural environment and that each may influence the breeding success of the Merlin (and other raptors).

The study of Nygård & Polder (2012) – see Chapter 4 for further details – showed that the levels of legacy pollutants continue to decline, and that the majority of eggs show concentrations below the believed critical levels, but that levels of PCBs have stabilised in some species. However, the level of DDE, which is known to be a significant eggshell-thinning contaminant, is higher in Merlins than in other birds of prey, and eggshell thicknesses have not yet returned to pre-organochlorine usage levels. Figure 279 shows the variation of some persistent contaminants, and also of mercury, in the eggs of Merlins over the period 1975–2010. Merlins, together with Peregrines and White-tailed Eagles, also have the highest levels of mercury. More worrying, as it took many years for the effect of organochlorine contamination to be understood, both brominated flame retardants and perfluorinated alkyl compounds are now being seen in raptor eggs. Levels are small, but little is known about the biological effects of these compounds, particularly in the longer term.

Recently concerns have been expressed over the increased usage of neonicotinoids, which have been linked with decreases in bee populations. For further information on the potential harm to falcons from these insecticides, see Chapter 2.

While lead contamination is chiefly associated with raptors which include waterfowl in their diet (see Chapter 4), Pain *et al.* (1995) found that six of 63 Merlins had concentrations of 6–15 ppm dry weight of lead in their livers (> 20 ppm dry weight is associated with lead-based mortality). Fifty-five per cent of the tested Merlins had non-detectable concentrations. Pain and colleagues considered it likely that the Merlins with high lead concentrations could have acquired the metal by consuming waders (Redshank or Snipe) which had survived being shot. The current regulations on the use of lead shot in North America and Europe have significantly reduced the likely threat in the future. However, Chandler *et al.* (2004) measured the lead levels in House Sparrows in Vermont, specifically to understand the potential effect this might have on Sharp-shinned

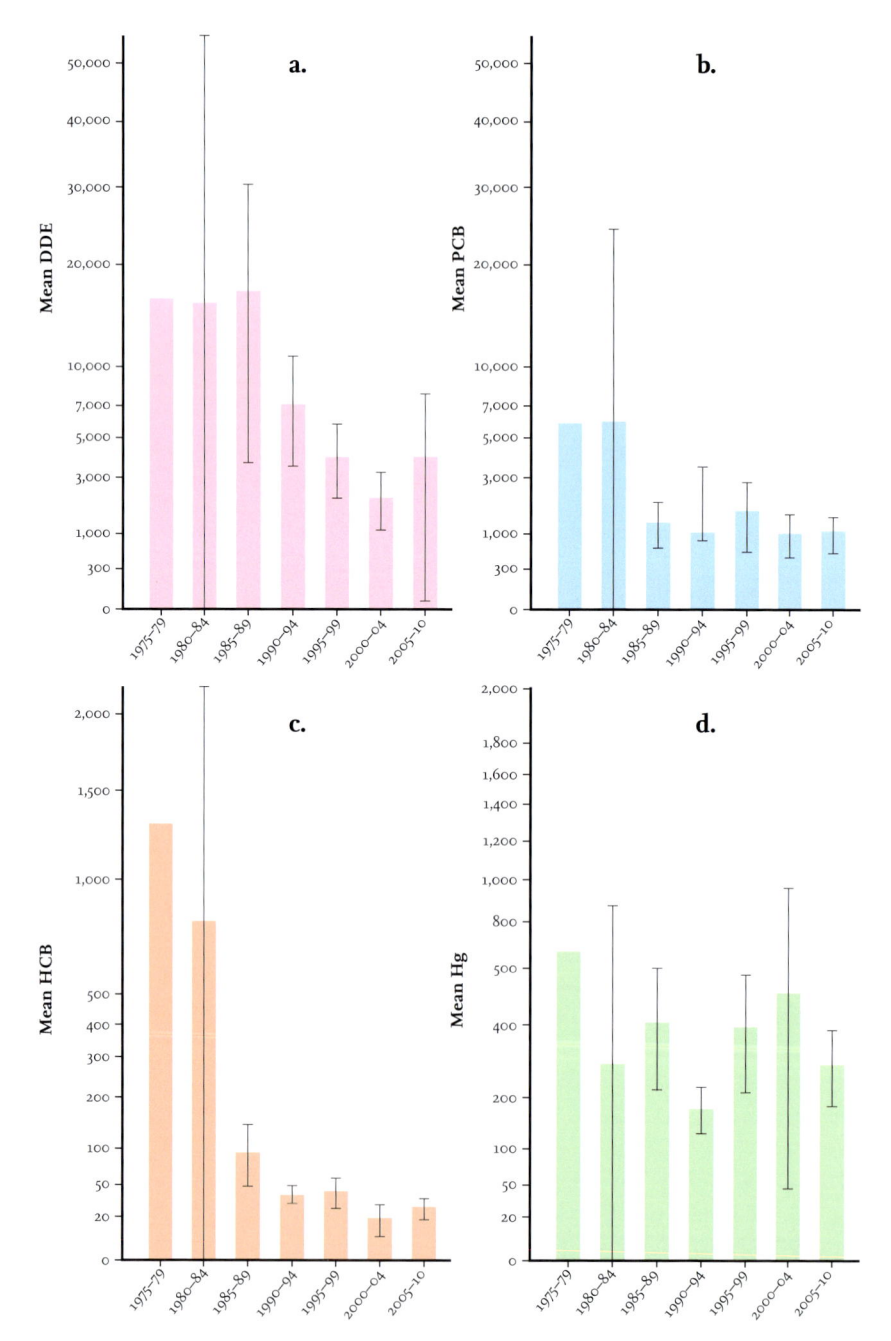

FIG 279. Variation of levels of contaminants in Merlin eggs in Norway (parts/billion fresh weight) for: (a) DDE (to be absolutely accurate, p', p' DDE); (b) PCB; (c) HCB; (d) mercury. Redrawn from Nygård & Polder 2012.

Hawks and Merlins. Each of the raptors has shown increased populations in urban areas, and while the increase in the hawk population is correlated with increased House Finch (*Carpodacus mexicanus*) numbers, it is known to take House Sparrows as well. Urban Merlins almost exclusively feed on House Sparrows. Despite the fact that using lead as an additive to petrol has now ceased, the researchers found elevated levels in urban House Sparrows and conjecture that this results from the ingestion of grit to aid digestion, lead being a persistent contaminant of the urban environment. The study indicated that in general the level of lead in House Sparrows was low, but that individual sparrows might carry significant burdens. Chandler *et al.* note that a small number of raptor deaths from lead poisoning have been identified in the USA, and consider that further work is warranted to identify the level of risk to urban-dwelling raptors.

Overall it seems that while pollutants have historically reduced the reproductive success of Merlins, and may still influence that success, at present they are unlikely to be a direct cause of death, though of course a contaminated bird may be more likely to succumb to disease or to starvation if its hunting ability is impaired. Identifying the case of death of recovered Merlins is difficult in most cases, as unless the cause is clear (e.g. the bird has flown into an object and sustained fatal injuries) the finders may not have the experience to discern causal effects, and most dead Merlins are not subject to autopsy. It is also inevitably the case that most recovered Merlins die close to human habitation (often as a direct result of human activity) because those that die in more remote areas may be subject to post-mortem predation and so are rarely recovered. Nevertheless statistics on recovered Merlins have been accumulated.

In his study of the recovery of Merlins ringed in the British Isles from 1911 to 1984, Heavisides (1987) provided data on the cause of death of 254 birds recovered dead or that were sick/injured at recovery but which subsequently died. In this study 37.8% were 'found dead' with no further explanation, 20.9% were killed by humans, 9.8% died after being recovered sick or injured, and the remaining 31.5% were classified as 'other', a category which included road casualties, flying into obstructions, starvation, killed by a cat, drowning in a water tank and 'found on a ship'. What is interesting about this 70-year study is the variation in the fraction of recovered Merlins which were 'killed by man'. This fell from 75% in the period 1911–1920 and 76% in 1921–1930, to 62% (1931–1940), 30% (1941–1950), 27% (1951–1960), then 16% (1961–1970), and around 5% after 1970. It is believed that most of the deaths in the earlier periods were from shooting. Prior to the passing of the 1954 Protection of Birds Act in Britain, the shooting of any raptor seen on a game bird estate was routine, the fact that Merlins could not take adult game birds and rarely took game chicks being an irrelevance. Rowan (1921–1922 part II) notes that on one occasion a gamekeeper was watching the area where he knew Merlins were nesting, waiting for the male to return with food so he could see the female rise to meet him and so reveal the nest position. The male Merlin flew in and, on seeing the keeper, dropped his prey in surprise, a grouse chick landing on the keeper's shoulder, doubtless reinforcing the view that all raptors were a threat to the grouse.

Disease and parasites

Only a single study on the causes of death from disease of Merlins by examination of dead birds has been identified. Cooper & Forbes (1986) examined 35 dead Merlins, all of which were captive birds, and also made clinical assessments of 13 live birds (11 of which were captive). Of the 35 dead birds, no diagnosis could be made of eight. Eight others had fatty liver–kidney syndrome, a condition which seems only to affect captive birds and may be associated with diet or inbreeding. Three birds died of enteritis/proventriculitis, three of coccidiosis. Three birds had peritonitis, two died of septicaemia and one of pneumonia. Two died of anaesthetic or surgical shock during treatment. Two birds died as a result of unidentified trauma, two had been poisoned, and one bird had been euthanised. Of the live birds, five had bumblefoot, the remainder having other minor problems.

FIG 280. A blood-sucking hippoboscid has attached to a female Icelandic Merlin. The fly is an *Ornithomya chloropus*, which has a most interesting life history. (Jóhann Óli Hilmarsson)

Following publication of the work of Cooper & Forbes (1986), the first recorded episode of lymphoid leukosis was observed in a three-year old captive male Merlin, one of a pair (Higgins & Hannam 1985). The disease was previously known in poultry, and was probably contracted from feedstuffs fed to the captive Merlins. The Merlin died, and autopsy revealed a lymphosarcoma in the liver.

Cooper & Forbes (1986) also found nematodes in three of the dead birds, and it is known that Merlins may also be infected by *Trichomonas gallinae*, which causes 'frounce' or 'canker' and can be fatal. The potential burden of other internal parasites in Merlins is unknown. Wright (2005) records finding parasitic louse flies on young Merlin chicks, but considers that the birds had rid themselves of them by the time they fledged. Other body parasites are also known, including screw-worm flies and Mallophaga lice. Maa (1969) and Matyukhin *et al.* (2012) also found the species *Ornithomya chloropus* on Merlins. While parasites may not kill the falcons they infest, they may weaken the bird and so be a contributory factor to death from other diseases or from starvation.

FRIENDS AND FOES

Friends

Cooperative behaviour between Merlins has already been considered, the species roosting communally during winter (see *Movements and wintering quarters*, above). Cooperative hunting has also been observed in both rural (Bengtson 1975) and urban-dwelling (Sodhi *et al.* 2005) Merlin populations. Dickson (1988, 1998c) reported two instances of Merlin and Hen Harrier hunting in close proximity, but it is not clear if this was cooperative, or if one raptor was using the prey confusion caused by the other. Dickson terms the behaviour 'association', which seems a more accurate description than true cooperation. There are also instances in which unrelated non-breeding adults (usually first-year males) will aid in both nest defence and food transfers to fledglings (see *Chick growth*, above).

While it can hardly be suggested as friendship, Newton *et al.* (1978) found a level of tolerance between Merlins and Kestrels, almost certainly due to the fact that they were not in competition for prey, feeding primarily on birds and mammals respectively. In some cases it was found that the two species would use particular nest sites in consecutive years and would also occasionally nest on the same cliff within 30 m of each other, the Kestrels using nest sites set higher on the face, the Merlins lower ones. I have also seen a site in Scotland at which a Kestrel pair was occupying a nest box less than 40 m from a Merlin pair which was raising chicks in an artificial nest. However, despite this tolerance and close association, attacks by Merlin on Kestrels have been recorded.

Suggesting considerably more than mere tolerance, in Scandinavia Fieldfares are occasionally seen to nest close to Merlins, and while it could be assumed that this was due to the thrushes seeking to gain advantage from the falcon's aggression towards corvids, the situation is much more complex and interesting. Since, in general, Merlins breed earlier than Fieldfares, it would seem that the main benefit here is to the thrushes, since they have a choice of nesting close to, or far from, the falcons. In a study in Arctic Sweden, Wiklund (1982) noted that Hooded Crows were the main predators of Fieldfare nests, mainly taking eggs. Merlins were extremely aggressive towards the crows, which were also a major predator of falcon eggs – not only in Sweden, but elsewhere in Europe, as noted by McElheron (2005) in Ireland, who comments that Merlins will not tolerate the crows near their nests. The Fieldfares clearly benefited from this aggressive behaviour.

In a study from 1978 to 1981 in a subalpine birch forest in central Norway, Hogstad (1981) found that 33 pairs of Fieldfares nesting close to breeding Merlins (in four colonies, average size 8.25 nests/colony) had higher reproductive success than 65 pairs (in 11 colonies, average size 5.91 nests/colony) which were not associated with Merlins, fledging an average of 1.73 fledglings per nest against 0.55 fledglings per nest. Hogstad also suggested an answer to another obvious question – if nesting close to Merlins is so advantageous, why are Fieldfare colonies not even larger? Hogstad suggests that because Fieldfares nest preferentially close to suitable feeding grounds, colonies can only grow to a limit imposed by intraspecific competition for food.

But Hogstad (1981) also noted that Fieldfares have developed communal nest defence strategies, which include not only mobbing of potential predators but 'defecation attacks' in which the mobbing birds eject fecal sprays which soil the plumage of avian predators. These attacks have been known to injure, and even kill, raptors and owls. In another Scandinavian study, this time in northern Sweden, Wiklund (1979) noted that 70 of 91 clutches laid by Merlins within a Fieldfare colony produced young, while only 13 of 34 nests outside colonies did so, a difference which is statistically significant at the 99.9% level. So the Merlins are also benefiting from nesting close to the Fieldfares. In a further study of Fieldfares, this time near Trondheim, Norway, Slagsvold (1979) noted a significant difference between predation of Chaffinch nests for those finches which nested close to and away from Fieldfare colonies, and also in the clutch and brood sizes of Bramblings that nested near the colonies. It would seem that the relationship between the Merlin, the Fieldfare and the other passerines is a fascinating example of commensal behaviour

Ivanovski (2012) has suggested, from studies in Belarus, that a similar relationship may exist between Wood Pigeons and Merlins, having found several instances of nests of the two within 30–50 m and on one occasion a pigeon nest only 1.5 m below Merlins breeding in an artificial nest. Such an association is known to exist between Wood Pigeons and Hobbies (see Chapter 6), giving credence to the idea.

Foes

Merlins are very aggressive to other birds which trespass onto their nesting territories during the breeding season, not only other species but conspecifics, and will also attack conspecifics in winter. When trespassers approach the nest, the male Merlin is usually in a position to give the first alarm call, and will give chase. The female will either sit tight or join in, depending on the age of the nestlings.

Wright (2005) noted Merlin attacks on both Peregrines and Goshawks, in each case the Merlin stooping on the larger raptor and hitting it hard. One female Goshawk rolled onto her back and attempted to catch the male Merlin in her talons, but was out-manoeuvred, and left the area at speed. There are also recorded attacks on Short-eared Owls, while Dickson (1988) recorded an attack on a Hen Harrier, and Ingram (1920) described a Merlin chasing a Peregrine. Wallen (1992) noted a series of attacks by a male Merlin on a Peregrine which ultimately resulted in the pair locking talons and tumbling towards the ground, separating only about 8 m above the ground. Corvids are chased throughout the Merlin's range (Note 7.4), and large, formidable birds have also been attacked. In Alaska's Denali National Park, Laing (1985) recorded Merlins chasing Golden Eagles and Gyrfalcons, while in northern Ontario, Lawrence (1949) observed an attack on a Great Blue Heron (*Ardea herodias*), a bird which stands 1.2 m tall and weighs around 25 kg. Merlins have also been seen attacking large gulls: Lusby *et al.* (2011), in Ireland, record an attack on a Great Black-backed Gull. Millais (1892) recorded a Merlin attacking a male Black Grouse in flight, knocking it down: the Merlin then rose, circled, and flew off.

Merlins suffer predation by some of the species they harass. Corvids will predate Merlin nests, and in his study in Iceland, Nielsen (1986) found that Merlins sharing territories with Ravens were less likely to produce fledglings than those falcons which were not – 74% success with Ravens present, 82% with no Ravens, across a five-year study period. Nielsen also found adult Merlins in prey remains at Raven nests, but was unable to be sure whether the Merlins had been preyed upon or scavenged. Other raptors will also predate Merlin nests.

Adult Merlins are not exempt from predation. Ratcliffe (1993) notes predation by Peregrines, while Roberts & Jones (1999) consider that the presence of Peregrines in an area historically favoured by Merlins can cause displacement

FIG 281. In the area around this nest there was a second Buzzard nest, and in successive years Merlin and Buzzard pairs alternated their occupation.

of the smaller falcon even if direct predation is not involved. It is suspected that Golden Eagles, Tawny Owls and Sparrowhawks also prey on Merlins, with varying degrees of success. Attacks by Buzzards are assumed, though the only recorded instance I am aware of is one on a falconry Merlin in which the falcon was killed. Interestingly, in a study area in Scotland, colleagues and I strongly suspect that in successive years Buzzards and Merlins swapped occupation of two Buzzard nests which were relatively close (less than 2 km apart), suggesting a degree of tolerance as long as respectful distances were kept.

Working on a seismic research vessel to the west of Shetland, Gricks (2005) noted the arrival of two Merlins and a Short-eared Owl in late September (the Merlins having perhaps arrived from Iceland). Over the next few days the Merlins killed and ate about ten Meadow Pipits, but then one disappeared. The same day the owl was seen to be eating the remaining Merlin, which it had presumably killed. Rebecca (1991) also noted predation by a Short-eared Owl, a dead female Merlin being found close to her nest. Owl feathers were scattered close by and the falcon had owl feathers in her talons. Eggshell fragments were stuck to the Merlin's brood patch, suggesting that she had been attacked while incubating.

In a study in northern England, Petty *et al.* (2003) found that 5.4% of the raptors taken by Goshawks were Merlins – the raptor fraction of the Goshawk diet was 4.5% by frequency, 2.5% by biomass; the remains of 13 Merlins were found in a total of 5,445 prey items. However, over time the effect of Goshawk predation has been to eliminate all Merlins from that particular area (A. Heavisides, personal communication).

Similar predation by larger raptors and owls occurs throughout the Merlin's range. In North America, Peregrine Falcons, Great Horned Owls, Cooper's Hawks (*Accipiter cooperii*) and Red-tailed Hawks are known to take Merlins (Palmer 1988, who specifically mentions Great Horned Owls killing Merlins in territorial disputes, though the falcon was not then eaten). It is suspected that Gyrfalcons will take Merlins, though an examination of 45,000 individual prey items in Icelandic Gyrfalcon nests over more than 30 years revealed the remains of only one Merlin (O. K. Nielsen, personal communication). Lindberg (1983) also records finding a Merlin in Gyrfalcon prey remains in Sweden: the remains constituted just one of 1,869 recovered items, representing 0.18% by number and 0.06% by biomass. These data suggest that attacks by Gyrfalcons are opportunistic and rare. While I was studying Gyrfalcons in Iceland, I once found a Merlin nest within 200–300 m of nesting Gyrfalcons and saw no aggressive encounters between the two. Woodin (1980) also found Gyrfalcons and Merlins nesting in close proximity in Iceland. Woodin saw aggression from the Merlins to the Gyrs, but not the reverse.

In Fennoscandia, Mikkola (1983) noted that both Eagle Owls and Tawny Owls preyed upon Merlins: Merlins represented 5 of 705 prey items in the diet of the larger owl, 1 of 33 prey items for the smaller owl. In a very interesting observation, Tømmeraas (1993) recorded the killing of a female Merlin by Golden Eagles in the Alta-Kautokeino region of Finnmark in northern Norway. A Merlin pair was nesting about 200 m from the Golden Eagle pair and regularly mobbed the eagles when they left their eyrie. One day the female Merlin was observed stooping on an eagle. After one stoop the Merlin gained height in order to stoop again: as it reached the top of its climb and effectively became momentarily motionless as

FIG 282. This young Goshawk may grow up to be a threat to neighbouring Merlins.

it turned to attack, the second eagle grabbed it from its blind side. Tømmeraas considered that the killing of the Merlin was an example of cooperative hunting, the first eagle acting as bait for the falcon with the second eagle waiting its moment to strike.

Merlins may also fall victim to mammalian predators such as Red Foxes, Pine Martens and other mustelids. MacIntrye (1936) records finding an Adder (*Vipera berus*) in a Merlin nest he had gone to inspect. He killed it and then found that three of the four eggs he knew had been laid were missing. He dissected the snake and found the contents of the three eggs. Records of Adder egg predation are rare, but Roberts & Green (1983) note that at a nest in their study area in north Wales one nestling was preyed upon by an Adder; Haffield (2012) reports a similar occurrence in south Wales, as does Shaw (1994) in southwest Scotland.

If humans approach a Merlin nest, an incubating female may simply fly off silently. Ground-nesting females usually respond in this way as well, the hope, presumably, being, of departure without drawing the intruder's attention to the nest. The female may then circle overhead, where she may be joined by the male. In such cases the birds may call, but may also remain silent. However, Merlin attacks on humans have been reported, attacks in North America including strikes and blood-letting (Craighead & Craighead 1940). In Asia Merlins have also been seen to feign injury in order to lead humans and their dogs away from nests (Karyakin & Nikolenko 2009).

In addition to the taking of eggs and deliberate destruction of nests, humans may be responsible for unwitting disturbance. In Scotland I am aware of one Merlin pair deserting a nest when walkers camped beside the tree in which it was set. In addition to the obvious disturbance of the campers themselves, a fire was lit which probably engulfed the nest in smoke. It is not known if the falcons attempted to breed elsewhere. Merlins are illegally poached in Russia, being collected during expeditions aimed primarily at gathering wild Gyrfalcons for sale in the West. Lobkov (2012) notes that among a 'cargo' of 58 falcons seized on a vessel near Kamchatka in late 2012 there were two Merlins and two Peregrines, the rest of the birds being Gyrfalcons; two other falcons were seen to have been thrown into the sea before the vessel was boarded by the Federal Security Services. At the same time a further 20 Gyrfalcons were found on another vessel and 14 Gyrs were seized at Vladivostock airport. All these birds had been captured in Kamchatka. Whether Merlins had been deliberately targeted or had been taken by mistake (just another falcon, as it were) is not clear. Also unclear is whether other Merlins are killed rather than released when taken during such operations when it is realised they are not as required. Sadly, adequate resources are not available to control the illegal poaching of falcons in Russia.

CHAPTER 8

Populations: Past, Present and Future

I**N THIS CHAPTER WE EXAMINE** the recent population history of each of the four falcons and consider the current position and the threats (or otherwise) to the species, before looking to the future.

PEREGRINE

As Ratcliffe (1993) notes, although the medieval age of falconry meant that the position of known Peregrine eyries was documented throughout the period from about 1200 onwards, the likelihood that this was a complete list is minimal, and the true British population before about 1900 cannot be computed. Once the coasts and wildernesses of Britain were more fully explored, the number of Peregrine eyries could be better established. Using data on the number of territories known to have been lost during the period 1880–1930, mainly due to disturbance by humans, Ratcliffe estimated that the population in the last years of the nineteenth century was about 1,365 pairs, and that this had declined to about 1,100 pairs before the outbreak of the 1939–1945 war. During the war, in order to protect carrier pigeons an order was made for the killing of Peregrines and the destruction of their nests, eggs and young (Note 8.1). As Ratcliffe (1993) notes, the order covered only certain counties (a rather odd collection). However, the effect was to virtually eradicate the falcons from southwest England and to deplete the population in other areas. Around 600 adult and juvenile falcons were killed in total with an unknown number of eggs and chicks destroyed;

482 · FALCONS

ABOVE: **FIG 283.** The Peregrine chicks in this nest box on top of a church tower in southwest England will soon be fledged.

FIG 284. Female Peregrine.

the best estimate is that the British population was reduced to perhaps 80% of the 1939 level.

The pesticide problem

Following the end of the Second World War, the government-sanctioned persecution of Peregrines ceased, and it is estimated that by the mid-1950s the population had returned to, or close to, the 1939 level. The population then crashed, though it was not until 1961 that the true extent of the collapse became apparent and an investigation was begun to identify the cause. By that time it is estimated that the Peregrine population had declined by at least 30%, an extraordinary reduction in so short a time. The investigation was led by Derek Ratcliffe (Note 8.2), whose book on the Peregrine has already been mentioned several times.

The investigation, begun in 1961, gathered data on Peregrines and Peregrine territories and found that, far from increasing, the population was actually in steep decline. The first evidence for a potential cause was in the large number of seed-eating birds which had been found dead during 1959–1960. Analysis showed that these birds had died after eating seeds treated with a new generation of pesticides which had quickly followed DDT onto the market. DDT, which had been discovered in 1939, had been used extensively as a pesticide during the latter years of the war. DDT was an organochlorine compound, as were the new chemicals. Compounds such as aldrin and dieldrin were highly effective against the insects and fungi they were supposed to target, but were far more dangerous to birds and animals than DDT had been. The pesticides were clearly killing birds which consumed treated seed, and, by implication, were also harming the predators which preyed on them. Analysis of unhatched eggs in Peregrine eyries showed that there were high levels of DDE (a residue of DDT produced by chemical breakdown of the original compound) and the newer pesticides. More importantly, it was found that the number of broken eggs in Peregrine nests was increasing. Ratcliffe (1970) noted that of 100 clutches examined in the period 1905–1950 only three had contained a broken egg or eggs, while of 163 clutches examined during 1951–1966, 51 had broken egg(s), an increase from 3% to 31%.

While it was clear that pesticides were killing adult birds and fatally contaminating some eggs, it also seemed that even viable eggs might be being lost as a consequence of changes to the eggshell itself which promoted breakage. Ratcliffe therefore needed a measure of the shell thickness, as, clearly, thinner shells were more vulnerable to breakage. He developed the equation (Ratcliffe 1967):

$$\text{eggshell thickness index} = \frac{\text{weight of shell (mg)}}{\text{shell length (mm)} \times \text{shell breadth (mm)}}$$

which is now known as the Ratcliffe index.

FIG 285. Peregrine nestling.

Use of the index allowed the shell thickness of museum specimens to be examined without damaging the eggs, so that changes over time could be established and the possibility of organochlorine-induced shell thickness identified as a problem. For a comprehensive review of Ratcliffe's work and the organochlorine contamination story, see Ratcliffe (1970) or Ratcliffe (1993).

Use of the Ratcliffe index is now widespread (Note 8.3), and it has been subject to testing by other researchers. Weighing eggs in the field, coupled with knowledge of the mean and range of embryo weights, allows the index to be calculated without the need to sample a clutch. In interesting work by Fox *et al.* (1975), the research team used β-particle backscatter to measure eggshell thickness, and the Ratcliffe index was shown to be highly correlated to the backscatter data, confirming the use of the index in the field. Perhaps more importantly, Fox (1979) presented data which allowed the level of DDE contamination in Merlin eggs to be assessed (within about 20%) by comparison with the Ratcliffe index, thus allowing a measure of contamination without the need for analysis, which requires expensive equipment and egg destruction (Fig. 286). To do this Fox measured the index for eggs from 110 nest attempts by Merlins between 1969 and 1973 in Alberta and Saskatchewan, Canada. The nests were then grouped according to index and the number of nestlings from each which reached the age at which they could be ringed was noted. The number of nests from which at least one nestling reached such an age, but which were not entirely successful, was also noted. The DDE contamination was also measured for eggs of each index. The result indicated not only the relationship between DDE level and the Ratcliffe index, but also the relationship between the index and Merlin breeding success.

Ratcliffe's findings on eggshell thickness were taken up in the USA, where it was soon shown that thinning to the same extent had taken place, and again the thinning was associated with the use of organochlorine pesticides. The unequivocal evidence of the impact of the chemicals, not only on Peregrines but on a large number of species, led to the phasing out of the pesticides, though dieldrin was not finally banned as a cereal seed dressing until late 1975. The falcon population began to increase (Fig. 287), though the persistence of

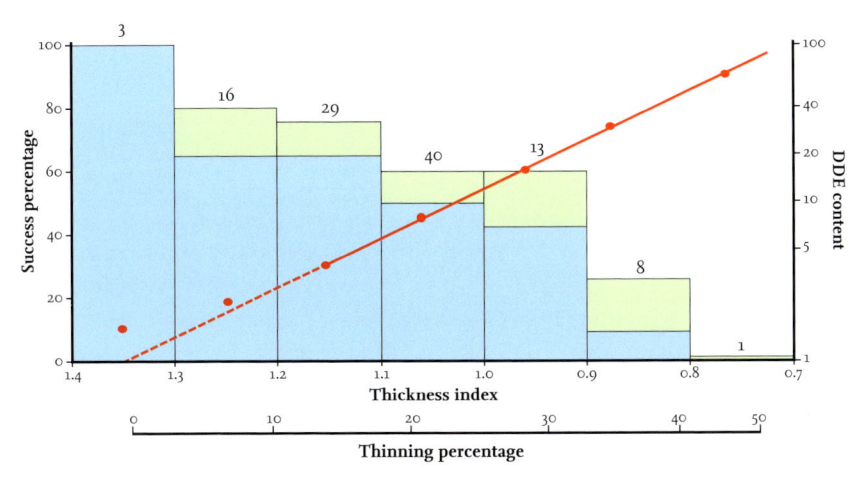

FIG 286. Variation of Ratcliffe index with DDE content (ppm wet weight) and nesting success for 110 Merlin nests during the period 1969–1973 in southern Canada. The blue histograms are the percentage of nests in which all eggs produced nestlings reaching ringing age. The pale green histograms are nests in which at least one nestling reached ringing age. DDE content for a given index class is represented by red dots. Numbers above histograms are the numbers of nests in each index group. Redrawn from Fox 1979.

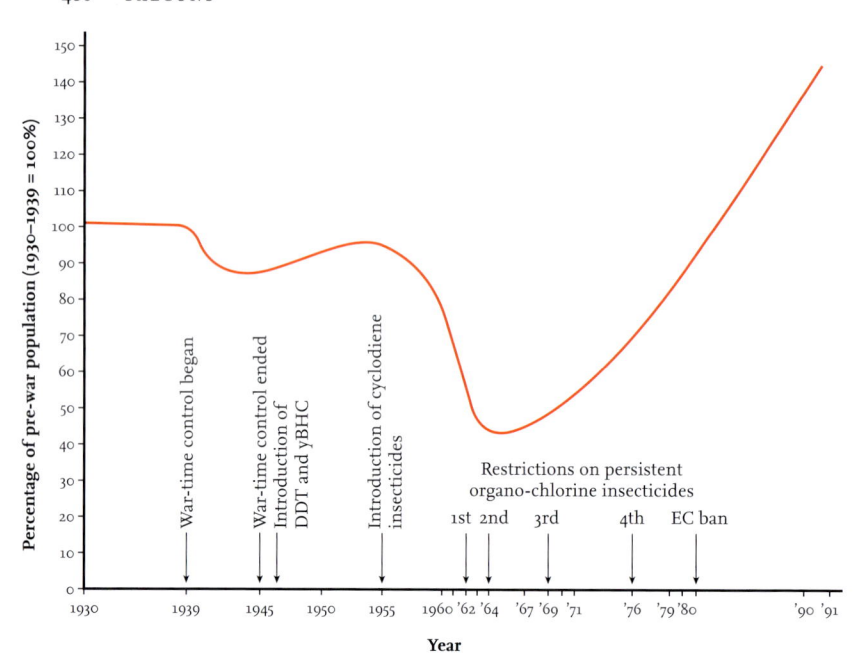

FIG 287. Variation of the British Peregrine population with time, assessed as a percentage of the 1939 population of 1,100 pairs. Redrawn from Ratcliffe 1993.

the chemicals in the environment meant that birds continued to be exposed to them, and some birds accumulated quantities sufficient to cause health problems and even death: Ratcliffe (1993) records that even in 1974 adult Peregrines were dying as a consequence of contaminant burden. However, the position is now much better, the immigration of Peregrines to British cities adding to a general increase in population. However, King (2008) saw a female Peregrine leaving the nest with a broken egg attached to her breast feathers. The female pecked the egg free, then bathed, presumably to clean her plumage. On investigating the nest, King discovered another broken egg. While this is not evidence of shell thinning rather than, say, clumsiness on the part of the female, it does give pause for thought.

The population increase was, at first, merely a recovery to the precontamination level, but after the early 1980s numbers began to exceed the assumed stable population of the 1930s. In 1991 it was estimated that there were 1,283 pairs, and this number had increased to 1,468 pairs by 2002 (Banks *et al.* 2010). The increase involved not only a recolonisation of ancient territories, but range expansion.

Availability of prey

Since, by definition, the population has to be sustained by available resources, this continuing increase cannot be maintained, particularly when the general trend in species populations in Britain is to remain stable or decline. Grouse-moor management can aid the Peregrines as long as persecution is minimal, and there is evidence to suggest that the racing pigeon population of Britain increased by about one-third between the mid-1970s and 1991, based on the number of rings issued annually by the governing body (the Royal Pigeon Racing Association), though the rate of rise has now decreased. Dixon & Richards (2003) investigated the probable kill rates of domestic pigeons in south Wales, concluding that the success rate of adult Peregrines was 0.19 kills per hour, but that adults with dependent young increase this to 0.29 kills per hour. Given the fraction of domestic pigeons in the diet of Peregrines, this represents a large number of birds, though, of course, in terms of the overall losses of pigeons from other causes, it is much less significant from the point of view of pigeon owners (see Chapter 2). For the Peregrines pigeons are a highly significant food resource, and a decline in popularity of the sport, coupled with a change in release points of racing pigeons, has been suggested as the main factor in the decline of Peregrines in central Wales (Dixon *et al.* 2010). Dixon and co-workers examined the diet of Peregrines during the racing pigeon season (April–September) and outside the season (October–March) and found that the percentage of domestic pigeons fell from 31.4% in season to 5.5% out of season. While the fraction of most other species remained essentially constant, the fraction of starlings and thrushes rose to compensate for the lack of pigeons.

A further change in potential prey populations is that of British waders. As already noted in Chapter 7, the latest Wetland Bird Survey (Austin *et al.* 2014) noted the significant fall in populations of some waders, including Dunlin and Redshank, which are important prey species for Peregrines overwintering at estuaries. These declines appear to be associated with increased agricultural intensity, which not only altered the habitat but also, when it involved cattle grazing, meant that many nests were trampled, or were preyed upon as a consequence of nest exposure due to grazing. In a study on the Ribble estuary, Lancashire, Sharps *et al.* (2015) found that an increase in cattle density from 0.15 to 0.82 animals per hectare increased the trampling rate from 16% to 98%, while nest predation rose from 28% with no grazing to 95% with 0.55 cattle per hectare.

In a study of tundra Peregrines in northern Canada, Court (1986) found that the population increased by 30% during a year when the rodent population reached a peak. Such peaks are a characteristic of the rodent populations of

FIG 288. In a remarkable display of flying ability, this female Peregrine seemed to hang in front of the photographer as though standing on a transparent perch.

the Arctic, and while Peregrines remained primarily bird feeders, they were sufficiently flexible in their hunting abilities and diet to take advantage of the rodent surplus. In Britain such rodent peaks do not occur. Neither do they occur in birds, and with environmental changes acting against prey species, for instance the degree of afforestation as well as the change in estuarine agriculture mentioned above, a Peregrine population ceiling was inevitable once grouse and pigeon numbers stabilised.

Current population estimates

The latest population data from the BTO (based on a 2014 survey) for the UK and the Isle of Man suggests that there has been a stabilisation of the Peregrine population since 2002. In 2002 Banks *et al.* (2010) estimated the number of breeding pairs at 1,437, while the latest survey suggests 1,505 for the same area. While the two estimates are essentially the same, the distribution of Peregrines has altered, with a significant increase in England (34%) and a much smaller increase in Northern Ireland (17%) being offset by reductions in Wales (12% – see, for instance, Dixon *et al.* 2010) and Scotland (11% – see, for instance, Etheridge 2013, who considered that the increase in driven grouse moors and consequent persecution was the probable cause). The BTO survey suggested that the breeding population of England was 628 pairs, with 96 pairs in Northern Ireland, 509 in Scotland, 249 in Wales and 23 in the Isle of Man (down from 31 pairs in 2002). In a study in Ireland, Mee (2012) concluded that the Peregrine population of Ireland (north and south) was 450–500 breeding pairs.

Birdlife International (www.birdlife.org) estimates that the world population of Peregrines is 100,000–500,000 mature individuals, considers the population is stable, and notes that the species is currently considered by the International Union for Conservation of Nature (IUCN) to be of 'least concern'. In their recent book on the Peregrine, White *et al.* (2013a) give estimates for each of the subspecies they identify, as well as for the Barbary Falcon (which they consider to be a subspecies). In some cases their estimates are wide, but summing across the subspecies produces a world population of 53,000–65,000 breeding pairs. This figure is comparable with the lower Birdlife International estimate, and as White and colleagues note, the number of individual birds always exceeds the number of breeding pairs multiplied by two, because of non-breeding adults and pairs which do not breed. White *et al.* also note that considerable uncertainties exist in the estimates of many of their subspecies.

Birdlife International estimates the European Peregrine population at 14,900–28,800 pairs. This is much closer to the estimate of White *et al.*, who estimate at least 16,000 pairs, split equally between the nominate subspecies (which breeds

FIG 289. Female Peregrine feeding a well-grown chick.

in Britain) and the 'Mediterranean' Peregrine (*F. p. brookei*). Assuming estimates of White and co-authors to be correct, then some 20% of the world population of the nominate subspecies breeds in Britain. It is therefore gratifying that the British population appears stable or even, perhaps, to be slowly increasing. However, the reductions in Scotland and Wales, where the mountainous inland areas and rugged coasts offer ideal Peregrine habitat, gives cause for concern, particularly with the continuing disquiet over the killing of raptors on managed grouse moors. It will be interesting to see whether the rise in the English population is due mainly to urban breeding, and whether this will lead to a movement of falcons towards traditional territories or the development of a truly 'urban' Peregrine stock.

KESTREL

In the *New Atlas* (Gibbons *et al.* 1993), Village noted that the Kestrel could be found in most parts of the British Isles. Saxby (1874) included the Kestrel in the birds of Shetland, but noted that it was migratory, arriving in small numbers to nest on the cliffs, especially those of Unst and Fetlar. As the human population declined, with a presumed reduction in the mouse population, Kestrels had to compete with Merlins for small birds. The latter was both far better able to hunt such prey and more abundant, and as a consequence Kestrels disappeared from the islands. They are still seen regularly as spring and autumn migrants, but are no longer considered a breeding species, though pairs did breed in 1905 and 1992. The species is also absent as a breeding species from the northern Outer Hebrides, and from much of western Scotland. It is found throughout most of England and Wales, though it is scarce across much of the latter and in England's Southwest Peninsula. This scarcity in western Scotland, Wales and western England could perhaps be due, in part, to high rainfall in those areas, which inhibits hunting more than it does in eastern Britain, though the *New Atlas* notes abundant Kestrels in the Lake District, which is also an area of high rainfall. Kestrels are also found on the Isle of Man and the Channel Islands. It is scarce in Ireland, from which its chief prey, the Field Vole, is absent.

Population estimates
In the first *Atlas* (Sharrock 1976) the population of Kestrels in Britain and Ireland was estimated at 100,000 pairs. Within a decade Newton (1984) had lowered this best estimate to 84,000 pairs. When the *New Atlas* (Gibbons *et al.* 1993) was published, the estimate had been revised downwards again, with Village

considering that 50,000 pairs was the best estimate for the British Isles as a whole (though accepting that the likely error on the calculation meant that the range was 25,000–89,000). Shrubb (1993a) reduced the probable population yet again, considering it to lie within a band of 35,000–40,000 pairs, though this was for Great Britain rather than the British Isles. Baker *et al.* (2006) considering the likely population to be 36,800 pairs for the United Kingdom, with a further 8,400 pairs in the Republic of Ireland – where Crowe *et al.* (2010) noted in their study of 52 species over the period 1998–2008 that the Kestrel was one of four showing the greatest rate of decline (the other three were the Swift, Skyark and Mistle Thrush). However, Mee (2012) in a review of data from the whole of Ireland, considered the total population of Ireland was 10,000, a figure in good agreement with that of Baker *et al.* (2006). Baker *et al.* considered their estimate to be '2' on a scale of '1' (good) to '3' (poor), having derived it by extrapolation from a combination of sample surveys and data from the BTO's Common Birds Census (CBC), later replaced by the Breeding Bird Survey (BBS), each of which involved large numbers of sample areas and counts by volunteers. Data from the latest BBS, combined with previous CBC/BBS data and earlier best estimates of Kestrel population, has allowed the population trend of Fig. 291 to be derived.

FIG 290. This Kestrel in Cornwall seems intent on having a close look at the photographer. (James Sellen)

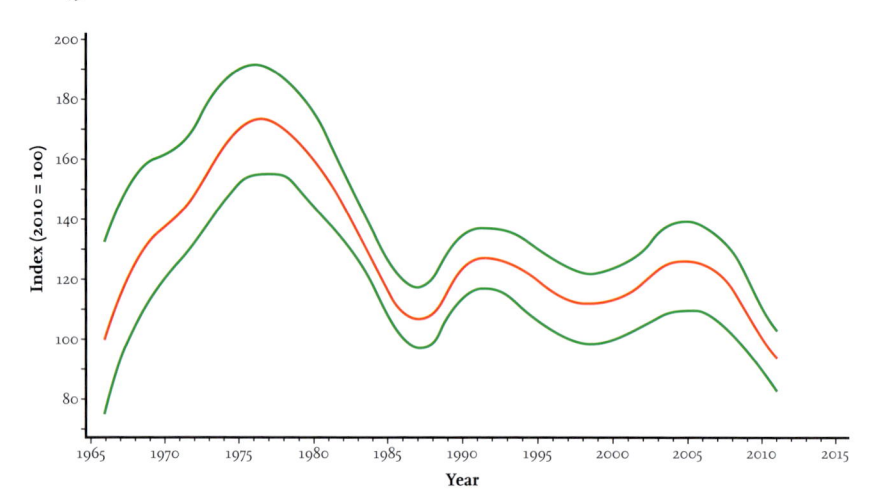

FIG 291. Kestrel population trend in the UK over the last 50 years. The probable upper and lower limits lie above and below the current best estimate. Redrawn from CBC/BBS data and earlier estimates.

However, it is worth noting that Clements (2008), extrapolating from studies made in several counties across England to define breeding densities in differing farmlands, urban and moorland areas, derived a total population of 53,000–57,500 pairs for Britain. This overall population estimate broke down as 43,000 (best estimate) in England, with ranges of 2,500–3,500 pairs in Wales and 7,500–11,000 pairs in Scotland. The estimate for Wales seems optimistic if the figures presented in the *Welsh Bird Reports* of the Welsh Ornithological Society over recent years are correct, as these indicate a breeding population of little more than 100 pairs at the latest. Even allowing for the possible limitations on data gathering – a small number of sample areas, and some counties not included, which makes such a low figure very unlikely to be realistic – it is likely that the Welsh Ornithological Society's view that the species is a 'rather scarce breeding resident' and the Kestrel's 'red-listing' in the Principality provide a more accurate view of the situation than Clements' estimate of the Welsh breeding population.

In Scotland, Riddle (2011) notes that the decline has been greater than that seen in England, quoting a 54% decline between 1995 and 2008. Musgrove *et al.* (2013) state a best estimate for the United Kingdom (i.e. including Northern Ireland but excluding the Republic of Ireland) of 46,000 pairs. Musgrove and co-workers also quote 45,000 for Great Britain, implying 1,000 pairs in Northern Ireland.

Population trends

But whatever the true population, there is little doubt that in recent years the Kestrel has been in decline throughout Britain, and that the rate of decline is increasing. The reduction has caused the BTO to place the Kestrel on its Amber list (species with a breeding population decline of > 25% but < 50%) for the country as a whole, and it is worth considering what the reasons might be.

Figure 291 notes the increase in Kestrel numbers following the decline due principally to the effects of organochlorine pesticides. In the 1980s there was another decline, initially, it is believed, caused by habitat loss due to agricultural changes. Riddle (2011) considers that Kestrel habitat was limited by reduction in land quality in Scotland, due to increased number of sheep and deer, increased sheep numbers in Wales, and afforestation in both countries, while farming practices (limiting the acreage of mixed farmland) in England may also have reduced available habitat.

Shrubb (1993a) noted that intensive sheep farming (the number of sheep in Wales, for instance, had almost doubled since the 1960s) had reduced the availability of rough grazing, the preferred vole habitat, and hence reduced vole (and therefore Kestrel) abundance. Subsequently, Shrubb (2003) noted the conclusion of Harris *et al.* (1995) that as Rabbit numbers recovered after the myxomatosis epidemic, vole numbers declined. The increase in agricultural monocultures has also caused a decline in vole habitat, as has the reduction in the number of hedgerows. It is now common to see crops harvested and, within a day or two, fields ploughed and then reseeded, allowing little time for small mammals to benefit from harvesting spillage. In a study of Kestrels in northern Italy, Costantini *et al.* (2014) noted that falcons breeding in areas of intense cultivation (areas with limited temporary or permanent grassland) bred later and had offspring with poorer body condition (measured by body mass and size). Such young Kestrels are less able to cope with the rigours of their first winter.

It is also true that the decline in Kestrels has occurred at the same time as there has been an increase in Buzzard, Peregrine and Goshawk numbers. Shrubb (2003) noted the increase in Buzzard numbers in Wales and considered these to have increased pressure on Kestrels, as the larger birds are resident and tend to claim the better territories. Buzzards take larger prey and, being better able to make a living in the landscape, will move Kestrels away from superior hunting areas. As noted in Chapter 5, the Buzzard's habit of hovering below flight-hunting Kestrels is a method of forcing the smaller bird to move elsewhere. The increase in Buzzard numbers is not restricted to Wales, and if the species is out-competing Kestrels in the Principality, it will presumably be doing the same in England and Scotland.

FIG 292. Going to inspect a Kestrel brood in a stick nest, we discovered a single fledged, but clearly poorly flying chick lying in the heather some distance from the nesting tree (a). Closer to the tree there was evidence of wild camping with a fire. It seems campers, probably unaware of the nest, had caused enough smoke and disturbance to cause the Kestrel chicks to fly. The chick we found had not made it far. Exhausted and dehydrated, the chick drank water from the palms of our hands. It was restored to its nest (b), where, to our relief, it was visited by the female a couple of hours later.

Petty *et al.* (2003), in a study in the Kielder Forest, Northumberland, noted that Kestrel numbers declined over a 23-year period despite voles remaining abundant (but with cyclic fluctuations). The decline in Kestrel numbers was positively correlated with the increase in Goshawk numbers, allowing for changes in vole population, the larger raptor having moved into the area in 1973 with numbers increasing until 1989 and then remaining stable (Fig. 293a). The number of Short-eared Owls, diurnal vole hunters as Kestrels are, also declined, while the numbers of Long-eared and Tawny owls (nocturnal vole hunters) stayed constant. Petty and co-workers therefore examined the diet of the Kielder Goshawks. The hawks fed mainly on birds, species including six raptors – Kestrel, Long-eared, Short-eared and Tawny owls, Sparrowhawk and Merlin. The raptors comprised 4.5% of the Goshawk diet, but Kestrels formed 58.2% of the raptor total – in other words, they contributed more to the diet than all the other raptors combined. Figure 293b suggests that the Goshawks took a progressively larger fraction of a declining Kestrel population.

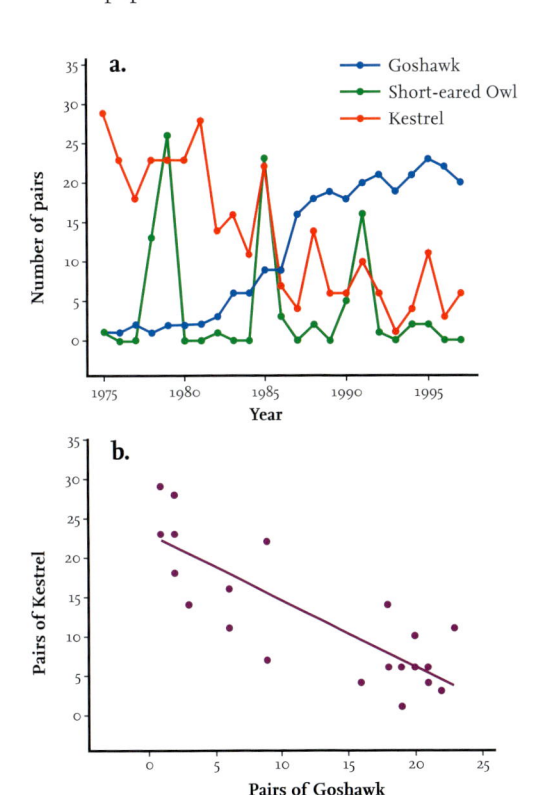

FIG 293. (a) Variation in numbers of pairs of Kestrels, Short-eared Owls and Goshawks over a 23-year period in Northumberland's Kielder Forest. (b) Variation in the number of pairs of Kestrels and Goshawks. The correlation in decline in Kestrel numbers with the increase in Goshawk pairs is statistically significant. Redrawn from Petty *et al.* 2003.

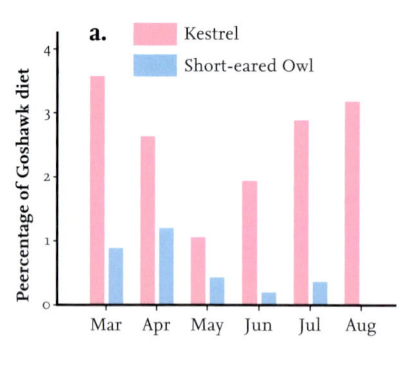

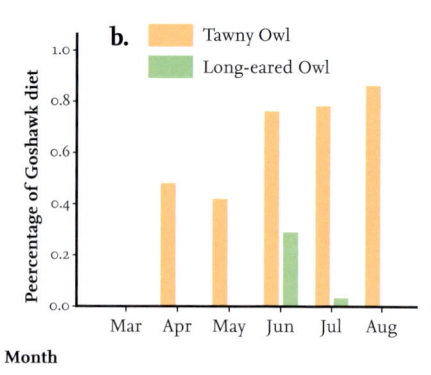

FIG 294. (a) Variation in fraction of Kestrel and Short-eared Owl remains in Goshawk diet from March to August, over a 22-year period in Northumberland's Kielder Forest. The variation from the expected fraction, based on population levels of the two species, is statistically significant: i.e. the Goshawks are preferentially taking the diurnal vole eaters at particular times. (b) Variation in fraction of Tawny and Long-eared owls in the Goshawk diet over the same period. In this case the expected fraction was not significantly different from that expected. The Goshawk predation increased during the late summer when they were able to take fledglings. Redrawn from Petty *et al.* 2003.

Kestrels were preyed upon more in spring and autumn than during the summer (Fig. 294), which implies that the Goshawks were killing unpaired Kestrels looking for territories prior to the commencement of breeding, predation which would have the greatest impact on the population, and during the autumn when the number of juveniles was high, predation which would have an impact on the population the following spring. Kestrels seem particularly vulnerable to attack, which, as Petty and co-workers note, is likely to be as a result of hovering flight, which allows a 'blind-side' attack. Short-eared Owls are vulnerable because their hunt method, slow quartering, is equally open to attack.

From the results of Petty *et al.* (2003) there seems little doubt that Goshawk predation of Kestrels is significant in reducing numbers in areas where both are found, and it is no surprise to find that both Shrubb (2004) and Riddle (2011) note the potential significance of Goshawk predation following population increases of the species in Wales and Scotland respectively. In a later study in the Kielder Forest on the predation of Tawny Owls by Goshawks, Hoy *et al.* (2015) found that the hawks preferentially took juvenile owls, but that within the adult population females, particularly older females, were taken most often. They noted that despite the predation the population of owls remained essentially stable, as the preference shown by the Goshawks was for owls of low reproductive potential and so represented the least harmful scenario. However, if the population of

FIG 295. A female Kestrel arrives with prey to feed her brood.

the prey species is under threat from other causes, as is likely for Kestrels in certain areas, a similar Goshawk preferential predation strategy could result in a significant population decline as the breeding stock was reduced due to an enhanced juvenile death rate. The Goshawk is a beautiful, but formidable, predator which is also thought to be responsible for the decline in Merlin numbers in areas where both species are found. In Austria, Goshawk predation is also considered to be responsible for a change in the nesting habits of the Honey-buzzard (Gamauf *et al.* 2014). However, Goshawk predation cannot be the reason for the decline in Kestrels observed in Ireland, as the Goshawk population there is believed to be less than ten pairs.

The population of Peregrines has increased slightly in recent years, and it is possible that they are out-competing Kestrels for nesting sites, particularly in urban areas (examples of the larger falcon ousting the smaller species from historic nesting sites being known), and reducing Kestrel numbers by direct predation. Red Kite numbers have also increased, creating pressure on Buzzards which may, in turn, have caused the latter to compete with Kestrels for territory, as well as possibly increasing direct predation. Red Kites are also mammal feeders and so may compete directly. But as Kestrel numbers have declined, Hobby numbers have increased, and while there is clearly no specific one-to-one comparison between the two smaller falcons, the implication is that predation by, or competition from, larger raptors cannot be the entire story.

There is evidence that the population of Field Voles, the main prey of Kestrels, is becoming less cyclic, which has raised concerns over the loss of ecosystem function. In a cooperative study by researchers across Europe, data on the annual variation in the population of *Microtus* species and other rodents was aggregated from sites which included northern England, central Europe (from western France to Poland) and northern Europe (Finland and northern Fennoscandia) since 1995 (Cornulier *et al.* 2013). Data analysis indicated that in 83% of the rodent populations which had been studied there had been a twofold decline in the spring-population cyclic amplitude, while in 67% of the studied populations there had been a decline in both spring and autumn cyclic amplitudes, though in these cases the spring decline was the most marked. Only in eastern Germany and Poland was there no evidence of a general pattern that vole population cycles were being dampened. Cornulier and co-workers note that there are three basic theories of why such cycle dampening occurs, and that all of these invoke environmental change, one involving random changes, the other two requiring sustained change. While Cornulier *et al.* are careful to avoid confirming a correlation between climate change and vole cycle decline, they do note that the evidence is suggestive of a climatic driver, as whatever the proximate cause of the decline it has coincided with a time of global environmental change, and it is known that a degradation of wintering conditions affects winter reproduction in voles and vole survival, while a reduction in winter population leads to a reduction in spring breeding and a dampening of any spring cycle. Cornulier *et al.* note that the decline, with its frequent prolonged periods of low-amplitude changes in vole (and other rodent) populations, would not preclude occasional peaks, such as that seen in Fennoscandia in 2011 (see Note 5.4), it would very likely result in a decline in the number of rodent predators, and that, inevitably, would mean a decline in Kestrel numbers. In Fennoscandia rodent populations live beneath the snow, which creates a 'blanket' shielding them from much colder ambient air temperatures as well as offering protection from predation while they forage. Warmer winters have caused the snow blanket to become less efficient, the thaw–freeze conditions which are now more normal creating a more difficult habitat with food occasionally encased in ice (see, for instance, Korslund & Steen 2006). While such winter conditions are not common in Britain, warmer, wetter winters are also likely to create difficult conditions for voles and so reduce winter survival.

FIG 296. Female Kestrel doing her best to brood five tired and fractious chicks.

There is some evidence to suggest that the numbers of mammal-eating predators may be influenced by pesticides. Walker *et al.* (2013) measured the concentrations of second-generation anticoagulant rodenticides (SGARs) in the livers of Barn Owl, Red Kite and Kestrel corpses collected across Britain. SGARs were developed to combat the pesticide resistance developed by, in particular,

Brown Rats, and include a number of compounds, most often difenacoum and bromadiolone. SGARs were detected in 94% of Red Kites and 84% of Barn Owls. While the concentrations were not shown to have been the direct cause of death in any of these birds, some of the kites showed signs of haemorrhaging, which may have been due to high liver concentrations. The study indicated that the incidence of SGARs in the livers of these two predators was rising. The position for Kestrels differs because although SGARs were found in the livers of 95% of dead birds, the sample size was small ($n = 20$). There was, therefore, no evidence that either the incidence or the concentration of SGARs had increased over previous studies. Nevertheless, the rise observed in the other two species implies that rodenticide concentrations in the livers of mammal-eating predators are on the increase and may be contributing to bird mortality.

The evidence for the reduction in vole population cyclicity might also help to explain why the Kestrel is a declining species across Europe. The European Bird Census Council notes a 38% reduction in the European Kestrel population since 1980, but a 42% reduction since 1990, the European population showing a similar trend to that of British Kestrels (PECBMS 2012). At present the European decline is considered 'moderate', meaning less than 5% per annum. Interestingly, one country in which the trend has been reversed is Finland, where the Kestrel population almost doubled from 1998 to 2009 (Honkala *et al.* 2012). There was a slight fall in 2010/11, but this seems to have been part of a three-year cycle which the population has shown consistently over the last 20 or so years, following a similar rodent population cycle. Since Finland is home to the Goshawk, this Kestrel increase seems surprising at first sight. The reduction in pesticide levels is considered to account for the initial rise in Kestrel numbers, while the later continuation of the rise resulted from the nationwide deployment of nest boxes to which the birds have rapidly become accustomed, coupled with a decline in the Finnish Goshawk population (P. Byholm, personal communication).

It is probable that the decline of Kestrels in Britain is due to a number of factors, including those mentioned above (and others: see the comment on wind turbine collisions under *Survival* in Chapter 5). The fluctuations in the population since the major decline of the late 1970s and early 1980s were not explicitly synchronised to vole population cycles, so unknown or poorly understood factors are responsible for changes in Kestrel numbers. However, the deeper decline since the last fluctuation peak of 2005 suggests that something more radical is occurring, and that the population will need more careful observation in the future to identify the need for conservation measures if the decline continues.

FIG 297. (a) An adult Hobby with a dragonfly is pursued by a hungry juvenile. (b) The juvenile grabs the dragonfly with its feet. (c) The juvenile has a good hold on the dragonfly … (d) … and finally the adult releases the dragonfly and the juvenile flies off with it. (Harry Albrecht)

HOBBY

Cramp & Simmons (1980) suggested a British population of about 100 pairs, a decrease in the nineteenth century due to human activity being followed by a century of fluctuating, but essentially stable, population. It is possible that during this period of stability the population might have grown, but the rarity of the Hobby during much of the twentieth century meant that it was the target for egg collectors, a practice which has now, thankfully, declined significantly.

The 100 pairs suggested by Cramp & Simmons may have been an underestimate at the time, but the population has increased substantially since, and at present there is no indication that it will not continue to do so as Hobbies extend their range and recolonise areas from which they were eliminated. What was once a species confined to the southern counties of England can now be found as far north as Inverness, and as far west as the borders of the Snowdonia National Park, though British Hobbies have not altered their habitat, and remain a lowland bird.

An indication of the extent of population increase can be seen in the study of Hobbies in Derbyshire (Messenger 2012), where the breeding density in a 100 km^2 study area in the south of the county increased from 3.00 pairs per 100 km^2 in 1992–1994 to 3.67 in 1999–2001 and then to 8.67 in 2010–2012. The rapid increase in the first decade of the new millennium saw an unsurprising decrease in the mean distance to the nearest neighbour of a Hobby nest from 5.60 km (1992–1994) to 2.10 km in 2010–2012. Messenger noted no substantive change in the mean number of young fledged by a successful pair during the 20-year period.

Hobbies are not only arriving in greater numbers, but are arriving earlier. In a study of data from the Portland Bird Observatory covering the 42-year period 1970–2011, Goodenough *et al.* (2015) found that the first arrival date of the falcons had advanced, though the mean arrival date had not (Fig. 298)

Figure 298 raises the question of what is driving the change in first arrival date, and why the majority of Hobbies are not responding to this driver. Clearly conditions in Britain will affect a Hobby's decision over whether to stay in an area or move northward, but changes in British climate can only influence early arrival if the falcons have a priori knowledge. Hobbies which bred the previous year could have such an understanding, but it would seem more likely that changes in conditions in the wintering quarters or along the migration route are responsible. However, a similar trend in earlier arrivals is not seen in those Merlins which migrate from Britain (Chapter 7, Fig. 275). It is therefore too early to come to definite conclusions.

The reasons for the range expansion are also still discussed, and it is likely that no single factor is at work. Prince & Clarke (1993) considered that the increased range of hawker dragonflies, particularly the Migrant Hawker, as a consequence of the increased number of gravel pits in central Britain might be a factor. Brownett (1998) questioned this causal link, wondering whether Hobbies and dragonflies have increased in tandem and have therefore come

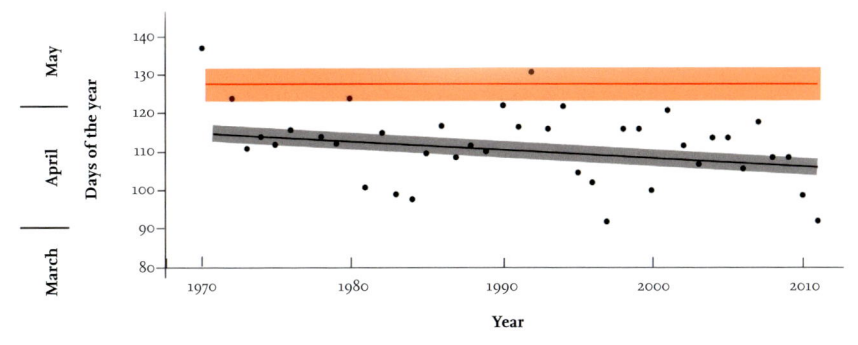

FIG 298. First arrival dates for Hobbies, as recorded by the Portland Bird Observatory, Dorset, for the years 1970–2011 inclusive. Note that a small number of years have been excluded because no falcons were observed. The y axis is the number of days of the year, with 1 January = 1, with allowance for leap years. The black line is a least squares fit to the first arrival date data, with the shaded block representing one standard deviation on the inter-year data. The red line is the least squares fit to the mean annual date, again with the shaded block at one standard deviation on the inter-year data. (With thanks to Dr Anne Goodenough of the University of Gloucestershire and Martin Cade of the Portland Bird Observatory.)

into contact more often, and that, as a consequence, predation was higher, rather than the falcon population increasing because of the availability of the prey resource. However, Messenger & Roome (2007) have echoed the view of Prince & Clarke, noting the increased frequency of both Migrant Hawkers and Common Darters in Derbyshire.

Global warming and the subsequent increase in airborne insects is also likely to be a factor (Note 8.4), while Sergio & Bogliani (1999) consider that the ability of the Hobby to adapt to modern agricultural methods (for instance an acceptance of habitat fragmentation and a willingness to move nest areas in response to the plant/fell cycle of conifer plantations), coupled with a tolerance of vehicles in the vicinity of nests, is another factor. The value of set-aside, which benefits invertebrates and therefore Hobby prey species, and the trend, particularly of 'small' farmers, to employ environmentally friendly practices, is of considerable help. Hobbies also have few competitors for their preferred hirundine prey species, and their preferred habitat lies away from those of Peregrines and Goshawks, which pose a predation risk: Goshawk numbers in Britain remain (relatively) low and the hawks, in general, are confined to specific areas. If the Goshawk were to become more widely distributed in Britain the effect on the Hobby could be dramatic: Klaus-Dietrich Fiuczynski (personal communication) noted a 40% reduction in Hobby breeding success around Berlin when Goshawks

504 · FALCONS

FIG 299. Hobbies hunting for insects over a lake in southwest England. (Dave Soons)

moved into their breeding area, while in the Netherlands there was a 50% reduction in the Hobby population in the previous decade (Bijlsma & de Vries 1997), which Boer & Hut (1997) considered was due to the prevalence of Goshawk attacks in the wooded areas which were their preferred habitat.

Boer & Hut (1997) consider that tree nesting in open farmland offers the Hobby the best protection against Goshawks, the implication being that open land reduces the possibility of surprise attack by the larger raptor and allows the Hobby to make better use of its flying abilities. It is an interesting suggestion, and has implications for Hobbies both in the Netherlands and in Britain. In many areas of Britain, trees in open country are used by the falcons, the studies of Fuller *et al.* (1985), Parr (1985) and Messenger & Roome (2007) all suggesting that Hobby nests in wooded areas account for only about 15% of the total. That percentage would imply that Hobby numbers would be little affected by an increase in the Goshawk population. However, nests in wooded areas are more difficult to locate, so this percentage may represent a minimum figure, and in southern England Clements & Everett (2012) found that the preferred habitat was woodland, which would increase the Hobby's vulnerability if the Goshawk distribution were to spread.

A. Messenger (personal communication, 2015) also notes that Buzzard numbers have increased in recent years, both in his Derbyshire study area and across Britain, the effect of this being that the Hobby–Buzzard inter-nest distance has decreased. Messenger notes that there is evidence that Buzzards take fledgling Hobbies, and surmises that they may also take nestlings, and that the higher Buzzard population is, the greater the time spent by Hobbies seeing off the larger raptor, an increase which may adversely affect breeding success.

Population estimates and trends

As a consequence of both the increased range of the Hobby and the increased breeding density in some established areas, Chapman (1999a) estimated the British population as 1,350 pairs in the late 1990s, and later estimates have increased this number to about 2,200 (Clements 2001). Musgrove *et al.* (2013) later used the data of Clements (2001) to derive the most recent best-estimate population of 2,800 pairs. Included in this is an estimate of 1–5 pairs in Scotland (Etheridge 2013 – Note 8.5). It is estimated that there were 30 breeding pairs of Hobbies in Wales in 2012 (Pritchard 2013), a population which is considered to have remained stable for the last decade. Breeding in Ireland has not as yet been confirmed, but there is anecdotal information to suggest that it has occurred irregularly in the past. However, Hobbies are regularly seen, and the numbers seen have been increasing in recent years (Fahy 2011), suggesting that breeding may perhaps be confirmed in the near future. It should be noted, though, that while Musgrove *et al.* (2013) consider their estimate to be '2' on a scale which runs from runs 1 to 3 (good to poor), Holling *et al.* (2015) consider the breeding population in 2013 to have been closer to 1,000 pairs.

The population increase has also been aided, in part, by the Hobby being much less susceptible than some other raptors to egg thinning as a consequence of organochlorine contamination, because of a significant difference in diet and the Hobby's migratory lifestyle (Ratcliffe 1970). Ratcliffe quotes a 19.1% decrease in eggshell weight (due largely to thinning) for Peregrines for the period 1947–1969 in comparison to the period 1901–1946. By comparison, over approximately the same periods, the decrease was 12.7% in Merlins, but 4.9% in Kestrels and 5.2% in Hobbies. Although a decrease in breeding success was noted in the Berlin population of Hobbies, Fiuczynski (1991), as already noted, considered the increase in Goshawk numbers and predation by the larger raptor to be responsible.

However, while use of organochlorine pesticides had much less impact on Hobbies than, for instance, on Merlins, the use of neonicotinoid pesticides could offer a greater threat – see the comments on this new class of pesticides in Chapter 2.

The population estimate for Britain of 2,800 breeding pairs (Musgrove *et al.* 2013 – but note the comment above regarding the lower estimate of Holling *et al.* 2015) – would make the Hobby the second most numerous British falcon after the Kestrel, a remarkable achievement for a bird which remains restricted in range (though that is becoming increasingly less the case) and elusive, and so is assumed to be rare by the casual birdwatcher. As a consequence of this population increase, specific conservation measures do not seem to be required. However, it is interesting to note that during the 1980s and early 1990s Hobbies were successfully reared and released into the wild (Woodland 1993). Injured Hobbies returned to health, but disabled and unable to be set free, were bred in captivity, the young from early breedings being placed in wild Hobby nests where they were successfully raised to fledge by foster-parents. The young from later breedings were hacked (Note 8.6). Of three hacked birds one definitely and a second probably returned to the hack box area the following year after successfully migrating. The experience suggests that, were it necessary, Hobbies could be reintroduced.

As A. Messenger notes (personal communication, 2015), the population and breeding density of Hobbies in Britain will, in due course, stabilise. So far, the lack of competition for hirundine prey in Britain has been one factor that has allowed the Hobby to profit from that resource, but sooner or later pressure

FIG 300. A female Hobby starts to dismember prey so as to feed her brood of three chicks.

FIG 301. A female Hobby feeds her single chick.

on hirundine numbers from the Hobbies themselves will result in a decrease in Hobby breeding success. It seems that this point has yet to be reached, but dramatic rises in the Hobby population similar to those seen in the last two decades are unlikely to be replicated in the future.

MERLIN

Nowhere throughout their range are Merlins common, but despite this the species is considered of 'least concern' in conservation terms, because of the vast area of the northern hemisphere in which they are found. Best evidence in North America suggests that the Merlin population is increasing, while across the rest of the range the population is considered to be either stable or slowly increasing. However, the difficulty of establishing Merlin populations with accuracy, because of the remoteness of much of the preferred habitat, means that although the

FIG 302. Female Merlin feeding a brood of four chicks.

FIG 303. Female Merlin feeding a brood of five chicks. In this photo, as in Fig. 302, the chicks were raised in old Buzzard nests.

position appears encouraging, at least in the short and medium term, it is open to question.

The pesticide problem

While present population evidence is reassuring, it is worth recalling that it was not always this way, the consequence of organochlorine contamination being a decline in Merlin populations across its range, though principally in the Nearctic and Europe, as there is much less agricultural land in the Merlin's Asian range. In a report on the status of breeding birds in Great Britain and Ireland, Parslow (1967) noted that over the previous 30–60 years there had been a general decline in the Merlin population, largely as a result of persecution, though no estimate of the population was made. Parslow also commented that in recent years the decline had been more marked. While the catastrophic effect of organochlorine contamination on Peregrines is well known, the effect was equally important in

TABLE 40 Mean clutch size and number of fledglings in Merlin nests in northern England during the period 1961–1976. From Newton et al. (1978).

Period	Mean clutch size	Percentage of nests in which at least one nestling fledged	Mean number of fledglings
1961–1970	4.44	50	3.00
1971–1973	4.33	60	3.06
1974–1976	4.42	75	3.57

the decline in breeding success of the Merlin: it was contamination which had precipitated the steepening of the decline referred to by Parslow.

That contamination was the major cause of the more rapid decline seen in the 1950s and 1960s can be seen in the data of Newton et al. (1978), who compared clutch size and fledging success over the years 1961–1976, a period which saw a decline in the usage of organochlorines (Table 40). While the mean clutch size did not vary over the 16-year period, the increase in the number of nests from which at least one nestling successfully fledged, and in the mean number of nestlings successfully fledged, was statistically significant, at the 99% and 95% levels respectively.

The data of Table 40 show the situation in northern England, and indicate the recovery in the 1970s from the losses which occurred in the preceding decades. Similar declines were seen across the British Isles.

However, while the reproductive success of the falcons had increased following the banning of the use of DDT and related pesticides, the decline of the Merlin continued. At one site in Wales where historically eight Merlin pairs had bred in the mid-1970s, only one remained in 1982 (Roberts & Green 1983). The researchers noted that in this case no single cause for the population reduction could be identified, the decline seemingly due to a combination of predation (largely by humans), fire and poor weather, along with organochlorine contamination. Roberts & Jones (1999) considered that a fire which had destroyed several preferred nest sites was responsible for a decline in their study area in northeast Wales.

Newton et al. (1981) noted that the Merlin had almost disappeared from the Peak District National Park where the general habitat was, in principle, ideal for the species. These researchers considered several potential causes of decline. One was the loss of heather (specifically *Calluna vulgaris*) cover in favour of grassland for sheep rearing. Heather is essential for ground nesting, and in the absence of trees (and, therefore, stick nests) Merlins in the park had traditionally

FIG 304. A juvenile Merlin on its first outing from the nest.

been ground nesters. However, counting prey species on heather and grassland suggested little change in prey density, and although it had been possible to identify lost nest sites in heather areas which had been used previously, but were now grassland, it was considered that overall the loss of heather had been marginal, and seemed not to be the cause of the population decline. Recreational use of the park was also considered. Since the 1960s there had been a significant rise in the numbers using the park for walking and other outdoor pursuits, numbers visiting the National Park Information Centre rising by almost 400% between 1965 and 1980. Disturbance by humans was therefore a possibility, but it seemed footpath use dominated, most visitors forgoing the 'pleasure' of walking through dense heather in favour of the less arduous grassy tracks. Overall Newton *et al.* (1981) were drawn to the conclusion that the effects of organochlorine contamination were largely responsible for the continuing Merlin population decline: that Merlins were contaminated by organochlorines was confirmed in a later study (Newton *et al.* 1982).

In a study of eggs gathered between 1964 and 1986, Newton & Haas (1988) provided further evidence that the Merlin was at risk from continuing contamination, with DDE, HEOD (from dieldrin and aldrin), PCBs and mercury all present. While levels of the organochlorine pollutants had fallen during the study period, the Merlin remained 'the most heavily contaminated of British raptors'. Newton & Haas noted that the Ratcliffe index was negatively correlated to DDE levels – confirming findings from other studies both in Britain (e.g.

Newton et al. 1982) and in North America (e.g. Hodson 1976) – while the overall burden of organochlorine contamination showed the same variation. In other words, DDE was the dominant contaminant with respect to shell thinning. Since DDE is also the most persistent of the organochlorines in the environment, this was a worrying finding.

However, Newton & Haas (1988) noted no negative correlation between organochlorine contamination and brood size, which is curious given the evidence of enhanced shell thinning, and concluded that organochlorine contamination was no longer the main reason for brood reduction, the continuing effect being outweighed by other factors. It was also noticeable that Merlin in areas which had not experienced significant use of organochlorine insecticides (e.g. the western Highlands of Scotland) were as contaminated as those from areas which had: the conclusion is that Merlins can pick up contamination from prey captured at wintering sites, and from summer prey which has wintered in contaminated areas. A later study confirmed that Merlins were the most contaminated of British raptors, but noted the continuing decline in organochlorine levels in Merlin eggs (Shore et al. 2002); see also the results of the Norwegian study of Nygård & Polder (2012) in Chapter 7.

While Newton & Haas (1988) had found no negative correlation between organochlorine contamination and brood size, they did find one between mercury levels and brood size. This was also the conclusion of studies in Orkney. There Meek (1988) found that mean reproductive success, defined as the proportion of Merlin pairs successfully raising one chick, fell from 48% (1975–1981) to 29% (1982–1986). Meek also found that the mean brood size in successful nests fell from 3.3 during 1975–1980 to 2.5 during 1981–1987. The species, once described as 'very common' (though this was, of course, a relative term), had reduced in numbers such that only five pairs nested in 1986 and none produced any fledglings.

Meek looked at the potential causes of the decline. In Britain the covering of large areas of upland land with conifer plantations in the 1960s and later years, continuing a trend which had begun half a century before, had potentially reduced the available habitat for the falcons. Orkney offered an opportunity to see if that could be an explanation, as there had been no commercial forestry. The islands were also free of mammalian predators (apart from feral cats, domestic dogs and Otters, though the latter are concentrated at the coast), which had been suggested as another possible cause for Merlin decline. Meek found that 48% of Merlin nests failed at the incubation stage, only 5% failing after hatching. As egg failure looked the likely cause of decline in reproductive success, Meek analysed sample eggs. The results showed organochlorine burdens, but at lower levels

FIG 305. Female Merlin in flight.

than were still occurring in mainland Britain. However, both Meek and Newton & Haas (1988) found mercury levels which were higher than those seen across most of the mainland. The Ratcliffe index was also low at 1.08 (mean for ten eggs in the period 1982–1986). Meek considered other potential causes for the population decline: there had been changes in land usage, with the ploughing of moorland to produce cattle pasture, but only one historical Merlin nest site had been lost; heather burning, for Red Grouse management and sheep rearing, had similarly altered land usage, but again with no apparent impairment of available Merlin nest sites. Human disturbance seemed minimal, and although there were known losses to feral cats, these too seemed minimal in comparison to predation of nests by Hooded Crows, which, though the crow population had increased, did not seem to account for nest losses. It was also the case that while the study period included a succession of cold springs, the weather overall was not unduly harsh. It therefore seemed most likely that contamination, particularly by mercury, was the cause of egg failures.

The diet of Orkney Merlins shows a much higher fraction of House Sparrows (17% of total biomass), and Meek noted that the barley traditionally grown there was treated with organomercury. Ellis & Okill (1990) also found very high levels of mercury in Merlins on Shetland (again confirming the result of Newton & Haas 1988). The Shetland Merlin population had declined by 50% in the years 1981–1983, with a breeding success of only 50% in 1982 (compared to an average of around 78% in the years 1976–1980). Ninety-seven per cent of nest failures occurred at the egg stage, with egg breakage apparently a major cause, shell fragments suggesting many breakages by the adult birds; some eggs were addled. The mean Ratcliffe index during the study period (1981–1985) was 1.14. Ellis & Okill considered adverse weather and predation as being unlikely causes of the decline, and noted that the levels of chemical contaminants other than mercury were lower in Shetland Merlins than in their British mainland cousins.

The Orkney and Shetland mercury results are curious. Newton & Haas (1988) found a negative correlation between mercury level in eggs and brood size for eggs gathered in mainland Britain, but the Orkney and Shetland results did not fit the regression: Merlin pairs on the islands have a range of brood sizes covering the entire spectrum of mainland pairs despite having mercury levels significantly higher. Newton & Haas could not explain this difference, though they did suggest it could have resulted from the specific mercury compound used in the two areas. In a later study Newton *et al.* (1999b) noted the decline in organochlorine levels in Merlin eggs collected from across Britain, but found that mercury levels, which had declined to the mid-1980s, had then increased before showing a further fall towards the mid-1990s. Looking at individual regions, the levels of mercury in eggs had remained essentially static in Orkney and Shetland (pre-1987 and post-1986) while those of several other regions – Wales, northeast England and north Scotland – had shown significant rises, the eggs from there having levels above those of the northern islands. The odd fluctuations in Merlin egg mercury levels will need continuing research to establish whether they are a cause for concern.

In their study of Merlin population decline, Newton *et al.* (1978) had also noted that while the loss of sites reduces the number available, there were no data on the number of sites which were not historically suitable, but had become so. The implication of this was that the species' requirement for a precisely acceptable habitat meant creation of Merlin habitat by chance was unlikely, with a further implication that in the absence of conservation measures Merlin numbers might continue to decline. But despite this concern, and the evidence of continuing high levels of egg contamination, by the 1990s the British Merlin population began to rise.

Population estimates and trends
Bibby & Nattrass (1986) estimated the Merlin population of Great Britain by asking fieldworkers to count birds in their areas. Coverage was not complete, but apart from mainland Scotland it did cover those areas which historically had been strongholds of the species (it was claimed to be complete in Orkney, Shetland and the Western Isles, in Wales and northern England, but patchy across Scotland and absent south of the Peak District National Park). The result was that the population in Wales was 40–45 pairs, with 180 pairs in northern England, and 100 pairs on the Scottish islands. On mainland Scotland 133 pairs were reported, but Bibby & Nattrass reasonably claimed that this likely underestimated the total by as many as 200–300 pairs because of the lack of coverage. Their estimate was therefore 550–650 breeding pairs in 1983/84, a figure that seemed to confirm a continuing decline.

Parr (1991) noted that the Merlin population of an area of central Wales had increased, from perhaps as few as 5–10 pairs in 1970–1975 to 10–20 pairs in 1986–1989, and that the reason was, in part, the use of stick nests in trees at the edges of forestry plantations. In this area the Merlins had historically used stick nests in moorland trees, but the new plantations were offering new opportunities. Parr considered that if the results were to be replicated across Wales then the population might have increased from the 40–45 pairs of Bibby & Nattrass (1986) to perhaps 60–70 pairs. Parr (1994) confirmed this estimate in a study from breeding areas across Wales, though Williams & Parr (1995) considered the population was 80–90 pairs on the basis of better survey coverage.

Little & Davison (1992) and Little *et al.* (1995) showed a similar change of nest site in a study in the Kielder Forest, Northumberland, where the Merlin population had increased from 10 pairs in 1982 to 29 pairs in 1991. Use of traditional sites (ground nests among heather, or nests on rock outcrops) had remained essentially static, the population increase being driven by stick-nest usage in forest-edge trees (Fig. 306), the nests being those of Carrion Crows, which began nesting in the Sitka Spruce trees once they had grown to 4–5 m in height. Interestingly, the use of forest-edge trees was associated with a shift in hunting habitat, the Merlins utilising not only the traditional heather moorland, but grass moorland close to the forest edge and, therefore, the new nesting sites (Fig. 307). By studying the nests of Merlins which used the different hunting habitats, Little and co-workers were able to show that there was no difference in the reproductive success of the pairs using either moorland habitat.

However, in a separate study in the Kielder Forest, Petty *et al.* (1995) found that Merlins did not respond to eruptions of Common Crossbills and Siskins arising

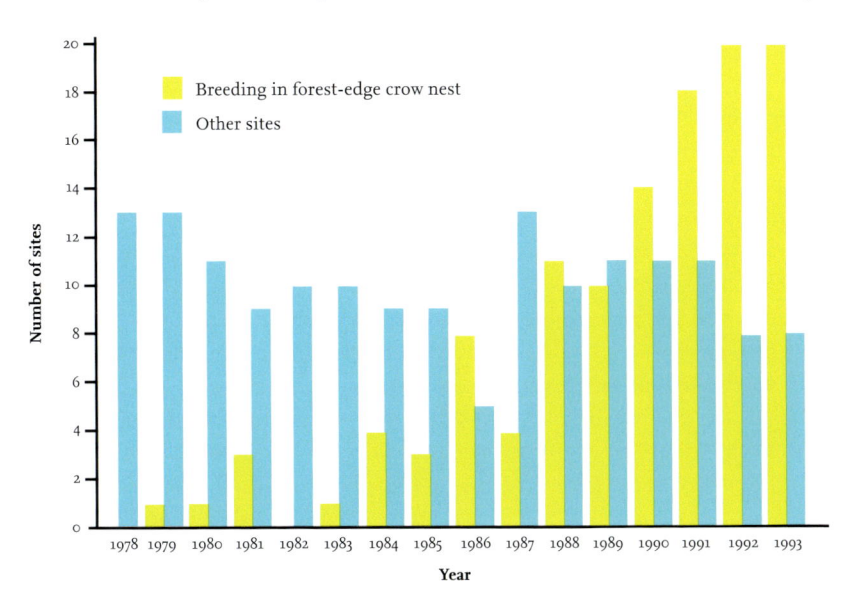

FIG 306. Merlin nest sites in the Kielder Forest, Northumberland, England during the period 1978–1993. Redrawn from Little *et al.* 1995.

516 · FALCONS

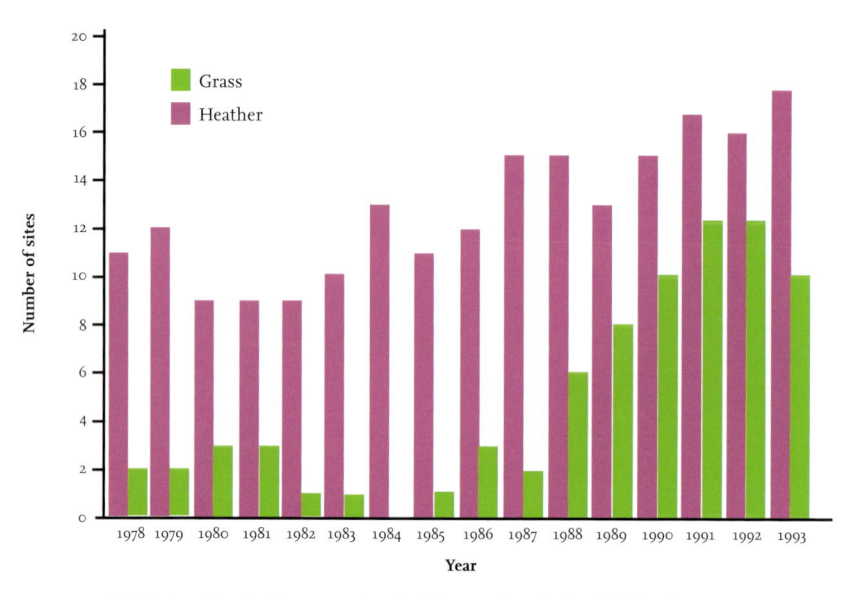

FIG 307. Merlin hunting habitat associated with nest sites in the Kielder Forest, Northumberland, England, during the period 1978–1993. Habitats are heather and grass moorland within 4 km of each nest site. Redrawn from Little et al. 1995.

as a consequence of peak conifer seed production in the forest, keeping to their 'normal' diet of moorland birds. A consequence of not taking advantage of this increased abundance of potential prey meant that the population of Merlins remained stable, whereas the population of the Sparrowhawk cycled in synchrony with the prey resource. A potential consequence of this finding is that while increased afforestation may offer Merlins new nesting sites at the forest edge, the falcon's hunting techniques are not adapted to forest dwelling and so they may not be able to take advantage of the potential prey species which breed in the bulk forest, preferring traditional moorland areas. This suggestion is in keeping with the findings of Newton et al. (1984) (Table 41).

Table 41 clearly shows that the observed increase in Merlins choosing stick nests at the edge of new forestry plantations has not been accompanied by a marked change in the falcon's diet: a continued spread of conifer plantations, which are usually planted on moorland rather than land which is more economically useful, may therefore increase nesting opportunities, but limit the availability of habitat for the falcon.

Rebecca & Bainbridge (1998) revised the population figure for Britain (England, Scotland and Wales), again using observers to count birds in areas

TABLE 41 Number and percentages of open-country and woodland species prey items in the diet of Merlins according to the predominant habitat found within 1 km of the nest during the period April to July. From Newton et al. (1984).

	Sheep grazing	Heather moor[1]	Mixed open land/forest	Forest plantation
	n (%)	n (%)	n (%)	n (%)
Open-country species	85 (88.5)	889 (88.0)	371 (80.8)	369 (84.6)
Woodland species[2]	11 (11.5)	121 (12.0)	88 (19.2)	67 (15.4)

1. The heather moorland was managed for Red Grouse.
2. Woodland species included those associated with scrub and woodland edges.
The difference in the two classes of prey species is statistically significant at the 99% level for all four habitats.

expected to hold breeding Merlin pairs. The estimate was 1,100–1,500 pairs (at the 95% confidence level), about double the 1983/84 estimate and a very encouraging outcome. Finally, Ewing et al. (2011) used the same surveying techniques as Rebecca & Bainbridge to revise the population figures up to 2008. The new estimates suggested 733 breeding pairs in Scotland (see also Etheridge 2013), 301 pairs in England, 94 pairs in Wales and 34 pairs in Northern Ireland for a total of 1,162 pairs in the United Kingdom, but with a range of 891–1,462 (at the 95% confidence level). However, the significant figures were that the population had reduced by 13% overall since the 1998 survey, with a 7% reduction in Scotland and a 25% decrease in England, but a 16% rise in Wales and no change in Northern Ireland. Ewing and co-workers discuss potential causes of the reduction in Merlin numbers. Petty et al. (2003) had noted that in the Kielder Forest Goshawks were considered a significant cause of decline in Kestrel numbers, but the fraction of Merlins in the Goshawk diet is much lower (see Chapter 7, *Friends and foes*), so this may not be a proximate cause of Merlin population decline. However, that view has since been challenged, as the Merlin population of the Kielder Forest has disappeared, and the reason is considered to have been the long-term effect of Goshawk predation (A. Heavisides, personal communication).

Ewing et al. (2011) state that the populations of the Merlin's primary prey species, in both summer and winter, have declined in Britain, with potential influences on the falcon's breeding success and winter survival. They also consider that heather burning for the management of moorland for grouse shooting may be having an impact, as may climate change, as the Merlin is at the southern end of its breeding range in Britain and so may be more susceptible to the effects of change. While the population decline is not as catastrophic as it was with

FIG. 308. Merlin chicks in a ground nest in northeast England.

organochlorine contamination, changes in land usage in an increasingly crowded Britain have the potential to cause further declines. As has been shown in North America, cultivation may cause a reduction in prey species, the Merlin being unable to breed in farmed areas which do not offer a habitat for primary prey.

In his study of Merlins on the Wicklow Mountains, McElheron (2005) noted that the less intensive agricultural practices in Ireland, in comparison to those of Britain, meant that less pesticide was used, but that the Merlin population still declined. A larger threat was that posed by the increase in subsidies for sheep farmers in the 1960s and 1970s, which resulted in the indiscriminate burning of large areas of heather moorland (McElheron refers to 'mindless destruction' by a 'small number of farmers') and a consequent reduction in the habitat of both the Meadow Pipit and the Merlin, depriving the latter of both prey and nesting sites: the few Merlins which remained turned to woodland species for prey, and stick nests in isolated tree clumps or at the forest edge for breeding. The concerns expressed by McElheron were echoed by data from a study, in which he collaborated, of the breeding ecology of Merlin across Ireland, including the Wicklow Mountains (Norriss *et al.* 2010). This showed that the productivity of the Wicklow Merlins was only 1.85 fledglings per breeding pair. The range of productivity across Ireland was 1.27–2.84, the lower figure from nests in County Kildare, the higher from those in an area of County Donegal. The mean across Ireland was 2.23.

Neither McElheron (2005) nor Norriss *et al.* (2010) quote a figure for the Irish Merlin population. Greenwood *et al.* (2003) suggested a total of 200 pairs in the Irish Republic, while Mee (2012), collecting data for all Irish raptors, considered it could be as high as 250 pairs (Republic of Ireland and Northern Ireland) based on data to 2010. However, Lusby *et al.* (2011) noted that the winter of 2009/10 was the most severe for 50 years and would likely have exacerbated a decline in passerine numbers, and particularly of the upland species (for instance Meadow Pipits) which form a significant fraction of the Merlin diet. Fernández-Bellon & Lusby (2011b) studied the breeding success of Merlins in 2010 and 2011, the years which followed the harsh winter, and found that at 14 nest sites only 0.7–1.3 chicks fledged, a breeding success rate which is below the 2.6 fledglings per breeding attempt that Bibby (1986) considered was required to maintain a stable population (though Rebecca *et al.* 1992 noted that the Scottish Merlin population seemed stable despite rearing only 2.2 fledglings per breeding attempt). The breeding success measured by Fernández-Bellon & Lusby (2011b) therefore raises concerns for the future of the Irish Merlin population, though the present best estimate is 200–400 pairs in the Republic of Ireland and a further 32 pairs in Northern Ireland (S. Newton, personal communication).

FIG. 309. Four well-feathered Merlin chicks line up for their photo in a basket nest in southern Scotland.

The wide range in the estimate for the Republic of Ireland is due, in part, to the difficulty of assessing the population, as Lusby *et al.* (2011) note. In a novel experiment, researchers tried to use the playback of conspecific calls to elicit a response from Merlin pairs and hence improve surveying results, but only 28% of pairs responded vocally, most responses being discreet and silent, so a negative response was not evidence of absence and the use of playback failed (Fernández-Bellon & Lusby 2011c).

Overall it seems the Merlin population of the British Isles is currently stable or increasing slowly, though with regional variations that mean the population is decreasing in places. Anecdotal evidence suggests that Merlins are now breeding at higher elevations, perhaps as a result of global warming, with a consequent decrease in range as the species is not showing the habitat flexibility of the Peregrine. In northeast Scotland, Rebecca (2006) found that the Merlin population declined as a consequence of commercial forestry at a time when populations in adjacent areas were considered stable, indicating the vulnerability of the species to changes in land usage. A further potential vulnerability was highlighted by the most recent Wetland Bird Survey (Austin *et al.* 2014) and the research of Sharps *et al.* (2015) – see *Peregrine*, above – which showed significant declines in the populations of Dunlin and Redshank on British saltmarshes. Each is an important prey species for Merlins overwintering at estuaries. While the indication of a stable or slightly increasing population is excellent news, the susceptibility of the species to so many factors means that with such a limited population the Merlin remains vulnerable. Indeed, the recently published report on the state of the UK's birds (Hayhow *et al.* 2015) noted the change of the Merlin from Amber to Red in Birds of Conservation Concern 4 (with a population estimate of 1100 pairs).

THE FUTURE

With the populations of two species stable, one increasing and the fourth declining (but from a relatively high level), the situation appears to be optimistic for the British falcons. However, with climate change, and an increasing human population putting pressure on both land and agricultural practices, there is no room for complacency. While populations may be stable or increasing, the total number of birds is limited, and history shows that apparently small-scale environmental events can have catastrophic effects on small populations. In a rapidly changing world there is a need for vigilance to ensure that Britain's falcons will still be present to enchant future generations.

Endnotes

Chapter 1
Note 1.1 Although the Peregrine Falcon and Barn Owl breed on six continents, they do not show a uniform pattern of breeding in those continents, a strange pattern for terrestrial species (though not as unusual in maritime species). The reason for such a 'staggered' breeding pattern is unknown, but is likely to be due to ecological factors or competition by established species which have prevented occupation.

Chapter 2
Note 2.1 For an assessment of the impact of raptors on grouse see Redpath & Thirgood (1999): this study suggested that the predation of grouse chicks by Hen Harriers was positively correlated with grouse density, while Peregrine predation was inversely correlated with grouse density. For cogent and insightful consideration of the conflicts generated by grouse-moor management on the one hand and species conservation (all species, not just raptors) on the other, see Thirgood *et al.* (2000, 2002), and *Inglorious*, the absorbing but disquieting book by Mark Avery (2015). For a view of the illegal persecution of raptors in England, see Holmes *et al.* (2000). This report was updated in 2003, though the main findings and conclusions did not change. There has been no further update in subsequent years.

Chapter 3
Note 3.1 While the work of Andersson & Norberg (1981) gives a good general understanding of the flight characteristics of falcons and other avian predators, a note of caution must be sounded for two reasons. Firstly, falcons have to be able to stop their prey and then carry it away (while eating at the point of capture is acceptable to an adult bird, breeding requires prey to be returned to the nest), both of which require a body mass which is comparable to that of the prey. Secondly, as already noted, there is more than physics to falcon flight, and while body mass is undoubtedly important (and wing loading probably more so) the power input to flapping flight might well influence linear acceleration and horizontal flight speed positively more than body mass influences it negatively. Hence the comment that for Merlins a quick take-off and

fast acceleration are important in surprise hunting. Physiology may also have a greater influence over the latter than body mass alone might indicate: a heavier bird may be able to accelerate fast at the expense of earlier exhaustion, favouring short, fast attacks followed by longer resting periods, as is often seen in hunting Merlins.

Note 3.2   In 1974 an aircraft collided with a Ruppell's Vulture (*Gyps rueppellii*) at a height of 11,400 m (Laybourne 1974). At such heights the air resistance to a free falling object is much lower than at sea level so the object's terminal velocity would be higher. In principle that means that the vulture, a much heavier bird than a falcon, could have reached a higher speed than a falcon was capable of, provided it had enough fall time in thin air. In practice the behaviour of vultures precludes such a possibility, and we can safely say that large falcons are the world's fastest creatures, though whether the accolade should correctly be assigned to the Peregrine, as it usually is, or to a hierofalcon, particularly the Gyrfalcon, which is usually significantly heavier, is a matter of debate.

Note 3.3   While the decelerations imposed on falcons at the end of fast stoops seem extremely high, very short-duration imposed forces of order 5 g are regularly experienced by the riders of the higher-speed roller coasters, and by Formula One drivers. The loads imposed on the heads of American footballers in tackles have recently been shown, by sensors inserted in their helmets, to occasionally exceed 100 g. While it might be assumed that such loads would inevitably lead to concussions, that is not the case, though the work has suggested that the footballers do sustain brain injuries (see, for example, http://www.purdue.edu/newsroom/research/2010/101007 NaumanFootball.html – retrieved 24 September 2014). The problem experienced by aircraft pilots who are usually sited in a discussion of imposed g-forces is that in a seated position the pilot cannot prevent blood being drained away from the brain when the heart fails to overcome the effect of negative g, loss of conscious following if the situation is prolonged. In much shorter duration events, blood draining does not occur.

Note 3.4   In addition to having more acute vision, falcons also have a higher flicker-fusion frequency (FFF) than humans. FFF is a measure of the ability to resolve rapid movements. Films are shown at a frame rate of 30 Hz, as below this humans are able to resolve the change from one frame to the next and so see the flicker of frame changes. Some humans can resolve higher frequencies, though few are able to detect the 50 Hz flicker of a fluorescent light. By contrast birds have an FFF which is at least 100 Hz, with some species having even higher rates. Such rates are required by both hunters and hunted: flying through woodland at speed, humans would collide with branches which birds easily avoid as their eyes, and, of course, brain, process visual information more quickly. While this ability is at a premium for woodland prey species and such predators as the Goshawk, falcons also need to be able to react quickly to changes in flight direction by fleeing prey, and to avoid lunges by captured prey.

Note 3.5   A related concern was raised by Sodhi *et al.* (1991a), who wondered if the radio-tagging of urban-breeding Merlins in Saskatoon was affecting breeding success or survival, particularly as other studies (on game birds) had noted reductions in both, as well as abnormal behaviour in tagged birds. The tags used weighed 4 g, representing 2.4% and 1.6% of the body weight of male and female Merlins respectively. In a study in which the breeding success of tagged and untagged males was measured, there was no difference between the two groups. In addition, survival rates of both males and females, as measured by the return rates of the birds the following year, were indistinguishable. By observation there was no discernible behavioural difference between tagged and untagged birds, though those fitted with tags (either to the underside of tail feathers or legs) tended to peck at the tags for a period and to preen frequently immediately after release. Sodhi *et al.* concluded that the small radio-tags were having no effect on the Merlins. This issue was irrelevant for the falconry birds used in the studies reported here, as the IMUs were not permanently attached. The harnesses/backpacks into which my IMUs clipped were permanently attached, so the birds were used to carrying them, and they weighed only about 1 g. The falcons were also used to carrying transponders, usually clipped to the harnesses, but occasionally attached to a leg or tail feather. Falconry birds fly with jessies attached to their legs, which hang free and undoubtedly affect the bird's aerodynamics. Falconry birds also fly less frequently than their wild cousins and so may not be as fit. Overall, therefore, speeds measured in falconry birds are probably lower than those in wild falcons. However, there is much less reason to assume that flight paths will be affected.

Note 3.6 Visible light is a very small range (in terms of wavelength) of the electromagnetic spectrum, a spectrum which also covers radio waves and x-rays. This is not the correct forum for a discussion on whether electromagnetic radiation is particle-like, wave-like or both at the same time: it is sufficient here to note that the spectrum is most conveniently considered by wavelength, and covers a range from radio, where the wavelength is measured in metres or fractions of a metre, to x-rays, where the wavelength is measured in nanometres (1 nm = 10^{-9}m, i.e. one thousand-millionth of a metre – 0.000000001 m). Beyond x-rays are γ-rays (gamma rays) with wavelengths measured in picometres (10^{-12} m, i.e. one million-millionth of a metre). Visible light is usually defined as covering the range 400–700 nm, with red light at the upper end and blue light at the lower, though it is worth noting that many people can see up to 1,000 nm and both children and young adults may see down to about 310 nm. The radiation at wavelengths below 400 nm is known as ultraviolet (the last colour of the 'rainbow' spectrum of visible light being violet) while at wavelengths above 700 nm it is known as infrared, which is often used to 'see' at night, as the heat produced by warm objects (including warm-blooded animals) is in the infrared part of the spectrum (though the idea that thermal radiation is only in the infrared part of the spectrum is a gross simplification). Ultraviolet (UV) is beneficial to humans as it allows the synthesis of vitamin D, but overexposure is also harmful, causing sunburn and, potentially, skin cancers. UV may also cause damage to the retina of the eye.

Note 3.7 The selection of prey by a predator which preys mainly on birds is complex. Baker & Bibby (1987) found that Merlins in Wales took prey in relation to its abundance rather than plumage colour, while Sodhi & Oliphant (1993) in Canada found that while there was some evidence to suggest that the falcons avoided cryptically coloured prey, the primary reason for selection was the time the prey species spent away from cover, i.e. how easy it was to spot and catch. When, inevitably, after the studies of Kestrel attraction to UV signalling by voles, interest in UV signalling by avian prey was considered, it was found in a study of Swedish songbirds that the plumage of the passerines was UV reflecting, but at shorter wavelengths than the UV sensitivity band of the raptors – the songbirds were using a private communication band that could not be intercepted by their predators (Håstad *et al.* 2005).

Of course, the finding that passerines are signalling to each other at wavelengths invisible to their avian predators raises the obvious question of why rodents do not do the same. Members of the Finnish team which had done much of the early work on vole UV scent trails suggested an immediate answer, Koivula & Korpimäki (2001) noting that for a vole the risk of predation from raptors is much lower than that from mustelids, which use olfactory clues rather than sight, so that UV signalling is not as dangerous as would first appear.

Note 3.8   In a study on prey choice by Kestrels in western Finland, Korpimäki (1985a) noted that in both spring and autumn the raptors took more male voles than female, a difference that was statistically significant in both seasons. This was considered to be due to the activity levels of males being higher at those times. The later finding by Koivula *et al.* (1999a) that reflectance was strongest (the urine tracks were brightest) in mature male voles suggested another reason why mature males might be preferentially predated, particularly if their urine trails were more frequent and across wider areas (as suggested by other studies) – if male voles were easier to find they would be easier to catch (all other things being equal). The concern over whether the hypothesis that hunting Kestrels are cueing off UV reflectance is correct casts doubt over the argument, but, of course, if the cueing is off UV fluorescence then again the higher level of scent marking of males would lead to higher predation.

Note 3.9   In a separate study, the Dutch team found summer success rates of 2.8 per hour when flight hunting, 0.3 per hour when soaring and 0.2 per hour when perching (Rijnsdorp *et al.* 1981). There are differences between the success data in each case, but the overall premise remains the same – flight-hunting is an efficient way of catching small mammals.

Chapter 4

Note 4.1   J. A. (John Alec) Baker (1926–1987) was the Essex manager of the Chelmsford branch of the Automobile Association (and later a manager for Britvic, the soft drinks manufacturer) with a passion for wildlife and the Peregrine in particular. In 1967 his book *The Peregrine* was published. It won the Duff Cooper Award that year, but was for many years largely the reserve of the specialist before being recognised as one of the great masterpieces of nature writing. The book describes Baker's observations of a Peregrine during a single winter and spring, October to April, though whether it was actually a single period (which some claim was the winter of 1962/63, a winter of such severity that it could definitely account for the descriptions of ice and snow) or the distillation of what is known to have been a ten-year study into a factional single winter is debated. He later wrote *The Hill of Summer*, which though less well known also draws admiration for its lyrical account of an English summer. In 2010, Collins, the publisher of the original book, published a compendium of *The Peregrine*, *The Hill of Summer*, and some of Baker's diaries from 1954 to 1961.

While there is no denying the beauty of Baker's prose and the depth of feeling between himself and the Peregrine, it has to be pointed out that there are sceptics who believe his accounts owe more to poetry than to observation. Baker saw Peregrines in an area where others never did and noted behaviour which others have not seen. Of the latter, the idea of Peregrines hovering behind ploughing tractors and eating the earthworms they bring to the surface has caused some to wonder whether he could actually distinguish between a Kestrel, which certainly does exactly that, and a Peregrine, which other observers have never seen doing either. However, hovering has in fact been seen: Roberts (1946) observed a Peregrine hovering above a Redshank nest (with rapid wing-beats at a height of about 9 m) before dropping down to pick up a chick. The answer of Baker's believers is that the time he spent and the intimate knowledge he therefore gathered explain why he could both observe Peregrines and log unusual behaviour. It is because of the existence of scepticism in some quarters that the 'health note' is attached to Table 11, though it seems to me that the data are so detailed and consistent with what is known about wintering Peregrines that they are correct.

As regards the provenance of the observations in Baker's book, doubtless the debate will continue. It will likely never be resolved, leaving us only with the joy of the writing.

Note 4.2 For further information on flocks as a defence mechanism against predation, and for other defence mechanisms employed by prey, see the section on hunting strategies in Chapter 3. In the light of the suggestion there that Dunlin may not be good at the tight flocking manoeuvres seen in other species, it is worth noting the work in Rome of Carere *et al.* (2009), who were able to show not only that the choreographed movements of Starling flocks were a defence mechanism, but that there was a social behavioural side to flocking. Each winter as many as 10 million Starlings congregate in Rome, arriving from all over northern Europe to enjoy the warmth of central Italy augmented by the heat of the city itself. The Starlings create wonderful choreographed patterns in the evening sky above the city, but rather less wonderful dropping masses which damage vehicle paintwork and make pavements treacherous. Of the vast number of birds, Carere and co-workers chose two flock areas to study, a city-centre square with rows of trees surrounded by buildings where about 20,000 birds collected, and a more open parkland area south of the city where 50,000 birds gathered. The predation risk from Peregrines was lower in the city-centre area than in the parkland. The researchers catalogued a series of flock forms, and found that larger, more compact forms were found in the high-predation-risk area, whereas smaller, looser flocks and singleton birds were found in the low-risk area. Peregrine success rates in the low-risk area were higher. While these findings are intuitively unsurprising, what was interesting was that the Italian researchers found that the behaviour of flocks at a distance from the roosts influenced local behaviour, i.e. if a distant flock showed anti-predator flock forms, the local birds adopted similar forms, implying that social information was being passed between flocks. (See also Hemelrijk *et al.* (2015) for interesting ideas on the generation of 'agitation waves', the choreographed movements in Starling flocks in the presence of predators.)

One additional anti-predation strategy that potential prey may use has been identified by Oro (1996) who studied Peregrines attacking Audouin's Gulls (*Larus audoiuinii*) at a colony at the Ebro Delta on the Mediterranean coast of Spain. Oro found that predation rates were lower for gulls nesting in small, dense subcolonies rather than in larger, looser colonies. Hunt (2012) also noted an unconventional defence mechanism from a Greenshank (*Tringa nebularia*) when it was attacked by a Peregrine, the shorebird landing close to a Mute Swan (*Cygnus olor*). The swan took no active part in the wader's defence, but its bulk limited the Peregrine's attacking options and eventually the falcon gave up.

Note 4.3 The implication of 'better-quality' Peregrines holding the most superior nesting sites implies that 'better' falcons are either more aggressive in the acquisition and defence of sites and/or more efficient hunters. The former may be true, but caution must be exercised as regards the latter. In a study of Peregrines in South Africa, Jenkins (2000) noted that falcons occupying higher cliffs (one definition of a 'better' site) had higher hunting success rates. However, while this implies higher efficiency, Jenkins noted that the height difference between the falcon and the prey was significantly correlated with hunting success. In other words falcons attacking from a higher start point, and probably achieving higher attack speed as well as greater surprise, had an enhanced success rate, which could imply that occupation of the 'better' site was as important, perhaps more so, than 'pure' hunting proficiency.

Note 4.4 Peregrine urban dwelling has a long history. Peregrines are recorded as breeding on Salisbury Cathedral in the early 1860s, tolerating not only street noise but the occasional bursts of bell-ringing, and Culver (1919) records a pair of Peregrines in the centre of Philadelphia in January 1918 (though noting they might have been present much earlier in the winter). The pair – Culver does not state whether they were actually male and female, but the recorded display flights suggest pair bonding or reinforcement – probably roosted on a tall tower in the centre of the city from which they flew to capture pigeons. (Such common roosting is often seen in breeding pairs prior to egg laying.) The falcons stayed until March, then left the city. While urban breeding might be assumed to be entirely dependent on the availability of nest sites, and therefore provision of nest boxes, an interesting study in South Africa found that the most important driver was immigration (Altwegg *et al.* 2014). Peregrines, it seems, have grown to love living in the city. The change appears to be a worldwide phenomenon, as Faccio *et al.* (2013) noted that after Peregrines had become extinct in New England in the 1960s a reintroduction programme had caused a rapid population expansion which soon filled the original range, with the falcons utilising many urban structures – buildings, bridges etc. – for breeding. While most Peregrines on first breeding tended to favour nest sites similar to their own natal habitat (i.e. cliff or building) there was significant cross-immigration of rural and urban populations. However, urban living is not without its hazards, fledglings in particular being at a higher risk of collisions than their rural cousins and being occasionally poisoned by pest control programmes. The breeding success rate, measured as fledglings per brood, is also lower than for rural pairs, though only marginally so, at 2.45 vs. 2.51 (Cade & Bird, 1990).

Note 4.5 It is generally assumed that female Peregrines lay eggs at 48-hour intervals. The British ornithologist Desmond Nethersole-Thompson (1908–1989) claimed that while Peregrines laid eggs at any time of day they were more likely to lay them in the early morning. Ratcliffe (1993), while restating the 48-hour interval, quotes Cade's view, based on North American captive Peregrines, that the laying interval was longer, 52–62 hours, which better accords with a 2- to 3-day interval. Nethersole-Thompson's view on the early-morning preference can be found in an article in *Oologists' Record* (Volume 11, pp. 73–80), a magazine written with egg collectors in mind. Nethersole-Thompson was himself an egg collector in his early days. The magazine ceased publication in 1969, by which time the collecting of eggs was both illegal and socially unacceptable. Nethersole-Thompson's many contributions to the *Oologists' Record* were published as a book (*In Search of Breeding Birds*, Peregrine Books, Leeds, 1992) which is now out of print. While some of the ideas expressed in the articles are now controversial, there is no doubting Nethersole-Thompson's significant contributions to the understanding of British birdlife, particularly his pioneering work on Hobbies.

Note 4.6   A North American Peregrine (probably *F. p. anatum*) ringed in northern Wisconsin in 1993, was recovered in Switzerland in 2008, a straight-line distance of 7,030 km from its natal site (Doolittle *et al.* 2013). Though the Atlantic crossing may have been weather-assisted and the falcon may have rested on ships, this still represents an extraordinary journey, particularly as the bird was 15 years old.

Chapter 5

Note 5.1   Recent work on mice has found that if the rodents are infected with *Toxoplasma gondii*, a protozoan parasite, of which they are a secondary host, they lose their fear of cat urine (Ingram *et al.* 2013). As cats are the primary host of the parasite this suggests the protozoan is influencing the behaviour of the rodent in order to aid its own life cycle. Such a remarkable, if alarming, finding may also have implications for other rodent parasites and their behaviour with other potential predators. One wonders, if Kestrels could read, whether they would currently be crossing their talons in the hope that some other parasite could persuade rodents to lose their fear of clear skies.

Note 5.2   With such attrition rates it might be supposed that voles would alter their behaviour, and specifically their breeding behaviour, but as there few, if any, areas in which vole populations are not predated this is not an option. To confirm this Klemola *et al.* (1998) set up an experiment in which caged voles were placed beneath active Kestrel nest boxes and, as a control, under empty nest boxes. Although the voles were not subject to predation, they were subject to the begging calls of hungry Kestrel nestlings, the excreted scats of those nestlings and the comings-and-goings of adult birds. There was no alteration in the breeding behaviour of the voles in comparison to those which were not subjected to such obvious signs of the presence of predators. Klemola and co-workers concluded that the presence of avian predators does not suppress vole breeding behaviour.

Note 5.3   The 'double-labelled water' method of energy expenditure calculation uses a specific form of heavy water, combining deuterium (D, heavy hydrogen, a hydrogen atom with a nucleus of a proton and a neutron, rather than the standard atom, the nucleus of which comprises a proton only) and oxygen-18 (^{18}O), an isotope of oxygen with ten neutrons rather than the eight found in the most abundant (99.8%) form. Each of the atoms (D and ^{18}O) is easily detected by mass spectrometry: the isotopes are both non-radioactive and non-toxic in the quantities used. A given amount of heavy water is injected into the blood of the subject (in our case a captured live Kestrel) and at the same time a blood sample is taken. The method works because of the body's partial conversion of inhaled oxygen to exhaled carbon dioxide. As a molecule of the latter has two oxygen atoms the body needs extra oxygen atoms in order to complete the chemical equation and obtains these from water molecules. Oxygen-18 can therefore leave the body through exhalation as well as through water loss (urine, sweat), whereas deuterium atoms can only leave through water loss. Blood sampling after a given time (in our case by recapturing the Kestrel) allows a comparison of the concentration of D and ^{18}O with that from the initial blood sample. The difference in concentrations allows the metabolic rate of the Kestrel to be accurately measured. The advantage of the test is accuracy, the disadvantage being that total energy expenditure is measured rather than the expenditure of specific activities.

Note 5.4 In his study in western Finland, Korpimäki (1985c) noted that there was no time lag between the populations of vole predators – Long-eared Owl, Short-eared Owl, Tengmalm's Owl, Hen Harrier and Kestrel – and their microtine prey. He noted that the ability of the predators to move into an area of high microtine density aided population stability by limiting rodent number peaks. He noted, too, the high degree of mobility of the predators, which aided a rapid response, and also that even at times of rodent scarcity there was invariably a small population of predators present. The result was confirmed in further work in Finland (Korpimäki 1994, Norrdahl & Korpimäki 1996).

The obvious question raised by the observed Kestrel breeding-density increase of Korpimäki (1985c), and the increase in Kestrels and Short-eared Owls noted by Riddle (2011), is how those predators that were not already resident in the area were able to recognise the increase in rodent population density. In their book on Snowy Owls, Potapov & Sale (2012) postulate that the owls move in loose congregations, which they term 'boids', with owls staying within about 5–7 km of each other so that visual signalling remains possible: a boid would be a congregation of several hundred owls spread out over an area with a long axis of 300–350 km. One owl finding a high lemming density would, by stopping and preparing to breed, alert and attract close members of the boid and hence a build-up of predator numbers would occur, later arrivals having to establish territories at the fringes of the peak lemming area, or to continue to search the tundra. The 'boid hypothesis' was set down in early 2011, but owing to unfortunate delays in production the book did not appear until early 2012, after the peak lemming year in Scandinavia in 2011 saw an influx of Snowy Owls after many years during which breeding had been entirely absent or spasmodic at best, the influx being in accord with the hypothesis. The Kestrels of the Scottish borders are partially migratory, and it is interesting to speculate whether something similar was happening in the early 1890s, with overwintering Kestrels discovering the increase in vole density and preparing to breed, and other Kestrels being visually alerted by this early breeding to the good vole year and, by chain reaction, increasing the local Kestrel population. While the boid hypothesis provides a potential explanation of the observed phenomena, obtaining proof would require the continuous tracking of large numbers of individual birds over many seasons, which is unlikely to be feasible on any reasonable timescale.

Chapter 6

Note 6.1 The derivation of *subbuteo* in the Hobby's name has a long history which is not easy to unravel, though Jobling (1991, 2009) has produced excellent groundwork which in large part is the basis of this note. Aristotle referred to a hawk which he called *hupotriorkhes*, which translates as 'near a bird of prey' or, more likely, 'near a buzzard', i.e. a bird which is similar to a buzzard. It is widely assumed that the hawk Aristotle was describing was the Hobby. Ulisse Aldrovandi (1522–1605), often referred to simply as Aldrovanus, was an Italian naturalist who produced two books on ornithology (1599 and 1600) in which he referred to the Hobby as *subbuteo*, translating the Greek form into Latin. It is likely that Linnaeus was aware of this work when compiling his own. The hobbies, as a group, have occasionally been classified as a subgenus *Hypotriorchis*, which is a 'Latinisation' of the original Greek form.

Note 6.2 A recent study of Barn Owl chicks has suggested that the chicks used vocal signals to compete for the next food item which would be delivered by a parent, and that these signals were not related to either age hierarchy or hunger level, but rather defined a turn-by-turn feeding regime (Dreiss *et al.* 2015). While there is evidence in some avian species for direct competition for food, the work of Dreiss and co-workers implies that if resources are not overly scarce, siblings may behave non-competitively. The chicks of all UK falcons are known to mantle prey once it has been acquired, but it would be interesting if future work were to discover that the lack of overt competitiveness in the species is also related to vocal signalling.

Note 6.3 In an article on the number of times escaped Budgerigars fall victim to Hobbies in the Netherlands, Grünhagen (1978a) suggested that it might result from the bright colours of the cage birds. Grünhagen noted that the escapees usually joined sparrow flocks, but would be highly conspicuous within them, and that the budgies seemed to form a disproportionately high percentage of prey in comparison to their numbers. Studies on whether raptors target prey on the basis of them being conspicuous rather than, say, choosing victims which appear dysfunctional in some way, or at random, have been carried out, though not apparently for Hobbies. It is of course possible the Hobbies are targeting the cage birds because they stand out within the flock, but it may also be that the budgies lack the streetwise skills of their wild flock-mates and so are easier to catch.

Note 6.4 The names of many agamas and geckos have changed over time. Roberts (1991) refers to *Agama nupta*, while Fiuczynski & Sömmer (2011) – and the original source of the information they quote – refer to *Gymnodactyulus russowi*. Both the familiar and scientific names quoted here are from a more recent work which deals with the etymology of reptiles of Iran (Mikaili & Shayegh 2011). Both species referred to in the text are to be found widely across north Africa/central Asia as well as in Iran.

Note 6.5 Edward Blair Michell (1843–1926) was Oxford born and Oxford educated, and became a barrister. He was a linguist, being fluent in French and Siamese, and a sportsman, winning several important rowing championships. He was also an expert falconer, particularly knowledgeable regarding the Merlin. *The Art and Practice of Hawking* (1900) is still regarded as one of the foremost books on falconry. Michell is somewhat scathing of the Hobby in the book, noting that he had twice tried to train a Hobby for lark-hawking (which involves ringing), failing each time. He points out that medieval falconers extolled the virtues of the Hobby, noting one authority as saying that the falcon is 'in all respects … as bold and hardy as any other hawk whatsoever' and wonders if Hobby training 'has become a lost art, or the Hobby has changed his nature entirely since he was thus eulogised.' Given Michell's enthusiasm for the Merlin, which takes to ringing flights with relative ease, it is tempting to ask if there was a degree of prejudice involved, though later in the book Michell is fulsome in his praise of the Hobby, noting that it will ignore the lure and stay in the air for the 'mere pleasure of flying'. It is difficult therefore to decide whether Michell thought the Hobby a poor or a strong flier.

Note 6.6 While it appears logical that the reason for males to arrive earlier than females is in order to claim better territories and therefore to be potentially more attractive to females and so enhance their reproductive chances, this hypothesis is still debated, the main point of contention being whether the cost to males arriving early (as this may require migration and arrival when resources are not optimal and so can threaten survival) – termed viability selection – is compensated for by increased mating opportunities (sexual selection). For a good review of how the factors compete see Morbey *et al.* (2012).

Note 6.7 The use of pylons is widespread in Germany (e.g. Fiuczynski & Sömmer 2011, and personal observation) and the Netherlands (e.g. Boer & Koks 1996) and also reported from other European countries. It is less prevalent in Britain, probably due to the method of construction: in continental pylons there is usually a flat plate in the crossbeam arms which offers an excellent base for the corvid nest builders, while the plate-free British form requires a much higher degree of structural engineering by the crows. The use of pylons as nest sites is not restricted to Hobbies: other falcons – Greater Kestrel, Lanner, Saker – throughout the world, and the Peregrine Falcon in Britain (first recorded in Lancashire in 1991) have also been recorded as using the structures. In the USA and Canada nesting platforms set on pylons have also been used by Bald Eagles, the choice of site deliberately aimed at providing additional protection to the species.

Note 6.8 The fact that the average clutch size of the Hobby is smaller than that for either the Kestrel or the Merlin, which are comparably sized falcons, might intuitively suggest that the rigours of long-distance migration result in female Hobbies having to reduce the bodily costs of egg laying. However, a recent study by Bruderer & Salewski (2009) found that the increased fecundity of non-migratory species was more likely a result of the harsh conditions of winter which result in a reduction of reproductive life. Evidence in terms of mean life for the three small British falcon species is less definitive. While it is the case that the mean lives quoted in this book suggest that Hobbies are longer-lived than either Kestrels or Merlins, there is considerable overlap in the age structures of the three populations, and longest recorded lives of each are comparable. It is, though, interesting to contemplate that for a small falcon the crossing of the Sahara Desert might actually be less daunting experience than a winter spent in Britain. However, in a study of American Redstarts (*Setophaga ruticilla*) in which the winter food of some birds was deliberately reduced, Cooper *et al.* (2015) found that those birds delayed the spring migration. As it is known that in this species each day's delay in arrival time at the breeding grounds reduces the likelihood of breeding success of a male redstart by 11%, the potential hazard of long migration is not negligible. As with so many aspects of the biology of birds, the comparative effects of migratory and non-migratory behaviour are complex.

Note 6.9 Greenwood (1980) noted that while many species of animals are faithful to their natal area, in birds the tendency is for males to be more philopatric than females, while the reverse is true for many mammals. That the degree of philopatry differs in the two sexes in either case reduces the likelihood of incest, which is clearly beneficial to the species. There is also evidence that female birds prefer philopatric males because occupation of a territory suggests both a willingness to defend it and an ability to withstand competition, and so points to the likelihood that resources will be available for breeding. Knowledge of a territory implies some understanding of local predators, which is also advantageous. These issues were neatly illustrated in an experiment in central Finland with three owl species – Eagle Owl, Ural Owl (*Strix uralensis*) and Tengmalm's Owl (Hakkarainen & Korpimäki 1996). Of the three, Tengmalm's Owl is by far the smallest and is predated by the larger two. However, the larger two owls cannot access the small tree holes used by breeding Tengmalm's Owls to take nestlings. Tengmalm's Owls are also out-competed by Ural Owls for the small rodents on which both prey. Eagle Owls take much larger prey and so are not direct competitors for resources. By erecting nest boxes in Eagle and Ural Owl territories Hakkarainen & Korpimäki were able to show that the breeding of Tengmalm's Owls was less affected in Eagle Owl territories than in territories of Ural Owls, where the smaller owls suffered both predation and competition for prey. Most breeding attempts of Tengmalm's Owls near Ural Owl territories failed during courtship, and those that succeeded saw clutches laid 11 days later, a delay which would inevitably have resulted in lower fledgling rates. Tengmalm's Owl pairs close to Ural Owls invariably consisted of younger males and females: experienced males were taking the best sites and experienced females were recognising the advantages they offered.

Note 6.10 The device fitted to the German female Hobby (Meyburg *et al.* 2011a) weighed 5 g and measured 24 × 14 × 7.5 mm, with a 178 mm antenna. The device was powered by solar cells and transmitted a signal at 41.650 MHz to the Argos satellite tracking system, allowing the bird's position to be registered on Google Earth. The device was attached to the bird with neck/body loops which formed a 'backpack' harness familiar to all falconers, as similar harnesses are used to attach transmitters to birds in order to locate them in the event they are lost. The harness weighs about 1 g. The total weight of the PTT was therefore 6 g. The female Hobby weighed 265 g, the PTT thus equating to 1.9% of body weight. The Scottish device seems to have been similar. Fewer details of the Swedish device (Strandberg *et al.* 2009a, 2009b) are given, but it used the same Argos tracking system and so was essentially the same. However it weighed 9.5 g (probably including the backpack) which was equivalent to 4.1% of body weight, which implies an average weight of 230 g for the four birds used in the study. For experiments in the UK, an ethics committee recommends that no device should be placed on a bird which weighs in excess of 5% of body weight: the German team imposed their own limit of 3% of body weight. However, in addition to the effect of the loading of experimental devices on a bird per se, the effect of an increase in drag coefficient on flight characteristics must be considered. Pennycuick *et al.* (2012) noted that in the particular case of a Rose-coloured Starling the effect of mounting a dummy transmitter on the bird was small in terms of mass loading and would increase only slightly with migration distance, but that the drag coefficient increased by 50% with implications for both performance and energy requirements. In terms of energy, the effect of the increase in drag coefficient by 50% would be to reduce the flight range for a given starting energy by 22% (for the specific bird in the experiment): an exact figure for mass loading is more difficult to assess but would likely be ≤ 5%. Such reductions in flight range, if seen at a comparable level in the Hobby, would more likely mean the bird having to 'refuel' at a higher rate at stops rather than reducing the distance flown or the speed travelled. However, Strandberg and co-workers claim that by observation the devices had no effect on flight behaviour or hunting performance, or on the timing of migration.

Note 6.11 The Zone is more commonly known as the Doldrums, the name given by sailors to the area of calm waters in the Atlantic and Pacific oceans close to the equator. In the time of sailing ships the area became infamous for being wind-free (hence the calm waters) and for becalming ships anxious to continue their trading journeys for long periods. The Zone appears as a band of clouds, these being responsible for southern African weather comprising wet and dry seasons as opposed to the hot and cold seasons of the high northern and southern latitudes. Movement of the zone north and south of the equator causes the rain fronts created by the cloud belt to shift across Africa.

Chapter 7

Note 7.1 Baker & Bibby (1987) were seeking to shed light on whether the evolution of bird plumage coloration was based primarily on predation avoidance or on sexual selection, the merits of these two theories still being debated, in part because of the difficulty of mounting experiments to test the theories, particularly as coloration which might reduce predation by one predator could actually increase likely capture rates by a different predator. The work of Baker & Bibby (on domestic cats as well as Merlins) suggested that cats primarily took prey which was cryptically coloured, whereas Merlins seemed primarily to hunt according to prey abundance. The work of Sodhi & Oliphant (1993) considered a further theory, that of optimal foraging, which suggests that prey should not be taken according to relative abundance, but relative profitability, usually defined by net energy intake, i.e. that some prey provides more energy input, relative to the energy requirement of capture. The overall conclusion of the two studies would seem to be that prey selection is very far from the simple equation intuition would suggest, and that more work is required before definite conclusions can be reached on prey selection, in either Merlins or other predators.

Note 7.2 In *The Art and Practice of Hawking* (1900), Michell states that a Merlin called Sis, a falconry bird, achieved a 97% kill rate against larks (59 of 61) including 'the extraordinary score of forty-one out of forty-two successful flights, the one miss being a ringer at which she was thrown off when the head of another lark was hardly down her throat – before she had shaken herself, or had time to look around.' Given Michell's standing in the falconry world, particularly with regard to Merlins, the veracity of this claim is hardly in doubt. While the larking season saw healthy Merlins flown against juvenile larks, in general falconry birds are likely to be less fit than wild birds, making the success rate astounding.

Note 7.3 Roberts & Jones (1999) calculated the mean volume of Merlin eggs in Wales assuming $V = LB^2$ and arrived at a figure of $38.9 \pm 0.2 cm^3$ for the mean (± standard error) across 145 eggs, which is in very good agreement with the value of Rebecca (2006) allowing for Hoyt's correction. Roberts & Jones noted that the mean volume of the eggs had fallen from 40.2 cm^3 (using their formula) for the pre-1983 period to 38.2 cm^3 for the period post-1983. They found no difference in the chick yield of nests in which eggs had above-average volume against nests with smaller eggs.

Note 7.4 As well as defending their nest site against corvids as potential nest predators, Merlins have been observed to chase them in the way that corvids will, for instance, mob Buzzards. Merlin pairs have been observed to chase corvids after the breeding season, but as there is little suggestion of mate fidelity this does not appear to be for reinforcement of pair bonding. Brewster (1925), recording observations at Lake Umbagog, Maine, USA, from a diary covering the period 1881–1889, notes an incident where having been thwarted in around 20 attempts to seize a victim from a flock of 'titlarks' (pipits) 'the mortification and disgust of the Pigeon Hawk, because of his ignominious failure … [he] flew listlessly across the marsh to a distant tree. Perhaps it was because of such lost self-respect and with some thought of thereby restoring it that he began harrying an unoffending crow not long afterwards, just as a human bully may correspondingly behave when similarly humiliated.' While today such anthropomorphism is frowned upon, Brewster's account does paint an entertaining scene.

Chapter 8

Note 8.1 Around 200,000 pigeons were employed by the British military during the war years, the birds being used for duties which ranged from bringing back information from agents in occupied Europe (in an irony doubtless lost on the birds themselves, the pigeons – more than 16,000 in total – were often carried into enemy-held lands by parachute) to being used by the crews of downed aircraft to alert the authorities of their position. Thirty-two pigeons were awarded the Dickin Medal (the equivalent of the Victoria Cross for animals) as a result of their activities during the war, seven related to downed aircraft, the remainder because of flights with messages from enemy-occupied lands.

Note 8.2 Derek Ratcliffe (1929–2005) was a leading British environmentalist and ornithologist who was appointed to head the official investigation into the status of the Peregrine Falcon in Britain after complaints by owners of homing pigeons – particularly owners in south Wales, who were especially vociferous in their objections to protecting a falcon which was, they claimed, killing increasing numbers of pigeons – that Peregrine numbers were increasing and that the protection of the species should be rescinded.

Note 8.3 Nygård (1999) noted that variation in the shape of eggs of different species meant that a correction to the standard Ratcliffe index was required in some cases. Nygård noted, for instance, that cormorants had long elliptical eggs which therefore had high eccentricity (defined in terms of egg length and breadth), while owls had short eggs with low eccentricity. Nygård also noted that the size of the blow hole in museum eggs affected the Ratcliffe index, and therefore proposed a correction based on species egg eccentricity and blow-hole size. For 585 eggs of six European raptor species the correction was small (about 3%), but it could be larger for other species.

Note 8.4   While an increase in the range of Hobbies as a consequence of global warming might seem an unexpected benefit, and will likely allow birdwatchers in Scotland and northern England to more frequently see a falcon which was once a rarity or which required a journey, the overall effect of warming will likely be less beneficial in Europe as a whole. In a study based on climate models, and resulting habitat (i.e. land-use) models, Barbet-Massin *et al.* (2012) looked at the probable effects of climate change on bird species in the western Palearctic and concluded that it would result in a range decrease in 71% of 409 species by 2050. The decline will be seen most markedly in southern Europe. In northern Europe, specifically Scandinavia and Russia, but also southern Ireland, species richness will increase, perhaps by as much as 12%. In southern Britain, species richness will probably also improve, but by a smaller fraction, while northern Britain will see little change. However, later work by Massimino *et al.* (2015) on populations in Great Britain alone suggests a different scenario. Choosing 80 native species defined by their occurrence in at least 100 observation squares during BTO Breeding Bird Surveys from 1994 to 2009, the researchers suggest that in the short term northward range expansion will not be accompanied by an alteration in the southern range limit. Northern Britain would therefore see an increase in species richness. That assessment has to be tempered with the observation that the Fulmar, Kittiwake and Puffin populations on St Kilda have declined dramatically in recent years as the warming of the sea has caused their chief prey to move northward (see Prior 2014 – the decline shown in that report was confirmed by the study in 2015 which was reported in the *Guardian* newspaper of 5 December 2015 based on the draft 2015 report).

Climate change is therefore a mixed blessing for the birdwatcher, and while an increase in species richness is welcome, the loss of populations of seabirds is not. There is also more significant bad news. In a study of 4,424 species from 1970–2009 Oliver *et al.* 2015 (see also Oliver *et al.* 2016) noted that a combination of habitat loss due to intensive farming and urbanisation, and climate change was leading to a reduction in biodiversity and the functioning of ecosystems. The reduction was seen in declines in carbon sequestration, decomposition, pest control and pollination, as well as the cultural value of thriving ecosystems. While birds and mammals constituted only 1.7% of the 4,424 species considered (the remainder were plants, insects, etc.) loss of biodiversity and ecosystem function will inevitably affect bird populations in the medium to long term.

Note 8.5   While the natural assumption would be that Hobbies are an essentially warm-climate falcon and so would be rare in northern climes, it is worth noting that in Finland Hobbies are the most numerous falcon to a latitude of about 63°N, and as numerous as Kestrels and Merlins as far north as the Arctic Circle. Only north of the Arctic Circle are they outnumbered by Merlins (Solonen 1994).

Note 8.6   Hacking is a falconry term for a form of raising young falcons either for release to the wild or for recapture for falconry. Young birds which have had minimum contact with humans are placed in a hack box, with a mesh front which allows a view of open country, where they are fed until a few days before fledging. The mesh is then removed, allowing the falcons to make excursions from the box as they would from a wild nest. After the falcons fledge and take their first flights, they return to the box, where they can find food and safety. Ultimately they disperse as they would in the wild.

References and Further Reading

Note: titles in square brackets have been translated from the original language.

Abuladze, A. (2013). Materials towards a Fauna of Georgia. Issue VI: Birds of Prey of Georgia, Ilia State University, Tbilisi.

Adair, P. (1891). The Short-eared Owl (*Asio accipitrinus*) and the Kestrel (*Falco tinnunculus*) in the vole plague districts. *Annals of Scottish Natural History*, 219–231.

Adair, P. (1893). Notes on the disappearance of the Short-tailed Vole (*Arvicola agrestis*), and some on the effects of the visitation. *Annals of Scottish Natural History*, 193–202.

Adriaensen, F., Verwimp, N. & Dhondt, A. A. (1997). Are Belgian Kestrels *Falco tinnunculus* migratory: an analysis of ringing recoveries. *Ringing and Migration*, **18**, 91–101.

Adriaensen, F., Verwimp, N. & Dhondt, A. A. (1998). Between cohort variation in dispersal distance in the European Kestrel *Falco tinnunculus* as shown by ringing recoveries, *Ardea*, **86**, 147–152.

Albuquerque, J. L. B. (1982). Observations on the use of rangle by the Peregrine Falcon (*Falco peregrinus tundrius*) wintering in southern Brasil. *Raptor Research*, **16**, 91–92.

Alerstam, T. (1987). Radar observations of the stoop of the Peregrine Falcon *Falco peregrinus* and the Goshawk *Accipiter gentilis*. *Ibis*, **129**, 267–273.

Altwegg, R., Jenkins, A. & Abadi, F. (2014). Nestboxes and immigration drive the growth of an urban Peregrine Falcon *Falco peregrinus* population. *Ibis*, **156**, 107–115.

Amar, A., Thirgood, S., Pearce-Higgins, J. & Redpath, S. (2008). The impact of raptors on the abundance of upland passerines and waders. *Oikos*, **117**, 1143–1152.

Amar, A., Court, I. R., Davison, M. *et al.* (2012). Linking nest histories, remotely sensed land use data and wildlife crime records to explore the impact of grouse moor management on Peregrine Falcon populations. *Biological Conservation*, **145**, 86–94.

Ambrose, R. E. & Riddle, K. E. (1988). Population dispersal, turnover, and migration of Alaska Peregrines. In *Peregrine Falcon Populations: Their Management and Recovery* (ed. T. J. Cade *et al.*). The Peregrine Fund, Boise, Idaho, pp. 677–684.

Andersen, H. H. (1975). [Lucky days in Crete.] *Felthorn*, **17**, 150–151.

Andersson, M. & Norberg, R. Å. (1981). Evolution of reversed sexual size dimorphism and role partitioning among predatory birds with a size scaling of flight performance. *Biological Journal of the Linnean Society*, **15**, 105–130.

Andersson, M., Wiklund, C. G. & Rundgren, H. (1980). Parental defence of offspring: a model and an example. *Animal Behaviour*, **28**, 536–542.

Aparicio, J. M. (1994a). The effect of variation in the laying interval on proximate determination of clutch size in the European Kestrel. *Journal of Avian Biology*, **25**, 275–280.

Aparicio, J. M. (1994b). The seasonal decline in clutch size: an experiment with supplementary food in the Kestrel *Falco tinnuculus*. *Oikos*, **71**, 451–458.

Aparicio, J. M. (1998). Individual optimization may explain differences in breeding time in the European Kestrel *Falco tinnunculus*. *Journal of Avian Biology*, **29**, 121–128.

Aparicio, J. M. (1999). Intraclutch egg-size variation in the Eurasian Kestrel: Advantages and disadvantages of hatching from large eggs. *Auk*, **116**, 825–830.

Aschwanden, J., Birrer, S. & Jenni, L. (2005). Are ecological compensation areas attractive hunting sites for Comon Kestrels (*Falco tinnuculus*) and Long-eared Owls (*Asio otus*)? *Journal of Ornithology*, **146**, 279–286.

Ashley, M. (1918). On the breeding habits of the Hobby. *British Birds*, **11**, 194–196.

Atherton, P. F. (1997). Baron Swallow giving specific alarm call for Hobby. *British Birds*, 90, 526.

Austin, G. E., Calbrade, N. A., Mellan, H. J. et al. (2014). *Waterbirds in the UK 2012/13: The Wetlands Bird Survey*. BTO/RSPB/JNCC, Thetford. (http://www.bto.org/volunteer-surveys/webs/publications/webs-annual-report).

Avery, M. (2015). *Inglorious: Conflict in the Uplands*. Bloomsbury, London.

Avilés, J. M., Sánchez, J. M. & Parejo, D. (2001). Breeding rates of Eurasian Kestrels (*Falco tinnunculus*) in relation to surrounding habitat in southwest Spain. *Journal of Raptor Research*, **35**, 31–34.

Baines, D. & Richardson, M. (2013). Hen Harriers on a Scottish moor: multiple factors predict breeding density and productivity. *Journal of Applied Ecology*, **50**, 1397–1405.

Baker, H., Stroud, D. A., Aebischer, N. J. et al. (2006). Population estimates of birds in Great Britain and the United Kingdom. *British Birds*, **99**, 25–44.

Baker, J. A. (1967). *The Peregrine*. Collins, London.

Baker, K. (1982). Hobby using a plucking platform. *British Birds*, **75**, 287.

Baker, R. R. & Bibby, C. J. (1987). Merlin *Falco columbarius* predation and theories of the evolution of bird coloration. *Ibis*, **129**, 259–263.

Balfour, E. (1955). Kestrels nesting on the ground in Orkney. *Bird Notes*, **26**, 245–253.

Ballard, J. W. O. & Whitlock, M. C. (2004). The incomplete natural history of mitochondria. *Molecular Ecology*, **13**, 729–744.

Banks, A. N., Crick, H. Q. P., Coombes, R. et al. (2010). The breeding status of Peregrine Falcons *Falco peregrinus* in the UK and Isle of Man in 2002. *Bird Study*, **57**, 421–436.

Barbet-Massin, M., Thuiller, W. & Jiguet, F. (2012). The fate of European breeding birds under climate, land-use and dispersal scenarios. *Global Change Biology*, **18**, 881–890.

Barnes, J. G. & Gerstenberger, S. L. (2015). Using feathers to determine mercury contamination in Peregrine Falcons and their prey. *Journal of Raptor Research*, **49**, 43–58.

Barrios, L. & Rodríguez, A. (2004). Behavioural and environmental correlates of soaring-bird mortality at on-shore wind turbines. *Journal of Applied Ecology*, **41**, 72–81.

Barton, N. W. H. & Houston, D. C. (1993). A comparison of digestive efficiency in birds of prey. *Ibis*, 135, 363–371.

Barton, N. W. H. & Houston, D. C. (2001). The incidence of intestinal parasites in British birds of prey. *Journal of Raptor Research*, **35**, 71–73.

Beaupre, E. (1922). The Duck Hawk. *Canadian Field-Naturalist*, **36**, 33–35.

Bednarek, W. (1986). [The relationship between climate, food requirements and kleptoparasitism in Hobbies *Falco subbuteo*.] *Jahrbuch des Deutschen Falkenordens*, **1986**, 43–46.

Beebe, F. L. (1960). The marine Peregrines of the northwest Pacific coast. *Condor*, **62**, 145–189.

Bélisle, E., Gahbauer, M. A. & Bird, D. M. (2012). Unusual behaviour by a juvenile Peregrine Falcon: interference, siblicide and incest. *Journal of Raptor Research*, **46**, 324–326.

Bell, D. A., Griffiths, C. S., Caballero, I. C., Hartley, R. R. & Lawson, R. H. (2014). Genetic evidence for global dispersion in the Peregrine Falcon (*Falco peregrinus*) and affinity with the Taita Falcon (*Falco fasciinucha*). *Journal of Raptor Research*, **48**, 44–53.

Bengtson, S.-A. (1975). [Hunting methods and prey of an Icelandic population of Merlins (*Falco columbarius*).] *Fauna och Flora*, **70**, 8–12.

Bennett, A. T. D. & Cuthill, I. C. (1994). Ultraviolet vision in birds: what is it for? *Vision Research*, **34**, 1471–1478.

Berezovikov, N. N. & Zinchenko, E. S. (1988). On the biology of the Hobby (*Falco subbuteo*) in the montane forest zone of the southern Altai. In *Bird Ecology and Behaviour* (ed. V. D. Ilychev). Proceedings of the All-Union Ornithological Society, Moscow, 70–75.

Bergman, G. (1961). The food of birds of prey and owls in Fenno-Scandia. *British Birds*, **54**, 307–320.

Bergmann, W. (1952). [A Hobby as a direct successor to Ravens.] *Vogelwelt*, **73**, 61–62.

Beukeboom, L., Dijkstra, C., Daan, S. & Meijer, T. (1988). Seasonality of clutch size determination in the Kestrel *Falco tinnunculus*: an experimental approach. *Ornis Scandinavica*, **19**, 41–48.

Beven, G. (1945). Hobby eating birds in the air. *British Birds*, **38**, 334.

Bibby, C. J. (1986). Merlins in Wales: site occupancy and breeding in relation to vegetation. *Journal of Applied Ecology*, **23**, 1–12.

Bibby, C. J. (1987). Foods of breeding Merlins in Wales. *Bird Study*, **34**, 64–70.

Bibby, C. J. & Nattrass, M. (1986). The breeding status of the Merlin in Britain. *British Birds*, **79**, 170–185.

Bijlsma, R. (1980). *De Boomvalk*. Kosmos, Utrecht/Antwerp.

Bijlsma, R. G. (1984). [On the breeding association between Wood Pigeons *Columba palumbus* and Hobbies *Falco subbuteo*.] *Limosa* **57**, 133–139.

Bijlsma, R. G. (1991). Migration of raptors and Demoiselle Cranes over central Nepal. *Birds of Prey Bulletin*, **4**, 73–80.

Bijlsma, R. G. & Beunder, C. (2007). Post-breeding Hobbies *Falco subbuteo* and dragonflies Odonata. *De Takkeling*, **15**, 222–232.

Bijlsma, R. G. & de Vries, C. (1997). [Breeding results and trends of raptors in Holland in 1996]. *De Takkeling*, **5**, 7–46.

Bijlsma, R. G. & van den Brink, B. (2005). A Barn Swallow Hirundo rustica roost under attack: timing and risks in the presence of African Hobbies *Falco cuvieri*. *Ardea*, **93**, 37–48.

Bijlsma, R. G. & van Diermen, J. (1986). (The Hobby *Falco subbuteo* as a breeding bird on the Dutch Wadden Sea Islands). *Limosa*, **59**, 135–137.

Bijlsma, R. G., van den Brink, B., de Roder, F. & Terpstra, K. (1994a). Some data on measurements and moult of flight feathers in raptors in Botswana. *Babbler*, **28**, 26–29.

Bijlsma, R. G., van den Brink, B., de Roder, F. & Terpstra, K. (1994b). Raptor predation on roosting Swallows. *Gabar*, **9**, 13–16.

Billett, D. F. & Rees, G. H. (1984). Falcons hunting close to harriers. *British Birds*, **77**, 482.

Bird D. M. & Aubry, Y. (1982). Reproductive and hunting behaviour in Peregrine Falcons, *Falco peregrinus*, in southern Quebec. *Canadian Field-Naturalist*, **96**, 167–171.

Bird, D. M., Weil, P. G. & Lague, P. C. (1980). Photoperiodic induction of multiple breeding seasons in captive American Kestrels. *Canadian Journal of Zoology*, **58**, 1022–1026.

Blezard, E., Garnett, M., Graham, R. & Johnson, T. L. (1943). *The Birds of Lakeland*. Transactions of the Carlisle Natural History Society, 6. Carlisle Natural History Society, Carlisle.

Boer, P. de & Hut, H. (1997). Can Hobbies *Falco subbuteo* prevent nest predation? *De Takkeling*, **5**, 47–51.

Boer, P. de & Koks, B. (1996). [Hobbies *Falco subbuteo* breeding on high voltage transmission towers in Groningen.] *De Takkeling*, **4**, 30–43.

Bogliani, G., Tiso, E. & Barbieri, F. (1992). Nesting association between the Wood Pigeon (*Columba palumbus*) and the Hobby (*Falco subbuteo*). *Journal of Raptor Research*, **26**, 263–265.

Bogliani, G., Barbieri, F. & Tiso, E. (1994). Hobby nest-site selection by the Hobby

(*Falco subbuteo*) in poplar plantations in northern Italy. *Journal of Raptor Research*, **28**, 13–18.

Bogliani, G., Sergio, F. & Tavecchia, G. (1999). Wood Pigeons nesting in association with Hobby falcons: advantages and choice rules. *Animal Behaviour*, **57**, 125–131.

Boileau, N. & Bretagnolle, V. (2014). Post-fledging dependence period in the Eurasian Kestrel (*Falco tinnunculus*) in western France. *Journal of Raptor Research*, **48**, 248–256.

Boileau, N. & Hoede, C. (2009). [Variations in egg size in the Common Kestrel *Falco tinnunculus*.] *Alauda*, **77**, 21–30.

Bond, R. (1936). Speed and eyesight of a Pigeon Hawk. *Condor*, **38**, 85.

Bonin, B. & Strenna, L. (1986). [On the biology of the Kestrel *Falco tinnunculus* in Auxois.] *Alauda*, **54**, 241–262.

Booms, T. L. & Fuller, M. R. (2003). Gyrfalcon diet in central west Greenland during the nesting period. *Condor*, **105**, 528–537.

Boratyński, Z. & Kasprzyk, K. (2005). Does urban structure explain shifts in the food niche of the Eurasian Kestrel (*Falco tinnunculus*). *Buteo*, **14**, 11–17.

Both, C., Bom, R. & Samplonius, J. (2013). Peregrine Falcon *Falco peregrinus* steals vole from Kestrel *Falco tinnunculus*. *De Takkeling*, **21**, 226–228.

Boyce, D. A. (1985). Merlins and the behaviour of wintering shorebirds. *Raptor Research*, **19**, 95–96.

Boyle, G. L. (1991). Skylark using car as refuge from Merlin. *British Birds*, **84**, 18.

Bradley, M. & Oliphant, L. W. (1991). The diet of Peregrine Falcons in Rankin Inlet, Northwest Territories: an unusually high proportion of mammalian prey. *Condor*, **93**, 193–197.

Bradley, M., Johnstone, R., Court, G. & Duncan T. (1997). Influence of weather on breeding success of Peregrine Falcons in the Arctic. *Auk*, **114**, 786–791.

Brambilla, M., Rubolini, D. & Guidali, F. (2004). Rock climbing and Raven *Corvus corax* occurrence depress breeding success of cliff-nesting Peregrines *Falco peregrinus*. *Ardeola*, **51**, 425–430.

Brambilla, M., Rubolini, D. & Guidali, F. (2006a). Factors affecting breeding habitat selection in a cliff-nesting Peregrine *Falco peregrinus* population. *Journal of Ornithology*, **147**, 428–435.

Brambilla, M., Rubolini, D. & Guidali, F. (2006b). Eagle Owl *Bubo bubo* proximity can lower productivity of cliff-nesting Peregrines *Falco peregrinus*. *Ornis Fennica*, **83**, 20–26.

Brewster, W. (1925). The Birds of the Lake Umbagog Region of Maine. *Bulletin of the Museum of Comparative Zoology*, **64**, 355–362.

Brown, L. (1976). *British Birds of Prey*. Collins, London.

Brown, L. E., Holden, J. & Palmer, S. M. (2014). Effects of Moorland Burning on the Ecohydrology of River Basins: Key Findings from the EMBER Project. University of Leeds, Leeds. http://www.wateratleeds.org/fileadmin/documents/water_at_leeds/Ember_report.pdf.

Brown, R. H. (1935). The food of certain birds of prey. *British Birds*, **28**, 257–258.

Brownett, A. (1998). Predation of adult *Anax imperator* Leach by the Hobby (*Falco subbuteo* L.) – how frequently does this occur? *Journal of the British Dragonfly Society*, **14**, 45–52.

Bruderer, B. & Boldt, A. (2001). Flight characteristics of birds: I. radar measurements of speeds. *Ibis*, **143**, 178–204.

Bruderer, B. & Salewski, V. (2009). Lower annual fecundity in long-distance migrants than in less migratory birds in temperate Europe. *Journal of Ornithology*, **150**, 281–286.

Bruderer, B., Peter, D., Boldt, A. & Liechti, F. (2010). Wing-beat characteristics of birds recorded with tracking radar and cine camera. *Ibis*, **152**, 272–291.

Bruinzeel, L. W. & van de Pol, M. (2004). Site attachment of floaters predicts success in territory acquisition. *Behavioral Ecology*, **15**, 290–296.

Buchanan, J. B. (1991). Two cases of carrion-feeding by Peregrine Falcons in western Washington. *Northwestern Naturalist*, **72**, 28–29.

Buchanan, J. B. (1996). A comparison of behaviour and success rates of Merlins and Peregrine Falcons when hunting

Dunlin in two coastal habitats. *Journal of Raptor Research*, **30**, 93–98.

Buchanan, J. B., Herman, S. G. & Johnson, T. M. (1986). Success rate of the Peregrine Falcon (*Falco peregrinus*) hunting Dunlin (*Calidris alpina*) during winter. *Raptor Research*, **20**, 130–131.

Buchanan, J. B., Schick, C. T., Brennan, L. A. & Herman, S. G. (1988). Merlin predation on wintering Dunlins: hunting success and Dunlin escape tactics. *Wilson Bulletin*, **100**, 108–118.

Buchanan, J. B., Hamm, K. A., Salzer, L. J., Diller, L. V. & Chinnici, S. J. (2014). Tree-nesting by Peregrine Falcons in North America: historical and additional records. *Journal of Raptor Research*, **48**, 61–67.

Burnham, W. A., Enderson, J. H. & Boardman, T. J. (1984). Variation in Peregrine Falcon eggs. *Auk*, **101**, 578–583.

Bustamante, J. (1994). Behavior of Common Kestrels (*Falco tinnunculus*) during the post-fledging dependence period in south-western Spain. *Journal of Raptor Research* **28**, 79–83.

Cade, T. J. (1960). Ecology of the Peregrine and Gyrfalcon populations in Alaska, *University of California Publications in Zoology*, **63**, 151–290.

Cade, T. J. (1982). *The Falcons of the World*. Cornell University Press, Ithaca; Collins, London.

Cade, T. J. & Bird, D. M. (1990) Peregrine Falcons, *Falco peregrinus*, nesting in an urban environment: a review. *Canadian Field-Naturalist*, **104**, 209–218.

Campioni, L., Delgado, M. D. M. & Penteriani, V. (2010). Social status influences microhabitat selection: breeder and floater Eagle Owls *Bubo bubo* use different post sites. *Ibis*, **152**, 569–579.

Carere, C., Montanino, S., Moreschini, F. et al. (2009). Aerial flocking patterns of wintering Starlings, *Sturna vulgaris*, under different predation risk. *Animal Behaviour*, **77**, 101–107.

Carlier, P. (1993). Sex differences in nesting site attendance by Peregrine Falcons (*Falco peregrinus brookei*). *Journal of Raptor Research*, **27**, 31–34.

Carlier, P. (1995). Vocal communications in Peregrine Falcons *Falco peregrinus* during breeding. *Ibis*, **137**, 582–585.

Carrillo, J. & González-Dávila, E. (2010). Geo-environmental influences on breeding parameters of the Eurasian Kestrel (*Falco tinnunculus*) in the western Palearctic. *Ornis Fennica*, **87**, 15–25.

Catley, G. P. (1994). More Hobbies nesting on pylons. *British Birds*, **87**, 335–336.

Cavé, A. J. (1967). The breeding of the Kestrel *Falco tinnunculus* L., in the reclaimed area Oostelijk, Flevoland. *Netherlands Journal of Zoology*, **18**, 313–407.

Chandler, R. B., Strong, A. M. & Kaufman, C. C. (2004). Elevated leadlevels in urban House Sparrows: a threat to Sharp-shinned Hawks and Merlins? *Journal of Raptor Research*, **38**, 62–68.

Chapman, A. (1999a). *The Hobby*. Arlequin Press, Chelmsford.

Chapman, A. (1999b). Barn Swallow giving specific alarm call for Hobby. *British Birds*, **92**, 51.

Charpentier, G., Louat, F., Bonmatin, J.-M. et al. (2014). Lethal and sublethal effects of imidacloprid, after chronic exposure, on the insect model *Drosophila melanogaster*. *Environmental Science and Technology*, **48**, 4096–4102. doi : 10. 1021/es405331c.

Charter, M., Izhaki, I., Bouskila, A. & Leshem, Y. (2007). Breeding success of the Eurasian Kestrel (*Falco tinnunculus*) nesting on buildings in Israel. *Journal of Raptor Research*, **41**, 139–143.

Chávez, A. E., Bozinovic, F., Peichl, L. & Palacios, A. G. (2003). Retinal spectral sensitivity, fur coloration, and urine reflectance in the genus *Octodon* (Rodentia): implications for visual ecology. *Investigative Ophthalmology and Visual Science*, **44**, 2290–2296.

Chesser, R. T., Banks, R. C., Barker, F. K. et al. (2012). Fifty-third supplement to the American Ornithologists' Union check-list of North American birds. *Auk*, **129**, 573–588.

Clarke, A., Prince, P. A. & Clarke, R. (1996). The energy content of dragonflies (Odonata) in relation to predation by falcons. *Bird Study*, **43**, 300–304.

Clarke, R. & Scott, D. (1994). Breeding season diet of the Merlin in County Antrim. *Irish Birds*, **5**, 205–206.

Clements, R. (2008). The Common Kestrel population in Britain. *British Birds*, **101**, 228–234.

Clements, R. J. (2001). The Hobby in Britain: a new population estimate. *British Birds*, **94**, 402–448.

Clements, R. J. & Everett, C. M. (2012). Densities and dispersion of breeding Eurasian Hobbies *Falco subbuteo* in southeast England. *Bird Study*, **59**, 74–82.

Clevinger, A. P. (1987). Atypical incubation rates at a New Mexico Peregrine Falcon eyrie. *Journal of Raptor Research*, **21**, 33–35.

Clifford, B. (1947). Hobby catching Green Woodpeckers. *British Birds*, **40**, 251.

Clum, N. J. (1995). Effects of aging and mate retention on reproductive success of captive female Peregrine Falcons. *American Zoologist*, **35**, 329–339.

Coath, M. (1992). Talon locking between Kestrel and Red-footed Falcon. *British Birds*, **85**, 496.

Cochrane, W. W. & Applegate, R. D. (1986). Speed of flight of Merlins and Peregrine Falcons. *Condor*, **88**, 397–398.

Cocker, M. (2007). Peregrine Falcon retrieving prey from a flock of Carrion Crows. *British Birds*, **100**, 307.

Collar, N. J. (1978). Association of nesting Wood Pigeons and Hobbies. *British Birds*, **71**, 545–546.

Collar, N. J. (2002). Insectivory and kleptoparasitism in Peregrine Falcons. *British Birds*, **95**, 142.

Combridge, P. (2008). Peregrine Falcon defending prey from flock of Carrion Crows. *British Birds*, **101**, 383–384.

Combridge, M. C. & Combridge, P. (1992). Red-footed falcon robbing Kestrels. *British Birds*, **85**, 496.

Combridge, P. & King, S. S. (2007). Hobbies fledging four young. *British Birds*, **100**, 624–625.

Cooper, J. E. (1984). Developmental abnormalities in two British falcons (*Falco* spp.). *Avian Pathology*, **13**, 639–645.

Cooper, J. E. (1993). Diseases in the Peregrine. In Ratcliffe, D., *The Peregrine Falcon*. Poyser, London, pp. 360–361 and Table 31.

Cooper, J. E. & Forbes, N. A. (1986). Studies on morbidity and mortality in the Merlin (*Falco columbarius*), *Veterinary Record*, **118**, 232–235.

Cooper, J. E., Redig, P. T. & Burnham, W. (1980). Bacterial isolates from the pharynx cloaca of the Peregrine Falcon (*Falco peregrinus*) and Gyrfalcon (*F. rusticolus*) (Bacteria from Falcons). *Raptor Research*, **14**, 6–9.

Cooper, N. W., Sherry, T. W. & Marra, P. P. (2015). Experimental reduction of winter food decreases body condition and delays migration in a long-distance migratory bird. *Ecology*, **96**, 1933–1942.

Cornulier, T., Yoccoz, N. G., Bretagnolle, V. et al. (2013). Europe-wide dampening of population cycles in keystone herbivores. *Science*, **340**, 63–66.

Corso, A. (2001). Raptor migration across the Strait of Messina, southern Italy. *British Birds*, **94**, 196–202.

Corso A. & Montrosso, G. (2000). [An undescribed dark variant of the Hobby *Falco subbuteo* and its distinction from Eleonora's Falcon *F. eleonorae*.] *Limicola*, **14**, 209–215.

Corso A. & Montrosso, G. (2004). Further comments on dark Hobbies in southern Italy. *British Birds*, **97**, 411–414.

Cosnette, B. L. (1984). Successive use of same site by two female Merlins. *Scottish Birds*, **13**, 118.

Cosnette, B. L. (1991). Apparent bigamy in Merlins and co-operation of two females with large young. *North-East Scotland Bird Report*, **1990**, 74–75.

Costantini, D., Dell'Omo, G., La Fata, I. & Casagrande, S. (2014). Reproductive performance of Eurasian Kestrel *Falco tinnunculus* in an agricultural landscape with a mosaic of land uses. *Ibis*, **156**, 768–776.

Court, G. S. (1986). Some aspects of the reproductive biology of tundra Peregrine Falcons. MSc thesis, University of Alberta.

Court, G. S., Gates, C. G. & Boag, D. A. (1988). Natural history of the Peregrine Falcon in the Keewatin District of the Northwest Territories. *Arctic*, **41**, 17–30.

Court, G. S., Bradley, D. M., Gates, C. G. & Boag, D. A. (1989). Turnover and recruitment in a tundra population of Peregrine Falcons *Falco peregrinus*. *Ibis*, **131**, 487–496.

Craib, J. K. (1994). Merlin follows prey underground. *Scottish Birds*, **17**, 236.

Craighead, J. & Craighead, F. (1940). Nesting Pigeon Hawks. *Wilson Bulletin*, **52**, 241–248.

Cramp, S. & Simmons, K. E. L. (eds.) (1980). *Handbook of the Birds of Europe, the Middle East and North Africa: The Birds of the Western Palearctic, Vol. 2*. Oxford University Press, Oxford.

Cresswell, W. (1993). Escape responses by Redshanks, *Tringa totanus*, on attack by avian predators. *Animal Behaviour*, 46, 609–611.

Cresswell, W. (1994). Song as a pursuit-deterrent signal, and its occurrence relative to other anti-predation behaviours of Skylark (*Alauda arvensis*) on attack by Merlins (*Falco columbarius*). *Behavioral Ecology and Sociobiology*, **34**, 217–223.

Cresswell, W. (1996). Surprise as a winter hunting strategy in Sparrowhawks *Accipiter nisus*, Peregrines *Falco peregrinus* and Merlins *F. columbarius*. *Ibis*, **138**, 684–692.

Cresswell, W. & Whitfield, D. P. (1994). The effects of raptor predation on wintering wader populations at the Tynghame estuary, southeast Scotland. *Ibis*, **136**, 223–232.

Crowe, O., Coombes, R. H., Lysaght, L *et al.* (2010). Population trends of widespread breeding birds in the Republic of Ireland 1998–2008. *Bird Study*, **57**, 267–280.

Cruickshank, R. A. (1980). European Hobby in the south-western Cape. *Ostrich*, **51**, 127.

Csermely, D., Bonati, B. & Romani, R. (2009). Predatory behaviour of Common Kestrels (*Falco tinnunculus*). *Journal of Ethology*, **27**, 461–465.

Culver, E. (1919). Duck hawks wintering in the centre of Philadelphia. *Auk*, **36**, 108–109.

Daan, S. & Dijkstra, C. (1988). Date of birth and reproductive value of Kestrel eggs: on the significance of early breeding. In Dijkstra, C., Reproductive tactics in the Kestrel *Falco tinnunculus*. PhD thesis, University of Groningen.

Daan, S., Dijkstra, C., Drent, R. & Meijer, T. (1988). Food supply and the annual timing of avian reproduction. In *Proceedings of the XIX International Ornithological Congress* (Ottawa), pp. 392–407.

Daan, S., Dijkstra, C. & Tinbergen, J. M. (1990). Family planning in the Kestrel (*Falco tinnunculus*): the ultimate control of covariation of laying date and clutch size. *Behaviour* **114**, 83–116.

Daan, S., Deerenberg, C. & Dijkstra C. (1996). Increased daily work precipitates natural death in the Kestrel. *Journal of Animal Ecology*, **65**, 539–544.

Dean, T. (1988). Merlin preying on Leach's Petrel. *British Birds*, **81**, 395.

Deane, C. D. (1962). Life of the wild. *Belfast Telegraph*, 19 September 1962.

Deerenberg, C., Pen, I., Dijkstra, C. *et al.* (1995). Parental energy expenditure in relation to manipulated brood size in the European Kestrel *Falco tinnunculus*. *Zoology*, **99**, 39–48.

Dejonghe, J. F. (1989). [Importance, structure, origins, biometrics and population dynamics of Kestrels *Falco tinnunculus* on spring migration at Cape Bon, Tunisia.] *Alauda*, **57**, 17–45.

Dekker, D. (1980). Hunting success rates, foraging habits, and prey selection of Peregrine Falcons migrating through central Alberta. *Canadian Field-Naturalist*, **94**, 371–382.

Dekker, D. (1988). Peregrine Falcon and Merlin predation of on small shorebirds and passerines in Alberta. *Canadian Journal of Zoology*, **66**, 925–928.

Dekker, D. (1995). Prey capture by Peregrine Falcons wintering on southern Vancouver Island, British Columbia. *Journal of Raptor Research*, **29**, 26–29.

Dekker, D. (1998). Over-ocean flocking by Dunlins, *Calidris alpina*, and the effect of raptor predation at Boundary Bay, British Columbia. *Canadian Field-Naturalist*, **112**, 694–697.

Dekker, D. (2003). Peregrine Falcon predation on Dunlins and ducks and kleptoparasitic interference from Bald Eagles wintering at Boundary Bay, British Columbia. *Journal of Raptor Research*, **37**, 91–97.

Dekker, D. & Bogaert, L. (1997). Over-ocean hunting by Peregrine Falcons in British Columbia. *Journal of Raptor Research*, **31**, 381–383.

Dekker, D. & Ydenburg, R. (2004). Raptor predation on wintering Dunlins in relation to the tidal cycle. *Condor*, **106**, 415–419.

Dekker, D., Out, M., Tabak, M. & Ydenberg, R. (2012). The effect of kleptoparasitic Bald Eagles and Gyrfalcons on the kill rate of Peregrine Falcons hunting Dunlins wintering in British Columbia. *Condor*, **114**, 290–294.

Dement'ev, G. P. & Gladkov, N. A. (eds.) (1966). *Birds of the Soviet Union.* Israel Program for Scientific Translations, Jerusalem. (The Russian original was published in Moscow in 1951.)

Dennis, R. H. (1970). The oiling of large raptors by Fulmars. *Scottish Birds*, **6**, 198–199.

Desjardin, D., Maruniak, J. A. & Bronson, F. H. (1973). Social rank in House Mice: differentiation revealed by ultraviolet visualisation of urinary marking patterns. *Science*, **182**, 939–941.

Devrient, I. & Wohlgemuth, R. (1992). [Observations of the behaviour of pylon breeding Hobbies *Falco subbuteo*.] *Charadrius*, **28**, 167–171.

Dickson, R. C. (1973). A Merlin roost in Wigtownshire. *Scottish Birds*, **7**, 288–292.

Dickson, R. C. (1987). Kestrels copulating in winter. *Scottish Birds*, **14**, 215.

Dickson, R. C. (1988). Habitat preferences and prey of Merlins in winter. *British Birds*, **81**, 269–274.

Dickson, R. C. (1989). Restricted winter range of a Merlin in west Galloway. *Scottish Birds*, **15**, 131–132.

Dickson, R. C. (1993). Hunting times by Merlins in winter. *Scottish Birds*, **17**, 56–58.

Dickson, R. C. (1994). Mating times of Merlins. *Scottish Birds*, **17**, 160–161.

Dickson, R. C. (1995). Nest reliefs and feeding rates of Merlin. *Scottish Birds*, **18**, 20–23.

Dickson, R. C. (1996). The hunting behaviour of Merlins in winter in Galloway. *Scottish Birds*, **18**, 165–169.

Dickson, R. C. (1998a). Cannibalism in a Merlin brood. *Scottish Birds*, **19**, 167.

Dickson, R. C. (1998b). Merlin's sunning behaviour in winter. *Scottish Birds*, **19**, 176.

Dickson, R. C. (1998c). Hunting associations between Merlins and Hen Harriers. *Scottish Birds*, **19**, 245.

Dickson, R. C. (1999). Size of Merlin pellets in winter and summer in Galloway. *Scottish Birds*, **20**, 31–33.

Dickson, R. C. (2000). Prey captured and attacked by Merlins in winter. *Scottish Birds*, **21**, 116–117, plus erratum in *Scottish Birds* (2001), **22**, 68.

Dickson, R. C. (2003). Sunning behaviour by a fledgling Merlin. *Scottish Birds*, **24**, 43.

Dickson, R. C. (2005). Female Merlin hunting in her nest area. *Scottish Birds*, **25**, 54.

Dickson, R. C. & Dickson, A. P. (1993). Kestrels feeding on road casualties. *Scottish Birds*, **17**, 56.

Dietz, M. W., Daan, S. & Masman, D. (1992). Energy requirements for molt in the Kestrel *Falco tinnunculus*. *Physiological Zoology*, **65**, 1217–1235.

Dijkstra, C. (1988). Reproductive tactics in the Kestrel *Falco tinnunculus*. PhD thesis, University of Groningen.

Dijkstra, C., Vuursteen, L., Daan, S. & Masman, D. (1982). Clutch size and laying date in the Kestrel *Falco tinnunculus*: effect of supplementary food. *Ibis*, **124**, 210–213.

Dijkstra, C., Daan, S. & Buker, J. B. (1990a). Adaptive seasonal variation in the sex ratio of Kestrel broods. *Functional Ecology* **4**, 143–147.

Dijkstra, C., Bult, A., Bijlsma, S. et al. (1990b). Brood size manipulations in the Kestrel (*Falco tinnunculus*): effects on offspring and parent survival. *Journal of Animal Ecology*, **59**, 269–285.

Dixon, A. & Richards, C. (2003). Estimating the number of racing pigeons killed at Peregrine (*Falco peregrinus*) territories in south Wales. *Welsh Birds*, **3**, 344–353.

Dixon, A., Richards, C., Haffield, P. et al. (2010). Population decline of Peregrines *Falco peregrinus* in central Wales associated with a reduction in racing pigeon availability. *Birds in Wales*, **7**, 3–11.

Doolittle, T. C. J., Berger, D. D. & Van Stappen, J. F. (2013). Easternmost recovery in Europe of a Peregrine Falcon banded in North America. *Journal of Raptor Research*, **47**, 75–76.

Dreiss, A. N., Ruppli, C. A., Faller, C. & Roulin, A. (2015). Social rules govern vocal competition in the Barn Owl. *Animal Behaviour*, **102**, 95–107.

Drewitt, E. J. A. & Dixon, N. (2008). Diet and prey selection of urban-dwelling Peregrine Falcons in southwest England. *British Birds*, **101**, 58–67.

Dronneau, C. & Wassmer, B. (1986). [The breeding of Hobbies *Falco subbuteo* on electricity pylons.] *Nos Oiseaux*, **38**, 363–366.

Dronneau, C. & Wassmer, B. (1987). [Bat hunting by Hobbies *Falco subbuteo*.] *Nos Oiseaux*, **39**, 159–162.

Dronneau, C. & Wassmer, B. (1989). [Adoption of fledglings in the Hobby *Falco subbuteo*.] *Nos Oiseaux*, **40**, 29–31.

Dronneau, C. & Wassmer, B. (2005). [Behaviour of juvenile Hobby *Falco subbuteo* after fledgling.] *Alauda*, **73**, 33–52.

Dronneau, C. & Wassmer, B. (2008). [Breeding ecology and hunting behaviour of the European Hobby *Falco subbuteo* in Alsace, France.] *Alauda*, **76**, 113–134.

Duncan, J. R. & Bird, D. M. (1989). The influence of relatedness and display effort on the mate choice of captive female American Kestrels. *Animal Behaviour*, **37**, 112–117.

Duncan, K. (1990). Merlin killing and retrieving a Dipper from a loch. *Scottish Birds*, **16**, 40.

Duquet, M. & Nadal, R. (2012). The capture of bats by raptors. *Ornithos*, **19**, 184–195.

Edwards, S. B. (1999). Barn Swallow giving specific alarm call for Hobby. *British Birds*, **92**, 51.

Ellis, D. H. & Groat, D. L. (1982). A Prairie Falcon intrudes at a Peregrine Falcon eyrie and pirates prey. *Raptor Research*, **16**, 89–91.

Ellis, P. M. & Okill, J. D. (1990). Breeding ecology of the Merlin *Falco columbarius* in Shetland. *Bird Study*, **37**, 101–110.

Enderson, J. H. (1969). Peregrine and Prairie Falcon Life Tables based on band-recovery data. In *Peregrine Falcon Populations: their Biology and Decline* (ed. J. J. Hickey). University of Wisconsin Press, Madison, pp. 505–509.

Enderson, J. H. & Craig, G. R. (1997). Wide ranging by nesting Peregrine Falcons (*Falco peregrinus*) determined by radiotelemetry. *Journal of Raptor Research*, **31**, 333–338.

Enderson, J. H. & Kirven, M. N. (1983). Flights of nesting Peregrine Falcons recorded by telemetry. *Raptor Research*, **17**, 33–37.

Enderson, J. H., Temple, S. A. & Swartz L. G. (1973). Time-lapse photographic records of nesting Peregrine Falcons. *Living Bird*, **11**, 113–128.

Espie, R. H. M., James, P. C., Warkentin, I. G. & Oliphant, L. W. (1996). Ecological correlates of molt in Merlins (*Falco columbarius*). *Auk*, **113**, 363–369.

Espie, R. H. M., Oliphant, L. W., James, P. C., Warkentin, I. G. & Lieske, D. J. (2000). Age-dependent breeding performance in Merlins (*Falco columbarius*). *Ecology*, **81**, 3404–3415.

Etheridge, B. (2013). Breeding raptors in Scotland: a review. *Scottish Birds*, **33**, 38–45.

European Commission (2013). Implementing Regulation (EU) No. 485/2013 of 24 May 2013 amending Implementing Regulation (EU) No 540/2011, as regards the conditions of approval of the active substances clothianidin, thiamethoxam and imidacloprid, and prohibiting the use and sale of seeds treated with plant protection products containing those active substances. *Official Journal of the European Union L*, **139**, 12–26.

Ewing, S. R., Rebecca, G. W., Heavisides, A. et al. (2011). Breeding status of Merlins *Falco columbarius* in the UK in 2008. *Bird Study*, **58**, 379–389.

Faccio, S. D., Amaral, M., Martin, C. J. et al. (2013). Movement patterns, natal dispersal, and survival of Peregrine Falcons banded in New England. *Journal of Raptor Research*, **47**, 246–261.

Fahy, K. (2011). Irish rare bird report 2010. *Irish Birds*, **9**, 283–314.

Fairley, J. S. (1973). Kestrel pellets from a winter roost. *Irish Naturalists' Journal*, **17**, 407–409.

Fairley, J. S. & McLean, A. (1965). On the summer food of the Kestrel in Northern Ireland. *British Birds*, **58**, 145–148.

Fargallo, J. A., Blanco, G. & Soto-Largo, E. (1996). Possible second clutches in a Mediterranean montane population of the Eurasian Kestrel (*Falco tinnunculus*). *Journal of Raptor Research*, 30, 70–73.

Fargallo, J. A., Blanco, G., Potti, J. & Viñuela, J. (2001). Nestbox provisioning in a rural population of Eurasian Kestrels; breeding performance, nest predation and parasitism. *Bird Study*, 48, 236–244.

Faulkner, R. C., Lee, R. F. & Rolls, J. C. (1968). Hobbies persistently preying on Starling roost. *British Birds*, 61, 134.

Feenders, G. & Bateson, M. (2013). Hand rearing affects emotional responses but not basic cognitive performance in European Starlings. *Animal Behaviour*, 86, 127–138.

Feldsine, J. W. & Oliphant, L. W. (1985). Breeding behavior of the Merlin: the courtship period. *Raptor research*, 19, 60–67.

Fernández-Bellon, D. & Lusby, J. (2011a). The feeding ecology of Merlin *Falco columbarius* during the breeding season in Ireland, and an assessment of current diet analysis methods. *Irish Birds*, 9, 159–164.

Fernández-Bellon, D. & Lusby, J. (2011b). *Irish Merlin Ecological Research, 2011 Report*. Report to the National Parks and Wildlife Service. BirdWatch Ireland, Banagher.

Fernández-Bellon, D. & Lusby, J. (2011c). The effectiveness of playback as a method for monitoring breeding Merlin *Falco columbarius* in Ireland. *Irish Birds*, 9, 155–158.

Fisher, D. (1978). Peregrine retrieving prey from sea. *British Birds*, 71, 461.

Fiuczynski, K. D. (1978). [The population ecology of the Hobby (*Falco subbuteo* L.).] *Zoologische Jahrbücher, Abteilung für Systematik*, 105, 193–257.

Fiuczynski, [K.] D. (1986). [Artificial nests for Hobbies, *Falco subbuteo*, in Berlin.] *Ornithologischer Bericht für Berlin (West)*, 11, 5–18.

Fiuczynski, K. D. (1991). [Predation and nest site limits as limiting factors in breeding density and brood success in the Hobby *Falco subbuteo*.] *Birds of Prey Bulletin*, 4, 63–71.

Fiuczynski, [K.] .D. & Nethersole-Thompson, D. (1980). Hobby studies in England and Germany. *British Birds*, 73, 275–295.

Fiuczynski, K. D. & Sömmer, P. (2000). Adaptation of two falcon species *Falco femoralis* and *Falco subbuteo* to an urban environment. In *Raptors at Risk* (ed. R. D. Chancellor & B.-U. Meyburg). World Working Group on Birds of Prey and Owls/Hancock House, pp. 463–467.

Fiuczynski, K. D. & Sömmer, P. (2011). *Der Baumfalke* Falco subbuteo. Die Neue Brehm-Bücherei, Westarp, Hohenwarsleben. (This book is an updated version of one produced by Fiuczynski alone, with the same title and publisher, produced in 1988.)

Fleet, D. M. (1993). Merlins stalking Dunlins on foot. *British Birds*, 86, 181.

Ford, B. (2007). Recovery of a Peregrine Falcon after hitting the sea. *British Birds*, 100, 304–305.

Formon, A. (1969). [A contribution to the study of Peregrine Falcons *Falco peregrinus* in eastern France.] *Nos Oiseaux*, 30, 109–139.

Fox, G. A. (1979). A simple method of predicting DDE contamination and reproductive success of populations of DDE-sensitive species. *Journal of Applied Ecology*, 16, 737–741.

Fox, G. A., Anderka, F. W., Lewin, V. & MacKay, W. C. (1975). Field assessment of eggshell quality by beta-backscatter. *Journal of Wildlife Management*, 39, 528–534.

Fox, R., Lehmkuhle, S. W. & Westendorf, D. H. (1976). Falcon visual acuity. *Science*, 192, 263–265.

Franklin, K. (1999). Vertical flight. *Journal of the North American Falconers Association*, 38, 68–72.

Fritz, H. (1998). Wind speed as a determinant of kleptoparasitism by Eurasian Kestrel *Falco tinnunculus* on Short-eared Owl *Asio flammeus*. *Journal of Avian Biology*, 29, 331–334.

Fritzsche, H. & Weise, W. (1963). [The biology of the Hobby.] *Falke*, 10, 193–194.

Frost, R. A. (1983). Insect food of Hobby. *British Birds*, 76, 449–450.

Fuller, R. J., Baker, J. K., Morgan, R. A., Scroggs, R. & Wright, M. (1985). Breeding populations of the Hobby *Falco subbuteo* on farmland in the southern Midlands of England. *Ibis*, **127**, 510–516.

Gahbauer, M. A., Bird, D. M., Clark, K. E. et al. (2015). Productivity, mortality, and management of urban Peregrine Falcons in northeastern North America. *Journal of Wildlife Management*, **79**, 10–19.

Galtier, N., Nabholz B., Glémin S. & Hurst G. D. (2009). Mitochondrial DNA as a marker of molecular diversity: a reappraisal. *Molecular Ecology*, **18**, 4541–4550.

Galushin, V. M. (1974). Synchronous fluctuations in populations of some raptors and their prey. *Ibis*, **116**, 127–134.

Gamauf, A., Tebb, G. & Nemeth, E. (2013). Honey Buzzard *Pernis apivorus* nest-site selection in relation to habitat and the distribution of Goshawks *Accipiter gentilis*. *Ibis*, **155**, 258–270.

Gamble, D. (1990). Hobby recovering prey from water. *British Birds*, **83**, 548–549.

Gamble, D. (1992). Aggression of Hobby towards other raptors. *British Birds*, **85**, 497.

Ganusevich, S. A., Maechtle, T. L., Seegar, W. S. et al. (2004). Autumn migration and wintering areas of Peregrine Falcons *Falco peregrinus* nesting on the Kola Peninsula, northern Russia. *Ibis*, **146**, 291–297.

Ganzeboom, P. D. (2014a). Copulation of Hobbies *Falco subbuteo* about three weeks after egg laying. *De Takkeling*, **22**, 124–126.

Ganzeboom, P. D. (2014b). Hobby *Falco subbuteo* dust bathing. *De Takkeling*, **22**, 127–128.

Garratt, C. M., Hughes, M., Eagle, G. et al. (2011). Foraging habitat selection by breeding Common Kestrels *Falco tinnunculus* on lowland farmland in England. *Bird Study*, **58**, 90–98.

Gentle, L., Gooden, D. & Kettel, E. (2013). Attempted predation by Common Kestrel at a House Sparrow nestbox. *British Birds*, **106**, 412–413.

Gibbons, D. W., Reid, J. B. & Chapman, R. A. (1993). *The New Atlas of Breeding Birds in Britain and Ireland: 1988–1991*. Poyser, London.

Gil-Delgado, J. A., Verdejo, J. & Barba, E. (1995). Nestling diet and fledgling production of Eurasian kestrels (*Falco tinnunculus*) in eastern Spain. *Journal of Raptor Research*, **29**, 240–244.

Glue, D. E. (1968). Bird predators feeding at autumn roosts. *British Birds*, **61**, 526–527.

Glutz von Blotzheim, U. N., Bauer, K. M. & Bezzel, E. (1971). *Handbuch der Vögel Mitteleuropas, Band 4: Falconiformes*. Akademische, Frankfurt.

Goater, B. (1948). Hobby attacking Green Woodpecker. *British Birds*, **41**, 22–23.

Goodenough, A. E., Fairhurst, S. M., Morrison, J. B. et al. (2015). Quantifying the robustness of first arrival dates as a measure of avian migratory phenology. *Ibis*, **157**, 384–390.

Goslow, G. E. (1971). The attack and strike of some North American raptors. *Auk*, **88**, 815–827.

Gray, A. P. (1958). *Bird Hybrids*. Commonwealth Agricultural Bureaux, Farnham Royal.

Greaves, J. W. (1968). Food concealment by Merlins. *British Birds*, **61**, 309–311.

Greenwood, J. J. D., Crick, H. Q. P. & Bainbridge, I. P. (2003). Numbers and international importance of raptors and owls in Britain and Ireland. In *Birds of Prey in a Changing Environment* (ed. D. B. A. Thompson, S. M. Redpath, A. H. Fielding, M. Marquiss, & C. A. Galbraith). Scottish Natural Heritage, The Stationery Office Scotland, Edinburgh.

Greenwood, P. J. (1980). Mating systems, philopatry and dispersal in birds and mammals. *Animal Behaviour*, **28**, 1140–1162.

Gricks, N. (2005). Short-eared Owl preying on Merlin. *British Birds*, **98**, 26.

Gricks, N. (2007). Hobby hunting European Storm-petrel. *British Birds*, **100**, 443.

Griffiths, C. S. (1994a). Syringeal morphology and the phylogeny of the Falconidae. *Condor*, **96**, 127–140.

Griffiths, C. S. (1994b). Monophyly of the Falconiformes based on syringeal morphology. *Auk*, **111**, 787–805.

Griffiths, C. S. (1997). Correlation of functional domains and rates of nucleotide substitution in cytochrome b. *Molecular Phylogenetics and Evolution*, **7**, 352–365.

Griffiths, C. S. (1999). Phylogeny of the Falconidae inferred from molecular and morphological data. *Auk*, **116**, 116–130.

Groombridge, J. J., Jones, C., Bayes, M. K., et al. (2002). A molecular phylogeny of African Kestrels with reference to divergence across the Indian Ocean. *Molecular Phylogenetics and Evolution,* **25**, 267–277.

Grünhagen, H. (1978a). [The budgerigar (*Melopsittacus undulatus*) as prey of the Hobby (*Falco subbuteo*).] *Charadrius,* **14**, 25–26.

Grünhagen, H. (1978b). [Hobby (*Falco subbuteo*) successfully rears crashed juvenile.] *Charadrius,* **14**, 26–27.

Grünhagen, H. (1983). [Hobbies bathing in foliage.] *Charadrius,* **19**, 124–125.

Haak, B. A. & Buchanan J. B. (2012). Bathing and drinking behaviour of wintering Merlins. *Journal of Raptor Research,* **46**, 224–226.

Hackett, S. J., Kimball, R. T., Reddy, S. et al. (2008). A phylogenomic study of birds reveals their evolutionary history. *Science,* **320**, 1763–1768.

Haffield, P. (2012). Merlin in mid and south Wales. *Birds in Wales,* **9**, 41–49.

Hagar, J. A. (1938). In Bent, A. C., *Life Histories of North American Birds of Prey (Part 2).* Smithsonian Institution, United States National Museum Bulletin 170. US Government Printing Office, Washington.

Hagen, Y. (1952). *Rovfuglene og Viltpleien.* Gyldendal Norsk Forlag, Oslo.

Hager, S. B. (2009). Human-related threats to urban raptors. *Journal of Raptor Research,* **43**, 210–226.

Hakkarainen, H. & Korpimäki, E. (1996). Competitive and predatory interactions among raptors: an observational and experimental study. *Ecology,* **77**, 1134–1142.

Hakkarainen, H., Korpimäki, E., Huhta, E. & Palokangas, P. (1993). Delayed maturation in plumage colour: evidence for the female-mimicry hypothesis in the Kestrel. *Behavioral Ecology and Sociobiology,* **33**, 247–251.

Hakkarainen H., Hunhta, E., Lahti, K. et al. (1996). A test of male mating and hunting success in the Kestrel: the advantages of smallness? *Behavioral Ecology and Sociobiology,* **39**, 375–380.

Hall, G. H. (1955). *Great Moments in Action: the Story of the Sun Life Peregrines.* Mercury Press, Montreal.

Hallmann, C. A., Foppen, R. P. B., van Turnhout, C. A. M., de Kroon, H. & Jongejans, E. (2014). Declines in insectivorous birds are associated with high neonicotinoid concentrations. *Nature,* **511**, 341–342.

Hambly, C., Harper, E. J. & Spea kman, J. R. (2004). The energy cost of loaded flight is substantially lower than expected due to alterations in flight kinematics. Journal of Experimental Biology, **207**, 3969–3976.

Hamlett, T. (1984). Hobbies feeding from water surface. *British Birds,* **77**, 74.

Harding, B. D. (1978). Hobbies hovering. *British Birds,* **71**, 189.

Härmä, O., Kareksela, S., Siitari H. & Suhonen, J. (2011). Pygmy Owl (*Glaucidium passerinum*) and the usage of ultraviolet cues of prey. *Journal of Avian Biology,* **42**, 89–91.

Harpum, J. (1983).The speed of a Hobby's stoop over Cheltenham. *Gloucestershire Bird Report,* **19**, 63–65.

Harris, S., Morris, P., Wray, S. & Yalden, D. (1995). *A Review of British Mammals: Population Estimates and Conservation Status of British Mammals Other Than Cetaceans.* Joint Nature Conservation Committee, Peterborough.

Hasenclever, H., Kostrzewa, A. & Kostrzewa, R. (1989). [The breeding biology of the Kestrel *Falco tinnunculus* in eastern Westphalia 1972–1987.] *Journal of Ornithology,* **130**, 229–237.

Håstad, O., Victorsson, J. & Ödeen, A. (2005). Differences in colour vision make passerines less conspicuous in the eyes of their predators. *Proceedings of the National Academy of Sciences of the USA,* **102**, 6391–6394.

Haverschmidt, F. (1948). [Bats as prey of the Hobby.] *Ardea,* **36**, 39–42.

Hayhow, D. B., Bond, A. L., Eaton, M. A. et al. (2015). *The State of the UK's Birds 2015.* RSPB, BTO, WWT, JNCC, NE, NIEA, NRW & SNH, Sandy.

Hayhow, S. J. (1988). Talon-locking between Hobby and Kestrel. *British Birds,* **81**, 324.

Hayman, R. W. (1979). Hobbies at home. *Devon Birds*, **32**, 18–20.

Hays, L. L. (1987). Peregrine Falcon nest defense against a Golden Eagle. *Journal of Raptor Research*, **21**, 67.

Heavisides, A. (1987). British and Irish Merlin recoveries, 1911–1984. *Ringing and Migration*, **8**, 29–41.

Heavisides, A. (1995). Analysis of prey taken by Merlins within the Lammermuir Hills 1984–1994. *Scottish Birds*, **18**, 88–94.

Hedenström, A. & Alerstam, T. (1995). Optimal flight speed of birds. *Philosophical Transactions of the Royal Society of London B*, **348**, 471–487.

Hedenström, A. & Rosén, M. (2001). Predator versus prey: on aerial hunting and escape strategies in birds. *Behavioral Ecology*, **12**, 150–156.

Heinroth, O. & Heinroth, M. (1927). *Die Vögel Mitteleuropas, Band 2*. Bermühler, Berlin.

Hemelrijk, C. K., van Zuidam, L. & Hildenbrandt, H. (2015). What underlies waves of agitation in Starling flocks. *Behavioral Ecology and Sociobiology*, **69**, 755–764.

Henningsson, P., Johansson, C. & Hedenström, A. (2010). How swift are Swifts *Apus apus*? *Journal of Avian Biology*, **41**, 94–98.

Henny, C. J. (1972). An analysis of the population dynamics of selected avian species. Bureau of Sport, Fisheries and Wildlife, Research Report 1. US Government, Washington DC.

Herbert, R. A. & Herbert, K. G. S. (1965). Behavior of Peregrine Falcons in the New York City region. *Auk*, **82**, 62–94.

Heukelen, C. van & Heukelen, E. van (2011). Kestrel *Falco tinnunculus* nest with 10 eggs. *De Takkeling*, **19**, 125–128.

Hewitt, S. (2013). Avian drop catch play. *British Birds*, **106**, 206–216.

Hickey, J. J. & Anderson, D. W. (1969). The Peregrine Falcon: life history and population literature. In *Peregrine Falcon Populations: their Biology and Decline* (ed. J. J. Hickey). University of Wisconsin Press, Madison, pp. 3–44.

Hie, H. de (2014). Replacement and adoption in a Hobby *Falco subbuteo* nest. *De Takkeling*, **22**, 133–147.

Higgins, R. J. & Hannam, D. A. R. (1985). Lymphoid leucosis in a captive Merlin (*Falco columbarius*). *Avian Pathology*, **14**, 445–447.

Hirsch, J. (1982). Falcon visual sensitivity to grating contrast. *Nature*, **300**, 57–58.

Hodson, K. A. (1976). Some aspects of the nesting ecology of Richardson's Merlin (*Falco columbarius richardsonii*) on the Canadian prairies. MSc thesis, University of British Columbia, Vancouver, Canada.

Hogstad, O. (1981). Improved breeding success of Fieldfares *Turdus pilaris*, nesting close to Merlins *Falco columbarius*. *Fauna Norvegica*, **5**, 1–4.

Holden, J., Chapman, P. J., Palmer, S. M., Kay, P. & Grayson, R. (2012). The impacts of prescribed moorland burning on water colour and dissolved organic carbon: a critical synthesis. *Journal of Environmental Management*, **101**, 92–103.

Holland, D. C. (1989). An instance of carrion-feeding by the Peregrine Falcon (*Falco peregrinus*). *Journal of Raptor Research*, **23**, 184.

Holling, M. & the Rare Breeding Birds Panel (2015). Rare breeding birds in the United Kingdom in 2013. *British Birds*, **108**, 373–422.

Holmes, J., Walker, D., Davies, P. & Carter, I. (2000). The illegal persecution of raptors in England. English Nature Research Report No. 343.

Honkala, J., Saurola, P. & Valkama, J. (2012). *Linnut Vuosikirja 2011* [Bird Yearbook 2011]. Finnish Museum of Natural History, Helsinki.

Honkavaara, J., Koivula, M., Korpimäki, E., Siitari, H. & Viitala, J. (2002). Ultraviolet vision and foraging in terrestrial vertebrates. *Oikos*, **98**, 505–511.

Hoy, S. R., Petty, S. J., Millon, A. *et al.* (2015). Age and sex-selective predation moderate the overall impact of predators. *Journal of Animal Ecology*, **84**, 692–701.

Hoyt, D. F. (1979). Practical methods of estimating volume and fresh weight of bird eggs. *Auk*, **96**, 73–77.

Hudec, K. & Cerny, W. (eds.) (1977). *Fauna CSSR (Animals of Czechoslovakia), Vol. 21, Birds*. Academia, Prague.

Huhta, E., Hakkarainen, H. & Lundvall, P. (1998). Bright colours and predation risk in passerines. *Ornis Fennica*, **75**, 89–93.

Huitu, O., Helander, M., Lehtonen, P. & Saikkonen, K. (2008). Consumption of grass endophytes alters the ultraviolet spectrum of vole urine. *Oecologia*, **156**, 333–340.

Huitzing, D. (2002). Probable kleptoparasitism between Kestrel *Falco tinnunculus* and Hobby *F. subbuteo*. *De Takkeling*, **10**, 255.

Hunt, B. S. (2012). Greenshank seeking protection during Peregrine Falcon attack. *British Birds*, **105**, 279.

Hunt, W. G., Driscoll, D. E., Bianchi E. W. & Jac kman, R. E. (1992). *Ecology of Bald Eagles in Arizona*. Report to U.S. Bureau of Reclamation, Nevada, Contract 6-CS-30-04470. BioSystems Analysis Inc., Santa Cruz. (The report is in four volumes; the information on the Bald Eagle attack is in Volume 2, pp. C-131–C-132.)

Hunt, W. G. (1998). Raptor floaters at Moffat's equilibrium. *Oikos*, **82**, 191–197.

Hyuga, I. (1955). [Breeding colonies of Japanese Kestrels.] *Tori*, **14**, 17–24.

Ingram, G. C. S. (1920). Nesting habits of Merlins in south Glamorganshire. *British Birds*, **13**, 202–226.

Ingram, W. M., Goodrich, L. M., Robey, E. A. & Eisen, M. B. (2013). Mice infected with low-virulence strains of *Toxoplasma gondii* lose their innate aversion to cat urine, even after extensive parasite clearance. *PLoS ONE*, **8**(9), e75246. Doi: 10.1371/journal.pone.0075246.

Insley, H. & Holland, M. G. (1975). Hobbies feeding on bats, and notes on other prey. *British Birds*, **68**, 242.

Ivanovski, V. (2003). The Merlin (*Falco columbarius*) in northern Belarus. *Buteo*, **13**, 67–73.

Ivanovski, V. (2012). *Birds of Prey of the Belorussian Poozerie*. Vitebsk State University, Vitebsk.

Izaaks, A. (2007). Breeding Hobbies *Falco subbuteo* in urban The Hague. *De Takkeling*, **15**, 87–88.

Jaarsveld, J. van (1988). African Goshawks and European Hobbies bat-hawking. *Gabar*, **3**, 29–31.

James, P. C. (1988). Urban Merlins in Canada. *British Birds*, **81**, 274–277.

James, P. C. & Oliphant, L. W. (1986). Extra birds and helpers at the nests of Richardson's Merlin. *Condor*, **88**, 533–534.

Jarvis, E. D. & 104 others (2014). Whole-genome analyses resolve early branches in the tree of life of modern birds. *Science*, 15 December, 1320–1331. (This article was the first in a series of ten which filled that issue of *Science* and which were all related to the work of the Avian Phylogenomics Consortium.)

Jenkins, A. R. (2000). Hunting mode and success of African Peregrines *Falco peregrinus* minor: does nesting habitat quality affect foraging efficiency? *Ibis*, 142, 235–246.

Jenkins, A. R. & Benn, G. A. (1998). Home range and habitat requirements of Peregrine Falcons on the Cape Peninsula, South Africa. *Journal of Raptor Research*, **32**, 90–97.

Jenkins, D., Watson, A. & Miller G. R. (1963). Population studies on Red Grouse, *Lagopus lagopus scoticus* (Lath.) in north-east Scotland. *Journal of Animal Ecology*, **32**, 317–376.

Jenkins, D., Watson, A. & Miller G. R. (1964). Predation and Red Grouse populations. *Journal of Applied Ecology*, **1**, 183–195.

Jobling, J. A. (1991). *A Dictionary of Scientific Bird Names*. Oxford University Press, Oxford.

Jobling, J. A. (2009). *The Helm Dictionary of Scientific Bird Names*. Christopher Helm, London.

Johnson, D. (2011). Peregrine Falcon nest relief at night. *British Birds*, **104**, 217.

Johnson, P. (2008). Peregrine Falcons feeding Common Kestrel chicks. *British Birds*, **101**, 327.

Johnstone, R. M. (1998). Aspects of the population biology of tundra Peregrine Falcons (*Falco peregrinus tundrius*). PhD thesis, University of Saskatchewan.

Jones, M. P., Pierce, K. E. & Ward, D. (2007). Avian vision: a review of form and function with special consideration to birds of prey. *Journal of Exotic Pet Medicine*, **16**, 69–87.

Jourdain, F. C. R. (1938). In Bent, A. C., *Life Histories of North American Birds of Prey*

(Part 2). Smithsonian Institution, United States National Museum Bulletin 170. US Government Printing Office, Washington.

Kane, S. A. & Zamani, M. (2014). Falcons pursue prey using visual motion cues: new perspectives from animal-borne cameras. *Journal of Experimental Biology*, **217**, 225–234.

Kane, S. A., Fulton, A. H. & Rosenthal, L. J. (2015). When hawks attack: animal-borne video studies of Goshawk pursuit and prey-evasion strategies. *Journal of Experimental Biology*, **218**, 212–222.

Karyakin, I. V. (2005). Anomalous late event of breeding the Kestrel in Volvograd District. *Raptors Conservation*, **2**, 61.

Karyakin, I. V. & Nikolenko, E. G. (2009). Merlin in the Altai-Sayan region, Russia. *Raptors Conservation*, **17**, 98–120.

Karyakin, I. V. & Nikolenko, E. G. (2010). Note of the Kestrel coming back on its birthplace and breeding in the nest where it was born. *Raptors Conservation*, **19**, 201–204.

Kellie, A., Dain, S. J. & Banks, P. B. (2004). Ultraviolet properties of Australian mammal urine. *Journal of Comparative Physiology A*, **190**, 429–435.

Kelly, G. M. & Thorpe, J. P. (1993). A communal roost of Peregrine Falcons and other raptors. *British Birds*, **86**, 49–52.

Kerlinger, O., Cherry, J. D. & Powers, K. D. (1983). Records of migrant hawks from the North Atlantic Ocean. *Auk*, **100**, 488–490.

Kerr, I. (1989). The Merlins in winter in Northumberland. *Birds of Northumbria*, **1988**, 91–94.

Kessler, S. C., Tiedeken, E. J., Simcock, K. L. et al. (2015). Bees prefer foods containing neonicotinoid pesticides. *Nature*, **521**, 74–76.

Kettle, A. (1990). Red-footed Falcon attacking and robbing Kestrel. *British Birds*, **83**, 548.

Kimball, R. T., Parker, P. G. & Bednarz, J. C. (2003). Occurrence and evolution of cooperative breeding among the diurnal raptors (Accipitridae and Falconidae). *Auk*, **120**, 717–729.

King, S. S. (2008). Peregrine Falcon egg breakage. *British Birds*, **101**, 326–327.

King, S. S. (2009). Peregrine Falcon robbing Hobby of prey. *British Birds*, **102**, 406.

Kirkwood, J. K. (1981). Bioenergetics and growth in the Kestrel. PhD thesis, University of Bristol.

Kirmse, W. (1989). [A Hobby chasing a Swift for four minutes.] *Falke*, **36**, 29.

Kirmse, W. (2001). Notes on restricted exchange between nest site types in the Peregrine (*Falco peregrinus*). *Buteo*, **12**, 85–88.

Kjellén, N. (1992). Differential timing of autumn migration between sex and age groups in raptors at Falsterbo, Sweden. *Ornis Scandinavica*, **23**, 420–434.

Kjellén, N. (1994). Differences in age and sex ratio among migrating and wintering raptors in southern Sweden. *Auk*, **111**, 274–284.

Klemola, T., Korpimäki, E. & Norrdahl, K. (1998). Does avian predation risk depress reproduction of voles? *Oecologia*, **115**, 149–153.

Kochanek, H.-M. (1984). The calls of the Kestrel *Falco tinnunculus. Charadrius* **20**, 137–154.

Koivula, M. & Korpimäki, E. (2001). Do scent marks increase predation risk of microtine rodents? *Oikos*, **95**, 275–281.

Koivula, M. & Viitala, J. (1999). Rough-legged Buzzards use vole scent marks to assess hunting areas. *Journal of Avian Biology*, **30**, 329–332.

Koivula, M., Koskela, E. & Viitala, J. (1999a). Sex and age-specific differences in ultraviolet reflectance of scent marks of Bank Voles *Clethrionomys glareolus. Journal of Comparative Physiology A*, **185**, 561–564.

Koivula, M., Viitala, J. & Korpimäki, E. (1999b). Kestrels prefer scent marks according to species and reproductive status of voles. *Ecoscience*, **6**, 415–420.

Korpimäki, E. (1984a). Food piracy between European Kestrel and Short-eared Owl. *Raptor Research*, **18**, 113–115.

Korpimäki, E. (1984b). Population dynamics of birds of prey in relation to fluctuations of small mammal populations in western Finland. *Annales Zoologici Fennici*, **21**, 287–293, 1984b.

Korpimäki, E. (1985a). Prey choice strategies of the Kestrel *Falco tinnunculus* in relation to available small mammals and other

Finnish birds of prey. *Annales Zoologici Fennici*, **22**, 91–104.

Korpimäki, E. (1985b). Diet of the Kestrel *Falco tinnunculus* in the breeding season. *Ornis Fennica*, **62**, 130–137.

Korpimäki, E. (1985c). Rapid tracking of microtine populations by their avian predators: possible evidence for stabilizing predation. *Oikos* **45**, 281–284.

Korpimäki, E. (1986a). Reversed size dimorphism in birds of prey, especially Tengmalm's Owl *Aegolius funereus*: a test of the 'starvation hypothesis'. *Ornis Scandinavica*, **17**, 326–332.

Korpimäki, E. (1986b). Diet variation, hunting habitat and reproductive output of the Kestrel *Falco tinnunculus* in the light of the optimal diet theory. *Ornis Fennica*, **63**, 84–90.

Korpimäki, E. (1987). Dietary shifts, niche relationships and reproductive output of coexisting Kestrels and Long-eared Owls. *Oecologia*, **74**, 277–285.

Korpimäki, E. (1988). Factors promoting polygyny in European birds of prey – a hypothesis. *Oecologia*, **77**, 278–285.

Korpimäki, E. (1994). Rapid or delayed tracking of multi-annual vole cycles by avian predators? *Journal of Animal Ecology*, **63**, 619–628.

Korpimäki, E. & Norrdahl, K. (1991). Numerical and functional responses of Kestrels, Short-eared Owls, and Long-eared Owls to vole densities. *Ecology*, **72**, 814–826.

Korpimäki, E. & Rita, H. (1996). Effects of brood size manipulations on offspring and parental survival in the European Kestrel under fluctuating food conditions. *Ecoscience* **3**, 264–273.

Korpimäki, E., Lahti, K., May, C. A. et al. (1996). Copulatory behaviour and paternity determined by DNA fingerprinting in kestrels: effects of cyclic food abundance. *Animal Behaviour*, **51**, 945–955.

Korslund, L. & Steen, H. (2006). Small rodent winter survival: snow conditions limit access to food resources. *Journal of Animal Ecology*, **75**, 156–166.

Kostrzewa, R. & Kostrzewa, A. (1990). The relationship of spring and summer weather with the density and breeding success of the Buzzard *Buteo buteo*, Goshawk *Accipiter gentilis* and Kestrel *Falco tinnunculus*. *Ibis*, **132**, 550–559.

Kostrzewa, R. & Kostrzewa, A. (1991). Winter weather, spring and summer density, and subsequent breeding success of Eurasian Kestrels, Common Buzzards, and Northern Goshawks. *Auk*, **108**, 342–347.

Kostrzewa, R. & Kostrzewa, A. (1993). *Der Turmfalke*. AULA-Verlag, Wiesbaden.

Kostrzewa, R. & Kostrzewa, A. (1997). [Breeding success of the Kestrel *Falco tinnunculus* in Germany: results 1985–1994).] *Journal für Ornithologie*, **138**, 73–82.

Krone, O. (2002). Fatal caryospora infection in a free-living juvenile Eurasian Kestrel (*Falco tinnunculus*). *Journal of Raptor Research*, **36**, 84–86.

Krone, O. (2007). Pathology: endoparasites. In *Raptor Research and Management Techniques* (ed. D. L. Bird & D. R. Bildstein). Hancock House, Blaine, WA, pp. 318–328.

Krüger, O. (2005). The evolution of reversed sexual size dimorphism in hawks, falcons and owls: a comparative study. *Evolutionary Ecology*, **19**, 467–486.

Kübler, S., Kupko, S. & Zeller, U. (2005). The Kestrel (*Falco tinnunculus* L.) in Berlin: investigation of breeding biology and feeding ecology. *Journal of Ornithology*, **146**, 271–278.

Kupko, S. & Kübler, S. (2007). Adoption of Common Kestrel nestlings *Falco tinnunculus* by a Peregrine Falcon *F. peregrinus*. *Vogelwelt*, **128**, 33–37.

Kurosawa, T. & Kurosawa, R. (2003). A helper at the nest of Peregrine Falcons in northern Japan. *Journal of Raptor Research*, **37**, 340–342.

Kuusela, S. (1979). [The Kestrel still hovers.] *Suomen Luonto*, **38**, 162–165.

Lack, P. (1986). *The Atlas of Wintering Birds in Britain and Ireland*. Poyser, London.

Laidlaw, T. G. (1893). Zoological notes. *Annals of Scottish Natural History*, **8**, 183.

Laing, K. (1985). Food habits and breeding biology of Merlins in Denali National Park, Alaska. *Raptor Research*, **19**, 42–51.

Langgemach, T., Sömmer, P., Kirmse, W., Saar, C. (1997). [First record of tree-nesting Peregrine Falcons *Falco p. peregrinus*, in

Brandenberg, Germany twenty years after the extinction of the European tree-nesting population.] *Vogelwelt*, **118**, 79–94.

Lawrence, L. de K. (1949). Notes on nesting Pigeon Hawks at Pimisi Bay, Ontario. *Wilson Bulletin*, **61**, 15–25.

Laybourne, R. C. (1974). Collision between a vulture and an aircraft at an altitude of 37,000 feet. *Wilson Bulletin*, **86**, 461–462.

Leckie, F. & Campbell, S. (2000). A new record of successful tree nesting Peregrines. *Scottish Birds*, **21**, 45–46.

Lee, Y.-F. & Kuo, Y.-M. (2001). Predation of Mexican Free-tailed Bats by Peregrine Falcons and Red-tailed Hawks. *Journal of Raptor Research*, **35**, 115–123.

Li Zhang, Yuyi Liu & Jie Song (2008). Genetic variation between subspecies of Common Kestrels (*Falco tinnunculus*) in Beijing, China. *Raptor Research*, **42**, 214–219.

Lieske, D. J., Oliphant, L. W., James, P. C., Warkentin, I. G. & Espie, R. H. M. (1997). Age of breeding in Merlins (*Falco columbarius*). *Auk*, **114**, 288–290.

Lima, S. L. (1993). Ecological and evolutionary perspectives on escape from predatory attack: a survey of North American birds. *Wilson Bulletin*, **105**, 1–47.

Lind, O., Mitkus, M., Olsson, P. & Kelber, A. (2013). Ultraviolet and colour vison in raptor foraging. *Journal of Experimental Biology*, **216**, 1819–1826, and corrigendum (Table S1 at http://jeb.biologists.org/content/216/10/1819/suppl/DCI).

Lindberg, P. (1977). [Peregrine ring recoveries in Sweden.] In *Pilgrimsfalk: Report of a conference on Peregrine Falcons at Grimsö, Sweden* (ed. P. Lindberg), pp. 39–42.

Lindberg, P. (1983). Relationship between the diet of Fennoscandian Peregrines *Falco peregrinus* and organochlorines and mercury in their eggs and feathers, with a comparison to the Gyrfalcon *Falco rusticolus*. PhD thesis, University of Gothenburg.

Linnaeus, C. (1746). *Fauna Svecica*. Laurentii Salvii, Stockholm.

Little, B. & Davison, M. (1992). Merlins *Falco columbarius* using crow nests in Kielder Forest, Northumberland. *Bird Study*, **39**, 13–16.

Little, B., Davison, M. & Jardine, D. (1995). Merlins *Falco columbarius* in Kielder Forest: influences of habitat on breeding performance. *Forest Ecology and Management*, **79**, 147–152.

Lobkov, E. G. (2012). The illegal capturing of Gyrfalcons *Falco rusticolus* L. in Kamchatka goes on unabated: the biggest batch of birds confiscated in 2012. *Far-Eastern Journal of Ornithology*, **3**, 67–72.

Lusby, J., Fernández-Bellon, D., Norriss, D. & Lauder, A. (2011). Assessing the effectiveness of monitor methods for Merlin *Falco columbarius* in Ireland: the pilot Merlin Study 2010. *Irish Birds*, **9**, 143–154.

Maa, T. C. (1969). A revised checklist and concise host index of Hippoboscidae (Dipteria). *Pacific Insects Monographs*, **2**, 261–299.

MacIntyre, D. (1936). *Wild Life of the Highlands: Shooting, Fishing, Natural History and Legend*. Philip Allan, London.

MacNally, L. (1979). Peregrine apparently killed by Golden Eagle, *Scottish Birds*, **10**, 234.

Manen, W. van (1995). [Bats as prey of Hobbies *Falco subbuteo*.] *De Takkeling*, **3**, 47–49.

Marques, A. T., Batalha, H., Rodrigues, S. *et al.* (2014). Understanding bird collisions at wind farms: an updated review on the causes and possible mitigation strategies. *Biological Conservation*, **179**, 40–52.

Marsden, A. (2002). Population studies of falcons using microsatellite DNA profiling. PhD thesis, University of Nottingham.

Martin, A. P. (1980). A study of a pair of breeding Peregrine Falcons (*Falco peregrinus peregrinus*) during part of the nesting period. BSc dissertation, University of Durham.

Martin, G. R. (1986). Shortcomings of an eagle's eye. *Nature*, **319**, 357.

Martin, R., Pepler, D., Martin, J. & Martin E. (1988). Observations on Hobby falcons in the Stellenbosch District: preliminary report. *Bo kmakierie*, **40**, 41–43.

Martínez-Padilla, J. & Millán, J. (2007). The prevalence and intensity of intestinal parasitation in a wild population of nestling Eurasian Kestrel *Falco tinnunculus*. *Ardeola*, **54**, 109–115.

Martínez-Padilla, J. & Viñuela, J. (2011). Hatching asynchrony and brood reduction influence immune response in Common Kestrel *Falco tinnunculus* nestlings. *Ibis*, **153**, 601–610.

Masman, D. (1986). The annual cycle of the Kestrel, *Falco tinnunculus*, a study of behavioural energetics. PhD thesis, University of Groningen.

Masman, D. & Klaassen, M. (1987). Energy expenditure during free flight in trained and free-living Eurasian Kestrels (*Falco tinnunculus*). *Auk*, **104**, 603–616.

Masman, D., Gordijn, M., Daan, S. & Dijkstra, C. (1986). Ecological energetics of the Kestrel: field estimates of energy intake throughout the year. *Ardea*, **74**, 24–39.

Masman, D., Daan, S. & Dijkstra, C. (1988a). Time allocation in the Kestrel (*Falco tinnunculus*), and the principle of energy minimization. *Journal of Animal Ecology*, **57**, 411–432.

Masman, D., Daan, S. & Beldhuis, J. A. (1988b). Ecological energetics of the Kestrel: daily energy expenditure throughout the year based on the time-energy budget, food intake and doubly labelled water methods. *Ardea*, **76**, 64–81.

Masman, D., Dijkstra, C., Daan, S. & Bult, A. (1989). Energetic limitation of avian parental effort: field experiments in the Kestrel (*Falco tinnunculus*). *Journal of Evolutionary Biology*, **2**, 435–455.

Massemin, S., Korpimäki, E., Pöyri, V. & Zorn, T. (2002). Influence of hatching order on growth rate and resting metabolism of Kestrel chicks. *Journal of Avian Biology*, **33**, 235–244.

Massimino, D., Johnston, A. & Pearce-Higgins, J. W. (2015). The geographical range of British birds expands during 15 years of warming. *Bird Study*, **62**, 523–534.

Mather, J. (1986). *The Birds of Yorkshire*. Croom Helm, London.

Matsyna, A. I., Matsyna, E. I. & Matsyna, A. A. (2010). Observations (of) Peregrine Falcon hunting habits along the coast of Iturp Island, South Kuril islands, Russia. *Raptors Conservation*, **18**, 184–185.

Matyukhin, A. V., Zabashta, A. V. & Zabashta, M. V. (2012). Louse flies (Hippoboscidae) of Falconiformes and Strigiformes in Palearctic. In *Birds of Prey in the Dynamic Environment of the Third Millenium: Status and Prospects* (ed. M. N. Gavriliuk). Proceedings of the 6th International Conference on Birds of Prey and Owls of North Eurasia, Kryvyi Rib.

Mayo, A. L. W. (1953). Magpies attacking Hobbies. *British Birds*, **46**, 415.

McElheron, A. (2005). *Merlins of the Wicklow Mountains*. Currach Press, Dublin.

McGrady, M. J., Maechtle, T. L., Vargas, J. J., Seegar, W. S. & Catalina Porras Peña, M. (2002). Migration and ranging of Peregrine Falcons wintering on the Gulf of Mexico coast, Tamaulipas, Mexico. *Condor*, **14**, 39–48.

McMillan, R. L. (2011). Raptor persecution on a large Perthshire estate: a historical study. *Scottish Birds*, **31**, 195–205.

Mead, C. J. & Pepler, G. R. M. (1975). Birds and other animals at Sand Martin colonies. *British Birds*, **68**, 89–99.

Mead, C. J. (1993). Peregrine ringing returns affecting Britain and Ireland. In D. Ratcliffe, *The Peregrine Falcon*. Poyser, London, pp. 259–266.

Mearns, R. (1982). Winter occupation of breeding territories and winter diet of Peregrines in south Scotland. *Ornis Scandinavica*, **13**, 79–83.

Mearns, R. (1983). Breeding Peregrines oiled by Fulmars. *Bird Study*, 30, 243–244.

Mearns, R. (1985). The hunting ranges of two female Peregrines towards the end of the breeding season. *Journal of Raptor Research*, **19**, 20–26.

Mearns, R. & Newton, I. (1984). Turnover and dispersal in a Peregrine *Falco peregrinus* population. *Ibis*, 347–355.

Mearns, R. & Newton, I. (1988). Factors affecting breeding success of Peregrines in south Scotland. *Journal of Animal Ecology*, **57**, 903–916.

Mebs, T. (1960). [Investigations of the moult order of wing and tail feathers in large falcons.] *Journal für Ornithologie*, **101**, 175–194.

Mebs, T. (1971). [Causes of death and mortality rates in German and Finnish Peregrines derived from ring recoveries.] *Vogelwarte*, **26**, 98–105.

Mebs. T. (2001). Ground-nesting Peregrine Falcons (*Falco peregrinus*) in Europe: situation in past and today. *Buteo*, **12**, 81–84.

Mebs, T. (2009). [The nocturnal hunting of Peregrine Falcons *Falco peregrinus* at buildings illuminated by powerful halogen floodlights: a review of documented cases in Europe.] *Vogelwelt*, **129**, 107–113.

Mee, A. (2012). An overview of monitoring for raptors in Ireland. *Acrocephalus*, **33**, 239–245.

Meek, E. E. (1988). The breeding ecology and decline of the Merlin *Falco columbarius* in Orkney. *Bird Study* **35**, 209–218.

Meese, R. J. & Fuller, M. R. (1989). Distribution and behaviour of passerines around Peregrine *Falco peregrinus* eyries in western Greenland. *Ibis*,**131**, 27–32.

Meier, A. J., Noble, R. E. & McKenzie, P. M. (1989). Observations of autumnal courtship behavior in Peregrine Falcons. *Journal of Raptor Research*, **23**, 121–122.

Meijer, T. (1988). Reproductive decisions in the Kestrel *Falco tinnunculus*. PhD thesis, University of Groningen.

Meijer, T. (1989). Photoperiodic control of reproduction and molt in the Kestrel *Falco tinnunculus*. *Journal of Biological Rhythms*, **4**, 351–364.

Meijer, T., Daan, S. & Dijkstra, C. (1988). Female condition and reproduction: effect of food manipulation in free-living and captive Kestrels. *Ardea*, **76**, 141–154.

Meijer, T., Masman, D. & Daan, S. (1989). Energetics of reproduction in female Kestrels. *Auk*, **106**, 549–559.

Meijer, T., Daan, S. & Hall, M. (1990). Family planning in the Kestrel (*Falco tinnunculus*): the proximate control of covariation of laying date and clutch size. *Behaviour*, **114**, 117–136.

Messenger, A. (2012). The status of the Hobby *Falco subbuteo* in Derbyshire – a continuing success story. *The Derbyshire Bird Report*.

Messenger, A. & Roome, M. (1994). Breeding Hobbies in Derbyshire. *The Derbyshire Bird Report*.

Messenger, A. & Roome, M. (2007). The breeding population of the Hobby in Derbyshire. *British Birds*, **100**, 594–608.

Messenger, D., Duckels, A. S., Pennington, M. & Taylor, J. (1988). Kestrel taking Leach's Petrel. *British Birds*, **81**, 395.

Mester, H. (1980). [On the pairing and sexual behaviour of Kestrels.] *Ornithologische Mitteilungen*, **32**, 150–152.

Meyburg, B.-U., Howey, P. W., Meyburg, C. & Fiuczynski, K. D. (2011a). Two complete migration cycles of an adult Hobby tracked by satellite. *British Birds*, 104, 2–15.

Meyburg, B.-U., Meyburg, C., Fiuczynski, K. D. & Hallau, A. (2011b). [The Hobby – wanderer between the continents.] *Falke*, **58**, 52–59.

Michell, E. B. (1900) *The Art and Practice of Hawking*. Methuen, London.

Mikaili, P. & Shayegh, J. (2011). The lizards of Iran: an etymological review of the families Gekkonidae, Eublepharidae, Anguidae and Agamidae. *Annals of Biological Research*, **2**, 22–37.

Mikkola, H. (1983). *Owls of Europe*. Poyser, London.

Mikula, P., Hromada, M. & Tryjanowski, P. (2013). Bats and Swifts as food for the European Kestrel (*Falco tinnunculus*) in a small town in Slovakia. *Ornis Fennica*, **90**, 178–185.

Milkovský, J. (2002). *Cenozoic Birds of the World. Part 1: Europe*. Ninox Press, Prague.

Millais, J. G. (1892). *Game Birds and Shooting-Sketches*. Henry Sotheran, London.

Mills, D. G. H. (1980). Hovering as hunting technique of Hobby. *British Birds*, **73**, 582.

Milsom, T. P. (1987). Aerial insect-hunting by Hobbies *Falco subbuteo* in relation to weather. *Bird Study*, **34**, 179–184.

Monneret, R.-J. (1974). [The behavioural display repertoire of Peregrine Falcons.] *Alauda*, **42**, 407–428.

Monneret, R.-J. (1983). [Helpers at the nests of Peregrine Falcons.] *Alauda*, **51**, 241–250.

Monneret, R.-J., Bulle, C. & Ruffinoni, R. (2009). [Predation of young Peregrines *Falco peregrinus* by a pair of Ravens *Corvus corax*.] *Nos Oiseaux*, **56**, 231–234.

Monneret, R.-J., Kery, M., Couerdassier, M. et al. (2015). [Consequences of artificial nest use by the Peregrine Falcon *Falco* *peregrinus* in the Jura range.] *Alauda*, **83**, 133–142.

Morata, G. (1971). [Observations on the reproduction of the Hobby *Falco subbuteo*.] *Ardeola*, **15**, 37–48.

Morbey, Y. E., Coppack, T. & Pulido, F. (2012). Adaptive hypotheses for protandry in arrival to breeding areas: a review of models and empirical tests. *Journal of Ornithology*, **153** (Supplement 1), S207–S215.

Morozov, V. V., Bragin, E. A. & Ivanovski, V. V. (2013). *Merlin*. Vitebsk State University, Vitebsk. (In Russian, with small English summary.)

Morrison, J. L., Terry, M. & Kennedy, P. L. (2006). Potential factors influencing nest defence in diurnal North American raptors. *Journal of Raptor Research*, **40**, 98–110.

Mueller, H. C., Mueller, N. S., Berger, D. D. et al. (2000). Age and sex differences in the timing of the fall migration of hawks and falcons. *Wilson Bulletin*, **112**, 214–224.

Müller, T. & Rohde, C. (1993). [Status of the Hobby in the Danube delta.] *Birds of Prey Bulletin*, **4**, 87–95.

Musgrove, A., Aebischer, N., Eaton, M. et al. (2013). Population estimates in Great Britain and the United Kingdom. *British Birds*, **106**, 64–100.

Nattrass, M., Clement, P. & Brown, A. (1993). *Status of the Merlin in England in 1992*. English Nature, Peterborough.

Naumann, J. A. & Naumann, J. F. (1905). Der Lerchenfalke, *Falco subbuteo* Linn. In *Naturgeschichte der Vögel Mitteleuropas* (ed. C. R. Hennicke), Vol. 5. Gera-Untermaus.

Negro, J. J., Ibáñez, C., Pérezjordá, J. L. & Delariva, M. J. (1992). Winter predation by Common Kestrel *Falco tinnunculus* on Pipistrelle Bats *Pipistrellus pipistrellus* in southern Spain. *Bird Study*, **39**, 195–199.

Nelson, R. W. (1970). Some aspects of the breeding behaviour of Peregrine Falcons on Langara Island, British Columbia. MSc thesis, University of Calgary.

Nelson, R. W. (1988). Do large natural broods increase mortality of parent Peregrine Falcons? In *Peregrine Falcon Populations: Their Management and Recovery* (ed. T. J. Cade et al.). The Peregrine Fund, Boise, Idaho.

Nethersole-Thompson, C. & Nethersole-Thompson, D. (1943). Nest site selection by birds. *British Birds*, **37**, 108–113.

Nethersole-Thompson, D. (1931a). Observations on the Peregrine Falcon (*Falco peregrinus peregrinus*). *Oologists' Record*, **11**, 73-80.

Nethersole-Thompson, D. (1931b). The field habits and nesting of the Hobby. *British Birds*, **25**, 142–150.

Nethersole-Thompson, D. (1931c). My observations of the Hobby (*Falco subbuteo subbuteo*) in 1931. *Oologists' Record*, **11**, 80–86.

Neumann, J. L., Holloway, G. J., Sage, R. B. & Hoodless, A. N. (2015). Releasing of Pheasants for shooting in the UK alters woodland invertebrate communities. *Biological Conservation*, **191**, 50–59.

Newton, I. (1979). *Population Ecology of Raptors*. Poyser, London.

Newton, I. (1984). Raptors in Britain: a review of the last 150 years. *BTO News*, **131**, 6–7.

Newton, I. (1986). *The Sparrowhawk*. Poyser, London.

Newton, I. (1995). Relationship between breeding and wintering ranges in Palearctic–African migrants. *Ibis*, **137**, 241–249.

Newton, I. (2008). *The Migration Ecology of Birds*. Academic Press, London.

Newton, I. & Haas, M. B. (1988). Pollutants in Merlin eggs and their effect on breeding. *British Birds*, **81**, 258–269.

Newton, I. & Rothery, P. (2001). Estimation and limitation of the numbers of floaters in a Eurasian Sparrowhawk population. *Ibis*, **143**, 442–449.

Newton, I., Meek, E. R & Little, B. (1978). Breeding ecology of the Merlin in Northumberland. *British Birds*, **71**, 376–398.

Newton, I., Robson, J. E. & Yalden, D. W. (1981). Decline of the Merlin in the Peak District. *Bird Study*, **28**, 225–234.

Newton, I., Bogan, J., Meek, E. R and Little, B. (1982). Organochlorine compounds and shell-thinning in British Merlins (*Falco columbarius*). *Ibis*, **124**, 328–335.

Newton, I., Marquiss, M. & Rothery, P. (1983). Age structure and survival in a Sparrowhawk population. *Auk*, **100**, 344–354.

Newton, I., Meek, E. R. & Little, B. (1984). Breeding season foods of Merlins *Falco columbarius* in Northumbria. *Bird Study*, **31**, 49–56.

Newton, I., Meek, E. & Little, B. (1986). Population and breeding of Northumbrian Merlins. *British Birds*, **79**, 155–170.

Newton, I., Bogan, J. A. & Haas, M. B. (1989). Organochlorines and mercury in the eggs of British Peregrines *Falco peregrinus*. *Ibis*, **131**, 355–376.

Newton, I., Wyllie, I. & Dale, L. (1999a). Trends in the numbers and mortality patterns of Sparrowhawks (*Accipiter nisus*) and Kestrels (*Falco tinnunculus*) in Britain, as revealed by carcass analyses. *Journal of Zoology (London)*, **248**, 139–147.

Newton, I., Dale, L. & Little, B. (1999b). Trends in organochlorine and mercurial compounds in the eggs of British Merlins *Falco columbarius*. *Bird Study*, **46**, 356–362.

Nicholson, D. (2010). Common Kestrel attempt to predate Hobby chicks at the nest. *British Birds*, **103**, 244.

Nielsen, O. K. (1986). Population ecology of the Gyrfalcon with comparative notes on the Merlin and the Raven. PhD thesis, Cornell University.

Nittinger, F., Haring, E., Pinsker, W., Wink, M. & Gamauf, A. (2005). Out of Africa? Phylogenetic relationships between *Falco biarmicus* and the other Hierofalcons (Aves: Falconidae). *Journal of Zoological Systematics and Evolutionary Research*, **43**, 321–331.

Nittinger, F., Gamauf, A., Pinsker, W., Wink, M. & Haring, E. (2007). Phylogeography and population surcture of the Saker Falcon (*Falco cherrug*) and the influence of hybridisation: mitochondrial and microsatellite data. *Molecular Ecology*, **16**, 1497–1517.

Norrdahl, K. & Korpimäki, E. (1996). Do nomadic avian predators synchronize population fluctuations of small mammals? A field experiment. *Oecologia* **107**, 478–483.

Norrdahl, K., Suhonen, J., Hemminki, O. & Korpimäki, E. (1995). Predator presence may benefit: Kestrels protect Curlew nests against nest predators. *Oecologia*, **101**, 105–109.

Norriss, D. W. (1995). The 1991 survey and weather impacts on the Peregrine Falcon *Falco peregrinus* breeding population in the Republic of Ireland. *Bird Study*, **42**, 20–30.

Norriss, D. W., Haran, B., Hennigan, J. et al. (2010). Breeding biology of Merlins *Falco columbarius* in Ireland, 1986–1992. *Irish Birds*, **9**, 23–30.

Nus, T. van (2003). Eurasian Hobby *Falco subbuteo* breeding in the city of Utrecht. *De Takkeling*, **11**, 151–154.

Nygård, T. (1999). Correcting eggshell indices of raptor eggs for hole size and eccentricity. *Ibis*, **141**, 85–90.

Nygård, T. & Polder, A. (2012). *Environmental Pollutants in Eggs of Birds of Prey in Norway: Current Situation and Time Trends.* Norsk Institutt for Naturforskning (NINA) Report 834.

Oakley-Martin, D. (2008). Juvenile Common Kestrel diving at female. *British Birds*, **101**, 383.

Odin, N. (1992). Merlins hunting at sea. *British Birds*, **85**, 467.

Oliphant, L. W. (1991). Hybridization between a Peregrine Falcon and a Prairie Falcon in the wild. *Journal of Raptor Research*, **25**, 36–39.

Oliphant, L. W. & Tessaro, S. V. (1985). Growth rates and food consumption of hand-raised Merlins. *Raptor Research*, **19**, 79–84.

Oliphant, L. W. & Thompson, W. J. P. (1976). Food caching behaviour in Richardson's Merlin. *Canadian Field-Naturalist*, **90**, 364–365.

Oliver, T. H., Isaac, N. J. B., August, T. A. et al. (2015). Declining resilience of ecosystem functions under biodiversity loss. *Nature Communications*, 6:10122. Doi: 10.1038/ncomms10122.

Oliver, T. H., Smithers, R. J., Beale, C. M. & Watts, K. (2016). Are existing biodiversity conservation strategies appropriate in a changing climate? *Biological Conservation*, **193**, 17–26.

Olsen, J. (2013). Reversed sexual dimorphism and prey size taken by male and female raptors: a comment on Pande & Dahanukar. *Journal of Raptor Research*, **47**, 79–81.

Olsen, P., Marshall, R. C. & Gaal, A. (1989). Relationships within the genus *Falco*: a comparison of the electrophoretic patterns of feather proteins. *Emu*, **89**, 193–203.

Olsen, P., Barry, S., Baker, G. B., Mooney, N. & Cam, G. (1998). Assortative mating in falcons: do big females pair with big males? *Journal of Avian Biology*, **29**, 197–200.

Orchel, J. (1992). *Forest Merlins in Scotland: their Requirements and Management*. Hawk and Owl Trust, London.

Oro, D. (1996). Colonial seabird breeding in dense and small sub-colonies: an advantage against aerial predation. *Condor*, **98**, 848–850.

Orr, N. (1996). Operation Hobby. *Hampshire Bird Report*, **1994**, 143–147.

Packham, C. (1985a). Bigamy by the Kestrel. *British Birds* **78**, 194.

Packham, C. (1985b). Role of male Kestrel during incubation. *British Birds* **78**, 144–145.

Pagel, J. E. & Sipple, J. (2011). Incident of full sibling mating in Peregrine Falcons (*Falco peregrinus*). *Journal of Raptor Research*, **45**, 97–98.

Pain, D. J., Sear, J. & Newton, I. (1995). Lead concentrations in birds of prey in Britain. *Environmental Pollution*, **87**, 173–180.

Paine, R. T., Wootton, J. T. & Boersma, P. D. (1990). Direct and indirect effects of Peregrine Falcon predation on seabird abundance. *Auk*, **107**, 1–9.

Palleroni, A., Miller, C. T., Hauser, M. & Marler, P. (2005). Prey plumage adaptation against falcon attack. *Nature* **434**, 973–974.

Palmer, R. S. (1988). *Handbook of North American Birds, Volume 5*. Yale University Press, New Haven.

Palokangas, P., Korpimäki, E., Hakkarainen, H. *et al.* (1994). Female Kestrels gain reproductive success by choosing brightly ornamented males. *Animal Behaviour*, **47**, 443–448.

Pande, S. & Dahanukar, N. (2012). Reversed sexual dimorphism and differential prey delivery in Barn Owls (*Tyto alba*). *Journal of Raptor Research*, **46**, 184–189.

Pande, S. & Dahanukar, N. (2013). Reversed sexual dimorphism and prey delivery: response to Olsen. *Journal of Raptor Research*, **47**, 81–82.

Parker, A. (1979). Peregrines at a Welsh coastal eyrie. *British Birds*, **72**, 104–114.

Parker, A. G. (1982). Hobby hunting close to Montagu's Harrier. *British Birds*, **75**, 286–287.

Parr, D. (1967). A review of the status of the Kestrel, Tawny Owl and Barn Owl in Surrey. *Surrey Bird Report*, **15**, 35–42.

Parr, S. J. (1985). The breeding ecology and diet of the Hobby *Falco subbuteo* in southern England. *Ibis*, **127**, 60–73.

Parr, S. J. (1991). Occupation of new conifer plantations by Merlins in Wales. *Bird Study*, **38**, 103–111.

Parr, S. J. (1994). Changes in the population size and nest sites of Merlins *Falco columbarius* in Wales between 1970 and 1991. *Bird Study*, **41**, 42–47.

Parslow, J. L. F. (1967). Changes in the status among breeding birds in Britain and Ireland. *British Birds*, **60**, 2–47, 97–123.

Parslow, J. L. F. (1992). Hobby [In systematic list]. *Cambridgeshire Bird Report*, **66**, 28–29.

PECBMS (Pan-European Common Bird Monitoring Scheme) (2012). *Population Trends of Common European Breeding Birds 2012*. Czech Society for Ornithology, Prague.

Pennycuick, C. J. (2008). *Modelling the Flying Bird*. Academic Press, London.

Pennycuick, C. J., Fuller, M. R., Oar, J. J. & Kirkpatrick, S. J. (1994). Falcon versus Grouse: flight adaptations of a predator and its prey. *Journal of Avian Biology*, **25**, 39–49.

Pennycuick, C. J., Fast, P. L. F., Ballerstädt, N. & Rattenborg, N. (2012). The effect of an external transmitter on the drag coefficient of a bird's body, and hence on migration range, and energy reserves after migration. *Journal of Ornithology*, **153**, 633–644.

Pepler, D. (1991). Diet of the Hobby falcon *Falco subbuteo* in the southwestern Cape. *Ostrich*, **62**, 74–75.

Pepler, D. (1993). Diet and hunting behaviour of the European Hobby (*Falco subbuteo*) in Africa. In *Biology and Conservation of Small Falcons: Proceedings of the 1991 Hawk and Owl Trust Conference* (ed. M. K. Nicholls &

R. Clarke). Hawk and Owl Trust, London, pp. 163–170.
Peter, D. & Kestenholz, M. (1998). [Stoops of Peregrine Falcon *Falco peregrinus* and Barbary Falcon *Falco pelegrinoides*.] *Ornithologische Beobachter*, **95**, 107–112.
Peter, H.-U. & Zaumseil, J. (1982). [Population ecology of the Kestrel (*Falco tinnunculus*) in a colony near Jena.] *Berichte der Vogelwarte Hiddensee*, **3**, 5–7.
Petty, S. J., Patterson, I. J., Anderson, D. I. K., Little, B. & Davison, M. (1995). Numbers, breeding performance, and diet of the Sparrowhawk *Accipiter nisus* and Merlin *Falco columbarius* in relation to cone crops and seed-eating finches. *Forest Ecology and Management*, **79**, 133–146.
Petty, S. J., Anderson, D. I. K., Davison, M. *et al.* (2003). The decline of Common Kestrels (*Falco tinnunculus*) in a forested area of northern England: the role of predation by Northern Goshawks (*Accipiter gentilis*). *Ibis*, **145**, 472–483.
Philips, J. R. (2000). A review and checklist of the parasitic mites (Acarina) of the Falconiformes and Strigiformes. *Journal of Raptor Research*, **34**, 210–231.
Philips, J. R. & Dindal, D. L. (1977). Raptor nests as a habitat for invertebrates: a review. *Raptor Research*, **11**, 86–96.
Piault, R., van den Brink, V. & Roulin, A. (2012). Condition-dependent expression of melanin-based coloration in the Eurasian Kestrel. *Naturwissenschaften*, **99**, 391–396.
Picozzi, N. (1983). Growth and sex of nestling Merlins in Orkney. *Ibis*, **125**, 377–382.
Piechocki, R. (1982). *Der Turmfalke*. Lutherstadt Ziemsen, Wittenburg.
Pike, G. V. (1981). Nesting Kestrels tolerating excessive disturbance. *British Birds*, **74**, 520–521.
Pikula, J., Beklová, M. & Kubík, V. (1984). The nidobiology of *Falco tinnunculus*. *Acta Scientiarum Naturalium Brno*, **18**, 1–55.
Plesník, J. & Dusík, M. (1994). Reproductive output of the Kestrel *Falco tinnunculus* in relation to small mammal dynamics in intensively cultivated farmland. In *Raptor Conservation Today: Proceedings of the IV World Conference on Birds of Prey and Owls* (ed. B.-U. Meyburg & R. D. Chancellor).
WWGBP/Pica Press, Mountfield, East Sussex, pp. 61–65.
Pokrovsky, I., Lecomte, N., Sokolov A., Sokolov, V. & Yoccoz, N. G. (2010). Peregrine Falcons kill a Gyrfalcon feeding on their nestling. *Journal of Raptor Research*, **44**, 66–69.
Ponting, E. D. (2002). Common Kestrel taking Canary from cage. *British Birds*, **95**, 23.
Ponton, D. A. (1983). Nest site selection by Peregrine Falcons. *Raptor Research*, **17**, 27–28.
Potapov, E. & Sale R. (2005). *The Gyrfalcon*. Poyser, London.
Potapov, E. & Sale R. (2012). *The Snowy Owl*. Poyser, London.
Potters, H. (1998). [Remarkable late onset of laying in Hobbies *Falco subbuteo* in 1997.] *De Takkeling*, **6**, 86–88.
Pounds, H. E. (1948). Wing-drumming of Hobby. *British Birds*, **41**, 153–154.
Prior, G. (2014). *Seabird and Marine Ranger Annual Report, St Kilda*. National Trust for Scotland.
Prince, P. & Clarke, R. (1993). The Hobby's range in Britain. What factors have allowed it to expand? *British Wildlife*, **4**, 341–346.
Pritchard, R. (ed.) (2013). Welsh Bird Report No. 26 for 2011. *Birds in Wales*, **10**, 8–178.
Probst, R., Pavlicev, M. & Viitala, J. (2002). UV reflecting vole scent marks attract a passerine, the Great Grey Shrike *Lanius excubitor*. *Journal of Avian Biology*, **33**, 437–440.
Pyle, P. (2005). First-cycle molts in North American Falconiformes. *Journal of Raptor Research*, **39**, 378–385.
Pyle, P. (2013). Evolutionary implications of synapomorphic wing-molt sequences among falcons (Falconiformes) and parrots (Psittaciformes). *Condor*, **115**, 593–602.
Pyman, G. A. (1954). Hobby in Essex in winter. *British Birds*, **47**, 308.
Quinn, J. L. (1997). The effects of hunting Peregrines *Falco peregrinus* on the foraging behaviour and efficiency of the Oystercatcher *Haematopus ostralegus*. *Ibis*, **139**, 170–173.

Quinn, J. L., Prop, J., Kokorev, Y. & Black, J. M. (2003). Predator protection or similar habitat selection in Red-Breasted Goose nesting associations: extremes along a continuum. *Animal Behaviour*, **65**, 297–307.

Rae, S. (2010a). Prey items of Merlins in the Lewis peatlands. *Scottish Birds*, **30**, 2–6.

Rae, S. (2010b). Density and productivity of ground-nesting Merlins on an island with no indigenous terrestrial predators. *Scottish Birds*, **30**, 7–13.

Ratcliffe, D. A. (1962). Peregrine incubating Kestrel eggs. *British Birds*, **55**, 131–132.

Ratcliffe, D. A. (1963). Peregrine rearing young Kestrels. *British Birds*, **56**, 457–460.

Ratcliffe, D. A. (1967). Decrease in eggshell weight in certain birds of prey. *Nature*, **215**, 208–210.

Ratcliffe, D. A. (1970). Changes attributable to pesticides in egg breakage frequency and eggshell thickness in some British birds. *Journal of Applied Ecology*, **7**, 67–115.

Ratcliffe, D. A. (1993). *The Peregrine Falcon* (second edition). Poyser, London. (First edition published 1980.)

Rebecca, G. W. (1987). Merlin dusting at roadside. *Scottish Birds*, **14**, 187.

Rebecca, G. W. (1991). Short-eared Owl killing a Merlin on the nest. *North-east Scotland Bird Report*, **1990**, 73.

Rebecca, G. W. (2004). Forest nesting Merlin apparently specialising on Barn Swallows. *Scottish Birds*, **24**, 46–48.

Rebecca, G. W. (2006). The breeding ecology of the Merlin (*Falco columbarius aesalon*) with particular reference to north-east Scotland and land-usage change. PhD thesis, Open University.

Rebecca, G. W. (2011). Spatial and habitat-related influences on the breeding performance of Merlins in Britain. *British Birds*, **104**, 202–216.

Rebecca, G. W. & Bainbridge, I. P. (1998). The breeding status of the Merlin *Falco columbarius* in Britain in 1993–94. *Bird Study*, **45**, 172–187.

Rebecca, G. W., Weir, D. N. & Steele, L. D. (1987). Bluethroats killed by nesting Merlins in Scotland. *Scottish Birds*, **14**, 174.

Rebecca, G. W., Cosnette, B. L. & Duncan, A. (1988). Two cases of a yearling and an adult Merlin attending the same nest. *Scottish Birds*, 15, 45–46.

Rebecca, G. W., Cosnette, B. L., Duncan, A., Picozzi, N. & Catt, D. C. (1990). Hunting distance of breeding Merlins in Grampian indicated by ringed wader chicks as prey. *Scottish Birds*, **16**, 38–39.

Rebecca, G. W., Cosnette, B. L., Hardey, J. J. C. & Payne, A. G. (1992). Status, distribution and breeding biology of the Merlin in north-east Scotland, 1980–1989. *Scottish Birds*, **16**, 165–183.

Redpath, S. M. & Thirgood, S. J. (1999). Numerical and functional responses in generalist predators: hen Harriers and Peregrines on Scottish grouse moors. *Journal of Applied Ecology*, **68**, 879–892.

Rees, G. (2009). More Peregrine kleptoparasitism. *British Birds*, **102**, 511.

Rejt, Ł. (2005).Utilisation of unhatched eggs by urban Kestrels (*Falco tinnunculus*). *Buteo*, **14**, 31–35.

Rejt, Ł., Rutkowski, R. & Gryczyńska-Siemiątkowska, A. (2004). Genetic variability of urban Kestrels in Warsaw: preliminary data. *Zoologica Poloniae*, **49**, 199–209.

Reymond, L. (1985). Spatial visual acuity of the eagle *Aquila audax*: a behavioural, optical and anatomical investigation. *Vision Research*, **25**, 1477–1491.

Reynolds, J. F. (1973). Hobbies preying on Swallows at winter roost. *British Birds*, **66**, 279.

Richards, C. & Shrubb, M. (1999). The prey of Peregrines *Falco peregrinus* in South Wales. *Welsh Birds*, **2**, 131–136.

Ricklefs, R. E. (1968). Patterns of growth in birds. *Ibis*, **110**, 419–451.

Ricklefs, R. E. (1969). Preliminary models for growth rates in altricial birds. *Ecology*, **50**, 1031–1039.

Ricklefs, R. E. (1973). Patterns of growth in birds II: Growth rate and mode of development. *Ibis*, **115**, 177–201.

Riddle, G. (2011). *Kestrels for Company*. Whittle Publishing, Dunbeath.

Riddle, G. S. (1987). Variation in the breeding output of kestrel pairs in Ayrshire 1978–85. *Scottish Birds* **14**, 138–145.

Riegert, J. & Fuchs, R. (2011). Fidelity to roost sites and diet composition of wintering male urban Common Kestrels *Falco tinnunculus*. *Acta Ornithologica*, **46**, 183–189.

Riegert, J., Fainová, D. & Bystřická, D. (2010). Genetic variability, body characteristics and reproductive parameters of neighbouring rural and urban Common Kestrel (*Falco tinnunculus*) populations. *Population Ecology*, **52**, 73–79.

Rijnsdorp, A., Daan, S. & Dijkstra, C. (1981). Hunting in the Kestrel *Falco tinnunculus*, and the adaptive significance of daily habits. *Oecologia (Berlin)*, **50**, 391–406.

Ristow, D. (2004). Exceptionally dark-plumaged Hobbies or normal Eleonora's Falcon? *British Birds*, **97**, 406–411.

Ristow, D. (2006). A European Hobby *Falco subbuteo* attacks a European Kestrel *Falco tinnunculus*. *Ornithologischer Anzeiger*, **45**, 175–176.

Roberts, E. L. (1946). Unusual hunting behaviour of Peregrine Falcon. *British Birds*, **39**, 318–319.

Roberts, J. L. & Green, D. (1983). Breeding failure and decline on a north Wales moor. *Bird Study*, **30**, 193–200.

Roberts, J. L. & Jones, M. S. (1999). Merlin *Falco columbarius* on a NE moor – breeding ecology (1983–1997) and possible determinants of density. *Welsh Birds*, **2**, 88–107.

Roberts, S. & Lewis, J. M. S. (1992). Observations of the Hobby nesting in Gwent. *Welsh Birds*, **6**, 84.

Roberts, T. J. (1991). *The Birds of Pakistan*. Oxford University Press, Oxford.

Robertson, D. (2012). Hunting behaviour of raptors targeting hirundine flocks. *Scottish Birds*, **32**, 134–135.

Robertson, I. S. (1977). Unusual feeding behaviour of Hobby. *British Birds*, **70**, 76–77.

Rogers, W. & Leatherwood, S. (1981). Observations of feeding at sea by a Peregrine Falcon and Osprey. *Condor*, **83**, 89–90.

Rolle, C. J. (1999). Merlin's sunning behaviour in summer. *Scottish Birds*, **20**, 39.

Rollie, C. & Christie, G. (2006). Peregrine Falcon catching and killing a bat in daylight. *Scottish Birds*, **26**, 45–46.

Romanowski, J. (1996). On the diet of urban Kestrels (*Falco tinnunculus*) in Warsaw. *Buteo*, **8**, 123–130.

Rosenfield, R. N., Schneider, J. W., Papp, J. M. & Seegar, W. S. (1995). Prey of Peregrine Falcons in west Greenland. *Condor*, **97**, 763–770.

Roulin, A., Brinkhof, M. W. G., Bize, P. et al. (2003). Which chick is tasty to parasites? The importance of host immunology vs. parasitic life history. *Journal of Animal Ecology*, **72**, 75–81.

Rowan, W. (1921–1922). Observations on the breeding habits of the Merlin. *British Birds*, **15**, 122–129, 194–202, 222–231, 246–253. The article was in four parts: I – General environment; II – Incubation; III – Rearing of the young; IV – The young.

Rozenfeld, F. M., Le Boulangé, E. & Rasmont, R. (1987). Urine marking by Bank Voles (*Clethrionomys glareolus* Screber, 1780: Microtidae, Rodentia) in relation to their social rank. *Canadian Journal of Zoology*, **65**, 2594–2601.

RSPB (2013). *The Illegal Killing of Birds of Prey in Scotland in 2012*. Royal Society for the Protection of Birds, Edinburgh.

RSPB (2014). *Birdcrime 2013: Offences Against Wild Bird Legislation in 2013*. Royal Society for the Protection of Birds, Sandy.

RSPB (2015). *Birdcrime 2014: Offences Against Wild Bird Legislation in 2014*. Royal Society for the Protection of Birds, Sandy.

Rudebeck, G. (1951). The choice of prey and modes of hunting of predatory birds with special reference to their selective effect. *Oikos*, **3**, 200–231.

RUG/RIJP (The raptor group of the University of Groningen and the Rijkdienst voor de IJsselmeerpolders, Lelystad, Holland) (1982). Timing of vole hunting in aerial predators. *Mammal Review*, **12**, 169–181.

Rundlöf, M., Andersson, G. K. S., Bommarco, R. et al. (2015). Seed coating with a neonicotinoid insecticide negatively affects wild bees. *Nature*, **521**, 77–80.

Runge, C. A., Watson, J. E. M., Butchart, S. H. M., Hanson, J. O. et al. (2015). Protected areas and global conservation of migratory birds, *Science*, **350**, 1255–1258.

Ruthven, G. (2013). Peregrine retrieving prey from water. *Scottish Birds*, **33**, 125.

Ruttledge, W. (1985). Captive breeding of the European Merlin (*Falco columbarius aesalon*). *Raptor Research*, **19**, 68–78.

Sale, R. (2006). *A Complete Guide to Arctic Wildlife.* Christopher Helm, London.

Sale, R. (2015). *The Merlin.* Snowfinch Publishing, Coberley.

Salvati, L. (2001). Does high population density affect reproductive value? Evidence from semicolonial Kestrels *Falco tinnunculus*. *Vogelwelt*, **122**, 41–45.

Salvati, L. (2002). Spring weather and the breeding success of the Eurasian Kestrel (*Falco tinnunculus*) in urban Rome, Italy. *Journal of Raptor Research*, **36**, 81–84.

Salvin, F. H. & Brodrick, W. (1855). *Falconry in the British Isles.* John Van Voorst, London.

Sammut, M. & Bonavia, E. (2004). Autumn raptor migration of Buskett, Malta. *British Birds*, 97, 318–322.

Sammut, M., Fenech, N. & Pirotta, J. E. (2013). Raptor migration in Malta. *British Birds*, **106**, 217–223.

Santing, J. (2010). Second clutch in Kestrel *Falco tinnunculus*? *De Takkeling*, **18**, 150.

Saxby, H. L. (1874). *The Birds of Shetland* (ed. S. H. Saxby). MacLachlan and Stewart, Edinburgh.

Schmid, H. (1990).]Breeding biology of Kestrels in Switzerland.] *Ornithologische Beobachter*, **87**, 327–349.

Schmidl, D. (1988). Dusting in falcons. *Journal of Raptor Research*, **22**, 59–61.

Schönwetter, M. (1967). *Handbuch der Oologie.* Akademie Verlag, Berlin.

Schuyl, G., Tinbergen, L. & Tinbergen N. (1936). [Observations of the behaviour of Hobbies (*Falco subbuteo* L.).] *Journal für Ornithologie*, **84**, 387–433.

Scott, R. E. (1968). Merlins associating with roosting Starlings. *British Birds*, **61**, 527–528.

Seacor, R., Ostovar, K. & Restani, M. (2014). Distribution and abundance of baling twine in the landscape near Osprey (*Pandion haliaetus*) nests: implications for nestling entanglement. *Canadian Field-Naturalist*, **128**, 173–178.

Sergio, F. & Bogliani, G. (1999). Eurasian Hobby density, nest area occupancy, diet and productivity in relation to intensive agriculture. *Condor*, **101**, 806–817.

Sergio, F. & Bogliani, G. (2001). Nest defense as parental care in the northern Hobby (*Falco subbuteo*). *Auk*, **118**, 1047–1052.

Sergio, F. & Newton, I. (2003). Occupancy as a measure of territory quality. *Journal of Animal Ecology*, **72**, 857–865.

Sergio, F., Bijlsma, R. G., Bogliani, G. & Wylie, I. (2001). *Falco subbuteo* Hobby. *BWP Update*, **3** (3), 133–156.

Sharps, E., Smart J., Skov, M. W., Garbutt, A. & Hiddink, J. G. (2015). Light grazing of saltmarshes is a direct and indirect cause of nest failure in Common Redshank (*Tringa totanus*). *Ibis*, **157**, 239–249.

Sharrock, J. T. R. (ed.) (1976). *The Atlas of Breeding Birds of in Britain and Ireland.* Poyser, Berkhamsted.

Shaw, G. (1994). Merlin chick killed by an adder. *Scottish Birds*, **17**, 162.

Shore, R. F., Malcolm, H. M., Weinberg, C. L. et al. (2002). *Wildlife and Pollution: 1999/2000 Annual Report.* Joint Nature Conservation Council Report 321, JNCC Peterborough.

Shrubb, M. (1993a). *The Kestrel.* Hamlyn, London.

Shrubb, M. (1993b). Nest sites in the Kestrel, *Falco tinnunculus*. *Bird Study*, **40**, 63–73.

Shrubb, M. (2003).The Kestrel (*Falco tinnunculus*) in Wales. *Welsh Birds*, **3**, 330–339.

Shrubb, M. (2004). The decline of the Kestrel in Wales. *Welsh Birds*, **4**, 65–66.

Simms, C. (1975). Talon-grappling by Merlins. *Bird Study*, **22**, 261.

Slagsvold, T. (1979). The Fieldfare *Turdus pilaris* as a key species in the forest bird community. *Fauna Norvegica, Series C., Cinclus*, **2**, 65–69.

Slagsvold, T. & Sonerud, G. A. (2007). Prey size and ingestion rate in raptors: importance for sex roles and reversed sexual size dimorphism. *Journal of Avian Biology*, **38**, 650–661.

Slijper, H. J. (1946). [Hobby hunting by moonlight.] *Limosa* **19**, 143.

Small, B. (1992). First-summer Hobbies in the New Forest. *British Birds*, **85**, 251–255.

Smallwood, J. A., Dudajek, V., Gilchrist, S. & Smallwood M. A. (2003). Vocal development in American Kestrel (*Falco sparverius*) nestlings. *Journal of Raptor Research*, **37**, 37–43.

Smit, T., Bakhuizen, T. & Jonkers, D. A. (1987). [Causes of death in Kestrels *Falco tinnuculus* in the Netherlands.] *Limosa*, **60**, 175–178.

Smith, A. R. (1978). The Merlins of Edmonton. *Alberta Naturalist*, **8**, 188–191.

Smith, M. B. (1992). Peregrines nesting beside Kestrels on urban chimney. *British Birds*, **85**, 498.

Sodhi, N. S. (1989). Attempted polygyny by a Merlin. *Wilson Bulletin*, **101**, 505–506.

Sodhi, N. S. (1991). Pair copulations, extra-pair copulations, and intra-specific nest intrusions in Merlin. *Condor*, **93**, 433–437.

Sodhi, N. S. (1993). Proximate determinants of foraging effort in breeding male Merlins. *Wilson Bulletin*, **105**, 68–76.

Sodhi, N. S. & Oliphant, L. W. (1992). Hunting ranges and habitat use and selection of urban-breeding Merlins. *Condor*, **94**, 743–749.

Sodhi, N. S. & Oliphant, L. W. (1993). Prey selection by urban-breeding Merlins. *Auk*, **110**, 727–735.

Sodhi, N. S., Warkentin, I. G., James, P. C. & Oliphant, L. W. (1991a). Effects of radiotagging on breeding Merlins. *Journal of Wildlife Management*, **55**, 613–616.

Sodhi, N. S., Warkentin, I. G. & Oliphant, L. W. (1991b). Hunting techniques and success rates of urban Merlins (*Falco columbarius*). *Journal of Raptor Research*, **25**, 127–131.

Sodhi, N. S., James, P. C., Warkentin, I. G. & Oliphant, L. W. (1992). Breeding ecology of urban Merlins (*Falco columbarius*). *Canadian Journal of Zoology*, **70**, 1477–1483.

Sodhi, N. S, Oliphant L. W., James, P. C. & Warkentin, I. G. (2005). Merlin (*Falco columbarius*). In *The Birds of North America Online* (ed. A. Poole). Cornell Laboratory of Ornithology, Ithaca, NY. http://bna.birds.cornell.edu/bna/species/044.

Solonen, H. (1994). Factors affecting the structure of Finnish birds of prey communities. *Ornis Fennica*, **71**, 156–169.

Sonerud, G. A., Steen, R., Løw, L. M., *et al.* (2013). Size-allocation of prey from male to offspring via female: family conflicts, prey selection, and evolution of sexual size dimorphism in raptors. *Oecologia*, **172**, 93–107.

Sonerud, G. A., Steen, R., Løw, L. M., *et al.* (2014a). Evolution of parental roles in raptors: prey type determines role asymmetry in the Eurasian Kestrel. *Animal Behaviour*, **96**, 31–38.

Sonerud, G. A., Steen, R., Selås, V., *et al.* (2014b). Evolution of parental roles in provisioning birds: diet determines role asymmetry in raptors, *Behavioral Ecology*, **25**, 762–772.

Sperber, I. & Sperber, C. (1963). Notes on the food consumption of Merlins. *Zoologiska Bidrag Fran Uppsala*, **35**, 263–268.

Spofford, W. R. (1947). A successful nesting of the Peregrine Falcon with three adults present, *Migrant*, **18**, 56–58.

Spofford, W. R. & Amadon, D. (1993). Live prey to young raptors – incidental or adaptive? *Journal of Raptor Research*, **27**, 180–184.

Sprunt, A. (1951). Aerial feeding of Duck Hawk, *Falco p. anatum*. *Auk*, **68**, 372–373.

Stager, K. E. (1941). A group of bat-eating Duck Hawks. *Condor*, **43**, 137–139.

Steen R., Løw, L. M., Sonerud, G. A., Selås, V. & Slagsvold, T. (2011). Prey delivery rates as estimates of prey consumption by Eurasian Kestrel *Falco tinnunculus* nestlings. *Ardea*, **99**, 1–8.

Steen R., Sonerud, G. A. & Slagsvold, T. (2012). Parents adjust feeding effort in relation to nestling age in the Eurasian Kestrel (*Falco tinnunculus*). *Journal of Ornithology*, **153**, 1087–1099.

Stephan, C. & Bugnyar, T. (2013). Pigeons integrate past knowledge across sensory modalities. *Animal Behaviour*, **85**, 605–613.

Strandberg, R. & Olofsson, P. (2007). [Hobbies: long-distance travellers with an unknown route.] *Var Fagelvärd*, **66**, 6–9.

Strandberg, R., Klaasen, R. H. G., Hake, M., Olofsson, P. & Alerstam, T. (2009a). Converging migration routes of Eurasian Hobbies crossing the African equatorial rain forest. *Proceedings of the Royal Society B*, **276**, 727–733.

Strandberg, R., Klaasen, R. H. G., Olofsson, P. & Alerstam, T. (2009b). Daily travel schedules of adult Eurasian Hobbies *Falco subbuteo* – variability in flight hours and migration speed along the route. *Ardea*, **97**, 287–295.

Strandberg, R., Klaasen, R. H. G., Hake, M. & Alerstam, T. (2010). How hazardous is the Sahara Desert crossing for migratory birds? Indications from satellite tracking of raptors. *Biology Letters*, **6**, 297–300.

Stresemann, V. & Stresemann, E. (1960). [Wing moults in raptors.] *Journal für Ornithologie*, **101**, 373–403.

Stubbert, D. (1943). Display of Merlin. *British Birds*, **37**, 17–18.

Stutchbury, B. J. (1991). Floater behaviour and territory acquisition in male Purple Martins. *Animal Behaviour*, **42**, 435–443.

Sulkava, S. (1968). A study on the food of the Peregrine, *Falco p. peregrinus* Tunstall, in Finland. *Aquilo*, **6**, 19–31.

Sumasgutner, P., Nemeth, E., Tebb, G., Krenn, H. W. & Gamauf, A. (2014a). Hard times in the city – attractive nest but insufficient food supply lead to low reproduction rates in a bird of prey. *Frontiers in Zoology*, **11**, 48.

Sumasgutner, P., Vasko, V. & Varjonen, R. (2014b). Public information revealed by pellets in nest sites is more important than ectoparasite avoidance in the settlement decisions of Eurasian Kestrels. *Behavioral Ecology and Sociobiology*, **68**, 2023–2034.

Šumrada, T. & Hanžel, J. (2012). The Kestrel *Falco tinnunculus* in Slovenia – a review of its distribution, population density, movements, breeding biology, diet and interactions with other species. *Acrocephalus*, **33**, 5–24.

Swan, D. C., Zanette, L. Y. & Clinchy, M. (2015). Brood parasite manipulate their hosts: experimental evidence for the farming hypothesis. *Animal Behaviour* **105**, 29–35.

Swann, R. L. (1998). Baby Stoat in Peregrine nest, *Scottish Birds*, **19**, 180.

Sweeney, S. J., Redig, P. T. & Tordoff, H. B. (1997). Morbidity and productivity of rehabilitated Peregrine Falcons in the upper Midwestern USA. *Journal of Raptor Research*, **31**, 347–352.

Szép, T. & Barta, Z. (1992). The threat to Bank Swallows from the Hobby at a large colony. *Condor*, **94**, 1022–1025.

Tempest, J. (2009). Owls and Kestrel share tenancy of nestbox. *British Birds*, **102**, 645.

Temple, D. (2008). Merlins plucking and eating dead young. *British Birds*, **101**, 687–688.

Thake, M. A. (1977/1978). Some aspects of Hobby (*Falco subbuteo*) migration over Buskett. *Il-Merill*, **19**, 1–4.

Thibault, J.-C., Vigne, J.-D. & Torre, J. (1993). The diet of young Lammergeiers *Gypaetus barbatus* in Corsica: its dependence on extensive grazing. *Ibis*, **135**, 42–48.

Thiollay, J.-M. (1977). [Population sizes of migratory raptors in the western Mediterranean.] *Alauda*, **45**, 115–121.

Thiollay, J.-M. (1989). Distribution and ecology of Palearctic birds of prey wintering in west and central Africa. In *Raptors in the Modern World* (ed. B.-U. Meyburg & R. D. Chancellor). WWGBP, London, pp. 95–107.

Thirgood, S. J., Redpath, S. M., Newton, I. & Hudson, P. (2000). Raptors and Red Grouse: conservation conflicts and management solutions. *Conservation Biology*, **14**, 95–104.

Thirgood, S. J., Redpath, S. M., Campbell, S. & Smith, A. (2002). Do habitat characteristics influence predation on Red Grouse? *Journal of Applied Ecology*, **39**, 217–225.

Thomas, B. (1992). Merlin feeding on rabbit carrion. *Scottish Birds*, **16**, 219–220.

Thompson, I. (2013). Raptor persecution in Scotland: an update. *Scottish Birds*, **33**, 46–48.

Tinbergen, L. (1940). [Observations on the division of labour in Kestrels (*Falco tinninculus*) during the breeding season.] *Ardea*, **29**, 63–98.

Tinbergen, N. (1932). [Observations of the Hobby.] *Journal of Ornithology*, **80**, 40–50.

Tomás, G. (2015). Hatching date vs laying date: what should we look at to study avian optimal timing of reproduction? *Journal of Avian Biology*, **46**, 107–112.

Tømmeraas, P. J. (1993). Golden Eagles *Aquila chrysaetos* killed a Merlin *Falco columbarius*, robbed a Wigeon *Anas penelope* nest and probably hunted Ring Ouzels *Turdus torquatus* in their territories. *Fauna Norvegica*, **C16**, 85–88.

Tordoff, H. B. & Redig, P. T. (1998). Apparent siblicide in Peregrine Falcons. *Journal of Raptor Research*, **32**, 184.

Tordoff, H. B. & Redig, P. T. (1999). Two fatal Peregrine Falcon territorial fights. *Loon*, **71**, 182–186.

Trainer, D. O. (1969). Diseases in raptors: a review of the literature. In *Peregrine Falcon Populations: their Biology and Decline* (ed. J. J. Hickey). University of Wisconsin Press, Madison, pp. 425–433.

Treleaven, R. B. (1977). *Peregrine: the Private Life of the Peregrine Falcon*. Headline Publications, Penzance.

Treleaven, R. B. (1980). High and low intensity hunting in raptors. *Zeitschrift für Tierpsychologie*, **54**, 339–345.

Trimble, S. A. (1975). Habitat management series for unique or endangered species: Report 15, Merlin *Falco columbarius*. USDI Bureau of Land Management Technical Note 271.

Trodd, P. (1993). Hobbies nesting on pylon. *British Birds*, **86**, 625.

Trollope, C. E. (2012). Hobbies take advantage of the gravy train. *British Birds*, **105**, 221.

Tucker. V. A. (1998) Gliding flight: speed and acceleration of ideal falcons during diving and pull out. *Journal of Experimental Biology*, **201**, 403–414.

Tucker, V. A. (1999). The stoop of a falcon: how fast, how steep, how high? *Hawk Chalk*, **38**, 58–63.

Tucker, V. A. (2000a). The deep fovea, sideways vision and spiral flight paths in raptors. *Journal of Experimental Biology*, **203**, 3745–3754.

Tucker, V. A. (2000b). Gliding flight: drag and torque of a hawk and a falcon with straight and turned heads, and a lower value for the parasite drag coefficient. *Journal of Experimental Biology*, **203**, 3733–3744.

Tucker, V. A., Cade, T. J. & Tucker, A. E. (1998). Diving speeds and angles of a Gyrfalcon (*Falco rusticolus*). *Journal of Experimental Biology*, **201**, 2061–2070.

Tucker, V. A., Tucker, A. E., Akers, K. & Enderson, J. H. (2000). Curved flight paths and sideways vision in Peregrine Falcons (*Falco peregrinus*). *Journal of Experimental Biology*, **203**, 3755–3763.

Tyler, S. J. & Ormerod, S. J. (1990). Mammals taken by Peregrines in mid-Wales. *Welsh Bird Report*, **4**, 57.

Uttendörfer, O. (1952). *Neue Ergebnisse über die Ernährung der Greifvögel und Eulen*. Eugen Ulmer, Stuttgart.

Vergara, P. & Fargallo, J. A. (2008). Sex, melanic coloration, and sibling competition during the postfledging dependence period. *Behavioral Ecology*, **19**, 847–853.

Vergara, P., Fargallo, J. A. & Martínez-Padilla, J. (2010). Reaching independence: food supply, parent quality, and offspring phenotypic characters in Kestrels. *Behavioral Ecology*, **21**, 507–512.

Videler, J. J. (2005). *Avian Flight*. Oxford University Press, Oxford.

Videler, J. J., Weihs, D. & Daan, S. (1983). Intermittent gliding in the hunting flight of the Kestrel *Falco tinnunculus*. *Journal of Experimental Biology*, **102**, 1–12.

Videler, J. J., Vossebelt, G., Gnodde, M. & Groenewegen, A. (1988a). Indoor flight experiments with trained Kestrels: I. Flight strategies in still air with and without added weight. *Journal of Experimental Biology*, **134**, 173–183.

Videler, J. J., Groenewegen, A., Gnodde, M. & Vossebelt, G. (1988b). Indoor flight experiments with trained Kestrels: II. The effect of added weight on flapping flight kinematics. *Journal of Experimental Biology*, **134**, 185–199.

Viitala, J., Korpimäki, E., Palokangas, P. & Koivula, M. (1995). Attraction of Kestrels to vole scent marks visible in ultraviolet light. *Nature*, **373**, 425–427.

Village, A. (1982). The home range and density of Kestrels in relation to vole abundance. *Journal of Animal Ecology*, **51**, 413–428.

Village, A. (1983a). Seasonal changes in the hunting behaviour of Kestrels. *Ardea*, **71**, 117–124.

Village, A. (1983b). Body weights of Kestrels in south Scotland. *Ringing and Migration*, **4**, 167–174.

Village, A. (1983c). The role of nest-site availability and territorial behaviour in limiting the breeding density of Kestrels. *Journal of Animal Ecology*, **52**, 635–645.

Village, A. (1985). Spring arrival times and assortative mating of Kestrels in south Scotland. *Journal of Animal Ecology*, **54**, 857–868.

Village, A. (1990). *The Kestrel*. Poyser, London.

Voous, K. H. (1961). Records of Peregrine Falcons on the Atlantic Ocean. *Ardea*, **49**, 176–177.

Waba, V. & Grüll, A. (2009). Common Kestrels *Falco tinnunculus* adopt Barn Owls *Tyto alba* breeding in the wild. *Vogelwelt*, **130**, 201–204.

Waddell, T. A. (1978a). Young Hobbies killed in nest. *British Birds*, **71**, 271.

Waddell, T. A. (1978b). Hobby apparently brooding chick on ground. *British Birds*, **71**, 271.

Walker, D. (1988). Peregrine taking Leach's Petrel. *British Birds*, **81**, 395.

Walker, I. (2012). More observations of an association between falcons and steam trains. *British Birds*, **105**, 626.

Walker, L. A., Chaplow, J. S., Llewellyn, N. R. *et al.* (2013). Anticoagulant rodenticides. In *Predatory Birds 2011: a Predatory Bird Monitoring Scheme (PMBS) Report and Addendum*. Centre for Ecology and Hydrology, Lancaster Environment Centre, Lancaster.

Wallen, M. S. (1992). Talon-locking between Merlin and Peregrine. *British Birds*, **85**, 496.

Wallin, K., Wallin, M. L., Jaras, T. & Strandvik, P. (1987). Leap-frog migration in the Swedish Kestrel *Falco tinnunculus* population. *Proceedings of the Fifth Nordic Ornithological Congress*, **1985**, 213–222.

Walpole-Bond, J. (1931/1932). The cries of the Hobby. *British Birds*, **25**, 200–202.

Walpole-Bond, J. (1938). *A History of Sussex Birds*. Witherby, London.

Warkentin, I. G. & Oliphant, L. W. (1985). Observations of winter food caching by the Richardson's Merlin. *Raptor Research*, **19**, 100–101.

Warkentin, I. G. & West N. H. (1990). Ecological energetics of wintering Merlins *Falco columbarius*. *Physiological Zoology*, **63**, 308–333.

Warkentin, I. G., James, P. C. & Oliphant, L. W. (1990). Body morphometrics, age structure and partial migration of urban Merlins. *Auk*, **107**, 25–34.

Warkentin, I. G., James, P. C. & Oliphant, L. W. (1991). Influence of site fidelity on mate switching in urban-breeding Merlins (*Falco columbarius*). *Auk*, **108**, 294–302.

Warkentin, I. G., James, P. C. & Oliphant, L. W. (1992). Assortative mating in urban-breeding Merlins. *Condor*, **94**, 418–426.

Warkentin, I. G., Curzon, A. D., Carter, R. E. *et al.* (1994). No evidence for extrapair fertilizations in the Merlin revealed by DNA fingerprinting. *Molecular Ecology*, **3**, 229–234.

Wassmann, R. (1993). [The Kestrel (*Falco tinnunculus*) as a ground nesting bird of open fields.] *Egretta*, 40–41.

Watson, G. (1982). A Hobby's kill. *Country Life*, 30 September 1982.

Weir, D. N. (1977). The Peregrine in N.E. Scotland in relation to food and pesticides. In *Pilgrimsfalk: Report of a conference on Peregrine Falcons at Grimsö, Sweden* (ed. P. Lindberg), pp. 56–58.

Weir, D. N. (1978). Wild Peregrines and grouse. *Falconer*, **7**, 98–102.

Weir, D. N. (2013). Ecological preferences of Speyside Merlins and relationship with Sparrowhawks. *Scottish Birds*, **33**, 218–228.

Wendt, A. M. & Septon, G. A. (1991). Notes on a successful nesting by a pair of yearling Peregrine Falcons (*Falco peregrinus*). *Journal of Raptor Research*, **25**, 21–22.

Wernham, C., Toms, M., Marchant, J. *et al.* (eds.) (2002). *The Migration Atlas: Movements of the Birds of Britain and Ireland*. Poyser, London.

Wheeler, B. K. (2003). Raptors of Western North America. Princeton University Press, Princeton, NJ.

White, C. M., Clum, N. J., Cade, T. J. & Hunt, W. G. (2002). Peregrine Falcon (*Falco peregrinus*). In *The Birds of North America Online* (ed. A. Poole). Cornell Laboratory of Ornithology, Ithaca, NY. http://bna.birds.cornell.edu/bna/species/660.

White, C. M., Cade, T. J. & Enderson, J. H. (2013a). *Peregrine Falcons of the World*. Lynx, Barcelona.

White, C. M., Sonsthagen, S. A., Sage, G. K., Anderson, C. & Talbot, S. L. (2013b). Genetic relationships among some subspecies of the Peregrine Falcon (*Falco peregrinus* L.), inferred from mitochondrial DNA control-region sequences. *Auk*, **130**, 78–87.

Wiebe, K., Korpimäki, E. & Wiehn, J. (1998). Hatching asynchrony in Eurasian Kestrels in relation to the abundance and predictability of cyclic prey. *Journal of Animal Ecology*, **67**, 908–917.

Wiebe, K., Jönsson, K. I., Wiehn, J. & Hakkarainen, H. (2000). Behaviour of female Eurasian Kestrels during laying: are there time constraints on incubation? *Ornis Fennica*, **77**, 1–9.

Wiehn, J. & Korpimäki, E. (1997). Food limitation on brood size: Experimental evidence in the Eurasian Kestrel. *Ecology*, **78**, 2043–2050.

Wightman, C. S. & Fuller, M. R. (2006). Influence of habitat heterogeneity on distribution, occupancy patterns, and productivity of Peregrine Falcons in central west Greenland. *Condor*, **108**, 270–281.

Wiklund, C. G. (1979). Increased breeding success for Merlins *Falco columbarius* nesting among Fieldfares *Turdus pilaris*. *Ibis*, **121**, 109–111.

Wiklund, C. G. (1982). Fieldfare (*Turdus pilaris*) breeding success in relation to colony size, nest position and association with Merlins (*Falco columbarius*). *Behavioral Ecology and Sociobiology*, **11**, 165–172.

Wiklund, C. G. (1990a). The adaptive significance of nest defence by Merlin, *Falco columbarius*, males. *Animal Behaviour*, **40**, 244–253.

Wiklund, C. G. (1990b). Offspring protection by Merlin *Falco columbarius* females: the importance of brood size and expected offspring survival for defense of the young. *Behavioral Ecology and Sociobiology*, **26**, 217–233.

Wiklund, C. G. (1995). Nest predation and life-span: components of variance in LRS among Merlin females. *Ecology*, **76**, 1994–1996.

Wiklund, C. G. (1996). Determinants of dispersal in breeding Merlins (*Falco columbarius*). *Ecology*, **77**, 1920–1927.

Wiklund, C. G. (2001). Food as a mechanism of density-dependent regulation of breeding numbers in the Merlin *Falco columbarius*. *Ecology*, **82**, 860–867.

Wiklund, C. G. & Larsson B. L. (1994). The distribution of breeding Merlins *Falco columbarius* in relation to food and nest sites. *Ornis Svecica*, **4**, 113–122.

Wiklund, C. G. & Village, A. (1992). Sexual and seasonal variation in territorial behaviour of Kestrels (*Falco tinnunculus*). *Animal Behaviour*, **43**, 823–830.

Williams, I. T. & Parr, S. J. (1995). Breeding Merlins *Falco columbarius* in Wales in 1993. *Welsh Birds*, **1**, 14–20.

Wimsatt, W. A. (1940). Homing instinct and profligacy in the Duck Hawk. *Auk*, **57**, 107–109.

Wink, M. & Sauer-Gürth, H. (2000). Advances in the molecular systematics of African raptors. In *Raptors at Risk* (ed. R. D. Chancellor & B.-U. Meyburg). World Working Group on Birds of Prey and Owls/Hancock House, pp. 135–147.

Wink, M., Seibold, I., Lotfikhah, F. & Bednarek, W. (1998). Molecular systematic of Holarctic raptors (Order Falconiformes). In *Holarctic Birds of Prey* (ed. R. D. Chancellor & B.-U. Meyburg). World Working Group on Birds of Prey and Owls/ADENEX, pp. 29–48.

Wink, M., Sauer-Gürth, H., Ellis, D. & Kenward R. (2004). Phylogenetic relationships in the *Hierofalco* complex (Saker-, Gyr-, Lanner-, Lagger Falcon). In *Raptors Worldwide* (ed. R. D. Chancellor & B.-U. Meyburg). World Working Group on Birds of Prey and Owls/MME, pp. 499–504.

Witherby, H. F., Jourdain, F. C. R., Ticehurst, N. F. & Tucker, B. W. (1939). *The Handbook of British Birds*, Volume 3. H. F. & G. Witherby, London.

Woodford, M. H. (1960). A Manual of Falconry, A&C Black, London. (The book has been revised several times, a 4th edition being published in 1987.)

Woodin, N. (1980). Observations on Gyrfalcon (*Falco rusticolus*) breeding near Lake Myvatn, Iceland, 1967. *Journal of Raptor Research*, **14**, 97–124.

Woodland, H. (1993). Captive breeding and release of Hobbies (*Falco subbuteo*) in the UK. In *Biology and Conservation of Small Falcons: Proceedings of the 1991 Hawk and Owl Trust Conference* (ed. M. K. Nicholls & R. Clarke). Hawk and Owl Trust, London, pp. 201–206.

Wrege, P. H. & Cade, T. J. (1977). Courtship behavior of large falcons in captivity. *Journal of Raptor Research*, **11**, 1–46.

Wright, P. M. (2005). Merlins of the South-east Yorkshire Dales. Tarnmoor, Skipton.

Wright, T. F., Schirtzinger, E. E., Matsumoto, T. *et al.* (2008). A multi-locus molecular phylogeny of the parrots (Psittaciformes): support for a Gondwanan origin during the Cretaceous. *Molecular Biology and Evolution*, **25**, 2141–2156.

Yalden, D. W. (1980). Notes on the diet of urban Kestrels. *Bird Study*, **27**, 235–238.

Yamada, I. (2001). [The status of Peregrine Falcons in the Setouchi District of western Japan.] *Goshawk*, **3**, 4–8.

Zabala, J. & Zuberogoitia, I. (2015). Breeding performance and survival in the Peregrine Falcon *Falco peregrinus* support an age-related competence improvement hypothesis mediated by an age threshold. *Journal of Avian Biology*, **45**, 141–150.

Zampiga, E., Gaibani, G., Csermely, D., Frey, H. & Hoi, H. (2006). Innate and learned aspects of urine UV-reflectance use in hunting behaviour of the Common Kestrel *Falco tinnunculus*. *Journal of Avian Biology*, **37**, 318–322.

Zampiga, E., Gaibani, G. & Csermely, D. (2008). Ultarviolet reflectance and female mating preferences in the Common Kestrel (*Falco tinnunculus*). *Canadian Journal of Zoology*, **86**, 479–483.

Zellweger-Fischer, J., Schaub, M., Müller, C. *et al.* (2011). Reproductibe success in Common Kestrels *Falco tinnunculus*: results from integrated population monitoring over five years. *Ornithologische Beobachter*, **108**, 37–54.

Zuberogoitia, I., Iraeta, A. & Martínez, J. A. (2002). Kleptoparasitism by Peregrine Falcons on Carrion Crows. *Ardeola*, **49**, 103–104.

Zuberogoitia, I., Martínez, J. A., Azkona, A. *et al.* (2003). Two cases of cooperative breeding in Eurasian Hobbies. *Journal of Raptor Research*, **37**, 342–344.

Zuberogoitia, I., Castillo, I., Azkona, A. *et al.* (2008). New evidence of dark Hobbies. *British Birds*, **101**, 207–208.

Zuberogoitia, I., Martínez, J. A., Azkona, A. *et al.* (2009). Using recruitment age, territorial fidelity and dispersal as decisive tools in the conservation and management of Peregrine Falcon (*Falco peregrinus*) populations: the case for a healthy population in northern Spain. *Journal of Ornithology*, **150**, 95–101.

Zuberogoitia, I., Martínez, J. A., González-Oreja, J. A., Calvo, J. F. & Zabala, J. (2013). The relationship between brood size and prey selection in a Peregrine Falcon population located in a strategic region of the Western European Flyway. *Journal of Ornithology*, **154**, 73–82.

Index

Page numbers in **bold** include illustrations. Since the production of this book, it has been decided that Northern and Hen Harriers are separate species, not subspecies. The Hen Harrier remains as *Circus cyaneus*, with the Northern Harrier now being *Circus hudsonius*.

Accipiter cooperii (Cooper's Hawk) 479
Accipiter gentilis (Goshawk) 34, 44, 48, 50, 64, 74, 302, 304, 345, 358, 384, 433, 477, 478, **479**, 493, 495, 496–7, 500, 503, 505, 506, 522, 517
Accipiter nisus (Sparrowhawk) 33, 34, 36, 37, 44, 50, 54, 85, 114, 123, 131, 134, 193, 213, 242, 296, 299, 304, 327, 328, 340, 384, 417–19, 421, 422, 423, 424–5, 467, 468, 478, 495, 516
Accipiter striatus (Sharp-shinned Hawk) 137, 471–3
Accipitridae (hawks) 2, 22
Acer pseudoplatanus (Sycamore) 341
Acheta domesticus (House Cricket) 330
Actitis hypoleucos (Common Sandpiper) 115, 116, 405, 407
Adder (*Vipera berus*) 480
Adolph, Peter 305–7
Aegithalos caudatus (Long-tailed Tit) 403, 404, 405, 407

Aegolius funereus (Tengmalm's Owl) 21, 431, 528, 531
Aeshna cyanea (Southern Hawker) **316**, 333
Aeshna grandis (Brown Hawker) 333
Aeshna mixta (Migrant Hawk) 333, 502–3
Africa 3, 4, 7, 8, 11, 15, 32, 48, 139–40, 181, 255, 256
migration to 33, 45, 47, 49, 199, 200, 210, 290, 312, 323–4, 331, 363–4, 366–74
Afroaves 3
Agama, Large-scaled Rock (*Laudakia nupta*) 319
Aglais urticae (Small Tortoiseshell) 402
Alauda arvensis (Skylark) 38, 63, 64, 114, 115, 116, 117, 118, 120, 134, 210, 320, 321, 397, 402, 403, 404, 405, 406, 407, 408, 410, 411, 415, 417, 418, 422, 423–5, 467

Albertus Magnus, *De Animalibus* 97
Alca torda (Razorbill) 117
Alcedo atthis (Kingfisher) 121
Alder (*Alnus glutinosa*) 341
Alectoris rufa (Red-legged Partridge) 82
Alle alle (Little Auk) 121
Alnus glutinosa (Alder) 341
American Ornithologists' Union 3
Ammophila arenaria (Marram Grass) 432
amphibians, as prey 37, 38, 210, 214, 316, 319, 402
Amphimallon solstitialis (Summer Chafer) 330, **327**
Anas creca (Teal) 115, 116, 120, 122, 126
Anas penelope (Wigeon) 115, 116, 124
Anas platyrhynchos (Mallard) 114, 115, 116, 118, 122, 129
Angola 367, 370, 373
Anguis fragilis (Slow Worm) 210
Anser anser (Greylag Goose) 111
Anthus pratensis (Meadow Pipit) **26, 27,** 38, 93, **94**, 114, 115, 116, 210, **211**, 321, **391**, 397, **398**, 402, 403, 404, 405–6, 407, 408, 412, **413**, 415, 416, **420**, 478, 518, 519
Anthus trivialis (Tree Pipit) 121, 321, 404
Apis mellifera (European Honeybee) 55
Apodemus sylvaticus (Wood Mouse) **208**, 215, 403
Apus affinus (Little Swift) 324, 332, 328
Apus apus (Swift) 32, 35, 114, 120, 313, 321, 322, 325, 365, 368, 374, 383, 407
Apus melba (Alpine Swift) 270
Aquila audax (Wedge-tailed Eagle) 70
Aquila chrysaetos (Golden Eagle) 34, 42, 50, 51, 52, 151, 193, 194, 304, 477, 478, 479–80

Ardea alba (Great Egret) 11
Ardea cinerea (Grey Heron) 44, 111, 242, 340, 384
Ardea herodias (Great Blue Heron) 477
Arenaria interpres (Turnstone) 404, 410
Aristotle 528
Arvicola amphibius (Water Vole) 114
Ash (*Fraxinus excelsior*) 341
Asio flammeus (Short-eared Owl) 34, 37, 50, 52, 116, 213, 250, 477, 478, 495, 496, 528
Asio otus (Long-eared Owl) 50, 114, **211**, 233, 495, 496, 528
Aspergillosis 189
Athene noctua (Little Owl) 114, 244, 294, 304
Atholl Estate, Pitlochry 50–1
Auk, Little (*Alle alle*) 121
Auklet, Cassin's (*Ptychoramphus aleuticus*) 131, 136, 146
Auklet, Rhinoceros (*Cerorhinca monocerata*) 136
Australaves 3
Australia 8, 10, 20, 75, 84, 149
Avian Phylogenomics Consortium 3
Avocet (*Recurvirostra avosetta*) 121
Ayrshire 250, 287, 288

Badger (*Meles meles*) 432
Baker, J. A. 524–5
Bat, Brown Long-eared (*Plecotus auritus*) 319
Bat, Daubenton's (*Myotis daubentonii*) 319
Bat, Lesser Horseshoe (*Rhinolophus hipposideros*) 319

Bat, Mexican Free-tailed (*Tadarida brasiliensis*) 112
Bat, Noctule (*Nyctalus noctula*) 113, 121, 318
Bat, Pipistrelle (*Pipistrellus* sp.) 318
Bat, Serotine (*Eptesicus serotinus*) 318
Bath 118, 120–1
bathing 22–4
bats, as prey 14, 27, 37, 39, 108, 112–3, 140–1, 212–13, 316, 319–20, 324, 329, 332, 355, 356, 397
beaks 16–17
Bedfordshire 336, 341
Beech (*Fagus sylvatica*) 341, 342
Belarus 440, 442, 447
Belgium 289, 363
Berlin 24, 35, 48, 219, 300, 301, 314, 317, 330, 334, 335, 341–2, 345, 358, 362, 367, 373, 374–5, 377, 384, 385, 502, 506
Betula pendula (Silver Birch) 332
Birch, Silver (*Betula pendula*) 332
Birmingham 246–7
Blackbird (*Turdus merula*) 114, 115, 116, 117, 120, 403, 404, 407, 410
Blackcap (*Sylvia atricapilla*) 121
Bluethroat (*Luscinia svecica*) 402, 405
body mass 19–22
Bombus terrestris (Buff-tailed Bumblebee) 55, 316
Bombycilla garrulus (Bohemian Waxwing) 36
Book of St Albans 12
Botswana 324, 370
Bracken (*Pteridium aquilinum*) 432
Brambling (*Fringilla montifringilla*) 116, 399, 403, 405, 407, 476
Branta canadensis (Canada Goose) 190

Branta leucopsis (Barnacle Goose) 75
Branta ruficollis (Red-breasted Goose) 190
Brassica napus (Oilseed Rape) 55
breeding 28–33, 41–8 *and see under individual falcons*
Bristol **40**, 91, 107, 118, 120–1
Bubo bubo (Eagle Owl) 32, 193, 304, 361, 384, 479, 531
Bubo scandiacus (Snowy Owl) 47, 190, 191, 250, 301
Bubo virginianus (Great Horned Owl) 193, 479
Bubulcus ibis (Cattle Egret) 11
Budgerigar (*Melopsittacus undulatus*) 121, 316, 402, 529
Bufo bufo (Common Toad) 210
Bullfinch (*Pyrrhula pyrrhula*) 114, 115, 116, 403, 404, 405, 407
Bumblebee, Buff-tailed (*Bombus terrestris*) 55, 316
Bunting, Corn (*Emberiza calandra*) 321
Bunting, Lapland (*Calcarius lapponicus*) 191
Bunting, Reed (*Emberiza schoeniclus*) 115, 321, 403, 404, 405, 407, 410
Bunting, Snow (*Plectrophenax nivalis*) 114, 116, 191, **398**, 403, 404, 405, 505
Buteo buteo (Common Buzzard) 2, 15, 34, 41, 42, 50, 52, 85, 114, 126, 151, 155, 187, 193, 199, 239, 242, **303**, 304, 305, 327, 340, 383, 384, 478, 493, 497, 505, 533
Buteo jamaicensis (Red-tailed Hawk) 41, 112, 479
Buteo lagopus (Rough-legged Buzzard) 83, 190, 362

Buzzard, Common (*Buteo buteo*) 2, 15, 34, 41, 42, 50, 52, 85, 114, 126, 151, 155, 187, 193, 199, 239, 242, **303**, 304, 305, 327, 340, 383, 384, 478, 493, 497, 505, 533

Buzzard, Rough-legged (*Buteo lagopus*) 83, 190, 362

Buzzard nests, use of 15, 41, 42, 155, 340, **435, 445, 447, 451, 453, 454, 462, 478, 508, 509**

'cadge' 98

Calcarius lapponicus (Lapland Bunting) 191

Calidris alba (Sanderling) 114, 116

Calidris alpina (Dunlin) 63, 114, 115, 116, 120, 130, 131, 132, 133–5, 136, 137–8, 317, 403, 404, 410, 416, 417, 418, 420–2, 487, 520

Calidris canutus (Knot) 114, 115

California 22, 113, 122, 138, 150, 421

Calluna vulgaris (Heather [Ling]) 432, 510

Cambridgeshire 137, 333, 335

Canada 30, 71, 112, 126, 130–7, 146, 148, 161–3, 173–4, 177, 179, 180, 181, 185, 193, 194, 393, 394, 395–6, 412, 413, 415, 425–8, 429–30, 436, 437, 438, 439, 443, 459, 464, 466, 470

    Saskatoon Merlin study 30, 393, 394, 395, 412, 413, 415, 425–8, 429–30, 436, 437, 438, 439, 443, 459, 464, 466, 470

Canary (*Serinus canaria*) 121, 212

Canary, Cape (*Serinus canicollis*) 324

Capercaillie (*Tetrao urogallus*) 50

Caprimulgus europaeus (Nightjar) 294

Carabus violaceus (Violet Ground-beetle) 316

caracaras 2

Carduelis cabaret (Lesser Redpoll) 121, 403, 405, 407, 410

Carduelis cannabina (Linnet) 114, 115, 403, 404, 405, 407, 410, 411

Carduelis carduelis (Goldfinch) 115, 120, 218, 403, 404, 405, 407

Carduelis chloris (Greenfinch) 114, 116, 120, 321, 403, 404, 405, 407, 410

Carduelis flammea (Common Redpoll) 191

Carduelis flavirostris (Twite) 34, 190, 402, 410, 411

Carduelis spinus (Siskin) 116, 403, 405, 407, 515

Caryospora 300

Carnus haemapterus 270

Carpodacus mexicanus (House Finch) 473

carrion, eating 213, 299, 397

'casting' 25

Catharus guttatus (Hermit Thrush) 146

Centrocercus urophasianus (Sage Grouse) 63–4

Cepphus grille (Black Guillemot) 117

Cerorhinca monocerata (Rhinoceros Auklet) 136

Certhia familiaris (Treecreeper) 115, 403, 404, 405, 407

Chafer, Summer (*Amphimallon solstitialis*) 330, **327**

Chaffinch (*Fringilla coelebs*) 114, 115, 116, 118, 120, 321, 402, 403, 404, 405, 406, 407, 408, 410, 467, 476

Charadrius hiaticula (Ringed Plover) 115, 118, 317, 402, 404, 410

Charadrius morinellus (Dotterel) 116

Cheltenham 94, 171

chicks 29 *and see under individual falcons*
Chiffchaff (*Phylloscopus collybita*) 121, 404, 407
Chough (*Pyrrhocorax pyrrhocorax*) 118
Chroicocephalus ridibundus (Black-headed Gull) 114, 115, 116, 120, 122, 123, 143, **304**, 326, **385**
Cinclus cinclus (Dipper) 114, 115, 116, 405, 421
Circus aeruginosus (Marsh Harrier) 371
Circus approximans (Australasian [Swamp] Harrier) 10
Circus cyaneus (Hen [Northern] Harrier) 50, 51, 52, 53, 137, 220, 406, 467, 475, 477, 521, 528
Circus pygargus (Montagu's Harrier) 38, 320, 327
claws 17–**18**
Coccothraustes coccothraustes (Hawfinch) 114
Cockatiel (Quarrion) (*Nymphicus hollandicus*) 75, 121
Cockchafer (*Melolontha melolontha*) 316
Coenagrion puella (Azure Damselfly) 333
Colorado 73, 139, 140, 144–5
Columba livia (Feral/Domestic Pigeon) 39, 45, 53–4, 101, 106, 114, 115, 116, 117, 118, 120, **121**, **122**, 123, 126–7, 133, 153, **155**, 171–2, 184, 389, 403
Columba livia (Rock Dove) 45, 106, 117, 122, 402, 404, 405
Columba oenas (Stock Dove) 114, 115, 116, 118, 212, 244, 403, 405
Columba palumbus (Wood Pigeon) 34, 44, 106, 114, 115, 116, 120, 123, 124, 129, 242, 340, 354, 358, 360, 379–83, 477
Coot (*Fulica atra*) 121

Cordulegaster boltonii (Golden-ringed Dragonfly) 316, 407
Corncrake (*Crex crex*) 121
Cornwall 106, 133, 141
Corvus brachyrhynchos (American Crow) 32, 395
Corvus caurinus (Northwestern Crow) 136
Corvus corax (Raven) 50, 123, 151, 192, 242, 340, 383, 384, 468, 477
Corvus cornix (Hooded Crow) 50, 114, 115, 116, 117, 381, 382, 432, 435, 476, 513
Corvus corone (Carrion Crow) 50, 114, 115, 116, 137, 151, 192, 193, 241, **243**, 313, 340, 357, 384, 419, 515
Corvus frugilegus (Rook) 114, 116, 124, 242
Corvus monedula (Jackdaw) 114, 115, 116, 117, 120, 244
Coturnix coturnix (Quail) 92, 121, 132, 359
courtship feeding 28 *and see under individual falcons*
Crataerina melbae (louse fly) 270
Crex crex (Corncrake) 121
Cricket, Garden (*Gryllus bimaculatus*) 332
Cricket, House (*Acheta domesticus*) 330
Crossbill, Common (*Loxia curvirostra*) 116, 403, 404, 405, 515
Crow, American (*Corvus brachyrhynchos*) 32, 395
Crow, Carrion (*Corvus corone*) 50, 114, 115, 116, 137, 151, 192, 193, 241, **243**, 313, 340, 357, 384, 419, 515
Crow, Hooded (*Corvus cornix*) 50, 114, 115, 116, 117, 381, 382, 432, 435, 476, 513

Crow, Northwestern (*Corvus caurinus*) 136
crows' and Ravens' nests, use of 13, 42, 141, 151, 155, 241, **243**, **276**, **277**, 313, 317, 340, 341, **347**, 361, 381, 435, 515
Cuckoo (*Cuculus canorus*) 38, 114, 115, 116, 118, 403, 405, 407
Cuculus canorus (Cuckoo) 38, 114, 115, 116, 118, 403, 405, 407
Curlew (*Numenius arquata*) 34, 114, 115, 116, 117, 118, 124, **301**, 403, 405, 407
Cyanistes caeruleus (Blue Tit) 114, 218, 321, 403, 407
Cygnus olor (Mute Swan) 525
Cyrtopodion russowii (Zarudny's Bent-toed Gecko) 319
Czech Republic 249, 255, 275, 288, 319

Damselfly, Azure (*Coenagrion puella*) 333
Dapritius 2
Darter, Common (*Sympetrum striolatum*) 333, 503
DDT/DDE 482–6
Delichon urbicum (House Martin) 94, 114, 313, 320, 321, **322**, **323**, 326, 327, 403, 404, 405, 407
Dendrocopos major (Great Spotted Woodpecker) 114, 116, **119**, 120
Derbyshire 48, 313, 316, 334, 336, 340–1, 343, 345, 357, 361, 502, 503, 505
Devon 106, 192, 302
Dicrostonyx groenlandicus (Northern Collared Lemming) 112
diet 36–41 *and see under individual falcons*
Dipper (*Cinclus cinclus*) 114, 115, 116, 405, 421

diseases 189–90, 300, 378, 474–5
displays 28 *and see under individual falcons*
Doldrums 532
Dor-beetle (*Geotrupes stercorarius*) 316, 355
Dotterel (*Charadrius morinellus*) 116
Dove, Collared (*Streptopelia decaocto*) 116, 120, 212
Dove, Rock (*Columba livia*) 45, 106, 117, 122, 402, 404, 405
Dove, Stock (*Columba oenas*) 114, 115, 116, 118, 212, 244, 403, 405
Dove, Turtle (*Streptopelia turtur*) 121, 210
dragonflies 209, 220, 316, 324, 325, 328, 332, 333, 355, 398, 402, 406, 502
Dragonfly, Golden-ringed (*Cordulegaster boltonii*) 316, 407
Duck, Ruddy (*Oxyura jamaicensis*) 121
Dunlin (*Calidris alpina*) 63, 114, 115, 116, 120, 130, 131, 132, 133–5, 136, 137–8, 317, 403, 404, 410, 416, 417, 418, 420–2, 487, 520
Dunnock (*Prunella modularis*) 120, 218, 321, 403, 404, 405, 407

Eagle, Bald (*Haliaeetus leucocephalus*) 39, 41, 131, 132, 137, 194
Eagle, Golden (*Aquila chrysaetos*) 34, 42, 50, 51, 52, 151, 193, 194, 304, 477, 478, 479–80
Eagle, Wedge-tailed (*Aquila audax*) 70
Eagle, White-tailed (*Haliaeetus albicilla*) 50, 187, 192, 471
earthworms 210, 215, 303
East Anglia 37, 106
East Lothian 131, 134, 417, 423

Eggar Moth, Northern (*Lasiocampa quercus callunae*) 316, 398, 402, 406, 407
Eggar Moth, Oak (*Lasiocampa quercus*) 316
eggs 46–8 *and see under individual falcons*
Egret, Cattle (*Bubulcus ibis*) 11
Egret, Great (*Ardea alba*) 11
Elm, English (*Ulmus minor* var. *vulgaris*) 340, 412
Emberiza calandra (Corn Bunting) 321
Emberiza citronella (Yellowhammer) 121, 405, 407
Emberiza schoeniclus (Reed Bunting) 115, 321, 403, 404, 405, 407, 410
Emperor Moth (*Saturnia pavonia*) 316, 398, 402, 406, 407
Endromis versicolora (Kentish Glory Moth) 402
energy balance study, Groningen University 224–32
Eptesicus serotinus (Serotine Bat) 318
Eremophila alpestris (Shore Lark) 92, 399
Erinaceus europaeus (Hedgehog) 432
Erithacus rubecula (Robin) 114, 115, 116, **210**, 403, 404, 405, 407
Essex 123, 124, 183, 302, 363
Exeter 118, 120–1, 126
eyas 1
eyes 1, 16, 69–73

Fagus sylvatica (Beech) 341, 342
Falco alopex (Fox Kestrel) 7, 198
Falco amurensis (Eastern Red-footed Falcon [Amur Falcon]) 7, 374
Falco araea (Seychelles Kestrel) 7

Falco ardosiaceus (Grey Kestrel) 7, 197, 198
Falco berigora (Brown Falcon) 10
Falco biarmicus (Lanner Falcon) 4–6, 60, 61, 157, 304
Falco cenchroides (Australian [Nankeen] Kestrel) 7, 198
Falco cherrug (Saker Falcon) 4–6
Falco chicquera (Red-necked/headed Falcon) 7
Falco columbarius, *see* Merlin
Falco colombarius richardsonii (Merlin) 30–1
Falco colombarius stuckleyi (Black Merlin) 24
Falco concolor (Sooty Falcon) 9, 60, 61, 374
Falco cuvierii (African Hobby) 8, 323, 324
Falco deiroleucus (Orange-breasted Falcon) 10
Falco dickinsoni (Dickinson's Kestrel) 7, 197, 198
Falco eleonorae (Eleonora's Falcon) 9, 46, 60, 61, 63, 304, 306, 311
Falco fasciinucha (Taita Falcon) 10
Falco femoralis (Aplomado Falcon) 10
Falco hypoleucus (Grey Falcon) 197
Falco jugger (Laggar Falcon) 4–6
Falco longipennis (Australian Hobby) 9
Falco mexicanus (Prairie Falcon) 4, 100, 157, 192, 194
Falco moluccensis (Moluccan [Spotted] Kestrel) 7, 198
Falco naumanni (Lesser Kestrel) 7, 10, 60, 199, 252, 303
Falco newtoni (Madagascar Kestrel) 7, 197, 198

Falco novaeseelandiae (New Zealand Falcon) 10, 41
Falco pelegrinoides (Barbary Falcon) 6–7, 60, 61, 65, 100
Falco peregrinus, see Peregrine
Falco peregrinus anatum 99, 527
Falco peregrinus babylonicus 99
Falco peregrinus brookei 99
Falco peregrinus calidus 99
Falco peregrinus cassini 99
Falco peregrinus ernesti 99, 100
Falco peregrinus furuitii 99
Falco peregrinus harterti 99
Falco peregrinus japonensis 99
Falco peregrinus macropus 99
Falco peregrinus madens 99
Falco peregrinus minor 99
Falco peregrinus nesiotes 99
Falco peregrinus pealei 99, 100
Falco peregrinus pelegrinoides 99
Falco peregrinus peregrinator 99
Falco peregrinus peregrinus 99
Falco peregrinus radama 99
Falco peregrinus submelanogenys 99
Falco peregrinus tundrius (Tundra Peregrine Falcon) 4, 11, 99, 100, 112
Falco punctatus (Mauritius Kestrel) 7
Falco rufigularis (Bat Falcon) 9–10
Falco rupicoloides (Greater [White-eyed] Kestrel) 7, 198, 199
Falco rusticolus (Gyrfalcon) 3, 4, 5, 10, 11, 12, 39, 65, 68, 71, 72, 100, 132, 138, 157, 194, 304, 477, 479, 480, 522
Falco severus (Oriental Hobby) 9
Falco sparverius (American Kestrel) 7–8, 41, 69, 198, 199, 258, 268, 296
Falco subbuteo streichi 307
Falco subbuteo subbuteo, see Hobby
Falco subniger (Black Falcon) 10
Falco tinnunculus, see Kestrel
Falco vespertinus (Western Red-footed Falcon) 7, 38, 60, 61, 213, 302, 309, 320, 333, 374, 378
Falco zoniventris (Madagascan Banded Kestrel) 7
Falcon, Amur (Eastern Red-footed Falcon) (*Falco amurensis*) 7, 374
Falcon, Aplomado (*Falco femoralis*) 10
Falcon, Barbary (*Falco pelegrinoides*) 6–7, 60, 61, 65, 100
Falcon, Bat (*Falco rufigularis*) 9–10
Falcon, Black (*Falco subniger*) 10
Falcon, Brown (*Falco berigora*) 10
falcon, derivation of word 1
Falcon, Eastern Red-footed (Amur Falcon) (*Falco amurensis*) 7, 374
Falcon, Eleonora's (*Falco eleonorae*) 9, 46, 60, 61, 63, 304, 306, 311
Falcon, Grey (*Falco hypoleucus*) 197
Falcon, Laggar (*Falco jugger*) 4–6
Falcon, Lanner (*Falco biarmicus*) 4–6, 60, 61, 157, 304
Falcon, Laughing (*Herpetotheres cachinnans*) 2
Falcon, New Zealand (*Falco novaeseelandiae*) 10, 41
Falcon, Orange-breasted (*Falco deiroleucus*) 10
Falcon, Prairie (*Falco mexicanus*) 4, 100, 157, 192, 194
Falcon, Red-necked/Red-headed (*Falco chicquera*) 7
Falcon, Saker (*Falco cherrug*) 4–6

Falcon, Sooty (*Falco concolor*) 9, 60, 61, 374
Falcon, Taita (*Falco fasciinucha*) 10
Falcon, Tundra Peregrine (*Falco peregrinus tundrius*) 4, 11, 100, 112, 161, 181, 185–6
Falcon, Western Red-footed (*Falcon vespertinus*) 7, 38, 60, 61, 213, 302, 309, 320, 333, 374, 378
Falconet, Spot-winged (*Spizipteryx circumcinctus*) 2
Falconidae family 2, 22
Falconiformes 2, 3
Falconinae 2
falconry 1, 12, 98, 198, 414
falcons and hawks, differences 2
feather care **22, 23**, 24–5
  parasites 24–5
feet 17–**18**
Fennoscandia 8, 23, 30, 38, 41, 46, 48, 55, 64, 82–3, 85, 98, 122, 123, 183, 199, 214, 216, 234, 236, 248, 250, 254, 256, 269, 283, 285, 290, 291, 292, 301, 307, 387, 389, 397, 398, 399, 410, 412, 414, 429, 437, 430, 442, 459, 461, 463, 464, 466, 470, 472, 476, 479, 498
Ficedula hypoleuca (Pied Flycatcher) 407
Fieldfare (*Turdus pilaris*) 34, 114, 115, 116, 117, 118, 120, 124, 125, 403, 404, 405, 407, 409, 476
filariasis 189
Finch, House (*Carpodacus mexicanus*) 473
Finland 35, 82, 85, 122, 153, 185, 212, 214, 236, 237, 248, 249, 254, 255, 256, 259, 264, 269, 283, 301, 307, 498, 500
fish, as prey 210, 319

Flea Beetle, Cabbage Stem (*Psylliodes chrysocephala*) 56
flight 19–20, 57–64 *and see under individual falcons*
'floaters' 32–3, 148, 150
flocking, by prey 63, 62, 419–23, 424, 525
fly, louse (*Crataerina melbae*) 270
Flycatcher, Pied (*Ficedula hypoleuca*) 407
Flycatcher, Spotted (*Muscicapa striata*) 405, 407
food caching **26**–7, 132, 141, 221, 222–4, 332, 411–13
forest falcons 2
fovea 16, 69
fowl cholera 189
Fox Moth (*Macrothylacia rubi*) 316, 403, 407
Fox, Arctic (*Vulpes lagopus*) 191, 196
Fox, Red (*Vulpes vulpes*) 112, 196, 304, 432, 433, 480
France 37, 48, 110, 112, 162, 166, 174, 213, 226, 255, 279, 290, 314, 316, 318, 319, 329, 330, 341, 364, 367, 373, 466, 498
Fratercula arctica (Puffin) 116, 117
Fraxinus excelsior (Ash) 341
Frederick II, *De Arte Venandi cum Avibus* 97–8
Fringilla coelebs (Chaffinch) 114, 115, 116, 118, 120, 321, 402, 403, 404, 405, 406, 407, 408, 410, 467, 476
Fringilla montifringilla (Brambling) 116, 399, 403, 405, 407, 476
Frog, Common (*Rana temporaria*) 402
frogs 319, 402
Fulica atra (Coot) 121
Fulmar (*Fulmarus glacialis*) 39, 117, 191–2

Fulmarus glacialis (Fulmar) 39, 117, 191–2

Gallinago gallinago (Snipe) 114, 115, 116, 117, 120, 135, 212, 403, 404, 405, 406, 407, 419, 471
Gallinula chloropus (Moorhen) 120, 124
game management 50–3, 433–4, 473–4, 487, 488, 490, 513
Garrulus glandarius (Jay) 114, 115, 116, 120, 224, 242, 317, 332
gastroliths 25
Gecko, Zarudny's Bent-toed (*Cyrtopodion russowii*) 319
Georgia 314, 317
Geotrupes stercorarius (Dor-beetle) 316, 355
Germany 10, 24, 33, 35, 44, 48, 60, 151, 155, 185, 219, 249–50, 252, 260, 283, 300, 301, 314, 322, 340, 344, 345, 356, 357, 362, 364, 368, 372, 373, 375, 377, 379, 498
Glaucidium passerinum (Pygmy Owl) 84
global warming 498, 503, 520
Gloucestershire 215
Godwit, Bar-tailed (*Limosa lapponica*) 121
Godwit, Black-tailed (*Limosa limosa*) 121
Goldcrest (*Regulus regulus*) 38, 112, 212, 316, 403, 404, 405, 407, **413**
Goldfinch (*Carduelis carduelis*) 115, 120, 218, 403, 404, 405, 407
Goosander (*Mergus merganser*) 115
Goose, Barnacle (*Branta leucopsis*) 75
Goose, Canada (*Branta canadensis*) 190
Goose, Greylag (*Anser anser*) 111

Goose, Red-breasted (*Branta ruficollis*) 190
Goshawk (*Accipiter gentilis*) 34, 44, 48, 50, 64, 74, 302, 304, 345, 358, 384, 433, 477, 478, **479**, 493, 495, 496–7, 500, 503, 505, 506, 517, 522
grasshoppers 209, 324
Grayling, Arctic (*Thymallus arcticus*) 113
Grebe, Black-necked (*Podiceps nigricollis*) 121
Grebe, Little (*Tachybaptus ruficollis*) 120
Greenfinch (*Carduelis chloris*) 114, 116, 120, 321, 403, 404, 405, 407, 410
Greenland 153, 194
Greenshank (*Tringa nebularia*) 114, 116, 525
Groningen, University studies 23, 74, 86–7, 88–90, 224–32, 258, 264–5, 275, 333, 425, 428
Ground Squirrel, Arctic (*Urocitellus parryii*) 71, 112
Ground Squirrel, California (*Otospermophilus beechyi*) 113
Ground-beetle, Violet (*Carabus violaceus*) 316
grouse moors 50–3, 433–4, 473, 487, 488, 490, 517
Grouse, Black (*Lyrurus tetrix*) 50, 115, 116, 405, 477
Grouse, Red (*Lagopus lagopus scoticus*) 50, 51, 64, 77–80, 114, 115, 116, 117, 118, 123, 403, 404, 405, 407, 409, 513, 517, 521
Grouse, Sage (*Centrocercus urophasianus*) 63–4
Gryllus bimaculatus (Garden Cricket) 332

Guillemot (*Uria aalge*) 113, 117
Guillemot, Black (*Cepphus grille*) 117
Gull, Audouin's (*Larus audoiuinii*) 525
Gull, Black-headed (*Chroicocephalus ridibundus*) 114, 115, 116, 120, 122, 123, 143, **304**, 326, **385**
Gull, Common (*Larus canus*) 114, 115, 116
Gull, Great Black-backed (*Larus marinus*) 111, 117, 196, 302, 477
Gull, Herring (*Larus argentatus*) 117, 129, 384
Gull, Lesser Black-backed (*Larus fuscus*) 116
Gull, Yellow-legged (*Larus michahellis*) 137
Gymnodactyulus russowi 529
Gypaetus barbatus (Lammergeier) 384–5
Gyps fulvus (Griffon Vulture) 299
Gyps rueppellii (Ruppell's Vulture) 522
Gyrfalcon (*Falco rusticolus*) 3, 4, 5, 10, 11, 12, 39, 65, 68, 71, 72, 100, 132, 138, 157, 194, 304, 477, 479, 480, 522

'hacking' 534
Haematopus ostralegus (Oystercatcher) 32, 33, 116, 117, 135, 405, 406
Haliaeetus albicilla (White-tailed Eagle) 50, 187, 192, 471
Haliaeetus leucocephalus (Bald Eagle) 39, 41, 131, 132, 137, 194
Hampshire 137, 367
Hare, Brown (*Lepus europaeus*) 115, 207–8
Hare, Mountain (*Lepus timidus*) 116
Harrier, Australasian (Swamp) (*Circus approximans*) 10

Harrier, Hen (Northern) (*Circus cyaneus*) 50, 51, 52, 53, 137, 220, 406, 467, 475, 477, 521, 528
Harrier, Marsh (*Circus aeruginosus*) 371
Harrier, Montagu's (*Circus pygargus*) 38, 320, 327
Hawfinch (*Coccothraustes coccothraustes*) 114
Hawk, Cooper's (*Accipiter cooperii*) 479
Hawk, Harris (*Parabuteo unicinctus*) 389
Hawk, Red-tailed (*Buteo jamaicensis*) 41, 112, 479
Hawk, Sharp-shinned (*Accipiter striatus*) 137, 471–3
Hawker, Brown (*Aeshna grandis*) 333
Hawker, Migrant (*Aeshna mixta*) 333, 502–3
Hawker, Southern (*Aeshna cyanea*) **316**, 333
Heather (Ling) (*Calluna vulgaris*) 432, 510
Hebrides 316, 404, 436
Hedgehog (*Erinaceus europaeus*) 432
Heron, Great Blue (*Ardea herodias*) 477
Heron, Grey (*Ardea cinerea*) 44, 111, 242, 340, 384
Herpetotheres cachinnans (Laughing Falcon) 2
Hertfordshire 98, 336
hierofalcons 4–6
Himalayas 314, 363
Hippolais icterina (Icterine Warbler) 374
Hirundo rustica (Barn Swallow) 56, 96, 121, 313, **317**, 320, 321, 323, 324, 326, 327, 328, 330–1, 332, **335**, 356, 403, 405, 406, 407, 416–7
Hobby, African (*Falco cuvierii*) 8, 323, 324

Hobby, Australian (*Falco longipennis*) 9
Hobby (*Falco subbuteo*) 8–**9**, 10, 14–15,
   309, **326**, **327**, **369**, **385**, **501**, **504** *see also* Hobby, female
 bathing 24
 breeding 14–15, 28, 29, 337–62
 chicks **47**, **311**, **318**, **351–3**, **361**, **376**
  calls 315
  diet 322–3
  feeding **318**, **322**, **323**, **328**, 334, **347**, **350**, **507**
  growth 346–57
  plumage 311, 348–9
 clutch size 47–8, 344–5
 and contamination 54
 copulation **342**–3
 courtship feeding 338
 death, causes of 377–8
 derivation of name 305
 diet and prey 14–15, 37–8, 316–25
 differences from other falcons 34–56
 dimensions and weight 307–8
 display 337–9
 eggs and egg-laying 45–6, 343–5
 energy balance 332–4
 feet 17–18
 flight **61**, 68, 94–6, 325–7
  mimicking 328
 food caching 332
 habitat 14–15, 34–5, 312–15, **313**, **314**
 hunting 94–6, 325–32
  cooperative 328
 incubation 346
 increase in numbers 502–5
 insect hunting strategies 324, 328
 juveniles **9**, 308–9, **310**, 333, 352–7, **354**, **355**, **356**, **377**, **501**
 and Kestrels 304, 320, 333–4, 378–9, 384
 kleptoparasitism 137, 320
 life expectancy 375–7
 mate fidelity 362
 migration and movement 15, 33, 45–6, 48, 96, 323–4, 327, 363–74
 moult 312
 nest sites 44, 340–2, 360–2, **361**, **376**
  fidelity 29, 360–2
 parasites 322, 378
 pellet analysis 316, 318
 and peregrines 320
 and pesticides 506
 plumage 308, 311–12, **335**, **338**
 population, estimates and trends 48, 501–8
 predators 34, 383–6
 range 306–7
  increase in 501–5
 success 336, 357–60
 survival 374–8
 territory 334–6
 urban dwelling 313
 voice 315
 and Wood Pigeons 379–83
Hobby, female **310**, **328**, **507**
 breeding behaviour 337
 calls 315
 chick care **318**, **322**, **323**, 346
 dimensions and weight 307–8
 displays 339
 egg-laying 343–4
 plumage 308
Hobby, Oriental (*Falco severus*) 9
Honeybee, European (*Apis mellifera*) 55
Honey-buzzard (*Pernis apivorus*) 192, 362, 371, 497

humans, disruption and persecution by 49–56, 118, 196, 304, 433–4, 473–4, 480, 494, 517–18
Hungary 331
hunting techniques 36–41 *and see under individual falcons*
Hydrobates pelagicus (European Storm Petrel) 130, 316–17

Ibis, Glossy (*Plegadis falcinellus*) 11
Iceland 317, 389, 397, 430, 437, 442, 458, 463, 467, 477, 478, 479
Inachis io (Peacock Butterfly) 403
incestuous relationships 153–4
Inclosure Act 1773 49
incubation 29 *and see under individual falcons*
India 181, 255, 363
insects, as prey 37, 38, 189, 209, 215, 217, 221, 307, 316, 322–4, 326, 328–30, 332–4, 346, 354, 355–7, 367, 373, 374, 397, 404, 416, 452
Ireland 12, 36, 98, 106–7, 135, 182, 187, 189, 215, 289, 387, 399, 406, 412, 435, 437, 455, 464, 476, 477
Ireland, Northern 408, 469
Israel 60, 248
Italy 56, 98, 153, 196, 208, 252, 290, 311, 335, 345, 358–9, 360, 363, 364, 370, 372, 373, 378, 381
Ixodes ricinus 270

Jackdaw (*Corvus monedula*) 114, 115, 116, 117, 120, 244
Japan 8, 98, 133, 150, 197, 252
Jay (*Garrulus glandarius*) 114, 115, 116, 120, 224, 242, 317, 332

Jynx torquilla (Wryneck) 113, 116, 315, 402

Kakapo (*Strigops habroptila*) 2
Kent 328, 336, 402, 411
Kentish Glory Moth (*Endromis versicolora*) 402
Kes (film) 285
Kestrel (*Falco tinnunculus*) 7–8, 14, **70**, **93**, **200**, **217**, **278**, **491**, **497** *see also* Kestrel, female
  aerial prey 210–13
  basal metabolic rate (BSR) 203
  bathing 23
  breeding 14, 29, 234–88
    cycle 228–30
  brooding **262**–5
  calls 197, 206–7
  captive 209, 258
  chicks **16**, **202**, 207, **209**, 242–3, 245, 269–82, **272**, 274–8, **494**
    brooding 261–3, 273–5, **499**
    feeding 270–1, **273**, **274**, **278**
    fledging 275–9, **280**
    growth 271
    parasites 279
    sex ratio 273
  clutch size 47, 250, 261–8
  conservation status 1
  copulation 253–1, **253**
  courtship feeding 239–40
  death, causes of 299–300, 499–500
  decline in numbers 490–500
  derivation of name 197
  diet and prey 14, 37, 199, 207–19, 493–9
  differences from other falcons 34–56

Kestrel *continued*
  dimensions and weight 14, 199–200
  diseases 300
  displays 238–40
  eggs and egg-laying 44, **46**, 252–61, **276**
  eggs, as food 210
  energy balance 224–32
  food caching 221, 222–4
  flight 74, 86–91
  habitat 14, 35, 204–6
  and Hobbies 304, 320, 333–4, 378–9, 384
  hovering 86–91, **92–3**, 197, 220, **223**
  and human interference 285, 299, 304
  and human landscapes 205
  hunting 82–91, 220–4
  incubation 265, 268–70
  juveniles **23**, **202**, 203–4, 217, 236, 239, 279–82, **283**, 288–9, 295, 297–8
  kleptoparasitism 213
  learning 84
  mate fidelity 287
  and Merlins 475–6
  moult 202–3, 258
  movement and migration 33, 48, 286–8, 288–94
  nest sites 44, **209**, 240–9
    boxes/baskets **209**, 241–3, 244, **272**
    buildings 246–9, **247**
    cliffs 241
    fidelity to 286
  pair formation 235–8
  pellet analysis 213–19
  perch hunting 220
  and Peregrines 193, 301–2

  plumage 200–4, 236
  polyandry 235
  polygony 234–5
  population estimates and trends 490–500
  predators 34, 493–8
  range 197–9
  roosts 123, 293–4
  similarities with other falcons 16–41
  subspecies 100, 198–9
  survival 33, 294–300
  territory 232–4
  vision 64, 82–6
  voice 197, 206–7
  wing 58
  winter acivity 289–94
Kestrel, American (*Falco sparverius*) 7–8, 41, 69, 198, 199, 258, 268, 296
Kestrel, Australian (Nankeen) (*Falco cenchroides*) 7, 198
Kestrel, Dickinson's (*Falco dickinsoni*) 7, 197, 198
Kestrel, female **8**, **201**, **262**, **278**, **499**
  aggression 233
  brooding 261–3, 273–5
  displays 238–9
  egg-laying and incubation 254–60, 264
  energy expenditure 228–32
  site and mate fidelity 286–7
  food consumption 217, 224–5, 239–40
  mating 235–8, 253–4
  migration 291–2
  plumage 201, 202–3
  weight and dimensions 199–200
Kestrel, Fox (*Falco alopex*) 7, 198

Kestrel, Greater (White-eyed) (*Falco rupicoloides*) 7, 198, 199
Kestrel, Grey (*Falco ardosiaceus*) 7, 197, 198
Kestrel, Lesser (*Falco naumanni*) 7, 10, 60, 199, 252, 303
Kestrel, Madagascan Banded (*Falco zoniventris*) 7
Kestrel, Madagascar (*Falco newtoni*) 7, 197, 198
Kestrel, Mauritius (*Falco punctatus*) 7
Kestrel, Moluccan (Spotted) (*Falco moluccensis*) 7, 198
Kestrel, Seychelles (*Falco araea*) 7
Kielder Forest 36, 394, 495, 496, 515–17
Kingfisher (*Alcedo atthis*) 121
Kite, Black (*Milvus migrans*) 358, 361, 379, 383
Kite, Red (*Milvus milvus*) 50, 52, 85, 497, 498, 499–500
Kittiwake (*Rissa tridactyla*) 116, 117
kleptoparasitic attacks 132, 137, 213, 320
Knot (*Calidris canutus*) 114, 115

Lacerta vivipara (Viviparous Lizard) **209**, 407
Lagopus lagopus scoticus (Red Grouse) 50, 51, 64, 77–80, 114, 115, 116, 117, 118, 123, 403, 404, 405, 407, 409, 513, 517, 521
Lagopus mutus (Ptarmigan) 50, 71, 116, 123
Lake District 20, 114, 123, 146–7, 176, 403, 490
Lammergeier (*Gypaetus barbatus*) 384–5
Lanius excubitor (Great Grey Shrike) 83, 92

Lanius minor (Lesser Grey Shrike) 374, 379
Lapwing (*Vanellus vanellus*) 37, 114, 115, 116, 117, 118, 120, 122, 123, 124, 212, 326, 402, 403, 404, 405, 407, 410, 416
Lark, Shore (*Eremophila alpestris*) 92, 399
Larus argentatus (Herring Gull) 117, 129, 384
Larus audoiuinii (Audouin's Gull) 525
Larus canus (Common Gull) 114, 115, 116
Larus fuscus (Lesser Black-backed Gull) 116
Larus marinus (Great Black-backed Gull) 111, 117, 196, 302, 477
Larus michahellis (Yellow-legged Gull) 137
Lasiocampa quercus callunae (Northern Eggar Moth) 316, 398, 402, 406, 407
Lasiocampa quercus (Oak Eggar Moth) 316
Latham, Simon 25
Laudakia nupta (Large-scaled Rock Agama) 319
lead contamination 187–9, 471–3
Leicestershire 326
Lemming, Northern Collared (*Dicrostonyx groenlandicus*) 112
Lemming, Norwegian (*Lemmus lemmus*) 38, 397
Lemmus lemmus (Norwegian Lemming) 38, 397
Lepus europaeus (Brown Hare) 115, 207–8
Lepus timidus (Mountain Hare) 116

lifetime reproductive success (LRS) 30, 461
Lime, Common (*Tilia europaea*) 341
Limosa lapponica (Bar-tailed Godwit) 121
Limosa limosa (Black-tailed Godwit) 121
Lincolnshire 341
Linnaeus, *Systema* 98
Linnet (*Carduelis cannabina*) 114, 115, 403, 404, 405, 407, 410, 411
Lizard, Viviparous (*Lacerta vivipara*) **209**, 407
lizards 210, 217, 222, 319, 397
logarithmic spiral 71–3, **72**
Loxia curvirostra (Common Crossbill) 116, 403, 404, 405, 515
Luscinia svecica (Bluethroat) 402, 405
Lutra lutra (Otter) 432
Lymnocryptes minimus (Jack Snipe) 121
Lyrurus tetrix (Black Grouse) 50, 115, 116, 405, 477

Macrothylacia rubi (Fox Moth) 316, 403, 407
Magpie (*Pica pica*) 50, 115, 116, 118, 120, 213, 242, 244, 303, 317, 379, 383, 468
Magpie, Black-billed (*Pica hudsonia*) 32, 395
Mallard (*Anas platyrhynchos*) 114, 115, 116, 118, 122, 129
Malta 363, 364, 367, 371–2, 373
Manchester 37, 218
Marram Grass (*Ammophila arenaria*) 432
Marten, Pine (*Martes martes*) 358, 385, 480

Martes martes (Pine Marten) 358, 385, 480
Martin, House (*Delichon urbicum*) 94, 114, 313, 320, 321, **322**, **323**, 326, 327, 403, 404, 405, 407
Martin, Purple (*Progne subis*) 32
Martin, Sand (*Riparia riparia*) 38, 212, 325, 331, 403, 405, 407
Mason Bee, Solitary Red (*Osmia bicornis*) 55
Melanitta deglandi (White-winged Scoter) 113
Meles meles (Badger) 432
Melolontha melolontha (Cockchafer) 316
Melopsittacus undulatus (Budgerigar) 121, 316, 402, 529
mercury 187, 471, 512–14
Merganser, Red-breasted (*Mergus serrator*) 116
Mergus merganser (Goosander) 115
Mergus serrator (Red-breasted Merganser) 116
Merlin (*Falco columbarius*) 10–12, **94**, **95**, **391** *see also* Merlin, female
basal metabolic rate (BMR) 425
bathing 24
breeding 15, 28, 29, 30–2, 429–64
chicks **42**, **393**, **433–5**, **445**, **447**, **451–4**, **457**, **461**, **462**, **478**, **518**, **519**
feeding **401**, **445**, 446–9, 454–5, **508**, **509**
growth 444–55
mortality 455–6
plumage 393
clutch size 48, 442–3
conservation status 1
contamination effects 471–4

cooperative behaviour 467–8, 475–7
copulation 437–8
death, causes of 471–5
derivation of name 388
diet and prey 38–9, 396–411
   sex differences 409–10
differences from other falcons 34–5
diseases 473–5
displays 430–2
eggs and egg-laying 44, 438–44, **451**
energy balance 425–8
in falconry 414
and Fieldfares 476
flight 59, 92–4, 414–18
   mimicking 417
food caching 411–13
habitat 15, 35–6, 394–6, **395**
human persecution and
   disturbance 49, 473–4, 80
hunting 92–4, 414–25
   success rates 418–19
incubation 443–4
juvenile **392, 411**, 450, **458, 511**
   moult 394
   mortality 469
   plumage 392
and Kestrels 475–6
kleptoparasitism 137
mate fidelity 463–4
moult 393–4, 466
movement and migration 48, 62, 464–8
nest sites 15, 41–2, 432–5
   baskets and boxes **401, 434**
   fidelity 29, 461–3
pair formation 429–30
parasites 475

pellet analysis 400–2
perch hunting 215
and pesticides 471–2, 509–14
plumage 391–2
population estimates and trends 514–20
prey, defensive tactics 420–5
predators 15, 34, 477–80
range 388–9
ringing flight 414
roosts 123, 468
shooting 473–4
similarities with other falcons 16–41
Starlings, association with 467–8
stooping 415
subspecies and hybrids 389
success rate 134
survival 33, 468–75
territory 428–9, 461–3
voice 396
weight and dimensions 389–90
wintering 464–8
and Wood Pigeons 477
Merlin (*Falco columbarius richardsonii*) 30–1
Merlin, Black (*Falco columbarius stuckleyi*) 24
Merlin, female **1, 59, 446, 453, 454, 474, 513**
   chick care 455, 460–1
   fidelity 462–4
   incubation 443–4
   migrating 464, 466
   plumage 392
   weight and dimensions 389–90
Mexico 163, 180, 181, 183
Michell, Edward Blair 529

Micrastur 2
Microhierax 2
Micromys minutus (Harvest Mouse) 37, 216
Microtus agrestis (Short-tailed Field Vole) 82, 83, 84, 85, 114, 115, 214, 215, 397, 402, 403, 490, 497, 498
Microtus arvalis (Common Vole) 125, 213, 214, 215, 221
Microtus arvalis orcadensis (Orkney Vole) 244
Microtus levis (Sibling Vole) 83
migration 33, 45–6, 48, 60–1 *and see under individual falcons*
Milvago 2
Milvus migrans (Black Kite) 358, 361, 379, 383
Milvus milvus (Red Kite) 50, 52, 85, 497, 498, 499–500
Mole (*Talpa europaea*) 37, 208, 318
Moorhen (*Gallinula chloropus*) 120, 124
mortality, differential 29–30
Motacilla alba yarrellii (Pied Wagtail) 120, 218, 317, 321, 403, 404, 405, 407, 410
Motacilla cinerea (Grey Wagtail) 114, 115, 116, 405, 407
Motacilla flava (Yellow Wagtail) 317
moult 2, 25 *and see under individual falcons*
Mouse, Harvest (*Micromys minutus*) 37, 216
Mouse, House (*Mus musculus*) 83, 216
Mouse, Wood (*Apodemus sylvaticus*) **208**, 215, 403
mtDNA analysis 3
Murrelet, Ancient (*Synthliboramphus antiquus*) 130, 131–2, 141, 146

Mus musculus (House Mouse) 83, 216
Muscicapa striata (Spotted Flycatcher) 405, 407
Mustela ermine (Stoat) 112, 432
Mustela nivalis (Weasel) 37, 207, 213
Myodes glareolus (Bank Vole) 83, 84, 85, 207, **208**, 216, 250
Myotis daubentonii (Daubenton's Bat) 319

Nautilus 71
neonicotinoids 54–6, 506
nest boxes 107–8, 247–8, 252
nest sites 41–4, 151–5
 cliffs 41, 42, 151, 341
 ground 41, 42, 153, 244–5, 341, 432–5
 pylons 248, 314, 334, 341, 386
 tree 42, 154, 241–4, 434–5
 urban 41, 42, 44, 155, 184, 246–9
Netherlands 23, 74, 86–7, 88–90, 213, 214, 220, 221, 224–32, 251, 255, 257, 258, 261, 263–7, 273, 275, 286, 289, 295–7, 298, 304, 314, 318, 333, 340, 344, 345, 346, 347, 357, 358, 363, 378, 379, 425, 428, 505
New Forest 317, 320–1, 328, 335, 412, 516
New Zealand 100
Nightjar (*Caprimulgus europaeus*) 294
North America 22, 24, 30, 36, 41, 46, 71, 73, 98, 100, 112, 113, 122, 126, 130–7, 146, 148, 149, 150, 151, 153, 157, 159–60, 161, 162–3, 173–4, 177, 180, 181, 185, 186, 189, 193, 194, 196, 300, 387, 389, 395, 396, 397, 398, 408, 411, 419, 421, 429, 430, 437, 440, 443, 449, 455, 463, 471, 479, 480

Northumberland 52, 394, 399, 402, 403, 404, 430, 432, 436, 442, 456, 467
Norway 186, 188, 216, 305, 341, 387, 399, 412, 442, 464, 472, 476, 479
Numenius arquata (Curlew) 34, 114, 115, 116, 117, 118, 124, **301**, 403, 405, 407
Numenius phaeopus (Whimbrel) 116
Nuthatch (*Sitta europaea*) 407
Nyctalus noctula (Noctule Bat) 113, 121, 318
Nymphicus hollandicus (Cockatiel [Quarrion]) 75, 121

Oceanodroma furcata (Fork-tailed Storm Petrel) 146
Oceanodroma leucorhoa (Leach's Petrel) 121, 130, 146, 212, 411
Ochotona alpina (Alpine Pika) 318
Ochotona hyperborea (Northern Pika) 318
Oenanthe oenanthe (Wheatear) 38, 114, 115, 116, 117, 190, 191, 397, **399**, 402, 403, 404, 405, 407
Oilseed Rape (*Brassica napus*) 55
organochlorines 54, 160, 187, 285, 299, 301, 442, 455, 456, 471, 483–6, 506, 509, 511, 512–14, 518
Orkney 106, 192, 244, 246, 390, 402, 446–7, 512–14
Ornithologia Britannica 98
Ornithomya frigillana 378, **474**, 475
Orthetrum cancellatum (Black-tailed Skimmer) 333
Oryctolagus cuniculus (Rabbit) 112, 114, 115, 116, 207, 244, 318, 397
Osmia bicornis (Solitary Red Mason Bee) 55

Osprey (*Pandion haliaetus*) 11, 50, 130, 371, 383
Otospermophilus beechyi (California Ground Squirrel) 113
Otter (*Lutra lutra*) 432
Ouzel, Ring (*Turdus torquatus*) 34, 114, 115, 190, 403, 404, 405, 407
Owl, Barn (*Tyto alba*) 11, 20, 37, 50, 115, 213, 244, 250, 270, 294, 302, 304, 324, 499–500, 521, 529
Owl, Eagle (*Bubo bubo*) 32, 193, 304, 361, 384, 479, 531
Owl, Great Horned (*Bubo virginianus*) 193, 479
Owl, Little (*Athene noctua*) 114, 244, 294, 304
Owl, Long-eared (*Asio otus*) 50, 114, **211**, 233, 495, 496, 528
Owl, Pygmy (*Glaucidium passerinum*) 84
Owl, Short-eared (*Asio flammeus*) 34, 37, 50, 52, 116, 213, 250, 477, 478, 495, 496, 528
Owl, Snowy (*Bubo scandiacus*) 47, 190, 191, 250, 301
Owl, Tawny (*Strix aluco*) 34, 50, 52, 114, 199, 244, 304, 357, 384, 433, 478, 479, 495, 496
Owl, Tengmalm's (*Aegolius funereus*) 21, 431, 528, 531
Owl, Ural (*Strix uralensis*) 531
Oxyura jamaicensis (Ruddy Duck) 121
Oystercatcher (*Haematopus ostralegus*) 32, 33, 116, 117, 135, 405, 406

Pacific Ocean 129–30
Pakistan 319

586 · FALCONS

Pandion haliaetus (Osprey) 11, 50, 130, 371, 383
Parabuteo unicinctus (Harris Hawk) 389
Parakeet, Rose-ringed (*Psittacula krameri*) 121
parasites 24–5, 85, 189–90, 270, 300, 322, 378, 469, 474–5
parasitic drag 66, 67, 68
parrots, link with falcons 2–3
Partridge, Grey (*Perdix perdix*) 81, 114, 115, **124**, 398, 403, 405, 444
Partridge, Red-legged (*Alectoris rufa*) 82
Parus major (Great Tit) 121, 212, 270, 321, 404, 405, 407
Passer domesticus (House Sparrow) 36, 37, 120, 210, 212, 218, 219, 317, 321, 396, 399, 400, 402, 403, 405, 407, 408, 426, 467, 471, 473, 513
Passer domesticus italiae (Italian House Sparrow) 383
Passer montanus (Tree Sparrow) 321, 383
Passerella iliaca (Fox Sparrow) 146, 406
Pastor roseus (Rose-coloured Starling) 75, 531
Peacock Butterfly (*Inachis io*) 403
pellet analysis 25–6, 213–19, 316, 318, 400–2
Pembrokeshire 20, 137, 182
Perdix perdix (Grey Partridge) 81, 114, 115, **124**, 398, 403, 405, 444
Peregrine (*Falco peregrinus*) **6**, 10–11, 13, **19**, **22**, **76**, **81**, **105**, **109** *see also* Peregrine, female
 aerial hunting 126
 and Barn Owls 302
 basal metabolic rate (BMR) 142–3

bathing 23
'binding' 127–8
breeding 13, 28, 29 148–180
 age 148–50
 density 146–8
 success 173–9
 captive 100, 128, 141–3, 155, 157, 159, 161, 177–8, 190, 200
 chicks 17, **43**, **104**, 110–11, 164–73, **168–70**, **177**, **482**
 feeding **165**, 166–71, **489**
 feet **18**
 growth 164–8
 teaching **171–2**
 sex ratio 164
 clutch size 46, 160–1
 conservation status 1
 copulation 158
 courtship feeding **156**, 157–8
 death, causes of 186–7, 482–6
 decline in numbers 481–8
 diet and prey 13, 46, 111–40, 487–8
 dimensions and weight 13, 101
 differences from other falcons 34–56
 diseases 189–90
 display 155–8
 distances travelled 138–9
 'dummy' or 'warm-up' attacks 132, 136–7
 earliest mentions 97–8
 eggs and egg-laying 45, 158, 159–60, 187
 energy balance 13, 36, 106–8
 fledging 167–8, 194
 flight **59**, 60, 64–82, **66**, 127–41
 food caching 141
 food passing **156**, **162**

habitat 13, 36, 106–8
and Hobby 320
hunting 64–81, 127–141, 418
incubation 161–4, **163**, 183
juveniles **103**–4, **107**, **171–3**
and Kestrels 301–2
kill 128, 140
kleptoparasitism 132, 137
mantling **79**, 166
mate fidelity 108
moult 105–6
mortality 184–90
movement and migration 48, 62, 181–4
name 97–8
nest sites 42, **43–4**, 151, **152**, 153–5
  artificial **154**, 174
  fidelity to 179–80
night hunting 131–2
pair hunting 129, 132, 137
persecution 49, 53–4, 481–3, 490
and pesticides 187, 483–6
plumage 101–6
population estimates and trends 481–90
predators 34
prey species tables 114–18
pursuit hunting 130–1
range 98, **99**, 100, 144–8
'ringing' 127, 131
seabirds, hunting 129–31
similarities with other falcons 16–41
speed 64–9
stooping (diving) **66**, **77**, 127
striking 128–9
survival 184–90
territory 144–8

urban dwelling 107–8, 118–21, 132, **171–3**, 526
vision 69–73
voice 108–11
wing 58
wintering 123–6
Peregrine, female **102**, **109**, **121**, **134**, **147**, **184**, **482**, **488**
mating 149–50, 157–8
call 108, 110
egg-laying and incubation 159–64
food consumption 141–2
plumage 102–3
range 145–6
reproductive success 177–9
site and mate fidelity 180–1
weight and dimensions 101
Peregrine Falcon, Tundra (*Falco peregrinus tundrius*) 11
Periparus ater (Coal Tit) 115, 403, 405, 407
Perlin **66**
Pernis apivorus (Honey-buzzard) 192, 362, 371, 497
pesticides and contaminants 54–6, 160, 187, 299, 301, 442, 455, 471–3, 483–6, 509–14
Petrel, European Storm (*Hydrobates pelagicus*) 130, 316–17
Petrel, Fork-tailed Storm (*Oceanodroma furcata*) 146
Petrel, Leach's (*Oceanodroma leucorhoa*) 121, 130, 146, 212, 411
Phalcoboenus 2
Phasianus colchicus (Pheasant) 49, 50, 80, 114, 115, 407, 302
Pheasant (*Phasianus colchicus*) 49, 50, 80, 114, 115, 407, 302

Phoenicurus ochruros (Black Redstart) 244
Phoenicurus phoenicurus (Redstart) 405, 407
Phylloscopus collybita (Chiffchaff) 121, 404, 407
Phylloscopus sibilatrix (Wood Warbler) 407
Phylloscopus trochilus (Willow Warbler) 121, 403, 404, 405, 407
phylogenetic analyses 2
Pica hudsonia (Black-billed Magpie) 32, 395
Pica pica (Magpie) 50, 115, 116, 118, 120, 213, 242, 244, 303, 317, 379, 383, 468
Picea abies (Norway Spruce) 341
Picea sitchensis (Sitka Spruce) 435, 515
Picus viridis (Green Woodpecker) 38, 114, 244, 332, 383
Pigeon, Feral/Domestic (*Columba livia*) 39, 45, 53–4, 101, 106, 114, 115, 116, 117, 118, 120, **121**, **122**, 123, 126–7, 133, 153, **155**, 171–2, 184, 389, 403
Pigeon, Wood (*Columba palumbus*) 34, 44, 106, 114, 115, 116, 120, 123, 124, 129, 242, 340, 354, 358, 360, 379–83, 477
pigeon racing 53–4
pigeons, carrier 118, 481
Pika, Alpine (*Ochotona alpina*) 318
Pika, Northern (*Ochotona hyperborea*) 318
Pine, Scots (*Pinus sylvestris*) 332, 340, 341, 367
Pinus sylvestris (Scots Pine) 332, 340, 341, 367
Pipistrelle, Common (*Pipistrellus pipistrellus*) 212–3

Pipistrellus pipistrellus (Common Pipistrelle) 212–3
Pipistrellus sp. 318
Pipit, Meadow (*Anthus pratensis*) **26**, **27**, 38, 93, **94**, 114, 115, 116, 210, **211**, 321, **391**, 397, **398**, 402, 403, 404, 405–6, 407, 408, 412, **413**, 415, 416, **420**, 478, 518, 519
Pipit, Tree (*Anthus trivialis*) 121, 321, 404
Plecotus auritus (Brown Long-eared Bat) 319
Plectrophenax nivalis (Snow Bunting) 114, 116, 191, **398**, 403, 404, 405, 505
Plegadis falcinellus (Glossy Ibis) 11
Plover, Golden (*Pluvialis apricaria*) 114, 115, 116, 117, 120, 124, 403, 404, 405, 416
Plover, Grey (*Pluvialis squatarola*) 121
Plover, Ringed (*Charadrius hiaticula*) 115, 118, 317, 402, 404, 410
plumage 22–5 *and see under individual falcons*
Pluvialis apricaria (Golden Plover) 114, 115, 116, 117, 120, 124, 403, 404, 405, 416
Pluvialis squatarola (Grey Plover) 121
Podiceps nigricollis (Black-necked Grebe) 121
Poecile montanus (Willow Tit) 321, 403
Poecile palustris (Marsh Tit) 321, 404, 407
Poland 218–19
Polihierax 2
polyandry 235
Polyborus 2
polygony 234–5
Portugal 48, 182, 307

predators 15, 34, 383–6, 493–8, 477–80
predatory adaptations 16–19
prey
   colour of 399
   escape tactics 62–4, 419–23, 424, 525
   and see under individual falcons
Progne subis (Purple Martin) 32
Protection of Birds Act 1954 50
Prunella modularis (Dunnock) 120, 218, 321, 403, 404, 405, 407
Psittacula krameri (Rose-ringed Parakeet) 121
Psylliodes chrysocephala (Cabbage Stem Flea Beetle) 56
Ptarmigan (*Lagopus mutus*) 50, 71, 116, 123
Pteridium aquilinum (Bracken) 432
Ptychoramphus aleuticus (Cassin's Auklet) 131, 136, 146
Puffin (*Fratercula arctica*) 116, 117
Puffinus puffinus (Manx Shearwater) 116
pulli 1–2
pygmy falcons 2
pylon-nesting 248, 314, 334, 341, 386
Pyrrhocorax pyrrhocorax (Chough) 118
Pyrrhula pyrrhula (Bullfinch) 114, 115, 116, 403, 404, 405, 407

Quail (*Coturnix coturnix*) 92, 121, 132, 359
Quarrion (Cockatiel) (*Nymphicus hollandicus*) 75, 121

Rabbit (*Oryctolagus cuniculus*) 112, 114, 115, 116, 207, 244, 318, 397
Rail, Water (*Rallus aquaticus*) 121, 132

Rallus aquaticus (Water Rail) 121, 132
Rana temporaria (Common Frog) 402
'rangle' 25
Rat, Brown (*Rattus norvegicus*) 121, 207, 500
Ratcliffe index 483–6
Rattus norvegicus (Brown Rat) 121, 207, 500
Raven (*Corvus corax*) 50, 123, 151, 192, 242, 340, 383, 384, 468, 477
Razorbill (*Alca torda*) 117
Recurvirostra avosetta (Avocet) 121
Redpoll, Common (*Carduelis flammea*) 191
Redpoll, Lesser (*Carduelis cabaret*) 121, 403, 405, 407, 410
Redshank (*Tringa tetanus*) 114, 115, 116, 117, 134, 135, 403, 404, 405, 410, 417, 418, 419, 423, 425, 471, 487, 520
Redstart (*Phoenicurus phoenicurus*) 405, 407
Redstart, American (*Setophaga ruticilla*) 530
Redstart, Black (*Phoenicurus ochruros*) 244
Redwing (*Turdus iliacus*) 114, 115, 116, 118, 120, 125, 126, 403, 404, 405, 407, 410
Regulus regulus (Goldcrest) 38, 112, 212, 316, 403, 404, 405, 407, **413**
reptiles, as prey 37, 38, 39, 214, 217, 316, 319, 324, 397
reversed sexual dimorphism (RSD) **19**–22
Rhinolophus hipposideros (Lesser Horseshoe Bat) 319
Riparia riparia (Sand Martin) 38, 212, 325, 331, 403, 405, 407

Rissa tridactyla (Kittiwake) 116, 117
Robin (*Erithacus rubecula*) 114, 115, 116, **210**, 403, 404, 405, 407
Rook (*Corvus frugilegus*) 114, 116, 124, 242
roosts, communal 123, 372, 431, 467, 468, 475
Russia 244, 252, 257, 300, 307, 318, 322, 363, 389, 480

Sahara Desert 290, 291, 356, 364, 366–9, 371, 372, 373, 377
Salisbury Cathedral 526
Salix sp. (willow) 341, 467, 468
salmonellosis 189
Sanderling (*Calidris alba*) 114, 116
Sandpiper, Common (*Actitis hypoleucos*) 115, 116, 405, 407
Sandpiper, Green (*Tringa ochropus*) 121
Sandpiper, Wood (*Tringa glareola*) 116
Saskatoon Merlin study 30, 393, 394, 395, 412, 413, 415, 425–8, 429–30, 436, 437, 438, 439, 443, 459, 464, 466, 470
Saturnia pavonia (Emperor Moth) 316, 398, 402, 406, 407
Saxicola rubetra (Whinchat) 321, 403, 404, 405, 407
Saxicola rubicola (Stonechat) 115, 321, 405, 407
Scandinavia, *see* Fennoscandia
Sciurus carolinensis (Grey Squirrel) 121, 242, 357
Sciurus vulgaris (Red Squirrel) 385
Scolopax rusticola (Woodcock) 114, 115, 116, 118, 120, 132, 317, 402
Scoter, White-winged (*Melanitta deglandi*) 113

Scotland 24, 39–40, 48, 51, 52, 77, 86, 87, 106–7, 112, 115–18, 123, 125, 129, 131, 134, 144, 146, 149, 151, 153, 155, 158, 159, 173–5, 176, 179, 182–3, 184, 185, 187, 214, 215, 240, 251, 252, 255, 256, 258, 271, 283, 286, 290, 389, 394, 397, 400, 402, 405, 406, 410, 412, 415, 416, 417–18, 422, 423, 425, 429, 430, 431, 434–8, 443, 446, 448, 463, 468, 470, 475, 478, 480
seriemas 3
Serinus canaria (Canary) 121, 212
Serinus canicollis (Cape Canary) 324
Setophaga ruticilla (American Redstart) 530
Shearwater, Manx (*Puffinus puffinus*) 116
Shelduck (*Tadorna tadorna*) 244
Shetland 106, 117, 128, 183, 387, 432, 478, 490, 513–14
Shrew, Common (*Sorex araneus*) 207, **208**, 214, 218, 219, 223, 250, 403
Shrew, Pygmy (*Sorex minutus*) 250, 402
Shrike, Great Grey (*Lanius excubitor*) 83
Shrike, Lesser Grey (*Lanius minor*) 374, 379
shrikes (Lanidae) 19, 92
Shropshire 289
Siskin (*Carduelis spinus*) 116, 403, 405, 407, 515
Sitta europaea (Nuthatch) 407
Skimmer, Black-tailed (*Orthetrum cancellatum*) 333
Skua, Arctic (*Stercorarius parasiticus*) 196
Skua, Long-tailed (*Stercorarius longicaudus*) 196

Skylark (*Alauda arvensis*) 38, 63, 64, 114, 115, 116, 117, 118, 120, 134, 210, 320, 321, 397, 402, 403, 404, 405, 406, 407, 408, 410, 411, 415, 417, 418, 422, 423–5, 467
Slow Worm (*Anguis fragilis*) 210
Snipe (*Gallinago gallinago*) 114, 115, 116, 117, 120, 135, 212, 403, 404, 405, 406, 407, 419, 471
Snipe, Jack (*Lymnocryptes minimus*) 121
Snowdonia 118, 502
Sopwell Priory 12
Sorex araneus (Common Shrew) 207, **208**, 214, 218, 219, 223, 250, 403
Sorex minutus (Pygmy Shrew) 250, 402
South and Central America 2, 3, 9, 10, 11, 100, 155, 181, 183
South Africa 199, 255, 319, 324, 328, 331, 332, 373, 374, 526
Spain 32, 48, 56, 111, 137, 149, 179, 181, 205, 209, 248, 252, 260, 266, 268, 279, 282, 290, 299, 303, 311, 464
Sparrow, Fox (*Passerella iliaca*) 146, 406
Sparrow, House (*Passer domesticus*) 36, 37, 120, 210, 212, 218, 219, 317, 321, 396, 399, 400, 402, 403, 405, 407, 408, 426, 467, 471, 473, 513
Sparrow, Italian House (*Passer domesticus italiae*) 383
Sparrow, Tree (*Passer montanus*) 321, 383
Sparrowhawk (*Accipiter nisus*) 33, 34, 36, 37, 44, 50, 54, 85, 114, 123, 131, 134, 193, 213, 242, 296, 299, 304, 327, 328, 340, 384, 417–19, 421, 422, 423, 424–5, 467, 468, 478, 495, 516
speed 58–69

spiral flight 71–4
Spizipteryx circumcinctus (Spot-winged Falconet) 2
Spruce, Norway (*Picea abies*) 341
Spruce, Sitka (*Picea sitchensis*) 435, 515
Squirrel, Arctic Ground (*Urocitellus parryii*) 71, 112
Squirrel, Grey (*Sciurus carolinensis*) 121, 242, 357
Squirrel, Red (*Sciurus vulgaris*) 385
Staphylococcus aureus 190
Starling (*Sturnus vulgaris*) 38, 41, 76, 114, 115, 116, 117, 118, **119**, 120, 126, 133, 210, 218, 251, 317, 332, 397, 403, 404, 405, 407, 408, 416, 467–8, 487, 525
Starling, Rose-coloured (*Pastor roseus*) 75, 531
Stercorarius longicaudus (Long-tailed Skua) 196
Stercorarius parasiticus (Arctic Skua) 196
Sterna albifrons (Little Tern) 121, 317
Sterna dougallii (Roseate Tern) 113
Sterna hirundo (Common Tern) 38, 114, 116, 118, 320, 331
Sterna paradisaea (Arctic Tern) 116, 117
Sterna sandvicensis (Sandwich Tern) 121
Stoat (*Mustela ermine*) 112, 432
Stonechat (*Saxicola rubicola*) 115, 321, 405, 407
Streptopelia decaocto (Collared Dove) 116, 120, 212
Streptopelia turtur (Turtle Dove) 121, 210
Strigiformes (Owls) 22
Strigops habroptila (Kakapo) 2
Strix aluco (Tawny Owl) 34, 50, 52, 114, 199, 244, 304, 357, 384, 433, 478, 479, 495, 496

Strix uralensis (Ural Owl) 531
Sturnus vulgaris (Starling) 38, 41, 76, 114, 115, 116, 117, 118, **119**, 120, 126, 133, 210, 218, 251, 317, 332, 397, 403, 404, 405, 407, 408, 416, 467–8, 487, 525
Subbuteo (game) 305, 307
Sussex 304
Swallow, Barn (*Hirundo rustica*) 56, 96, 121, 313, **317**, 320, 321, 323, 324, 326, 327, 328, 330, 331, 332, **335**, 356, 403, 405, 406, 407, 416–7
Swan, Mute (*Cygnus olor*) 525
Sweden 30, 48, 55, 64, 85, 111, 133, 137, 161, 168, 181, 183, 185, 255, 290, 291, 305, 364, 372, 410, 414, 459, 461, 463, 466, 470, 476, 479
Swift (*Apus apus*) 32, 35, 114, 120, 313, 321, 322, 325, 365, 368, 374, 383, 407
Swift, Alpine (*Apus melba*) 270
Swift, Little (*Apus affinus*) 324, 328, 332
Switzerland 60, 153, 196, 205, 255, 256, 270, 361, 383
Sycamore (*Acer pseudoplatanus*) 341
Sylvia atricapilla (Blackcap) 121
Sylvia borin (Garden Warbler) 402, 407
Sylvia communis (Whitethroat) 121
Sympetrum striolatum (Common Darter) 333, 503
Synthliboramphus antiquus (Ancient Murrelet) 130, 131–2, 141, 146

Tachybaptus ruficollis (Little Grebe) 120
Tadarida brasiliensis (Mexican Free-tailed Bat) 112
Tadorna tadorna (Shelduck) 244
Talpa europaea (Mole) 37, 208, 318
tapeworm 190

Teal (*Anas creca*) 115, 116, 120, 122, 126
termites 210, 323–4, 370
Tern, Arctic (*Sterna paradisaea*) 116, 117
Tern, Common (*Sterna hirundo*) 38, 114, 116, 118, 320, 331
Tern, Little (*Sterna albifrons*) 121, 317
Tern, Roseate (*Sterna dougallii*) 113
Tern, Sandwich (*Sterna sandvicensis*) 121
Tetrao urogallus (Capercaillie) 50
'third party' birds 335, 337, 356
Thrush, Hermit (*Catharus guttatus*) 146
Thrush, Mistle (*Turdus viscivorus*) 38, 114, 115, 116, 118, 328, 403, 404, 405, 406, 407
Thrush, Song (*Turdus philomelos*) 114, 115, 116, 117, 118, 120, 133, 403, 404, 405, 407
Thymallus arcticus (Arctic Grayling) 113
tiercel (tercel) 1
Tilia europaea (Common Lime) 341
Tit, Blue (*Cyanistes caeruleus*) 114, 218, 321, 403, 407
Tit, Coal (*Periparus ater*) 115, 403, 405, 407
Tit, Great (*Parus major*) 121, 212, 270, 321, 404, 405, 407
Tit, Long-tailed (*Aegithalos caudatus*) 403, 404, 405, 407
Tit, Marsh (*Poecile palustris*) 321, 404, 407
Tit, Willow (*Poecile montanus*) 321, 403
Toad, Common (*Bufo bufo*) 210
Tortoiseshell, Small (*Aglais urticae*) 402
Treecreeper (*Certhia familiaris*) 115, 403, 404, 405, 407
Trichomonas gallineae 475
trichomoniasis 189

Tring, Natural History Museum 98
Tringa glareola (Wood Sandpiper) 116
Tringa nebularia (Greenshank) 114, 116, 525
Tringa ochropus (Green Sandpiper) 121
Tringa tetanus (Redshank) 114, 115, 116, 117, 134, 135, 403, 404, 405, 410, 417, 418, 419, 423, 425, 471, 487, 520
Troglodytes aedon (House Wren) 399
Troglodytes troglodytes (Wren) 34, 121, 190, 316, 403, 404, 405, 407
tuberculosis, avian 189, 300
Tunstall, Marmaduke 98
Turdus iliacus (Redwing) 114, 115, 116, 118, 120, 125, 126, 403, 404, 405, 407, 410
Turdus merula (Blackbird) 114, 115, 116, 117, 120, 403, 404, 407, 410
Turdus philomelos (Song Thrush) 114, 115, 116, 117, 118, 120, 133, 403, 404, 405, 407
Turdus pilaris (Fieldfare) 34, 114, 115, 116, 117, 118, 120, 124, 125, 403, 404, 405, 407, 409, 476
Turdus torquatus (Ring Ouzel) 34, 114, 115, 190, 403, 404, 405, 407
Turdus viscivorus (Mistle Thrush) 38, 114, 115, 116, 118, 328, 403, 404, 405, 406, 407
Turnstone (*Arenaria interpres*) 404, 410
Twite (*Carduelis flavirostris*) 34, 190, 402, 410, 411
Tyto alba (Barn Owl) 11, 20, 37, 50, 115, 213, 244, 250, 270, 294, 302, 304, 324, 499–500, 521, 529

Ulmus minor var. *vulgaris* (English Elm) 340, 412

Uria aalge (Guillemot) 113, 117
urine trails, tracking 82–6
Urocitellus parryii (Arctic Ground Squirrel) 71, 112
UV light 82–6

Vanellus vanellus (Lapwing) 37, 114, 115, 116, 117, 118, 120, 122, 123, 124, 212, 326, 402, 403, 404, 405, 407, 410, 416
V-flight 238–9
Vipera berus (Adder) 480
vision 69–73 *and see under individual falcons*
Vole, Bank (*Myodes glareolus*) 83, 84, 85, 207, **208**, 216, 250
Vole, Common (*Microtus arvalis*) 125, 213, 214, 215, 221
Vole, Orkney (*Microtus arvalis orcadensis*) 244
Vole, Short-tailed Field (*Microtus agrestis*) 82, 83, 84, 85, 114, 115, 214, 215, 397, 402, 403, 490, 497, 498
Vole, Sibling (*Microtus levis*) 83
Vole, Water (*Arvicola amphibius*) 114
voles as prey 82–5, 205, 207–8, 213, 214–18, 220–2, 225, 229, 232–3, 234, 235, 244, 250–9, 264, 269, 283–5, 290, 293, 295, 296, 298, 301, 318, 397, 402, 403, 410, 412, 490, 493, 495, 496, 498, 500
Vulpes lagopus (Arctic Fox) 191, 196
Vulture, Griffon (*Gyps fulvus*) 299
Vulture, Ruppell's (*Gyps rueppellii*) 522

Wagtail, Grey (*Motacilla cinerea*) 114, 115, 116, 405, 407

Wagtail, Pied (*Motacilla alba yarrellii*) 120, 218, 317, 321, 403, 404, 405, 407, 410

Wagtail, Yellow (*Motacilla flava*) 317

Wales 24, 35, 36, 48, 52, 106, 112, 118, 128, 137, 146, 151, 167, 176, 182, 187, 206, 216, 262, 282, 304, 389, 394, 397, 399, 406, 407, 408, 432, 433, 435, 436, 440–2, 444, 456, 480, 487, 488–9, 490, 492–3, 502, 505, 510, 514–15, 517

Warbler, Garden (*Sylvia borin*) 402, 407

Warbler, Icterine (*Hippolais icterina*) 374

Warbler, Willow (*Phylloscopus trochilus*) 121, 403, 404, 405, 407

Warbler, Wood (*Phylloscopus sibilatrix*) 407

Warwickshire 327

water, hunting over 129–31

Waxwing, Bohemian (*Bombycilla garrulus*) 36

Weasel (*Mustela nivalis*) 37, 207, 213

Wheatear (*Oenanthe oenanthe*) 38, 114, 115, 116, 117, 190, 191, 397, **399**, 402, 403, 404, 405, 407

Whimbrel (*Numenius phaeopus*) 116

Whinchat (*Saxicola rubetra*) 321, 403, 404, 405, 407

Whitethroat (*Sylvia communis*) 121

Wigeon (*Anas penelope*) 115, 116, 124

willow (*Salix* sp.) 341, 467, 468

Wiltshire 317

wind turbines 299–300, 385–6

wing design 57–9

Woodcock (*Scolopax rusticola*) 114, 115, 116, 118, 120, 132, 317, 402

Woodpecker, Great Spotted (*Dendrocopos major*) 114, 116, **119**, 120

Woodpecker, Green (*Picus viridis*) 38, 114, 244, 332, 383

Wren (*Troglodytes troglodytes*) 34, 121, 190, 316, 403, 404, 405, 407

Wren, House (*Troglodytes aedon*) 399

Wryneck (*Jynx torquilla*) 113, 116, 405, 315, 402

Yellowhammer (*Emberiza citronella*) 121, 405, 407

Yorkshire 52, 403, 412, 435, 436, 438, 442, 443, 447

The New Naturalist Library

1. *Butterflies* — E. B. Ford
2. *British Game* — B. Vesey-Fitzgerald
3. *London's Natural History* — R. S. R. Fitter
4. *Britain's Structure and Scenery* — L. Dudley Stamp
5. *Wild Flowers* — J. Gilmour & M. Walters
6. *The Highlands & Islands* — F. Fraser Darling & J. M. Boyd
7. *Mushrooms & Toadstools* — J. Ramsbottom
8. *Insect Natural History* — A. D. Imms
9. *A Country Parish* — A. W. Boyd
10. *British Plant Life* — W. B. Turrill
11. *Mountains & Moorlands* — W. H. Pearsall
12. *The Sea Shore* — C. M. Yonge
13. *Snowdonia* — F. J. North, B. Campbell & R. Scott
14. *The Art of Botanical Illustration* — W. Blunt
15. *Life in Lakes & Rivers* — T. T. Macan & E. B. Worthington
16. *Wild Flowers of Chalk & Limestone* — J. E. Lousley
17. *Birds & Men* — E. M. Nicholson
18. *A Natural History of Man in Britain* — H. J. Fleure & M. Davies
19. *Wild Orchids of Britain* — V. S. Summerhayes
20. *The British Amphibians & Reptiles* — M. Smith
21. *British Mammals* — L. Harrison Matthews
22. *Climate and the British Scene* — G. Manley
23. *An Angler's Entomology* — J. R. Harris
24. *Flowers of the Coast* — I. Hepburn
25. *The Sea Coast* — J. A. Steers
26. *The Weald* — S. W. Wooldridge & F. Goldring
27. *Dartmoor* — L. A. Harvey & D. St Leger Gordon
28. *Sea Birds* — J. Fisher & R. M. Lockley
29. *The World of the Honeybee* — C. G. Butler
30. *Moths* — E. B. Ford
31. *Man and the Land* — L. Dudley Stamp
32. *Trees, Woods and Man* — H. L. Edlin
33. *Mountain Flowers* — J. Raven & M. Walters
34. *The Open Sea: I. The World of Plankton* — A. Hardy
35. *The World of the Soil* — E. J. Russell
36. *Insect Migration* — C. B. Williams
37. *The Open Sea: II. Fish & Fisheries* — A. Hardy
38. *The World of Spiders* — W. S. Bristowe
39. *The Folklore of Birds* — E. A. Armstrong
40. *Bumblebees* — J. B. Free & C. G. Butler
41. *Dragonflies* — P. S. Corbet, C. Longfield & N. W. Moore
42. *Fossils* — H. H. Swinnerton
43. *Weeds & Aliens* — E. Salisbury
44. *The Peak District* — K. C. Edwards
45. *The Common Lands of England & Wales* — L. Dudley Stamp & W. G. Hoskins
46. *The Broads* — E. A. Ellis
47. *The Snowdonia National Park* — W. M. Condry
48. *Grass and Grasslands* — I. Moore
49. *Nature Conservation in Britain* — L. Dudley Stamp
50. *Pesticides and Pollution* — K. Mellanby
51. *Man & Birds* — R. K. Murton
52. *Woodland Birds* — E. Simms
53. *The Lake District* — W. H. Pearsall & W. Pennington
54. *The Pollination of Flowers* — M. Proctor & P. Yeo
55. *Finches* — I. Newton
56. *Pedigree: Words from Nature* — S. Potter & L. Sargent
57. *British Seals* — H. R. Hewer
58. *Hedges* — E. Pollard, M. D. Hooper & N. W. Moore
59. *Ants* — M. V. Brian
60. *British Birds of Prey* — L. Brown
61. *Inheritance and Natural History* — R. J. Berry
62. *British Tits* — C. Perrins
63. *British Thrushes* — E. Simms
64. *The Natural History of Shetland* — R. J. Berry & J. L. Johnston

65. *Waders* — W. G. Hale
66. *The Natural History of Wales* — W. M. Condry
67. *Farming and Wildlife* — K. Mellanby
68. *Mammals in the British Isles* — L. Harrison Matthews
69. *Reptiles and Amphibians in Britain* — D. Frazer
70. *The Natural History of Orkney* — R. J. Berry
71. *British Warblers* — E. Simms
72. *Heathlands* — N. R. Webb
73. *The New Forest* — C. R. Tubbs
74. *Ferns* — C. N. Page
75. *Freshwater Fish* — P. S. Maitland & R. N. Campbell
76. *The Hebrides* — J. M. Boyd & I. L. Boyd
77. *The Soil* — B. Davis, N. Walker, D. Ball & A. Fitter
78. *British Larks, Pipits & Wagtails* — E. Simms
79. *Caves & Cave Life* — P. Chapman
80. *Wild & Garden Plants* — M. Walters
81. *Ladybirds* — M. E. N. Majerus
82. *The New Naturalists* — P. Marren
83. *The Natural History of Pollination* — M. Proctor, P. Yeo & A. Lack
84. *Ireland: A Natural History* — D. Cabot
85. *Plant Disease* — D. Ingram & N. Robertson
86. *Lichens* — Oliver Gilbert
87. *Amphibians and Reptiles* — T. Beebee & R. Griffiths
88. *Loch Lomondside* — J. Mitchell
89. *The Broads* — B. Moss
90. *Moths* — M. Majerus
91. *Nature Conservation* — P. Marren
92. *Lakeland* — D. Ratcliffe
93. *British Bats* — John Altringham
94. *Seashore* — Peter Hayward
95. *Northumberland* — Angus Lunn
96. *Fungi* — Brian Spooner & Peter Roberts
97. *Mosses & Liverworts* — Nick Hodgetts & Ron Porley
98. *Bumblebees* — Ted Benton
99. *Gower* — Jonathan Mullard
100. *Woodlands* — Oliver Rackham
101. *Galloway and the Borders* — Derek Ratcliffe
102. *Garden Natural History* — Stefan Buczacki
103. *The Isles of Scilly* — Rosemary Parslow
104. *A History of Ornithology* — Peter Bircham
105. *Wye Valley* — George Peterken
106. *Dragonflies* — Philip Corbet & Stephen Brooks
107. *Grouse* — Adam Watson & Robert Moss
108. *Southern England* — Peter Friend
109. *Islands* — R. J. Berry
110. *Wildfowl* — David Cabot
111. *Dartmoor* — Ian Mercer
112. *Books and Naturalists* — David E. Allen
113. *Bird Migration* — Ian Newton
114. *Badger* — Timothy J. Roper
115. *Climate and Weather* — John Kington
116. *Plant Pests* — David V. Alford
117. *Plant Galls* — Margaret Redfern
118. *Marches* — Andrew Allott
119. *Scotland* — Peter Friend
120. *Grasshoppers & Crickets* — Ted Benton
121. *Partridges* — G. R. (Dick) Potts
122. *Vegetation of Britain & Ireland* — Michael Proctor
123. *Terns* — David Cabot & Ian Nisbet
124. *Bird Populations* — Ian Newton
125. *Owls* — Mike Toms
126. *Brecon Beacons* — Jonathan Mullard
127. *Nature in Towns and Cities* — David Goode
128. *Lakes, Loughs and Lochs* — Brian Moss
129. *Alien Plants* — Clive A. Stace and Michael J. Crawley
130. *Yorkshire Dales* — John Lee
131. *Shallow Seas* — Peter J. Hayward

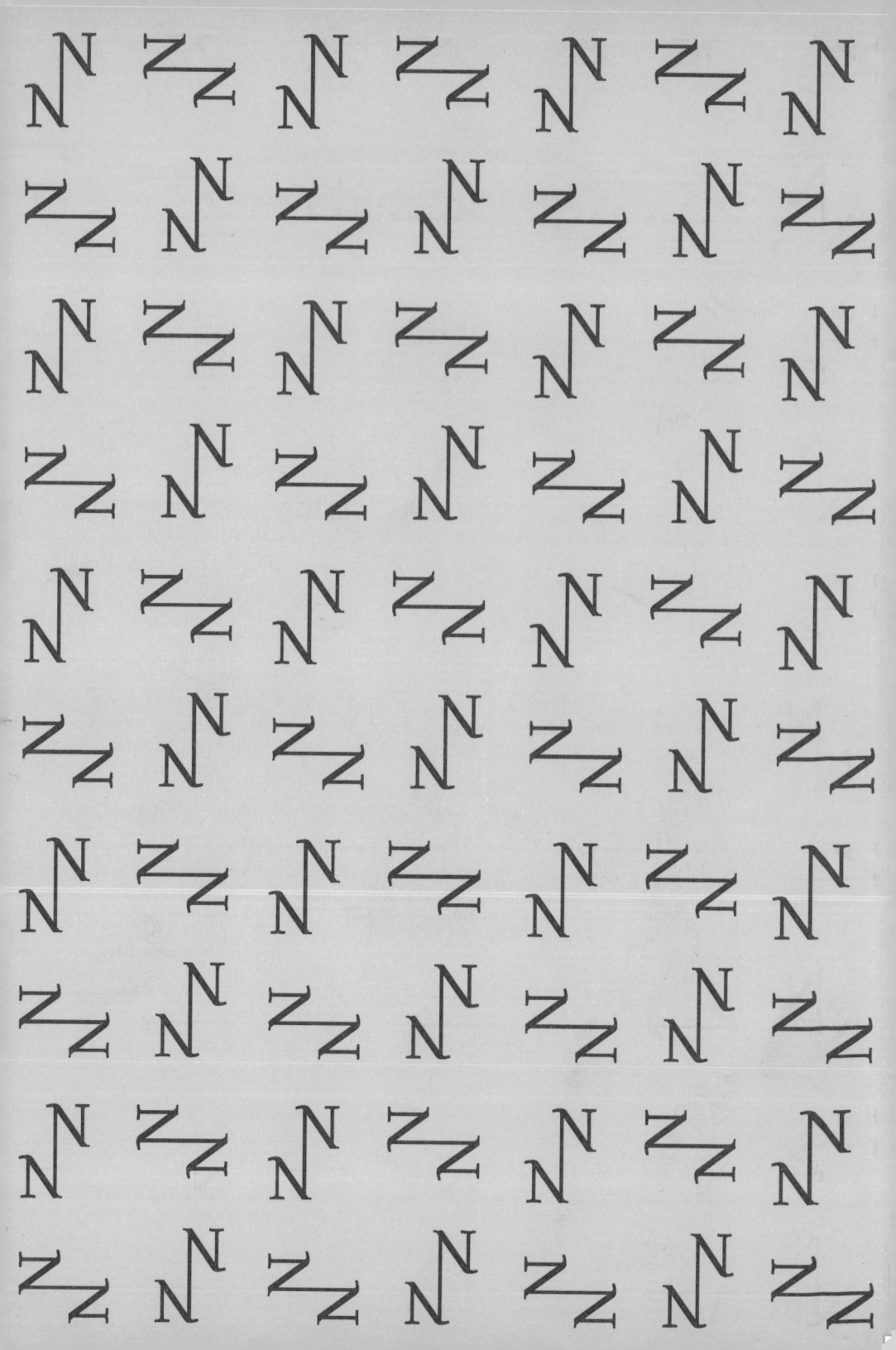